MEDIA, FEMINISM, CULTURAL STUDIES

The Sacred Cinema of Andrei Tarkovsky
by Jeremy Mark Robinson

Stepping Forward: Essays, Lectures and Interviews
by Wolfgang Iser

Genius and Loving It! Mel Brooks
by Thomas Christie

The Comic Art of Mel Brooks
by Maurice Yacowar

Marvelous Names
by P. Adams Sitney

Cixous, Irigaray, Kristeva: The Jouissance of French Feminism
by Kelly Ives

Jean-Luc Godard: The Passion of Cinema / Le Passion de Cinéma
by Jeremy Mark Robinson

Liv Tyler
by Thomas A. Christie

The Cinema of Richard Linklater
by Thomas A. Christie

John Hughes
by Thomas A. Christie

Walerian Borowczyk
by Jeremy Mark Robinson

The Art of Katsuhiro Otomo
by Jeremy Mark Robinson

Wild Zones: Pornography, Art and Feminism
by Kelly Ives

'Cosmo Woman': The World of Women's Magazines
by Oliver Whitehorne

Andrea Dworkin
by Jeremy Mark Robinson

Sex in Art: Pornography and Pleasure in Painting and Sculpture
by Cassidy Hughes

Erotic Art
by Cassidy Hughes

*The Erotic Object: Sexuality in Sculpture
From Prehistory to the Present Day*
by Susan Quinnell

Women in Pop Music
by Helen Challis

Julia Kristeva: Art, Love, Melancholy, Philosophy, Semiotics
by Kelly Ives

Luce Irigaray: Lips, Kissing, and the Politics of Sexual Difference
by Kelly Ives

Helene Cixous I Love You: The Jouissance *of Writing*
by Kelly Ives

Detonation Britain: Nuclear War in the UK
by Jeremy Mark Robinson

Akira: The Movie and the Manga
by Jeremy Mark Robinson

The Art of Masamune Shirow (3 vols)
by Jeremy Mark Robinson

FORTHCOMING BOOKS

Legend of the Overfiend
Death Note
Naruto
Bleach
Hellsing
Vampire Knight
Mushishi
One Piece
Nausicaä of the Valley of the Wind
Tsui Hark
The Ecstatic Cinema of Tony Ching Siu-tung
The Twilight Saga
Jackie Collins and the Blockbuster Novel
Harry Potter

PASOLINI

IL CINEMA DI POESIA/
THE CINEMA OF POETRY

PASOLINI

IL CINEMA DI POESIA/
THE CINEMA OF POETRY

Jeremy Mark Robinson

CRESCENT MOON

Crescent Moon Publishing
P.O. Box 1312, Maidstone
Kent, ME14 5XU, Great Britain
www.crmoon.com

First published 2024.
© Jeremy Mark Robinson 2024.

Set in Times New Roman 10 on 14pt.
Designed by Radiance Graphics.

The right of Jeremy Mark Robinson to be identified as the author of this book has been asserted generally in accordance with sections 77 and 78 of the Copyright, Designs and Patents Act 1988.

All rights reserved. No part of this book may be reprinted or reproduced, stored in a retrieval system, or transmitted, in any form or by any means, electronic, mechanical, photocopying, recording or otherwise, without permission from the publisher.

British Library Cataloguing in Publication data available for this title.

ISBN-13 9781861718419
ISBN-13 9781861719218

CONTENTS

Acknowledgements ❖ 9
Abbreviations ❖ 9

PART ONE ❖ PIER PAOLO PASOLINI

1   Introduction ❖ 16
2   Pier Paolo Pasolini: Biography ❖ 17
3   The Works of Pier Paolo Pasolini ❖ 51
4   Aspects of Pasolini's Cinema ❖ 69

PART TWO ❖ THE FILMS

5   *Beggar* ❖ 115
6   *Mamma Roma* ❖ 135
7   *Curd Cheese* ❖ 157
8   *The Gospel According To Matthew* ❖ 165
9   *The Hawks and the Sparrows* ❖ 220
10 *Oedipus Rex* ❖ 232
11 *Theorem* ❖ 255
12 *Pigsty* ❖ 282
13 *Medea* ❖ 305
14 *Notes Towards an African Oresteia* ❖ 319
15 *The Decameron* ❖ 334
16 *The Canterbury Tales* ❖ 361

17 *The Arabian Nights* ✤ 377
18 *Salò* ✤ 419
19 Other Films and Documentaries ✤ 470
20 Unmade Projects ✤ 478

Appendices
    Quotes By Pier Paolo Pasolini ✤ 493
    Notes On Renaissance Artists ✤ 495
    The Big Night and *A Violent Life* ✤ 498
    The Grim Reaper ✤ 504
    Sergio Citti: Two Films ✤ 509
Filmography and Bibliography: Pier Paolo Pasolini ✤ 515
Bibliography ✤ 519

ACKNOWLEDGEMENTS

To the authors and publishers quoted.
To the copyright holders of the illustrations.

ABBREVIATIONS

ES Enzo Siciliano, *Pier Paolo Pasolini*
PP *Pasolini On Pasolini*

For Danny

Poetry is more philosophical and of higher value than history.

Aristotle, *Poetics*

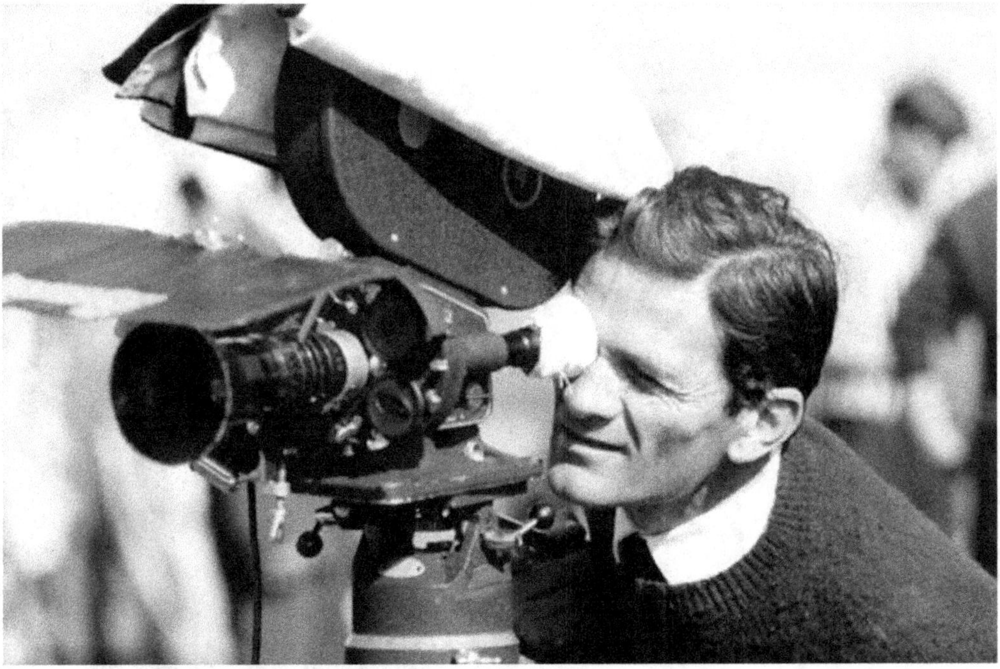

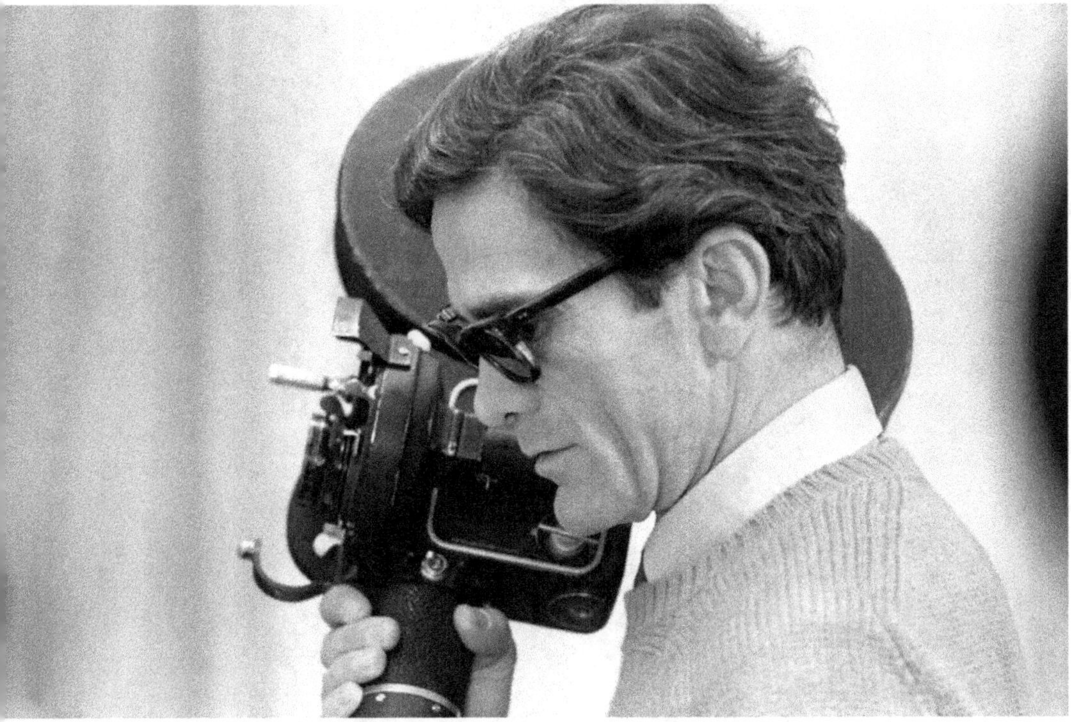

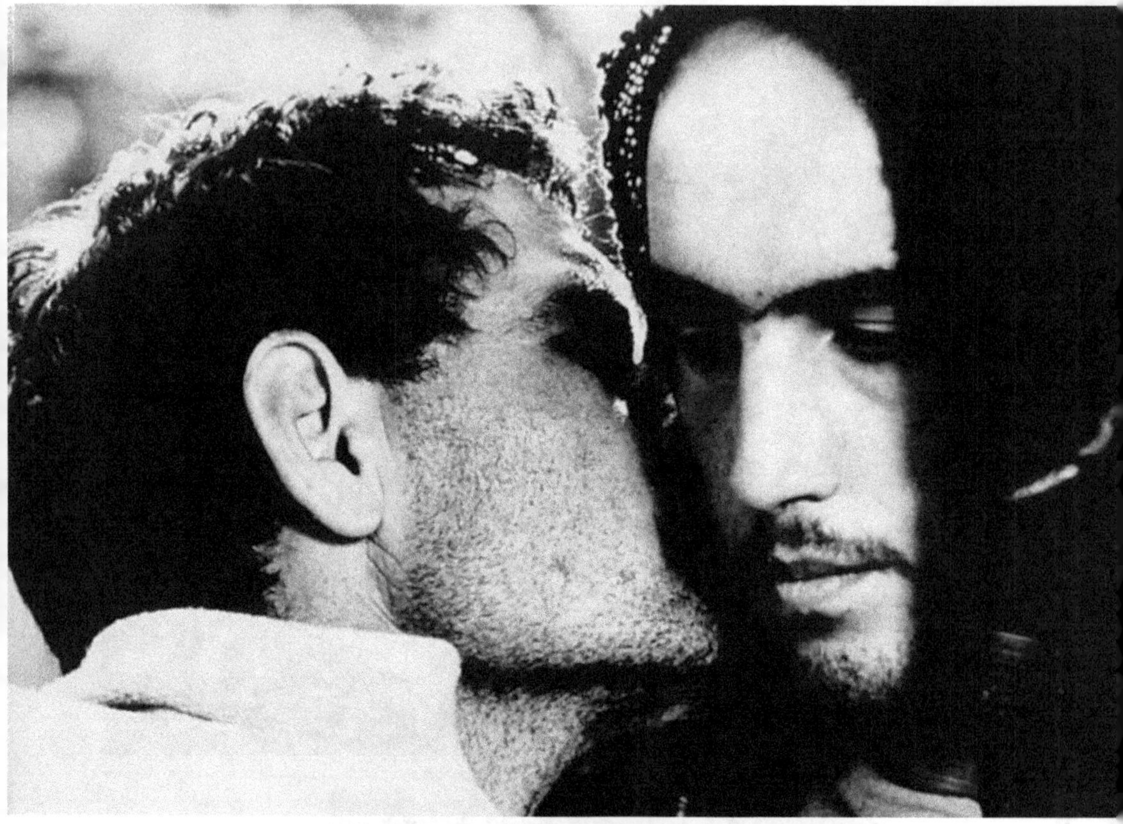

ALFREDO BINI
PRESENTA
PIER PAOLO PASOLINI
IL
VANGELO
SECONDO
MATTEO
ARCO FILM
LUX CIE CINEMATOGRAFIQUE
FRANCE

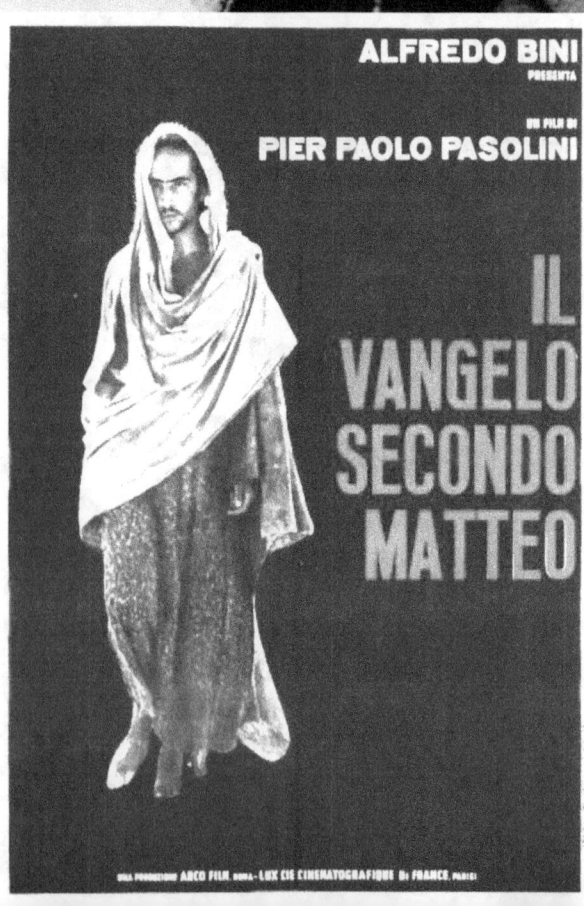

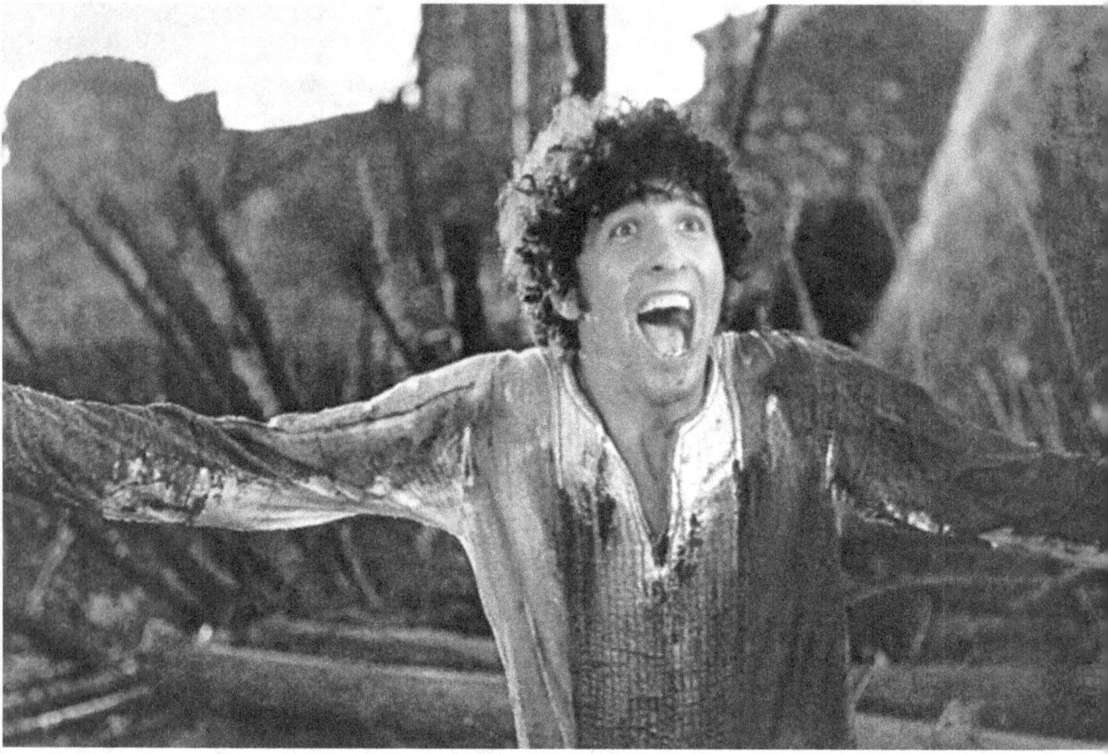

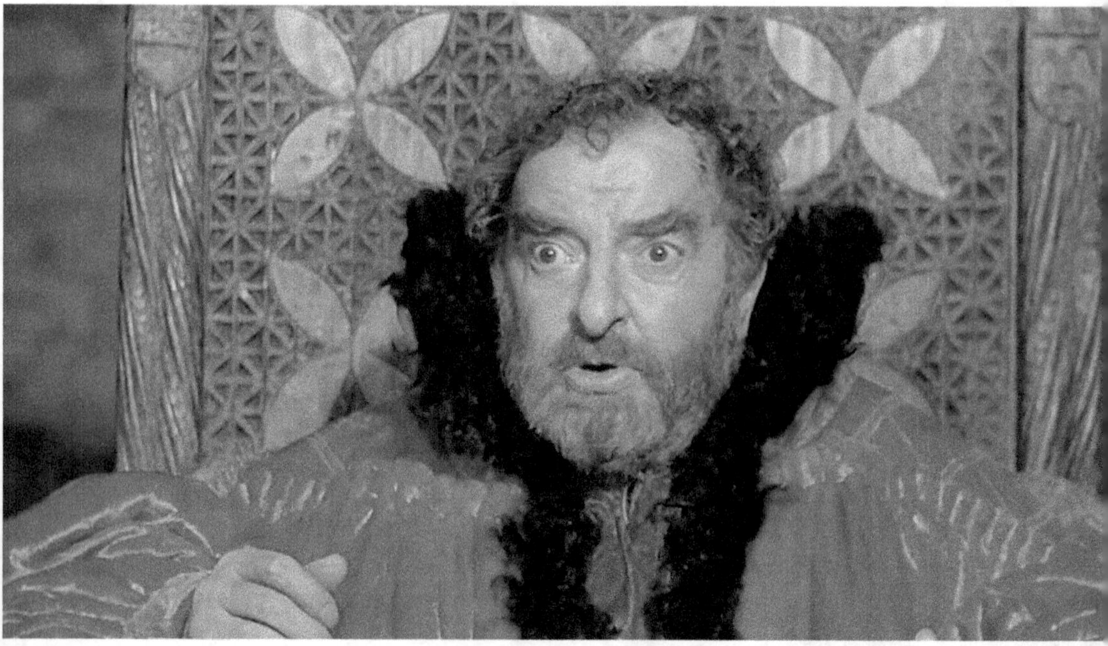

PART ONE
⊕
PIER PAOLO PASOLINI

Oso alzare gli occhi
sulle cime secche degli alberi:
non vedo il Signore, ma il suo lume
che brilla sempre immenso.

(Daring to lift my eyes
towards the dry treetops,
I don't see God, but his light
is immensely shining.)

Pier Pasolo Pasolini, 'Mystery' (1945)[1]

---
1 Trans. A.P. Nicolai, C.U.N.Y., Brooklyn.

1

INTRODUCTION

This study focusses on the films directed by Pier Paolo Pasolini, but it should be remembered that he was also a poet, novelist, essayist and playwright. Indeed, there is still a huge interest in Pasolini as a poet and writer, and there are as many articles and books about Pasolini's writing as there are about his cinema. (For many, it is Pasolini the poet who is more valuable culturally than Pasolini the filmmaker – which's a *very* unusual situation for a film director who's regarded as a major player in Italian and European cinema). But Pasolini is one of those filmmakers, like Orson Welles or Jean-Luc Godard, who is so enormously talented and full of life, they produced major works in a number of areas, not only in cinema.

There are plenty of approaches to the work of Pier Paolo Pasolini – I have focussed on the cinema, and Pasolini as a filmmaker. Another obvious approach is to consider the gay, queer and homosexual elements in Pasolini's work (as I have done so much of this elsewhere, I have left that approach aside).

I began this book in the early 2000s, and added to it over the years, including in 2011, 2015 and 2017 (when it was nearly complete). It has been difficult to finish – partly because Pasolini is a fascinating filmmaker and artist, and there always seems to be more to say about his work. Also, I wanted to track down and see pretty much everything he produced in cinema, which takes time. Most of Pasolini's films are easily available, but some are not. The book has been rewritten and expanded numerous times, and has demanded an enormous amount of work to complete.

2

PIER PAOLO PASOLINI: BIOGRAPHY

LIFE.

Pier Paolo Pasolini was born on March 5, 1922, in Bologna, Italy. He died on November 2, 1975, in Ostia, Rome (he was buried in Casarsa, in his beloved Friuli). Italy, by the way, has a population of 57 million (in 1997), and a land mass of 116,341 square miles. The country was re-unified in 1870.

Pier Paolo Pasolini looks like one of the characters in his movies: the suave, chiselled, sometimes gaunt features (beautiful cheekbones!), the short, dark hair, and those beady eyes that don't miss a thing. Pasolini comes across in interviews (and in his films) as an aristocrat – an artist, surely, but debonair, sophisticated and clever. He appears highly educated, intellectual, out-spoken, but also mischievous and very individual (people compared him to a priest – and of course he played priests in his movies).

He was a slim, rangy guy, 5' 6" (with those prominent cheekbones and piercing dark eyes, he was often compared to actor Jack Palance: the street kids of Roma called him *Giacche Palànce*).[2] He prided himself on keeping active into middle-age, and being able to play soccer.[3]

Later, when he was a film director (starting late, at age 39), Pier Paolo Pasolini was certainly an intimidating presence, with a formidable reputation – like Cecil B. DeMille, Erich von Stroheim or Akira Kurosawa. Very confident, very smart, a great talker and interviewee, a leader

---

[2] Jack Palance in his red Alfa Romeo in *Contempt* (1963) is strikingly reminiscent of Pier Paolo Pasolini.
[3] Tho', like everybody, he also disliked ageing (the bad teeth, the thinning hair), and dressed younger than his years.

on set, with no doubts from anyone about who was the primary creator and author.

It's clear, if you know anything about Pier Paolo Pasolini, that he was a very bright guy from an early age. He doesn't seem to have been afflicted by a lack of self-confidence – certainly with regard to his own work (which affects writers almost as a matter of course). Pasolini happily, in his twenties, takes on any big subject he likes.

Pasolini's background was bourgeois – ironic, considering how passionately he detested the bourgeoisie. His mother, Susanna Colussi, was born in 1891 and died in 1981. His father Carlo Alberto Pasolini (1892-1958)[4] was a lieutenant in the Italian Army (consequently, like many military families, they moved around a good deal). They married in 1921. For Pasolini, his father was 'overbearing, egoistic, egocentric, tyrannical and authoritarian' (PP, 13).

Pier Paolo Pasolini's relationship with his mother Susanna Colussi, and hers with him, has been described as unhealthily eroticized: according to Enzo Siciliano, Susanna invested far too much in her son emotionally: she gave Pasolini what she withheld from her husband Carlo Alberto (ES, 33). The theme of (hints of) incestuous relations between mothers and sons crop up in Pasolini's work (in *Mamma Roma*, obviously; some Pasolini movies, such as *Theorem*, play the incestuous fantasy literally and explicitly).

Pier Paolo Pasolini's brother Guidalberto (b. 1925) died in WWII (in 1945), when he was part of the Resistance. In the war, Pasolini was taken prisoner by the Germans, but escaped back to Friuli. WWII looms very large over all of Pasolini's work.

Pier Paolo Pasolini described himself as a child as stubborn, capricious, naïve, credulous, easily enthusiastic, and also shy and awkward (ES, 45). As a boy, Pasolini lived in Bologna, Belluno, Conegliano, Casarsa della Delizia (in Friuli), Cremona, Scandiano and Reggio Emilia.[5] From 1950, Pasolini made Rome[6] his home (PP, 19).

Apart from literature[7] (he formed a literature club at high school), Pier Paolo Pasolini enjoyed football. As a child Pasolini studied music (piano and violin) briefly.

Pier Paolo Pasolini worked as a teacher in the late 1940s and early 1950s. Pasolini had a number of teaching posts, and the teacher in him

---

[4] His father had once prevented an assassination attempt on Benito Mussolini.
[5] As a youth, Pier Paolo Pasolini said he grew up in Bologna, Parma, Conigilano, Belluno, Sacile, Idria, Cremona and other towns in Northern Italy (PP, 11).
[6] Pasolini bought a country retreat at Chai, near Viterbo, which Dante Ferretti had re-modelled for him.
[7] Pasolini's early literary idols included Rimbaud, Dostoievsky, Tolstoy, Shakespeare, Novalis and Coleridge.

never left – it was always a part of his movies, for instance (indeed, a character such as the talking bird in *The Hawks and the Sparrows* was entirely a teacher figure). And in interviews, Pasolini can't help coming across at times like an instructor.

That Pier Paolo Pasolini was a highly, passionately politicized artist is obvious: his passion for political issues runs throughout his movies and his poetry, his interviews, his essays, and pretty much everything he did or said publicly. Pasolini is always talking about Italian society, Italian culture, about Communism in Italy, about how Italy is becoming modernized, about Italy losing something when it embraces new technologies, etc. If there's an opportunity for ruminating on contemporary, Italian culture and society, Pasolini will take it.

Among the important friends in Pier Paolo Pasolini's life were:
Laura Betti (1927-2004).
Alberto Moravia (1907-1990).[8]
Elsa Morante (1912-1985).
Franco Citti (1938-2016).
Sergio Citti (1933-2005).
Susanna Colussi, mother (1891-1981).
Ninetto Davoli (b. 1948).

One of Pier Paolo Pasolini's first lovers was the fourteen year-old Tonuti Spagnol, whom Pasolini had met in Versuta (where he and his mom Susanna Colussi had retreated during the bombings of WW2). Pasolini tended to go for much younger lovers (like Ninetto Davoli later, 26 years younger than him).

Way before Pier Paolo Pasolini began to write for movies and then to direct them, he was deeply into poetry, into writing, and into literature. Way back in the 1940s, when Pasolini was in his twenties (and during WWII), he was already publishing poetry, writing essays,[9] reviews, and memorials (such as for his brother Guido who died in the war at the hands of Communists).

Another of Pier Paolo Pasolini's passions, long before he became enamoured of cinema, was Friuli: Friuli the place, the landscape, and the local people (and, later, the Friulian dialect). Pasolini moved away from Bologna (which he associated with his father) to Friuli.

Pier Paolo Pasolini had grown up around Casarsa, near Pordenone, in the Friuli-Venezia Giulia region, right up in the Northern corner of Italy. Yugoslavia is not far off to the East, with the Alps to the North; Venice

---
[8] The *dolce vita* set included Federico Fellini, Pier Paolo Pasolini, Luchino Visconti, Alberto Moravia *et al.*
[9] In his essays and articles for magazines over the years Pier Paolo Pasolini discussed Giuseppe Ungaretti, Umberto Saba, and Gianna Manzaini.

isn't too far away (the Venice Film Festival looms large in Pasolinu's career). Friuli is a region that prides itself on being somewhat distanced from Italy. Friuli is known for its peasant culture, which Pasolini revered (tho' it has been disappearing for many decades).

Pier Paolo Pasolini was thus a kid from the sticks, not a city kid at all, not the sophisticated urbanite of Italy's great cities (Milan, Bologna,[10] Venice, Rome, nor the Southern country that he later loved – Napoli, Sicily). Rather, it was a world of small towns and villages and the countryside, bicycle rides, flirting with girls, reading books, writing poetry in dialect ('peace and quiet, girls, mental concentration, fields, idleness, drink', Pasolini noted in a letter of 1940, when he was 18).

But it was also the Friulian dialect (*friulano*) that Pier Paolo Pasolini fell in love with, and Friulian culture. Pasolini was a keen connoisseur of dialects; he composed works in dialect (such as his early poetry), and also employed dialects in his cinema.

Pier Paolo Pasolini was a devotee of language like many modern poets and writers. One thinks of Rainer Maria Rilke, André Gide, Lawrence Durrell, Henry Miller, Alain Robbe-Grillet, Samuel Beckett, etc – writers for whom language and communication itself was a mysterious and utterly compelling force in their lives. Language, as French feminist Hélène Cixous remarked, is the key. For Cixous (who is loved and loathed by feminists nearly as energetically as Andrea Dworkin or Princess Diana), writing is absolutely crucial, and central. Writing is oxygen to Cixous, she must write to live. Cixous asserted in "Difficult Joys" that

> writing, writing poetically, treating language as one of the most important things in the world, today sounds mad. Yet for human beings it is the first most important thing.[11]

Pier Paolo Pasolini was one of those filmmakers who, had he been unable to continue to make movies, would've been quite happy writing (Woody Allen and Ingmar Bergman come to mind).[12] Jean-Luc Godard also took that view: for him, filmmaking and writing were part of the same thing anyway. Writing was 'already a way of making films,' Godard said in 1962 of his time as a film critic, 'for the difference between writing and directing is quantative not qualitative'.[13] Godard often said he

---
10 Tho' he was born in Bologna.
11 "Difficult Joys", in H. Wilcox, 1990, 23.
12 There are, of course, some famous film directors who found writing very difficult to do – Steven Spielberg, David Lean, Stanley Kubrick – filmmakers who couldn't write their own scripts, who had to have collaborators and writers. But of course most directors *do not* write their own scripts at all.
13 *Godard On Godard*, 171.

wouldn't stop creating if cinema died: he would move into TV, and if that disappeared, he would move into writing again (ibid., 171).

Other areas which Pasolini might've explored had he lived longer would include opera – several of his contemporaries took up directing live opera performances (Luchino Visconti, Ken Russell, Andrei Tarkovsky, Robert Altman – and even Federico Fellini, who disliked opera, came around to it. Fellini claimed that he only liked Nino Rota's music, and didn't like anything else. In the 1980s, however, Fellini decided he liked opera after all).[14]

Another area was pop promos – maybe too capitalist for Pier Paolo Pasolini, but the right pop act and the right deal might've attracted Pasolini to direct some pop videos. (One of the appeals was that they could be done in a single day, often had a decent budget, and were guaranteed exhibition and an audience).

DVD, Blu-ray and home releases of movies seem an ideal platform for Pier Paolo Pasolini to talk about his works. Some of the most valuable contributions that film directors make are to audio commentaries about their movies (such as Ken Russell, Oliver Stone, Werner Herzog, Mamoru Oshii and Stephen Sommers). Pasolini relating the stories of making *The Gospel According To Matthew* and *The Arabian Nights* would be a treat. (However, some film directors pointedly refuse to talk in audio commentaries about their films, such as Steven Spielberg and Woody Allen. For them, the works speak for themselves).

PASOLINI AND HIS FATHER

The revolt against the Father, against his own father Carlo Alberto Pasolini, was a violent one for Pier Paolo Pasolini, and it coloured much of his work. 'The public aspect of Pasolini's poetry will take the form of a struggle against all repressive and authoritarian conventions', remarked Enzo Siciliano (ES, 43), and it was his father that inaugurated that rebellion. (It was the loss/ rejection of the father, Siciliano reckoned, that was fatal for Pasolini, a loss and a pain that never left him).

Pier Paolo Pasolini associated his father and the father image with

---

[14] *And the Ship Sails On* (1983) featured an opera star along with other singers, and many other references to opera, and Fellini planned a documentary about opera in 1987 (there were invitations to direct operas, such as at Covent Garden and in Milan).

'all the symbols of authority and order, of fascism, of the bourgeoisie'.[15] Pasolini defined his father as 'a nationalist and a fascist', and conventional (PP, 14).

According to his biographer, Pier Paolo Pasolini's father Carlo Alberto was stricken by his son's gay lifestyle:

> he was overwhelmed by the drama of Pier Paolo, by the "scandal," and accepted it with grief. It brought him to a kind of insanity. He drank more and more, and at night cried out that his wife did not love him. (ES, 40)

As Pier Paolo Pasolini put it, he had placed himself 'in a relationship of rivalry and hatred towards my father', which made it easier for him to examine that relationship, compared to that with his mother, which was more latent (PP, 119). For Pasolini, 'everything ideological, voluntary, active and practical in my actions as a writer depends on my struggle with my father' (ibid., 120). Pasolini was thus conscious of using his deep-seated feelings as engines for his creative work (in the way that André Gide said that everything could be material or fuel for a writer. Famously, Gide remarked that as he was living his life he was also considering how it could be exploited in his writing).

According to Sam Rohdie, Pier Paolo Pasolini associated Northern Italia and Bologna with his father, with the bourgeoisie, with fascism, with technology, with capitalism, and with the Law of the Father. That was not the Italy that Pasolini enshrined, but the one he wanted to move away from. Pasolini's Italy was of the South, of Rome and Napoli and Calabria: the South was alive, it was peasants, it was a link to the past, it was non-technological, it was not capitalist (13). However, Bologna has long been a stronghold for the Italian Communist Party (it has held the city since 1945).

That Pier Paolo Pasolini's cinema exhibits a major father complex is clear to all. The ambiguous, anxious attitude towards fathers, father figures, the Sins of the Fathers, and the older generation, is everywhere. In *Pigsty,* the only words spoken in the 15th century tale are when the chief protagonist (Pierre Clementi) announces just as he's about to die: 'I killed my father, I ate the flesh of humans, I shivered with joy' (or something similar). Killing the father – the atmosphere of *Oedipus Rex* and *Theorem* was still in the air, perhaps (these movies – *Pigsty, Theorem, Medea* and *Oedipus Rex* are perhaps Pasolini's most concentrated attacks on the figure of the father).

---

15 Quoted in J. Duflot, 22.

POETRY AND LITERATURE

Pier Paolo Pasolini was writing poetry and articles from an early age: it's as if, as with poets such as Emily Dickinson or William Shakespeare, he had always written poetry. It was one of the fundamental creative activities in his life. He became disillusioned with politics, with the cultural life in contemporary Italy, with intellectuals, with the passing of the old world (as he saw it – but it had been decaying for 100s of years), yet his poetry remained central to his existence.

Pier Paolo Pasolini's poetry is in free verse – long, rambling lines and stanzas in the modernist tradition (recalling poets such as Walt Whitman and D.H. Lawrence, who preferred to write in lengthy, loose lines).

Pier Paolo Pasolini's first artistic efforts in the public arena included publishing a literary magazine (in 1941), and his own poems (*Versi a Casarsa*, 1941). He was editor of *Il Setaccio* (*The Sieve*).

By the late 1940s, Pasolini was writing and publishing regularly: *The Diaries*; *Quaderni Rossi*; the play *Il Cappellano*; and *The Cries*, a poetry book. Pasolini's novels (still in print) include *Ragazzi de Vita* (1955)[16] and *Una Vita Violenta* (1959) (both of which have been filmed).

Pier Paolo Pasolini's novel *Ragazzi di Vita* was 'a succès de scandale, drawing positive reviews, heated sales, hostile editorials, and even legal action for obscenity', remarked Shawn Levy in *Dolce Vita Confidential* (190). *Boys of Life* had a run-in in 1956 with the public prosecution office for being 'obscene'. Among the defenders of Boys of LIfe were Giuseppe Ungaretti, Carlo Bo, Pietro Bianchi and Livio Garzanti.

Reviewing *Una Vita Violenta*, Mario Montanana (a Communist senator), wondered that

> Pasolini does not like poor people, that he despises in general the inhabitants of the Roman shantytowns, and despises our party even more. The hero, Tommasino, is in reality a juvenile delinquent of the worst kind: thief, robber, pederast.

Enzo Siciliano called Pier Paolo Pasolini a

> frantically manneristic writer – and of a baroque mannerism, a lover of asymmetry, of tormented versifications of topical matter, who made of his style a shining example of the forbidden, who delighted in a "poetics of regression" in order to break the gilded trappings of twentieth-century academicism. (ES, 398)

---
16 Andrea Di Marco sued Pier Paolo Pasolini for libel in relation to *Ragazzi di Vita* in April, 1962.

An unfinished novel (of 1948), *Amado Mio*, contained autobiographical resonances, coalescing around its central character, Desiderio. In *Amado Mio*, Pasolini secreted 'the meaning of his own obsession,' according to Enzo Sciliano: 'to become father to his boy, so that the latter would mirror, by returning his embrace, all his unsatisfied longings for a son' (114).

The early work, *Amado Mio*, contains a pæan to Rita Hayworth in *Gilda*, as it plays to a cinema of rowdy, young Italians, by moonlight, in the open-air, with the boisterous crowd getting turned on. As the narrator of *Amado Mio* tells it,

> before the image of Gilda something wondrously shared enveloped all the spectators... Rita Hayworth with her huge body, her smile, her breasts of a sister and a prostitute – equivocal and angelic – stupid and mysterious with that nearsighted gaze of hers, cold and tender to the point of languor...

Pasolini was a passionate advocate of Friuli – he was a member of the Friulian Language Academy, the Association for the Autonomy of Friuli, and contributed to the magazine *Stroligùt di cà da l'aga*. Pasolini learnt how to speak Friulian as an adult – it wasn't part of his upbringing: it became part of his poetry – 'I learnt it as a sort of mystic act of love' (PP, 15).

Among Pier Paolo Pasolini's early influences were William Shakespeare (*Macbeth*), whom he discovered at 14,[17] and of course Italy's two giant poets, Francesco Petrarch and Dante Alighieri. Other favourites were André Gide (such as his novel *The Immoralist*[18]), Barbey d'Aurevilly, Niccolò Tommaseo, Johann Wolfgang von Goethe, Lautréamont and *Les Chants de Maldoror* (inevitably), Arthur Schopenhauer (his pithy, proto-Existential philosophy is a favourite with many European intellectuals), Villiers de l'Isle-Adam, and Daniell Bartoli (*Uomo al punto*).

As a youth, Pier Paolo Pasolini said he had consumed adventure stories, like many other children, but in his mid-teens discovered Fyodor Dostoievsky, William Shakespeare, Arthur Rimbaud, and authors who were somewhat regarded as rebellious, standing outside of the fascist society of Italy (PP, 17).

There are so many references to the work of Dante Alighieri in Pier

---

[17] With *Macbeth* Pasolini entered the world of books, visiting the stalls in the Portici della Morte in Bologna to buy used books.

[18] A novel tailor-made for Pasolini, evoking a spiritual journey from Northern Europe to the South, the breakdown of a marriage, the discovery of homosexual encounters in North Africa, and the development of an Existential, outsider persona. Classically, André Gide begins his tale with the anti-hero's father's death, a very Pasolinian device (instantly adding a welter of œdipal associations and an evocation of the Law of the Father). Pasolini didn't need to adapt *The Immoralist* – he lived it (tho' it would have been fascinating to see Pasolini take on Gide).

Paolo Pasolini's output it's a wonder that he didn't produce a feature film of the *Divina Commedia* (or at least a TV documentary). However, there *are* elements of *The Divine Comedy* in *The Decameron*, in the finale of *The Canterbury Tales,* with its devils, the traveller and his guide (in *The Hawks and the Sparrows* and the 'trilogy of life' films), and of course the *tableaux* from Renaissance art in *La Ricotta* and *The Gospel According To Matthew*.

The significance of Pier Paolo Pasolini's works are often interpreted as a group, and in relation to one another, rather than taken as single pieces to be seen in isolation. Thus, *Accattone* is always related to Pasolini's novels of the rough Roman youth, and the Marxism in *The Gospel According To Matthew* and *Oedipus Rex* is related to Pasolini's political statements. (This inter-connectedness was of course encouraged by the maestro himself).

'THE BOURGEOISIE ARE ALWAYS WRONG': MARXISM AND ANTI-BOURGEOIS POLITICS

> I don't think you can make an unpolitical movie. Your politics are going to show by permission or omission, so that the best you can do is to try and focus on them in some way in your movie, organise it so that it doesn't happen totally by accident.
>
> Warren Beatty

Only Jean-Luc Godard among comparable filmmakers has a deeper and more visceral loathing of the bourgeoisie than Pier Paolo Pasolini. Oh, how Pasolini *hated* everything bourgeois! – 'I nourish a visceral, deep, irreducible hatred for the bourgeoisie, its self-importance, its vulgarity; it is an ancient hatred, or if you like, a religious one', Pasolini asserted.[19]

As with Jean-Luc Godard, an ingredient of Pier Paolo Pasolini's politics is not so much Marxism as anti-bourgeoisism, anti-capitalism, and anti-consumerism. It is – again like Godard – partly *against things* for the sake of it: *against* the bourgeoisie, *against* consumerism.[20] And it's a politics that is *for* revolution, *for* change, for the sake of it, to turn things upside-down, and to oppose whatever's on offer. (But *how* would

---
19 Quoted in J. Duflot, 22.
20 However, Pasolini was happy to drive flashy sports cars, one of the loudest symbols of consumer-capitalism.

Pasolini stem the tide of consumerism and the social decline of his beloved Italy? He doesn't say – because he can't say – because no one can say. Pasolini offers nothing to replace contemporary, capitalist society. His utoptian project is about rewriting or enshrining the past, or the 'Third World').

Pasolini acknowledged that Marxism was a system imposed from the top down by an *élite*, like other political/ philosophical systems. But it gave the illusion that an individual mattered, or had an effect on the system. Andrew Sarris reckoned that 'Italian cinema as a whole – is primarily a Marxist cinema with a deep sense of doubt' (D. Georgakas, 236).

The aim of shocking the bourgeoisie (that childish goal of too many leftist/ Marxist artists), may derive in part from the attempt at reaching a realm where the bourgeoisie and their ideals do not go. That is, to go beyond the limits of what is accepted by bourgeois society, into the crude, the ultra-violent, the bestial.

It's typical that Pier Paolo Pasolini would side with the policemen in the political unrest of 1968, rather than with the student protesters. Why? Because Pasolini thought the students were bourgeois, and the cops were true working class people.

However, that part of the Pasolini Legend isn't the whole story: Pasolini's famous views about the police (expressed in a poem) were modified by his sceptical views of the police as enforcers of the law in Italy, and his sympathies with the political aspects of the counter-culture (Pasolini, the subject of many run-ins with the Italian authorities, held a sceptical view of the *carabineri*).[21] Subsequently, Pasolini's verses were employed by right-leaning groups and commentators., and twisted around, missing the irony and paradox that Pasolini was exploring.

On his Marxism, Pier Paolo Pasolini reminded Oswald Stack that in Italy everybody is a Marxist, and everybody is a Catholic (PP, 22). 'Pasolini's Marxist critique is sadly too narrow in its view of bourgeois neurosis as a symptom of class decadence under advanced capitalism', according to John Orr in *Contemporary Cinema* (1998, 8).

It's ironic for a left-wing and Marxist radical author like Pier Paolo Pasolini that often for his material he took on very traditional, conservative and right-wing texts and authors: the *Bible*, Ancient Greek mythology, Islamic stories, Geoffrey Chaucer and Giovanni Boccaccio. In fact, historical cinema tends to be conservative at the least, and often right-wing, too (this conservatism doesn't only reflect the markets of

---

[21] See an interesting article by Luca Peretti on Pasolini and Communism: "Remembering Pier Paolo Pasolini" (jacobinmag.com).

commercial cinema).

The decline of the ideological investment in Communism, socialism and Marxism in the 1970s, following the height of the idealism and activism of the late 1960s, was something that many intellectuals and artists had to face. Hayao Miyazaki, Jean-Luc Godard, Milos Forman, and many Eastern European filmmakers, as well as Pier Paolo Pasolini, confronted the fact that in some societies Communism and Marxism were not only not working, they were becoming as damaging as the mythologies and ideologies they opposed to, or were created in opposition to (such as Western capitalism).

The dream was over. Between the heady days of 1968 (manning the barricades, the student/ youth riots, the anti-Vietnam War protests, the civil rights marches), and the mid-1970s, it was a rapid decline.

'Pasolini's interventions were extreme and unflagging, pleasing to practically nobody across the political spectrum, and, uniquely, were intricately inscribed with the fact of his sexual difference', noted Gary Indiana (14).[22] True – left-wingers and Communists found just as much to get irritated by in Pasolini's pronouncements in the political arena as right-wingers and conservatives. (And Pasolini likely secretly enjoyed the fact that his views wound up leftists as well as rightists).

SOUTHERN ITALY

Pier Paolo Pasolini had a very idealized view of Southern Italy, or rural Italy, or pre-industrial Italy, of peasant Italy, of an Italy before television, cars and two World Wars. It was an Italy that never really existed, but which he wanted to exist. It was an Italy that he loved – the Italy of regions, and regional dialects and languages. It was if Pasolini saw himself as born out of his time – he might've been happier in the mediæval era, say, or the Renaissance (I think Pasolini would've got along just fine in the Ancient Roman period – and so would Federico Fellini and Walerian Borowczyk!).

A Northern Italian (he was born in Bologna), Pier Paolo Pasolini revered the South, of Naples, of Calabria. Of course he spent most of his adult life in the Eternal City; yet he always maintained the links to the

---

[22] For Indiana, Pier Paolo Pasolini was the wrong sort of gay artist – a Marxist who criticized the political system who wasn't like Franco Zeffirelli, a raging queen (and thus harmless).

countryside (keeping a Summer house, for instance).

It was no surprise that Pasolini opted to stage his most well-known movie, *The Gospel According To Matthew*, in Southern Italy, using many non-actors who were chosen by the maestro and his casting team for their interesting faces (as with Federico Fellini).

Accattone had inaugurated numerous approaches to cinema which Pier Paolo Pasolini would pursue throughout his career: a cast of unknowns and non-actors, low budgets, filming on location (and adapting existing settings), and employing recorded music, often classical (rather than specially composed scores).

Choosing unknown performers was about achieving some kind of reality, or a non-fictionalized, non-embellished reality: Pier Paolo Pasolini said in 1973:

> I pick actors whose sheer physical presence suffices to convey this sense of reality. I do not pick them at random but in order to offer examples of reality.[23]

Pasolini wanted the real thing, without making it pretty or cute. I can't think of another filmmaker who so loved extras, or who gave more screen time in terms of close-ups to extras – except perhaps Federico Fellini. And Pier Paolo Pasolini was especially fond of anybody who looked odd – terrible teeth, warts on lips, wall eyes, scars, and faces wrinkled by the Southern Italian sunshine.

The casting directors on Pier Paolo Pasolini's movies deserve all the credit coming their way for gathering such an extraordinary collection of actors and amateurs (such as Alberto di Stefanis, who cast *The Decameron*). Using non-actors is part of the Neo-realist film tradition – such as the Roberto Rossellini film *Francesco* (1950), co-written by Fellini. Movies like *Francesco* showed Pasolini how you could adapt a religious subject for the cinema without stars or professional actors.

Pasolini was happy to direct non-professional actors thru scenes, beat-by-beat, in the Italian cinema manner (by coaxing them from beside the *macchina fotografica*). It worked wonders – Enrique Irazoqui as Jesus in *The Gospel According To Matthew*, for instance. But sometimes it failed: Giuseppe Gentile might possess the sportsman's physique to look like the mythical hero Jason in *Medea*, but he sure can't act.

For Sam Rohdie, the extras in the 'trilogy of life' movies didn't need to act, they just needed to 'be', to appear on camera – their appearance was their characterization and their performance. (It's a version of Pasolini's notion of 'realism' – you simply show reality, and show

---
23 P. Pasolini, *The Guardian*, Aug 13, 1973.

people as people, and the process of cinema does the rest).

'A SEARCH FOR MAGIC': TRAVELS WITH PASOLINI

Pier Paolo Pasolini's is a cinema of journeys and voyages, eternally restless – films as a continuous search for locations (and as what we could term location scouting movies, Pasolini's are some of the finest). But also a search for the sacred, 'a search for magic', a search for mythology. And it's a quest for a place where those things still hold sway. A search for a time, too, an era of magic and the poetic.

Certainly the exotic is a big draw in Pier Paolo Pasolini's cinema, and for the director too. He did not shoot in North America (tho' he enjoyed visiting it), but took his productions to North Africa, the Middle East, India and Nepal (as well as the wildly alien, end-of-the-line wildernesses of dear, old England!).

Always Pier Paolo Pasolini goes South and East – to Africa, the Middle East, India (and Southern Italy), rather than North, to Germany, Scandinavia, Russia... Some have associated the North in Pasolini's æsthetics to his father, and the Law of the Father (i.e., Northern Italy, Bologna, etc).[24] The journey East and South, when taken from Europe, is towards the sun, to heat, to the desert, to the exotic, to the ancient world, to Islam, to old religions, to old mythologies.

As well as India, Pier Paolo Pasolini also visited Africa several times: Kenya in Jan, 1961 and Jan, 1962 (as well as Sudan); Ghana, Guinea and Nigeria in 1963; Africa again in 1970 (for the *Oresteia* film); and Israel and Jordan in 1963 (when he was planning to film *The Gospel According To Matthew* in the Holy Land).

When Pier Paolo Pasolini and his writer chums Alberto Moravia and Elsa Morante visited India in December, 1960, it wasn't for a particular film or book project (tho' a book, *The Scent of India,* duly appeared, as well as a short documentary later, *Notes For a Film In India,*1969).

---

[24] Pasolini's beloved Friuli was in the North, of course, but not grouped with the North for Pasolini – it was beyond-the-North.

PASOLINI THE POET

Was Pier Paolo Pasolini a believer or a non-believer? In what? – in God? Love? Death? Art? Life? Terms like belief, or atheism, or agnosticism, or non-belief, just don't do justice to Pasolini's multi-faceted personality and works. The man and his art were much more complicated than that (also, there are many levels of 'belief', and ways of 'believing').

Pier Paolo Pasolini was a mass of contradictions only to the extent that many (most?) humans are contradictory. Can a Marxist believe in God? What is the relation between Marxism and materialism to religion and the spirit? These and many other questions have been discussed in relation to Pasolini. As he put it in 1966:

> If you know that I am an unbeliever, then you know me better than I do myself. I may be an unbeliever, but I am an unbeliever who has a nostalgia for a belief.

You only have to look at a couple of movies directed by Pier Paolo Pasolini to see there is a wealth of romance, nostalgia, spirituality, desire and yearning. What was Pasolini's 'religion'? What did he 'believe in'?

Poetry.

If there *are* contradictions, that's because Pier Paolo Pasolini was certainly a contradictory personality. Like Orson Welles, Rainer Fassbinder, Jean-Luc Godard and Andrei Tarkovsky (among filmmakers), Pasolini was a complex person – no single view, no one opinion, no philosophy on its own can sum him up, or condense his views into a coherent whole. (Indeed, every single biographical sketch online, in documentaries, books and newspapers always stresses the seemingly contradictory elements of the Pasolini Legend: religion plus Marxism plus homosexuality plus radical cinema, etc etc etc etc etc).

If there's one single word I would use for Pier Paolo Pasolini, it is poetry. He poeticizes life, poeticizes the world and everything in it. 'To make films is to be a poet', he asserted (PP, 154). 'Pasolini's defence of poetry was a political act of complete committment' (S. Rohdie, 89). Poetry and the poet's life sums up many aspects of Pasolini's personality, and also his approach to art, and to cinema, but it doesn't crystallize everything. With Pasolini, you are always aware of depths and levels below the surface. He may talk a lot in interviews, he may appear forthcoming and affable on camera in interviews (or as the interviewer in his own movies, when he won't shut up or let the interviewee get a word in edgeways), but there are whole oceans of things you don't know about, whole continents where acts, thoughts, ideas and gestures are hidden, or will never be found out, and as everybody who knew Pasolini personally eventually dies as the years pass, we won't know.

With Pier Paolo Pasolini, the legend has become enormous, and of course Pasolini fed it no end in his lifetime, as with filmmakers such as Orson Welles, Alfred Hitchcock, Ken Russell, Jean-Luc Godard and Werner Herzog. Those filmmakers liked nothing better than talking about themselves and their work. There should be a sub-category of film directors who luxuriate in their own eccentricities, in rattling out the same stories and anecdotes. The brief moments of self-deprecation (Ingmar Bergman, Woody Allen, Andrei Tarkovsky, Steven Spielberg) don't fool us for a moment.

In Enzo Siciliano's 1978 biography, Pier Paolo Pasolini comes across as a *very* complex individual: he was a mass of contradictions. Nothing could be simple with Pasolini. There were always a number of levels to consider at the same time.

Pier Paolo Pasolini's relationship with his father Carlo Alberto Pasolini was ambiguous, anxious and filled with conflicting emotions. Pasolini spoke of loving his father until his was three years-old; then came a crisis, and he fell out of love, forever. It was during the time that Susanna was pregnant with Pasolini's brother Guido. What exactly happened isn't clear; certainly it is a classic case of oedipal rebellion, with the father as the erotic rival with the boy for the mother's love (it may have been the Freudian primal scene, Enzo Siciliano wondered, of stumbling upon his parents making love in the kitchen). And it is also a (jealous) rivalry with the younger brother.

There's no need to explore the love-hate relation with the father and the Law of the Father in P.P. Pasolini's art here, because it's plastered all over his films and his poetry. Pasolini's movies are in part a psychoanalytical investigation into the relationship with the father figure. The movies are their own therapy, their own psychoanalytical cases. The depictions of fathers and the Sins of the Fathers is so obvious it doesn't require any gloss here.

Ditto with his mother – there's no need to explore Pier Paolo Pasolini's relation with his beloved mother, Susanna Colussi Pasolini. That Pasolini adored his mom comes over strongly in his poetry and cinema.

> The mark which has dominated all my work is this longing for life, this sense of exclusion, which doesn't lessen but augments this love of life. (Interview in a documentary, late 1960s)

PASOLINI AND RELIGION

> I suffer from the nostalgia of a peasant-type religion, and that is why I am on the side of the servant. But I do not believe in a metaphysical god. I am religious because I have a natural identification between reality and God. Reality is divine. That is why my films are never naturalistic. The motivation that unites all of my films is to give back to reality its original sacred significance.
>
> Pier Paolo Pasolini (1968)

Whatever he may have said in interviews or written in essays and poetry, Pier Paolo Pasolini was certainly fascinated by many aspects of religion and Catholicism. The imagery and themes of Catholicism, for instance, run throughout his movies – and not because he was Italian, or because he was brought up amongst Catholicism.

You can think of Pier Paolo Pasolini's 'religion' as being poetry; but even here, the crossovers between religion and poetry are numerous, and have been explored by 1,000s of commentators. Enzo Siciliano called Pasolini 'a profoundly religious man, but in his religion the vocative "God" was absent' (ES, 396).

As commentators have noted, Pier Paolo Pasolini's religious faith wasn't in Catholicism, it was in Communism. For him, Communism was natural, inevitable, essential, a way of looking at the world that explained (and fed) his nostalgia for the peasant world, his dissatisfaction with modern life, his hatred of advanced capitalism, his sympathy with the under-class, and his distrust of authority. And there was a social aspect to Communist politics for Pasolini: it brought him together with intellectuals, of course, but he also 'frequented the dance halls on the "red" outskirts of the city' (as Enzo Siciliano explained [162]). Pasolini continued to vote for the Partito Comunista Italiano (Italian Communist Party) and contribute to its publications (though his relationship with the Partito Comunista Italiano was troubled at times).

Of course, being an intellectual and highly educated observer, Pier Paolo Pasolini was inevitably highly critical of the Church, but he was also intrigued by many issues that the Church was linked to. Social control, and State authority, for instance, or issues such as morality and sexual ethics, or the role that Catholicism had in the political and social formation of young people. (And of course, Pasolini was steeped in Catholic art, to the point where it would have probably been absolutely impossible for him to eradicate all traces of that cultural absorption).

In 1971, he said:

> The Church will probably be able to continue for centuries to come if it creates an ecclesiastic assembly that continually negates and re-creates itself. My criticism is against the Church as power as it is today. I said that when I was a boy I believed, I prayed… but it wasn't anything very serious. I think there're some facets in my character that have something of a mystifying quality. I'd say this is a part of the trauma that dominates my existence. Nature doesn't seem natural to me, it is a sort of an act between me and the naturalness of nature. (1971)

Whether Pier Paolo Pasolini personally 'believed' or not is not the issue, is not important, and is not even interesting. It's what Pasolini *did* with those beliefs or non-beliefs that's valuable, it's how Pasolini engaged with institutions such as religion, Catholicism, the State, education, Communism, Marxism, and capitalism that's interesting. But even those big issues are not especially compelling on their own, unless, at least for commercial cinema, they are combined with or put into drama, fiction, stories and characters.

'Christianity was part of his moral reasoning, the part that obliged him to interrogate himself (albeit in the guise of a country priest) on the unrelenting demands of the body', Enzo Siciliano noted, *pace Amado Mio* (121).

Pier Paolo Pasolini said he tended to see the world in too reverential, too childlike terms – if he had any religion, he remarked, it would be a vague mystical response to the world (including objects and nature as well as people [PP, 14]).

PASOLINI THE OUTSIDER

The feeling of not fitting in anywhere in the modern world can be found throughout Pier Paolo Pasolini's writings and films (and it makes his work appealing to modern audiences). You can see how Pasolini would be right at home in the Middle Ages (as an assistant to Dante Alighieri or Giotto, say, or in the Ancient Roman world, as a poet rival to, say, Petronius or Ovid) – yet, even here, Pasolini would probably still feel that he didn't fit in, would still have that consuming, near-tragic experience of otherness. Pasolini is an exile in his own life, where his poems and films offer a commentary, a layer, a musing on the discontinuities between his life and his art, his life and his heart, his life and his relationships.

We are all exiles, says French philosopher Julia Kristeva. Her experience of displacement (from her homeland of Bulgaria) was an ingredient in her notion of the 'cosmopolitan' individual, the 'intellectual dissident'. As Kristeva knew, strangeness or otherness (being a foreigner) is fundamental to being human: as Kristeva put it, *étrangers à nous-mêmes* (we are strangers to ourselves).[25]

Some of the forerunners of Pier Paolo Pasolini's lifestyle, which combined outsider status, an eccentric and highly individual cultural trajectory, and a homosexual lifestyle, included Oscar Wilde and André Gide. A touchstone for Pasolini, Gide (1869-1951) was cited by Pasolini as an important influence. Easy to see why: early Gide works such as *The Immoralist* and *Fruits of the Earth* are like early Pasolini movies,[26] with their Existentialist, outsider protagonists, their fashionable (French) avant gardism, their depictions of older, white, European guys falling for young, Arab boys (plus the inevitable guilt and post-coital self-loathing), their Catholic/ post-Catholic *milieu,* their high culture and literary allusions, and their enshrinement of the poetry of being alive.

If you enjoy Pier Paolo Pasolini's movies, you will love André Gide's novels (and vice versa). As Pasolini was a 'filmmaker's filmmaker' (like Orson Welles, F.W. Murnau or Sergei Paradjanov), so Gide was very much a 'writer's writer' (as with Rainer Maria Rilke, Francesco Petrarch or Samuel Beckett). C.P. Cavafy, the 20th century Greek poet of lyrical, homoerotic nostalgia, is another reference point for Pier Paolo Pasolini (there are numerous affinities between the two).

PASOLINI THE ICONOCLAST

A controversial figure even today, Pier Paolo Pasolini had run-ins with the Italian authorities many times (he was brought to trial on several occasions). His works were condemned for their blasphemy and obscenity. An early encounter with the authorities occurred when he was accused of pædophilia and homosexuality – with the Ramuscello boys in

---

25 In *Strangers to Ourselves,* Julia Kristeva describes the foreigner as the 'cold orphan', motherless, a 'devotee of solitude', a 'fanatic of absence', alone even in a crowd, arrogant, rejected, yet oddly happy (4-5). The stranger is always in motion, doesn't belong anywhere, to 'any time, any love' (7).
26 *The Immoralist* is ideal for the Pasolinian treatment. Indeed, *Theorem* has the feel of *The Immoralist.*

Casarsa. It was this incident that partly encouraged Pasolini to leave Bologna and to live in Rome (see below).

Altho' critics and admirers found some of Pier Paolo Pasolini's writing and movie-making extreme, it wasn't, compared to some authors: William Burroughs, Marco Vassi, Henry Miller, or even Paul Bowles.

There's no doubt that part of Pier Paolo Pasolini enjoyed shocking people, or simply winding them up – he did it in his newspaper articles, in his poetry, in his movies, and in his documentaries. And he succeeded many times: the number of controversies that Pasolini was involved with is very high – compared to most of his contemporaries (either in literature or cinema). Things seemed to happen to Pasolini.

> Wholly a man of his time [wrote Enzo Siciliano], he chose to live in the enemy camp, launching polemics and accusations, pushing his intolerable personal situation to the point of paradox, and not troubling himself about anything else. (ES, 399-400)

Pier Paolo Pasolini saw himself as something of an outsider in Italian culture, a 'disturber of the peace', someone whose contributions were unwanted. Yes – but that didn't stop Pasolini pouring out pronouncements and movies and poems and books! Pasolini wasn't going to hurry home, slam the door and vow never to talk to the press or anyone else again for the rest of his life! He was not someone who could keep quiet. (Instead, Pasolini glorified in attention of all kinds: he was one of those filmmakers who revel in the attention – look at his interviews – you see the same enjoyment of adulation in Orson Welles, in Jean-Luc Godard, in Steve Spielberg, in Francis Coppola, etc).

Pier Paolo Pasolini was involved in a brawl in Rome, at nighttime in a rough part of the city (Via di Panico). The case came to trial on Nov 15, 1961 (around the time that *Accattone* opened in cinemas). Pasolini was charged with 'aiding and abetting', but was fully acquitted.[27] Enzo Siciliano speaks of this period as having 'a climate of persecution', when 'hysteria grew around the public figure of Pasolini' (248).

Yet another brush with the law occurred when Pier Paolo Pasolini was accused of holding up a gas station with a gun (!). The accusations came from Bernardino De Santis, a boy working at the garage, who said that Pasolini had used a black pistol to hold up the garage. The trial took place in Latina on July 3, 1962. (Once again, Pasolini's defence used the concept of research – Pasolini often defended himself by saying that he

---

[27] According to Laura Betti in the *Who Says the Truth Shall Die* documentary, Pasolini was accused some 33 times of different crimes but he was always acquitted. Yet the Italian press kept going after him.

was researching places and people for future projects). Further scandals are noted below.

Few Italian artists in the same era were attacked and criticized more than Pasolini. 'Pasolini remained uninterruptedly in the hand of judges from 1960 to 1975', as Stefano Rodotà put it in *Pasolini: Judicial Report, Persecution, Death* (1977). Magazines and newspapers such as *Il Borghese, Oggi, Gente* and *Lo Specchio* regularly slandered him. Among Pasolini's loudest critics were Maria Predassi (writing as Gianna Preda) and Giose Rimanelli (writing as A.G. Solari).

But why? asked Wu Ming in a 2016 article:

> Why such a persecution? Because he was homosexual? He was certainly not the only one amongst artists and writers. Because he was homosexual and communist? Yes, but this isn't enough either. Because he was homosexual, communist and expressed himself openly against the bourgeoisie, government, Christian Democracy, fascists, judges and police? Yes, this is enough. It would have been enough anywhere, let alone in Italy, and in that Italy.

PASOLINI AND HOMOSEXUALITY: THE PERCEPTION OF PASOLINI'S IDENTITY

It's striking how many commentators on the work of Pier Paolo Pasolini mention his sexual identity (i.e., his homosexuality). As if they are now professional, psychoanalytical experts on sexuality and gender (almost all critics are not). There is something patronizing about this, as well as something of the tabloid journalist's pig's nose for snuffling out sensationalism (yes, and the bastard was gay, too!). As if to be gay is automatically to be weird, 'other', or perverted.

Every frigging biographical sketch I've read about Pier Paolo Pasolini mentions his sexuality. Yes, even those critics who are supposed to be (1) intellectual, (2) well-read, and (3) critical/ perceptive. And they often depict Pasolini's sexual preferences as 'dark', or exotic, or odd. Were they? And how can anybody know?! Why is his sexual identity seen as such a big deal? Hell, maybe Pasolini just liked sex! As Spike Milligan said: 'people like to fuck'.

The issue of homosexuality in relation to Pasolini's media persona is very minor compared to his public critiques and attacks on institutions such as the Christian Democrat party in Italy, on the bourgeoisie, on consumer capitalism, etc.

There are so many assumptions and damaging views in the way that the personality of Pier Paolo Pasolini has been discussed. However, it's true that in some respects the media image of Pier Paolo Pasolini conforms to the stereotype of the ageing homosexual who preys upon boys. Many observers have attested to that, how, according to the Pasolini Legend, he would go out night after night in search of rough trade (often in one of his sports cars). Boys that hung around the Termini railroad station in the centre of Roma, or in the *borgate*, or the bathhouses along the River Tiber (such as the Ciriola below Castel Sant' Angelo).[28] Boys that wouldn't be brought back home, because home meant his beloved Mamma. (His preference was for *ragazzi* with a roguish smile, curly hair on their foreheads, plenty of vitality, and often a reputation as bad boys, as petty criminals).[29]

Famous filmmakers who were homosexual include F.W. Murnau, Jean Cocteau, Andy Warhol, Rainer Werner Fassbinder, Kenneth Anger, George Cukor, James Whale, and more recently, James Ivory, Joel Schumacher, and Pasolini's fellow Italians Luchino Visconti and Franco Zeffirelli (also, Visconti and Zeffirelli didn't, as with Pasolini, hide their sexual identity[30]).

Discussing the idea of the romantic couple in 1970, Pasolini pointed out that societies reject what challenges the norms and the rules – and that includes homosexuality:

> Homosexuality is a threat to society. It is inconceivable in any organisms or community, no matter how free. (1970)

Enzo Siciliano in his biography portrays Pier Paolo Pasolini as someone tormented by his passions, his predilections for young, raw boys. 'Pasolini lived in the torment of not being able to give it [his eros] what it demanded of him. And the demand was obscure, indeed dark and nocturnal' (ES, 391).

In 1948, Pier Paolo Pasolini described his homosexuality as something other:

---

[28] Pier Paolo Pasolini was sometimes accompanied by his friend Sandro Penna: they had a joky contest over who could tup the most boys.
[29] In Great Britain, in legal history, male homosexuality has been the subject of several laws, including the law on sodomy of 1533 (in Henry VIII's reign), the 1861 and 1885 laws on sodomy and gross indecency; the 1898 Vagrancy Act, the Sexual Offences Act of 1967, and the Criminal Justice Bill of 1991 (however, lesbianism has been largely invisible and unacknowledged).
[30] However, Visconti and Zeffirelli didn't loudly criticize the State, the Church and other Italian institutions like Pasolini.

> I was born to be calm, balanced, natural: my homosexuality was something added, it lay outside, it had nothing to do with me. I've always seen it as something beside me like an enemy, I've never felt it to be within me.

Pier Paolo Pasolini revered the rugged, working class *ragazzi* of Rome, Calabria and Friuli, but however much he liked to hang around with them (and have sex with them), he was never one of them. Pasolini was always the intellectual, always the poet, always the guy who wrote newspapers columns and directed movies. He was never a street kid, was never one of the tough, poor *ragazzi* that he liked to cruise at night.

For some observers, Pier Paolo Pasolini was the classic predatory homosexual, the older, gay man who takes to exploring the streets of cities and towns at night looking for willing youths to share the momentary pleasures of sex. It was a habit that Pasolini found hard to break: he enjoyed the danger of it, as well as the ecstasy (he would return from his secretive nighttime jaunts battered and bruised sometimes). According to Enzo Siciliano, most times the erotic encounters consisted of fellatio and masturbation.

Sometimes Pier Paolo Pasolini had to be rescued from his nightly adventures, sore and bleeding (producer Alfredo Bini and production manager Eliseo Boschi would respond to telephone calls to go get Pasolini from some nocturnal spree that'd turned sour – in Africa and the Middle East as well as in Rome). 'I'm leading not a violent but an extremely violent life', Pasolini wrote in a letter of Oct 5, 1959 (ES, 141).

Pier Paolo Pasolini did have heterosexual experiences. One was with a young mother from Viterbo. Another was with a girl at the beach. Another was with Mariella Bauzano in the early 1950s. And as a kid Pasolini had flirted with girls (and referred to them in his letters). However, Enzo Siciliano wondered if some of these 'girls' were in fact boys (ES, 52).

There were also a number of social and criminal scandals, some of which involved under-age youths and sexuality – which were linked to Pasolini's homosexual practices.

When he was 19, Pier Paolo Pasolini was accused by a neighbourhood child's father of pederasty, when he offered the child some ice cream (this occurred in Bologna in 1941). Pasolini insisted that his intentions were innocent.

One of the biggest scandals in Pier Paolo Pasolini's life, and one which changed the course of his life, occurred in 1949 in Casarsa (his home), when Pasolini (then 27) was overheard talking to some 16 year-old lads in Ramuscello (outside of San Vito al Tagliamento). What happened with the boys at Ramuscello ('probably mutual masturbation', Enzo Siciliano reckoned [135]), which Pasolini had enjoyed (he called it an unforgettable evening), became public when complaints were made to the *carabineri*. In December, 1950, the court acquitted Pasolini of the charges of corrupting minors, but he was convicted of committing lewd acts. In April, 1952, the appeals court absolved Pasolini due to insufficient evidence (ES, 135).

Pier Paolo Pasolini trotted out a defence he used again in later scandals a few times: he was conducting research for a novel, he claimed: 'I was trying an erotic and literary experiment, under the influence of a book I had been reading'. Even if he cited a big cultural name like André Gide, it seems a pretty flimsy excuse.

Pier Paolo Pasolini's erotic encounter with the Ramuscello boys had other repercussions – such as Pasolini's ousting from the Communist Party, which he found very upsetting (he revered Communism). Pasolini lost his teaching job (as well as the financial security it brought).

The scandal tore into Pier Paolo Pasolini's family – his father went ballistic, raging all night about his son, and his mother locked herself in her room ('Yesterday morning my mother almost went out of her mind, my father is in an unbearable state – I heard him weeping and moaning all night', Pasolini wrote to Ferdinando Mautino). To a friend called over for solace, Giuseppe Zigaina, Pasolini confessed he wanted to kill himself (ES, 137). It was the repercussions of this event that precipitated the move to Roma with his mother, where he remained for the rest of his life.

The pattern of this early scandal of 1949 – Pier Paolo Pasolini preying upon young boys, the social intolerance of homosexuality it evoked, and Pasolini's intellectual defence of his actions – would be repeated a few times in his life.

Another incident involving young boys occurred on July 10, 1960, in Anzio, when Pier Paolo Pasolini was thought to have propositioned some boys in the harbour (the parents of the boys filed a complaint). One of the striking aspects about the career of Pier Paolo Pasolini is that he didn't give up in the face of several scandals.

HOMOSEXUALITY IN PASOLINI'S CINEMA

Critics have noted that although he was a gay filmmaker, homosexuality is not often portrayed in Pier Paolo Pasolini's cinema. Well, there are obvious instances, such as the condemned, male homosexuals in the witchhunting sequence in *The Canterbury Tales*, where one of the victims is publicly burnt to death (while an older one buys himself out), and in *Theorem,* homosexual relationships are explored in more depth (but in *Theorem* the homosexuality is with a visitor who is part-god, part-devil – not an 'average' relationship at all!).

But when you look closer, there are further levels of homosexual elements in Pier Paolo Pasolini's cinema. The preponderance of male brotherhoods, for instance, of men being men together, which you can see in *The Canterbury Tales*, *The Decameron*, *Accattone* and, yes, in *The Gospel According To Matthew*. The homosocial relationships are right in the foreground from Pasolini's debut (*Accattone*) onwards. Indeed, *Accattone* is a very gay movie from that perspective (even down to the way that women are treated – their maltreatment further bolsters the homosocial bonds of the guys).

And look at the way that Pier Paolo Pasolini includes so many rough and ready youths in his movies (the *ragazzi* of his 1950s novels), and how the camera lingers over them at length. Pasolini is very fond of close-ups of young *ragazzi* smiling into the camera, as part of the conventional shot-reverse-shot editing pattern of cinema, yes, but the amount of screen time given over to close-ups of attractive, macho young men is very striking.

Brotherhoods and male bonding are fundamental to many other filmmakers' work – it's central to Westerns, to the crime and gangster genres, to the war genre, to action cinema, and is a key element in the cinema of Sam Peckinpah, Howard Hawks, John Woo, Ringo Lam, Martin Scorsese, Francis Coppola, etc etc.

I'm reminded of Michelangelo Merisi da Caravaggio,[31] probably *the* painter (at least in Italy), of beautiful, tough, young men. The homosexuality of Caravaggio is another aspect, of course, but in terms of the art itself, Caravaggio's work is certainly a forerunner of this element in Pier Paolo Pasolini's cinema. And the other artist is of course Michelangelo Buonarroti, the towering genius of the Renaissance, who made the male nude the most sublime, erotic thing you've ever seen (visit the

---

[31] Other writers have noted the affinities between Pier Paolo Pasolini and Caravaggio: Cesare Garboli drew attention to the similarities, with the art historian Roberto Longhi as the intermediary (Longhi had organized an important exhibition of Caravaggio in Milan in 1951).

Musée de Louvre to see the *Dying Slave* sculptures, truly orgasmic works of art).

And Pier Paolo Pasolini and his crews did film many men nude. Within the context of heterosexual encounters, that male nudity has a justification. And Pasolini was unusual among many film directors is putting an equal amount of male nudity on screen as female nudity in love scenes (male actors can be more reluctant to disrobe completely – and of course, there are double standards in most cinema, where an actor will stay partially clad, while an actress is fully naked).

As well as nudity,[32] Pier Paolo Pasolini and the camera teams also focussed on the male genitals. In *The Arabian Nights* there are quite a few close-ups of genitals (as well as the usual thrusting butts of heterosexual cinema in sex scenes). *The Arabian Nights* probably contains the most male nudity in Pasolini's cinema, along with *Salò*.

Despite the beauty of Pasolini's imagery, his exaltation of bodies (and men in particular), there isn't much erotic pleasure in some of his works, and sexuality is tied, via his personality, 'to a realm of suffering' which 'inflects his work with melancholy and morbidity', according to Gary Indiana (16).

Pasolini identified with the victim, not the perpetrator, some observed; his masochism was to sympathize with the down-trodden – in Italia, that meant the sub-proletariat (Pasolini invested his social hopes in the sub-proletariat).

Feminists have discussed the male gaze (voyeurism, the look, etc), and wondered if there can be a female gaze in cinema. That there is a homosexual, lesbian, queer and bisexual gaze – or, I would prefer to call it a multi-sexual gaze (why stop at two or three genders?) – is clear from the films of Pier Paolo Pasolini, Walerian Borowczyk and Ken Russell.

I'm not talking about the sexual preferences of the filmmakers, but of the gaze, the looks, the desire and the structure of their works. For example, although Ken Russell, Francis Coppola, Martin Scorsese, Bernardo Bertolucci and Michael Powell were heterosexual (at least according to their autobiographies and colleagues and wives and girl-friends), some of their works are supremely gay, queer, lesbian and homosexual.

Pier Paolo Pasolini, though, was not particularly interested in fore-grounding that aspect of his personality in his cinema. What does come across, though, and very strongly, is the aspect of *desire*. Sexual desire, desire for life. Which's often intensely romantic and poetic, sometimes

---

[32] Nobody can miss the fact that Pier Paolo Pasolini's last four films are jammed with nudity and sex. (And also in *Theorem* and *Pigsty*).

nostalgic, sometimes ironic, sometimes masochistic, and sometimes vitriolic.

The most unbridled expression of desire in Pier Paolo Pasolini's work occurs in the three 'life' movies, 1971, 1972 and 1974. But the desire on display is nearly all heterosexual (*Salò* explores desire within an eccentric, S/M environment).

PASOLINI CRITICISM

A huge amount of articles, essays and books have appeared about the works of Pier Paolo Pasolini, focussing on his poetry, his novels, his essays/ statements and his movies. In short, Pasolini has been taken *very* seriously, with critics and journos assuming that he is an important figure with significant things to say. I would imagine that Pasolini himself would be stunned, delighted, and perhaps embarrassed by the number of pieces written about his work, and how he has been placed in the same company as many of his cultural heroes.

I would recommend, as the first point of call, the amazing biography by Enzo Siciliano (sadly out of print). Among the studies of Pier Paolo Pasolini's films, Sam Rohdie, B. Babington, Pamela Grace, Philip Kolker, John Orr, A. Pavelin, and Gary Indiana are useful.

There are far fewer biographies of Pier Paolo Pasolini in print than one might think. In fact, for years no biographies have been in print in English. The biography by Enzo Siciliano, *Pasolini,* published in 1978 by Rizzoli (in Italian), is among the finest (it was translated in 1982, and published in 1987). Retrospectives of Pasolini's work were mounted at the Museum of Modern Art in 2012 and the British Film Institute in 2013.

Enzo Siciliano concentrates very much on Pier Paolo Pasolini the public figure in Italian cultural life, and on Pasolini's poetry: there is far less in his biography on Pasolini's cinema, for instance, than on Pasolini's poems (Siciliano quotes from the poetry at length). Siciliano also employs the poems in a problematic manner: to illustrate Pasolini's thoughts and even some of his experiences. Assessing and explaining someone's life through their poetry is full of difficulties, filled with assumptions about what poetry is, how it works, how poets write poems, and how poetry relates to the poet's life.

In short, poetry is not autobiography, or documentary, or history. Very often it has no relation to the poet's life whatsoever. Robert Graves called poetry a 'spiritual autobiography', but even that is not always the case.

With Pier Paolo Pasolini, however, some of his poems definitely do reflect upon his experiences, and many poems do express his own views. But it's still a very stylized, literary kind of mirror, reflecting back only what the poet chooses.

Pier Paolo Pasolini has been discussed widely in cinema circles, but when you look into it, there are far fewer really good books about Pasolini's cinema than one might expect (certainly compared to contemporaries such as Jean-Luc Godard or Orson Welles). And many of the best studies are now out of print (including Enzo Siciliano's essential biography).

In studies of the cinema of Pier Paolo Pasolini's cinema, the context and the references tend to be Neo-realism, and to that select band of Italian filmmakers who have been exported and critically revered: Fellini, Rossellini, Visconti, Antonioni, de Sica, Bertolucci, etc.

Sure – those are the great artists of Italian cinema of the 1950s to 1970s. But they are not really representative of Italian cinema of that era. Rather, cinema in Italy of the 50s through 70s was a thriving industry of remakes, sequels, rip-offs, exploitation movies, *mondo* movies, populist comedies (hugely popular), *James Bond* cash-ins, and endless genre movies (Spaghetti Westerns, *gialli* (horror/ thriller), crime, erotica, and of course the *peplum/* sword & sandal movies), plus the many visiting productions from North America (resulting in the 'Hollywood On the Tiber' cycle). If a movie – from anywhere – was successful, Italian cinema dived in and had a cash-in movie filmed and released within weeks (same with the Hong Kong film business).

We don't think of Pasolini as a director of sequels and franchises, but he *did* sequelize his own movies: *Mamma Roma* follows up *Accattone*, *The Hawks and the Sparrows* led to further collaborations with Totò (in the short films for anthologies, and a feature-length sequel to *The Hawks and the Sparrows* was planned), *Medea* is a follow-up to *Oedipus Rex,* and the 'trilogy of life' pictures can be regarded as a film series.

Pier Paolo Pasolini distanced himself from Neo-realist cinema; while Neo-realism was dead in Italy, it had migrated to England and France, Pasolini noted (PP, 137). He didn't like the British version of the New Wave at all (very few Europeans did!), tho' of course he greatly admired

Jean-Luc Godard.

Inevitably, Pasolini would be critical of Neo-realist cinema and distance himself from it (as Federico Fellini and Bernardo Bertolucci did), partly because we know that Pasolini (and Fellini and Bertolucci) didn't like being part of a group, or being pigeon-holed and labelled.

However, Pasolini, like Fellini, certainly employed some of the formal approaches of Neo-realism (even if he denied using them): in her 2005 essay on *Rome: Open City*, Marcia Landy listed some of the styles and subjects of Neo-realist cinema:

> a predominant use of location shooting, deep-focus and long-take photography, non-professional actors, a loose form of narration, and a documentary look, plus in the intermingling of fiction and nonfiction, the privileging of marginal and subaltern groups, and a focus on contemporary situations. (J. Geiger, 404)

The decline of the Neo-realist form of cinema coincided with the changes in Italian society after WWII. As David Cook explained in *A History of Narrative Film*:

> In practice, it was a cinema of poverty and pessimism firmly rooted in the immediate postwar period. When times changed and economic conditions began to improve, neorealism lost first its ideological basis, then its subject matter. (453)

Another factor was the Andreotti Law, instituted in response to the glut of North American movies in Italy in 1949. The Andreotti Law taxed imported films and promoted home-grown products. (Several European nations have attempted to control American cultural imports and promote their national arts).

CRITICS ON PASOLINI

For David A. Cook (in *A History of Narrative Film*), at his best Pier Paolo Pasolini 'succeeded in creating an intellectual cinema in which metaphor, myth, and narrative form all subserved materialist ideology' (1990, 633).

Gary Indiana described Pasolini as:

> Indefatigably productive, ingenious, exasperating, narcisstically didactic, slyly self-promoting, abject, generous, exploitative, devoted to the wretched of the earth with honest fervor and deluded romanticism...

Pierre Leprohon, in one of the standard books on Italian cinema (1972), was suspicious of the merits of Pier Paolo Pasolini's work: 'originality, violence, controversiality and a taste for (often confused) symbols', Leprohon asserted, with anachronistic music, and it's deliberately, irritatingly mystifying (207).

For David Thomson (an idiosyncratic and not always reliable film critic), Pier Paolo Pasolini's films weren't up to the level of his theories and poetry: there was too much portentousness in Pasolini's imagery, Thomson reckoned, adding:

> His strident compositions were clumsy and monotonous, and his appetite for faces often overrode the ability to edit shots together fluently. The style was top-heavy, just as the meanings of his films were too literary, too immediate, and too inconsistent. (1995, 575-6)

Of course I don't agree with any of that. 'Monotonous'?! Hardly. And why is being 'too immediate' a problem? But you could agree that some of the imagery and the *mise-en-scène* didn't match up with the grand themes and issues, that sometimes the imagery is too grandiose for the stories and the characters (or vice versa).

THE DEATH OF PIER PAOLO PASOLINI

> How would I define myself? It's like asking the definition of infinity. There's an interior infinity and an exterior infinity. When I think of myself, I think of something infinite. It's impossible to define myself. For you I'm definable but for me I'm infinite. I'm the mirror of exterior infinity, it's impossible for me to define myself. I could create... some slogans, a few funny things in conversations, in salons, perhaps... I could quote something Elsa Morante said about me: "I'm a narcissistic individual who has a happy love of myself." I must add that I have an unhappy love for the world. Or maybe, I could say I'm a true devil, not a false devil like Sanguineti or the *avant garde* writers.
>
> Pier Paolo Pasolini (1966)

The death of Pier Paolo Pasolini at age 53 has loomed large in his legend (as with the deaths of figures such as Marilyn Monroe, Jim Morrison, Jimi Hendrix and Bruce Lee). The details are still shrouded in mystery and controversy. No one knows precisely what happened, or will confess the truth. (It does seem as if some people *do* know who was responsible, but refuse to say). Anyway, nobody can agree exactly what went on that fateful night of November 1-2, 1975.

Some of the events of the night of Nov 1 and Nov 2, 1975 are agreed upon: that Pier Paolo Pasolini picked up the 17 year-old hustler Giuseppe Pelosi in Rome; that they ate in a restaurant; and that they drove in Pasolini's sports car to Ostia (a typical evening for Pasolini, thus far).

After that, there are many versions of what happened. That Pasolini was beaten and run over by his own car seems certain.

Other details of the murder have come to light:
- the green sweater that didn't belong to Pasolini in the car;
- the bloody handprint on the roof of the car;
- that witnesses claimed they saw at least one motorbike and possibly a car following Pasolini's vehicle;
- that a skinny kid could not have killed the bigger, athletic Pasolini;
- that Pelosi didn't have any blood on him;
- that the damage sustained by Pasolini was far beyond what Pelosi could have inflicted;
- that, if other people were involved, the murder seems inept;
- that the motives are obscure – for Giuseppe Pelosi, but also for other groups (such as a local gang).

Giuseppe Pelosi confessed to Pier Paolo Pasolini's murder (and was duly imprisoned). Pelosi claimed that Pasolini had proposed things that he didn't want to do (including, preposterously, sodomy with a wooden stake). Pelosi's motives for the murder have never been explained satisfactorily.

In 2005, Giuseppe Pelosi retracted his confession, which he claimed had been made due to threats to his family. Pelosi gave more names in 2008.

Several high profile members of Italian society have asked that the case be re-opened, including former mayors and lawyers, as well as journalists.

When the case was re-opened in 2005, Sergio Citti, Pier Paolo Pasolini's long-time lover and colleague, said that Pasolini had been going to meet someone who had stolen reels of the film *Salò* (with a view to extorting money). Others have also reckoned that film canisters stolen on Aug 27, 1975 from the Technicolor lab in Rome might've been involved (as well as *Salò*, some of the negatives of *Casanova* were taken – 74 cans of film. Some have suggested that the thieves mistook the negatives of *Salò* for those from *Casanova*. Producer Alberto Grimaldi (he was producing both films) refused to pay the thieves the half a billion Lire they demanded).

The extortion scenario doesn't make total sense – not least because it's the producers, the production companies and the studios who control the money in the film industry, not directors. Also, killing someone means you won't get the money you're extorting. That Pasolini would go to meet some small-time crooks intent on extracting some Lire out of him at night in a lonely spot like Ostia seems unconvincing.

Several theories have been proposed for the death of Pier Paolo Pasolini. That he irritated some groups (and institutions) is well-known – that his views were not welcome in some quarters of Italian society; that he was known as a Marxist and Communist who criticized the social and political status quo; that he wrote articles published in Aug, 1975 which criticized Christian Democrats and other right-wing organizations for the decline of Italian society, etc. But then, many writers and artists have stirred up controversy (and some were louder and more outspoken than even Pasolini). And being a Communist in Italy is common (Pasolini remarked that everyone in Italy was a Catholic, and a Communist).

Anyway, one or more neo-fascist groups have been put forward as possible culprits, plus a local criminal gang (partly because witnesses said several people (perhaps five) murdered Pier Paolo Pasolini, not Giuseppe Pelosi on his own. Laura Betti and others have claimed that a car containing four people followed Pasolini's vehicle). Links have also been suggested between neo-fascist groups and the Italian secret services. (The neo-fascist connection makes sense – it was neo-fascist groups that caused trouble at screenings of Pasolini's films in the early 1960s. In a famous incident, Adriano Romualdi (son of the Member of Parliament Pino Romualdi), tried to run down some of Pasolini's friends outside the Casa dello Studente, Rome, in 1964).

For Bernardo Bertolucci and others, it was a kind of public execution, an over-the-top act of punishment, probably backed by conservative groups in Italy who wanted Pasolini silenced, or to make an example of him. Bertolucci wondered if the perpetrators even knew what they were doing, or if they knew of the real motives behind the murder they were hired to carry out.

The death of Pier Paolo Pasolini has provided plenty of speculation and gossip-mongering. Inevitably commentators refer to his homosexuality, to his habit of cruising or seeking out rough trade, to his apparent sadomasochism (even with suggestions of a kind of suicide), to the brutality of his last film, *Salò,* and so on. But the sex/ masochism angle, though sensational, isn't the whole story by any means.

With its combination of spectacle, sex and mystery, Pasolini's murder is a 500-word newspaper piece that writes itself. When you add in aspects such as conspiracy, or extortionists, or neo-fascist groups, or political organizations such as Christian Democrats, you have an explosive cocktail that damns segments of Italian society. Pretty much every piece on Pasolini mentions his sensational demise.

Even philosophers such as Julia Kristeva have had their say (in *Tales of Love*):

> Masochism, which, we are told, is essentially and originally feminine, is a submissiveness to the Phallus that the soulosexual knows well and can assume until death in order to become the "true" woman – passive, castrated, nonphallic – that his/ her mother was not. Mishima, mistaking himself for Saint Sebastian, and even Pasolini, allowing himself to be executed by a hoodlum on an Italian beach, carry to the limit the slavish moment of male eroticism appended to a deathful veneration of the Phallus. (78)

Pasolini on set:
with opera superstar Maria Callas during Medea (above).
And with Enrique Irazoqui during The Gospel (below).

Pasolini and Welles during Curd Cheese (1963).

3

THE WORKS OF PIER PAOLO PASOLINI

I love life fiercely, desperately... Love of life for me has become a more tenacious vice than cocaine. I devour my existence with an insatiable appetite.

Pier Paolo Pasolini[1]

Pier Paolo Pasolini directed thirteen feature films (one is a documentary), and also many shorter pieces, including contributions to anthology movies. His feature movies are:

Beggar (*Accattone*, 1961)
Mother Rome (*Mamma Rome*, 1962)
Love Meetings (a.k.a. *Lessons In Love* = *Comizi d'Amore*, 1964)
The Gospel According To Matthew (*Il Vangelo Secondo Matteo*, 1964)
The Hawks and the Sparrows (*Uccellacci e Uccellini*, 1966)
Oedipus Rex (*Edipo Re*, 1967)
Theorem (*Teorma*, 1968)
Pigsty (*Porcile*, 1969)
Medea (*Medea*, 1969)
The Decameron (*Il Decamerone*, 1971)
The Canterbury Tales (*I Racconti di Canterbury*, 1972)
The Arabian Nights (*Il Fiore Delle Mille e Una Notte*, 1974)

---

1 In L. Valentin, "Tête-à-Tête avec Pier Paolo Pasolini", *Lui*, April, 1970. Andrea Dworkin used that Pasolini quote – 'I love life so fiercely, so desperately' – in her novels.

Salò, or The 120 Days of Sodom (*Salò, o le Centoventi Giornate di Sodoma*, 1975)

Pier Paolo Pasolini's contributions to episode or anthology[2] movies are:

The Anger (*La Rabbia*, 1963)
Curd Cheese (*La Ricotta*, episode in *RoGoPaG*, 1963)
The Earth Seen From the Moon (*La Terra Vista Dalla Luna*, episode in *The Witches* = *Le Streghe*, 1967)
What Are the Clouds? (*Che Cosa Sono le Nuvole?*, episode in *Caprice Italian Style* = *Capriccio all'Italiana*, 1968)
The Sequence of the Flower Field (*La Sequenza del Fiore di Carta*, episode in *Love and Anger* = *Vangelo '70/ Amore e Rabbia*, 1969)

Pier Paolo Pasolini's shorter works include:

Location Hunting In Palestine (*Sopralluoghi in Palestina Per Il Vangelo Secondo Matteo*, 1965)
Notes For a Film In India (*Appunti Per un Film Sull'India*, 1969)
Notes For a Garbage Novel (*Appunti Per un romanzo dell'immondizia*, 1970)
Notes Towards an African Oresteia (*Appunti Per un'Orestiade Africana*, 1970)
The Walls of Sana'a (*Le Mura di Sana'a*, 1971)
12 December 1972 (*12 Dicembre 1972*, 1972)
Pasolini and the Shape of the City (*Pasolini e la forma della città*, 1975)

*

Pier Paolo Pasolini's 1955 novel *Ragazzi di vita* was adapted into a movie by Jacques-Laurent Bost and Pasolini: *La Notte Brava* (a.k.a. *Bad Girls Don't Cry*, a.k.a. *The Big Night*, Mauro Bolognini, 1959). It was produced by Antonio Cervi and Oreste Jacovini for Ajace Film and Franco-London Film. In the cast were: Rosanna Schiaffino, Laurent Terzieff, Jean-Claude Brialy, Franco Interlenghi, Antonella Lauldi, Mylène Demengeot and Elsa Martinelli.

A chapter from *Ragazzi di vita* was adapted in *La Canta dell Marane* (1960, dir. Cecilia Mangini). It was produced by Giorgio Patara.

---

2 Advantages for filmmakers with anthology movies included: they didn't have to originate them or raise the cash – the producer did all of that; they could be filmed in one or two weeks; they could dig out unmade ideas; they could write their own scripts or come up with their own ideas; and they often had more freedom than with a feature film.

Una Vita Violenta (*A Violent Life,* dirs. Paolo Heusch and Brunello Rondi) was adapted by Ennio De Concini, Franco Brusati, Paolo Heusch, Brunello Rondi and Franco Solinas in 1962. *A Violent Life* was produced by Aera Films/ Zebra Film.

*

Pier Paolo Pasolini worked on about 15 scripts b4 directing his first feature, *Accattone*, in 1961. As a screenwriter, Pasolini contributed to movies (working with many other writers) such as:

- *La Donna del Fiume* (1954, with 5 other writers: Bassani, Franchina, Vancini, Altovitti and Soldati),
- *Il Prigioniero della Montagna* (1955, with Trenker and Bassani),
- *Nights of Cabiria* (1956, alongside 3 other writers: Fellini, Flaiano and Pinnelli),
- *Marisa la Civetta* (1957, with 2 writers: Demby and Bolognini),
- *A Farewell To Arms* (1957, with Ben Hecht and John Huston),
- *Giovani Mariti* (1958, with 5 other writers: Currelli, Martino, Bolognini, Franciosa and Camanile),
- *La Notte Brava* (1959, with Jacques-Laurent Bost),
- *Marte di un Amico* (1960, with 5 other writers: Berto, Biancoli, Rossi, Guerra and Riganti),
- *I Bell'Antonio* (1960, with Brancati, Bolognini and Visentini),
- *La Lunga Notte del '43* (1960, with Bassani, Vancini and Concini),
- *La Giornata Balorda* (1960, with Moravia and Visconti),
- *Il Carro Armato dell'8 Settembre* (1960, with Baratti, Bertolini and Questi),
- *La Ragazza In Vetrina* (1961, with Cassuto, Emmer, Sonego, Martino and Marinucci),
- *The Grim Reaper* (1962, a.k.a. *La Commare Secca*,[3] with Citti and Bertolucci),

He also co-wrote with Sergio Citti the films *Ostia* (1970) and *Storie Scellerate* (1973), both of which Citti directed.

*

Pier Paolo Pasolini's books of poetry include:
Poesie e Casarsa (1942)
Diarii (1945)
Tal cour di un frut (1953/ 1974)

---

[3] Pier Paolo Pasolini had conceived *The Grim Reaper* (writing a five-page treatment), but decided to make *Mamma Roma* instead. Producer Antonio Cervi had bought the project from Pasolini, and decided to let Bernardo Bertolucci have a go at directing it, after seeing the script he had commissioned from Bertolucci and Sergio Citti. Bertolucci admitted that his first film as director (he was only 21), *The Grim Reaper*, was made very much in the Pasolinian mold.

La Meglio gioventù (1954)
Le Ceneri di Gramsci (1957)
L'Usignolo della chiesa cattolica (1958)
La Religione del mio tempo (1961)
Poesia in forma di rosa (1964)
Trasumanar e organizzar (1971)
La Nuova gioventù (1975)
and *Roman Poems* (1986)
Pier Paolo Pasolini's fiction and narratives include:
Amado Mio - Atti Impuri (1948/ 1982)
Ragazzi di vita (*The Ragazzi*, 1955)
Una Vita Violenta (*A Violent Life*, 1959)
A Dream of Something (1962)
Roman Nights and Other Stories (1965)
Reality (*The Poets' Encyclopedia*, 1979)
Petrolio (1992)

Pier Paolo Pasolini's volumes of essays and writings include: *Passione e ideologia* (1960), *Canzoniere italiano, poesia popolare italiana* (1960), *Empirismo eretico* (1972), *Scritti corsari* (1975), *Lettere luterane* (1976), *Le belle bandiere* (1977), *Descrizioni di descrizioni* (1979), *Il caos* (1979), *La pornografia è noiosa* (1979) and *Lettere (1940–1954)* (*Letters, 1940-54*, 1986).

Pier Paolo Pasolini directed plays. In Turin he directed a version of *Orgia* in November, 1968. The cast included Laura Betti, Luigi Mezzanotte and Nelide Giammarco.

Pier Paolo Pasolini's theatre work includes: *Orgia* (1968), *Porcile* (1968), *Calderón* (1973), *Affabulazione* (1977), *Pilade* (1977), and *Bestia da stile* (1977).

Films/ TV shows/ documentaries have been made after Pier Paolo Pasolini's death from his works (some have quoted from his poems and plays), including:

Laboratorio teatrale di Luca Ronconi (1977)
Mulheres... Mulheres (1981)
Calderon (1981)
Die Leiche murde nie gefunden (1985)
L'altro enigma (1988)
Who Killed Pasolini? (1995)
Complicity (1995)
Il pratone del casilino (1996)
Le bassin de J.W. (1997)

Una disperata vitalità (1999)
Orgia (2002)
Salò: Yesterday and Today (2002)
Pasolini prossimo nostro (2006)
'Na specie de cadavere lunghissimo (2006)
La rabbia di Pasolini (2008)
Pilades (2016)

Of the thirteen features directed by Pier Paolo Pasolini, only one is an acknowledged masterpiece: *The Gospel According to St Matthew* (taking its place alongside meisterwerks such as *8 1/2, The Searchers, Sunrise, Ran, Rashomon, Ordet, Persona, Vertigo, The Magnificent Ambersons, Citizen Kane* and *The Godfather*). Some Pasolini pictures are highly regarded (*Theorem, Salò, Accattone*), some are minor (*Mamma Roma*), some deserve to be much better known (*The Arabian Nights, Medea, Oedipus Rex*), some are almost wilfully obscure (*The Canterbury Tales, Theorem*), some are very patchy (*The Hawks and the Sparrows*, parts of the 'trilogy of life' films), only parts of *Pigsty* are any good,[4] and one is a disaster (*Love Meetings*). But only *The Gospel According To Matthew* has become an out-and-out classic, that can take its place in the top ten lists of the critical academy. *The Gospel According To Matthew* is no. 30 in *Sight & Sound*'s 2012 poll of top movies among directors, and is included in the Vatican's list of important films (which the Pontifical Council For Social Communications produced in 1995, for the 100th anniversary of cinema). Other Italian films on the Vatican's list are *Rome: Open City, Bicycle Thieves, The Road, 8 1/2, The Leopard* and a forerunner of *The Gospel, Francesco*.

And of Pier Paolo Pasolini's short fiction films (for anthology movies), most are disappointing (*The Witches, Capriccio all'Italiana, Love and Anger*), with only two attaining greatness (*Curd Cheese* and *The Anger*).

However, some critics and filmmakers have put *Salò* into their top ten lists, and Bernardo Bertolucci places *Accattone* in there (as have some other critics). Occasionally a film like *The Arabian Nights* or *Oedipus Rex* makes it into a critic's top ten. (The Italian movies that regularly crop up in top ten movie lists include *The Leopard, The Road, Bicycle Thieves, La Dolce Vita, The Conformist, Voyage To Italy* and *Rome, Open City*. The single most beloved Italian movie around the world for

---
4 Yes, we know that *Pig Fry* is a poetical-political-polemical fable, a savage satire about survival and being human and capitalist consumerism and why aren't there any cafés on Mount Etna where you get a cheeseburger and a decent cup of coffee?

film critics and film directors is definitely *8 1/2,* the astonishing and enormously entertaining exploration of a modern film director in crisis helmed by Federico Fellini – closely followed by *La Dolce Vita*).

One should note, too, that directing 13 pictures over 15 years (from 1961-1975) is very productive (plus the anthology pieces and the documentaries). I wish that Pier Paolo Pasolini had started directing earlier (he was 40 when *Accattone* was released), and also that we might have seen the incredible work that Pasolini would no doubt have created from 1975 onwards (his *St Paul*, his *Socrates* – even, maybe, his *Terms of Endearment 3*, his *X-Men 6*, his *Star Trek 9*).

PASOLINI AS EUROPEAN *AUTEUR*

Although Pier Paolo Pasolini is classed with other European *auteurs* as a maker of small-scale art films (as if only North American or internationally-financed pictures could be 'epic' or large scale), in fact many of Pasolini's films as director have an enormous scope (and they were also part-financed by American companies). Sure, some of Pasolini's pictures are intimate and small-scale, but many of them happily contend with hundreds of extras, props, animals, costumes and a huge number of different locations and sets. In many movies directed by Pasolini the frame is teeming with human life – in the mediæval trilogy and in *The Gospel According To Matthew*. Pasolini, in some ways, is the European equivalent of Cecil B. DeMille or D.W. Griffith as a creator of historical epics.

Of course, there have been plenty of European, costume epic films over the years, but Pier Paolo Pasolini's films are very different from those international movies which are usually co-productions between, say, French, Italian, German, Spanish, Swedish or British film companies. Pasolini's films do not have the style, flavour or feel of the typical 'Euro-pudding' with their starry casts, glamour, and self-conscious apeing of Hollywood cinema.[5] Instead, Pasolini goes completely his own way, doesn't pander to creating star parts or scene-stealing cameos, doesn't cast U.S. actors, doesn't have easy-to-follow plots, doesn't shoot in English (or mid-Atlantic), and his cinematic approach is instantly recognizable

---

5 However, Pasolini's later films were part-financed by American companies.

(and has proved inimitable – very few film directors have the vision, the guts, the energy, the sheer stubbornness or, crucially, the *patience* to pursue that kind of grand, vast filmmaking).

Some of Pier Paolo Pasolini's Italian contemporaries produced large-scale historical films: Federico Fellini, Bernardo Bertolucci and Luchino Visconti, for instance. But Bertolucci's historical epics, from *1900* to *The Last Emperor* and *The Sheltering Sky*, were always commercial, European-American productions (in style and casting, if not in financing). Incredible as many of Bertolucci's later movies were, they were always slickly and glossily turned out, more than half in love with the creation of finely-crafted visuals (what Jean-Luc Godard called the cinema of Max Factor, his comments *pace Schindler's List*. Pasolini thought that Bertolucci had sold out to commercialism with *Last Tango In Paris*). Luchino Visconti's later films also have that eager eye on the international market. (Notice too that Pasolini doesn't do the usual thing of recreating the past accurately of historical movies: no, he preferred to produce characters and settings by analogy. Thus, the *Bible* wouldn't be filmed in Israel or Palestine, but in Calabria and Sicily).

Comparing the cinema of Pier Paolo Pasolini with that of Bernardo Bertolucci,[6] Bruce Kawin and Gerald Mast (in *A Short History of the Movies*) assert that Pasolini's movies are

> more abstract, more elliptical, more complexly structured, and more ferociously aggressive moral-political investigations, enlivened and propelled by dazzling bursts of unforgettable imagery... (338)

In his history of Italian cinema, Gian Brunetta remarked that

> Of the entire generation of 1960s filmmakers, none stood out like Pier Paolo Pasolini. He was a postwar one-man band, capable ot transforming everything he touched into gold, from painting, poetry, and narartive to cinematography. Even his life and death were works of art. (238)

Somehow, Pier Paolo Pasolini's films remained stubbornly his own, far more idiosyncratic and eccentric than most of his contemporaries, except filmmakers such as Federico Fellini (Fellini's films were always highly self-conscious and comical in their evocations of history – *Fellini Satyricon*, for example, or *Roma*). Sometimes reaching for camp eccentricity appears laboured and clunky in cinema; for Pasolini, as for Fellini, Walerian Borowczyk and Ken Russell, it seems almost effortless (indeed, it is their natural habitat; when people drew attention to the vulgarity, the eccentricity, the eroticism and the silliness of their movies,

---
[6] Pier Paolo Pasolini remarked that Bertolucci's 'real master is Godard' (*Pasolini On Pasolini*, 138).

they would reply, eh? I don't know what you mean. Because for them, it was natural to make movies like that!).

No doubt Pier Paolo Pasolini was a powerful talent in cinema, but let's not forget that he was aided by some of the greatest artists in Italian cinema, some of whom have been called geniuses: Danilo Donati (costumes), Dante Ferretti (production designer), Nino Baragli (editor), Sergio Citti (writer/ director), Giuseppe Rotunno and Tonino Delli Colli (photographers) and Ennio Morricone (composer).

There must have been times when Pier Paolo Pasolini's producers pleaded with the *auteur* to at least include some big names in some cameos, or to cast one or two star actors. But no, Pasolini simply didn't. However, he and his casting directors did put some well-known faces into his movies, include Silvana Mangano, Anna Magnani, Terence Stamp, Orson Welles, Totò, Hugh Griffith, Jean-Pierre Léaud, and Maria Callas. (And of course Pasolini helped to make Franco Citti a star, at least in Italy).

But I'm sure some of Pier Paolo Pasolini's producers wished he'd used plenty more stars, or used them in the conventional way (that would be the instinct of Italian producers such as Dino de Laurentiis and Carlo Ponti). There would be all sorts of factors involved here, not least money – the budgets of some of Pasolini's movies were small, compared to big, international co-productions, and to Hollywood A-pictures. Also, I would guess that some film stars wouldn't want to appear in the kind of movies that Pasolini was making (and also, they wouldn't do some of the things that the movies required, such as nudity. Sure, Marlon Brando might bugger Maria Schneider in *Last Tango In Paris*, but he did it fully clothed!).

It's intriguing to note that Pier Paolo Pasolini made three ancient world movies: *The Gospel According To Matthew*, *Medea* and *Oedipus Rex*, and three Middle Ages movies: *The Arabian Nights*, *The Decameron* and *The Canterbury Tales*. He was very happy in distant history (most filmmakers, if they film historical periods, go back to the mid or early 20th century (often their early years, or that of their parents), or to the 19th century[7] at most). Indeed, the last significant work that Pasolini produced that was set in the contemporary period in feature movies was one half of *Porcile* (the other half was set in the 15th century). His next four films after 1969 were historical pieces.

You can easily discern the influence of the cinema of Pier Paolo

---

[7] Pier Paolo Pasolini's works are steeped in Victoriana – the hysterical melodrama, the Gothicism and Romanticism, the early Industrial Revolution, the emerging metropolises, the industrialization of desire in mass prostitution, early capitalism, etc.

Pasolini on filmmakers such as Sergei Paradjanov (a huge admirer of Pasolini), Federico Fellini, Francis Coppola, Oliver Stone, Terry Gilliam (and the Monty Python team),[8] Derek Jarman, Peter Greenaway, Bernardo Bertolucci, Martin Scorsese, Jeunet and Caro, Guillermo del Toro and Abel Ferrara. In 2003 Gian Brunetta noted Pasolini's continuing impact on Italian filmmakers such as Mario Martone, Luigi Faccini, Nico d'Alessandria, Aurelio Grimaldi, Pappi Corsicato, Daniele Ciprí and Franco Maresco (239).

> Pasolini's life's work and his cinema continue to speak to us thanks to his cultural nomadism, his ability to mix and hybridize all codes, his asystematic working method, and his ability to tap into the pulse and capture the soul of minorities and regional identity. (239)

FIRST WORKS IN CINEMA

In Bologna, Pier Paolo Pasolini saw some of the classics for the first time: Charlie Chaplin, Jean Renoir, René Clair, etc. 'That's where my great love for the cinema started' (PP, 30). Films like *Rome, Open City* and *Bicycle Thieves*[9] made a big impact on the young Pasolini (ibid.).

Pier Paolo Pasolini had written his first film script in 1945 (aged 23), called *I calzon* or *Lied*. When he arrived in Roma (in 1950), he began writing movie scripts professionally. Some of the early screenplays were co-written (such as *La Donna del Fiume*, with Giorgio Bassani).

In the mid-1950s, Pier Paolo Pasolini was working in movies as a scriptwriter. He published his key works in this period – such as *Ragazzi di vita* and his poetry book *La Meglio gioventù*.

When Pier Paolo Pasolini was dating Sergio Citti in the mid-1950s, he became friendly with many of the *ragazzi* of the *borgate*, the real-life street kids who would become non-professional actors in his first movies, from *Accattone* onwards.

Pier Paolo Pasolini was most productive in the years prior to his entry into film production, according to his biographer Enzo Siciliano: from 1953 to 1961. This was the period when he published novels

---

[8] One can see the influence of Pier Pasolini Pasolini in the Ancient Greek sequence in *Time Bandits* (Terry Gilliam, 1981), or in Monty Python's *Life of Brian* (the desert sequences in both films also allowed the two Terrys (Jones and Gilliam) to recreate Pasolini, whom they loved, as well as a bit of the Biblical epics – *Ben-Hur* and *The Ten Commandments*).

[9] He went to Udine (from Casarsa) specially to see *Bicycle Thieves*. He wasn't so young, tho' – *Bicycle Thieves* was released in 1948, when Pasolini was 26.

(*Ragazzi di Vita, Una Vita Violenta*), poetry (*La Ceneri di Gramsci, La Religione del mio tempo*), 13 film scripts, translations (*Oresteia*), and magazine articles (such as for *Officina*).

SCRIPTS

All of the movies that Pier Paolo Pasolini wrote before taking up directing with *Accattone* were *co*-written: Pasolini was *not* the sole screenwriter on *La Donna del Fiume, Il Prigioniero della Montagna, Le Notti di Cabiria, Marisa La Civetta*, etc. Instead, he was part of writing teams which included Basilio Franchina, Florestano Vancini, Antonio Altovitti and Mario Soldati (*La Donna del Fiume*), Luis Trenker, and Giorgio Bassani (*Il Prigioniero della Montagna*), Federico Fellini, Ennio Flaiano and Tullio Pinelli (*Nights of Cabiria*), etc. Other films Pasolini contributed to were: *The Big Night, La Giornata balorda, Giovani mariti, Morte di un amico, Il Carro armato dell '8 settembre, La Ragazza in vetrina* and *La Cantata delle marane*. Pasolini worked with Bassani (1916-2000) on several films, including *Una Notte del' 43*. Bassani dubbed Orson Welles in *Curd Cheese,* and he wrote the novel *Il Giardino dei Finzi-Contini* (later filmed by Vittorio de Sica).

It's also worth noting that before he started to direct with *Accattone,* Pier Paolo Pasolini had already had some of his works made into movies – though he didn't direct them. A chapter of the important Pasolini novel *Ragazzi di Vita* was adapted in *La Canta dell Marane* (1960, dir. Cecilia Mangini), and *Ragazzi di Vita* was made into a movie in 1959, as *La Notte Brava* (= *The Big Night,* dir. Mauro Bolognini), and *Una Vita Violenta* (= *A Violent Life*) was filmed by Ennio De Concini, Franco Brusati, Paolo Heusch, Brunello Rondi and Franco Solinas in 1962 (*Una Vita Violenta*, dir. Paolo Heusch and Brunello Rondi).

*

Only a very few filmmakers write and direct their movies. I don't mean co-write, I mean who are the sole writers of their films. And even fewer filmmakers write and direct *from their own ideas* (i.e., they come up with the fundamental concept). Because most movies are adapted from existing material, whether it's comicbooks, plays, books, computer games, TV shows, musicals, newspaper articles, or even theme park rides (plus remakes, sequels, reboots, etc).

And Pier Paolo Pasolini is no different: although we think of him as an *auteur*, writing and directing his movies (each one with the possessive credit: '*un film scritto e diretto da*'), in fact maybe half of his movies are based on existing material. They do not come from ideas and stories that Pasolini has conceived himself. Instead, they are adaptations – usually of classic literature: mediæval literature in three movies (the 'trilogy of life' series), three ancient world sources (*The Gospel According To Matthew*, *Medea* and *Oedipus Rex*), and the Marquis de Sade (*Salò*). So Pasolini didn't invent the concepts, the characters, the stories, the situations, the themes, the settings, the interactions, the relationships or many other elements of those adaptations.

The movies that are based on Pier Paolo Pasolini's own ideas and stories include: *The Hawks and the Sparrows, Accattone, Mamma Roma, Theorem, Curd Cheese, The Earth Seen From the Moon* and *Pigsty*. Also, Pasolini did *not* write everything himself: he co-authored his scripts with writers such as Dacia Maraini, Pupi Avati, Giorgio Bassani, and Sergio Citti.

Pier Paolo Pasolini didn't take up pot-boilers, sleazy novels, airport fiction, computer games, theme park rides, TV comedies, sit-coms, radio shows, comicbooks or the backs of cereal packets to adapt into movies: he took up the very greatest literature, heavyweight authors like Sophocles, Euripides, Aeschylus, the *Bible*, Giovanni Boccaccio, Geoffrey Chaucer, the Marquis de Sade and *The Thousand and One Nights*. Well, that's a *very* impressive list! Nobody can doubt the high ambition or the seriousness of the master's approach!

For Jean-Luc Godard, all of the work in making a film is *already done* before the cameras started rolling. The real work of making the film was the scriptwriting and the preparation. 'Most people think they work only when the camera is rolling, but that's not it. When the camera rolls, everything is done already'.[10] That certainly applies to Pasolini – it's all about the conception and the writing.

---

10 *Interviews*, 1998, 174.

FLAWS IN PASOLINI'S CINEMA

I am writing about the movies directed by Pier Paolo Pasolini primarily as movies, as movie experiences, in a deliberately simple and direct manner. But of course there are *thematic* and *narrative* and *political* and *psychological* and *theoretical* perspectives to these films which are rich and inspiring.

However, there are times in watching a Pasolini movie when you think:

This is twaddle.[11]

I don't care if he's a major poet and political rebel and cultural iconoclast! It's as if Dante Alighieri directed *Deep Throat*!

Observers of the Legend and Cult of Pasolini in the early 1970s might've looked at the 'trilogy of life' movies with exasperation and dismay: when is Pasolini, they might've thought, going to stop bothering with these silly saucy frolics and get back to something worthy of his immense talents, like *Medea* or *Oedipus Rex*? (Well, Pasolini *did* come back to something very serious after the three Middle Ages romps, but it was *Salò, or The 120 Days of Sodom*! – a film that was so far in the other direction, it wasn't what audiences were expecting, and probably not what the Pasolini admirers wanted).

Unfortunately, with the less-than-successful movies in the Pier Paolo Pasolini canon – such as *Love Meetings, The Hawks and the Sparrows, Pigsty* and *The Canterbury Tales* – it becomes more difficult to sustain the hi-falutin' theoretical approach. I mean, if you didn't know that Pasolini directed *The Canterbury Tales,* would we even be discussing it today? Wouldn't it have been relegated to the marginal critical discourses of cult movies or *mondo* cinema? An entertaining, weird, over-the-top slice of 1970s kitsch, but ultimately small potatoes?

Not *everything* by a great filmmaker has to be 'great' (or can be 'great'), does it?[12] Orson Welles completed twelve features (a comparable number with Pier Paolo Pasolini's thirteen features): seven are masterpieces, by my reckoning – *Kane, Ambersons, Othello, Touch, Macbeth, F For Fake* and *Shanghai* – but his 1955 movie *Mr Arkadin* (a.k.a. *Confidential Report*) was, by his own admission, a failure (whichever you look at, in whichever botched, public domain version you get to see it, *Mr Arkadin* is incredibly disappointing). *Mr Arkadin* was an important

---

[11] This thought – am I watching piffle? – occurs with many directors who are highly critically acclaimed – Steven Spielberg, Sergio Leone, Billy Wilder, Martin Scorsese, John Woo, Vincente Minnelli, even Alfred Hitchcock, John Ford and D.W. Griffith.

[12] Like many filmmakers (such as Woody Allen, Tim Burton and Hayao Miyazaki), Pier Paolo Pasolini said he never went to see his own films (PP, 108). Sometimes he saw them at film festivals, but he'd never dared to go see one of his movies in a public theatre.

personal project for Welles, but the post-production had been unhappy (a recurring motif in Welles' film career), and the film had been re-cut by the producer (Louis Dolivet).

Or take Francis Coppola: an all-round filmmaker with few peers and a truly colossal talent, Coppola has directed at least three masterpieces (*The Godfathers 1* and *2* and *Apocalypse Now*, though some would include *The Conversation*, and I would include more), but many critics found *Jack* (1996) perplexingly lightweight, and Coppola's two early movies – *Finian's Rainbow* (1968) and *You're a Big Boy Now* (1966) – are uneven (some would say mis-conceived and very dissatisfying – certainly *Finian's Rainbow*, as a Fred Astaire musical, is underwhelming).

To a degree, Pier Paolo Pasolini suffered like Orson Welles and Francis Coppola from a similar problem, seen in conventional critical terms: they were very successful early in their careers. Everything Welles did after *Citizen Kane* was compared with *Citizen Kane*, and his films never escaped that blinkered view from critics.[13] And Coppola is routinely satirized by critics as the man who directed *The Godfather* but went into artistic 'decline' in the 1980s with *The Cotton Club* and *One From the Heart*.

Rubbish, of course, but persistent rubbish.

Pier Paolo Pasolini, meanwhile, launched a filmmaking career with a minor masterwork, *Accattone*, and produced the staggering, 100% classic *The Gospel According To Matthew* three years later. As with Orson Welles and Francis Coppola and other filmmakers, early successes mean other movies can get made, but the stigma of early triumphs can colour the critical reception of later works. And in the case of Welles and Coppola, critics' emphasis on the early triumphs becomes obsessive (both Coppola and Welles became completely exasperated by everybody harking on about those early works, even while they appreciated that at least people were talking about them!).

I'm sure that the later films of Pier Paolo Pasolini tried the patience and devotion of even his most ardent admirers (as with the later work of Jean-Luc Godard, Walerian Borowczyk, Ken Russell and Terry Gilliam). You can imagine Pasolini-worshippers turning up to theatres to see *Pigsty* in 1969 or *The Canterbury Tales* in 1972, and wondering if their Freudo-Marxo-Poetico God was losing his marbles. Jean-Pierre Léaud getting freaky with pigs in a film about cannibalism? Eh?! Hugh Griffith humping on top of Charlie Chaplin's daughter in a movie stuffed with spotty,

---

[13] Which is also applied all the time to Woody Allen, where audiences prefer his early, funny films.

greasy, British non-actors?

*

When you watch the films of Pier Paolo Pasolini again and again, some of the technical aspects and the flaws do rankle: the shaky, handheld camera,[14] the patchy sound, the endless shots of people walking, and too much Ninetto Davoli.

There is a *lot* of filler in Pier Paolo Pasolini's later films. Filler meaning, for example, shots of people walking in landscapes and towns. Now, the Pasolini sympathizers can point out the atmospherics, the mood, the Existential loneliness, the exquisitely-poised, ontological *ennui*, etc, of a shot of a guy walking across a volcano (*Pigsty*) or thru an anonymous, Middle Eastern town (*The Arabian Nights*). But Pasolini detractors can rightly criticize such images as pointless, redundant, or dramatically, poetically empty – the characters have already been established, the story is already in progress, the chief locales have been explored, so four shots of a guy getting from A to B are not necessary, and even harm the narrative flow.

Take a movie everybody has seen – *Jaws* (1975): do we need to watch Police Chief Brody driving for 15 minutes down to the dock where he joins the crew of the *Orca* boat? No – we cut straight to it. Do we need to see all fifteen hours of the connecting flights from the U.S.A. to the island off the coast of Costa Rica in *Jurassic Park* (1993) – plus four hours waiting in the terminal at Panama? No – we cut straight to the island. (An Ancient Greek text might say, 'And then he went to Thebes'. But that doesn't mean we need to see five lengthy shots of a guy walking to Thebes!).

Endless shots of people walking are a sure sign that a filmmaker is out of ideas. Yes, even a hyper-super-mega-genius like Pasolini. There's no juice in such shots (even isolated, Existential, metaphysical, ontological, outsider-ish juice). The filmmaker has admitted to the audience: *I have no idea how to dramatize the script or the story.* (This occurs even in *The Gospel According To Matthew*).

---

14 Pier Paolo Pasolini operated the *macchina* himself sometimes. Unfortunately, he's no Stanley Kubrick, Ridley Scott or Ken Russell. He can't hold a camera. (One of the reasons for his terrible camerawork might be that he's yelling instructions at his actors at the same time!)

ANTI-CINEMA

When you consider all of the films of Pier Paolo Pasolini, sometimes it seems as if these movies *don't* want to be liked, or enjoyed (at least in the usual manner). As if, as with Carl-Theodor Dreyer, Robert Bresson and Andrei Tarkovsky, Pasolini wasn't going to make it easy for the viewer. And sometimes it can appear as if Pasolini's movies are being deliberately off-putting. Not 'offensive' or 'obscene', just plain difficult or obscure. A kind of anti-cinema, where expectations are wilfully, stubbornly scuppered. (Yes, there is definitely in Pasolini a delight in being difficult for the sake of it, as with Jean-Luc Godard).

For example, how would a Pier Paolo Pasolini movie play in a big cinema multiplex today? Reactions might run from laughter, scorn and ridicule to dismay and walk-outs. These are not movies that're going to preview well! They would die a death in the preview process, where unreleased movies are shown to invited audiences from the general public, getting a near-zero rating from the score cards. (Pasolini's personality, his financial contracts – and his reputation – would mean his films would be exempted from the preview process. Is a Pasolini movie going to be screened before an audience culled from shopping malls in San Diego who're then going to 'judge' his movie? I don't think so!).

They are not funny when they're meant to be funny, they are not scary when they're meant to be scary, they are not thrilling when they're meant to be thrilling, they are not dramatic when you expect/ hope them to be dramatic, they are not romantic when you think they might be romantic. They don't do what audiences would expect them to do. The technical aspects let Pier Paolo Pasolini's movies down, from the sound (the crude voice dubbing, the lack of sound effects (or 'immersion'), and the poor sound mixes),[15] to the picture (the too-shaky camerawork, and the sometimes indifferent staging).

There's an impossible-to-miss self-analysis in Pier Paolo Pasolini's cinema, a love-hate relationship with the material: as with the movies of Jean-Luc Godard, you can feel Pasolini's films arguing with themselves, simultaneously loving as well as distrusting the material, the themes, even individual shots. Like all artists, Pasolini wants to have it all ways: to evoke a scene of, say, extras in exotic costumes in a dusty, Mediterranean setting, but also to critique the subject and the very idea of

---

[15] Oh, how I wish that Alfredo Bini or Franco Rossellini or Alberto Grimaldi, the principal producers of Pier Paolo Pasolini's movies, had said, OK, we will use some of the budget to buy some decent sound equipment. This time it's live sound for us! Direct sound! Sound recorded on the set! *Si, si*, no more crappy dubbing at Cinecittà for us! (But the maestro of course preferred to deal with the sound in post-production).

making a movie in the first place.

This restlessness and dissatisfaction permeates not only Pier Paolo Pasolini's cinema but also his poetry, and his whole work. And his personality, too, as those who knew him attest. Pasolini, everybody agrees, was a very complicated person.

*

The cinema of Pier Paolo Pasolini does not do many other things that audiences expect from movies. They do not employ conventional dramaturgy, for example. They avoid the conventions of rising action and cause and effect. So the flow of the drama and the narrative from scene-to-scene of your average movie is negated. Pasolini's movies do not build and build with suspense or tension or drama. Many scenes are self-enclosed, with little relation to scenes before or after.

And when you couple that avoidance of conventional dramaturgy with the intense stylizations of Pier Paolo Pasolini's cinematic approach – the flattened, static, *tableau* approach, for instance, or the paucity of dialogue or exposition – it creates a cinema that can be tough-going for some viewers. You can't slide thru a Pasolini movie easily, quickly and cheaply (with no investment): you have to *work*. It's not easy-to-digest television, like *C.S.I.* or *Friends*.

Pier Paolo Pasolini wasn't interested in action, either, or staging impressive spectacles (the 1st A.D.s would organize a vast array of extras, animals and props, which would then be filmed with a single, wobbly, handheld shot from a single viewpoint).[16] Like Jean-Luc Godard, Pasolini was indifferent to action (Godard famously filmed action as quickly as possible; he just couldn't be bothered with it). Pasolini wasn't interested in the glamour of cinema, or in making people look gorgeous, like the Hollywood Dream Factory (tho' he would insist on very extravagant costumes and hats. Which would then be filmed somewhat casually – unlike Walerian Borowczyk, who has probably the most acute and sensual feeling for clothes in all cinema).

---

16 No multiple cameras, either, or additional takes for safety, to make sure that a scene had been captured.

DOCUMENTARIES

Sam Rohdie noted that 'Pasolini's documentaries were feigned. His past was not real, but a fragment framed, cut out. Reality was mutilated to make it all the more beautiful' (1995, 109). Pasolini realized that his essay/ documentary pieces were for a minority, intellectual audience (PP, 140).

Pier Paolo Pasolini's documentaries are niche, certainly, and they are let down by misguided concepts, some dubious ideology, and poor technical aspects. But with the right producer, or maybe the right commissions from television companies, I reckon that Pasolini might've been amongst the finest documentary filmmakers in cinema. He possessed all of the skills required to deliver some great material, except for the discipline and rigour to really make the material fly. Plus, with a major TV company behind him, he could have drawn on the resources necessary to complete the ambitious projects he wanted to make. (But he would also need a very strong TV producer who could say 'no' to his face).

Take the documentary made in Africa and Italy about staging an African version of Aeschylus' *Oresteia – Notes Towards an African Oresteia* (1970). The concept is full of ideological holes, and the execution is scrappy at best, and downright dreadful at worst.

So dump all of that material, and start again with a decent team of filmmakers and decent resources, and put the director himself in the picture (it's silly to squander a striking and well-known personality on camera like Pasolini, and have him hide behind a microphone back in Roma. Put Pasolini front and centre. And let's also see Pasolini directing his cast of amateurs in Africa).

Compare Pier Paolo Pasolini's documentaries with two geniuses of the medium in the same Euro-art arena: Werner Herzog and Jean-Luc Godard. Herzog has produced a striking and lively set of documentaries and film essays, often about exotic subjects in far-flung places (the Amazon, Africa, caves, etc). Like Pasolini, Herzog often appears in his documentaries, exploring places and interviewing people. He is a far more sympathetic interviewer than Pasolini, who tended to dominate his interviewees, and to ask them rhetorical questions (as if he'd already decided what he wanted his documentary to say). Herzog's documentaries are quirky and very distinctive (Herzog's German-accented voiceovers identified them as thoroughly Herzogian).

Jean-Luc Godard, meanwhile, is a master of the film essay form – half of his fiction movies, for example, might be characterized as film essays. Godard produced several fascinating film essays about his feature films, which he called notes for films (and Godard can talk about cinema as few people can, including Pasolini. Godard is a formidable intellectual talent). And with *Histoire(s) du Cinéma,* Godard created an epic history of cinema (between 1989 and 1998). *Histories of Cinema* was a major work, and has generated a good deal of critical comment. As well as being a history of cinema, it was also a history of the age – and a history of Godard himself.

DOCUMENTARIES ABOUT PASOLINI

Pier Paolo Pasolini has fascinated TV documentary producers – there was a documentary of 1970 (filmed with Pasolini's co-operation), and *Who Says the Truth Shall Die* (Phil Bregstein, 1981). Several documentaries have appeared on *Salò – Fade To Black* (2001), *Salò: Yesterday and Today* (2002), *Enfants de Salò* (2006, French), *Pasolini Prossimo Nostro* (2006, Italian) and *The End of Salò* (2008). Pasolini's murder was explored in *Who Killed Pasolini?* (1995). A ficionalized account of Pasolini was released in 2014 (with Willem Dafoe as the great man).

PASOLINI.
Pasolini (Abel Ferrara, 2014) was a biographical portrait of the last days of Pier Paolo Pasolini. Starring Willem Dafoe, Maria de Medeiros, Ninetto Davoli, Adrianna Asti and Riccardo Scamarcio, produced by Thierry Lounas and Fabio Massimo Cacciatori for the production companies Urania Pictures/ Dublin Films/ Belgacom/ Canal Plus, and scripted by Maurizio Braucci, *Pasolini* was a curiously flat and unengaging take on an incendiary filmmaker and poet. For Pasolinians, there was not only nothing new here, and the opportunities for depicting a complex and compelling artist were squandered. *Pasolini* took a de-dramatized approach, flattening the aspects of this passionate artist into a series of boring images and boring dialogues.

We see: Pasolini working on the post-production of *Salò;* a snippet of Pasolini's home life (with his mother Susanna prominent (played by Pasolini regular Adriana Asti – she was Amore in *Accattone*)); an interview with a journalist; a visit from an effervescent actress;[17] and extracts from a novel that Pasolini was working on.

Pasolini was one of those works in which nothing much happens – either visually, narratively, dramatically, psychologically or philosophically. More like notes for a possible movie about Pier Paolo Pasolini (in the Godardian manner). It's scrappy. Bitty.

Time passes... *Pasolini* ends... a pointless group of images and sounds. Cinema at its worst.

Pasolini came alive a tad when Ninetto Davoli entered the frame – sort of playing himself (and shadowed by his former self, played by Riccardo Scamarcio), in an illustration of an unmade film idea from Pasolini about a spiritual journey/ religious skits, which included a visit to a gay and lesbian Sodom and Gomorrah (a festival where couples tup and the audience around them jeers and cheers. Presumably this is meant to be the 1973 unmade film project *Porno-Teo-Kolossal*). Not a patch on what Pasolini himself would've done with a modern-day Sodom and Gomorrah scenario, of course.

Pasolini recreated the night in November, 1975, when the director was murdered after picking up a youth. This played out as expected, but without the political/ ideological/ blackmailing motives (instead, the three youths who round on Pasolini attack him partly for homophobic reasons, yelling insults as they kick him. That fudged the issue, avoiding an opportunity to explore the more controversial issues surrounding Pasolini's demise).

---

17 Is that meant to be Laura Betti? (Played by Maria de Medeiros).

4

ASPECTS OF PASOLINI'S CINEMA

PIER PAOLO PASOLINI AND ITALIAN CINEMA

Pier Paolo Pasolini made his thirteen feature movies as a film director between 1961 and 1975, the years of a boom in the Italian film business, and of the European New Wave (but he had been working on co-written scripts thru the Fifties). This period of Italian cinema was marked by the regeneration of production after WW2, with movements such as the development of Neo-realism (embodied in productions such as *Rome: Open City,* Roberto Rossellini, 1945 and *Bicycle Thieves,* Vittorio de Sica, 1948). However, Neo-realist cinema was not popular in Italy itself, but overseas (especially North America). The significant filmmakers of this period were, with Rossellini and de Sica, Luchino Visconti and Alberto Lattuada. North American companies increasingly used Italian studios (such as Cinecittà): they followed the money, which couldn't be repatriated. When M.G.M. made *Quo Vadis* in Italy in 1950, other U.S. studios followed (and the Yanks visited Italy throughout the 1960s).

Actually, how 'Italian' is Italian cinema? Pasolini's and Federico Fellini's later films, for example, were backed by North American companies (such as United Artists). It was the same with Luchino Visconti and Michelangelo Antonioni, as director Glauber Rocha of Brazil's New Cinema pointed out in the mid-1960s: 'Italy does not really have a national film industry, a truly Italian cinema, anymore' (in D. Georgakas, 17).

In the 1960s, Federico Fellini, Michelangelo Antonioni, Bernardo Bertolucci, Marco Bellocchio, Sergei Leone and the Tavianis were among the key film directors in Italy, as well as Pier Paolo Pasolini. The film stars included Marcello Mastroianni, Monica Vitti, Anna Magnani, Gina Lollobrigida, Sophia Loren, Vittorio Gassman, Totò and Silvana Mangano (Pasolini used Totò and Mangano the most). Among film producers of the period, such as Alberto Grimaldi and Alfredo Bini (who produced Pasolillni's films), two stand out in the Italian industry: Carlo Ponti[18] (married to Loren) and Dino de Laurentiis (married to Mangano); Pasolini worked with all of them). The 1960s, according to Gian Brunetta,

> would prove to be the years of the greatest experimentation, freedom, and expressive riches. Not everything in the cauldron was made of gold, but the average qualitative level was the highest of all time. (171)

The Italian film industry reacted swiftly to any big hit movie, hurrying copies and sequels into production. Thus, successful movies such as *Spartacus* (1960), *Cleopatra* (1963), *Ben-Hur* (1959), and *Hercules* (1958) led to instant cash-ins. As Howard Hughes noted in *Cinema Italiano*:

> The story of Italian cinema is essentially a series of creative explosions, interspersed with fallow periods of audience exhaustion. If a film was popular, literally dozens of imitations would be made to cash-in at the domestic and international box office. This intense technique often resulted in each fad enjoying rather limited longevity, as the glut quickly satisfied audience interest. (ix-xi)

Thus, there was a craze of musclemen movies with mythological or ancient world settings, inaugurated by *Hercules*[19] (1958),[20] which lasted from 1958 to 1964. The Spaghetti Western fad, sparked by the *Dollars* films starring Clint Eastwood, ran from 1965 to 1970 (but continued into the 1970s). The *James Bond*-inspired spy cycle ran from 1963 to 1967. Gothic horror flicks were popular from 1960 to 1965 (and again in the 1970s with the *gialli*). 1960 was a triumphant year for Italian cinema, with *Rocco and His Brothers* and *La Dolce Vita* becoming big critical and commercial successes. Pasolini's cinema had its own cash-ins (the

---

18 Carlo Ponti (1912-2007) is one of the legends of the Italian film industry. Ponti produced some 140 movies, including many film classics, such as *La Strada, Boccaccio '70, Doctor Zhivago, War and Peace, Closely Watched Trains, Cléo From 5 To 7*, and three Michelangelo Antonioni flicks, *The Passenger, Blow-Up* and *Zabriskie Point.*
19 The Italian 1958 *Hercules* (the first one), starring Steve Reeves (Mr Universe) and helmed by Pietro Francisci, was so successful it inaugurated a series of Italian 'muscle-men', sword-and-sandal epics – some 180 films. *Hercules* cost $120,000 and made $20 million, and was released in 1959 thru Warners (producer Joe Levine had paid $120,000 for the rights). Its budget was less than 1% of that of Hollywood's *Ben-Hur* or *The Ten Commandments*, yet it made somewhere between 1/8th and 1/3rd as much (a producer's dream!). Levine launched *Hercules* with $1.1 million of advertizing, including on television ('the most aggressive campaign any film ever had', as William Goldman put it).
20 The couple in *A Violent Life* go to see a *Hercules* movie at the cinema.

'trilogy of life' movies were obvious candidates for rip-offs, which were released rapidly following the success of *The Decameron*. Producers saw that they could deliver sex romps much cheaper, by leaving out the elaborate set-pieces with extras and animals).

Along with Germany, Spain, Holland and of course France, Italy has been one of the most significant film production territories in Europe. The number of productions made each year and the number of tickets sold (i.e., punters going to the cinema) is among the highest in Europe.

Pier Paolo Pasolini benefited from the boom years of Italian film production, when it was making more movies per year than Hollywood: 242 films were produced in 1962, for example, compared to 174 in North America. 245 films in Italy in 1966, compared to 168 in the U.S.A. 237 productions in 1974, compared to 156 in America (the recession hit Hollywood badly in the early 1970s).

In the 1960s and the 1970s, the period when Pier Paolo Pasolini was active as a film director, Italy made more movies than any other European country, including France (which since then has become the premier country for production *and* consumption), and more people went to the cinema in Italy than in any other nation (this's if you exclude Russia from Europe – which most people did in the Cold War era).

So film culture is immensely significant in Italy (even though de-regulated, hyper-capitalist television in the Silvio Berlusconi era has overshadowed it). And the star filmmakers, like Federico Fellini, Luchino Visconti, Bernardo Bertolucci, Michelangelo Antonioni and Pier Paolo Pasolini, have become well-known outside film circles. And Dino de Laurentiis is a legendary mogul whose movies (and those produced by his daughter Raffaella) have generated billions.[21]

Dino de Laurentiis (1919-2010) was probably the most well-known Italian producer of recent times, a formidable mogul who moved from Italian movies (*Il Bandito, Bitter Rice, Anna, Europa '51, La Lupa, La Strada*), to North American co-productions (*War and Peace, Ulysses*), to international movies (*Barabbas, Bandits In Rome, Serpico, Barbarella, Three Days of the Condor* and *The Valachi Papers*), and epics (*The Bible, Waterloo, The Bounty* and *Dune*). De Laurentiis produced all-out commercial ventures (such as *King Kong, Death Wish, Hurricane, Orca the Killer Whale, Flash Gordon, Conan the Barbarian, Year of the Dragon, Body of Evidence* and *Hannibal*), but also movies by art maestros like Ingmar Bergman, Federico Fellini, Luchino Visconti,

---

21 Jean-Luc Godard sent up Italian producers such as Carlo Ponti and Dino de Laurentiis (whom he's worked with), in his film *Passion* (1982), who always turn up with a beautiful woman on their arm. The producer in *Passion* yells: 'where's my money?', 'what have you done with my money?' It's one of the recurring phrases in the film business (usually yelled out, as of course it should be).

Michael Cimino, Milos Forman, David Lynch, Vittorio de Sica and Robert Altman (such as *Buffalo Bill, Desperate Hours, Face To Face, Lo Straniero,* and *Blue Velvet*). In North America in the 1980s, de Laurentiis founded D.E.G. (De Laurentiis Entertainment Group) in North Carolina, which flourished until it ended in 1988 (with, some said, debts of $200 million).

Dino de Laurentiis' career is truly remarkable – and long-running (he began producing during the German Occupation of Italy). He formed Real Cine in 1941 (when he was 23), produced *Il Bandito* (Alberto Lattuada, 1946), when he was 28, and married actress Silvana Mangano (who appeared in Pier Paolo Pasolini's *Theorem, The Decameron, The Witches* and *Oedipus Rex*, among others). With Carlo Ponti, de Laurentiis formed Ponti-De Laurentiis in 1950 (they owned the Farnesina Studios in Rome). De Laurentiis created Dinocittà outside Rome, where *The Bible, The Great War* and *Barabbas* were based. (Dinocittà has since become a movie theme park).

PASOLINI AND FELLINI

In the late 1950s, Pier Paolo Pasolini became part of Federico Fellini's court.[22] They had met at the Canova (Franco Rossi had brought them together). They took to wandering around Roma at night, with Pasolini introducing Fellini to some of the locations he drew inspiration from: Idroscalo, Tiburtino Terzo, Pietralata and Guidonia. The maestro had brought in Pasolini (and his partner, Sergio Citti) to help with some of his scripts (such as advising on the dialect in *Nights of Cabiria*[23] – dialect being one of Pasolini's passions). Pasolini wrote about 40 pages of the screenplay, according to Moraldo Rossi, but Fellini hardly used any of it.[24]

Federico Fellini later invited P.P. Pasolini to sit in on auditions at Cinecittà for projects such as *La Dolce Vita* (1960). Although some in the Fellini camp resented the maestro becoming so close to Pasolini, it was not a long-lasting friendship.[25] Fellini's wife Giulietta took 'an

22 Totò parodied *La Dolce Vita* in *Totò, Peppino and La Dolce Vita* (1960).
23 The settings of *Nights of Cabiria* – the outskirts of Roma, the scrubland and the caves – were employed several times in Pasolini's early films.
24 Quoted in *Fellini On Fellini* 1995, 50.
25 It was a lively friendship, tho', according to Enzo Siciliano, 'a deep human attachment' (ES, 223).

immediate dislike to the homosexual Pier Paolo as a corruptor of innocent young souls'),[26] and Fellini's regular screenwriter, Ennio Flaiano, refused to work with Pasolini on *La Dolce Vita*. Flaiano (known as a cynical, spiky writer) wrote a skit about it – "*La Dolce Vita* According to Pasolini" (which Fellini begged him not to publish).

Pier Paolo Pasolini had hoped that Federico Fellini (and his new company, Federiz, formed with the publisher Angelo Rizzoli), would back his first movie as director, *Accattone*[27] (Fellini and Rizzoli were also planning movies by Vittorio De Seta, Ermanno Olmi, Marco Ferreri and of course Fellini. But in the end, Fellini wasn't bothered about becoming a movie mogul – he only wanted to make his own films).

Tests for *Accattone* were shot (in September, 1960),[28] including two scenes: at via Fanfulla da Lodi, in the pine woods, and outside Castel Sant'Angelo. Pasolini later recalled meeting with Fellini to discuss them (after hearing nothing from the maestro): but it became apparent that Fellini and Rizzoli were not going to get behind *Accattone* (which in the event was produced by Alfredo Bini[29] – it was Bini who persuaded Pasolini to make *Accattone*).[30] According to Moraldo Rossi, Pasolini 'had staked everything on Fellini, but Fellini had dropped him'.[31] And from that point, Fellini and Pasolini fell out, sniping at each other's projects in the press.

---

26 Quoted in T. Kezich, 178.
27 *Accattone* announces its quirkiness from the outset: after those Renaissance-elegant opening titles, and the breezy, rarefied tones of J.S. Bach, what is the first shot of the movie? A pretty aerial view of the Eternal City? Oh no, this is not going to be a film featuring dignified professional actors spouting Shakespeare or Petrarch! Instead, it's a close-up of the ugly mug of Fulvio, joshing with the lads in their customary position: sitting outside the café in the side street. The final shot of *Accattone* is of Balilla, crossing himself as he looks down at the dying Accattone.
28 This was Pier Paolo Pasolini's first experience of being a film director, at least with his own material. His model was the 'absolutely simplicity of expression' in *The Passion of Joan of Arc*, directed by Carl-Theodor Dreyer. Another influential film for Pasolini was the 1950 *Francesco*, the portrait of St Francis and his followers directed by Roberto Rossellini using all non-professional actors (except for Aldo Fabrizi).
29 Mauro Bolognini saw photographs of the tests, and suggested the project to Bini.
30 E. Siciliano, 227.
31 Quoted in C. Constantin, 1995, 50.

PIER PAOLO PASOLINI'S COLLEAGUES

Critics typically talk about Pier Paolo Pasolini's movies in awed, auteurist terms, as if the director did *everything* in his movies. He didn't, though: he directed them, sometimes appeared in them in cameos, and wrote or co-wrote most of them (Pasolini did, however, believe in the *auteur* theory, unlike almost every filmmaker).[32] Thus, his films usually have the credit:

> *scritto e diretto da*
> or: *un film scritto e diretto da*

But one must always remember that Pier Paolo Pasolini was surrounded by some legends in Italian cinema – such as designers Dante Ferretti and Danilo Donati, DPs Giuseppe Rotunno and Tonino Delli Colli, producers Alfredo Bini and Alberto Grimaldi, and composer Ennio Morricone. And numerous others: by the 1960s, when Pasolini started to direct features, the Italian film industry boasted some of the finest, most imaginative and skilled technicians and talents in the world. (Italian cinema was on a high, an up, a boom in this period).

The *auteur* credit, the 'un film de' credit, is dishonest and dumb. Who drew up all of the contracts (sometimes thousands for big movies)? Who oversaw the insurance, taxes, and liabilities? Who bought the cloth for the costumes? Who built the sets? Who booked the hotels? Who carried the lights up ten flights of stairs?[33] Who drove the actors to the locations? Who created the opticals for the titles? Who logged all of the rushes and takes? Who rented the vehicles? Who processed the exposed celluloid?[34] And who does 100s of other jobs in movie production?

Not the director.[35]

The producers of Pier Paolo Pasolini's movies included Alfredo Bini, Alberto Grimaldi, Franco Rossellini (brother of Roberto Rossellini), Carlo Lizzani, Dino de Laurentiis, and Gian Vittorio Baldi. Bini produced the early works, Rossellini the middle period pictures (late 1960s), and Grimaldi the later ones.[36]

---

32 Pasolini insisted that he 'always thought of a film as the work of an author, not only the script and the direction, but the choice of sets and locations, the characters, even the clothes. I choose everything – not to mention the music' (PP,32).
33 No elevators in some of those old buildings.
34 I could go on!
35 This is a simplistic argument of who does what in movies, but *auteur* theory has also been disparaged on ideological, political, social, philosophical and cultural grounds.
36 The only problems he had with producers, Pasolini said, were *Pigsty* and *Medea*, which were flops.

ALFREDO BINI (Dec 12, 1926-Oct 16, 2010)[37] is a hugely important figure[38] in the cinema of Pier Paolo Pasolini.[39] That he not only produced Pasolini's movies (and took a chance on him with his first film as director), but also supported the movies and stood behind them (when they attracted controversy), is also not to be under-estimated. Producing Pasolini's films wasn't the easiest gig in town, I would imagine, adding all sorts of unforeseen challenges that went beyond your run-of-the-mill producing duties. I bet you had to be on top of your game to keep up with Pasolini.

> Bini had confidence in me at a time when that was extremely hard: I knew nothing about the cinema, and he gave me *carte blanche* and let me work in peace. (PP, 138)

Alfredo Bini formed Arco Film in 1960, and later the companies Finarco and Gerico Sound. Bini produced most of Pier Paolo Pasolini's earlier movies (such as *RoGoPaG, The Gospel According to St Matthew, Mamma Roma* and *Accattone* and, later, *Oedipus Rex*). Bini's other producer credits included films helmed by Mauro Bolognini (*The Mandrake*, 1965), *El Greco* (1966), a rival version of *Satyricon* to the Federico Fellini film (1969), *Simon Bolivar* (1969), *Gli Eroi* (*The Horse*, 1973), *Lancelot du Lac* (Robert Bresson, 1974), and adaptations of theatrical plays aimed at the video market. He was married to actress Rosanna Schiaffino.

ALBERTO GRIMALDI (Mch 28, 1925-Jan 23, 2021, born in Naples) produced Pasolini's last four films, from *Il Decamerone* to *Salò*. Grimaldi was a lawyer from Naples; he had formed Produzioni Europee Associate S.p.A. in Roma in 1961. He had made plenty of $$$$ by producing the *Fistful of Dollars* Spaghetti Westerns starring Clint Eastwood. Grimaldi went on to become a big cheese in the Italian film industry – producing several Federico Fellini films, for instance, plus *Last Tango In Paris, 1900, Burn!, Trastevere, Man of La Mancha* and *Bawdy Tales*. One of Grimaldi's last producing jobs was *Gangs of New York* (2002). Grimaldi had a distribution deal with United Artists (hence, the films were released thru U.A. in North America, including the Pasolini productions).

United Artists was investing, like other North American studios in the 1960s, in European productions (brokering deals with Dino de

---

37 Pasolini was four years older than Bini.
38 Occasionally you see snipes at Bini – but that goes with the territory of being a film producer. It doesn't detract from Bini's significance in Pasolini's film career.
39 'My contemporary from Gorizia | red-haired, hands in his pockets, | heavy as a paratrooper after mess-hall', as Pasolini characterized Bini in a poem in *Il padre salvaggio*.

Laurentiis as well as Alberto Grimaldi and other Italian producers). United Artists wanted prestige pictures – 'more complex, larger-scale pictures' than Spaghetti Westerns (see below).

The films produced by Alberto Grimaldi often had erotic content – in the 1970s alone, there was *Last Tango In Paris*, the 'trilogy of life' films, *Salò, Novecento* and *Casanova* (dir. Federico Fellini, 1976). But that also reflects the era, when eroticism meant box office.

Many of Pasolini's later films were backed by Les Productions Artistes Associées along with Alberto Grimaldi's Produzioni Europee Associate (so they were Italian and French co-productions). Les Productions Artistes Associées had been founded in 1963 in Paris. Their movies included *Last Tango In Paris, Le Cage aux Folles, The Night Porter, 1900, Man of the East, The Story of Adele H., Roma, The Train, Burn!,* and *Moonraker* (the *James Bond* film).

UNITED ARTISTS. In the early Seventies, United Artists was known as one of the more adventurous of the Hollywood studios, and backed some of the more eccentric or left-of-centre productions. (U.A. was instrumental in forging the 'New Hollywood' cinema, for instance). From its early days, United Artists was known as a filmmaker-friendly studio, on the side of the filmmaker-as-artist. It was set up by Mary Pickford, Charlie Chaplin, Douglas Fairbanks and D.W. Griffith in 1919, where it was known as a company that would control marketing and distribution of the artists' products, rather than a conventional film studio (it didn't have sound stages and production facilities, didn't own cinemas, and didn't have a roster of stars).

By the 1960s, among United Artists' successes were the *Pink Panther* franchise (led by Blake Edwards and Peter Sellers), the Beatles films (*A Hard Day's Night* and *Help!*), and the ever-reliable *James Bond* franchise. (There were flops in the 1960s, however, such as the very costly picture *The Greatest Story Ever Told* (1965) – $20 million, and disappointments such as *Chitty Chitty Bang Bang* (1968, cost: $10m), *Battle of Britain* (1969, cost: $12m) and *The Private Life of Sherlock Holmes* (1970, cost: $10m). These productions were part of the over-spending cycle of the late Sixties.)

In the 1970s, *Rocky* was an important franchise for U.A. – the Chartoff-Winkler movies were sequelized several times. Chartoff and Winkler made a *ton* of money from United Artists' *Rocky* series (the first *Rocky* movie cost $1.5 million and took $55.9 million in North American rentals alone – equivalent to $487m in 2005 dollars). Among Chartoff and Winkler's productions was the controversial movie *The Last*

Rex, *Pigsty*, *Salò* and the 'trilogy of life' movies. For Federico Fellini, Donati designed *Satyricon* (1969), *The Clowns* (1971), *Roma* (1972), *Armarcord* (1973), *Casanova* (1976), *Ginger and Fred* (1986) and *Intervista* (1987). As well as working for Visconti, Fellini and Pasolini, Donati also provided costumes for films such as *The Taming of the Shrew* (1967), *Romeo and Juliet* (1968), *Bawdy Tales* (1973), *Caligula* (1979), *Flash Gordon* (1980), *Red Sonja* (1985), *Nostromo* (1996), *Life Is Beautiful* (1997) and *Pinocchio* (2002).

On a Pier Paolo Pasolini production, costume designers were often encouraged to go all-out, and not hold back from outrageous designs. A huge challenge were the ancient world and mediæval movies – especially the ones set in archaic societies. Not least among the challenges would be getting all of the costumes to those remote locations in Africa or Turkey (or even Southern Italia). No doubt quite a few costumes were manufactured near the set, using local workers (which would require a whole new way of working). For some of the historical productions, the wardrobe dept also had to clothe huge numbers of extras – and on budgets that were a fraction of their Hollywood equivalents. Yet each Pasolini movie has a look in costume design that's unique: a single frame, or a single still photograph from a Pasolini movie is instantly recognizable as coming from Danilo Donati. If there was a touring exhibition of costumes from Pasolini's movies, I would be first in line. (You can see some of Donati's costumes today at Cinecittà).

DANTE FERRETTI (b. 1943) is one of the superstars of production design in recent cinema. His list of credits is extraordinary by any standards. Ferretti worked with Pier Paolo Pasolini as production designer on *Medea, The Arabian Nights, The Decameron, The Canterbury Tales* and *Salò* (and as an assistant on earlier pictures, such as *The Gospel According To Matthew*). Ferretti also designed for Federico Fellini – *City of Women, And the Ship Sails On, The Voice of the Moon* and *Ginger and Fred,* and films such as *The Night Porter, Tales of Ordinary Madness, The Name of the Rose, Hamlet, Titus, The Adventures of Baron von Munchausen, Bram Stoker's Dracula, Sweeney Todd* and *Interview With a Vampire*; Ferretti worked with Martin Scorsese on *The Age of Innocence, The Aviator, Kundun, Bringing Out the Dead* and *Casino,* and with directors such as Tim Burton, Francis Coppola, Terry Gilliam, Jean-Jacques Annaud and Marco Ferreri

Pier Paolo Pasolini would research the designs for his films from paintings, Ferretti said. Ferretti recalled that he was

Temptation of Christ (1988), which they had set up with Paramount in the early 1980s.

And let's not forget editor NINO BARAGLI (1925-2013), who cut nearly all of Pier Paolo Pasolini's features. Thus, Baragli (three years younger than the maestro), is one of the most important figures in Pasolini's cinema, and in Italian cinema of recent times (yet some film critics don't even mention him). Baragli worked with all of the major Italian filmmakers, including Federico Fellini, Luchino Visconti, Sergio Leone, Bernardo Bertolucci, Damiano Damiani, Mauro Bolognini, Massimo Troisi, Alberto Lattuada, Tinto Brass and Roberto Benigni, and directors such as Gabriele Salvatores and Margarethe von Trotta (for many of those directors, Baragli worked on many of their projects).

Editing is always underrated by film critics, even critics you'd think would know better (partly because critics don't really know what editing is. I think film critics should spend a day or so with a film editor, to learn exactly what the job entails). Among Baragli's credits were important collaborations with Sergio Leone (the *Fistful* Spaghetti Westerns and *Once Upon a Time In America*), *Ginger and Fred* and *The Voice of the Moon* (Federico Fellini), and *Mediterraneo*.

Editing a Pier Paolo Pasolini production, though, meant working with intuitive, spontaneously-shot material, where eyelines didn't match, where inserts and close-ups were often not filmed (plus all of the other 'coverage' of a scene of a typical movie), where non-naturalistic and discontinuous images had to be welded together. Pasolini didn't arrive on set with a regular shot list, and didn't approach scenes in a conventional manner. Editing a Pasolini film would be a challenge, with different requirements from your average film or TV show. Luckily, Nino Baragli was a master editor – some critics have called him a genius.

As for costumes, in DANILO DONATI (1926-2001), Pier Paolo Pasolini had one of the great costume designers (and set designers) of recent times: Donati's feeling for costume is simply astonishing.[40] Solely in the realm of *hats* and *headgear*, Donati has few peers. If you want to study the history of costume in cinema, you have to include lengthy research into Danilo Donati, or the cinema of Federico Fellini and Luchino Visconti. (In many ways, in Pasolini's cinema, as with Vincente Minnelli, Walerian Borowczyk and Ken Russell, it's all about the clothes).

For Pier Paolo Pasolini, Danilo Donati designed *RoGoPaG, The Gospel According To Matthew, The Hawks and the Sparrows, Oedipus*

---

[40] Pier Paolo Pasolini praised Donati's genius with costume – 'he does all that, extremely well, with excellent taste and zest' (PP, 32).

always a little intimidated by Pasolini. He was like a poet or a priest, and his approach to filmmaking was architectural: his shots were always like geometrical *tableaux*, with the camera dead centre. (P. Ettedgui, 49)

TONINO DELLI COLLI (1923-2005) began, with *Accattone,* a long-running collaboration with Pier Paolo Pasolini that must rank as one of the finest in recent cinema – alongside Federico Fellini and Giuseppe Rotunno, Bernardo Bertolucci and Vittorio Storaro or Jean-Luc Godard and Raoul Coutard. Delli Colli (a year younger than Pasolini) was the cinematographer on eleven out of the maestro's thirteen feature films[41] (plus the episodes for anthology films). He was also DP for Federico Fellini, Roman Polanski, Jean-Jacques Annaud, Claude Chabrol and Sergio Leone (you can see Delli Colli at work with Fellini in *Interview*, 1987).[42] Delli Colli was known for subsuming his style into the material, and what the director wanted. He didn't impose his style on the movie, he served the movie. (He was described by Enzo Siciliano as short, Roman, nervous and given to uncontrollable rages, but was gentle with Pasolini.[43] From Delli Colli Pasolini learnt much of the art and practice of cinema).

> Come on, Tonino, come on,
> set it at fifty, don't be afraid
> of the light sinking – let's take
> this unnatural shot![44]

Tonino Delli Colli recalled: 'Our relations were perfect. [Pasolini] was an incredibly sweet and kind person, and he had respect for everyone on the set.' In terms of camera movement and style, Pier Paolo Pasolini preferred a simple visual approach: Pasolini was not interested in tricks, gimmicks or the 'magic' of cinema (even the greatest of filmmakers are full of tricks and gimmicks: Orson Welles, D.W. Griffith, F.W. Murnau, Jean Cocteau, Akira Kurosawa, Ingmar Bergman and Jean-Luc Godard. And Federico Fellini, of course, used every trick available).[45] Pasolini liked the 50 mil lens, Delli Colli said,[46] which gave a slightly compressed, squashed image, but approximated to the field of vision of the naked human eye.

GIUSEPPE ROTUNNO (1923-2021) is one of the great cinematographers of Italian cinema: he was DP on many classics, including the

---

[41] And Tonino Delli Colli would've shot the other movies if it weren't for scheduling conflicts.
[42] He filmed the famous Spaghetti Westerns, for instance.
[43] Delli Colli was described by Gideon Bachmann as a 'small, wiry man'.
[44] Pasolini, *La Poesie*, 337.
[45] Sergio Citti, in the 1970 documentary on Pier Paolo Pasolini, insists that *he* didn't use zooms or dollies or other trickery on his movies, as Pasolini did.
[46] Delli Colli said that Pasolini liked to use either long lenses or wide angle lenses.

incredible *The Leopard* (1963), and worked for Federico Fellini (as his chief cameraman, from the late 1960s to the end of Fellini's life), Luchino Visconti,[47] Terry Gilliam (*Baron Munchausen*), Bob Fosse (*All That Jazz*) and John Huston (*The Bible*). Rotunno also lit films such as *Candy, The Secret of Santa Vittoria, Carnal Knowledge, Popeye, Red Sonja* and *Five Days One Summer*. Solely for his work for three Italian maestros – Fellini, Pasolini and Visconti – Rotunno should be regarded as one of the greats among photographers.

SERGIO CITTI (1933-2005) was a very important collaborator in the cinema of Pier Paolo Pasolini – he worked on the scripts, on the dialogue, and was an assistant director (as well as having a relationship with the maestro). Born in Rome, Citti was one of the longest-serving members of the Pasolini Movie Circus, following the master everywhere.

In 1970, Sergio Citti stepped up to become a film director: Pier Paolo Pasolini co-wrote Citti's first two films as director: *Ostia* (1970) and *Bawdy Tales* (1973). If anyone could step in to direct in Pasolini's absence, it would be Citti.

Sergio Citti's subsequent films included: *Beach House* (1977), *Happy Hobos* (1979), *Il Minestrone* (1981), *Mortacci* (1989, *We Free Kings* (1996), *Cartoni Animati* (1997), *Vipera* (2001) and *Fratella e Sorello* (2005). *Sogni e Bisogni* (1985) was a TV mini-series.

SILVANA MANGANO. One of Pier Paolo Pasolini's favourite actresses was Dino de Laurentiis' wife Silvana Mangano (1930-89): she appeared in *Theorem, The Decameron, The Earth Seen From the Moon* (the episode in *The Witches*), and *Oedipus Rex*. As well as films helmed by Pasolini, she was in *Ulysses, Barabbas, Black Magic, Mambo, Tempest, Il Processo di Verona, Gold of Naples, Five Branded Women, Conversation Piece, Dune* and *Death In Venice* (many of those movies were produced by de Laurentiis). Like Sophia Loren, Gina Lollobrigida, Anna Magnani and Alida Valli, Mangano was an icon of Italian cinema; her face, which could melt the camera, was instantly recognizable (she was a hit aged nineteen in *Bitter Rice* (1949), walking in rice fields with her skirt up around her thighs).

LAURA BETTI (1927-2004) was another of Pier Paolo Pasolini's special actresses, appearing in many of his films (and providing the voice in others). Betti was one of his most important friends. The bond between Betti and Pasolini could be fiery, however – she would yell at him, hurling insults, and Elsa Morante, listening, would interject: 'If you two want to make love, stop doing it in words' (ES, 261). Betti was

---

[47] Rotunno started out on Visconti productions such as *Senso* and *White Nights*.

possessive over her friendship with Pasolini, pushing away anyone who threatened it (such as Maria Callas).

ALBERTO MORAVIA (1907-1990, born in Rome) was a favourite author with Italian filmmakers – most of his fiction was adapted into movies (including *The Conformist, La Romana, Agostino, Gli Indifferenti*, etc). Moravia also wrote films.

Novelist ELSA MORANTE (1912-85) was an valued advisor and encourager for Pier Paolo Pasolini, and influenced several of his film projects (such as advising on the music for *The Gospel According To Matthew* and others). Morante's husband, author Alberto Moravia, was a fellow colleague and traveller (he appeared in *Love Meetings* and went on trips with Morante and Pasolini, such as to India in 1960).

FRANCO CITTI

Apart from six Pier Paolo Pasolini movies, Franco Citti (1938-2016) has also appeared in mainly Italian movies – by Bernardo Bertolucci (*La Luna*), Sergio Citti, Sergio Pastore, Elio Petri, Franco Rossi, Antonio Bido, Antonio Avati, and two *Godfather* movies.

While Nino Davoli represented the lighter side of Pasolini's art, the Charlie Chaplin aspects which mocked existence, Franco Citti, from *Accattone* onwards, embodied the murky, egotistic, and degenerate sides of the Pasolini persona, with its tendency towards self-loathing, violence and depression. Citti played Pasolini's grandiose but doomed hero Oedipus (his finest role for the maestro, along with Accattone), a ruthless crook (in *The Decameron*), a fellow cannibal (in *Pigsty*), the Devil in *The Canterbury Tales,* an enigmatic demon (in *The Arabian Nights*), and an arrogant pimp (in *Mamma Roma*).

Franco Citti's characters operate on the wrong side of the law, are introspective and difficult, and see themselves as Existential rebels (who feel that the whole world is against them). They want an easy life (they think they deserve it), and they can't understand why everybody isn't falling over themselves to do their bidding. They are charismatic and independent (which makes them initially attractive), but they implode under pressure (and arrogance).

NINETTO DAVOLI

While actors such as Franco Citti might be associated with Pier Paolo Pasolini's cinema in its arty, handsome, dramatic mode, just as significant were actors such as Ninetto Davoli (b. 1948, Calabria).[48] With his toothy grin and frizzy hair, Davoli is terrific as hapless, lusty, rather dim youths on the make. Energetic, naïve, indefatigable, cowardly, Davoli is an unlikely leading man: he can never be the romantic lead, he is always the ordinary guy looking for the easiest way out.

Enzo Siciliano portrays Davoli as having a

> slight and skinny build, pimples on his face, kinky hair, and incredibly "merry" eyes... His voice was raucous, his physicality pliant and emaciated. His histrionics had a melancholy tinge and conveyed from the depths an inexpressible emotional anxiety. (284-5)

Ninetto Davoli was also Pier Paolo Pasolini's lover (from 1963, when Davoli was 15) – and they lived together for years after they'd ceased being lovers. So Davoli plays a special role in Pasolini's cinema on many levels[49] (he is also, like Franco Citti, a manifestation of the street kid from the Roman shanty towns, the kind of youth that Pasolini liked to hang out with).

Enzo Siciliano characterized the relationship of Pier Paolo Pasolini and Ninetto Davoli after the eroticism had gone as a male friendship of near-equals (tho' Pasolini was 26 years older). Pasolini wasn't a father figure to Davoli, Siciliano reckoned, and they were not dependent on each other. But Pasolini was in despair when Davoli wed (in January, 1973).

In the midst of filming *The Canterbury Tales* Ninetto Davoli told Pier Paolo Pasolini that he was getting married (during shooting in Bath in the West Country). According to Enzo Siciliano, Pasolini was distraught: 'Pier Paolo's despair was uncontainable. He wanted to die' (ES, 338). The high emotion behind the camera may have coloured the movie (Pasolini composed many poems about his relationship with Davoli).

In a 1965 poem, Pier Paolo Pasolini wrote:

> Ninetto is a herald
> and overcoming (with a sweet laugh
> that blazes from his whole being
> as in a Muslim or a Hindu)

---

[48] Davoli's parents were Calabrian peasants.
[49] 'Pasolini deserves credit for foregrounding his relationship... with Davoli, who was not from the class in which the director's chic friends thought he should look for a boyfriend, and for his public frankness about this infatuation', commented Gary Indiana (91).

And that's exactly how Pasolini cast him in some films: in *Theorem*, he's the angelic messenger who visits the morose Milanese family; in *Oedipus the King*, he's the herald who guides Oedipus to the Sphinx.

However, altho' Pier Paolo Pasolini became infatuated with Ninetto Davoli and put him in quite a few films following *The Hawks and the Sparrows*,[50] he is a somewhat limited actor in terms of range (Davoli on screen tries the patience of even the most committed Pasolinian devotees). But Pasolini was quite enamoured of Davoli – especially when Davoli was teamed up with Totò (after *The Hawks and the Sparrows*, Pasolini cast Davoli in a series of films alongside Totò, including the episodes in *The Witches* and *Love and Anger*).

MAKING A FILM WITH PASOLINI

I imagine that Pier Paolo Pasolini, though a perfectionist in some areas of filmmaking, would not push his actors to numerous takes.[51] It seems as if Pasolini and the team are searching for the spontaneity of performances that *haven't* been rehearsed and blocked at length. There must be times when Pasolini would ask for many takes, but I bet in general he would shoot one or two takes then move on.

'I always shoot very short takes' (PP, 132). Pier Paolo Pasolini's cinema is constructed from short pieces of film – not for him lengthy takes where the camera and the actors're hitting many marks, and seven minute takes run thru numerous beats. 'I never use the long take (or virtually never). I hate naturalness. I reconstruct everything' (ibid.). And he didn't shoot a single master shot to cover a scene – 'I never do a whole all in one take' (ibid.). However, there *are* many examples of lengthy takes in Pasolini's films (or lengthy by the standards of today's cinema).

Sometimes Pasolini would shoot a scene with both actors in shot, and ask them not to get too close, so that he wouldn't have to film a reverse angle. That way, a scene could be covered with a single shot (Pasolini like to move fast, and get shots done quickly).

Like George Lucas in the age of digital filmmaking (and the *Star Wars* prequels), Pier Paolo Pasolini spoke of shooting as 'collecting

---

[50] And a brief cameo in *The Gospel*.
[51] Sometimes Pasolini would ask for retakes with the camera still running – asking his actors to do the scene repeatedly without cutting.

material': he was gathering content that he would shape later into a movie (in the editing room). Thus, there were opportunities for spontaneity and improvization from the non-professional actors, and later in post-production the best bits from the takes would be selected and put together.

While crews complain about being cold and wet on locations, I wonder if Pier Paolo Pasolini's crews moaned about the heat (Pasolini and co. filmed in hot, dry climes far more than in rainy, chilly regions). I bet a Pasolini shoot moved fast, too – I bet the crew didn't sit around on the grass, drinking and chatting and dancing to Euro-pop as depicted in *La Ricotta*, either. Instead, I bet it was one or two takes for each set up, then swiftly on to the next set up.

Filming a Pier Paolo Pasolini movie would provide many opportunities for cinematographic challenges for DPs – candlelight, firelight, magic hour, sunrise, sunset, plus lighting all sorts of existing locations, some of which would probably be miles from the nearest town, and with no power nearby (thus, many of the African and distant European locations in Pasolini's movies were filmed during daytime, using available light augmented by lamps. Because filming at night in remote locations is tough – and expensive).

Camera operators on a Pier Paolo Pasolini movie would need to be physically fit, too – there would be much clambering over rocks in hot sun to reach that perfect spot under an over-hanging cliff, or climbing Mount Etna[52] yet again in gales or heat. And Pasolini often preferred to have the cameras handheld, so the operators would be shouldering heavy cameras all day.[53] (On the plus side, most scenes would be filmed in one or two takes – no going to 12,457 takes like Jackie Chan, Michael Cimino or Stanley Kubrick for Pasolini!).

Pasolini was fond of staging scenes as *tableaux*. Carl-TheodorDreyer often used the frontal, *tableau* style – in *Ordet* (1955), for instance.[54] Walerian Borowczyk used it in all of his films. Theo Angelopoulos took it up in films like *Ulysses' Gaze* (1995). Sergei Paradjanov was a master of the form (in *The Color of Pomegranates*, 1969). Werner Herzog exploited the *tableau* approach in movies such as *Aguirre, Wrath of God*

---

52 A favourite Pasolini location.
53 Thus, tripod shots were dispensed with – no need to carry a tripod if the shot's going to be handheld anyway.
54 Many of the compositions in *Ordet* are flattened, with the performers arranged in a tight, flat space at right angles to the camera. It's a frontal, *tableau* approach to composition that Carl-Theodor Dreyer favoured in other movies. You might say that action is staged this way in *Ordet* because it derives from a theatrical play, and the film set is a replica of a stage. No. That has nothing to do with it: this is how some filmmakers like to block their actors (Walerian Borowczyk was the same, and so was Sergei Paradjanov).

(1972)[55] and *Heart of Glass* (1976 – in which he also hypnotized the cast!).

For the first features, Pier Paolo Pasolini and his DP Tonino Delli Colli filmed in black-and-white (Delli Colli, like many cinematographers, spoke nostalgically of b/w, and preferred it in many respects to colour film). By the Sixties, tho', colour film stock was cheaper, and distributors and television wanted colour (everybody wants colour except for filmmakers). Pasolini stuck with monochrome longer than necessary, perhaps (as did filmmakers like Federico Fellini and Ingmar Bergman), tho' the pressure of the marketplace prevailed, and from around 1966 onwards, his movies were in colour.

Colour was more complicated for Pier Paolo Pasolini, and it took more planning. Pasolini's approach to colour films was to take out all of the colours he didn't want: there are too many colours in real life, Pasolini remarked. He said he chose to shoot *Oedipus Rex* in Morocco[56] 'because there are only a few main colours there – ochre, rose, brown, green, the blue of the sky' (PP, 63). That's one reason why some filmmakers preferred to film in the studio, where the settings could be controlled entirely.

The running times of Pier Paolo Pasolini's films as director tend to be in the 80-110 minute range (with *Accattone* and *The Gospel According To Matthew* and others going over slightly). One wonders what sort of movies Pasolini might've made in the era of the 1990s, 2000s and after, when movies (and not only prestige productions), ran to 140 and 150 minutes. We might've seen longer, perhaps more rambling pictures (Pasolini was headed that way, though, with the 'trilogy of life' movies).

Compared with his contemporaries, it's striking how much of Pier Paolo Pasolini's output is comical: his first three fiction features were dead serious, but for his fourth feature, *The Hawks and the Sparrows,* Pasolini and the team attempted a comedy (with mixed results). Short films of the period, such as in the anthologies *RoGoPaG* and *The Witches*, were also comedies. And large parts of the 'trilogy of life' pictures were humorous (or they tried to be). A good reason for making the 'trilogy of life' series was to tackle something upbeat and positive after the gloom and seriousness of *Medea, Pigsty* and *Theorem.*

However, contemporaries of Pasolini's such as Federico Fellini and Jacques Tati were far more skilled with comedy, and Pasolini's attempts at humour are often badly conceived and badly executed (excellent editing

---

[55] *Aguirre* employed stylized *tableaux,* scenes which were consciously staged as paintings or portraits.
[56] *Edipo Re* was shot in Italy and Morocco (including San Petronio, Bologna).

is absolutely foundational for screen comedy, and Pasolini's films really do lack that, even with cutting by the great editor Nino Baragli). Pasolini is also *way* too indulgent with his performers (with Totò and Ninetto Davoli in particular. Totò is a great screen clown, but you can see even him struggling with the material and the situations. Davoli, meanwhile, relies too much on charm, energy and enthusiasm. Pasolini's comedies hope to get by on Marx Brothers-type clowning around, but it doesn't work. Mel Brooks and the Zucker-Abrahams-Zucker team insisted that the performers or the director shouldn't try to be funny – it was the script, the situations and the characters that were funny. And that was what Pasolini's comedies lacked – amusing characters and situations).

Indeed, it's curious that Pier Paolo Pasolini persisted in attempting to direct (and write or co-write) movies in a comical mode, when they clearly were not working. Surely people in Pasolini's entourage pointed out to him that his so-called comedies were not funny – and worse, they might damage Pasolini's reputation as a world-class director? (Or did no one dare to voice their opinion to the director? Would *you* have the guts to tell Pasolini to his face that his comedies stank?[57]).

Well, anyway, the maestro kept going, from *The Hawks and the Sparrows* and the anthology movies of the mid-Sixties onwards, to the mediæval trilogy. (It's possible that nobody dared to suggest to the maestro that the comedies weren't amusing. And anyway, *The Decameron* had been a big hit in Italia in 1971, encouraging the production of further historical comedies).

One of the chief reasons why the comedy of the 'trilogy of life' films and others can seem laboured, or haphazard, or incomprehensible is due to that issue that irks so many TV broadcasters and film distributors: cultural translation. Humour is often difficult to translate not only into different languages but different cultures and societies. Thus, comedy stars can be huge in Asia (Stephen Chow Sing-chi, for example), but almost unknown in the Western world (Stephen Chow is *very* funny – *Royal Tramp, Fight Back To School, Shaolin Soccer, The Mad Monk*, etc – but nobody knows who Chow is in the West, and he's rarely celebrated).

---

57 Not if you wanted to keep all of your fingers! Just kidding.

Some of the producers of the films directed by Pier Paolo Pasolini. Alberto Grimaldi (left). Franco Rossellini (below), and Alfredo Bini (bottom).

Pasolini with Totò during The Hawks and the Sparrows (top).
And with Anna Magnani during Mamma Roma (above).

ACTORS AND ACTING

Like Tim Burton, Woody Allen and Ken Russell, Pier Paolo Pasolini preferred actors who just 'got it' straight away, without needing lots of discussion, coddling, encouragement, and analysis. No lengthy sessions of questions and answers between actors, producers and directors, and no arguments about the characterizations. 'I choose people for what they are and not for what they pretend to be', Pasolini remarked (PP, 49).

> In general, I choose actors because of what they are as human beings, not because of what they can do. Terence Stamp was offended by this because I never asked him to demonstrate his acting ability. It was like stealing from him, using his reality. I had a similar experience with Anna Magnani on 'Mamma Roma.' She also felt I was stealing from her. (1968)

Actors were given the screenplay, but Pasolini preferred to talk them through their roles. As with many directors (such as Ken Russell), it was in the chats before filming that Pasolini really did much of his directing. The scripts might be adjusted slightly during shooting, usually in response to what an actor was doing.

The trouble with the non-acting, Robert Bressonian approach to film performance is that it can too easily come over as wooden, uninspired or just plain *boring*. There are instances in the cinema of Pier Paolo Pasolini, as well as Robert Bresson, Michelangelo Antonioni and Carl-Theodor Dreyer (four of the key exponents of the non-performance performance style), where any heat/ juice/ drama/ tension/ suspense in a scene is deflated or negated. Yes, that may be one of the goals of Bresson, Antonioni, Dreyer and Pasolini, but there are trade-offs with every performance style. (More recent proponents of po-faced non-acting include Mamoru Oshii and Theo Angelopoulos).

*

You have to admit that Pier Paolo Pasolini's appearances in his own movies were, like those of many other film directors, not especially special (quite a few film directors are convinced they can act). He was no Orson Welles or John Huston. But at least he didn't deliberately send his movies up, like Jean-Luc Godard did in his cameos in his own films.[1] And Pasolini is a significant presence in his documentaries, too – he had no problem appearing before the camera, interviewing people (or simply talk-talk-talking), or providing voiceovers (which sometimes sound like he is making it up on the spot).

---

[1] Jean-Luc Godard's best cameo is in *First Name: Carmen*, where he plays a director who commits himself to hospital because he can't – or won't – make movies anymore. And Godard's worst cameo is in *King Lear*, in which he sports a wig of electrical cables and plugs, chomps on a cigar permanently, and speaks out the side of his mouth like a would-be wise guy. It's *so* bad!

SAINTS, SINNERS AND STRANGERS (OUTSIDERS)

Filmed like mediæval saints[2] (or martyrs) in the modern world, Pier Paolo Pasolini's characters – Accattone, Stracci, Zumurrud, Ninetto – were ancient souls, who didn't fit into contemporary society, as Sam Rohdie explained in his book on the *maître*: they were outsiders, eternally at odds with their society; they are useless in terms of economy and capitalist production; they are innocents in a corrupt land; they are otherworldly, and as such were revolutionary: 'their otherworldliness, essentially their uselessness, made of them revolutionary in *this* world' (123), but not because they existed within this world, but because they refused it, they didn't compromise with it.

And yet the Pasolinian sanctification of these subproletarian characters was æsthetic and artistic, not practical or even social: that is, it was a sacralization of the subproletariat that could only take place in cinema and poetry and similar arts. As Sam Rohdie commented, Pier Paolo Pasolini gave his characters

> a sacred halo, as if they were sanctified angels. He made them into Masaccio saints, Caravaggio apostles, a Mantegna Christ, a Piero della Francesca Madonna, the Christs of Pontormo and Rosso Fiorentino. (123-4)

THE POETRY OF CINEMA

> The cinema should always be the discovery of something. I believe that the cinema should be essentially poetic.
>
> Orson Welles[3]

Pier Paolo Pasolini was a poet: his aim was to be 'purely poetical and natural'.[4] Pasolini remarked that he was 'the least Catholic of all the Italians I know' and that his religion was 'probably only a form of psychological aberration with a tendency towards mysticism'. Pasolini said he saw the world in childlike, reverential ways (PP, 14).

Poetry was an early love of Pier Paolo Pasolini's – he started to write poems in the Friulan dialect, poems of the hermetic, Symbolist kind (he

---
2 In *Accattone*, they refer to themselves as saints. What they really mean is martyrs.
3 O. Welles, interview, in A. Sarris, 1969.
4 In A. Pavelin, 33.

cited Stéphane Mallarmé, Giuseppe Ungaretti, Eugenio Montale and Rainer Maria Rilke as influences [1969, 15]). He began publishing his books of poetry in the mid-1940s (with *Poesie e Casarsa* in 1942 and *Poesie* in 1945).

Instead of one recognizable style, as with Robert Bresson or Orson Welles, underneath Pasolini's cinema was his own recognizable tone. 'You can always feel underneath my love for Dreyer, Mizoguchi and Chaplin – and some of Tati, etc, etc' (PP, 28). Of Dreyer, Mizoguchi and Chaplin,[5] Pasolini said: 'all three see things from a point of view which is absolute, essential and in a certain way holy, reverential' (PP, 43). (Notice that Pasolini cites big, serious names in cinema, not commercial, exploitation directors such as Roger Corman or William Castle.) You can't cheat in style, Pasolini maintained, but you could cheat with the content (PP, 83).

'One sees, often, an *idea* of sensuality instead of sensuality, a *concept* of comedy', Gary Indiana commented (20). Pier Paolo Pasolini's films come across as essays or notes for movies that might be made. They are films of ideas, of possibilities for future projects. The comedies aren't funny, but they contain seeds that might be explored in further works.

Pier Paolo Pasolini defends himself in this respect by insisting that his films are not finished works: rather, they are questions. 'My films are not supposed to have a finished sense, they always end with a question. I always intend them to remain suspended' (PP, 56-57).

> I've never wanted to make a conclusive statement. I've always posed various problems and left them open to consideration. (1971)

'I don't want to be paternalistic, or pedagogical, or engage in propaganda, or be an apostle', Pasolini insisted in 1970 (yet part of his personality couldn't help being a teacher).

Jean-Luc Godard was greatly admired by Pier Paolo Pasolini – to the point where some of Pasolini's films are infused with the spirit of Godard (such as *Pigsty, Theorem* and *Salò, or The 120 Days of Sodom*). Most committed filmmakers in the 1960s in Europa were inspired by Godard's films: Godard's 1960s movies remain one of the most extraordinary groups of works in cinema history.

And so many filmmakers have tried to put some Jean-Luc Godard on the screen as well as Pier Paolo Pasolini: Francis Coppola, George Lucas, Oliver Stone, Martin Scorsese, Luc Besson, Jean-Jacques Beineix,

---

[5] Charlie Chaplin and silent movie comedy was a touchstone for Pasolini, according to Sam Rohdie; Chaplin is *hommaged* in many Pasolini movies. But what did Chaplin himself think of the often very strange tributes to him in Pasolini's films?

Bernardo Bertolucci, Terence Malick, Donald Cammell, Abel Ferrara, Rainer Werner Fassbinder, Wim Wenders, Peter Greenaway, and Robert Altman. But not even cinema giants like Coppola or Pasolini have managed it as successfully as the maestro himself. As they say, Godard is still the Man.

Pier Paolo Pasolini said he wasn't much fond of North American cinema (PP, 136), and the American films he did like were directed by Europeans who had moved to the U.S.A. (such as Fritz Lang and Ernest Lubitsch). Among American directors Pasolini has cited John Ford and Orson Welles.

Though he regarded himself as 'born from the Resistance' and a Marxist, Pier Paolo Pasolini was inevitably drawn to what he called 'irrational' and 'decadent' literature.

Pier Paolo Pasolini's form of cinema was (like that of Andrei Tarkovsky or Walerian Borowczyk) the 'cinema of the image', one of André Bazin's two definitions of cinema (the other was the 'cinema of reality').[6] Pasolini had more in common with Soviet silent cinema than with Italian Neo-realism, with Dziga Vertov and Sergei Eisenstein rather than Roberto Rossellini.[7]

Pier Paolo Pasolini used the formal aspects of cinema (quotation, pastiche, parody, analogy, repetition, rhyme) to foreground its construction, its writing, to make the viewer aware of the process of fictionality. Terence Stamp (*Theorem*) said Pasolini made films in a particular way which could be called 'using the camera to write poetry'.[8]

> To watch Pasolini's films [commented Sam Rohdie] is to watch a parable, a type of non-fictional fiction, evidently made up and false, yet whose falsity is there to express a truth. (1995, 3)

Orson Welles made the same distinction: like Pier Paolo Pasolini, Welles advocated a theatrical, abstract, expressive kind of cinema. Welles' take on the realism vs. artificiality debate was simple: his films might be 'unreal', might be 'theatrical' and 'baroque', but they were 'truthful'.[9] Welles' goal was to make something that wasn't necessarily 'real', but was 'true'. It could be unreal, stylized and theatrical, but it had to be true to life.

'Cinema represents reality with reality; it is metonymic and not metaphoric' (PP, 38). Yes but exactly what 'reality' is, and what 'reality'

---

6 A. Bazin, 1960, 9f, 23f.
7 S. Rohdie, 1995, 3.
8 M. Cousins, *Scene By Scene*, Laurence King, 2002, 83.
9 'In my case, everything has to be real', Pier Paolo Pasolini insisted, 'even if only by analogy' (PP, 90).

is in cinema, is difficult to define, Pier Paolo Pasolini admitted. The first question to ask when people use terms like 'reality' or 'realism' is: *whose reality? Whose realism?*

Alain Robbe-Grillet's comments (made at the time of 1962's *Last Year At Marienbad*) summarize the position of Pier Paolo Pasolini neatly:

> I don't think either the cinema or the novel is for explaining the world. Some people believe there's a certain definite reality and all that a work of art has to do is pursue it and try to describe it... I don't think believe a work of art has reference to anything outside itself. In a film there's no reality except that of the film, no time except that of the film... The only reality is the film's, and as for the criterion of that reality, for the author it's his vision, what he feels. For the spectator, the only test is whether he accepts.[10]

For Pier Paolo Pasolini, cinema was not an image but 'an audio-visual technique in which the word and the sound have the same importance as the image' (PP, 146). Pasolini said that it was easy to see, by looking at a page, if a text was in poetry or prose, but in cinema it was more difficult. A cinema of poetry could be produced by particular techniques. For Pasolini, certain sounds could get closer quicker to the mystery of reality than written poetry.

> Even a sound image, say thunder booming in a clouded sky, is somehow infinitely more mysterious than even the most poetic description a writer could give of it. A writer has to find oniricity through a highly refined linguistic operation, while the cinema is much nearer to sounds physically, it doesn't need any elaboration. All it needs is to produce a clouded sky with thunder and straight away you are close to the mystery and ambiguity of reality. (PP, 150)

For Pier Paolo Pasolini, cinema was 'substantially and naturally poetic', because it was dream-like,[11] and because things in themselves were 'profoundly poetic':

> a tree photographed is poetic, a human face photographed is poetic because physicity is poetic in itself, because it is an apparition, because it is full of mystery, because it is full of ambiguity, because it is full of polyvalent meaning, because even a tree is a sign of a linguistic system. But who talks through a tree? God, or reality itself. Therefore the tree as a sign puts us in communication with a mysterious speaker. (PP, 153)

Even the most banal films could contain the poetry of cinema, Pier Paolo Pasolini said, but the cinema of poetry proper was a cinema 'which

---

[10] A. Robbe-Grillet, *The Observer*, Nov 18, 1962.
[11] 'Cinema is already a dream' (PP, 150)

adopts a particular technique just as a poet adopts a particular technique when he writes verse' (PP, 153). In short: 'to make a film is to be a poet'.

Pier Paolo Pasolini believed in the notion of the author of a film. He said he was the author not only of the script[12] and the direction, but of everything else (such as the choice of sets, locations, characters and costumes [PP, 32]). True, Pasolini's stamp is all over his movies, but he could not have made them without a large group of collaborators, such as regular actors like Ninetto Davoli, Silvana Mangano, Laura Betti, and Franco Citti, and production crew such as Nino Baragli (editor), Tonio Delli Colli (DP), Umberto Angelucci (assistant director), Ennio Morricone (music), Dante Ferretti (production designer), Alfredo Bini, Franco Rossellini, and Alberto Grimaldi (producers).

Once again, let's not forget the actors: no matter how well a script is written, or the concept of the film is conceived, it is actors on set who have to express it all. So Pasolini *did not* do everything himself! (But his reputation persists even today in overshadowing everybody else).

In Pier Paolo Pasolini's poetics of cinema, reality and cinema commingle, as a system of signs.

> The cinema is a language which expresses reality with reality. So the question is: what is the difference between the cinema and reality? Practically none.

To express people, Pier Paolo Pasolini used people; to express trees, Pasolini used real trees, as he found them in reality. In a interview in the *New York Times* (1968), Pasolini stated:

> the cinema forced me to remain always at the level of reality, right inside reality: When I make a film I'm always in reality, among the trees and among the people; there's no symbolic or conventional filter between me and reality as there is in literature. The cinema is an explosion of my love for reality. I have never conceived of making a film that would be a work of a group, I've always thought of a film as a work of an author, not only the script and the direction but the choices of sets and locations, the characters, even the clothes. I choose everything, not to mention the music. (PP, 29)

No veils or no distantiation between the filmmaker and reality – and no metaphors either.

Reality doesn't need metaphors to express itself... In the cinema it is as

---

12 Many of Pasolini's scripts didn't alter much during production. And the filmmakers shot pretty much what was in the script. For *The Hawks and the Sparrows*, a sequence was filmed but cut (for running time). For *Accattone*, a scene was cut because the film was too long.

though reality expressed itself with itself, without metaphors, and without anything insipid and conventional and symbolic. (ib., 38)

However, despite Pier Paolo Pasolini's penchant for realistic, non-metaphorical or non-symbolic cinema, he did not like naturalism. He aimed for realism, not naturalism. 'I believe deeply in reality, in realism, but I can't stand naturalism', he asserted (PP, 39).

Pier Paolo Pasolini repositioned himself *vis-à-vis* the Neo-realism tradition (in Italian cinema) and the films of Roberto Rossellini, saying that the naturalistic, credulous and crepuscular everyday reality of Neo-realist cinema was not his style. The detachment, warmth and irony of Neo-realism were 'characteristics which I do not have', commented Pasolini (PP, 109). Maybe – but Pasolini's cinema, and not only his early works, exhibit many of the elements of Neo-realist cinema. In the late 1960s, Pasolini said he did not go to the cinema anymore for entertainment, unless he could be sure the film was going to be worth seeing (PP, 136).

PASOLINI AND PAINTING

Pier Paolo Pasolini is known as a Mannerist (the same accusations have been made of Bernardo Bertolucci, Walerian Borowczyk and Peter Greenaway). Sometimes critics also use the term 'Baroque' (yes, even film critics, God bless them!, don't know their art history as well as they should). Yet altho' the Mannerist artists – Pontormo, Michelangelo, Rosso, Mantegna – were cited often by the maestro, he also revered the Early Renaissance artists (Giotto, Duccio, Piero, Masaccio, Angelico, etc).

Pier Paolo Pasolini was something of a 'Renaissance' man, in the sense of being happy to work in a number of disciplines: poetry, painting, criticism/ essays, short stories, novels, films, reportage and theatre. He was 'Renaissance' in another sense, taking much of his inspiration from (mainly Italian) Renaissance art (in the deployment of religious imagery in *The Gospel According To Matthew*, for example).

The two favoured periods of painting in Pier Paolo Pasolini's cinema were the Early Renaissance (Giotto di Bondone, Duccio Buoninsegna, Masaccio and Piero della Francesca), and the High Renaissance,

Mannerism and Baroque (Michelangelo Buonarroti, Jacopo Pontormo, Sebastiano del Piombo, Giovanni Battista Rosso and Andrea del Sarto). Pasolini spoke of being deeply influenced by the Early Renaissance masters like Giotto and Masaccio – to the point where, in cinema, he automatically composed shots using their visual techniques (where 'man stands at the center of every perspective', as Pasolini put it). Even moving shots were like the lens was moving over a painting. 'I always conceive the background of a painting, like a stage set, and for this reason I always attack it frontally' (and even tho' he sometimes fought against the Renaissance pictorial approach, he could never lose it completely, because it was so deeply embedded in his psyche). Books of art were used on the set to help with setting up shots.

STYLE

> One can cheat in everything except style.
>
> Pier Paolo Pasolini

Pier Paolo Pasolini said he didn't have a cinematic style of his own, like Charlie Chaplin or Jean-Luc Godard: his style was made up of many influences and inspirations; he was a *pasticheur*, he said (among the filmmakers that Pasolini cited were Jacques Tati, Carl Theodor Dreyer, Kenji Mizoguchi, Chaplin and Godard). The dream in *Wild Strawberries* (1957) was admired by Pasolini – 'remarkable, it comes very close to what dreams are really like' (PP, 150). Anyway, what counts, Pasolini insisted, wasn't the form or even the content, but the violence and intensity of the work, 'the passion I put into things' (PP, 28). Tsui Hark, a dragon emperor among film directors, said a similar thing: sometimes, it's not the characters, or the stories, or the themes that interest a filmmaker, but the *attitude* of the piece. In 2011, Tsui said (in *Twitch*):

> The best thing actually to do is write according to what you feel. If you feel your heart would take you to the point where you would want to express something to do with the story or the film. Sometimes it's not the story; sometimes it's the way you tell the story. Sometimes it's the attitude you have with the story. The attitude is something you build and you accumulate for a long time for no reason and no logic, it's there. When you write that way, you might want to make it that way.

Pier Paolo Pasolini's cinema is full of conventional and clichéd elements. Some are so obvious that they're seldom remarked upon, as if Pasolini is somehow exempt from being treated like any other filmmaker, as if he soars above narrative conventions (in the legend that is Pasolini the Poet, Pasolini the Saint). He doesn't: the motif of the death of the hero is a good example: films like *Accattone, Mamma Roma, Pigsty, Theorem* as well as the tragedies close with the demise of the main characters.

*

Not known as a technically brilliant filmmaker, or rather, a filmmaker for whom technique was an end in itself, or something that had to be got absolutely right, as with F.W. Murnau, Andrei Tarkovsky or Alfred Hitchcock, Pier Paolo Pasolini could nevertheless orchestrate the technical arsenal of cinema to do anything he wanted. But Pasolini is the opposite of a technical film director, the polar opposite of someone like Jackie Chan or Stanley Kubrick, who would shoot take after take until they got what they were looking for.[13] But for directors like Pasolini and Jean-Luc Godard, that approach to filmmaking would be ridiculous, wasteful, and pointless (Godard, like Werner Herzog, preferred to shoot one or two takes. No more were necessary).

Pier Paolo Pasolini did share one thing with perfectionists like Jackie Chan, Michael Cimino, Fritz Lang and George Lucas of course: total control. I bet there was no question as to who was the top guy on set in a Pasolini movie. Pasolini regarded cinema as the work of one man, an author. Terry Gilliam commented that in Italy the director is treated like a maestro (*à la* Luchino Visconti and Federico Fellini). Consequently, when Gilliam was shooting *The Adventures of Baron Munchausen* in Roma in 1988, one of the things he couldn't get used to was that production crew were reluctant to offer suggestions, and Gilliam preferred to work as a team.

---

[13] The final shot of *The Shining*, the slow tracking shot towards the hotel wall and the 1920s photograph, took ages to film. Stanley Kubrick wanted it to be as fluid as possible. The camera crew tried changing the dolly cart; they put it on a track; they took it off the track; they loaded it with more weight; they put more people on it (in V. LoBrutto, 1997, 444).

The idea of re-shooting that tracking shot again and again, until it was as smooth and perfect as possible, just wouldn't occur on a Pier Paolo Pasolini set! (Or a Jean-Luc Godard set!). Forget it!

PASOLINI: THEMES AND ISSUES

Consider the works of Pier Paolo Pasolini in print, theatre, TV or cinema (and in numerous interviews), and a host of concerns and themes will pop out time after time:

• Politics is part of pretty much everything that Pasolini did or said in the public arena.

• Communism – Pasolini was in constant dialogue with Communism, and with the Partito Comunista Italiano (which he voted for and was once a member[14]).

• Pasolini celebrated peasants, the under-class, and never lost his reverence for them.

• Southern Italy and its peasants were very important for Pasolini (he linked the area and its inhabitants to the Third World).

• The love of the Friulian dialect is part of Pasolini's exaltation of all things sub-proletarian and working class.

• The progress of Italy towards being a modern, capitalist nation was a recurring concern for Pasolini (in particular how modern technology would affect his beloved peasant class).

• For Pasolini, consumerism[15] was nothing less than 'a real anthropological cataclysm', and 'pure degradation'.

• Pasolini venerated his mother, and had a very ambiguous relationship with his father.

• Pasolini had a vision/ theory of cinema as poetry, as a means of mythicizing life.

• Pasolini was searching for the epic and the mythological in everyday life (and said he saw it everywhere).

• Sexuality – altho' many commentators always draw attention to Pasolini's homosexuality, it actually plays a much smaller role in his works than the Pasolini Legend would suggest.

*

Nothing is resolved to a point of bliss or unity in the cinema of Pier Paolo Pasolini: his art is one of eternal strife and dissatisfaction. There is a conflict between opposites, and the oppositions are instantly familiar:

Male	Female
Men	Women
Masculine	Feminine
Father	Mother

---

[14] He had been thrown out of the Communist Party following the sex scandal in 1949.
[15] Pasolini said he detested consumerism 'in a complete physical sense'.

Present	Past
Youth	Age
Realism	Fantasy
Reality	Poetry
Heterosexuality	Homosexuality
North (Europe/ Italy)	South (Europe/ Italy)
Bologna	Rome
Italy	Third World
Europe	Asia/ Africa
Christianity	Communism
Capitalism	Marxism
Wealth	Poverty
Bourgeoisie	Proletariat

PRE-MODERN, PRE-INDUSTRIAL, PRE-CAPITALIST

Pier Paolo Pasolini enshrined pre-industrial Italy, the Italy of his youth, which he reckoned was being eroded in the modern era, with its advanced (North American/ Western) capitalism, its technology, its science. By the 1960s, much of the world that Pasolini yearned for was rapidly disappearing underneath concrete and tenements (it was a similar story of suburbanization all over the developed world).[16] Pasolini neglects to recognize that young people in the Western world embraced all things American with incredible fervour. They *wanted* America, even more than America or the Americans did! (As director Elio Petri remarked, America had already been colonizing Italy culturally from the 1930s – via Hollywood cinema).

In short: after the war, *teenagers in Europe wanted all things American.*

They *yearned* for the U.S.A. following World War Two. The choice was: America or Europe? Dreary, war-torn, impoverished Europe or glitzy, out-size America? Pop acts in Britain such as the Beatles and the Rolling Stones opted for the Great American Dream. The coolest youth culture was American. The clothes. The music. The movies. The cars. The places. The language…

---
16 Yet if you visit Italy today it can still feel archaic.

As Paul McCartney put it, Route 66 and the American South in the blues music that he and John Lennon loved sounded so much more glamourous than dear, old England:

> We know about the Cast-Iron Shore and the East Lancs Motorway but they never sounded as good to us, because we were in awe of the Americans. Even their Birmingham, Alabama, sounded better than our Birmingham.[17]

Let's remember that after WWII much of Italy was in pieces and it received around $1.2 billion in aid (from the Marshall Plan and other initiatives) from the U.S.A. (only France and Britain received more U.S. assistance). Like it or not, Italy and America were intimately linked politically and ideologically as well as economically and socially in the postwar era.

Anyway, these yearnings of Pier Paolo Pasolini's for earlier times which were thought to be better (even if they actually weren't), occur in many artists. Fifty years before Pier Paolo Pasolini, for instance, D.H. Lawrence (1885-1930) had spoken with incredible fury of the ugly, industrial Midlands, and how his England ('England, My England') was being destroyed by modern social and industrial forces (the Midlands is far worse today than in Lorenzo's time). And before Lawrence, Thomas Hardy had decried the advances of the modern era and the Industrial Revolution.

And so it goes, back and back, so that artists and writers can never reach that Eden, that Paradise, when all was better, richer, deeper, purer, juicier. No it wasn't. This is age talking, this is growing up to become an adult talking. Because if you are an eighteen year-old today, in the 21st century, I bet you could be having a *fantastic time*! But in thirty years, you'd look back and think, darn, things were cooler thirty years ago!

You can't win, because you can't turn back time. You can't be 17 again. What? Did Pier Paolo Pasolini want to return to the 1920s, the decade of his birth? Or – why hold back? – why not go back to the 1810s (pre-industrialization)? Or the 1580s, the height of Pasolini's beloved Renaissance era? Or, hell, why not go back to the Roman Empire?!

Truth is, Pier Paolo Pasolini's comparisons of then and now, of the 1930s with the 1960s, are simply more of his dualistic worldview, his penchant for oppositions, for automatically and violently slamming two eras, two political views, two artforms, two whatevers together. That's how Pasolini made art, by setting something up he could kick against (whether it was capitalism, or consumerism, or technology, or fascism, or

---
17 B. Miles. *Paul McCartney*, Secker & Warburg, London, 1997, 201.

old age, or poverty, or concrete jungles). With Pasolini, it's always 'us and them', 'me and that', 'I and those'.

Pier Paolo Pasolini knew that his mythical, ancient past didn't exist, and probably had never existed. But, as with God, or belief, or religion, an Eden was necessary for his existence.[18] He needed to believe that primitive cultures were more in touch with nature, or more 'authentic', or more substantial as communities, even if they weren't, even if nothing like his idealized, utopian communities ever existed.

The *idea* of the ancient world – and the Third World – is thus vital to Pier Paolo Pasolini's project: it might never have had any 'reality', outside of essays, and discussions, and films, and poems (the past as cultural imaginary), but that didn't matter. Because it was useful for Pasolini to have an invented, mythical past with which to accuse the present day (for falling short of his ideals, his utopia). The utopian, idealized past was also a realm, as Sam Rohdie pointed out (1995, 110), in which Pasolini could play and explore, and in which he was in control.

Pier Paolo Pasolini's utopias were not to be found in the real, contemporary world, which was too capitalist, too bourgeois, too consumerist and too superficial for him. Instead, he looked to exotic climes (to Southern Italia), to the Third World (particularly to Africa, the Middle East and India), and to the distant past (of the ancient world). The notion of *ancestors*, then, is crucial – Pasolini explored the idea of people living today who had ancestors going back to the ancient world.

The exaltation of peasant, primitive societies in Pier Paolo Pasolini's philosophy has a right-wing, regressive and racist component, as Sam Rohdie noted: this nostalgia for archaic, pre-modern societies (communities which Pasolini claimed to have found in Africa and the Middle East), chimes with the writings of Claude Lévi-Strauss, with D.H. Lawrence and Gustave Flaubert, with Marguerite Duras' novels of the Orient, and, most problematically with racist and Nazi theorists such as Ernest Renan and Arthur de Gobineau.

Pier Paolo Pasolini might've known what was wrong with contemporary society in the West, but he didn't know how to put it right, or how to make his utopian visions come to fruition. Of course. It's much easier to attack, to identify targets and hit them, than it is to build a whole new world. (No artist of recent times has come up with a complete, complex, and convincing vision of how a utopia/ paradise/ new world would work).

Artists complain about modern society, and in TV and films super-

---

[18] One of the recurring motifs in the 'trilogy of life' movies (and in other Pasolini movies) is the notion of miracles. Many times characters are speaking in awed tones of a *miracolo*. And in Fellini's cinema.

villains are always destroying the world (or trying to). But *no one* has any idea at all what to put in its place. (We could get into a really fascinating topic here – the formation of alternative communities or societies in the modern era. For example, communities that have been developed along women-only, or feminist and lesbian lines (several female communes/ communities have been founded in the U.S.A.). Many would-be utopias tend to be very small, and often last only as long as the lifetimes of the original founders. When the creators die, or leave, alternative communities often go into decline and break up).

PASOLINI AND AMERICA

Pier Paolo Pasolini remained a European film director, and didn't leave for North America like some of his contemporaries. Nor did he venture into co-productions with North American companies. And he tended to cast from European (mainly Italian) actors, and didn't use North American actors, like many of his contemporaries. He also didn't take up North American subjects: his movies stay in Italy, or they venture into the Middle East, Africa, Britain or India (whereas a filmmaker such as Jean-Luc Godard has explored probably the most passionate love-hate relationship with the U.S.A. in all of cinema). Pasolini's films are Italian, made by and for Italians, even when their subjects are Ancient Greek or Arabian. However, thru producer Alberto Grimaldi and his distribution deals with United Artists, Pasolini was linked to the North American movie business (and some of his movies were financed with U.$. dollars; this occurred throughout the Italian film industry).

Pier Paolo Pasolini visited Gotham in October, 1966, for a retrospective of his cinema organized by Richard Roud, an important showcase for Pasolini's work in the New World. Pasolini loved N.Y.C. (it was his first trip to the U.S.A.).

> I'm in love with New York. I have a passion beyond words for it. Like Romeo and Juliet – love at first sight. It is the most beautiful city in the world. I love the huge mingling of enormous amounts of people, races. The mixture of cruelty and innocence. New York is a piece of mythical reality, as beautiful as the Sahara Desert.

ON EROTICISM AND VOYEURISM

A significant ingredient in the cinema of Pier Paolo Pasolini is the emphasis on voyeurism: every movie contains sequences of people looking and being looked at. And, like the cinema of Tsui Hark, Alfred Hitchcock or Orson Welles, Pasolini is a master at orchestrating the network of looks and camera angles: consider the angles and the viewpoints that Pasolini and the DPs select, for instance, or how editor Nino Baragli cuts those shots together.

It's not only the erotic aspect of voyeurism and scopophilia that Pier Paolo Pasolini's cinema activates – power and the relationship of power between the observer and the object are more to the point than sex. 'Desire' is a better term than sex or eroticism – 'desire' with all its philosophical associations with the Lacanian lack, with loss, with distance, with Kristevan abjection, with Foucauldian power. Yes – *distance* – the looking and looked-at-ness in Pasolini's cinema emphasizes the sadness and loss evoked by the distance between people. Looking is not pleasurable in Pasolini's work – the observers are not getting off on looking: rather, looking reminds them of their own loneliness, their separateness from everything. Pasolini made a remark about sex in cinema that resonates here, how seeing sex emphasizes sadness and distance.

As for sex, titillation, nudity – well, Pier Paolo Pasolini didn't use *those* particular ingredients the same way anyone else did, either. Sex and nudity are some of the tried and tested and above all *cheap* means of getting an audience's attention (maintaining it is something else). Hence so much of exploitation cinema, *mondo* cinema, cult cinema, and European (art) cinema, has used the genres of horror, fantasy and thriller (all cheap genres to produce), and included plenty of naked bodies. Or any scenario where characters can disrobe and get freaky. Sex and nudity are simply easier to market than, say, abstract concepts like Ludwig Wittgenstein's philosophy of language or the notion of pessimism in the philosophy of Arthur Schopenhauer.

So if Pier Paolo Pasolini wasn't going (to be persuaded) to use stars in his movies, a producer might think, at least we'll have some T. and A. to be able to market the picture – something for the film poster and the trailers (in the way that producers Joe Levine and Carlo Ponti asked Jean-Luc Godard to shoot some nude scenes featuring Brigitte Bardot in

Contempt.[19] As Levine told Godard, the 1963 movie 'didn't have enough ass in it'. So Godard, Raoul Coutard and co. duly filmed B.B. naked[20]).

But Pier Paolo Pasolini wouldn't do that! Yes, there *would* be naked bodies and people Doing The Deed in his movies, but the sex would be either desperate or off-the-wall, or the bodies wouldn't be slinky, European vixens and handsome, buff men.

HANDHELD CAMERA

Sometimes, the over-use of handheld camera can be irritating in the films of Pier Paolo Pasolini. So much effort has clearly gone into the production design, the costume design, the props, the art direction, the casting, the hair and make-up, the lighting and the visuals of Pasolini's films, it seems wasteful or irresponsible (at first) that all that hard work should be captured with a shaky camera (a *very* shaky camera at times – there are many ways of doing a handheld shot!). But the viewer soon gets used to it, and the handheld camera becomes a cinematic device that Pasolini and the camera operators employed repeatedly to achieve a sense of poetic immediacy and urgency to their narratives.[21] The handheld camera becomes a tool of someone totally confident about capturing the action in front of the lens. (One can't imagine studio executives in a Hollywood studio being satisfied with that kind of loose, improvized camerawork if they had been financing Pasolini's films. Of course, self-consciously shaky camerawork has become fashionable in TV and movies since the 1990s, but it's fake, simulating *cinéma verité*, and is never as haphazard as the handheld camerawork in Pasolini's movies).[22] (You can see Pasolini at work filming *Salò*, where it seems that he operated the *macchina* himself sometimes, and you can see that he is wobbling the camera at times).

Other *auteurs* employed handheld camerawork far more than usual –

---

[19] Joe Levine and Carlo Ponti, wanted Brigitte Bardot to be seen nude in *Le Mépris*. Levine demanded reshoots of Bardot nude, and Godard drew up a budget which he thought Levine might not pay, being twice what it should be. But Levine OK-ed it and the scenes were filmed: Bardot nude with Michel Piccoli, Bardot nude on different coloured rugs, Bardot running by a lake, and Bardot with Jack Palance (dressing after sex, tho' this wasn't used).
[20] That must've been a tough day of filming: 'OK, Brigitte, now you take your clothes off, *bien*?'
[21] Enzo Siciliano has rationalized the shaky camerawork by saying that it expresses 'the sign of his hand, the visual possibility of his retina. Style tries to be life, life in its entirety' (240).
[22] The actors are always in focus and framed nicely and well-lit, for a start. The framing is traditional, even if the camerawork seems shaky. And the self-conscious, wobbly camerawork is always integrated into familiar editing patterns and dramatic structures. Not so with Pasolini's cinema.

Walerian Borowczyk comes to mind, and also Ken Russell (which Russell often operated himself – his camerawork is instantly recognizable). In their movies, the handheld camera isn't used to evoke a 'documentary' approach, or to emulate an actor's movement or viewpoint, it is a whole stylistic manner bound entirely to the material and the drama.[23]

SOUND

One reason given for the tradition of dubbing in Italian cinema is the lack of decent equipment following WWII (and the absence of it during the war). Yes, true, you could use that excuse at the start of the 1960s, but not by the end of the 1960s, when so many hit movies had been filmed in Italy. And movies that shot in Cinecittà, such as 1963's *Cleopatra*, used direct sound (when Italy was the biggest film production centre in Europa). Besides, the cost of a Nagra tape recorder, a couple of mics, a boom and some electrical cables isn't really *that* much (even provincial film schools have them).

There are other reasons, however: one is that Italian sound stages could be noisy (and were not constructed to the same sound-proofed standards of state-of-the-art studios. Cinecittà, for instance, might possess the largest stage in Europe, but it had only had one indoor restroom). Another reason is that the casts of Italian movies often comprised actors who spoke different languages. A key reason is probably the cinema distributors and exhibitors, who wouldn't want to pay the extra costs for sound editing and mixing (with looping, actors can sit in a studio and dub their lines in a few hours). Also, apparently, Benito Mussolini (a big influence on Italian cinema), didn't want to hear foreign languages in movies, so they were dubbed in Italian.

For overseas versions of his films, Pier Paolo Pasolini said he preferred subtitles rather than dubbing (PP, 40). Jean-Luc Godard preferred dubbing to subtitling for foreign prints – he thought it was more honest. As Godard noted in *Histoire(s) du Cinéma*,[24] postwar Italian cinema was filmed without sound – instead, the great Italian poetry

---

[23] And also for speed – Borowczyk liked to use the handheld camera to get shooting quickly once everything was ready.
[24] Pier Paolo Pasolini appears in *Histoire(s) du Cinéma*, with Jean-Luc Godard intercutting a photograph of the maestro with a painting by Piero della Francesca (from *The Legend of the True Cross*).

(Ovid, Dante) replaced the sound.

And not only is the sound added afterwards in all Italian cinema after WWII, it's often a completely new cast. As in any industry which relies on voices, like radio, or TV commercials, or feature animation, producers and directors will have their favourite voice actors (often they're also the actors who dub Hollywood movies for Italian distributors). Pasolini would have likely certain voice actors in mind when he was casting their screen counterparts, for example.

Pier Paolo Pasolini followed the example of Federico Fellini in the use of sound. For Fellini, direct sound wasn't a big deal, and he didn't think highly of the fetishization of it in North American movies. In short, Fellini much preferred to add the sound on after shooting. It was also because Fellini liked to talk to his actors during takes (or, as U.S. director Elia Kazan observed on a visit to a Fellini set: he 'yelled at the actors'). So a take on a Fellini film often had the maestro telling his actors what to do. Famously, Fellini had his performers simply recite numbers if they didn't know the text.

The point is, when you are replacing the entire soundtrack to a movie, and not using any live sound recorded on set at all, there is an enormous *potential* for exploring some really interesting things in sound and music and dialogue. Unfortunately, the films directed by Pier Paolo Pasolini don't often take advantage of that (compared to the king of post-synchronized soundtracks, Orson Welles. And even when some of Welles' experiments were spoilt by technical faults, as in *Othello* or *Macbeth*, and interference from studios or producers, the results are still fascinating). The truth is, Pasolini as a film director is far less compelling in the realms of sound compared to some other filmmakers (even tho' he thought of cinema not as simply an image, but as an audio-visual experience). Part of this is attributable to the poor technical facilities in sound in Italian cinema.

Pier Paolo Pasolini preferred to dub voices on later: he reckoned that dubbing 'while altering a character, also makes it more mysterious; it enlarges and enriches it. I'm against filming in sync' (PP, 39). It was part of Pasolini's penchant for pastiche and anti-naturalism: 'I believe deeply in reality, in realism, but I can't stand naturalism' (ibid.).

It was also because many of the actors in Pier Paolo Pasolini's films were non-professionals, and weren't used to the rigours of acting, such as remembering cues and dialogue (so their voices were replaced by professional actors back in Roma). And Pasolini also liked to direct actors during takes (like Federico Fellini), from behind the camera (again, this is also partly due to using non-professionals, who needed more guidance than professional actors).

Often even the professional actors in a Pier Paolo Pasolini movie didn't dub their own voices.[25] Pasolini liked this – and he liked to have two non-professional actors create a character: one to perform it on set, and one in the dubbing theatre.[26] In fact, Pasolini would travel to parts of Italy to hire actors who weren't Roman or part of the film business, because he was after unaffected, untrained, working class voices, or a particular regional accent. (Thus, the performances in Italian cinema are actually a double act: the actor *and* the voice actor).

MUSIC

Too many film critics had (and still have) little idea about the music that Pier Paolo Pasolini included in his movies – particularly what is now known as 'world music'. After several decades of 'world music' circulating in the media and popular culture, we can spot particular sounds and musics, we are used to hearing those sounds – but critical accounts of the 1960s tended to flounder (but musical appreciation is often way down the list for film critics, and they also don't have the intellectual capabilities to assess it. Also music can be fiendishly challenging to *really* describe (try describing the physical sound of a piano). Hence, critics talk about everything else – the musicians, the singers, the lyrics, the celebrities, the fashions, the concerts; anything but the actual music).

Notice that the classical music composers that Pasolini liked to use in his films tended to be German/ Austrian – Bach, Mozart, Webern, Orff, etc – rather than Italian. Pasolini did employ Antonio Vivaldi, but often neglected the big names of Italy, such as Verdi, Rossini, Puccini, Monteverdi, etc.

Sometimes the music in a Pier Paolo Pasolini-directed movie is allowed to burble along, without editing, punctuation or dramatic significance: altho' Pasolini is often described as a genius with putting music in movies, occasionally the underscore meanders thru scenes at a low volume for too long (this usually occurs with existing recordings). And

---

25 The voice dubbing actors in *The Gospel* include Enrico Maria Salerno, Cesare Barnetti, Gianni Bonagura, Pino Locchi and Emanuela Rossi.
26 Pier Paolo Pasolini also said that he wasn't interested in actors who depended on their voices (PP, 40).

his films do that with genius composers such as Vivaldi, Bach and Mozart (for musos, this is sacrilege, demeaning, a crime against music, turning music into muzak).

Also, the music is often mixed far too low – this may be due to the unsatisfying sound mixes on the home entertainment releases of movies. (Sometimes movies are remixed for DVD and video releases, but often they're not: the sound mixes of the films directed by Pier Paolo Pasolini, stemming from 1961-1975, will probably all be the original mono mixes).

There are times in Pasolini's movies when you wish that some effort had been undertaken during pre-production (1) to select the *final* pieces of music for a film, and (2) to clear the rights to use the music. Adding the music later often doesn't work in sections featuring singing and dancing. There are wonderful scenes captured in the historical movies (*Medea, Oedipus Rex, The Arabian Nights*, etc) of players playing and singers singing which have completely different music dubbed over them.

PASOLINI, BOROWCZYK AND JARMAN

The cinema of Walerian Borowczyk (1923-2006) has many affinities with that of Pier Paolo Pasolini: both come from the same highly intellectual, highly educated, European backgrounds which valorize *avant garde* art, philosophy (Existentialism), Surrealism, de Sade, etc. Both were mavericks, who worked on the fringes of commercial cinema. Both produced controversial, Euro-art movies which included plenty of eroticism and nudity as well as politically provocative subject matter. Borowczyk's debut feature, *Goto: Island of Love*, was seen as an allegory about a Communist state, echoing Borowczyk's own experience of growing up in Poland. It amused Borowczyk, for example, that *Goto: Island of Love* was banned in fascist Spain as well as Eastern Bloc nations. In the truly remarkable *Immoral Tales* (1974), Borowczyk attacked European fascism in the 20th century, with his take on the 'Countess Dracula' myth – in which Countess Báthory collects and slays a group of virgins in order to bathe in their blood (*Erzsébet Báthory* was set in Eastern Europe in 1610, and starred Pablo Picasso's daughter Paloma in her only film role). With its scenes of mass degradation and nudity, of naked victims being herded and controlled like concentration camp inmates, *Immoral Tales* chimes closely with *Salò*.

Derek Jarman (1942-1994) was one of a number of filmmakers who cited Pier Paolo Pasolini as an inspiration. Jarman worked with Ken Russell in the early 1970s (on *The Devils* and *Savage Messiah*). Jarman came to critics' attention with the gay film *Sebastiane* (1976), a totally Pasolinian piece. Jarman wanted the film to be like Pasolini, but it turned out (or was sold or consumed) as gay soft porn (though it wasn't). Jarman spoke of a 'romance in the camera' that he saw 'all over the Pasolini films – something vulnerable, an archaic smile. I see it in our films, nowhere else. This is all I really want to film' (1991, 143).

Attempting a film in the manner of Pier Paolo Pasolini on one's first feature was very ambitious (Derek Jarman had already made many short Super-8 films by 1976). But Pasolini is by far the greater artist than Jarman in every respect. None of Jarman's films come close to even Pasolini's middling efforts. There is simply a welter more life, more humour, more emotion, more imagination and more invention in Pasolini's cinema than in Jarman's cinema. Take the use of non-actors, which both directors liked to do a lot: Pasolini could compose a poetry of unusual faces and characters from the simplest means, while in Jarman's pictures the non-actors drift about aimlessly. Pasolini had a genius for choosing fascinating people and orchestrating them within sequences, and putting them in amongst his professional actors which's pretty much unique in cinema. Absolutely no other filmmaker employs extras like Pasolini. By contrast, too often the non-professional actors in Jarman's movies are dull people doing dull things.

Pasolini making documentaries in Africa (top) and India (above).

Filming The Arabian Nights in Isafahan (left).
Filming Salò (below).

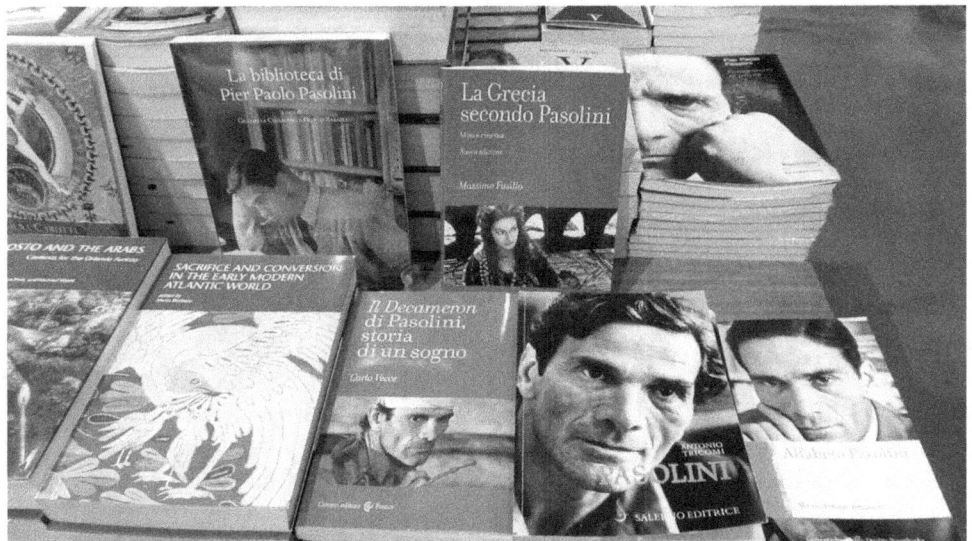

Pasolini's books and films on display in Rome's biggest bookstore

PART TWO
✳
THE FILMS

...to make films is to be a poet.

Pier Paolo Pasolini

5

ACCATTONE

BEGGAR

THE PRODUCTION.
Aged 39, Pier Paolo Pasolini began his impressive feature film directing career (of 14 years) with *Accattone* (Arco Film, 1961), an amazingly assured debut set in the working class districts of Rome (however, by 1961, he was already an accomplished artist, fully rounded creatively, and the author of many works, some of which had been critically lauded (while others had been controversial).) So Pasolini wasn't a newbie in any sense, and he had already been contributing scripts for movies, right back to at least 1954 (so he'd been working in cinema for at least seven years). Indeed, in 1960 alone, Pasolini contributed to around five film scripts (including *Marte di un Amico, I Bell'Antonio, La Lunga Notte del '43, La Giornata Balorda* and *Il Carro Armato dell'8 Settembre*). Pasolini said he became a scriptwriter because he needed the money[1] [PP, 31]). The move from screenwriter to director is one that many filmmakers have taken – famous examples include Woody Allen, Billy Wilder and Barry Levinson.

Accattone was a story of pimps, whores, thieves and unemployed men in modern-day Roma. Pasolini had been disappointed with aspects of the movies adapted from his fiction (*The Big Night/ La Notte Brava* and *La Canta dell Marane*): *Accattone* is the maestro's reply to those adaptations: *Accattone* announces that *this* is how his novels should be filmed.

---
[1] He had lost his teaching job in 1949 due to a sexual scandal.

Franco Citti (born in 1938 – 23 at the time) was brilliant in the role of the title character, Vittorio 'Accattone'[2] Cataldi; it is another dual role, however, because Citti was dubbed – by Paolo Ferraro (Pasolini later regretted dubbing Citti, yet he had Ferraro dub Citti again – in *Oedipus Rex* in 1967).

Pier Paolo Pasolini wrote the script for Franco Citti:[3] 'I wrote every line for him, and the script in the film is exactly as I wrote it, down to the last comma' [PP, 135]). Some critics regard *Accattone* as a version of Pasolini's novels *Boys of Life* and *A Violent Life* (indeed, the adaptation of *A Violent Life*, released not long after *Accattone*, has numerous affinities with *Accattone*, including the crew and of course the lead role of a disenfranchised youth played by Citti). Sergio Citti, Pasolini's lover and long-time collaborator, was Franco Citti's real brother, and played his brother in the film.

Accattone is a stunning film debut: Pier Paolo Pasolini steps right up to the mark and delivers a scorching piece for his first movie as director (tho' not his first as writer). It's a fully confident film, that knows what it's doing, that has something to say, and knows how to say it. (It is also a long film (it's constructed in four acts), again stemming from that confidence. It's not a 70 or 80 minute piece which runs out of things to say. However, *Accattone* is not solely the story of the young crook Accattone – secondary characters carry subplots).

It wasn't all Pier Paolo Pasolini on his own making *Accattone*, of course: he had some talented collaborators, including the genius director of photography Tonino Delli Colli, editor Nino Baragli, producers Alfredo Bini and Cino Del Duca, the art director was Flavio Mogherini, Carlo Rustichelli arranged the music, and as the first A.D., the twenty year-old Bernardo Bertolucci. Released Nov 22, 1961. 120 minutes.

Accattone had been set up first with Federico Fellini's new company, Federiz. But Fellini wasn't convinced by the tests that Pier Paolo Pasolini and a crew filmed. (Conditions hadn't been ideal, however – the camera didn't work properly, there wasn't enough raw stock, the actors were new, etc). Anyway, Federiz were reluctant to back anyone else's work apart from that of Fellini.

There were other producers who were interested in working with Pier Paolo Pasolini – Sandro Jacovini and Tonino Cervi (they had produced *The Big Night* in 1959, adapted from *Ragazzi di Vita*). When they lost interest, Fellini was the next stop. When Fellini cooled on *Accattone*,

---

[2] Accattone is a nickname which means 'beggar' or 'scrounger'. And Vittorio prefers to be called 'Accattone': there are lots of 'Vittorios', he claims, but only one 'Accattone'.
[3] The brother of his lover, Sergio Citti, Pasolini had known Franco since he was a small boy (PP, 38).

Pasolini tried to get Jacovini and Cervi interested again. At this point, Alfredo Bini approached Pasolini (director Mauro Bolognini had pointed Bini in Pasolini's direction after seeing photos of the screen tests).

Accattone also began filmmaking associations that would be key for Pier Paolo Pasolini: producer Alfredo Bini, DP Tonino Delli Colli, editor Nino Baragli, music arranger Carlo Rustichelli, and Elsa Morante. Plus of course actors such as Franco Citti, Adele Cambria, Stefano D'Arrigo, Adriana Asti, etc. As with many filmmakers, including many of your favourites, gathering a group around them of like-minded and dedicated collaborators is *absolutely fundamental* to the continuing success of their cinema. This group was instrumental in creating the cinema of Pasolini (and many worked with him right up to the final film).

The rest of the cast of *Accattone* included: Franca Pasut as Stella, Silvana Corsini as Maddalena, Paola Guidi as Ascenza (voiced by Monica Vitti), Adriana Asti as Amore, Luciano Conti as Il Moicano, Luciano Gonini as Piede D'Oro, Renato Capogna as Renato and Alfredo Leggi as Papo Hirmedo.

Several in the cast of *Accattone* pop up in later Pasolini films: one of the Napoli crew is Amerigo Bevilacqua, who was Herod in *The Gospel According To Matthew*; one of the police line-up guys is Otello Sestili, who played Judas in *The Gospel*; Mario Cipriani (playing Balilla) was the lead in *RoGoPaG* (in *Curd Cheese*); and Silvana Corsini, who plays Maddalena, takes a similar role in *Mamma Roma*.

Accattone boasts a cast of unknowns, who are terrific. The performances are naturalistic, yet also stylized. Some of the situations and the characterizations stretch belief at times, but the non-actors inhabit this world beautifully. You can buy into these characters in these settings.

As a production, *Accattone* inaugurated numerous approaches to cinema which Pier Paolo Pasolini would pursue throughout his career: a cast of unknowns and non-actors, low budgets, filming on location (and adapting existing settings), and using employing existing (classical) music (rather than specially composed scores).

✳

Aside from the obvious influences of Roberto Rossellini, Federico Fellini and Vittorio De Sica on *Accattone*, critics also discerned Kenji Mizoguchi and Carl-Theodor Dreyer, both favourites with the maestro (E. ScIliano, 227). You could also add Orson Welles, Jacques Tati, Jean Cocteau, Charlie Chaplin and John Ford.

Accattone displays many of the aspects of Pier Paolo Pasolini's cinema that would become central to the later movies:

- The title sequence: black letters (in Bodoni font) over bright, white cards, accompanied by classical music. (That would be Pasolini's preference, for titles: they are like a brand, like the main titles of Woody Allen and Ingmar Bergman, who used the same credits each time in white letters in a traditional, post-Renaissance font over black. Pasolini's titles emphasize that this is a prestige, serious production. All of the crew credits are placed upfront, so each Pasolini movie ends with the simple word 'FINE' = the end).
- using large, mainly non-professional casts.
- using existing locations[4] where possible (including his beloved Roman shanty towns and the *borgate*).[5] Pasolini seems to have made the *milieu* of Rome's streets and the under-class life instantly his own, with this first picture as director.
- classical music (and using music in an unusual manner). The use of classical music, and Johann Sebastian Bach in particular, automatically gives *Accattone* a grandeur.[6] This, among other elements, looks forward to *The Gospel According To Matthew* (the idea of placing the *St Matthew Passion* by Bach in a street brawl is extraordinary: it fits perfectly, but was something audiences hadn't seen before).[7]
- references to (Renaissance) painting.[8]
- shooting in a loose, apparently spontaneous style. (But of course it's not).
- poetry: although a first feature directed by Pier Paolo Pasolini, *Accattone* is confident enough to open with a quote from Italy's national poet, Dante Alighieri (the quote is from Canto V of *Purgatory*); Pasolini went on to quote from Dante many times in his film career (and satirically in *The Hawks and the Sparrows*).

However, even tho' *Accattone* is based on an original script by the maestro, many of the films he directed subsequently were adaptations.

Accattone is also a fascinating document of postwar Italy, how it was rebuilding itself after WWII: there are new tenements in the distance, for instance, but on the suburban edges of Rome, the characters live in run-down buildings (the population of Rome in 1960 was 2.3 million – large

---

[4] *Accattone* was filmed to the East of Rome, around the Pigneto area, the slums of Via Fanfulla da Lodi, and the Appian Way (where Stella meets the pimp).
[5] The *borgate* were formed in Rome's surrounding areas in the mid-20th century, often from people coming in from the country or from the South (Pier Paolo Pasolini came to the capital from Friuli).
[6] According to Robert Kolker, it was probably *Un Condamné à mort s'est échappé* (*A Man Escaped*, Robert Bresson, 1956) that suggested the use of Bach (1985, 16).
[7] However, there are some scenes where Bach's music is used as wallpaper – it burbles along underneath scenes, and isn't melded with the drama.
[8] Pasolini said he only thought of Masaccio directly in filming *Accattone* (plus some Giotto and Romanesque sculpture).

for a European city). In both *Accattone* and *Mamma Roma,* the in-between zone of the *borgate* is explored: new tenements rising in the midst of empty land, where poverty is rife, where the postwar dream in reality means that life is as harsh as it always was.

Bernardo Bertolucci said he was very lucky in meeting Pier Paolo Pasolini when he was young (and being introduced to Pasolini's friends, such as Alberto Moravia and Elsa Morante). And then Bertolucci helped Pasolini with *Accattone,* or as Bertolucci put it:

> In 1961 I had the great chance, as first assistant on *Accattone,* to see Pier Paolo directing his first film, or I would say, inventing cinema.[9]

That was a common notion at the time: throughout the 1950s, any time that Jean-Luc Godard wanted to praise his latest favourite film, he crowed that it was re-inventing cinema. 'For Pasolini each shot, each zoom,' Bernardo Bertolucci remarked, 'was the first in the history of the cinema'.[10]

As Bernardo Bertolucci told *Cineaste* magazine in 1972:

> It was a kind of new birth of cinema because Pasolini, never having made a movie himself before, was inventing the cinema as if for the first time. When he made a close-up, the film, for me, discovered the close-up. It seemed like the first close-up in movie history because it was the first time for Pier Paolo. (D. Georgakas, 34)

After *Accattone,* Pier Paolo Pasolini had planned to make *The Grim Reaper,* but he decided to do *Mamma Roma* instead; Pasolini's 5-page treatment was bought by producer Tonino Cervi and given to Bernardo Bertolucci. *The Grim Reaper* became Bertolucci's first feature film as director.

✢

THE STYLE OF *ACCATTONE.*

Often, Pier Paolo Pasolini had his camera crew use a fixed camera on a tripod for *Accattone,* with little camera movement. It was a conscious attempt to return to the roots of cinema (though a particular kind of cinema, of course – in D.W. Griffith's cinema, the camera isn't fixed). Quite a few filmmakers have gone back to basics like that now and again – as if a camera on a tripod is somehow less gimmicky or self-conscious than a camera on a dolly or a crane (it isn't, tho' – a camera is a far more complex and highly technological item than anything it's mounted on).

But wait, there *are* mobile shots, of course in *Accattone* – in fact,

---

9 Quoted in I. Halberstadt, *Pix*, 2, British Film Institute, 1997.
10 B. Bertolucci, *Newsweek*, Feb 12, 1973.

very many, and in most scenes (filmed with a dolly, but also from a vehicle). Typically the camera is tracking with Accattone as he prowls Rome's shanty towns (and often the camera is ahead of Accattone, and he walks towards it. But he can never catch up, never overtake it – he will always be someone lagging behind. In *The Gospel According To Matthew*, it's the opposite: the camera is hurrying to keep up with Jesus, who strides ahead).

The signature shot in *Accattone* is of the anti-hero sloping through the sun-lit backstreets of Rome – exhausted, though not from work, from life itself. He's beaten down and dejected by just existing. (It's bright and sunny, but it's too harsh, and the sun and the light mean absolutely nothing to Accattone.)

Technically, *Accattone* is an assured work: thankfully, DP Tonino Delli Coll has enough lamps to illuminate the night scenes decently, without resorting to the unsatisfying lighting of *Mamma Roma* the following year. And the camera is on a tripod and a dolly, so the shoddy handheld shots haven't taken over yet in Pasolini's cinema.[11]

Accattone prefigures *The Gospel According To Matthew* in many ways, from the use of classical music (Johann Sebastian Bach), to the poetic realist approach to filmmaking, the use of non-professional actors, the ensemble playing, groups of men, and even the sub-proletarian settings. It really isn't too much of a stretch from the ancient world of the Middle East to the 20th century slums of Naples and Rome. (That was part of Pasolin's project – to recreate Ancient Palestine in modern Italy).

And it's inevitable to seek comparison between Accattone and his chums in Roma and Jesus and his disciples, though that comparison is bound to be outrageous for some. (Some of the cast did appear in *The Gospel According To Matthew*).

The Catholic religion is evoked ironically often in *Accattone*,[12] and often in a visual manner: for ex, one of the early Stella and Accattone scenes takes place in front of a church (but there's nothing comforting about the image). A telling shot tilts up the wall of a church from the characters on the street below: the enormous wall looms over them makes the church look more like a forbidding fortress. (Actually, many churches are like that in Italy: the attractive West fronts, which you see in the tourist brochures, have surrounding walls that are plain, blank, and imposing).

---

11 Thankfully, *Mamma Roma* was filmed before Pier Paolo Pasolini became enamoured of shaky handheld camerawork, so the camera is on a tripod or a dolly, and this gives *Mamma Roma* a much smoother, more professional look.

12 Characters refer to themselves as saints (both Accattone and his brother do – the brother compares himself to St Sebastian).

THE POETRY OF CINEMA.

But what's so striking about *Accattone* is the *poetic style* that Pier Paolo Pasolini seems to have minted from nothing. You can see the derivations from Italian Neo-realism, of course, and the combination of the cinematic style with the sub-proletariat subject matter (i.e., the filmic approach and the subject matter feed into each other). The simultaneous rejection of Neo-realist approaches, but also the seemingly inevitable use of them.(And there's Jean Cocteau, Charlies Chaplin, Ingmar Bergman and Carl-Theodor Dreyer in there, too).

Accattone has many of the hallmarks of Neo-realist cinema, even tho' it is made partly as a critique of the form, and a swansong for it: the contemporary setting, the location shooting, the sentiment, the working class *milieu* and characters, the non-professional cast, the simple visual style, the long takes, the documentary-style approach to viewpoint, etc.

But *Accattone* announces a *poetry of cinema* from the outset: if you put aside the story and the characters for a moment (though they are hugely compelling, and it's difficult to let go of them), and focus on the images and sounds, and the flow of the editing, you have such a poetry here in *Accattone*. It's as if Pier Paolo Pasolini is re-inventing cinema (which's what Bernardo Bertolucci said). It might not be on the same grand scale of *Citizen Kane* (but what movie is?). But it is a re-invention, or a creation from scratch.

Or rather, *Accattone appears* to be a re-invention, on its own terms, because D.W. Griffith, Cecil B. Mille, Géorges Méliès and the other founding fathers of cinema had already done *everything* by 1915. And yet this film is also often *not* an invention or a re-invention: there is nothing here that Ozu, Dreyer, Bergman, Kurosawa, Murnau, Ford, Renoir, Lang, and Fellini hadn't already done.

Bernardo Bertolucci remarked of Pier Paolo Pasolini at the time of *Accattone*:

> Pier Paolo's films are imbued with a special kind of spirituality. It's a deeply religious cinema that shuns any contact with bourgeois culture and that feeds on his own blend of innocence (with respect to the cinema that he was only then beginning to know) and a concept of space within the frame that was instinctual and unique. (29)

Pier Paolo Pasolini remarked:

> I made my first film, *Accattone*, with a lot of feeling. I chose my style by following my own feelings. Technique is a myth. The technique of filmmaking is very easy. Perhaps there are classifications and restrictive prosody, so there may be difficulties in editing but these difficulties are

not as terrible as we tend to think they are. Sometimes it's enough to follow the instinct of the rhythm in the editing. In *Accattone*, I tried to simplify the technique. I shot the film very simply. I used close-ups and very few camera movements. I had to do that partly because I knew nothing about technique. I didn't even know what panoramic meant. I didn't know there were different lenses. The reason for my simplicity wasn't my battle with technique. It was deeper. It's my way of seeing reality as a sacred apparition. Sacredness is simple.

Accattone is certainly a movie about making a movie, about how a movie could be made, and about what a movie could be about. It's impossible to disregard that the French New Wave was exploding at precisely this period. *Accattone* is certainly of its time in that respect – a movie shot in Europe by an Italian intellectual and poet in 1961.

But, like the classics of the early era of the French New Wave – *The 400 Blows, Don't Shoot the Piano Player, Vivre Sa Vie, A Woman Is a Woman* and above all, *Breathless* – *Accattone* also seemingly effortlessly transcends its time. *Accattone* lunges into the sunlight on those dusty, Roman backways just like Franco Citti as Vittorio Cataldi does, a film and a character that are archetypally Pasolinian – a movie and an anti-hero that's both blasé and preoccupied, both cool and doomed, both uncaring and tender, both driven and lazy.

For Enzo Siciliano, Pier Paolo Pasolini's anguished nature was in *Accattone* 'expressed cinematographically in a form of severity, austerity, and visual pauperism that would seem to be opposed to the author's frantic sense of style' (228).

ACCATTONE THE OUTSIDER.

The filmmakers give Accattone a surprising number of negative, unappealing attributes: he's lazy, he doesn't work, he's a loser, he's vindictive, he puts others down, he's aggressive and violent, he's intolerant, he's loudly arrogant, he has a foul temper, he's a chauvinist, he's dim, he drinks, he's spineless, he wallows in self-pity, he's a pimp,[13] he's a thief, and his self-loathing is second to none. This is a guy who orders his girlfriend Maddalena to work as a hooker at night even when she's had an accident and can barely walk! And when she's in the slammer, he persuades another girl to earn money for him, because he simply will *not* work like everyone else. It's as if the filmmakers were trying to prove that they could conjure up the lowest, sneakiest, shittiest anti-hero in contemporary cinema. (Some film anti-heroes are given a handful of unfavourable characteristics, but Accattone suffers from more

---

[13] Accattone is a pimp, but he's at the bottom of the ladder in the Roman underworld. No tailor-made Italian suits and flashy cars for him – he only has one employee, Maddalena. (As one of the charas (Fulvio) notes, in jail pimps are despised).

than most.[14] It's overkill – but typical of Pasolini).

Accattone is yet another addition to the roster of alienated, European outsiders, a direct inheritor of the fiction of Albert Camus, André Gide and Knut Hamsun. No explanation is necessary: we know who Accattone is from the first few scenes. Existential, yes, alienated, yes, an outsider, oh most definitely yes.

Accattone is a rebel without a cause, of course,[15] and he's as detached from himself as he is from the people around him. He is surrounded by people but remains fatally lonely. Self-doubt troubles him and, worst of all, self-hatred.

And Accattone knows he's a loser, that he's weak. But he isn't giving up: underneath the *braggadocio* amongst his comrades (he is a young, Italian male, after all), who hang out in the sunshine, everyday, in a side street, there's a terrified desperation. It's an ambition, if not to be 'somebody' (in the North American manner – 'I'm gonna be somebody one day!'), then to at least survive.

To survive.

But Accattone is not going to kill himself. He is not so lost in self-pity to do that: the early scene when he dives off the bridge into the River Tiber and boasts afterwards that the water isn't going to take his life, demonstrates that. He is a tough survivor. (The scene also shows that Accattone is something of a leader, or at least he's admired, amongst the band of drifters and petty criminals. But it's an ambiguous favouritism at the least, and it's constantly being contested. In this so-macho world, you've got to keep proving yourself all the time.)

Accattone is the first manifestation in a feature-length movie of the intense anger in much of Pier Paolo Pasolini's cinema (and his poetry). And this rage didn't subside and become kindly, forgiving old age: in his last film, *Salò*, the hostility of *Accattone* continues to flourish. Only filmmakers such as Jean-Luc Godard seem angrier than Pasolini.

What makes it worse for Accattone is that there's no one to blame (or he doesn't possess the language to articulate a socialist/ Marxist deconstruction of his predicament). Whether it's the society, or the law, or postwar neo-capitalism, Accattone can't say. But he does tell Stella that if he had gun, there'd be no one left alive.

✣

And yet, in the scene in the bar, where Accattone first rants and then breaks down, he is depicted weeping at length, while his new chums

---
14 No doubt some viewers in Italy objected to a film which painted such a rotten portrait of modern youth.
15 Several of the youths in the picture are James Deans, and sport North American hairstyles and clothing. By 1961, North America's cultural dominance was being felt throughout Europa.

(Carmine and company, from Napoli) look on with indifference. He's young, but it's as if his life is already over. (It's another instance where Accattone, who often talks about pride, loses it and seems shameless in his lack of pride).

It's just that Accattone is one of those people who talk about changing things, and about changing themselves, but can't quite do it, or can't be bothered to do it (like all of us!). Sure, if someone came along and waved a magic wand, or if he won the lottery, Accattone wouldn't complain. But is he going to make it happen? No.

Accattone is one of those people who are their own worst enemy. He's stubborn, too, and wilful; he won't admit defeat even tho' he's already displayed it to everybody. And he's also someone who can't quite see the effect he has on the people around him. Self-destructive he certainly is: the face-off at the street where his ex-wife Ascenza (Paola Guidi) lives with her father (Romolo Orazi) and brother (Massimo Cacciafeste) demonstrates that big time.

In this scene, brilliantly staged by all concerned, there's a point where Accattone would do far better to back off and admit defeat. He's just not going to win here, at this time (or perhaps at any time: his ex-wife has just told him, in no uncertain terms, to get the hell away from her – in a very lengthy tracking[16] shot along the road as she walks home from work with her baby in her arms. That says it all: Ascenza has just done a day's work, and Accattone hasn't, and she's carrying their child, and Accattone walks a few paces behind her, classic staging for emotional distance). He talks about her giving him a second chance, and he mentions getting a job (with no absolutely intention of doing so) – it's another vivid scene of Accattone's pitiful degradation.

But still Accattone thinks everyone is against him. He doesn't get it.

This scene is a tremendous and vivid demonstration of Pier Paolo Pasolini's powers as a film director: this is world-class filmmaking. In fact, it's much more satisfying than many similar scenes of high drama and confrontation in Pasolini's later movies (where often a careless, throwaway attitude diminishes the dramatic possibilities).

The 1961 film captures the wilful, stubborn, self-destructive nature of the young masculinity, how the anti-hero enters enemy territory, alone, and won't back down, or retreat (but it's not bravery: it's a twisted kind of pride, as if Accattone is sure he can prove that he's superior to these people whom he derides as hicks – particularly Ascenza's father, who *really* loathes him).

---

16 And bumpy – it's filmed on a cobbled street.

But Accattone just can't help making matters worse. The brawl is the self-conscious polar opposite of Hollywood, of dignified duelling, of spectacle: it's a rough wrestle in the dirt. No choreographed fisticuffs and stunts here! The fight is eventually broken up and this has to be one of Accattone's lowest points in the story – slinking away, defeated, while the guys behind him shout, 'Pimp!'

Accattone holes up with Nannina (Adele Cambria) and her brood of very young children; unusually, he never once raises his voice against her (as does with his ex-wife, and his two hookers). And he puts up with all those kids.

Accattone is terrific at evoking the joking camaraderie among the unemployed guys, the mock-serious insults hurled at each other all the time:

'the cemetery's that way, Accattone!'

'the food stall is this way, Accattone!'

There are some hints of homosocial elements in *Accattone*, apart from the obvious one of the quasi-brotherhood of pals who hang out together day in, day out, in the side street, outside a little café. One is Balilla, the guy who happily mocks Accattone's fate, who is seen with a young boy; another is the scene at the river in act one, where no one can miss the fact the screen is teeming with lads in swimsuits.

There are several other gangs of guys apart from the unemployed loafers that Accattone associates with: Carmine and his thugs from Napoli are visiting the capital to enact revenge on Maddalena for putting away one of their own, Ciccio. Once they've soundly beaten the prostitute in act one, they disappear – but Accattone dreams of them as corpses near the end of the film.

Another crew is a band of thieves led by the rat-faced Cartagine (Roberto Scaringella); they spend most of their time playing cards in a local bar (where Accattone meets the Napoli gang), bragging about beating up hookers, and joshing with other gangs. Cartagine is mistakenly accused by Maddalena of attacking her, which sends her to prison (Cartagine rails loudly at Accattone for this). And Cartagine is one of the thieves in the finale, along with Balilla, who goes with Accattone to the city to steal a van.

Meanwhile, there are several prostitutes who form a Greek chorus of sorts, commenting on the narrative (the theme was reprised in *Mamma Roma*). They are all weary veterans – principal among them is Amore, played by Adriana Asti (a Pasolini regular, Asti appeared in *Where Are the Clouds?* and others).

The scene where the pimp Carmine and his cronies beat up the prostitute (Maddalena, who works for Accattone) on a piece of waste ground at night is truly shocking: four men against one woman (they are getting revenge for their buddy Ciccio). The act condemns them utterly, but the movie isn't as simple as that. (Robert Kolker noted the shoddy treatment of female characters in *Accattone*: the film is 'as perverse as its characters, intensely anti-female and anti-humanist' (1985, 16). The maltreatment of women in the movies of Pier Paolo Pasolini is not confined to *Accattone*, but crops up throughout his cinema.)

✢

Accattone is an unusual movie in several respects; it is full of oppositions. For instance, the opening credits have the most sublime music created in the Western world played over them – by Johann Sebastian Bach. Plus those elegant white titles – we might be about to see a serious, thoughtful adaptation of a William Shakespeare play (and Bach is played at least five times in the first act of *Accattone*). Yet this is a movie set in the slums and shanties of Rome, with a cast of layabouts, thieves and prostitutes.

And what climaxes act one of *Accattone*? Only the truly horrific attack on a woman at night on waste ground, one of the nastiest scenes that Pier Paolo Pasolini and company filmed, and no doubt one of the contributing factors in the controversy that *Accattone* attracted on its release. Four men kicking and punching a prostitute,[17] then abandoning her (reminding us, as the quote from Dante Alighieri in the credits hinted, that we are in Hell. Notice, too, that the authorities are ineffectual in *Accattone* – everyone is left to their own devices. In this movie, everyone is condemned. You go to the police for help (as Maddalena does), and you're branded as a traitor).[18]

The scene looks forward to the pointless violence in Pier Paolo Pasolini's most controversial work as a director, *Salò o Le 120 Giornate di Sodoma*. Pointless, and not much fun, either – the weariness and the desperation of the act, even its casual portrayal and staging, enhance the sorrow.

These bullies are filth – *Accattone* is designed to take the audience down to the dregs of humanity. (What happens to Maddalena is foreshadowed in the café scene, where some of the youths sitting near Accattone and his new chums claim they went with a hooker the night before and beat her up. The arrogant bragging about such a revolting act

---

[17] Her name, Maddalena, is another of numerous Christian allusions in *Accattone*.
[18] In this world of small-time crooks, pimps and whores, anyone in authority is an enemy.

further condemns these brutes).[19]

The attack on Maddalena, for Pasolini watchers, is also disturbingly prescient of the circumstances of the director's death fourteen years later (not only the attack with its sadomasochistic elements, with one of the characters being a prostitute, but the driving out from Rome to waste ground at night, and the assault occurring near the car).

✦

However, the movie does not judge Accattone at all – of course not, because Pier Paolo Pasolini is *far* too sophisticated a filmmaker for anything as simplistic as that.[20] No moralizing, no judgement – that withdrawal of an easily discerned point-of-view (or moral stance) can frustrate some audiences. But you can see immediately how any kind of moral assertions on the part of the filmmakers or the movie itself would reduce its power and impact considerably. It's not that *Accattone* doesn't need that kind of point-of-view (though it doesn't), it's that such ethical or social or political pressure on the movie would unbalance it and weaken it.

✦

Though an ensemble piece – which characterizes Pier Paolo Pasolini's cinema throughout his career (that is, he is a very sociable filmmaker, happy to populate his scenes with plenty of characters, and many onlookers – any time anything happens in *Accattone*, people gather to watch) – *Accattone* is also very much Franco Citti's movie. It's one of those rare parts in cinema where the character is not only in nearly every scene, but is being given dramatically challenging things to do in most every scene.

But this is no star vehicle in the Hollywood tradition, where a big movie star demands to be in most of the scenes. It's a completely different sort of picture. And Franco Citti has no problem with playing a thoroughly unlikeable, weasly, oafish, idle character.

Around the edges of *Accattone* there are many vivid vignettes – like the short, stocky guy (Balilla – Mario Cipriani – he was the lead in *La Ricotta*), who sarcastically berates Accattone from time to time[21] (we see Balilla talking to a child carrying a lute, like a street urchin out of Michelangelo da Caravaggio's art, with hints of homosexual predation).

✦

Hunger and poverty is a difficult topic to sustain as a basis for stories

---

19 This particular gang is seen teasing Maddalena on the streets at night before she meets Carmine and his cohorts from Naples. This is the gang that Maddalena wrongly fingers in the police line-up, which leads to her incarceration. (They did tease her on that fateful night, but it was the gang from Napoli who beat her).
20 Altho' in some of his later films his sophistication seems to have disappeared.
21 Once a thief, always a thief, he asserts.

in the affluent social environment of some countries: *Accattone* uses it as a major motivation amongst this group of working class guys (or, rather, these not-willing-to-work working class guys).[22] But when filmmakers influenced by Pier Paolo Pasolini, such as Martin Scorsese, came to make their own movies about bunches of lower class men hanging out, they didn't use hunger and poverty as key motivations.[23]

Accattone contains numerous scenes featuring food – to highlight the theme of survival, and poverty, and the fundamental needs of being alive. Many characters refer to food (and money), and several scenes illuminate what a louse Accattone is: when the lads have snaffled some pasta (and boast about being charitable!), and visit their pal, Fulvio, to cook it, Accattone's first thought is to trick the others to leave, because there won't be enough. (And he does, stirring up trouble with the cunning of a crooked lawyer in order to hurry back and guzzle the chow with Fulvio. However, at this point, another meal ticket materializes, picking her way over the waste ground: Stella, the girl he recently met).

✦

WORK OR NO WORK?

For Sam Rohdie, *Accattone* and *Mamma Roma* and Pier Paolo Pasolini's movies of the lumpenproletariat, filmed in Rome's *borgate*, were not working class movies, movies with working class heroes. Rather the subproletariat and their society was pre-industrial, pre-capitalist, linked to Italy before the rise of the bourgeoisie. Pasolini asserted that the Catholicism in *Accattone* was 'pre-bourgeois, pre-industrial' and mythical (PP, 47-48). The revolutionary nature of Pasolini's peasant films was precisely because it was associated with a world before industrialization and mercantile capitalism. As Rohdie put it:

> Its characters, like Accattone, are part of Pier Paolo Pasolini's 'aristocracy of labour', *because they do not work*. They refuse to be integrated into the productive process. They are pimps, thieves, layabouts, whores, the unemployed. Their elitist position is not as skilled workers in a Marxist heaven, the true aristocracy of labour, but as unemployed parasites in a Pasolinian Utopia. They are useless. (121)

And their aristocracy, their uselessness, makes them analogous to poets, and their lifestyle is poetic (ibid.). *Accattone* is revolutionary in a different sense, then, from the socialist statements made by Sergei Eisenstein and Soviet propaganda cinema, and it was a Marxism that was

---

22 The youths are not shown drinking much, or smoking (is that a comment on not being able to afford it?). Their portrayal is also a lot less crude than it might be.
23 In New York? Forget it! Scorsese's Italian-Americans all have big mammas back home who cook them plenty of pasta.

poetic, and in a way impractical.

Accattone also raises the important issue of the ethical and moral aspects of labour. Accattone denounces work, and those who work, in a key speech (his cohorts likewise look down on those who have jobs – when Accattone's brother walks past, returning from a day's work, the youths gathered in the usual spot in the back street mock him).[24]

And when Accattone *does* try to work, it nearly kills him (so he takes to thieving). The question is: why is work valued so highly, in a moral and ethical sense? In terms of mercantile capitalism, of production and consumption, work and workers are essential. Indeed, workers are bred and trained in schools – in the Western world, you go to school, then you work (or you go to college or university, but after that, you must work).

But the capitalist, the social, the political and the legal aspects of labour aren't the province of *Accattone*: the movie raises the issue from a moral and ethical standpoint, and asks: why is work valued so highly? Why is it regarded as essential to existence? (The despising of labour as dishonourable also comes from the Surrealist movement: the Surrealists regarded work as feeding the capitalist pigs.)

Existential philosophy certainly informs *Accattone* – the height of the popularity of Existentialism in Europe was probably the 1950s and early 1960s, the period of *Accattone* (it was linked to the Beat Generation and the Bohemians, for instance, with their black, turtleneck fashions, their jazz music, and their *avant garde* poetry). Accattone is another in a long line of European, Existential outsiders, stretching back thru Albert Camus (*The Stranger*), Jean-Paul Sartre (*Nausea*), Knut Hamsun (*The Hunger*), André Gide (*The Immoralist*), Lawrence Durrell (*The Alexandria Quartet*), Aldous Huxley (*Eyeless In Gaza*), Henry Miller (*Tropic of Cancer*), Géorges Bataille (*The Story of the Eye*) – back to J.-K. Huysmans (*Against Nature*) and to the Marquis de Sade.

The Existential outsider is typically white, educated, bourgeois, privileged, intellectual, manic depressive, self-absorbed (and selfish), acutely sensitive (yet boorish and socially inept), alienated, disaffected, an exile (a king without a kingdom), lazy, aloof/ superior, self-loathing, a loner and a lost soul. Accattone ticks pretty much all of the boxes of the Existential stranger (though he is the working class version, lacking the inherited wealth or rich family background).

---

[24] Every scene is played out in the open – this is a Mediterranean world, warm, sunny, and as soon as anything happens, people are gathering outside to watch (such as when the cops come to pick up Accattone, or when he brawls with his ex's brother). City life in Italia is a soap opera – or a grand opera.

STEALING TO LIVE.

One of Accattone's lowest acts is to steal his 6 year-old son Iaio's necklace, so he can buy clothes and shoes for his new prostitute, Stella. He returns to his ex-wife Ascenza's digs, waits for her to leave, then snaffles the necklace as he kisses his son. The concept of working for the money to invest in his latest protegé Stella simply doesn't figure in Accattone's noggin. (Again, the scene is brilliantly staged – the boy is playing alone outside (not with fancy toys, but empty bottles and a rock), and Accattone's single fatherly act is to steal from his own son!).

Life is there for the taking – you just have to steal it.

Or: 'once a pimp, always a pimp' (Or: 'once a thief, always a thief').

So Accattone grooms the naïve, sweet Stella as his next streetwalker (after Maddalena has been jailed for a year following the botched police line-up scene; Maddalena, tho', has the wits not to finger Accattone). Stella (a brave, touching performance by Franca Pasut) isn't so innocent that she doesn't know what's going on (she tells Accattone that her mother walked the streets too, to look after her, after her pa died in the war). Stella receives a new dress, shoes, and jewellery (from Accattone, and his buddy Pio – Piero Morgia), and accepts her first clients.

The film portrays Accattone's mixed emotions (he's fallen for Stella a little), and his jealousy over her; when he's drunk, he threatens to jump into the Tiber again. He's watched some guys making a move on her: the camera cuts in closer to reveal a guy's wandering hands, while Accattone looks on morosely. Yet this is what he's groomed Stella for. (Incredibly, Accattone berates Stella the following day for allowing the guy to do more than dance with her. In this scene Accattone also complains to Stella that he was doing great before he met her, had a car and all. They both know these are lies, and that Accattone persists in taking out his frustrations on her).

One of Stella's first clients (who's a regular for Amore), drives her away into the night, but Stella balks, and is roughly pushed out of the car. (She returns afoot, along the Appian Way – yes, the *real* Appian Way, scene of many an Ancient Roman epic movie in the '50s and '60s.[25] But no Hollywood flick filmed the Appian Way like this, with lonely hookers lost in the night).[26]

Meanwhile, *Accattone* depicts the circle of youths who discuss Accattone falling for Stella with contempt, and bet on when he'll persuade her to go hooking (to them, Accattone's acts, like everything in

---

[25] The hookers joke about *Quo Vadis*.
[26] It's as if Italian filmmakers of the Neo-realist sort, such as Fellini and Pasolini, enjoyed depicting the 'real' Rome, in grainy black-and-white, in contrast to the brash, Technicolor Rome of Hollywood fantasy.

life, are a joke, something to laugh at, mere entertainment. They also relish the fact that Accattone seems to worse off than them).

To illustrate Accattone's desperation – now he's even attempted to do an honest day's work! and it was a disaster – the 1961 film has him launching himself at his own friends (and when he's exhausted after said work). Even tho' Accattone knows that hurling insults and jokes is the group's way of getting through the crushing boredom of the day, he rises to their jibes, and dives in (after throwing his shoe, a great touch of another hissy fit). Well, ten guys versus one guy is not going to end well.

Accattone's self-loathing is almost as strong as his instinct for survival. *Almost* – because Accattone doesn't hurl himself off the bridge to die, but continues to struggle, no matter how much he despises himself. Franco Citti plays all of this marvellously, vividly evoking the desperation and the self-degradation. Bini and Pasolini must've been delighted with Citti's performance – it's dead-on.

THE FINALE.

Accattone's fourth act (4 of 4) is fascinating: first, Maddalena is brought back into the narrative (as she's in jail, we thought we'd seen the last of her. And certainly Accattone isn't the kind of character who'd visit her, so there's no scene of Accattone going to see Maddalena in prison). Instead, Maddalena learns that Accattone has shacked up with a new girl (the hooker Amore tells her).[27] This piece of news encourages Maddalena[28] to set in motion a new plot: the surveillance of Accattone, because Maddalena insists to the prison authorities that he is a pimp. Thus, Accattone is followed by a guy (there are giant close-ups of his eyes[29] – the Eyes of God, of authority, of society).

Next, extraordinarily, Accattone actually takes up the offer of a job! But he doesn't last even a single day! Humping heavy iron in a builders' yard is too much for this useless, would-be aristocrat, and he wimps out and collapses. In a vicious comment, Accattone gripes to his pal that this seems like Buchenwald. Well, comparing a regular job to being in a concentration camp is pretty extreme![30]

Yes – one aspect of Accattone's character is very obvious: he is a first-rate whinger. He complains about, well, everything. For the Existential outsider, nothing is good enough, all of society stinks, everybody's

---

27 Elsa Morante, Pasolini's regular collaborator, is the other woman in the prison cell.
28 She might be a little jealous, maybe, but it's likely more to do with Maddalena hearing that Accattone's new girlfriend has been put on the streets, and Maddalena nearly died from being beaten. So she wants Accattone stopped.
29 Re-used many times.
30 It's a Godardian quip, but not even Godard makes that comparison!

an idiot (especially those who work for a living!), and Accattone looks down on one and all. (Inevitably, Accattone's choice of work is exaggerated – heavy, manual labour. Of course he doesn't take a job as a runner in an office of pretty girls, where he can slack off, drink coffee and maybe exploit some of the women).

Next, there's a sequence that might have been borrowed from the cinema of Ingmar Bergman or Federico Fellini, a sequence which's perhaps the only false note in *Accattone* – he dreams of his own funeral (this was foreshadowed in the funeral procession thru the streets in act two). It's been done before and since – *Vampyr* (1932) is one of the greatest examples, and Ken Russell and Woody Allen are fond of the motif. (The dream seems directly influenced by *Wild Strawberries*).

But in *Accattone* the nightmare seems too pedestrian, too plain and – fatally – it is too long (at this point in the story). The dream sequence outstays its welcome, and runs beyond the dramatic or poetic requirements of the movie.

However, the dream does contain some unusual elements, such as Carmine and his crew from Naples as naked corpses (with gravel strategically strewn to cover those parts of the body that God Himself created, but which now are permanently shameful following the Fall of Man and the Expulsion from Paradise. Or something).

Lastly, Accattone dies – this sequence concludes the film, and takes up half of the fourth act of *Accattone*. One day of working is too much for Accattone, and he asks Balilla (the owner of the bar) if they can set up a theft (because it's easier and better to steal than to work). Aided by the cocky Cartagine, who'd once threatened to kill Maddalena, off the lads go to downtown Rome, pulling a cart (as if they're ancient world peasants in the modern city).

Like many of the set-pieces in *Accattone* (and in Pier Paolo Pasolini's cinema), the sequence has the air of fairy tale and fantasy as well as dusty, earthy, hard-bitten reality. The death of Accattone has been foreshadowed several times in the movie (from his leap off the bridge in the first act (where plenty of joshing about dying and passing on possessions occurred), to his self-hating comments, to seeing a funeral procession, to the nightmare, etc).

The ingredients of the ending sequence of *Accattone* can be viewed as everyday or as symbolic or as ideological as you like. You can read pretty much anything you want into it: the laughter and camaraderie before the cops show up, the (stolen) motorcycle,[31] the van, the setting (a bridge),

---

[31] When Accattone races off on a motorcycle to pick up Stella, abandoned on the Appian Way, it foreshadows his death on a motorbike.

the theft of food (what else could it be in this film but meat?), and the alien setting of downtown Rome. (The crash on the motorbike isn't shown – there may be several reasons for that, but it might also be a common one: it's cheaper to use a sound effect than spend half a day setting up and staging a stunt).

Death isn't really a proper ending to a story comments Fritz Lang in *Contempt* (1963) – it's Jean-Luc Godard acknowledging that he used death as the capper to so many of his movies in the 1960s.[32] And it isn't in *Accattone*, either. Except that, unlike Godard, Pier Paolo Pasolini and company have actually done plenty of narrative work to set up the anti-hero's demise. It doesn't come out of nowhere, isn't tacked on as a quick and easy way of exiting the story, and it does fit the thematic/ philosophical/ spiritual issues of the piece.

You could argue, too, that there is a grandeur or tragic aspect to *Accattone* which justifies the application of the artistic elements of classical, literary tragedy. Not that *Accattone* is *Oedipus Rex* quite yet, but it is getting there. 'Whom God wants to destroy, he first makes mad,' remarked Euripedes famously in the 5th century B.C.E, and there is an element of that, of Accattone being pursued by the Furies. (You could also re-align *Accattone* not with Catholicism (which's referenced throughout the film), but with a more primitive, ancient, and pre-Christian set of beliefs, the world of Gods, Titans, and Furies who hover over mere mortals, which Pasolini would explore in his subsequent movies. So that the allusions to Christianity[33] are simply used in the film to suggest the even older themes).[34]

The death of Accattone is a martyrdom, for sure, but it also has elements of an Existential demise – pointless, valueless, an inconclusive death (and it echoes the ending of *Breathless*). The elements of heroism – dying in broad daylight on the city streets (and symbolically next to the river), surrounded by onlookers and friends – are only part of this downfall.

THE RECEPTION OF *ACCATTONE*.

Accattone was a hit, and a controversial one: the critical success, plus the controversy, was key in launching Pier Paolo Pasolini's film career (it was typical of Pasolini to open his film directing career with a bang! His first film has a pimp as the main character, and the second film has a

---

32 Fritz Lang was 'astonished' that Jean-Luc Godard didn't show the car crash that closes *Contempt*, as any Hollywood film would do, and Lang himself had done in a movie.
33 Sarcastically referring to religion is a recurring motif in the dialogue among the disaffected youths in *Accattone* (as if this is a modern version of a Biblical morality play).
34 So that it was easier and quicker to refer to God, St Sebastian and Jesus, in a film set in Italy in the early Sixties, than to the Furies or the Gods of Ancient Greece).

prostitute! Ah, but the protagonist of his third movie was Jesus Christ, no less).

'*Accattone* was the crucial one. It didn't do super well, but good enough for a beginner', Pasolini remarked in relation to its commercial performance (2012). Indeed – had *Accattone* been a flop economically, it would have been a set-back in his film career, but it would not have ended it: because Pasolini already had several films released (or in the works) based on his fiction and his scripts. And at this buoyant time in the Italian film business, Alfredo Bini or another producer would have hired Pasolini to direct.

In Italy, *Accattone* was banned for under-18s; it made a huge impact at the Venice Film Festival in Sept, 1961. *Accattone* had its premiere on Nov 23, 1961, in Rome's Cinema Barberini (a protest group, 'Nuova Europa', disrupted the screening with ink, stink bombs, throwing around seats and attacking punters). The film's producers were sued by Salvatore Pagliuca, who reckoned he had been maligned in the movie (the case, heard on Feb 22, 1965, was rejected by the judge, but the filmmakers were ordered to pay material damages, and to remove the name Pagliuca from the soundtrack).

Enzo Sciliano described Pier Paolo Pasolini as combining 'an anomalous fury, a fury that is anti-humanist, anti-Renaissance, and profoundly rural Catholic' in *Accattone* (228).

Hayao Miyazaki says in one of his magazine articles that you only need to see a few minutes of a really great movie to know you're watching something special: you can feel the filmmakers' resolve, their intentions, their talent. You can certainly feel that in *Accattone*, and in later Pasolini films such as *Il Vangelo Secondo Matteo* and even the outrageous *Salò*.

6

MAMMA ROMA

MOTHER ROME

Mamma Roma was produced by Alfredo Bini for Arco Film, Sergio Citti co-wrote the dialogue (and was an A.D.), Tonino Delli Colli was DP, Nino Baragli was editor, Carlo di Carlo was 1st A.D., Flavio Mogherini was art director, set decorator was Massimo Tavazzi, Marcello Ceccarelli (make-up), Amalia Paoletti (hair), sound by Renato Cadueri and Leopoldo Rosi, and music was by Antonio Vivaldi and Cherubini-Bixio (Carlo Rustichelli was music arranger). The cast included Anna Magnani, Ettore Garofolo,[35] Franco Citti,[36] Silvana Corsini, Luisa Orioli, Vittorio La Paglia, Piero Morgia, Franco Ceccarelli, Marcello Sorrentino, Sandro Meschino, Franco Tovo and Paolo Volpone. Filming began on April 19, 1962, in and around the Eternal City. Released: Aug 31, 1962 (Venice Film Festival). 106 minutes.

I eventually saw *Mamma Roma* (1962), Pier Paolo Pasolini's second feature movie, late. I didn't know what to expect. But the title *Mamma Roma* does prepare you a little for the theme of this picture. Forget the story, the characters, the themes, the issues, the settings, the filmmaking and everything, *Mamma Roma* is undoubtedly foremost of all a pæan to actress Anna Magnani (1909-1973), the 'Mother Rome' of the title, one of the icons of 20th century Italian cinema (the star of films directed by Roberto Rossellini, Federico Fellini, Jean Renoir, William Dieterle,

---

[35] Pier Paolo Pasolini said he found Garofolo waiting tables in a restaurant, 'carrying a bowl of fruit just like a figure in a Caravaggio painting' (PP, 51). The script was written for Garofolo.
[36] Franco Citti appears as one of Mamma's early lovers, a total reversal emotionally of his role in the previous year's *Accattone*.

Sidney Lumet, Stanley Kramer, George Cukor, and Luchino Visconti, among others – including *Roma, The Secret of Santa Vittoria, The Fugitive Kind, Wild Is the Wind, L'Amore, Bellissima, Rome: Open City,* and *The Golden Coach. The Rose Tattoo* (1955) was written for her by Tennessee Williams, which won her an Oscar). A larger-than-life personality, Magnani started out in cabaret and variety, moving into movies in the Thirties. She had affairs with Rossellini and Visconti. In *Dolce Vita Confidential* (highly recommended), Shawn Levy described Magnani as

> a volcano, a tempest, a devastating performer who seemed to live and breathe her art and whose best performances would rank among the most vivid and immediate and emotion-rich ever filmed. She was born in Rome in 1908 (and would die there in 1973), and she was a living symbol of the city: its she-wolf, its spirit goddess, the voice of its streets, the face and body of its native population. (105)

That *Mamma Roma* is Anna Magnani's movie (she was then 53) goes without saying: from the opening scene at Carmine's wedding, Magnani dominates (and owns) this picture. In a North American movie, this would be an automatic Oscar win. And when she's not on screen, you wonder what the hell's going on, and why the movie suddenly dissolves into something shambling and far less interesting (when, for instance, it follows her son, Ettore (Ettore Garofolo), in the second act).[37]

Indeed, the *story* of *Mother Rome* is far less compelling than the screen presence of Anna Magnani (and the other characters barely make an impression). Magnani's Mamma Roma is a force of nature, larger than life, earthy, bawdy, brassy, full of energy and *chutzpah*.[38] She might be a hooker, she might run a market stall, but all of that is by the by. (But Pasolini later remarked that he hadn't directed Magnani in a way that suited the material: he should've had her play a petite bourgeoisie instead of a working class woman with petit bourgeoisie aspirations [PP, 49]).

Bravely, Anna Magnani allows herself to be filmed looking less than glamorous; and in many scenes, she is teetering on the verge of collapse (or she's about to blow her top). When Carmine returns she weeps almost immediately; when Ettore proudly swans around the restaurant, she cries a mother's cry of losing her child (now he's got a job); as she shambles thru the last of the long, dark nights[39] of the soul (when she's hooking),

---

[37] 'Anna Magnani's body is forever bursting its boundaries in *Mamma Roma*: laughter, anger, hysteria, dancing, song, grimaces, tears, anguish', as Sam Rohdie put it (78).
[38] 'Fears and lusts and griefs cascaded organically across her face, through her eyes and voice, in her very posture and gait. She was protean, mercurial, profound, and deeply original', Shawn Levy wrote of Magnani's acting style (106).
[39] What was the point of it all? Mamma Roma wonders as she streetwalks for the last time: she is a philosopher of the streets, in the manner of left-wing theatre (so that some of her speeches are too eloquent, too cleverly written for her character).

she weeps.

Who does Pier Paolo Pasolini pair Mother Rome up with? Friends her own age? Rivals? Her father? Mother? Daughter? Work colleagues? Husband? Ex-husband/ lover? No. A teenage son! And the viewer is free to interpret that anyway they like[40] – and no doubt some viewers have linked the veneration of the mother figure, of the idea and the reality of mothers and motherhood, of the domineering and controlling aspects of the mother (and her possessiveness over her son), and of the child's and the son's relationship with the mother, to Pasolini's own life, and his own relationship with his mother, Susanna Colussi (which some observers found unhealthy. Freudians, post-Freudians and psychoanalysts can dive into the 1962 movie to explore mothers and sons and incest and taboos. But there's no need: Pasolini's movies come fitted with their own commentaries and meta-texts).

Meanwhile, Ettore Garofolo bravely steps into a prominent role in a dramatic movie made by an iconoclastic film director/ poet, playing opposite an Oscar-winning national treasure. Not easy for a 16 year-old boy! And you can see that Garofolo isn't always comfortable in the role; but if you let Anna Magnani run the show, in acting terms, all eyes will be on her. And they are.

The concept of *Mamma Roma* – an ex-prostitute muses on her life, with her son's life as a pretext – seems old-fashioned and clichéd, recalling left-wing plays by Bertholt Brecht or George Bernard Shaw (like Shaw's *Mrs Warren's Profession*). There's a smug self-righteous about the socialist politics in *Mamma Roma* – the movie simply assumes the audience will be on its side as it targets the ills of modern society (from the point-of-view of one of life's working class strugglers and sufferers). It can do that partly due to the presence of Anna Magnani – she brings plenty of goodwill towards her in this story. The socialist politics in *Mamma Roma* are just too simplistic, too pat. What raises the movie above this is the strength of Magnani's performance and her compassionate core. As North American screenwriters would say, Mamma is the 'heart' of the picture.

Mamma Roma is also about single mothers – and, to enhance the drama, a single mother who's a hooker. It's over-cooked, but Pier Paolo Pasolini is not a filmmaker to hold back! He'll use narrative clichés all the time, knowing they're clichés, and often doing nothing to disguise them. His cinema can be as schmaltzy as the goofiest, Hollywood junk, but, if you shoot it in black-and-white, if you use non-professional actors,

---

[40] 'A tragedy of maternal love, the son a lamb sacrificed to the ferocity of the world' (E. Siciliano, 251).

and if you sprinkle some Vivaldi or Bach over it, even highly educated film critics will buy it as serious drama.[41]

That Mamma Roma is a controlling, possessive, jealous and overly-protective mother is clear to all. And she is still hooking (but doesn't want Ettore to know). She wants the best for her child, and will go to considerable lengths to do so. (Mamma is a working class woman with upwardly mobile aspirations: she scorns her working class origins, hopes to escape them, to enter the social realm of the bourgeoisie, and wants her son to have a better life than she did).[42]

So Mamma Roma is a woman who'll do anything for her son Ettore, even coming up with a bizarre blackmailing scheme that involves help from a fellow prostitute, Biancofiore (Luisa Loiano), and a local pimp, Zaccaria (played by Luciano Gonini). In the dog-eat-dog world of Roma's *borgate*, the only way to obtain Ettore a decent job is for his mother to resort to petty crime and blackmail. Well, this *is* Italy we're talking about! (And, true to ethnic stereotypes, the scene where the Zaccaria and Mamma Roma burst in on Biancofiore and the sap (Vittorio La Paglia) is played as a spoof on hot-blooded Latins shouting and yelling and brandishing knives).

The condemnation of prostitution is everywhere in *Mamma Roma*. Yet it's also an issue that's explored with sensitivity and nuance. That this is a Marxist director using the issue of prostitution to critique modern, European capitalism goes without saying. That the 1962 film uses many of the clichés of the prostitution movie sub-genre is also expected (for instance, the film concentrates on one particular prostitute, on her relationships with her family, and her former pimp, Carmine, and her desire to better herself, and to leave hooking behind).

It's interesting to compare *Mamma Roma* with *Vivre Sa Vie*, also released in 1962, Jean-Luc Godard's film of prostitution in Paris starring his wife Anna Karina. Both were early movies from the directors. Both were filmed on low budgets in real, urban locations. Both were condemnations of the exploitation and degradation of prostitution. Both drew on Italian Neo-realism. And both came from a left-wing/ Marxist perspective.

However, I think that *Vivre Sa Vie* is a masterpiece: it's brilliantly controlled, technically inventive, highly imaginative, and wilfully idiosyncratic. As a vehicle for Anna Magnani, *Mamma Roma* is superb and piquant, but it's not at the level of *Vivre Sa Vie* (but Pier Paolo Pasolini's next film, *The Gospel According To Matthew*, would be).

---

41 I mean, it must be 'high art' if it's got Bach in it, right?
42 Mamma looks darkly on the youths hanging out on the stairs, or around her son; she doesn't want him to be like them, or for him to spend time with them. These are the boys who will grow up to be the men seen at the wedding.

There are other issues in *Mamma Roma* – such as: can you escape your past? (Answer: *no*). Such as the 'Sins of the Fathers' (here, it's mothers – but the impact of fathers on the next generation is just as significant when they are absent[43]). Such as: youth vs. old age, and children vs. parents. Such as: what is the family? Such as: what is life? Such as: what is sacred? Such as: what makes life poetic? (These last, Existential questions are posed in most Pasolini movies).

In several respects, *Mamma Roma* is like a sequel to *Accattone*, or a sister movie to that 1961 production. It employs some of the same motifs (pimps and prostitution, for instance, and survival, and money, and Rome's under-class, and Rome's suburbs), some of the same locations, and some of the same actors.[44] But now, instead of the camera tracking as it follows Accattone wearily shuffling thru the outskirts of Rome, it's with Mamma Roma on the streetwalking circuit.

(If you watch *Mamma Roma* back-to-back with *Accattone*, you'll see just how much *Mamma Roma* retreads and reworks the same sort of material and *milieu*. We're hanging out with pimps and prostitutes again, for instance, but now it's from a new perspective: a female one. But it's a worldly-wise, veteran female perspective – Mamma Roma isn't the sort of woman who'll be beaten by clients and meekly let herself be led to jail. And the film that Pasolini might've made instead of *Mamma Roma* – which Bernardo Bertolucci took on – *The Grim Reaper* – has a similar *milieu*)

Comparing *Mamma Roma* with *Accattone*, Pier Paolo Pasolini called it 'less accomplished, less beautiful and that's because it is less dream-like' (2012).

> When I shot *Accattone*, it was the first time I laid my hands on a movie camera. I hadn't even taken a photograph. To this day, I cannot take good pictures. (2012)

When *Accattone* was shown on Italian television after 15 years, 'We realized it is not a realist film at all. It's a dream, it's an oneiric movie' (2012). Maybe *Accattone* is a dream, but it's an incredibly angry, violent and desperate dream.

As with many of his other films, Pier Paolo Pasolini doesn't employ a composer to score the 1962 movie, but selects existing recordings of music (all classical), including *Concert In C Major* by Antonio Vivaldi (one of his favourite composers) and *Violino Tzigano* by Cherubini-Bixio

---

[43] When Ettore brings up the subject of his father (as they dance), Mamma is immediately despondent.
[44] Such as Silvana Corsini, Franco Citti and some of the extras.

(sung by Joselito and arranged by Carlo Rustichelli). *Violino Tzigano* is the gypsy-like popular song that appears in a number of guises (including ironically. Mother and son dance to it in the first act. The music is also foreshadowing – Ettore steals his mom's records later, to sell for Lire, and the merchant who buys the records plays it, and comments on it. And, bitterly, one of the guys in the prison hospital sings it, tormenting Ettore with memories of his mother).

✢

Mamma Roma opens with a wedding. But no ordinary wedding! Mamma Roma is allowed to dominate it completely (she starts off by shoo-ing some piglets into the banqueting room!). Visually, it's composed as yet another reference to *The Last Supper* in Milan by Leonardo da Vinci. So, the guests are all seated, chatting, laughing, and Mamma, loud, very drunk, and certainly uncontrollable (nobody would dare to quieten her![45]), is lurching about, making jokes, being crude and in-your-face. And then, in an unusual dramatic turn, she embarks on a lengthy sing-a-thon, a call-and-response exchange of songs (with her former lover, and even the subdued[46] and rather plain bride, Maria Bernardini, has a go).[47]

It's as if Pasolini was challenging himself to deliver a wedding scene that didn't emulate any others. So we've got piglets running about, the characters sing to each other, and the whole thing is designed as a platform to introduce the movie star, Anna Magnani, and let her rip.

And it's not only Mamma Roma's personality that is striking in this scene, but the way the people around relate to her, indulging her, being amused by her. Anna Magnani plays the scene broad and close to being the obnoxious wedding guest that everybody wishes would leave (the Last Supper allusions enhance Mamma's vulgarity).

> The bodily excess of the characters, which is a linguistic-stylistic excess of the film, is a feature of the composition of the scene which contaminates high art with low life, the figurative and the cinematic, the spiritual and the terrestrial, the diegetic and the extra-diegetic

according to Sam Rohdie (79).

The subtext of the scene is slippery (as it often is in Pier Paolo Pasolini's cinema – it's one of the aspects that makes his work so unpredictable and forceful): that is, sometimes it is the unspoken but

---

[45] There are no patriarchs here with the authority to silence Mamma.
[46] The bride is understandably subdued – you can't compete with Mamma Roma when she's on a roll (and also, when you know your husband-to-be sitting next to you had a relationship with Mamma).
[47] Poor Carmine – Mamma gatecrashing your wedding is a nightmare come true.

clearly at one time powerful relationship that Mamma had with Carmine, the groom, but sometimes it is the veneration of Mamma as the Crude and Rude Queen of the Suburbs.

That Mamma Roma is keen to move upwards socially is emphasized: she is determined to escape her working class origins (the locals are referred to as 'hicks' in the subtitles). She promises a better life (in Roma) for her son Ettore. It's classic drama, then, that Carmine (Franco Citti), her former pimp,[48] (and one-time lover), should call soon after the wedding and ask for help with money for some shady scheme (so Mamma goes streetwalking again, to raise the cash, for two weeks). Thus, she can't escape her origins as easily as she thought (Carmine also appears towards the end of the picture, as an angel of death from the past; Mamma offers him a place to sleep and food, but she also loathes him. As soon as he appears and announces he's back, she breaks down and weeps. Then she attacks him with a knife. Carmine is portrayed as a rather weak character, looking like Accattone aged up (with a moustache);[49] for instance, he weeps as he recounts his view of the history of their failed relationship (in the scene after the wedding). Mamma Roma isn't having any of it: she won't even invite him in).

✦

Among the most intriguing scenes in *Mamma Roma* are the very lengthy sequences of Mamma Roma walking the streets at night. These are essentially long monologues, covered with tracking shots, as the camera (on a truck) faces back at Anna Magnani walking towards it. She talks, and punters or acquaintances come and go, chatting to her. She's been doing this for 30 years, with no enthusiasm for this lifestyle at all anymore (if she had any in the first place). Why is she a nobody? she muses as she walks. The camera follows her into shadows, with very little light on her,[50] and swerves around corners. Lamps dot the background.[51] It's stagey,[52] but it works – largely due to the force of Magnani's screen presence.

The streetwalking scenes are also exposition scenes – and very obviously exposition scenes – where a character speaks in monologues. Except that Anna Magnani *bellows* her speeches, and laughs in between –

---

[48] Carmine was the name of the arrogant pimp in *Accattone*, so the Franco Citti character is a sort of continuation.
[49] So Franco Citti is playing older than his 24 years at the time, whereas in *Accattone* he was playing younger than his age of 23.
[50] Technically, it's patchy – many Italian productions of this era struggled to light night scenes. It's not one of Delli Colli's finest moments. Maybe the production couldn't afford extra lamps; or maybe another film was using the only ones available.
[51] The location seems to have been chosen specifically for those street lights, which enliven the black background with points of light.
[52] The monologue scenes feel a little synthetic, as if Pasolini was apeing Tennessee Williams.

as if she's playing to the gods in a theatre, not to the characters who drift in and out of the frame. Certainly there's no performance like this in the rest of Pasolini's cinema. (One wonders if Pasolini and Magnani disagreed about how to play Mamma Roma; it does seem as if it was *Magnani's* way, after all. The non-professional actors would never dare to openly contradict Pasolini, but a veteran like Magnani might. After all, she had worked many big director names, and won an Oscar).[53]

The exposition takes up much of the second half of act one of *Mamma Roma,* after the characters of mother and son have been established. We learn about Mamma Roma's colourful past (such as her arranged marriage to an ageing fascist from Benito Mussolini's time when she was only 14.[54] That was, we find, her parents' doing – but now they're dead, tho' the old rascal is still alive).

✛

Yet, altho' Anna Magnani is allowed to dominate *Mamma Roma,* this is also a Pier Paolo Pasolini movie. As such, it contains many of the elements we are familiar with in Pasolini's cinema: the dusty, lower middle class and sub-proletarian districts of suburban Rome, lengthy sections of classical music (Antonio Vivaldi), Ettore and the gangs of *ragazzi* (hanging out, playing cards in stairwells, getting into petty crime, and, of course, talking about sex and women).

✛

Act 2 of *Mamma Roma* shifts the focus to Ettore (tho' Mamma Roma appears several times – hooking, selling vegetables in the market, and visiting the Priest). Ettore is a regular kid in many respects: he hangs out with a bunch of local kids, plays soccer, rides motorcycles, etc. But he's also his mother's son, barely remembers his father (Mamma Roma said he was a petty criminal), doesn't like school, but doesn't want to work, either (when he finally gets a job, he acts smilingly proud – for his mom's benefit, maybe, when she comes to watch him at work, then weeps as she realizes her li'l bambino is growing up. But he soon walks out on waiting tables).

Ettore is also something of an Existential, outsider figure, in the manner of Albert Camus, André Gide and Knut Huysmans (like Accattone before him). He doesn't fit in with the gang completely (there is always friction), he doesn't want to work, he doesn't worship his mom, doesn't care for his absent father, and so on. He has no purpose, no direction, no hobbies, no passions (the film includes some very lengthy shots, at the start of act two, of Ettore doing not much of anything,

---

[53] Yet Magnani also felt that Pasolini was stealing from her life.
[54] Hints of the storytellers in *Salò*.

wandering around the in-between zone beyond the tenements, which is where Bruna finds him. These are images of a lost soul, but do we need to see two shots (lasting 45 seconds together) of Ettore loafing about aimlessly? The dramatic content of the shots is established after 5 seconds, or 10 seconds tops).

Like many teen characters in many youth movies, Ettore is *against everything*. You name it, he's against it (as Groucho Marx might say), and he's rebelling (as Marlon Brando said in *The Wild One*). However, Ettore is not an angry, resentful, teenage kid in the explosive, fiery, North American manner (Mamma Roma absorbs and gives out all of the fire in this movie). He's no James Dean or young Dennis Hopper. He's much more subdued than that, much more, like, uhh, whatever, hands in the pockets, head hanging down, lowered eyes, gangly and awkward (he would fit right in to a 1990s grunge band, or a Generation X or Generation Y computer gaming club[55]).

Which of course makes his persecution and scapegoating all the more vicious. That this harmless, relatively nice and friendly kid should die young, and in extreme circumstances (alone, cold, strapped to a table), is gruesome. It's another of Pier Paolo Pasolini's middle fingers to society, to the forces of capitalism, to pointless, superficial consumerism (the white radio, the new motorbike), and the Italian authorities who were wrecking the ancient world, the pre-industrial Italy that Pasolini loved. (The maestro would be kicking against those capitalist/ fascist targets right up until his final movie, *Salò*).

> Italy as a whole is moving towards a consumer civilization [Pasolini complained], it's turning into a horrible petit bourgeois world, so my flash of optimism is buried under the most profound pessimism. (PP, 25)

Ettore's first erotic encounter is with Bruna (Silvana Corsini – she played Maddalena in *Accattone*, and it's the same sort of role), a 24 year-old woman (with a baby) that, according to the guys, everybody has been with (and Mamma Roma doesn't like that one little bit! She laughs heartily when she hears about it, but also resolves to make Ettore forget all about Bruna with one of her fellow ladies of the night, Biancofiore. Parts of *Mamma Roma* come across like an 18th century sex farce, or as if Pier Paolo Pasolini is already plotting to do *The Decameron* or *The Canterbury Tales*). Again, the Freudian, incestuous subtexts are writ large (and the erotic rivalry between an older woman who feels threatened by a younger woman. It's *Snow White and the Seven Dwarfs*, where the

---

[55] Indeed, Ettore is a teenager in the era before cel phones and computer games. Like, what did kids *do* before TVs or computers or cel phones?

Wicked Queen is furious about encountering a younger, prettier rival).

It's significant that the two women in Ettore's life are both hookers, and that Ettore's first sexual experience should be with a woman who, if she isn't a prostitute, is regarded as such in the neighbourhood (and in some scenes is depicted as such. Anyway, the denizens of Roma don't differentiate between the two).

But 16 year-old Ettore is besotted with Bruna – indeed, the first time we see him moving into the world of petty crime, it's stealing his mom's records to sell for money at a used goods store to buy a gold chain[56] for Bruna. (As soon as he meets Bruna, he's giving her a token, and then shyly promising to buy her a gold chain. At this meeting, she approaches him, notice – and he is flattered. Bruna's not the world's greatest mom, either – she says she's left her baby asleep back home).

In a later scene, Bruna and Ettore are heading for the disused building again, to fool around. The boys in the gang, lost for something to do, follow them. As the jibes and insults escalate to a fight, Bruna is grabbed by the *ragazzi*, while the frail, skinny Ettore is beaten up[57] (no one comes to his aid, they just watch). While Ettore slinks away, the movie shows Bruna and the lads heading for the abandoned building. Now she's walking beside them, the struggle is forgotten (a revealing touch, how the kids shift from fighting to chatting instantly, as if it's all a game), and presumably she's going to do what they want, as she has probably done before. That *Mamma Roma* depicts what could be coercive sex or possibly gang rape in such a throwaway, casual fashion, and abruptly switches the tone, is typical of Pier Paolo Pasolini's cinema.

✦

Meanwhile, the Mamma Roma-related scenes in the second act of *Mamma Roma* include Mamma streetwalking (again), and putting plans in motion to help her son Ettore: first, she asks Biancofiore to seduce Ettore and cure him of his infatuation with Bruna. Second, she enlists a favour from a local pimp (Zaccaria) she knows (and Biancofiore, too) for a blackmailing scheme, in which the owner of a local restaurant will be framed and shamed into giving Ettore a job.

We saw earlier how Mamma Roma denounced Carmine, her former lover, when he came to see her, but she has taken up his scheme of selling dodgy vegetables in the local market. (So she's a single mom with two jobs – Ettore's father is very absent, never seen, and, when he's mentioned, Mamma wallows in self-pity).

And there's a scene of Mother Rome reaching out to, of all places,

---

56 A reprise of Accattone and the chain he steals from his son.
57 Thus, Ettore is the flipside of a character like Accattone, who gets into street brawls frequently.

the Catholic Church. Here Mamma seeks help for finding a job for her son Ettore from the Priest (Paolo Volpone) and receives the standard response from society, from authority, from the law, from mercantile capitalism: the lad must study, must learn a trade. It's what careers advisers in schools say, it's what governments say, and *it's what no kid wants to hear* (and not Pasolini, neither!). Is that the only option, to become just another worker, a cog in the capitalist machine? (Ettore, like Accattone before him, thinks it's beneath him to work for a living; he'd rather steal).

Thus, *Mamma Roma* critiques contemporary, European society, and its narrow-minded, boring opportunities for work, for life, among the younger generation. But, like all political critiques, it can offer *nothing* in its place: it has utopian desires, but it cannot come up with realistic, practical and achievable means of creating a utopia.

Yes – Godard, Bergman, Fassbinder, Buñuel, Pasolini and whoever can criticize (or viciously lambast) modern society for its flaws, its stupidities, its brutalities, but they do not (indeed, they *cannot*) show how everything can be fixed, or how a utopia could be achieved.

Maybe movies with a political analysis of contemporary society should spend half of the movie telling a story, raising issues, asking questions, etc (and whingeing), and the second half coming up with answers, solving problems, and setting out exactly how their utopia would work.

✢

So Carmine returns, the shadow of the past that Mamma Roma wishes would disappear forever. What she fears is that he'll tell her son about her shady past, and that she's still a prostitute – knowledge which is a key factor in Ettore's psychological collapse.

Their ride on the new motorcycle she bought for him is their last moment of mother-son bonding, before the finale and Ettore's demise. But in true Pasolinian style, it isn't particularly enjoyable or fulfilling. While cheesy, Hollywood cinema would milk this scene for all of its pathos, in Pasolini's hands it's an experience shared, but Mamma still finds things to complain about, has already realized that she can't buy her son's affection, and the symbol of teenage freedom and rebellion – the motorcycle – has been paid for by the thing that Mamma is most ashamed of, selling her body.

THE FINALE.

Pier Paolo Pasolini conjures a huge cheat in the final act of *Mamma Roma* (actually, it a series of cheats). It's easy to spot, and it's as manipulative and cheesy as the most sentimental, saccharine Hollywood romance. Pasolini physically separates Mamma and her son Ettore, as Ettore is caught stealing[58] and put in jail.[59] Yet the doting mother isn't seen. At all. No sign of her. Anywhere. Even tho' she's a mother so possessive and protective of her offspring she makes Jewish moms look like laidback hippies!

This is a mom who concocts an elaborate blackmailing scheme in order to further her son's career, and gets him a job waiting[60] tables[61] at a posh restaurant. This is a mom who lavishes affection on her child all the time (buying him a 250,000 Lire motorcycle, for instance). This is a mom so keen on controlling every aspect of her kid's life, she will ask one of her fellow hookers to tup the kid, to make him forget about the neighbourhood harlot Bruna. (And we saw her in the previous scene leaving her market stall and tailing Ettore and his pals,[62] seemingly unable to let him live his life, and make all of the mistakes that everybody makes. Mamma Roma can't let go, so when we see her at home, separated from Ettore by the magic of cinema (i.e., parallel cutting), it doesn't convince). As Biancofiore put it, Mamma would get nailed to a Cross for her son.

Yes, Mamma Roma isn't shown visiting Ettore in jail or hospital once! Come on! This is a mom who would storm the Fortress of Doom of sword-and-sorcery stories (very loudly), carrying bundles of food and gifts for her child in her teeth as she climbs the Jagged Cliffs of Catastrophe. This is a mom who would berate the prison authorities for their incompetence and sadism in jailing a 17 year-old boy for stealing a five dollar radio! This is a mom who would seduce the lawyer, the judge, and anybody else, to get her boy out of court or out of prison!

Ettore's crime – filching a little, white radio from an old man's bedside – seems deliberately trivial compared to his punishment and persecution. The scheme that the gang[63] of boys cook up is ridiculous – visiting people on their deathbeds in hospital so they can swipe items

---

58 When the kids from school meet the crooks, and the notion of stealing from the sick in hospitals is introduced, Ettore is told to wait a moment. He walks to one side, in a step-motion shot, while a very loud police siren is heard: it's a not-so-subtle piece of foreshadowing of Ettore's capture and imprisonment.
59 It was drawing on a real case, where Marcello Ellisei died in prison a year b4 Pasolini wrote the script (PP, 51).
60 Co-writer and A.D. Sergio Citti has a cameo as a waiter.
61 A nod to where Pasolini found actor Garofolo.
62 Now Ettore has his own life with his friends, and Mamma Roma is excluded.
63 A great touch has Ettore moving up in the gang's hierarchy – now it seems as if he is one of the leaders.

which wouldn't fetch a dollar fifty in a yard sale! Talk about *petty* crime! (How low can you get?).

That the local *ragazzi* in the *borgate* are dim and haven't got a clue (yet they act with a macho, jeering strut, like they know it all) is part of the point, of course. The way that the theft scene is filmed is deliberately overly-dramatic (how the guy on the bed notices the snaffle instantly, for example, or how Ettore is physically manhandled out of the room, where a simple apology or gesture would've fixed everything). This is one of many over-cooked elements in the finale of *Mamma Roma*.

The 1962 Italian movie then cuts directly to Ettore in bed in the prison hospital. No scenes of Ettore with the authorities, no scenes of courts and judges and cops. And, of course, no scenes of Mamma Roma, the force of nature herself, wading in with her foghorn voice and her coarse, earthy ways, wrapping her arms around the boy as he sits meekly and dumbly, listening to a cop or lawyer or court official dress him down, and giving back as good as she gets.

The finale of *Mamma Roma* is thus a highly contrived piece of storytelling, designed to wring the maximum amount of sentiment from the characters, the situation and the audience (notice how the music – *Concert In C Major* by Antonio Vivaldi – is allowed to dominate the sound mix, in order to really push home the attempts at high drama and tragedy).

According to Pier Paolo Pasolini, Ettore finding out that his mom is a hooker sends him into a trauma: 'so he has a collapse, a real crisis, which eventually takes him to his death' (PP, 55). Yet that key moment when Ettore finds out isn't shown.[64]

Notice too that Bruna is still on the scene, and Ettore pushes her to the ground, which seems out of character. In fact, Pasolini's direction of Garofolo changes in the finale – he is portrayed as cocky and arrogant at times, masking his inner turmoil over finding out that his mom is a hooker. In the Bruna scene, it seems that *she*, not Carmine, told Ettore about it.

However, Ettore does change somewhat: now he's rejecting his mother publicly, pushing Bruna away, acting the angry/ angsty teenager, and even, in an intriguing reversal, seems to become the leader of the local gang.[65] Much of that doesn't quite convince, dramatically, narratively or performatively (Ettore Garofalo isn't really at home portraying rebellious, furious energy; he's no Robert de Niro or Al Pacino).

It's persecution all the way, in this dry-run for *The Gospel According*

---

[64] One of many curious elisions in the finale of *Mamma Roma* occurs here: it's a scene we'd expect to see, but it occurs off-screen: Bruna telling Ettore about her mother's hooking.
[65] It's Ettore who persuades them to try thieving at the hospital again.

To Matthew (as with *Curd Cheese* the following year). At the level of 'realism', Ettore is feverish, but that's a side issue (tho' it does explain why he dies). What Pier Paolo Pasolini, Sergio Citti and the team are really depicting is the vindictive treatment of an innocent and harmless person by a society that doesn't understand him, or like him, or want him, that can't integrate him (he won't work – he leaves the restaurant job), and so casts him aside. (*Si, si*, it's the socialist/ Marxist interrogation of the violence inherent in the system, how left-wing philosophy sees societies and political systems as corrupt and aggressive, just as much as people or groups. If a caption came up at the end of *Mother Rome* – 'VOTE COMMUNIST!' – 'THE PARTITO COMUNISTA ITALIANO WANTS YOUR VOTE!' – we wouldn't be surprised)[66]

Another addition to the over-cooked melodrama has Ettore is suffering in a bed from a fever, while a guy nearby recites from Dante Alighieri's *The Divine Comedy* to a group of guys (who dissolve into mirth, as if the *Divina Commedia* was really a laugh-a-thon. No wonder Ettore goes nuts, and tries to escape (this is where he's grappled by the guys, and is taken to the hospital's equivalent of a dungeon).

The repeated, low angle tracking shots of Ettore strapped to a bed alone in a dark room, with the overhead lighting reminiscent of the religious paintings of Michelangelo Merisi da Caravaggio or Rembrandt van Rijn, which emphasize that this is a *Dead Christ* image (*à la* Andrea Mantegna[67] or Masaccio), aren't necessary. We get the allusion already!

We can see that poor Ettore is strapped to the table in a crucifixion pose, we can see he is looking upwards towards the grating above him like Jesus in his final moments in Golgotha, we can see the pleading look, the whispered imprecations to his mother, we can see the sweat on his brow, and that nobody comes, there's no one to save him, including the one person we know would insist firmly to be there, his mom. (*Mamma Roma* stops just short of having Ettore yelling out the famous words from the *New Testament*: '*Eli, Eli, lama sabachthani?* = 'My God, why hast thou forsaken me?').

So, where's mom, then? Only after a *lengthy* period with the Ettore persecution sequence does editor Nino Baragli cut back to Mamma Roma. Finally! And what is she depicted doing? Shaking her head in worry and bewilderment over her son[68] as she makes a cup of coffee and dips some bread in it *back at her apartment*. Not sitting outside the prison, not walking to the jail, and not battering on the dungeon doors backed up by

---

66 Mamma Roma denounces Communism of course.
67 Andrea Mantegna's *Lamentation* may be a reference here.
68 Following yet another imploring glance at the distant church dome, as if an angel is going to burst out of it, fly to her, and together they'll swoop into the gaol and rescue the beloved Ettore.

a crowd of Rome's rowdiest proletariat demanding to see her child!

So there are scenes that are cleverly avoided, or passed over. Instead of moving from A to B, *Mamma Roma* skips onwards, to F and G, the final scenes. These are, tho', impressively played and they begin to attain that inevitable and implacable momentum which great tragedies possess in their final moments. No, *Mamma Roma* isn't Sophocles or Molière, it is not high tragedy, or even authentic tragedy, but it does nod towards those dramatic forms (five years later, with *Oedipus Rex*, Pasolini would tackle the classical form of tragedy far more successfully).

The finale of *Mamma Roma* has its cinematic moments, too: for instance, in the scene where Mamma Roma hears that her son has died in jail, she is depicted in deep shadow, and surrounded by people.[69] Perhaps this is an allusion to the Madonna, who suffered with her son during the Crucifixion, in some versions of the Christian story. That was used for *The Gospel According To Matthew* (with repeated cuts between the mother and the son). And the very last scene, at the window of Mamma's apartment, the editor's gift for orchestrating point-of-view shots to generate high emotion is marvellously evoked: the 1962 movie cuts from medium shots of Mamma to reverse angles of what she's looking at (out of the window, we see more tenements over rough ground, and on the horizon, a church dome – Basilica di San Giovanni Bosco).

And here is where the reason you cast a great actor comes good, as Anna Magnani's face conveys a host of feelings, from sorrow to desperation to shock to fury to confusion (without needing dialogue). Her instinct is to throw herself from the window, but the people from the market stalls have followed her into her apartment, and gather round her, holding onto her. (It's another slightly false moment, as if this is a Bertholt Brecht play on a stage where the chorus gathers in the final moments, rather than a post-Neo-realist movie).

Why that image of a church and the tenements? It's a multi-purpose symbol or image. Is it because Mamma Roma turned to the Church (discussing her son with the Priest)? And because the Church let her down, in the end? Is the church included in the final shot because it is, ultimately, without value, without function, in this post-WW2, post-Nietzschean, God-less world? (Yet there are at least three scenes in a church, during ceremonies, and the dome of Basilica di San Giovanni Bosco is framed in several other scenes). Is it the Church as Mother (Mother Church, Mother Rome), as a sanctuary, a protectress? (we note that the hemisphere dome looks like a breast). Is the church shown to

---

[69] This scene looks as if some parts were cut out.

indicate the pointlessness of authority, of worship, of social structures? (Because the Catholic Church is linked to the authorities who persecuted Ettore).

✛

THE RECEPTION OF *MAMMA ROMA*.

Mamma Roma was another controversial movie for some audiences. That it took on the issue of prostitution was more than enough for some viewers. That it attacked contemporary Italian society and that it included a little swearing didn't help. There are no sex scenes or nudity in *Mamma Roma,* as they were would be plenty of in Pier Paolo Pasolini's later works, but there are numerous indications of sex (Mamma Roma with her clients at night, for instance, and the whispered suggestions). And Ettore and Bruna are seen entering a disused building, about to do the deed.

Mamma Roma was condemned on its release as being obscene by the Lieutenant Colonel of the *carabinieri* in Venice (where it was showing at the Venice Film Festival, on Aug 31, 1962). Farting and words like shit and piss enraged the cops. The case was heard on Sept 5, 1962, but didn't go anywhere.

Another scandal involving *Mamma Roma* occurred at the Roman premiere (Sept 22, 1962), when some of the student members of right-wing organizations Giovane Italia and Avanguardia Nazionale attacked Pier Paolo Pasolini in the foyer. Already, then, Pasolini's films had a knack for attracting trouble – protesters disrupted a screening of *Accattone* in Roma, for instance. (Ideologically, *Mamma Roma* seems pro-Communist and left-wing, and contains material and views that wouldn't endear themselves to right-wing groups).[70]

---

[70] It's possible that some of the outraged right-wing groups from this period or linked to later groups were involved in Pasolini's death.

Beggar (a.k.a. Accattone, 1961).
This page and over.

Cino Del Duca Films presenta

un film di
PIER PAOLO PASOLINI
ACCATTONE

Prodotto da Alfredo Bini per la Cino Del Duca Films - Arco Film (Roma)

Mamma Roma (1962).
This page and over.

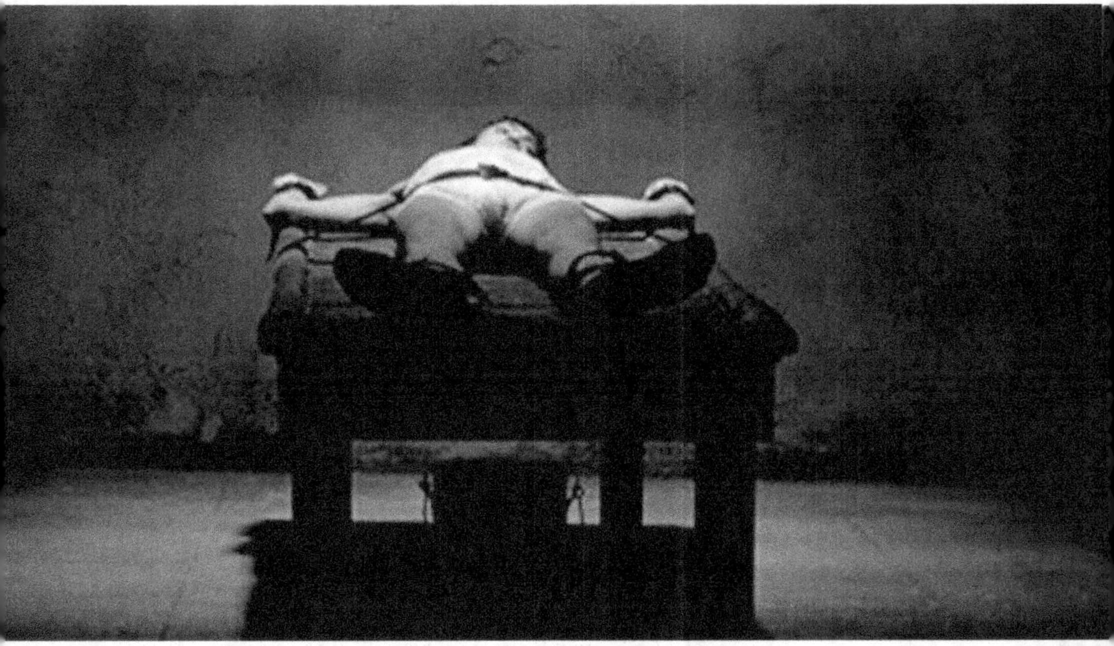

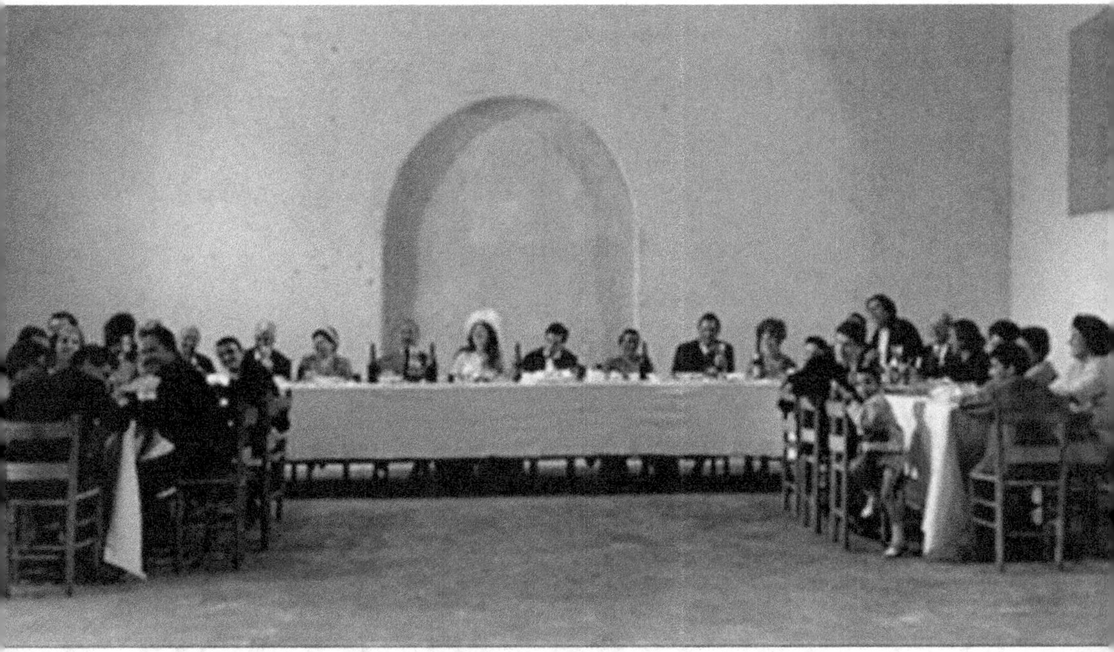

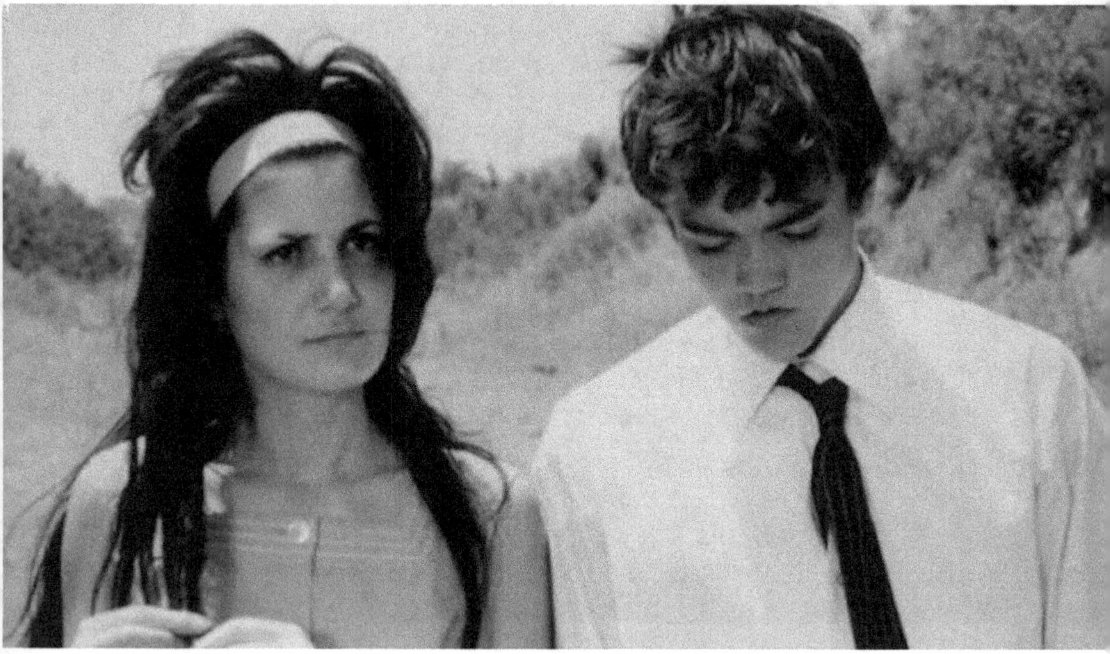

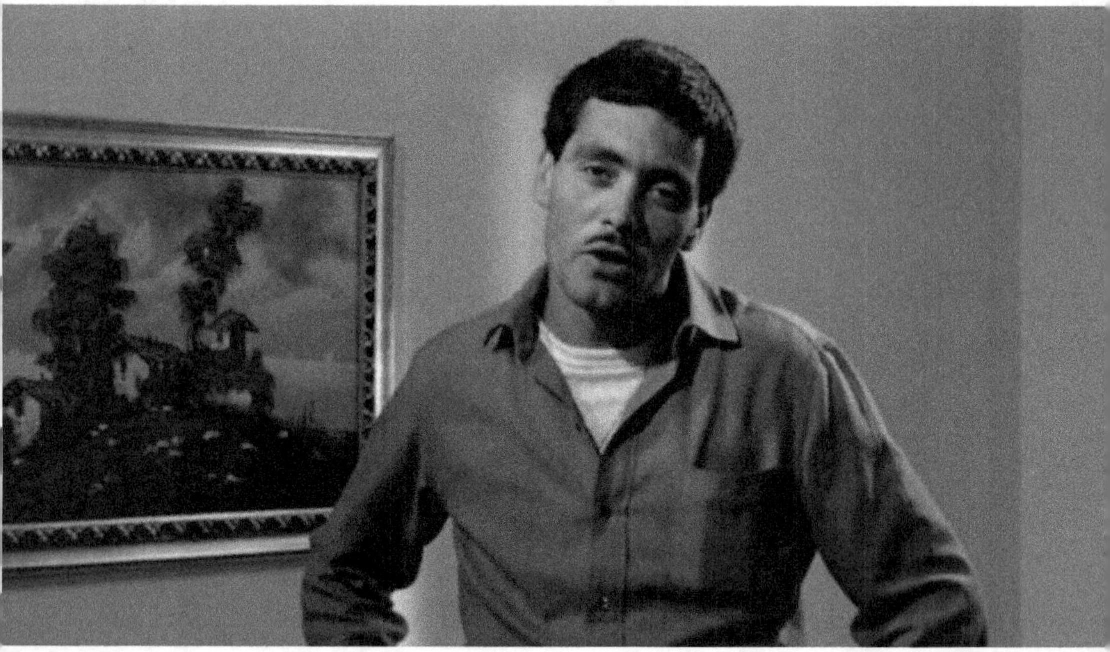

7

LA RICOTTA

CURD CHEESE

The Gospel According To Matthew wasn't the first time that Pier Paolo Pasolini had put Jesus on film. In 1963 he contributed a segment (the best, with Jean-Luc Godard's episode, *The New World*) to producer Alfredo Bini's oddly-titled episode film *RoGoPaG*[1] (the other directors were Godard, Roberto Rossellini and Ugo Gregoretti. The film was released under the title *Let's Wash Out Our Brains,* a title not much better than the ugly *RoGoPaG*).

RoGoPaG was part of a fashion in Italian and European cinema for anthology movies (others included *Siamo donne* (1953 – Visconti, Rossellini, Francolini and Zampa) and *Amore In Città* (1953 – Fellini, Antonioni, Lattuada, Lizzani, Maseli and Risi). Pasolini contributed to others, such as *The Witches* and *Caprice Italian Style.* Many of the well-known directors in Italy were part of anthology films during their career.

Anthology films were producer-driven projects. A producer would come up with an idea for a movie, go to Ingmar Bergman, telling him that Federico Fellini and Jean Renoir had already signed up to do it (they hadn't). When Bergman agreed, the producer'd go to Fellini and Renoir, and so on. (Producers recognized that an anthology movie needed a name director for advertising – and stars, too).

La Ricotta (= *Curd Cheese*) was filmed near Rome (Via Appia Antica, Via Appia Nouva), in Autumn, 1962. Flavio Morgherini was art director, Nino Baragli was editor, the A.D.s were Sergio Citti and Carlo di Carlo, Tonino Delli Colli was DP, music by Carlo Rustichelli, and

---

1 *La Ricotta* had been written for another producer ('but they mucked about with it because they were afraid; they thought it was too violent' [PP, 59]).

costumes were by Danilo Donati. Several actors in the Pasolini Circus appear in *La Ricotta*, including the lovely Rossana Di Rocco (the Archangel in *The Gospel According To Matthew*),2 Ettore Garofolo from *Mamma Roma*, Mario Cipriani (the bar owner in *Accattone*), and Pasolini's friend Laura Betti playing the Film Star. (In the other films were Rosanna Schiaffino, Ugo Tognazzi, Emonda Aldini and Gianrico Tedeschi). Released: Feb 19, 1963. 122 mins.

Pier Paolo Pasolini's 35-minute episode *La Ricotta* was one of the better things he produced in film. Gian Brunetta called it 'one of the greatest moments of creativity in postwar art' (238). It starred Orson Welles as a Film Director making a Biblical epic on the outskirts of Rome (or what *appears* at first to be a sword-and-sandal or life of Christ movie). Shot in black-and-white (and colour, for the film-within-a-film), *La Ricotta* is partly a broad comedy which sends up many targets, including Pasolini himself, Marxism, cinema and his views on cinema.

Orson Welles is insouciant, mysterious, with the famous smile (think *The Third Man*) flickering at the edges of his mouth. Throughout the film he sits apart from the cast and crew, issuing orders to lackeys who relay them on a tannoy or bark them to each other. Welles has little to do in *Curd Cheese* except to play the impassive, cool, aloof Film Director (which he can do better than anybody else).3 He does call 'action', though, and also answers some (inane) questions from a visiting reporter (Vittorio La Paglia – the duped restaurant owner in *Mamma Roma*) (with deliberately mystifying or pretentious answers – he is asked about his film, about his politics and, yes, about Federico Fellini (remember that Pasolini and Fellini had fallen out).4 His answer?: 'Fellini dances'.5 Welles also reads aloud (at length) what appears to be a book entitled *Mamma Roma* by one Pier Paolo Pasolini). Welles sports a heavy, black coat, despite the Italian Summer. He is also the Bastard Director – let them remain nailed to the crosses, he tells his assistants, referring to the actors (when there's no need at all, because they're tied on with rope! We know that film directors sometimes dislike extras, but this is highly exaggerated).

---

2 Rossanna Di Rocco is part of Stracci's family, picnicking nearby (they visit him near the set, where he seems to have promised them free food). She also appeared as Nino Davoli's possible girlfriend in *The Hawks and the Sparrows*, and as one of Noah's family in *The Bible*, the giant Dino di Laurentiis production of 1966.

3 Altho' some directors found Orson Welles intimidating to direct, Pier Paolo Pasolini found the North American genius easy to work with, because Welles was a director himself. 'I think directors understand this better than anybody' (PP, 135).

4 The comic goings-on in *La Ricotta* appear sometimes as if Pasolini were sending up the cinema of Federico Fellini.

5 Pier Paolo Pasolini must've got fed up by this time with questions about Fellini. In *Toby Dammit*, Fellini got his own back, by having a producer character define his movie as 'situated between Pasolini and Dreyer with a *coupçon* of Ford'.

It is the complete opposite of what Orson Welles was like as a film director of course: actors absolutely loved him and he absolutely loved actors. And the *last* thing that Welles would be doing on a film set would be sitting apart from everyone else – he liked to be at the centre of the action. (Similarly, Pasolini as a film director was nothing like this).

Curiously, Orson Welles was dubbed by Giorgio Bassani, even tho' Welles could speak many languages, and was an expert with no peers when it came to dubbing actors (for some movies, such as *The Trial*, *Chimes At Midnight* and *Mr Arkadin,* he dubbed many characters). Welles said he '*played* it in Italian' (which you can see in the film).[6]

As for working with Pier Paolo Pasolini, Welles enthused:

> Terribly bright and gifted. Crazy mixed-up kid, maybe – but on a very superior level. I mean Pasolini the poet, spoiled Christian, and Marxist ideologue. There's nothing mixed up about him on a movie set. Real authority and a wonderfully free way with the machinery. (ibid., 270)

Among the many delights in *Curd Cheese* are the two scenes shot in the lurid Technicolor of sword-and-sandal epic movies of the period (1950s and early 1960s). These are the rushes of the film that Orson Welles' Director is shooting. The two scenes are *Depositions From the Cross*: Christ is surrounded by characters such as Joseph of Arithemea and several Marys and Marthas. Everything in these scenes visually derives from Italian Renaissance painting: the flattened space, the blue cyclorama, the robes, the colours, the poses (the reference is to Rosso Fiorentino's *Deposition of Christ*, 1521). But the scenes are played for broad comedy: there are cock-ups, actors forget their lines or corpse, an assistant director frantically shouts instructions, and the sound guy keeps playing trashy pop songs instead of the sober Domenico Scarlatti that the director wants (while the A.D. or director splutters about blasphemy and lack of respect (it's as if Pasolini and Bini were anticipating the controversy that *The Gospel* might attract, so they satirized themselves in advance. A kind of pre-emptive satirical strike). Italian films of the era were shot wild (without sound): do you think the film sets had A.D.s or directors screaming instructions at the actors?). A year or so later, when Pasolini returned to the same subject, of Christ on the Cross, the approach would be utterly sombre and reverent.

Orson Welles' Film Director, though, isn't at the centre of *La Ricotta* – that is Mario Cipriani, who plays Stracci, one of the thieves being crucified beside Christ. He is a hapless Any Guy, non-descript, well-meaning and simple-minded (and he's over-weight). His one goal is

---
6 Quoted in O. Welles, 1992, 270.

to get some food (he dresses up (badly!) as a female extra in order to obtain an extra lunch hand-out. One of the legends of Cinecittà was extras dressing up in several outfits a day in order to obtain multiple lunches or pay envelopes).[7] His colleagues tease him (somewhat cruelly) about his obsession with eating. He sells the Film Star's dog for 1,000 Lire and dashes off down the road to buy some cheese. With all his running around, and pigging out on cheese and bread, Stracci over-indulges and expires on the cross. It's self-consciously heavy-handed satire (and hasn't aged well in some respects), but it is produced with a great verve. (Some of the analogies with the Christian story require some clumsy script-writing: for example, the scene where a bunch of actors and crew gather to laugh at Stracci wolfing down food in speeded-up motion, echoing the jeering of the mob during the Crucifixion).

What sort of movie is the Film Director making? It seems to be a Felliniesque fantasy, rather than a Biblical tale, with bits that don't match up. The three crosses are only one element – there's a table decorated with a still life of food out of Baroque painting, and actors in costume who don't seem to have any roles. Meanwhile, the *tableau* of the *Descent From the Cross*, which the Film Director appears to be directing, is obviously filmed in a studio, while the reverse angles, depicting the crew, are back on the outdoor set, lit by the familiar, hard Roman sunlight.

Further inconsistencies in *Curd Cheese* include: the extras on the crosses are carried some way off in between takes, for no apparent reason (and left to bake in the sun!). Costumes are hung on some rails, but no one looks after them, or dresses anyone. There are no make-up or hair people in sight (even tho' hair, make-up and wardrobe folk are everywhere on a historical movie set). There is little to no activity on the set: filmmaking means waiting around (as we know too well!), but there's usually someone preparing something somewhere.

Curd Cheese depicts the lengthy periods in between rolling the cameras – the waiting about, the focus on food, and nothing much seems to be happening. The crew spends its time loafing around, persuading one of the actresses (Maria Bernardini) to strip (which she does), playing nasty pranks on the hapless Stracci, or doing the twist to rotten pop songs.[8]

Stracci dies on the cross in the middle of a filmmakers' worst nightmare – the film producers,[9] dignitaries, journalists and an entourage

---

[7] S. Levy, 104. Food is definitely one of the main considerations of film extras. Yes, and the crew. And the actors.

[8] It's 1963, but the Beatles and the British invasion hasn't hit Rome yet. In so many would-be cool European movies, the pop music chosen to be 'trendy' is utterly terrible!

[9] Alfredo Bini, the producer of the movie, is one of the visiting dignitaries.

of hangers-on arriving to watch the shooting.[10] The Film Director (after calling for 'action!' several times), offers Stracci's tombstone eulogy: he had to die to make us realize he was alive.

> The theme is complex and profoundly Christian. It does violence to the clericalism of any church. The blasphemy of the repeated cries – "get those crucified characters out of here" – is the sign of an ancient despair at not seeing the everlasting urgency of religion matched by the world. (E. Siciliano, 253)

Pier Paolo Pasolini wasn't the only European art film director to use the big budget, ancient world, epic film as an ironic background for a meditation on art and filmmaking. In *Contempt*, Jean-Luc Godard had Fritz Lang shooting a version of *The Odyssey* in Italy (*Contempt*, regarded as one of the finest films about films, was made in 1963, around the same time as *RoGoPaG*). The ancient world movie was very lucrative and widespread in world cinema at the time (1950s and 1960s): Hollywood came to Spain and Italy to make movies about Europe's ancient past, and European film companies responded by churning out movies about its own past for the international (and American) market.

✢

RoGoPaG was another controversial entry[11] in the Pier Paolo Pasolini Legend: it was condemned for its depiction of the Catholic religion. For 'publicly maligning the religion of the state', as the legalese put it (the film had been taken by the authorities on March 1, 1963, on the grounds of insulting the State, with a writ signed by the public prosecutor, Giuseppe De Gennaro).[12] Pasolini received a four month suspended sentence in prison (in Rome, the Appeals Court on May 6, 1964 revoked the charge, 'because the act does not constitute a crime').[13] Pasolini said: 'I was slandered week after week, and for two or three years I lived under a kind of unimaginable persecution' (PP, 63).

All of that might've put off some filmmakers from attempting a feature-length portrayal of Jesus – but not Pier Paolo Pasolini and Alfredo Bini! They steamed ahead with *The Gospel According To Matthew*! (Altho' *The Gospel According To Matthew* was released after *Curd Cheese*, Pasolini had already written *The Gospel According To Matthew* before making *Curd Cheese*). And all credit to Bini for backing *The*

---

10 In a bizarre gesture, the filmmakers have set up the three crosses and place the actors on them, in front of a table laid with food (*à la* Leonardo da Vinci's *Last Supper*). And when Stracci is supposed to say his one line of dialogue, he expires.
11 Cuts were made to *Curd Cheese*, and the opening caption was changed.
12 Pier Paolo Pasolini deliberately wound up the authorities by including a character called Pedoti, referring to one of the magistrates in the prosecutor's office. Producer Alfredo Bini was furious when Pasolini insisted on keeping the character's name. Pasolini could be stubborn at times.
13 *RoGoPaG* was re-released as *Laviamoci il Cervello*, with *La Ricotta* re-edited.

Gospel According To Matthew, knowing that it would probably ruffle feathers, as most (no, all) of Pasolini's movies had already done up to that time.

GODARD'S EPISODE IN *ROGOPAG*.

For Jean-Luc Godard's segment in *RoGoPaG*, entitled *The New World* (a.k.a. *Le Nouveau Monde/ Il Nuovo Mondo*), many regular Godardians joined the crew (Charles Bitsch, Agnès Guillemot, etc). Jean Rabier was DP. The cast included: Jean-Marc Bory, Alexandra Stewart, Michel Delahaye and Jean-André Fieschi. It was filmed in b/w and ran for about 20 minutes.

Jean-Luc Godard's *The New World* is typical Godard: a man (Jean-Marc Bory), a woman (Alexandra Stewart), a neurotic relationship, and Paris… all very Godardian (but made in Italian), though not his most satisfying work by any means. It's *Breathless Revisited* for the *n*-th time. It must have been a kick for Godard to be included alongside heroes like Roberto Rossellini and Orson Welles in the same movie.

So the background story for *The New World* has an atomic bomb exploding over Paris (but 80 miles up),[14] which changes the city, but subtly, psychologically, socially: *The New World* looks forward to *Alphaville* (1965) with its evocations of the strange city of the present day/ near future, where the inhabitants act odd (here they take pills)[15] and regular logic is disrupted. (This was how Godard described the sketch, in a *Cahiers du Cinéma* interview: 'things are the same, but different'). The nuclear bomb and the futuristic elements are delivered in the familiar cheapo manner of low budget filmmaking: with sound effects, with newspaper photos, and with a *lot* of voiceover explaining what's happened.

Anyhoo, the atom bomb and sci-fi elements in *The New World* are simply a pretext (as in *Alphaville*), because the 1963 short evokes yet another romantic couple in the Godardverse, yet another relationship on the skids, yet another story where the man is perplexed/ confused/ irritated by the woman.

Yes, it's the *Godard Soap Opera Show* once again: he loves her, she 'ex loves' him; he makes a date with her, she doesn't appear; he follows her to a swimming pool[16] (more stalking from the Godard male), and observes her kissing a guy; quizzed about it later, the woman doesn't know what he's talking about (fed up, he pushes her roughly).

We've seen this soap opera *à la* God-Art many times before and since

---

14 Don't ask why (or how) a bomb was detonated 80 miles above the planet – this is Godard!
15 One of the few instances of drug-taking in a Godard movie – outside of tobacco and alcohol.
16 Cue gratuitous images of women in bikinis.

The New World. The atom bomb going off is used as an explanation for people acting weirdly, and Alessandra not showing up for their rendezvous is explained by her living with a different logic to the husband (that's what he reasons to himself). But in a Godard movie, women always baffle men! They always live to/ in/ with a different logic or poetry from men!

For the rest, *The New World* is Godard operating on autopilot: he could send out a second unit team to get:

(1) a shot of a woman standing by a window (the first shot of the movie – of course, she's smoking a cigarette);

(2) shots of a man and woman sitting opposite each other at a table (talking, smoking);

(3) shots of a man driving a car seen from inside;

(4) shots of Paris by day;

and (5) shots of women in bikinis.[17]

---

[17] Yes, Jean-Luc, we know that the name 'bikini' comes from Bikini Atoll, an atomic bomb connection.

Curd Cheese (1963).

8

IL VANGELO SECONDO MATTEO

THE GOSPEL ACCORDING TO MATTHEW

> Philosophically, nothing that I have ever done has been more fitted to me than *The Gospel According To Matthew* because of my tendency always to see something sacred, mythical and epic quality in everything, even in the most simple and banal objects and events.
>
> Pier Paolo Pasolini (1971)

INTRODUCTION.

Among the most successful and satisfying of the portrayals of Christ's story is *The Gospel According To Matthew* (*Il Vangelo Secondo Matteo*, 1964, Italy/ France),[1] directed by Pier Paolo Pasolini (Pasolini did not want the prefix 'St' to be inserted in his title for *The Gospel According To Matthew*, which was added by the British distributors). I first saw *The Gospel According To Matthew* on television, on April 20, 1984. In the *Sight and Sound* list for top 100 films in 2012, *The Gospel According To Matthew* is 30th in the directors' list.

Alfredo Bini, Pier Paolo Pasolini's regular producer of the era, and an enormously important member of the Pasolini operation, produced *The Gospel According To Matthew*. It was Bini who saw the possibilities of the movie straight away, and who worked very hard to get *The Gospel According To Matthew* made – it was going to be an expensive and

---

[1] There is a colourized version of *The Gospel According To Matthew*, but it's shorter (running at 91 minutes, compared to the 142 minutes of the standard version). The film was intended to be around 150-165 minutes.

complex production, and b4 it was filmed it was already viewed with suspicion in the public arena (E. Siciliano, 26). The movie took a long time to prepare, but that probably worked in its favour (movies of this scale are made in pre-production, as everyone knows).

Some in the Italian industry (and in the Catholic Church) thought that Alfred Bini, Pier Paolo Pasolini *et al* were crazy in taking on the *Gospel*s. Crucially, *The Gospel According To Matthew* was originated by Pasolini – it didn't come from a producer/ writer/ production company/ studio, etc (Pasolini took the idea to Bini, and Bini loved it straight away, jumping out of his chair). However, *The Gospel According To Matthew* is also a product of its time: more religious movies were made in the 1950s and 1960s than any other time in film history.

We have to remember that the Italian film industry was churning out a huge number of ancient world movies and Biblical movies during one of its busiest periods – copycat versions of Hollywood spectaculars like *Cleopatra, Ben-Hur, Alexander the Great et al*, the *Hercules* craze (begun in 1958), which included loads of Ancient Greek and mythological flicks, and plenty of historical films, including Ancient Roman and mediæval films. Everybody in the Italian film industry, it seems, was in a toga, gladiator armour, or the long robes of Ancient Palestine.

Pier Paolo Pasolini – and his crew – would've been very conscious of all of those movies coming out of Rome and Cinecittà (indeed, many in the crew of *The Gospel According To Matthew* worked on them). So you can see how *The Gospel According To Matthew* was conceived very much *in opposition*[2] to the schlocky, melodramatic historical movies, to *Hercules* flicks and to Biblical movies, the bread and butter of the Italian film business at the time.

✢

The Gospel According To Matthew was a film of austerity, simplicity, lyricism and profundity. It is one of the greatest religious films (only one or two films are in the same league, such as *The Seventh Seal* and *The Passion of Joan of Arc*).

The *conception* of *The Gospel According To Matthew* is brilliant, quite, quite brilliant. The movie has an extraordinary self-assurance – it really knows what it's doing. It has something to say and it knows how to say it (I mean, it *really* has something to say). The combination of music, images, acting, casting and action is inspired and inventive – it's miraculous like a sacred act in itself.

Atom Egoyam said that Pier Paolo Pasolini 'is one of the few

---

2 *Contempt* (1963) is a Euro-art movie that's partly a commentary on the ancient world movie bonanza.

directors who have communicated the true nature of transcendent experience on film', and cited the 'brilliant depiction of Christ' in *The Gospel According To Matthew* as an example.³

As that opening quote illustrates, Pier Paolo Pasolini plus the *Gospels* was a perfect match: 'Philosophically, nothing that I have ever done has been more fitted to me than *The Gospel According To Matthew* because of my tendency always to see something sacred, mythical and epic quality in everything'. *The Gospel According To Matthew* is the perfect embodiment of Pasolini's notion of the cinema of poetry, and of poetic cinema. Consider any two-minute stretch of *The Gospel* movie and you can appreciate instantly how beautifully the filmmakers were suited to the material, and how the elements – the script, the cast, the acting, the music, the images, the sounds – plus of course that incredible story – all fit together.

A match made in heaven.
Made in Italy.
Same thing.

LOCATION HUNTING IN PALESTINE.

The documentary on *Il Vangelo Secondo Matteo, Sopraluoghi In Palestina* (1965, a.k.a. *Location Hunting In Palestine*), had come about when the producers at Arco Film asked Pier Paolo Pasolini to put together the footage that had been filmed in the Middle East to show to distributors and Christian Democrats. It was produced by Alfredo Bini, with camerawork by Aldo Pennelli, Domenico Cantatore and Otello Martelli, and sound by Domenico Cantatore. *Sopraluoghi In Palestina* was shown at the Spoleto Festival in Summer, 1965. Pasolini provided a commentary to the footage that had been cut to 55 minutes without his supervision (PP, 73).⁴

When Pier Paolo Pasolini and don Andrea Carraro and his team went to Palestine in 1963, a cameraman (Aldo Pennelli) joined them – the idea at that point was to film some material as research for *Il Vangelo Secondo Matteo*, rather than with the intention of making a documentary.

As well as scenes of Pier Paolo Pasolini in his neat, white suit speaking to camera about his film project, there are also interviews with Andrea Carraro, the Italian priest who joined him on the trip.⁵

In the documentary, we see the River Jordan, Capernam, the hill of the Sermon on the Mount, Nazareth, Bethlehem, the Dead Sea, Mount

---
3 In J. Boorman, 1995, 65.
4 Pier Paolo Pasolini was accompanied by Don Andrea Carraro, of Pro Civitate Cristiana, on the research trip to Israel.
5 The interviews do have a slightly stilted, rehearsed quality.

Tabor and of course Jerusalem. Pasolini writing in a notebook. Pasolini studying a map in the car. Pasolini observing farmers at work. Pasolini greeting a bunch of kids. Donkeys. Camels. Roads. Small towns.

Location Hunting In Palestine is a rare item: nowadays, cameras following filmmakers around on set and elsewhere are familiar, and on television behind-the-scenes shows are common (turning every part of life into 'reality TV'). Back then, it was unusual to see a major film director visiting potential locations in this manner, and in this depth (many 'making of' films of the 1950s and 1960s were usually short, fluffy publicity pieces made for talk shows or as little info pieces for cinema, like extended trailers of 3 minutes. They might show a bit of filming, but not pre-production). Ah, if only there were similar documentaries showing F.W. Murnau discussing how he was going to make *Sunrise*, or D.W. Griffith visiting the colossal sets for *Intolerance*, or Orson Welles in the R.K.O. Studios for *Citizen Kane*...

Location Hunting In Palestine is in part a record of an essential aspect of filmmaking – searching for locations. For some filmmakers (such as Ken Russell), this is one of the most enjoyable parts of film production: it consists of driving around in a car with one or two colleagues, and a map, and stopping at suitable locations and visiting buildings and taking lots of photographs. The filmmakers are away from the city and the film studio, so the pressure is off a little, and they are seeking out places to make their movie (so they are imagining and planning scenes in their heads).

Indeed, most location scouting trips involve taking 100s of photographs – but bringing a movie camera along for the journey and filming the filmmakers is more unusual (tho' more common today with video). In this period, though, Pier Paolo Pasolini had made some documentaries, and was used to filming as he travelled about (for *Love Meetings,* for instance, in the same year – which was also in part another location scouting trip for the *Gospel* film).

By the time that Pier Paolo Pasolini recorded the narration for *Location Hunting In Palestine*, *The Gospel According To Matthew* had been produced. But even during the visit to Israel and Palestine in 1963, Pasolini had already realized that he couldn't make his movie of Jesus there. Altho' the terrain had the familiar deserts and mountains, it was altogether too built-up, too industrialized, and too heavily populated. Pasolini pointed out that the geography of the *Bible* was too small and too modest for the grander visions he had from reading the *Gospels*, and for his movie. (Locations such as Jerusalem, Bethlehem and the Dead Sea are not very far from each other).

Another consideration was the supply of suitable extras: Pier Paolo Pasolini was after a certain look, and planned to play much of the Christ movie off people's faces. Why? Because the *reactions* of people to Jesus and his ministry are absolutely fundamental to this movie – and to many religious movies. (Pasolini discusses Jews and Arabs in the documentary – in a way that some viewers have found racist).[6]

While most of the landscapes in Palestine were too domesticated and too modest for Pasolini's elevated vision for his Christ movie, the desert and hills near the Dead Sea possessed the requisite spectacle. In the end, *The Gospel According To Matthew* recreated the desert on the slopes of Mount Etna[7] and parts of Calabria. Which, as the documentary shows, are not as vast as the canyons, ridges, and rocky screes of the shores of the Dead Sea.

Professional location managers could probably have informed Pier Paolo Pasolini beforehand that filming in Palestine and Israel wouldn't be a great idea for a feature film, but the trip was useful in many other ways. Such as: visiting the real places where the fantastical events in the *New Testament* occurred; thinking about the events and how to film them; and meeting the people who lived in those places (and contemplating how they might relate to the people who lived 2,000 years ago, something that concerned Pasolini. He was fascinated by the idea that people today were related to their ancestors hundreds or even thousands of years ago).

THE PRODUCTION.

Il Vangelo Secondo Matteo was dedicated to the memory of Pope John XXIII (Angelo Roncalli, 1881-1963). Pier Paolo Pasolini (then 40) had been invited to Assisi by Pro Civitate Cristiana, along with other filmmakers and artists, to discuss Jesus.[8] Pasolini had read the *Gospels* in his hotel while visiting Assisi, as a guest of the Citadella. The idea for *The Gospel According To Matthew* grew steadily, Pasolini explained, as he read the *Bible*, eventually overwhelming all of the other ideas he was contemplating. He chose Matthew's *Gospel*, rather the others, because it had a 'national-popular epic' quality, and 'Mark's seemed too crude, John's too mystical, and Luke's sentimental and bourgeois' (1964, 297).

Pier Paolo Pasolini described in February, 1963 how the film production came about:

---
6 For instance, Pasolini explains that he doesn't want Arab extras, because they come from a pre-Christian, pagan culture.
7 Mount Etna became a favourite spot for Pier Paolo Pasolini. The volcano pops up in all sorts of places – footage of the eruptions appeared in *Star Wars: Revenge of the Sith* (2005), for example.
8 Pro Civitate Christiana regarded cinema as potentially a modern form of sacred art.

> One day the Pope arrived in the city. The whole place was in a ferment. I didn't fancy going out in all that confusion and decided to stay in my room. Not knowing how to pass the time, I picked up a copy of St Matthew's Gospel. I was remarkably impressed and enthusiastic.
> When I returned to Rome, I spoke to producer Alfredo Bini about it. I told him I wanted to make a film out of the Gospel. He was so excited about the project that he jumped out of his seat.[9]

Pope John XXIII was famous for inaugurating the Second Vatican Council (1959-1964); he was elected Pope in 1958;[10] and for updating (*aggiornamento*) some of the Church's activities and ideas (and introducing liberalization). The links to Popes (the movie is dedicated to Pope John XXIII) and Pro Civitate Cristiana gives *The Gospel According To Matthew* surprising connections to distinctly right-wing and conservative institutions. You can't get much more establishment and traditional than the Catholic Church,[11] can you?[12] Yet Pier Paolo Pasolini and the film movement of the European New Wave is usually thought of as radical and non-conformist and left-wing (it would be associated with the man-the-barricades idealism and political activism of the years leading up to 1968, for instance). And Pasolini's previous movies *Accattone, Curd Cheese* and *Mamma Roma* had irritated right-wing political groups.

> I want to create a pure work of poetry [Pasolini wrote to his producer, Alfredo Bini], risking even the periods of æstheticism (Bach and Mozart as musical accompaniment; Piero della Francesca and in part Duccio for pictorial inspiration; the basically prehistory and exotic reality of the Arab world as background and setting). (1964, 20)

Sam Rohdie suggested that one of the inspirations for Pier Paolo Pasolini to make the film was Orson Welles, who had narrated *King of Kings* (released in the early 1960s), and who had appeared in Pasolini's *Curd Cheese,* which had depicted Christ's Passion (1995, 25).

Many filmmakers have ached to make a film of Christ but didn't – Carl Theodor Dreyer, Paul Verhoeven, Ken Russell and Orson Welles (it's possible that Welles might've discussed his Jesus film with Pasolini). While we might lament that we never got to see Dreyer's *Christ* or Welles' modern version of the life of Jesus, we do have *The Gospel According To Matthew*. And, in a way, *The Gospel According To Matthew* does many of the things that modern directors were keen to do,

---
9 P. Pasolini, in *Scene*, Feb 19, 1963.
10 If Pope Pius XII (1939-58) had lived on for another 3 or 4 years, Pier Paolo Pasolini said he would never have been able to make *Il Vangelo Secondo Matteo* (PP, 75).
11 *The Gospel* is a wholly Catholic movie – of course. Protestantism didn't really exist in the same way as it does in Northern Europe (PP, 46).
12 As Sam Rohdie put it, Pasolini was now working with 'the Father, the Pope, the Church, Authority, Society' (1995,156).

or something approximating to them. (There's more than one director who has looked at *The Gospel According To Matthew* and admitted, darn it, I was going to do that!).

The Gospel According To Matthew examines the ideals and values of Pier Paolo Pasolini's youth, according to Enzo Siciliano – as if Pasolini is exploring what it means to him to live by (Christian) values.

The budget of *The Gospel According To Matthew* was small, the actors mostly amateurs, yet the film, which could easily have been disastrous (there are many things that could've gone wrong), is magnificent. Pier Paolo Pasolini explained his thinking behind the casting in 1969:

> I was obliged to find everything – the characters and the ambience – in reality. And so the rule that dominated the making of the film was the rule of analogy. That is, I found settings that were not reconstructions, but were analogous to ancient Palestine.[13]

So Pier Paolo Pasolini and co. picked peasants from Southern Italy's rural communities, and the disciples from the ruling classes. Danilo Donati dressed Herod's men as Knights Templar, soldiers from Paolo Uccello paintings, and fascist hoodlums. (Pasolini remarked that he was very happy with the cast of *The Gospel According To Matthew;* it is a production that meticulously selected the actors).

The disciples in this version of the *Gospels* are: Peter, Simon, Judas, Andrew, Thaddeus, John, James, James son of Alphæus, Philip, Thomas, Bartholomew, and of course Matthew. The casting of the disciples presents a range of faces and types; many are in their twenties or thirties; they are working class people (in the main), not intellectuals, scribes or poets.

The Apostles are not given much characterization beyond what the actors themselves bring to the part. Some have more to do than others, and many have only one or two lines in the film. The daily lives of the disciples are not depicted – in most scenes they are following Jesus (tho' there are domestic scenes, such as a moment when they buy some food and eat it).

The decision to let the text speak for itself, and to avoid psychology and conventional characterization, suits this film very well, and reinforces the concept that this is an 'anti-Hollywood' interpretation of the Christian story. (However, in many Hollywood versions of Christ's life, Jesus remains a mysterious figure, ultimately unknowable).

Enzo Siciliano (who played Simon) recalled that Pier Paolo Pasolini

---
[13] In J. Leyda, 346. True, but there is some material filmed in the studio.

was tireless in directing *The Gospel According To Matthew*, and they worked all day (ES, 274). Pasolini didn't want 'acting', and told his cast to just use their normal expressions (relying on the process of cinema to do the rest of the work. Because for Pasolini cinema was *already a dream*. The actors thus didn't need to 'do' anything – the magical apparatus of cinematography would do it all).

Low budget *The Gospel According To Matthew* might have been (by Hollywood terms),[14] but it had a large cast, a huge number of locations, hundreds of costumes, a welter of props and practical effects, animals, and other expensive items. Historical films are usually more costly to produce than those set in contemporary times. And shooting on location can be more expensive than shooting in the studio: all of those actors and extras, for instance, had to be bussed out to the locations, put in costume, and fed (and some would stay in hotels). Had it been made within the Hollywood system at the time, *The Gospel According To Matthew* would have cost millions – *The King of Kings* of 1961 would be a budgetary comparison for a Christ movie, as would *The Greatest Story Ever Told* of 1965. (You can see that some of those locations were probably difficult to reach – the crew would've had to schlepp heavy gear up the volcano at Mount Etna, for instance, by hand. No Hollywood helicopters on this shoot. Mount Etna is in Sicily, near Messina and Catanbia. It's 10,912 feet (3,350m) high).

THE CAST AND THE CREW.

Among the cast were Margherita Caruso as the young Mary, and Susanna Pasolini as the elder Mary;[15] Marcello Morante[16] (Elsa Morante's brother) was Joseph; Mario Socrate was the Baptist;[17] Settimio Di Porto was Peter; Otello Sestili[18] was Judas; Ferruccio Nuzzo was Matthew;[19] Giacomo Morante was John; Amerigo Bevilacqua was Herod I; Francesco Leonetti[20] was Herod II; Alfonso Gatto was Andrew; Luigi Barbini[21] was James; Giorgio Agamben was Phillip; Elio Spaziani was Thaddaeus;

---

14 One wonders what Pier Paolo Pasolini might've done with a colossal budget – something with the $$$$ of Cecil B. De Mille or the epic movies of the 1960s.
15 Susanna Pasolini is probably too old – if Mary was in her late teens (in movie terms) when she had Jesus (in the *Bible*, she is 14 or 15), she would in her late forties when the adult Jesus is encountered.
16 Morante was dubbed by Gianni Bonagura.
17 Socrate was dubbed by Pino Locchi.
18 He was an extra in *Accattone*. Pier Paolo Pasolini said he cast an intellectual to play Matthew.
19 Matthew is cast as a young man (perhaps to tie in with the date of the *Gospel*'s composition, many decades later).
20 Playwright Leonetti was a regular in the Pasolini Circus – he's the crow's voice in *The Hawks and the Sparrows*, Laius' servant in *Oedipus Rex*, and in *Che Cosa Sono la Nuvole?* he's the puppet-master.
21 Barbini pops up in later Pasolini films – he's the youth that Massimo Girotti stares at in Milan station in *Theorem*, for instance.

Enzo Siciliano was Simon; Guido Cerretani was Bartholomew; Rosario Migale was Thomas; Marcello Galdini was James, son of Alphaeus; Juan Rodolfo Wilcock was Caiaphas; Alessandro Clerici was Pontius Pilate; Franca Cupane was Herodias; Paola Tedesco was Salomé; Rossana Di Rocco was the Angel of the Lord; Renato Terra was the Possessed One; Eliseo Boschi was Joseph of Arimathea; Natalia Ginzburg was Mary of Bethany (her real husband, Gabriele Baldini, played her husband); and Ninetto Davoli was a Shepherd.[22] Released: October 2, 1964. 142m.

Some of the cast of *The Gospel According To Matthew* were played by intellectuals and authors that Pier Paolo Pasolini knew: Giorgio Agamben (Phillip) was a philosopher, Enzo Siciliano[23] (Simon) and Alfonso Gatto (Andrew) were writers, and Natalia Ginzburg (Mary of Bethany) and Juan Rodolfo Wilcock (Caiaphas) were poets.[24]

Many of the actors in *Il Vangelo Secondo Matteo* only appeared in this film and in no others (such as Margherita Caruso). It is truly a cast of unknowns – even if you watch Italian television and movies, you won't have seen most or any of these actors before.[25] Or since. Only Pier Paolo Pasolini and producer Alfredo Bini are familiar names in this production (but even many Italians wouldn't haven't heard of Pasolini or Bini at the time of the movie's theatrical release). And many actors didn't do much at all in movies afterwards (Morante, Irazoqui, etc). This is quite common when employing non-actors: they appear in just one movie, and in nothing else (because they're not interested in acting). And sometimes, when they are so good, it's a pity. Margherita Caruso (the young Virgin), for instance, has a face that could launch a thousand movies, and she is stunning as the Madonna, but I think her only appearance on celluloid is *Il Vangelo Secondo Matteo*.

Using a cast of total unknowns (and proper unknowns, not like the 'unknowns' of North American and European movies, who aren't 'unknowns' at all, but just happen to have appeared in TV and movies already, and have agents and/ or managers), works for one simple reason: the story, the characters, the themes, the settings – in short, the everything – in *The Gospel According To Matthew* are so well-known. The story of Jesus, Mary, Joseph, and the twelve disciples and all the rest don't need a guest star as Joseph or the older Mary, because it is all so familiar. (There is only one star in *The Gospel According To Matthew* – and that's the director, Pasolini. And, after the film was released, Enrique

---

22 Pasolini put Davoli in as 'kind of screen-test' (PP, 103).
23 Enzo Siciliano is Pasolini's brilliant biographer.
24 But the minor characters were played by the agricultural proletariat of Southern Italy, as Pasolini described them (PP, 77).
25 Many of the extras were hired from where the movie was shot (as usual in movies) – in places like Barile, Matera and Massafra.

Irazoqui, perhaps. But, in truth, the true star is the movie itself).

The acting in *The Gospel According To Matthew* ranges from Enrique Irazoqui's histrionic, gestural style (no doubt encouraged by the maestro – Pier Paolo Pasolini would be keen to elicit the right sort of performance from Irazoqui), to the minimal expressions of the non-professional extras (the *sensei* seems to have told them to simply stand there and look in this direction; if an actor or extra breaks the fourth wall and glances at the camera, it only adds to the verisimilitude of the film – and several do). On a production like this, with such a large cast, and so many people to organize in the frame, and in so many locations, the assistant directors do a lot of the work: the A.D.s were Maurizio Lucidi, Paolo Schneider and Elsa Morante.

✦

As well as Tonino Delli Colli, another important Italian cinematographer worked on *The Gospel According To Matthew*: Giuseppe Ruzzolini (as camera operator). With so many shots featuring the camera shifting around the actors very intimately, Ruzzolini can he regarded as a key contributor to the film. (Ruzzolini acted as DP for some of Pasolini's later films).

The crew on *The Gospel According To Matthew* also included: Luigi Scaccianoce, production designer, Andrea Fantacci, set decorator, Dante Ferretti, assistant production designer, costumes by Danilo Donati, Manolo Bolognini, production manager, editing by Nino Baragli, sound by Mario Del Pozzo, sound mixing by Fausto Ancillai, make-up by Marcello Ceccarelli, hair by Mimma Pomilia, and script girl Lina D'Amico (many in the crew worked often with Pasolini).

On a historical movie like this, hair and make-up are absolutely vital – not only for the principals, but to organize hair and make-up assistants to dress and prepare all of those extras.

Most of *The Gospel According To Matthew* is filmed during the day, including night scenes (such as the Agony in the Garden). Because night shoots are more expensive, and some would be logistically tough in some of those locations (like lighting large outdoor areas far away from electricity supplies).

CASTING CHRIST.

Casting Christ is a daunting task. Christ in *The Gospel According To Matthew* was played by a young Spanish[26] student from Barcelona, Enrique Irazoqui (born July 5, 1944, Barcelona), that Pier Paolo Pasolini

---
26 Irazoqui's mother is Italian, however.

found by chance. As a student, Irazoqui had read Pasolini's *Ragazzi di vita* (unusual – but that would endear Irazoqui to Pasolini); Irazoqui asked to meet Pasolini when he was visiting Rome. As soon as the maestro saw Irazoqui, he was cast in the role of a lifetime. Pasolini recalled:

> And then one day I came back to the house and found this young Spaniard, Enrique Irazoqui, sitting here waiting to see me and as soon as I saw him, even before he had a chance to start talking, I said: 'Excuse me, but would you act in one of my films?' – even before I knew who he was or anything. He was a serious person, and so he said 'no'. But then I gradually won him round. (PP, 78)

Following his portrayal of Jesus, Irazoqui had his passport confiscated, his career at university suspended for a year, and spent 15 months in the National Service.[27]

Pretty remarkable, though, isn't it? Enrique Irazoqui had little acting experience, is only 20 years-old, and next minute he's playing Jesus in a big Italian movie! And he does a brilliant job: and Christ, as actors have found over the years, is a tough acting gig on many levels. (And Irazoqui was Spanish, and probably one of the few Spaniards in this Italian production).

It was a huge risk – casting a non-actor in a lead role is a big deal; added to that was the large and complex production, plus it was a prestige production by a famous director. As if that wasn't pressure enough, this was also the story of Christ – a formidable subject, and a very challenging role for any actor.

Enrique Irazoqui wasn't Max von Sydow or Jeffrey Hunter, who also played Jesus in films of this period; they were established actors who'd worked in some important movies directed by masters (John Ford, Nicholas Ray, Ingmar Bergman, etc). Irazoqui had to trust Pasolini's faith in him.

Enrique Irazoqui was dubbed by Enrico Maria Salerno,[28] an Italian actor: so Irazoqui's performance is a double act (by two Enriques/ Enricos); it's not only Irazoqui alone. Indeed, in the scenes where Christ is a figure off in the distance, it's Salerno we're listening to, not Irazoqui we're watching. Salerno is vitally important to the success of *The Gospel According To Matthew* – if this were an animated movie, audiences would be applauding Salerno for his performance as the voice of Christ.

Thus, Jesus was *not* wholly an unknown, non-professional actor –

---

[27] Following *The Gospel According To Matthew*, Irazoqui appeared in *Noche de vino tinto* (José María Nunes, 1966, Spain), *Dante no es únicamente severo* (Jacinto Esteva and Joaquim Jordà, 1966, Spain) and *A la soledat* (2008, José María Nunes, Spain). Rather than acting, Irazoqui became a lawyer.

[28] He had appeared in *A Violent Life*.

because he is voiced by Enrico Maria Salerno. When they hired Enrique Irazoqui, Bini and Pasolini knew they would be replacing his voice (and they probably had Salerno in mind).

Enrico Salerno (1926-1994) appeared in numerous films and TV series, and also directed films and plays. He worked for many well-known Italian directors, such as Fellini, Zeffirelli, Argento, Bolognini, Monicelli, Rossellini, Risi and Magni. (Salerno voiced many other characters in Italian cinema, including dubbing Clint Eastwood in the Spaghetti Westerns, and Richard Basehart for Federico Fellini). Salerno's films included: *Three Nights of Love, Six Days a Week, Casanova 70, Le Masque de Fer, Escape By Night, Seasons of Our Love, The Strange Night, Candy, The Bird With the Crystal Plumage, The Swinging Confessors, The Sicilian Checkmate, The Assassination of Trotsky, City Under Seige, Gambling City, Dianry of a Passion,* and *An Ideal Adventure.*

✦

Christ was initially going to be African, part of Pier Paolo Pasolini's modernization of the myth, with Christ as 'the true 'savage father'' (Pasolini had visited Africa several times in the early 1960s, and the idea, the culture and the reality of Africa subsequently remained fundamental to his art).

Then Pier Paolo Pasolini considered using a poet or an intellectual to play Christ – after going through all the poets Pasolini came up with Jack Kerouac and Yevgeny Yvetushenko (one can't help thinking that Kerouac would have been disastrous). The movie demonstrates that to *play* a *poetic* Christ, you don't need to have an *actual* poet (let's face it, writers make some really bad actors – even worse than directors!). At another time, Pasolini had considered using a German actor. He also said that he had spent more than a year looking for the right person to play Jesus (PP, 78).

Why didn't Pier Paolo Pasolini choose Franco Citti, probably the obvious choice at the time? Dunno. In *Accattone*, Pasolini and Citti had already explored Christ-like themes. Probably one reason was to have an unknown – even though an untried actor is a big gamble, and the role is very demanding – and very physical. Also, Citti had played anti-social characters in Pasolini's films – a pimp and a thief. (It can't have been an age issue, as Citti was 26 at the time).

As well as casting Christ, there are so many other roles in *The Gospel According To Matthew* to fill: and *The Gospel According To Matthew* is much bigger than some Jesus movies, which focus on the

Holy Family, the disciples, and secondary figures. *The Gospel According To Matthew* took in temple elders, Pharisees, Sadducees, priests, courtiers, soldiers, people to be healed... the list is endless. So part of the decision of where to shoot must take that into consideration: where you film the life of Christ, you need *a lot* of extras (and you need a *choice*, too, not just one actor for each role).

Thus, the casting director on *Gospel* was hugely important (Pier Paolo Pasolini's name overshadows all of the other collaborators in *The Gospel According To Matthew*, and the casting director[29] is seldom cited in film criticism. But when you've done some casting yourself (as I have), you realize how vital the role is. The film crew didn't just roll up in Matera and grab some people out of the onlookers nearby and throw them into a scene!).

PASOLINI THE UNBELIEVER.

Certainly Pier Paolo Pasolini was an unusual film director to decide to make a film of Jesus. As everyone discussing the production has noted, he was an atheist and a Marxist (and a radical). Pasolini's personality contained seemingly contradictory ingredients for a director who would be dealing with Christian themes and the story of Christ. But if you know about Pasolini's previous movies, and his poetry, and his views, it isn't so surprising.

Of *The Gospel According To Matthew*, Pier Paolo Pasolini said he did not believe in the divinity of Christ, and the film was not a practising Catholic's film (in fact, it was 'an unpleasant and terrible work, at certain points outright ambiguous and disconcerting, particularly the figure of Christ'). However, it was religious; Pasolini said the film fitted philosophically into his 'tendency always to see something sacred and mythic and epic in everything, even the most humdrum, simple and banal objects and events' (PP, 77).

> I've never been religious unless you can count a very ridiculous religious crisis at fourteen years of age, I was still very innocent. Then from one day to the next, I didn't believe anymore. I was born Catholic by mere chance because I was born in Italy, but I was never particularly Catholic and I came to my criticism of the Church as every Italian intellectual has. I had a very agnostic upbringing; this led me to Marxism so therefore I arrived at it in the most obvious and natural way. The Church in Italy has always been an instrument of power but I don't think it's an ideological power as opposed to its practical power, as any influence over the Italian peasant. An Italian's not religious. I don't want

---

[29] There is no credit for the casting director on *The Gospel According To Matthew* – Pier Paolo Pasolini said he chose all of the extras himself – but they were ordinary people from the area, not film extras (PP, 40). Of course, assistants would've helped.

to say pagan because that would be generic but he's pre-Catholic in as much as he's remained in the state in which Catholicism found him, above all, in the South. It is a superficial cross over the Italian people and I believe it would only take a strong confrontation to destroy these ideals. (1971)

'I don't believe in God,' P.P. Pasolini stated, as if it was necessary to remind everyone. But he did believe in the cult of love of Christianity, or at least, reckoned that the Christian form of love was going to crop up in his films inevitably.

Externally, Pier Paolo Pasolini said, *The Gospel According To Matthew* may have been a Catholic film, but internally it was aligned with his mythic, sacred view of the world ('making *The Gospel* was to reach the maximum of the mythic and the epic' [ibid.]). Pasolini did not believe Christ was the Son of God. He was not interested in reconstructing the history of Christ; as he was not a believer, he did not want to turn Christ's life into that of one of the thousands of saints preaching in Palestine at the time (PP, 83). But he was concerned with transmitting his view of life as sacred and mythic.

Pier Paolo Pasolini said, however, that he did not want to deconsecrate Christ: 'this is a fashion I hate, it is *petit bourgeois*. I want to re-consecrate things as much as possible, I want to re-mythicize them' (PP, 83). My Christ, Pasolini explained, would take into account two thousand years of Christian mythicizing and history. 'My film is the life of Christ plus two thousand years of storytelling about the life of Christ' (ibid.). And Pasolini acknowledged that the two thousand years of Christianity were his heritage and culture: 'I know that in me there are two thousand years of Christianity'.

No need to point out the elements of persecution in the story of Jesus as presented in *The Gospel According To Matthew* and how that relates to Pier Paolo Pasolini's own life at the time. In this early 1960s era, the notoriety of Pasolini grew, and he seemed to draw attention and trouble to himself with an unconscious skill. It's an era of several court cases and accusations – against Pasolini as a sexual predator as well as a filmmaker who irritated the authorities (and neo-fascist groups) in Italy with controversies like *La Ricotta* and *Mamma Roma*. (Lesser filmmakers might've been put off making a movie of the *Gospels*, or to shelve it for a few years until the memories of the controversies faded. Not Pasolini!).

A CONFIDENT MOVIE.

In *The Gospel According To Matthew*, the filmmakers have clearly relied a good deal upon the audience already knowing the story in detail (you could follow *The Gospel According To Matthew* without knowing anything about Christianity or the story of Christ, but I would imagine that most of the people who've seen the movie would know something about Christianity. Certainly the initial main audience for the movie – Italy – partly defined how the movie was produced; this is an Italian movie – made by Italians, in Italy and in Italian – speaking first of all to fellow Italians).

Hence the filmmakers could employ the *tableau*-style of presentation within scenes (as to staging), and could emphasize those *tableaux* with montages of close-ups of faces. Or, to put it another way: *The Gospel According To Matthew* could have been edited, like any movie, many different ways. But the two approaches – montages of *tableaux* and more conventional dramatic scenes– fused perfectly with the material.

The movie is long – 142 minutes – that is, it's long compared to the average Italian flick of the period (but *not* long compared to movies in the 21st century, when going over two hours is commonplace, resulting in too many bloated, saggy movies). However, for a religious or historical epic movie, this was *not* long: historical epics, including the Biblical flicks, often went over two hours (and some, such as *Ben-Hur* and *The Ten Commandments*, were famously very long, up to three hours). Audiences accepted the long running times – these movies were often prestige films or they were super-productions, where everything is big, big, big. (However, most Italian films of the period were not prestige productions, and had regular running times).

But *The Gospel According To Matthew* does not out-stay its welcome, as too many movies of today do. There's no padding in here, no unnecessary scenes, and no scenes that drift on aimlessly. It's a pacey film; it doesn't meander or linger. In *The Gospel According To Matthew*, the filmmakers have got something important to say, and they say it (very different from so many contemporary movies, which have little to say, and no idea how to say it).

The Gospel According To Matthew is a masterful piece of cinema: you are in the hands of great artists, who really know what they're doing. It's confident, too: Pier Paolo Pasolini and his team must have been feeling *very* confident to take on this big subject.[30] Consider, for instance, that up to this time (1964), Pasolini had only made three theatrical

---

[30] A really successful film has to have everyone in each department working at their best (or at least appearing to do so).

features: *Accattone* (1961), *Mamma Roma* (1962) and *Comizi d'Amore* (1964 – though this was a documentary), and some shorter pieces, such as *The Anger* (1963), the *Curd Cheese* segment of *RoGoPaG* (1963), and *Location Hunting In Palestine* (1964). And certainly those films and documentaries are much more modest in scale and scope than *The Gospel According To Matthew* (some, like *The Anger*, are editing jobs done by someone else). To leap from two fiction features into a Biblical epic production seems especially bold.

Even Jean-Luc Godard, for me one of the two or three most significant filmmakers of the period from 1960 to the present day, felt humbled and unsure about filming the life of the Virgin Mary in his 1985 movie *Hail, Mary*. In *The Gospel According To Matthew*, you've got an actor who's impersonating Jesus and you're recreating events from the *Bible*. And that isn't easy. You've got to be feeling self-assured to be able to do that, and to know what you're doing.

FILMING THE DIVINE.

The film does not question Christ's divinity, as some later films have done. Whatever the filmmakers may personally believe, *The Gospel According To Matthew* presents a divine Jesus: this is a man who walks on water and performs miracles. For Pier Paolo Pasolini, Jesus was divine – that is, as a supreme manifestation of humanity: 'in him humanity is so lofty, strict, and ideal as to exceed the common terms of humanity', as Pasolini put it in his letter to Lucio S. Caruso of the Pro Civitate Christiana of Assisi (ES, 270).

Pier Paolo Pasolini wrote to Lucio S. Caruso in February, 1963:

> My idea is to follow the *Gospel According to St Matthew* point by point, without making a script or adaption of it. To translate it faithfully into images, following its story without any omissions or additions. The dialogue too should strictly be that of St Matthew, without even a single explanatory or connecting sentence, because no image or inserted word could ever attain the poetic heights of the text. (P. Pasolini, 1964)

How do you make a film from one of the *Scriptures*? Have a look at the text of *The Gospel According To St Matthew* and ask the basic questions:

Where is this going to take place?
Who are you going to cast in the lead roles?
What will the actors wear?
What will they look like?
What will they say?

How will the characters relate to each other?
How much exposition is required?
How will you depict an angel?
How does an angel interact with a human being?
What will the dialogue be?
What is divinity?
How do you portray it on film?

And so on and on. The questions are endless (they are the sorts of questions that are fired at a film director continuously during pre-production and on set). In short, creating the script and concept of *The Gospel According To Matthew* was not simply a case of transcribing the *Gospel* into cinema. You don't carry the *Bible* onto the set and yell, 'action!'

Certainly, as Pier Paolo Pasolini stated above, the film was on the whole 'faithful' to the text of *St Matthew's Gospel* – but as numerous commentators have noted, and many filmmakers have found out, being 'faithful' to a text is not only not desirable most of the time, it's not even possible.

Yet *The Gospel According To Matthew* gives the *impression* of being a 'faithful' representation in images and sounds and music of the text of *The Gospel of St Matthew* written two thousand years ago. That's the trick – and a mighty, mighty trick it is, too.

Cinema is entirely fakery and lies, as everyone knows, but the skill is to persuade the audience to believe in the world of the movie for two hours. It's all lies in cinema, as the Japanese director Hayao Miyazaki stated in 1979, it's all a fabrication of something that the filmmakers want the audience to believe is real:

> Even if the world depicted is a lie, the trick is to make it seem as real as possible. Stated another way, the animator must fabricate a lie that seems so real viewers will think the world depicted might possibly exist.[31]

Audiences *want* to believe, of course. They *yearn* to think that some fantasy world can really exist. And they want to go there.

Or put it like this: *The Gospel According To Matthew* is a highly stylized, highly artificial movie made in the mid-1960s in a particular place and time, under particular financial and labour conditions, using a particular cast and crew, with a particular form of technological equipment, within a particular social and political context, based on a script by an Italian poet-turned-director that was in turn based on a text written two

---

[31] H. Miyazaki, *Starting Point, 1979-1996*, tr. B. Cary & F. Schodt, Viz Media/ Shogakukan, San Francisco, CA, 2009, 21.

thousand years ago that was originally perhaps written in Aramaic but later translated into Greek (and Pasolini presumably used an Italian translation), and the original text was written many years after the extraordinary events that may or may not have happened.

In other words, the 1964 movie *The Gospel According To Matthew* is a highly stylized and self-conscious production subject to countless constraints and social contexts, and what it purports to be about is something that is both historical and religious, that might have happened, but might not (whatever the 'truth' of a historical event, we are *very* far from it here). So the trick is make what happens in front of the camera in *The Gospel According To Matthew* seem as if it's really happening, even though the audience knows it is a trick upon a trick upon a stylization upon a cliché upon a literary text upon multiple translations upon events that may or may not had some basis in history or reality.

We always need to remind ourselves that *everything* in movies is technological, everything is fake, everything is a highly sophisticated cultural form created by humans for mass entertainment.

And Christianity, like civilization and technology, is constantly evolving. For instance, the Catholic Church has had an ambiguous attitude towards the Madonna, as Julia Kristeva commented in her outstanding 1977 essay on the Virgin Mary, "Stabat Mater":

> Mary's function as guardian of power, later checked when the church became wary of it, nevertheless persisted in popular and pictural representation, witness Piero della Francesca's impressive painting, *Madonna della Misericordia,* which was disavowed by Catholic authorities at the time. And yet, not only did the papacy revere more and more the christly mother as the Vatican's power over cities and municipalities was strengthened, it also openly identified its own institution with the Virgin: Mary was officially proclaimed Queen by Pius XII in 1954 and *Mater Ecclesiæ* in 1964. (1986, 170)

So as recently as 1954 and 1964, the Vatican has altered its official stance on the Virgin Mary: thus *The Gospel According To Matthew* was being produced in a political atmosphere where issues that might seem to be 'eternal' and 'fixed' were still being negotiated.

Not many Biblical films explored the early life of the Madonna. One is *The Gospel According To Matthew*; the other one is *Jesus of Nazareth*, the all-star, blockbuster TV series of 1977, which depicts the young Virgin and her life with Joseph (an Italian production from R.A.I. TV).

There have been further TV shows about the Madonna. For instance, the Italian company Lux Vide has produced a *Bible Collection* of TV movies centred on figures such as Jesus, Mary Magdalene, Judas, Simon, etc. The Hollywood *Nativity Story* (2006), distributed by New Line Cinema, depicted the early life of Mary in detail. And the *Da Vinci Code* (2006) phenomena, plus the surprise success of *The Passion of the Christ* (2004), has spearheaded renewed, millennial interest in Christian themes in movies (production of Christian movies reached a high in 2006). New outlets such as direct to DVD/ video, online/ streaming, and satellite/ cable TV have encouraged film companies, too.

The Italian film and TV industry has a long tradition of producing religious/ Biblical/ Christian works. Recently, from the 1990s onwards, companies such as Lux Vide and Five Mile River have been active in religious movie production. Lux Vide, for example, made a film about St Paul, which had been one of Pasolini's long-cherished projects.

POETRY AND POLITICS IN *THE GOSPEL ACCORDING TO MATTHEW*.

Il Vangelo Secondo Matteo is described as having a Marxist approach. The combination of Marxism and Catholicism, Communism and Christianity, makes for a fascinating mix. Yet, *The Gospel According To Matthew* isn't a Marxist movie in any way, really: any Marxist politics it contains seems to derive more from the perception of Pier Paolo Pasolini as a Marxist artist. A purist Marxist approach would presumably be thoroughly materialist, and would debunk any religious or spiritual aspects; it would analyze the events in social and political terms. There would be no miracles in a purist's Marxist interpretation of the *Gospels*, would there? The spiritual elements would be ignored, or rationalized into nothing.

The director might be a Marxist (but many in the crew probably were, too – though not as out-spoken as Pasolini!), but the resultant movie isn't Marxist (Pasolini often downplayed his Marxism). It doesn't want to be. There is an emphasis on *materiality*, certainly, on the physicality of the ancient world, but that sensuality is not seen in Victorian, industrial, Marxist terms (or in modern Marxist or Communist terms, either).

As to the ideology and the politics[32] within *The Gospel According To Matthew*, one could just as well see them as *radical* and *anarchist* as *Marxist*. The individuality, the poetry, the sensuality and artistic aspects of Pier Paolo Pasolini's cinema also seem to me to come out triumphant above politics and ideology, Marxist or otherwise. Pasolini is a mass of contradictions, which's partly what makes him such a fascinating film-

---

[32] Because it used analogy, rather than direct historical reconstruction, Pier Paolo Pasolini said, 'I have left out objectively important political and social factors' (PP, 82).

maker to study (and his Christ is 'not bad in fact, he is just full of contradictions' [PP, 87]).

Pier Paolo Pasolini's Christ fights against the establishment like a political activist: he is an angry, passionate Christ, a fiery, Southern, Mediterranean peasant rebel, a social reformer, a world away from the pale, passive Anglo-Saxon Jesuses of Hollywood cinema (where Jesus is usually cast from white, American or European actors – whereas the historical Jesus was a Jewish man from the Middle East). But Christ's polemical ferocity is tempered by the 1964 film's incredibly tender lyricism. Jesus in *The Gospel According To Matthew* isn't always storming about yelling about baptisms of fire and inciting his disciples to use the sword ('Think not that I am come to send peace on earth: I came not to send peace, but a sword' [*Matthew,* 10: 34]); clearly a political firebrand, Pasolini's Jesus also has plenty of scenes of contemplation and gentleness.

✢

Martin Scorsese wrote that Pier Paolo Pasolini's film 'really worked beautifully, the film is so joyous: he was a great poet' (M. Scorsese, 138). Scorsese wrote of the miracles:

> I love the way Pasolini did the miracles; for example, when Jesus cures the leper, with the Leadbelly steel guitar on the soundtrack. Just a simple cut, and it's so shocking and beautiful: he's looking into the eyes of Christ, who says, 'Go now yourself to the high priest.' (ib., 136)

Pier Paolo Pasolini's Jesus was for the sacred and the poetic, in the midst of the profane and the banal. Pasolini emphasized the rebellious aspect of Christ because for him Christ had been crucified by the fathers, the State, the Pharisees and Philhistines. Christ was instrumental in the revolution against the Law of the Father which was part of Pasolini's project.

> The fathers who killed Christ had killed Oedipus, had tried to kill Pasolini's poetry. Christ crucified therefore was a revolutionary sign of the sacred against the profane of authority. It was the idea made fact and made flesh.

as Sam Rohdie put it (1995, 164). Pier Paolo Pasolini's Christ appears 'revolutionary',[33] something of an agitprop or radical leader. Pasolini maintained that this 'revolutionary' character was not something he added or exaggerated: it was already there in Matthew's *Gospel*.

---

[33] 'Christ going round Palestine is really a revolutionary whirlwind: someone who walks up to a couple of people and says 'drop your nets and follow me' is a total revolutionary' (PP, 95)

The quiet self-assurance of Jesus in *The Gospel According To Matthew* is striking – how he walks up to Simon and Peter hauling in their fishing nets on a beach and says simply, 'follow me'. There is never a question of doubt – either for Jesus, but also not for his disciples. They simply leave right away, as if they've always been waiting for him. This Jesus doesn't command, or persuade, or implore, he simply says – and quietly – what must be said, and what must be done: 'follow me'.

THE GOSPEL AS A BIBLICAL MOVIE.

The Gospel According To Matthew is a commentary on the religious film genre, of course, and it employs many New Wave and modernist cinematic techniques, and it has elements of Marxism and radical politics – but aside from all of that, *The Gospel According To Matthew* is a very traditional movie. It has all of the elements of the conventional religious movie: deserts, low, one-storey stone buildings, horses and donkeys, palm trees, hordes of extras in Biblical dress, and plenty of choral music.

The Baptism, for example, takes place in one of those shallow riverbeds, with rocks in the water, and onlookers dotted around the bank. While the Baptist may be angrier than previous incarnations of the role, the scene itself is very traditional, complete with the initiates looking up to Heaven after they've been baptized.

The visual aspects of *The Gospel According To Matthew* are instantly recognizable as belonging to the Biblical or religious movie. It's often in the *invisible elements* of movie-making that *The Gospel According To Matthew* reveals its modernism, its departure from the conventional religious movie. The editing, for instance, and the music. The simple decision of putting modern blues music like Blind Willie Johnson on the soundtrack was far-reaching, and automatically distances *The Gospel According To Matthew* from your average sword-and-sandal flick. Similarly, and also part of post-production, was the editing, the use of jump cuts, irregular parts of shots, and rapid montages.

It's as if Pier Paolo Pasolini and his team thought, well, you've seen a Biblical movie before, but we are going to do it in a very different way. Because the more you contemplate what Pasolini and co. are doing in *The Gospel According To Matthew*, you realize how startlingly different it is from what had gone on before. The French New Wave and Neo-realist approach had been taken with other subjects (such as the crime genre in *Breathless*, or the romantic comedy drama in *Jules et Jim*), but not in the religious movie genre.

RECEPTION.

The Gospel According To Matthew was premiered at the Venice Film Festival on September 4, 1964 (where earlier Pasolini-directed films, like *Accattone* and *Mamma Roma,* had made such an impact). However, neo-fascist groups once again attempted to disrupt the screening (insulting the audience, throwing leaflets, and attacking the film critic Palo Valmarana and painter Renato Guttuso). The critical response was inevitably strong, and divided (it's a film that demands you have an opinion), but the movie immediately drew support, and won the Grand Jury Prize in Venice (and 3 Nastro d'Argento Awards).

Il Vangelo Secondo Matteo was awarded a prize by the Ufficio Cattolico Internazionale del Cinema. The jury praised its simplicity and Pier Paolo Pasolini's humility, making it 'far superior to earlier, commercial films, on the life of Christ. It shows the real grandeur of his teaching stripped of any artificial and sentimental effect'.[34] It was nominated for 3 Oscars. It has subsequently been praised by religious organizations, including official Vatican publications, and regularly appears in top ten lists of films and religious films.

In Italy, according to Pasolini, *The Gospel According To Matthew* was perceived as a

> disconcerting and scandalous novelty, because no one expected a Christ like that, because no one had read Matthew's *Gospel*. (PP, 79)

Critics objected to the Marxism of *The Gospel According To Matthew*; its avoidance of the living conditions of Ancient Israel; the 'haughty, prophesying and violent transgression' translated onto Jesus (N. Greene, 78). Not 'Marxist' enough, then! Or the 'wrong kind' of 'Marxism'!

Pier Paolo Pasolini changed his mind about the film. Sometimes he thought the compound of styles – *cinema vérité*, handheld camera, zooms, long lenses, and so on – was a hotch-potch but worked (it *is* an uneven mix of cinematic styles). At other times, he found *The Gospel According To Matthew*

> a violently contradictory film, profoundly ambiguous and disconcerting, particularly the figure of Christ – at times he is almost embarrassing, as well as being enigmatic. (PP, 87)

But it's almost impossible to make a film about Christ without falling into embarrassment or awkwardness at some point, and not a

---
34 Museo Nazionale del Cinema, Turin.

single one of the greatest religious films have avoided that completely.

When Pier Paolo Pasolini saw the picture after he'd finished it, he wondered if perhaps it did, in the end, have a stylistic unity – which derived from 'my own unconscious religiousness, which came out and gave the film its unity'. So, Pasolini mused, 'therefore I probably do believe after all' (PP, 87).

The miracles Pier Paolo Pasolini later found (in the 1969 interviews) 'repellent', 'disgusting pietism', because they were faked. Pasolini wanted them to be real, but the artificial aids made the fakery obvious (PP, 90). Pasolini wondered if he should have invented 'completely new miracles', such as

> the sense of miraculousness each of us can experience watching the dawn, for example: nothing happens, the sun rises, trees are lit up by the sun. Perhaps for us this is what a miracle is. (PP, 91)

I think that Pier Paolo Pasolini is being too hard on himself, or on his movie, which is an authentic masterpiece, almost a miracle in itself. (Besides, all of cinema is fakery, and the miracles in the 1964 movie are just one kind of fakery out of 1,000s. Computer-aided imagery and green screen visual effects look just as fake today as any other effects in film history).

But then, many filmmakers have been doubtful about their achievements. To take one example: one of Pier Paolo Pasolini's key influences, Jean-Luc Godard, for my money one of the two or three most significant filmmakers of the 1960-2010 period (Ingmar Bergman and Akira Kurosawa would be the others), often remarked that he didn't think his movies were that good:

> John Cassavetes, who was more or less my age – now he was a great director. I can't imagine myself as his equal in cinema. For me he represents a certain cinema that's way up above. (2000)

And Godard told Andrew Sarris in 1994 that he didn't think he'd

> succeeded in making any really good films. There are moments, scenes, whole movements that sing. It has all added up to a cinema of sorts, even though I'm still learning my art. (1994)

And this is the man who wrote and directed films such as *Breathless, Pierrot le Fou, Weekend, Contempt, Vivre Sa Vie, Hail Mary, Passion, Masculin/ Féminin, La Chinoise, Tout Va Bien, Alphaville, Two or Three Things I Know About Her, Histoire(s) du Cinéma, Notre Musique,*

Éloge de l'Amour and *Bande à Part*!

One thing's for sure about *The Gospel According To Matthew*: anyone contemplating a movie based on the *Gospels* has to see it. And they have: Mel Gibson, Martin Scorsese, Atom Egoyam and Abel Ferrara are among many who have cited *The Gospel According To Matthew* as an influence (there must be 100s more filmmakers). But how can you *not* be influenced by *The Gospel According To Matthew* if you've seen it? The picture has such an impact, it's impossible to ignore it.

CRITICS.

For David A. Cook in *A History of Narrative Film*, *The Gospel According To Matthew* is a 'stark but brilliant work', and 'stands today as the most dynamic version of the gospel story ever filmed' (1990, 632).

Pamela Grace calls *The Gospel According To Matthew* 'spare, laconic, almost ritualistic in form... demanding and profoundly moving' (105). Greg Way (in *Movietone News* in 1976) found the film's pace breakneck and uncompromising, and very unexpected in a Jesus film. The viewer hurries to keep up with Jesus like the camera does.

Bosley Crowther, film critic for the *New York Times* (and tough to please), raved about *The Gospel* when it opened in Gotham in 1966, praising its 'extraordinary blending of black-and-white reality and the literalness of St Matthew's Gospel'; 'it is neither transcendent nor mundane, neither extravagant nor banal' (Feb 18, 1966).

THE LOOK AND THE STYLE

THE LOOK.

Jesus in *The Gospel According To Matthew* is depicted in a white robe (white pops out of the wilderness landscapes of much of the movie – many of the characters wear white), with bare feet and a black hood and cloak made from coarse[35] material. His hair is pulled back and shoulder length. He sports stubble which at times becomes a stubbly beard. Jesus's look is right out of Renaissance paintings: he might've stepped out of an

---

[35] Many of Danilo Donati's costumes are about texture and weave – for this and other Pasolini movies.

altarpiece by Piero della Francesca[36] or Albrecht Dürer.

As for colour, Pier Paolo Pasolini said there were too many colours in real life (PP, 63), and he chose particular locations because they eliminated the many colours he didn't need (as with Morocco for *Oedipus Rex*). The black-and-white in *Il Vangelo Secondo Matteo* does seem to fit its stark, earthy, austere interpretation of the Christian story[37] (interestingly, the other time Pasolini staged the Passion story, in *La Ricotta*, was in lurid Technicolor made to look trashy. That is, if he was going to use colour, Pasolini seemed intent on deliberately exaggerating the colour).

In developing the shooting style for *The Gospel According To Matthew*, the filmmakers started off principal photography by using the reverential technique of *Accattone*. This did not work for the theme and subject of the *Gospels*, so they jettisoned that approach.

During the filming of the Baptism scene (near Viterbo and Orte), DP Tonino Delli Colli and Pier Paolo Pasolini began using zooms, and different camera movements which were 'not reverential, but almost documentary' (PP, 84). Thus, Pasolini and his team were mixing Godardian and *cinema vérité* techniques with a traditional, religious subject.[38] It worked. The combination of filmic styles did not make for a stylistic unity, as Pasolini said: 'the unity comes from a mixture of styles' (PP, 87). The false continuity shots and many zooms, Pasolini said, recalled Jean-Luc Godard.

Pier Paolo Pasolini spoke of using the zoom lens to achieve close-ups from a distance, with the zoom set on 250mm, so they looked like Masaccio's paintings (i.e., a flattened sense of space and perspective). (And of course zooms are cheaper – and quicker – to set up than a tracking shot).

There is a significant advance, however, in terms of the handling of the camera, from Pier Paolo Pasolini's first two features to *The Gospel According To Matthew*: Pasolini and Tonino Delli Colli step away from using the standard 50mm lens, for instance, and use much longer focal lengths. They also employ wide angle lenses, much fancier camera angles, and tracking shots. (However, the camera is most often on a tripod, or handheld – dolly shots are used minimally).

---

36 *Histoire(s) du Cinéma*, directed by Jean-Luc Godard, puts Pasolini together with Piero della Francesca on screen (a portrait of Pasolini is combined with part of Piero's *Legend of the True Cross*).
37 But that's easy to say, because there isn't a colour version of *The Gospel According To Matthew* to compare it with. Actually there was a colourized version (a version was released on DVD in 2007).
38 Pasolini: 'the style in *The Gospel* is very varied: it combines the reverential with almost documentary moments, an almost classic severity with moments that are almost Godardian' (PP,84).

The early days of Christ's ministry are depicted with handheld shots following just behind Jesus, as if the camera takes the viewpoint of one of the disciples. Meanwhile, Jesus looks over his shoulder as he leads the way, speaking urgently.

The costumes (by Danilo Donati) are the first examples of what would become a staple of Pier Paolo Pasolini's historical cinema: coarse textures that can be read by the camera, clothing that seems handmade by the wearer, and many out-of-period elements, such as mediæval/ Renaissance outfits for some groups of characters (such as Herod's henchmen), and of course the mandatory giant hats which Donati and Pasolini were very fond of (used for the Pharisees). With so many officials, soldiers, courtiers and priests to dress, the costuming is not all of the era (the approach was the same with the settings).

PHOTOGRAPHIC STYLE.

Il Vangelo Secondo Matteo was lensed (by Pier Paolo Pasolini's regular cameraman Tonino Delli Colli and camera operator Giuseppe Ruzzolini) in a Neo-realist/ New Wave style – a documentary style, with handheld camera, natural lighting and much camera movement (yet much of the film is also very straightforward, with a camera on a tripod with a standard (50mm) lens and no camera movement). The miracles (the curing of the lepers, the loaves and the fishes, the raising of the dead) are done with straight cuts by editor Nino Baragli (some of them are match cuts and some are jump cuts, straight out of Jean-Luc Godard's cinema, which jolt the viewer).[39] Healing a man's disfigured face, for example, is achieved with a cut from Jesus to the leper (wearing special make-up by Marcello Ceccarelli to distort the nose and eyes), his face now healed, accompanied by a leap into an African spiritual song. The moment is from *Matthew* 8:1-4:

> When he was come down from the mountain, great multitudes followed him. And, behold, there came a leper and worshipped him, saying, Lord, if thou wilt, thou canst make me clean. And Jesus put forth his hand, and touched him, saying, I will; be thou clean. And immediately his leprosy was cleansed. And Jesus saith unto him, See thou tell no man; but go thy way, shew thyself to the priest, and offer the gift that Moses commanded, for a testimony unto them.

The miracles were transparently 'false' (or self-consciously theatrical), as with the other visual effects, in which the mechanisms of cinema were

---

[39] I say out of Godard's cinema – but Godard and editor Agnès Guillemot did not invent the jump cut, of course. However, in *The Gospel According To Matthew* the editing techniques draw heavily on the French New Wave.

deliberately exposed.40

The straight cut works so well, though, doesn't it? It's as if you don't want to see how it was done, how Jesus might have healed a leper. Excessive (and expensive) movie trickery, of the Hollywood kind (digital effects, for instance, which could blend a Before and After face together slowly), wouldn't be nearly so effective and *right* as a simple cut. That fits, because a god healing someone instantly, in a millionth of a second, seems correct.41

There are two sorts of close-ups in *Il Vangelo Secondo Matteo*: those of the by-standers and crowds, filmed with long lenses that pan from face to face or linger over them (with the camera zoomed in from further away, so it isn't physically right in the face of the non-professional actors, which can be off-putting for newbies). Shots are left in by the editor (Nino Baragli) where the camera operator (Giuseppe Ruzzolini) searches for a face in a group, and occasionally the focus slips, as the focus puller struggles to keep the shots sharp.42 *The Gospel According To Matthew* keeps coming back to this cinematographic device: actors are blocked in loose rows or semi-circles, and the camera searches for them in medium close-ups. The technique emphasizes the concept of seeing these people for the first time (as the viewer discovers them with the lens).

The second type of C.U. is usually handheld, with the camera very close to the actors. This approach is typically employed for dramatic scenes, and most memorably for the scenes where Jesus is speaking to his disciples (very effective in the Sermon on the Mount sequence).

Another technique the filmmakers employed was having the camera follow Jesus as if it were one of the disciples, walking behind him, while he turns his head and talks over his shoulder into the lens. That helps to give the film its hurried pace. As Martin Scorsese put it, Irazoqui 'doesn't act walking, he is walking; it's not self-conscious and yet it's very determined' (1990, 136). It's surprising just how many of the sayings of Jesus are delivered in this manner, over-the-shoulder, with Christ in quarter-profile, to his disciples (but we don't see the reverse angles much).

The handheld technique gave *The Gospel According To Matthew* an immediacy and *casualness* that was entirely lacking in religious movies and in particular films about Christ up until that time, when Jesus was

---

40 S. Rohdie, 1995, 8.
41 It doesn't matter a jot, either, that the continuity here is up the spout: when the leper walks towards Jesus, he's on his own, with nobody around him. But when he's healed, he runs into a throng of celebrating onlookers.
42 Parts of these shots would be instantly discarded by a conventional editor. One wonders if Ruzzolini was happy with having what appear to be mistakes left in the film.

always filmed reverentially,[43] and never *casually*, as if he just happened to be walking down some steps in Jerusalem and talking to his disciples over his shoulder (and then he will stride ahead of them, still declaiming).

The Gospel According To Matthew delivered a Jesus as a flesh-and-blood man, part of the real world, not a distanced, aloof, obviously divine personality. In *The Gospel According To Matthew,* Christ was really there, saying those things, walking that way.

The typical shot in *The Gospel According To Matthew* is a handheld shot of Enrique Irazoqui's Christ walking through stony hills, all the time declaiming rapidly from the *Scriptures,* followed by his disciples. Although he *acts* in a naturalistic or realistic manner (as well as a highly stylized manner), the look of Jesus is conventional: for example, the costumes that Jesus wears are traditional ones, instantly recognizable from all of cinema's previous Biblical, epic movies. So Jesus has the flowing robes, the hood or cowl (dark-hued), the long hair, the beard, etc. He might have stepped out of a fresco by Duccio or Massacio.

Of his general cinematic technique, Pier Paolo Pasolini said he tried to emphasize frontality; symmetry; characters moving against a background: these æsthetics derive from painting. When a tracking shot or pan was employed, for example, Pasolini said it referred to the camera moving over a canvas. There were few tricky dolly shots in *The Gospel*, and no characters entering or exiting the frame. Pasolini said (*pace Mamma Roma*) that he was trying for a Renaissance painterly approach. Pasolini was much impressed by Masaccio and the Quattrocento painters: background not landscape, figures on a background, not an empty field or landscape.

The Gospel According To Matthew, though, employs plenty of cinematic techniques, including dolly shots, handheld shots, long lens shots, overhead shots, jump cuts, zooms, crash zooms, rapid montage, film library footage (such as buildings collapsing), and practical effects such as fire, wind and smoke.

And there are many formal shots, including wide angle, establishing shots filmed from a tripod, where the camera doesn't move, and many shots where the actors are arranged within the frame formally. The tracking shots are also generally formal. For obvious reasons, in many locations where laying dolly tracks isn't possible (such as atop Mount Etna), movement is often captured with a handheld camera.

---

[43] Pier Paolo Pasolini wondered if he'd been too stylized and too reverential in his filmic approach to *Il Vangelo Secondo Matteo* (PP, 83). Some viewers who found the film irreverent and too casual would say the opposite.

PAINTING AND *THE GOSPEL ACCORDING TO MATTHEW*.

The visual style of *Il Vangelo Secondo Matteo* alluded, as so often in Pier Paolo Pasolini's cinema, to painters such as Paolo Uccello (the battle scenes, opulent robes and the large hats), Masaccio, Piero della Francesca (the use of static *tableaux,* the pregnant Madonna, and the Pharisees' costumes), Byzantine icons, and Georges Rouault[44] (for Christ's face).[45]

The references to painting may have been obvious, Pier Paolo Pasolini remarked, but that didn't detract from the film. Painting was an important element of *The Gospel According To Matthew* for Pasolini's view of the *Gospel,* because in the Italian cultural tradition painting contributed much to Christianity, and Pasolini wanted to make 'the story of Christ plus two thousand years of Christianity' (PP, 91). And of course painting – and Renaissance painting in particular – was central to the *Curd Cheese* episode in *RoGoPaG.*

Pier Paolo Pasolini was also aware that the references to painting could unbalance the narrative:

> whenever I realized from behind the camera that something might recall the composition of a painting, I destroyed it immediately. I sought to do everything the most cinematographically possible. Naturally there are some painterly echoes – there's Duccio, there's Mantegna – but certainly not a precise painting or school, simply generic references.

The conscious effort to avoid painting on Pier Paolo Pasolini's part, and in particular Renaissance and mediæval painting, of course reveals his deep immersion in art, and in religious art, and also the pitfalls of wanting to relate cinema too closely to painting. As Pasolini acknowledges, some allusions to painting seem inevitable. Pasolini recognizes that in the West audiences have been aware of how the Christian story has been portrayed visually for centuries – and by some of the greatest artists. Pasolini realizes that cinema is a late addition to Christian art, and is inevitably inflected by the thousands of images that have preceded it.

But *The Gospel According To Matthew* does not feel like it is bogged down by the references to paintings at all: it is not overly self-conscious, and does not show off its painterly allusions like other movies (the films of Peter Greenaway, Derek Jarman and Martin Scorsese come to mind).

---

44 Like Lovis Corinth, James Ensor, Egon Schiele and Emil Nolde, Georges Rouault was an Expressionist artist who explored Christian themes, producing anguished, modern versions of Christian iconography. Rouault's *Crucifixion* (c. 1918, collection: H.P. McHenny, Philadelphia), for instance, is a moving, stained glass-like picture in bright colours, marked out by the thickest black outlines in Expressionism.

45 For Sam Rohdie, *Il Vangelo Secondo Matteo* drew not from reality but from art – it was Masaccio, Piero della Francesca, Giotto *et al* who formed the inspirations for the world of *Il Vangelo Secondo Matteo,* not the real world (1995, 60).

THE SETTINGS AND LOCATIONS.

Instead of modern Palestine, which did not evoke Ancient Palestine for Pier Paolo Pasolini and the team, the director and producer chose to film in modern Calabria, in which the Biblical past (or an equivalent for it) was still alive. 'Calabria now contains the sacred of the Gospel which the modern had obliterated in Palestine and would obliterate again in Calabria', Pasolini said in *Location Hunting In Palestine*.[46] At first, Pasolini had thought that modern Israel, which was where Jesus had preached, would be ideal, but there was 'something too modern, too industrial in the countryside' (it was also a turbulent time in the Middle East, and not the easiest (nor the most financially viable) time to produce the movie). Using Southern Italy enabled the production to 'remake the Gospel by analogy', without having 'to reconstruct it either archæologically or philologically' (PP, 82). His research film *Sopralluoghi In Palestina* came to be used for documentation – the production team had already decided to use Southern Italy.

The use of found locations in *The Gospel According To Matthew* is stunning, easily as accomplished as in any film ever made (and would have required weeks of location scouting – this is a production that filmed in many, many different places. The cast and the crew would be constantly getting in and out of cars and vans, and riding in cars and vans all over Southern Italy). Mary's village; the hill town near Jesus's home; Herod's palace; the coastal town, with its ruined castle (Aci Castello, Sicily), where the Baptist is held captive; Golgotha, overlooking the hill town (which doubles for Jerusalem); the plains of Massafra in Puglia; and the rocky hills in the desert (filmed in Calabria, up in the Sila massif, tho' avoiding the huge forests, of course).

Every time I watch *The Gospel According To Matthew* I am struck by how modern and 20th century many of the locations are: they *look* old, from a distance, but on closer inspection they clearly display many modern features (iron railings on a staircase, for instance, or concrete blocks, and the houses use cement and building materials in a modern fashion. (True, the Ancient Romans had forms of concrete and cement, but not used in this way.)

But it works. You forget about the very contemporary-looking locations for many reasons: the story is utterly compelling, the filmmaking is so brilliant, the performances are so engrossing, and there's so much going on. Even tho' the art directors might've taken down a few TV aerials, and covered up a shop sign with a sheet, or hung a rug in

---

46 In S. Rohdie, 1995, 164.

front of a glass doorway (for the scenes where Christ walks thru a town), it doesn't matter.

The Baptism was the first scene to be shot (in Spring, 1964), near Orte and Viterbo (the Fosso Castello Waterfalls, Soriano nel Cimino); the Mount of Olives (staged near Hadrian's Villa and Tivoli) was next; then Matera[47] and Crotone (the two towns formed Capernaum). Satan's temptation was staged on Mount Etna (using the familiar black, volcanic earth which crops up in a few Pier Paolo Pasolini movies).[48] Bethlehem was filmed in Barile, Apulia. Some of the locations (such as Matera, Massafra and Crotone) had been discovered during the filming of the documentary *Love Meetings*. Other locations included: Potenza, Basilicata; Aci Castello, Acireale, Catania in Sicily;[49] and Canale Monterano, Rome.

Bethlehem in *The Gospel According To Matthew* is a cluster of dwellings built into the hillside, virtually like caves, modest, small, and lit by fires only – very different from the usual Biblical movie setting of free-standing buildings, where Joseph, Mary and Jesus live in relative comfort (filmed in Barile, Apulia). Of course, people have been living in caves for at least three million years (depending on what you class as 'human').

It's striking how much of *The Gospel According To Matthew* is set by the ocean: Jesus is often filmed against the sea, and there are many scenes staged on beaches: the loaves and the fishes, Jesus walking on water, the castle (the exterior of Herod's palace), and of course the scenes where Jesus finds Peter and Andrew. (Calabria is only twenty miles across in some parts, so the Ionian Sea and the Tyrrhenian Sea are never far away, and it's well-known for its memorable coastal spots. And the sea doesn't date or age! – if you point a camera at the ocean, it probably looks the same as it did 2,000 years ago).

The Gospel According To Matthew was not all filmed on location – the cell for the Baptist, for instance, is a set, and parts of the *Sermon On the Mount* sequence were filmed in the studio (in Incir De Paolis Studios in Roma).

The settings in *The Gospel According To Matthew* are simple, earthy, dusty, and mainly found rather than constructed sets. The settings are not only presumably cheap (as they had to be), they also suit the

---

47 Matera is famous for its *sassi*, the buildings constructed in tiers in a ravine. Now mainly abandoned, they were populated by the poorest of the poor, living in squalor that Carlo Levi's sister compared to Dante's *Inferno*. Matera was also used for *The Passion of the Christ* (2004).
48 Another filmmaker was fond of the black soil of volcanoes – Akira Kurosawa. To the point where the *sensei* staged entire battles with horses and soldiers on Mount Fuji – such as in the incredible 1985 epic *Ran*. Kurosawa's films also influenced *The Gospel*.
49 The castle on the beach.

pared-down visual style (one of the reasons big budget, Hollywood epics look unreal is because of their over-elaborate sets, or, more accurately, the way that those sets are lit and filmed). Some of the settings are anachronistic, and clearly mediæval (and some have elements, such as doors, which are 19th or 20th century).

At the same time, the locations in *The Gospel According To Matthew* were also obviously art directed (props were added, but also taken away: many of the settings would have had to be cleared of material that wasn't analogous with the ancient world). The art department (Luigi Scaccianoce, Andrea Fantacci and Dante Ferretti) created a wholly convincing ancient look, that appeared lived-in, dusty, dirty, and real. It was a world of old stone walls, uneven and worn steps, mats and low tables. Everything looked ancient and well-used. (For some filmmakers, such as Ken Russell, that's a mistake when recreating a historical period on celluloid: those times and places would have often been relatively new: instead of a crumbling, mediæval castle, if a castle had been recently built, it should look new. That was the approach that Russell and his team took with *The Devils* (1971), for instance).

There is a wonderful sense of landscape in *The Gospel According To Matthew*; the film contains many panoramic shots of mountains, rocks, fields, the camera drifting slowly to the right, accompanied by the sound of wind, or birds (that particular sound of the breeze crops up in many films of Federico Fellini too – it seems to be a sound effect that many Italian filmmakers employed at the time. Maybe it was the only wind sound effect they had at Cinecittà).

MUSIC.

Besides keeping the imagery earthy and simple (like Ingmar Bergman and Andrei Tarkovsky), *The Gospel According To Matthew* employed highly emotive music: Johann Sebastian Bach,[50] 1685-1750 (used more than any other composer in *The Gospel*),[51] Sergei Prokofiev, Wolfgang Amadeus Mozart, Anton Webern, the Congolese *Missa Luba*, spirituals ("Sometimes I feel like a motherless child"), Russian revolutionary songs, and Blind Willie Johnson.

The pieces of music in *The Gospel According To Matthew* include:

• Johann Sebastian Bach: *St Matthew Passion* (1727).[52] Number 78: *Wir setzen uns mit Tränen nieder* and number 47: *Erbarme Dich.*

• Johann Sebastian Bach: *Concerto For Violin and Oboe In D Minor*

---

50 Jean-Luc Godard commented that you can put Bach's music with anything and it works.
51 Orchestrated by Carlo Rustichelli.
52 The *St Matthew Passion* (1727/ 79), like the *B Minor Mass* and the *Goldberg Variations*, was composed in Leipzig, where Bach moved in 1723 (where he was the Cantor of St Thomas's Church).

(BWV 1060). Number 2: *Adagio*.

• Johann Sebastian Bach: *Fugue (Ricercata)*, A 6, Number 2 (arranged by Anton von Webern). From *Das Musikalische Opfer* (BWV 1079).

• Johann Sebastian Bach: *High Mass* (BWV 232). *Agnus Dei* (*Dona nobis pacem*).

• Johann Sebastian Bach: *Concerto For Violin In E Major* (BWV 1042). Number 2: *Adagio*.

• Wolfgang Amadeus Mozart: *Maurerische Trauermusik In C Minor* (KV 477). *Quartet For Two Violins, Altviolin and Cello, Number 19 In C major*.

• Wolfgang Amadeus Mozart: *Dissonant-Quartet* (KV 465).

• Sergei Prokofiev: *Cantate 'Alexander Nevsky', Number 1*.

• *Gloria* from the *Missa Luba* (a Congolese work by Father Guido Haazen, 1958).

• Odetta: "Sometimes I feel like a motherless child".

• Blind Willie Johnson: 'Dark Was the Night, Cold Was the Ground' (1927).

The score of *The Gospel According To Matthew* is a library score, an off-the-shelf score. It is nearly all found music. As such, it also one of the finest found or bought scores in all cinema.

However, there is some incidental music composed and arranged specially for the movie (by Luis Bacalov), and some of the existing pieces were orchestrated by Carlo Rustichelli.

Billie Holiday is sometimes wrongly credited on the soundtrack of *The Gospel According To Matthew* – the confusion perhaps comes from the song "Sometimes I feel like a motherless child", which is sung by Odetta not Holiday. Odetta (1930-2008) was known as 'the Queen of American folk music' (as Martin Luther King called her).

"Sometimes I feel like a motherless child" is used a couple of times in *The Gospel According To Matthew* – over the Nativity scene with the three Kings, and during the Baptism. It is a Negro spiritual song that has been covered by everybody from Paul Robeson to Prince:

> Sometimes I feel like a motherless child
> Sometimes I feel like a motherless child
> Sometimes I feel like a motherless child
> Long way from my home
>
> Sometimes I wish, I could fly
> Like a bird up in the sky
> Oh, sometimes I wish, I could fly
> Fly like a bird up in the sky

> Sometimes I wish, I could fly
> Like a bird up in the sky
> Little closer to home

Nina Power, in a 2013 article ("Subversive Pasolini"), commented:

> This spiritual can be read in the film as a comment on Jesus of course, albeit with the roles reversed – the virgin birth makes him a "fatherless child" in a human, though not divine, sense – but as a comment on slavery and the diasporic nature of the lives of black people kidnapped into work, Odetta's refrain is stark, and the dissonance between the modernity of the recording and the historical legacy of slavery fused with the gospel is, to my mind, one of the most striking things about the film. (2013)

Some observers have confused Blind Willie Johnson with Leadbelly (the slide guitar perhaps adds to the confusion). Johnson (1897-1945) was a Texan bluesman best-known for 'Jesus Make Up My Dying Bed', 'John the Revelation', 'It's Nobody's Fault But Mine' and the song used here, 'Dark Was the Night, Cold Was the Ground'. Johnson has influenced and been covered by Bob Dylan, Led Zeppelin, Tom Waits, Eric Clapton and Fairport Convention.

Luis Bacalov was the music arranger of *The Gospel According To Matthew*, as well as the composer of some pieces (for Salomé's dance, for example, and some of the folky flute music). So although P.P. Pasolini is credited as the grand *auteur* of this masterpiece of 1964 (Pasolini's contribution to his movies tends to overshadow everyone else's efforts), Bacalov's input was vital – when we're not hearing famous classical music by Bach or Mozart, we are hearing Bacalov's music. (Also, Elsa Morante helped with selecting music – she discussed the music at length with her friend Pasolini, and her choices of J.S. Bach, W.A. Mozart, Leos Janácek, etc).

Italian-Argentian Luis Bacalov (1933-2017) was a veteran composer of numerous movies and TV shows. He scored movies such as *City of Women, Blood and Diamonds, The Sicilian Cross, Seduction, The Man Called Noon, Catch As Catch Can, Django, Sea of Dreams, The Postman, Mother Theresa, Woman On Top, The Love Letter, Polish Wedding* and *The Truce,* and many TV series and TV movies.

One of many great touches in *The Gospel According To Matthew* is the use of music within scenes (diegetic music), played by youths on flutes and pipes[53] (for instance, as the boats row out on the water, there's a piper playing). The boys who play music on the edge of a scene in Pier

---
[53] Tho' dubbed, of course.

Paolo Pasolini's cinema might've stepped out of a painting by Michelangelo da Caravaggio.

Music is also used in *The Gospel According To Matthew* to enlarge scenes – folk music (often with choral vocals), is heard, not as accompaniment or mood music, but to suggest that people are singing off-screen. Like the spot sound effects (horses neighing, bird calls, sheep), they expand the scope of the picture.

The mix of music works brilliantly. The soundtrack of *The Gospel According To Matthew* is simply remarkable. Combined with the filmmakers' extraordinary feeling for faces (faces which are so individual and direct, faces which recall those painted by Hieronymous Bosch, Rembrandt van Rijn, Albrecht Dürer and Francisco de Goya), and the passionate music, the result is tremendous.

In fact, the first time you see *The Gospel According To Matthew* and *hear* the African spiritual and "Sometimes I feel like a motherless child" by Odetta in the early section of the movie, the effect is staggering. Because this sort of music had *never* been deployed in a Biblical movie before. You could say that the use of the music is an even more striking departure from the usual kind of Christian movie than many other elements in *The Gospel According To Matthew* – like portraying an angry Christ, or the use of extras and faces, or the desacralizing, *cinéma verité* approach.

I'm sure some people would've found the music difficult to accept, because up until that time, scoring accompanying Christ on screen was always reverential, slow, solemn music. And the opening credits play with Johann Sebastian Bach, which audiences would've found very suitable. Imagine, for example, that *The Gospel According To Matthew* had *opened* with "Sometimes I feel like a motherless child" (but there is an African spiritual song also in the opening credits).

In its radical deployment of music, particularly laying modern popular music such as Willie Johnson on top of traditional, religious scenes, *The Gospel According To Matthew* reminds me of *Scorpio Rising* (1963), Kenneth Anger's cult movie which makes an instant impression with its combination of bikers, leather, homosexuality, hints of S/M, and the outrageous fusion of 1960s pop songs with religious movies. (It's like a flashy, American version of a Pasolini film).

Scorpio Rising is a classic cult movie in every sense: it displays anti-establishment and rebellious attitudes, acute fashion-consciousness, an exploration of subcultures (Hell's Angels and biker culture), and a terrific soundtrack (which includes Elvis Presley, the Randells, the Angels,

Bobby Vinton, Ray Charles, the Crystals, Kris Jensen, Claudine Clark, Gene McDaniels, the Surfans and Little Peggy March). If you made a list of the elements that a cult movie should have, *Scorpio Rising* has them in spades. (Certainly the mix of pop music and visuals was influential: Martin Scorsese and David Lynch have been influenced by *Scorpio Rising*, for Andy Medhurst, in pictures such as *GoodFellas, Mean Streets* and *Blue Velvet*).[54]

Using Sergei Prokofiev's music for *Alexander Nevsky* (1938) inevitably gives the 'Massacre of the Innocents' scene in *The Gospel According To Matthew* a specific cultural context. That Pier Paolo Pasolini would cite the cinema of Sergei Eisenstein seems inevitable, Eisenstein being a firm favourite with critics and filmmakers, and *Alexander Nevsky* has inspired many subsequent filmmakers.[55] (*Alexander Nevsky* is ideologically problematic, tho', being a State-endorsed production, made at the height of the repressive regime of Joseph Stalin's administration; the same goes for much of Eisenstein's cinema and its alignment with Stalin and the Soviet authorities. Maybe the *Alexander Nevsky* music works ideologically, despite being a quote from another movie, because it grew out of the period of Communism when it had fascistic under-pinnings – and the act of King Herod ordering the death of children who threaten his rule is supremely fascistic).

EDITING.

Pier Paolo Pasolini said he did all his own editing, with the technical help of Nino Baragli. '[Baragli] is full of good sense, and he is a Roman, so he has a sense of irony, so I use him to keep a rein on some of my excesses' (PP, 139).

The editing in *The Gospel According To Matthew* is such an important ingredient to its overall success. Yes, this is true of many movies, but in a movie like *The Gospel According To Matthew,* film critics tend to always emphasize the visuals, and it's true that visually *The Gospel According To Matthew* is stunning. But it requires the editing of Nino Baragli to maintain the pacing, knowing when to move on and when to linger, when to introduce a montage of shorter shots, and when to stay on a lengthier shot.

But because editing is invisible, very few critics remark upon it. But it's editing that dictates how the images unfold, how one scene relates to the one coming next and the one before it, and how the story is told.

In spite of its occasional radical innovations, *The Gospel According*

---

54 A. Medhurst, in J. Romney, 1995, 75.
55 *Ivan theTerrible* is in there, too.

To Matthew is actually cut in the usual shot-reverse-shot manner. For instance, scenes often open with a simple establishing shot. Or that other favourite device of editors: a close-up of a symbolic object, before going wider and back to regular continuity editing.

There *are* more unconventional editing choices, such as jump cuts and rapidly repeated shots – which pop out more because of the context of a religious movie about Christ. When Christ walks on the water, for ex, Nino Baragli cuts in several crash zooms, from the Apostles' point-of-view. (The jump cuts that occur in *Breathless*, released four years earlier, for instance, seem more part of the piece, the genre (gangsters), and the loose, handheld approach. But *Breathless* made the old device of jump cuts seem startling again).

More radical than jump cuts in *The Gospel According To Matthew*, however, in terms of editing, are the montages – particularly the Sermon on the Mount montage, and the *Psalms* sequence. To chop up the speeches of Jesus Christ seems a more drastic departure from the conventional cinematic techniques of a religious movie.

Meanwhile, the two trials of Jesus do away with the expected close-ups, to cross the distance between the onlookers (such as the disciples Peter and Matthew), and the Saviour and the officials in the distance. Precisely when the agony that Christ is suffering is intensifying, the 1964 movie does something very unexpected and, for some viewers, probably very frustrating, by staying back (especially when for much of the time the camera has been right next to Jesus).[56]

ADAPTING THE *GOSPEL*.

There is plenty of material in the *Gospel* authored by St Matthew that was left out of the Italian, 1964 production – most of the parables, for instance: in the *Scriptures*, Jesus tells many parables. A movie, even one that's two hours and 22 minutes long, just doesn't have time for all of those stories (it's striking just how much Jesus is a storyteller). Some of the parables are simply summed up in a sentence or two. Not all of the quotations are from St Matthew's *Gospel*; some are from *Isaiah*.

Who was (St) Matthew? He was famously a tax collector, one of Jesus's disciples, who supposedly wrote the *Gospel* in 60-65 A.D. (some say later, 80-85 A.D.) – 30 or 50 years after the events, then. *The Gospel According To St Matthew* was the first *Gospel* to be written, and it opens the *New Testament*.

Pier Paolo Pasolini said he preferred *The Gospel of John*, but 'I

---

[56] The device was employed in the 'trilogy of life' movies.

thought Matthew's was the best for making a film' (P, 95). However, a TV mini-series of *The Gospel of John* was produced in 2003 (it was an attempt at a 'faithful' interpretation (impossible to achieve) of the *Bible*).[57] A film based on *The Gospel of Luke* was produced in 1979. Matthew's *Gospel* has also been used for stage musicals (such as *Godspell*, which opened Off Broadway in 1971[58]).

The Gospel According To Matthew doesn't adapt all of St Matthew's *Gospel*, either: the opening chapter involves one of those long lists of 'so-and-so begat so-and-so':

> And Judas begat Phares and Zara of Thamar; and Phares begat Esrom; and Esrom begat Aram; (4) And Aram begat Aminadab; and Aminadab begat Naasson; and Naasson begat Salmon; (5) And Salmon begat Booz of Rachab; and Booz begat Obed of Ruth; and Obed begat Jesse; (6) And Jesse begat David the king; and David the king begat Solomon of her that had been the wife of Urias; (7) And Solomon begat Roboam; and Roboam begat Abia; and Abia begat Asa; (8) And Asa begat Josaphat; and Josaphat begat Joram; and Joram begat Ozias; (9) And Ozias begat Joatham; and Joatham begat Achaz; and Achaz begat Ezekias…

There's a lot of begetting in the *Bible*.

Scenes filmed but dropped from *Il Vangelo Secondo Matteo* included some of the miracles, and the possessed people, which were taken out 'because it was really horrible', Pasolini said (PP, 97).[59]

The Gospel According To Matthew follows the chronology of the *Gospel* of St Matthew pretty much, but not entirely. For instance, there are a few switches from the main story of Jesus and his ministry to John the Baptist in prison. The scenes with the Baptist are only brief, but they serve to remind the viewer of this parallel plot. In the scriptural text, the Baptist and his fate is important – Jesus discusses the Baptist at length, for instance. *The Gospel According To Matthew* brings together Jesus and the Baptist with the scenes on the beach, in front of the fortress of Aci Castello in Sicily: Jesus discusses the Baptist with his disciples, and also talks to the Baptist's followers. *The Gospel According To Matthew* also includes the scene where Jesus, hearing of John's death, leaves: 'When Jesus heard of it, he departed thence by ship into a desert place apart' (14:

---

[57] Directed by a 73 year-old Brit (Philip Saville (d. 2016) – he had helmed the rival production of *Oedipus Rex*, in 1968), *The Gospel of John* was produced by Garth Drabinsky and Chris Chrisafis and executive producers Sandy Pearl, Joel B. Michaels, Myron Gottlieb and Martin Katz for Think Film and Visual Bible, Inc, a Canadian company who had previously produced word-for-word versions of *The Gospel of Matthew* and the *Acts of the Apostles*. It was written by John Goldsmith, with Henry Ian Cusick as Jesus, and narrated by Christopher Plummer (who had been Oedipus in 1968).

[58] *Godspell*'s book was by John-Michael Tebelak, with music and lyrics by Stephen Schwartz. *Godspell* was filmed in 1973, and opened on Broadway in 1976.

[59] He used some students, Pier Paolo Pasolini recalled, 'but you could see they were students from the film school, the reality came out, it was awful, so I got rid of it' (PP, 97).

13).

And notice how the fate of the Baptist stops Jesus in his tracks: up to this point, in movie terms, he has been a force of nature, a charismatic leader. As he contemplates the Baptist's fate, he is depicted sitting, dejected.

One character familiar from many film adaptations of the *Gospels* is featured only briefly in *The Gospel According To Matthew*: Mary Magdalene. In St Matthew's *Gospel,* the Magdalene is only mentioned three or so times, as one of the women who tended to Christ after the Crucifixion (she plays a larger role in the apocryphal *Gospels*).

The world of *The Gospel According To Matthew* is thoroughly patriarchal; the movie contains only two women with prominent roles: Mary and Salomé (Herodias has a minor role as Salomé's mom). Later film versions of the Christian story sometimes try to bump up the presence of women in key parts (the Magdalene, for instance), for obvious reasons. (However, in non-speaking roles, there are many women in *The Gospel According To Matthew*, as onlookers).

DIALOGUE.

The dialogue in *The Gospel According To Matthew* is straight out of the Evangelists[60] (in many ways, despite its modernist, New Wave techniques and loose, apparently improvisatory approach, *The Gospel According To Matthew* is a very traditional film). The dialogue is of course very famous, and there are numerous sequences in *The Gospel According To Matthew* which quote the well-known phrases of the *Bible*. You will recognize these phrases:

> Man shall not live by bread alone. (4:4)
> I will make you fishers of men. (4:19)
> Blessed are the poor in spirit: for theirs is the kingdom of heaven. (5:3)
> Love your enemies. (5:44)
> Give us this day our daily bread. (6:11)
> Lead us not into temptation, but deliver us from evil. (6:13)
> Where your treasure is, there will your heart be also. (6:21)
> Ye cannot serve God and mammon. (6:24)
> Consider the lilies of the field, how they grow; they toil not, neither do they spin: And yet I say unto you, that even Solomon in all his glory was not arrayed like one of these. (6:28)
> Seek ye first the kingdom of God, and his righteousness; and all these things shall be added unto you. (6:33)
> Judge not, that ye not be judged. (7:1)
> Ask, and it shall be given you; seek, and ye shall find; knock, and it shall be opened unto you. (7:7)
> Strait is the gate, and narrow is the way, which leadeth unto life, and

---
60 The dialogue comes straight out of the *Gospel*, with Salomé's dance from the *Gospel* of Mark.

few there be that find it. (7:14)
> By their fruit ye shall know them (7:20)
> I can not to send peace, but a sword. (10:34)
> He that is not with me is against me. (12:30)
> Be of good cheer; it is I; be not afraid. (14:27)
> O thou of little faith, wherefore didst thou doubt? (14:31)
> Get thee behind me, Satan. (16:23)
> Let him deny himself, and take up his cross, and follow me. (16:24)
> Except ye be converted, and become as little children, ye shall not enter into the kingdom of heaven. (18:3)
> Thou shalt love they neighbour as thyself. (19:16)
> It is easier for a camel to go through the eye of a needle, than for a rich man to enter into the kingdom of God. (19:24)
> My house shall be called the house of prayer; but ye have made it a den of thieves. (21;13)
> Many are called, but few are chosen. (22:14)
> Before the cock crow, thou shalt deny me thrice. (26:34)
> My God, my God, why hast thou forsaken me? (27:46)

With so many wonderful speeches and phrases to include in the film, it's no wonder that at times Jesus in the 1964 movie speaks rapidly, in order to cover them all,[61] particularly during the Sermon on the Mount episode (which incorporates many of those famous phrases), and when he's talking to his disciples.

You'll notice, too, that the Virgin Mary does not speak in *Il Vangelo Secondo Matteo* – neither as a young woman, nor as an older woman (and neither does Herodias in the scenes with Salomé. Indeed, how many women have speaking parts in *The Gospel*? One or two speak when Christ returns home). And neither does Joseph speak. Indeed, a great deal of *Il Vangelo Secondo Matteo* is accomplished without dialogue. Of course, it's Christ who has the most dialogue in *Il Vangelo Secondo Matteo*, and sometimes he is rattling off many pages of the script (as in the Sermon on the Mount sequence). This is a Jesus who is never lost for words, and he can argue with the best of them (yet there are also segments where he is silent and withdrawn).

That comes from partly from the *Gospels*, which gives Jesus lengthy monologues, but little or nothing to Mary or Joseph (one of the challenges that Jean-Luc Godard set himself when he tackled the Christian story in his 1985 movie *Hail Mary* was to imagine what Mary and Joseph would have said to each other).[62]

The sound teams of Pier Paolo Pasolini's movies preferred to dub the dialogue of the actors, rather than use direct sound (common practice in Italian cinema, and in nearly all of Pasolini's movies). Although it wasn't

---

61 As you have to with William Shakespeare's plays, if you want to include all of the lines.
62 Myriem Roussel watched *The Gospel According To Matthew* in preparation for playing the Virgin in *Hail Mary* in 1985, at Godard's behest, and also a film Godard loved, *The Passion of Joan of Arc*.

as 'naturalistic' as synchronized sound, it could be more 'realistic'. For Pasolini, dubbing 'enriches a character; it is part of my taste for pastiche; it raises a character out of the zone of naturalism' (PP, 39). It can be off-putting at first (when you can see that the extras in *The Gospel* are clearly mouthing different dialogue), but, as with the work of Federico Fellini, one soon gets used to it.

On set, the sound of the takes in *The Gospel According To Matthew* would have included Pier Paolo Pasolini directing the actors, sometimes beat for beat. You can tell in some scenes that the actors, many of whom had never appeared in front of a camera before, are being cued and guided by the director. As in the films of Federico Fellini, Pasolini would direct the actors from near to the camera, asking them to move over there, or look this way. Directors had been doing that since the origins of cinema, and all through the silent movie era.

The sound in *The Gospel According To Matthew* (by Mario Del Pozzo and Fausto Ancillai), skilfully employs off-screen sound to enlarge the cinematic space:[63] horses, sheep, goats, dogs, birds (swifts and swallows), cockerel's cries (for dawn scenes), and the sound of the breeze and high wind. The spot sound effects are judiciously employed: horses, for instance, in the scenes in King Herod's palace (the horses are nearby), but suggesting wealth and military power. Loud gale noises for the forty days in the desert. Birdsong (with swifts prominent) over many of the early scenes of Mary and Joseph (as if the parents are part of the natural order of things, and as if Jesus's early life took place in a kind of Paradise or Eden). The quality of the soundtrack, however, can be a little rough: you can hear the scratches on the vinyl records used for the music, for instance (but olde schoole musos might find that even that enhances the piece).

FACES.

The Gospel According To Matthew is a film of faces: it's one of the great films of faces in cinema – the wizened, wrinkled faces of the peasants and onlookers; the sweet, pure lines of the young Virgin Mary, straight out of the Renaissance art of Sandro Botticelli or Fra Filippo Lippi; the youthful, beguiling charm of Salomé; the haunting eyes of the beautiful, androgynous archangel Gabriel; Joseph's bewildered, tender expression; the aged Madonna's agony; the craggy, grizzled faces of the older disciples; the cute faces of grinning children; the haunted look of the ill and the disabled; and of course Jesus's intensity and poetry.

---

[63] And more imaginatively than in some of Pier Paolo Pasolini's later films, where the sound design can be pedestrian.

The filmmakers filmed the expressive faces using simple close-ups, often with a long lens, lingering on them as they stood still and looked silently at the scenes unfolding before them. In a lesser director, these static, simple shots of Italian peasants and extras might appear dull; but in the hands of this group of filmmakers, they are full of mystery, and so moving.

There is a huge variety of human life portrayed in *The Gospel According To Matthew*, from babies, through children and youths, to older folk. The 1964 movie is particularly strong on aged men and women, faces with lifetimes of experience etched into them. And just as important are the groups of children which the production surrounds Jesus with many times. It's a reminder of how life is lived out on the streets and in the open in warmer climes, in Mediterranean and Middle Eastern countries. It's a totally different kind of society from Northern communities, where everyone scurries home as soon as possible, and the place's dead after four or five p.m.

The extras and non-professionals are not used in a condescending fashion in *The Gospel According To Matthew*, but are filmed with a deep sense of empathy and respect. The close-ups of extras take up a far larger proportion of screen time than one would expect from many another filmmaker (and for a story which has so many events to pack in): it's as if the filmmakers assumed that the audience would have a pretty good idea about what was going on from moment to moment, because each event in the *Scriptures* was so well-known. Thus, the filmmakers spend as much time showing the *reactions* of onlookers to what Christ and his disciples are doing, rather than the events themselves (and if you want to show that something is amazing, scary, funny or whatever, the easiest option is to cut to observers reacting appropriately).

The typical approach to each scene in *The Gospel According To Matthew* is a *tableau* form – editorially as well as visually. That is, the scene frequently begins with a montage of close-ups of extras before moving into the dramatic or narrative segment of the scene. The *tableau* approach derives in part from painting, of course. The scenes are often deliberately (and stubbornly) *static*: the filmmakers have arranged the extras and lead actors in *tableaux*, flat spaces of figures against backgrounds. The lengthy close-ups of the actors and extras are filmed with either one close-up cut in after another, or with the camera wandering from face to face (sometimes in a deliberately loose fashion – shots which many another producer and director would reject from the rushes).

It's as if the film is taking its time, and is looking at everyone involved in the scene before beginning the dramatic action. And it's as if the landscape of this particular movie is the human face as well as the desert or the mountains or the dusty towns and villages of Palestine and Israel.

And no one is saying anything in these close-ups of extras and actors, and often the montages have no music. *The Gospel According To Matthew* exists in a special space cinematically, very different from your average movie. For Pasolini, faces were enough, and the act of photographing a face was enough in a movie:

> ...a tree photographed is poetic, a human face photographed is poetic because physicity is poetic in itself, because it is an apparition, because it is full of mystery, because it is full of ambiguity, because it is full of polyvalent meaning, because even a tree is a sign of a linguistic system. But who talks through a tree? God, or reality itself. Therefore the tree as a sign puts us in communication with a mysterious speaker.

Pier Paolo Pasolini's cinema was not one of long takes. Pasolini associated the long take with Neo-realism and naturalness, which he hated. He did not like having people acting out everyday interchanges in lengthy takes. Thus, Pasolini did not use master shots of a whole scene, but had each actor say their piece to the camera. Pasolini's is thus a montage cinema, a poetic heap of broken images, rather than a chain of Wellesian sequence shots. One supposes that many of the scenes were filmed in one or two takes.

MULTITUDES.

In the *Bible*, there are many multitudes – not just crowds, but always 'multitudes' (such as on the shore, listening to Jesus, whole multitudes stood on the shore (*Matthew*, 13:1)). If you're a god, maybe you can speak to thousands of people at the same time (maybe they all heard Jesus speaking inside their minds). In realistic situations, it's more difficult, if Jesus was a man with a regular human voice – and some filmmakers have explored how to portray that.

In *The Gospel According To Matthew*, the solution is very simple: there are no casts of thousands listening to sermons or parables (as in many Hollywood versions). There are hundreds of extras, of course, but in most of the scenes where Christ is addressing a crowd, the crowd is not huge. In the loaves and fishes episode, for instance, there is no multitude of five thousand sitting on the grass.

> And when it was evening, his disciples came to him, saying, This is a desert place, and the time is now past; send the multitude away, that they may go into the villages, and buy themselves victuals. But Jesus said

unto them, They need not depart; give ye them to eat. And they say unto him, We have here but five loaves, and two fishes. He said, Bring them hither to me. And he commanded the multitude to sit down on the grass, and took the five loaves, and the two fishes, and looking up to heaven, he blessed, and brake, and gave the loaves to his disciples, and the disciples to the multitude. And they did all eat, and were filled: and they took up of the fragments that remained twelve baskets full. And they that had eaten were about five thousand men, beside women and children. (14: 15-21)

However, in some of the last scenes where Christ is preaching, the crowds have become very large: the shots are composed like Renaissance paintings, and make use of verticality and perspective, for the simple reason that when you have a large crowd you either get up high to see them from above (the most extreme solution being the famous images in *Intolerance* from the special crane built to film the Gates of Babylon), or you range them across slopes or tiers or bleachers.

Thus, in some images, the filmmakers and the assistant directors (Maurizio Lucidi, Paolo Schneider and Elsa Morante) spend some time arranging the extras across hillsides, with the camera lower down, looking up at them. Meanwhile, Christ is way off in the distance, preaching his heart out, and everybody listens quietly.

STAGING *THE GOSPEL*.

The staging of scenes and the blocking of actors in *The Gospel According To Matthew* often uses simple vertical symmetry: Christ is often in the middle of the frame, with people grouped around him. The camera is often below shoulder level, looking up at Jesus. And *The Gospel According To Matthew* employs the traditional set-up of Jesus standing separate from his followers – either walking ahead of them, or turning to address them. In this treatment of the life of Christ, the Saviour is always shown walking ahead of his disciples, always in the lead, never lagging behind them. This is a dynamic Jesus, striding ahead, and often addressing his followers over his shoulder (so that they have to struggle to keep up).

The tactic is used time and again in *The Gospel According To Matthew*, and it gives the religious *Scriptures* a real feeling of urgency. It's as if Jesus has thought of what he's going to say right at that moment, and doesn't wait to stop and talk to his disciples in a formal fashion, so that they can all hear him (or debate the issues). Instead, he calls over his shoulder, looking past the camera. It really is as if, as some commentators have noted, that the cameras were right there, capturing the events as they occurred, and followed Jesus as he rattles off parables and psalms and pithy phrases.

The problem is, the middle section of the *Gospel* text of Matthew (and the other *Gospels*), can be interpreted *dramatically* as a series of conversations: Jesus talks... his disciples listen... Putting Jesus in motion like this is a dynamic motif that activates the whole movie.

Nobody bursts into song, and nobody (except Salomé) dances, but much of *The Gospel According To Matthew* is actually staged and blocked like a musical movie. The minimal dialogue, the *tableau* staging, the central characters surrounded by crowds, it looks like a stage musical. (That *Jesus Christ Superstar* turned up seven or so years later seems inevitable. *Jesus Christ Superstar* opened in Gotham on Oct 12, 1971, and was controversial, with demonstrations outside the Mark Hellinger Theater).

There are millions of ways of staging the Christian story: one absolutely key decision, as far as the visual approach went, was to keep Jesus in motion in many scenes. That automatically separates *The Gospel According To Matthew* not only from previous interpretations of the Christian story, but also from the history of art. It's as if the filmmakers decided to celebrate one of the things that cinema can do, often more compellingly than painting or sculpture: show people in motion.

✦

Pier Paolo Pasolini and the team didn't construct the 1964 film as a conventional piece of drama, with the components of a traditional film script: rising action, cause and effect, sub-plots, foreshadowing, pay-offs, motivations, back-story and the like. Instead, the scenes from Matthew's *Gospel* are portrayed pretty much as they appear in the text; in other words, there are no conventional transitions between scenes or sequences, and characters disappear and reappear in a non-dramatic fashion.

There is some back-story, but it's largely scriptural – that is, it comes from references to earlier events, such as those referenced in the *New Testament* (often by Jesus). There is some foreshadowing, of course: Jesus in the latter part of the film points out those who will betray him, and those who will deny him. And there are some minor sub-plots, though they are not the conventional ones: the fates of Judas and Peter, for instance, following Christ's capture, are kind of sub-plots, but not really, as they are functions of the central plot.

However, altho' the filmmakers relied on the audience knowing the story very well and in detail, they *did* construct a conventional film script from the *Gospels*. You can't carry the *Bible* onto the set and just start shooting. Scenes need to be staged, shots planned, props and costumes created, actors rehearsed, etc.

The story of Christ in the *Gospels* is for some people *the* story, it's the Ultimate Story. For J.R.R. Tolkien, the author of *The Lord of the Rings* and *The Hobbit,* for example, it was the ultimate story, and it was true, and every other story was in imitation of it, a pale reflection of the original story.

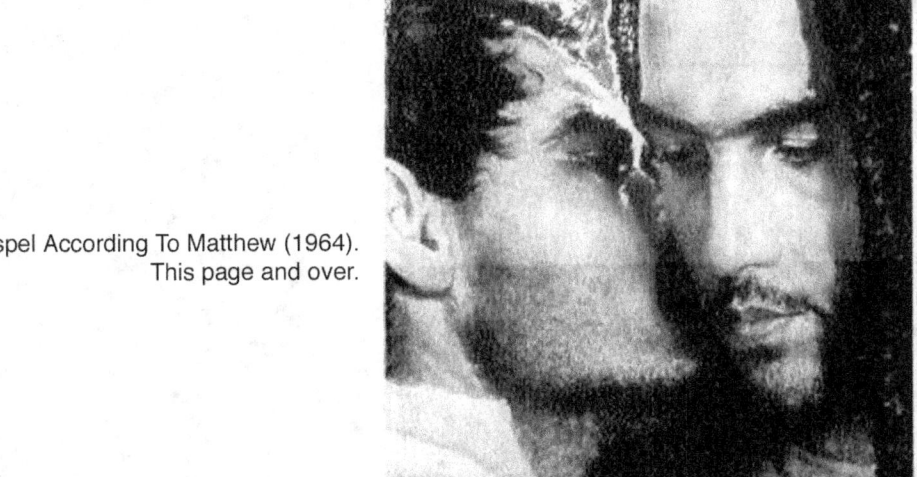

The Gospel According To Matthew (1964).
This page and over.

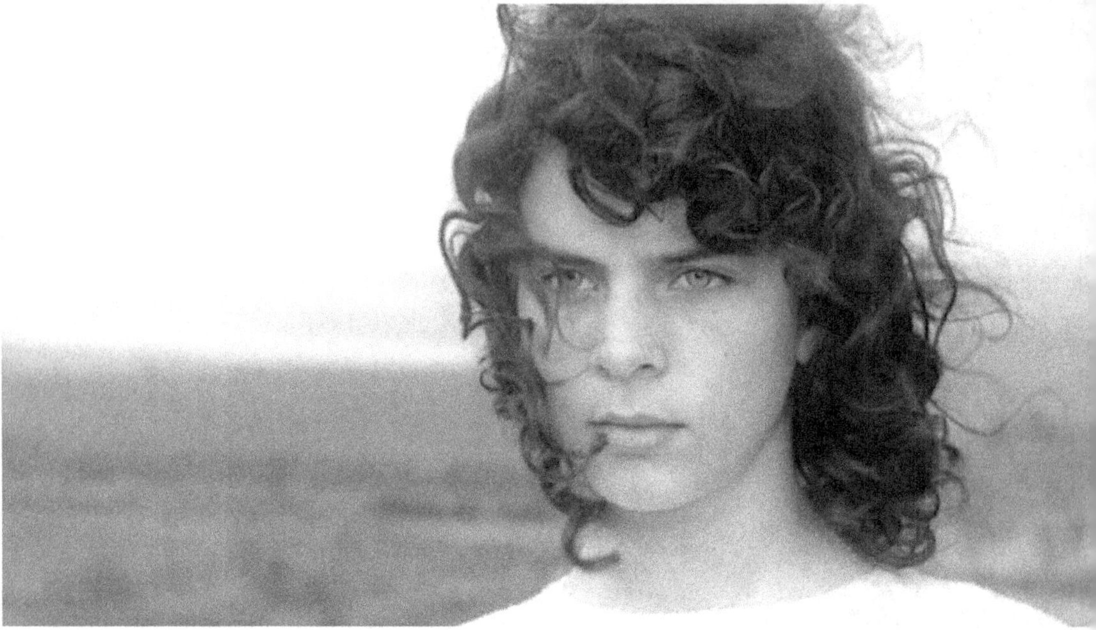

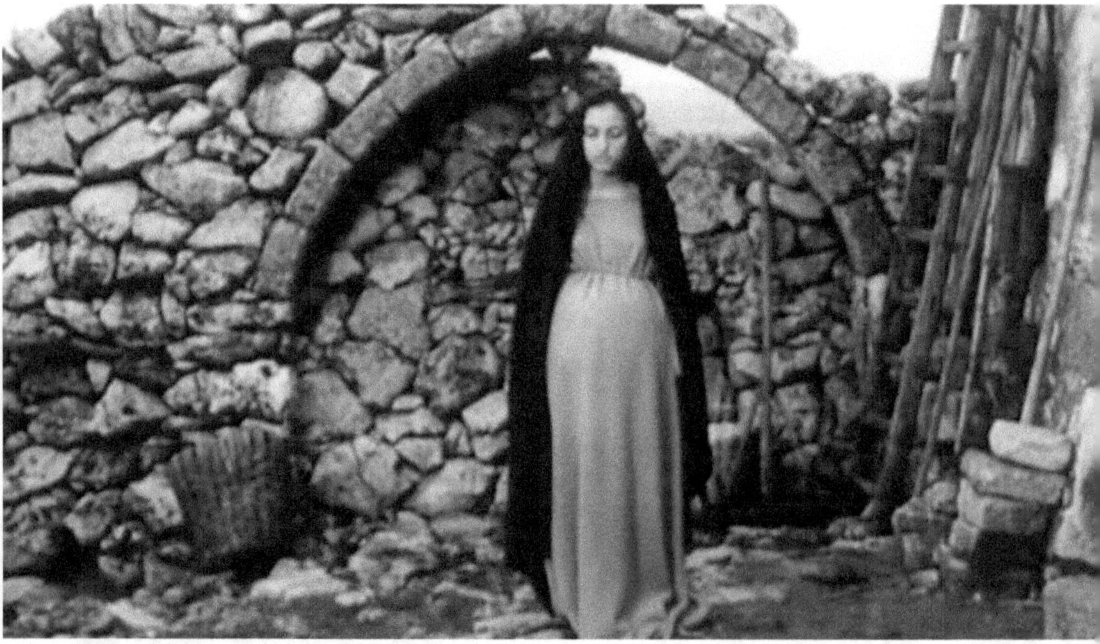

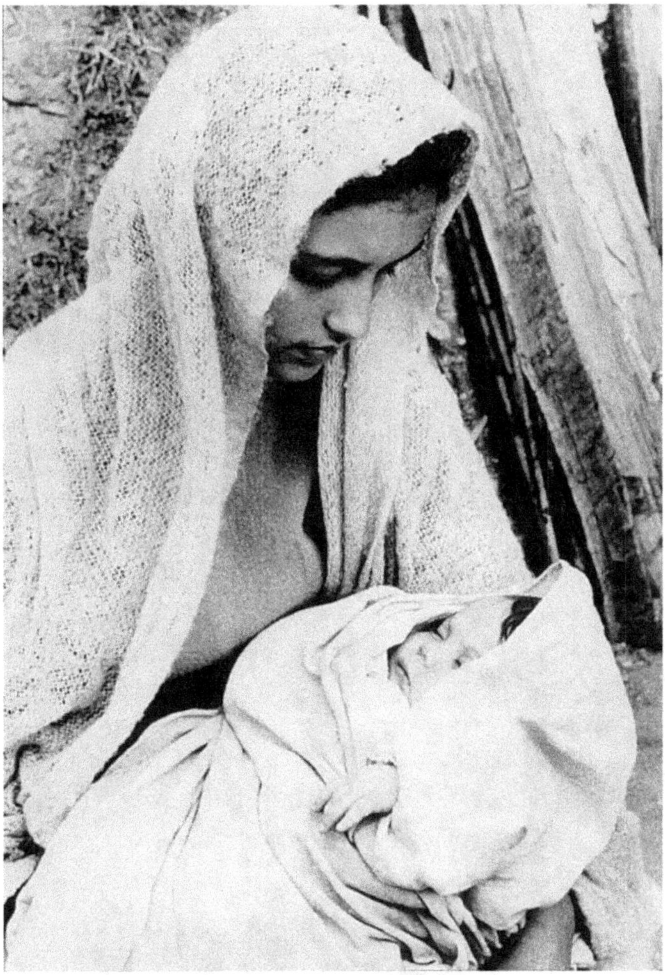

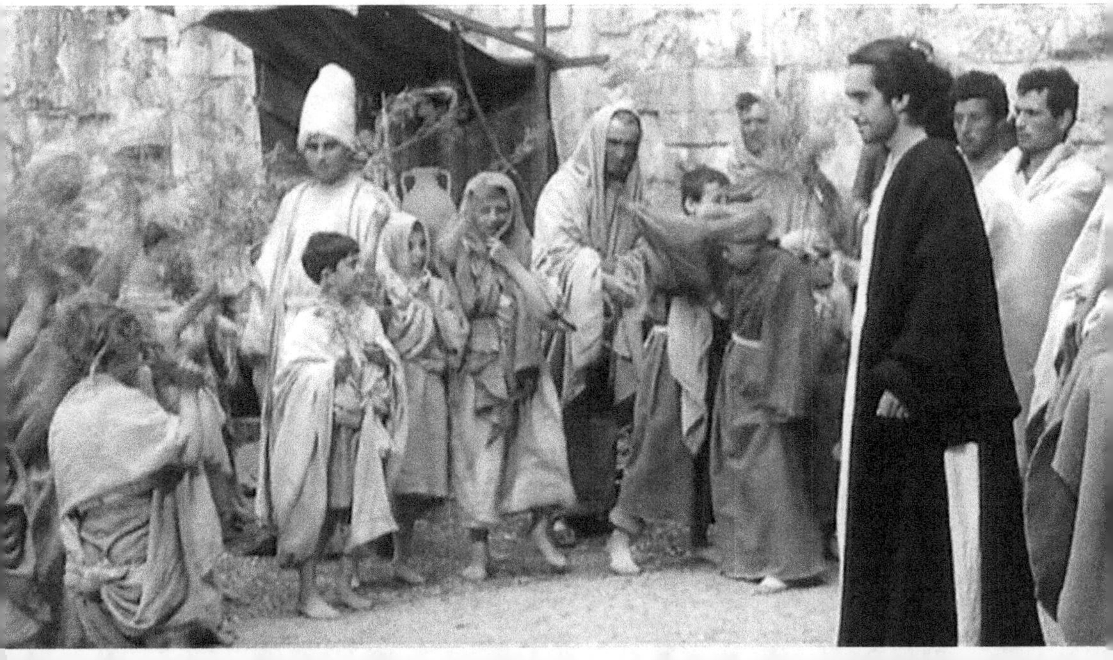

Making The Gospel According To Matthew.
This page and over.

Location Hunting In Palestine(1965).

9

UCCELLACCI E UCCELLINI

THE HAWKS AND THE SPARROWS

The fifth feature directed by Pier Paolo Pasolini was *The Hawks and the Sparrows* (*Uccellacci e Uccellini*) in 1966. The crew comprised Pasolini regulars: Alfredo Bini (prod.), Sergio Citti (A.D.), Nino Baragli (ed.), Tonino Delli Colli and Mario Bernardo (DPs), Danilo Donati (costumes), Luigi Scaccianoce (prod. des.), Ennio Morricone (m),[1] Vincenzo Cerami (A.D.), Vittorio Biseo (make-up), Adriana Cassini (hair), Pietro Ortolani, Franca Silvi and Emilio Rosa (sound), etc. Dante Ferretti[2] is credited with co-writing. Released May 8, 1966. 88 minutes.[3]

The cast of *The Hawks and the Sparrows* featured only two main players: the ageing, Italian comedian Totò[4] (as the father/ Innocenti Totò/ Brother Ciccillo) and Pier Paolo Pasolini's new lover, the irrepressible, eternally grinning, frizzy-haired Nino Davoli (as the son/ Innocenti Ninetto/ Brother Ninetto). Also in the cast were: Femi Benussi, Umberto Bevilacqua, Renato Capogna, Alfredo Leggi, Renato Montalbano, Flaminia Siciliano, Giovanni Tarallo and Vittorio Vittori (some of the bit players you'll recognize from Pasolini's earlier features).[5]

The film was taken to Cannes in 1966. It was filmed around Rome

---

[1] Domenico Modugno sings over the credits; Toto sings 'Carme Carme'.
[2] Credited also as associate production designer.
[3] An episode was filmed but dropped from *The Hawks* – it was yet another satire on the bourgeoisie from Pasolini: Totò taught an eagle how to become a petit bourgeois, but becomes an eagle himself in exchange. When the scene was shortened, to reduce the running time, it didn't work, so it was left out altogether (PP, 107).
[4] That Totò suffered from heart attacks didn't stop Pier Paolo Pasolini making him run and run in some scenes, or clamber up mounds of dirt, or crawl thru fields of crops.
[5] It was filmed near the E.U.R., in Fiumicino, and Tuscania.

(including Viterbo and the airport), in de Paolis Studios, and in Assisi.

Totò (Antonio De Curtis, 1898-1967) was a veteran of numerous films and TV shows, a much-loved clown/ comedian in Italia; this was one of his last films – he died the following year. Wikipedia summed up Totò's persona in cinema thus:

> His personal story (a prince born in the poorest *rione* (section of the city) of Naples), his unique twisted face, his special mimic expressions and his gestures, created an inimitable personage and made him one of the most beloved Italians of the 1960s.

Among Totò's more recent movies were *Totò of Arabia* (1965), *Totò Against the Black Pirate* (1964), and *Totò Against Maciste* (1961). Totò also starred in a Federico Fellini parody (*Peppino and La Dolce Vita*, 1960). After the war, Totò made over 100 films: not all of them were potboilers: Totò also worked with Roberto Rossellini, Vittorio de Sica, Mauro Bolognini, Alessandro Blasetti, Zampa, Aldo Fabrizi, Steno, and Mario Monicelli. Apart from being famous and adored by audiences, another thing in Totò's favour for Pier Paolo Pasolini was that he was born in Naples.[6]

Clowns have been a part of Italian cinema since the early days, and every silent film studio had one: Cretinetti at L'Italia, Polidor at Pasquali, and Tontolini, Lea, Kri Kri and Coco at Cines.

It's understandable that Pier Paolo Pasolini might opt for something lighter and more whimsical after helming three pretty intense movies – *Accattone*, *Mamma Roma* and *The Gospel* (which had also been controversial, with releases troubled by protesters). *The Hawks and the Sparrows* also shows Pasolini happy to send himself up, and his media image as the political iconoclast.

A rambling, episodic, wistful, wry movie, *The Hawks and the Sparrows* centres around the double act of Ninetto Davoli and Totò. They schlepp, they talk, they drift from place to place (once again, filmed around the beloved *borgate* regions of Roma), they encounter people, meet a talking crow, and not much happens. It's Sancho Panza and Don Quixote, Laurel and Hardy,[7] Bob Hope and Bing Crosby in the *Road* movies, the clown and the straight man...

...However, comedy is not Pier Paolo Pasolini's cinema's strongest attribute, and tho' *The Hawks and the Sparrows* does have its comical moments, it is not by any means a successful or even enjoyable film

---

[6] Today images of Totò can be found on the streets of Napoli.
[7] The bickering duo is also reminiscent of Didi and Gogo in *Waiting For Godot* by Samuel Beckett. But, again, not as funny (or as well-written).

viewed as a comedy (and certainly not in the same realm as Laurel and Hardy or the *Road* movies). The humour tends to be somewhat abstract and cerebral, and the physical comedy hasn't aged that well. (I would imagine that being in a packed audience in Rome in 1966 might've been a different story, where the film might've been received warmly. Actors such as Totò generated the sort of good will in an Italian audience of a much-loved comic).[8]

What genre is *The Hawks and the Sparrows*? At times it resembles one of the comedies of Luis Buñuel, where the Spanish master sent up Catholicism in the form of a stroll thru the contemporary, European landscape. But Buñuel's comedies weren't that funny, either (1969's *The Milky Way* comes to mind, where Buñuel, Jean-Claude Carrière (co-writer) Serge Silberman (producer) and others spend a huge amount of time and effort sending up Catholic religion in all its forms (it also features two guys[9] in a road movie format) but the end result is remarkably unfunny). *The Hawks and the Sparrows* is also reminiscent of some of the sillier Jean-Luc Godard movies of the mid-1960s, but not as amusing[10] (Godard's wit was way sharper and more merciless than Pasolini's).

So *The Hawks and the Sparrows* could be seen as a philosophical comedy, a religious comedy, or maybe it's a new genre, a 'Pasolinian comedy' (the maestro had to admit: 'I agree it is not very funny' [PP, 107]). In part, *The Hawks and the Sparrows* is sending up Pasolini's previous work, and how it was perceived by Italian audiences.

The central section of *The Hawks and the Sparrows* is a historical episode where Nino Davoli and Totò play a pair of ordinary monks in the Middle Ages in Italia who're charged with praying to the birds of the world by no less a personage than St Francis himself. I guess two men kneeling on the grass and praying to hawks in a tree or sparrows on the ledge of a crumbling church might be laugh-out-loud good if it was edited sharply, and written well, and staged adroitly (it draws on the band of monk followers in *Francesco*, 1950, a film that Pasolini admired). But the mediæval episode just drags on and on (it's a television skit clumsily extended with little feeling for pace or timing).[11] Yes! We get the point! It's tough being a Catholic monk and being ordered by St Francis to pray to a bunch of birds! Can't we go back to the earlier scene, where Davoli chats up some girls?! (In that too-brief scene (entitled 'Nino and His

---

8 Possibly Pier Paolo Pasolini fancied a change of tone and style with *The Hawks and the Sparrows* from his previous feature, *The Gospel According To Matthew*.
9 Some in the cast worked with Pasolini – Laurent Terzieff, Michel Piccoli and Pierre Clémenti.
10 A road sign which says, 'Cuba, 13,257 km' is stolen wholesale from Godard. There are further gags in the signage in the background of shots.
11 When the birds speak in the subtitles, it is amusing. But consider what the Zucker-Abrahams-Zucker team did with subtitle jokes in *Airplane!* Or the *Scary Movie* series.

Girls'), the beautiful and striking Rossana Di Rocco appears (she was the Archangel Gabriel in *The Gospel According to Matthew*). She plays a girl that Ninetto is keen on, and asks out for a date. In a reference to *The Gospel According to Matthew*, she is being dressed in an angel's outfit (for a local performance for some nuns), and she appears in the windows of a nearby house (to taunt Ninetto even further).) In a nod to the prevalence of pop culture, there's a scene early on of some *ragazzi* dancing to pop music[12] outside the Bar Las Vegas, before they hurry off to chase after the bus.

A brilliantly trained,[13] large, black crow [14] appears in *The Hawks and the Sparrows,* as a sort of surrogate for Pier Paolo Pasolini ('the crow is extremely autobiographical: there is almost total identity between me and the crow' [PP, 100]), another of his teacher figures[15] (but this time voiced by his friend Francesco Leonetti (tho' he sounds like Pasolini), who was Herod in *The Gospel According To Matthew* and a puppeteer in *Caprice Italian Style,* among other roles in Pasolini's films). The crow (or is it a raven? I've been told how to tell them apart, but I forget!), talks, and lectures his charges at length. The father and the son walk, and the bird hops along beside them, prattling on. He introduces a story (yes, you're going to hear a story, whether you like it or not), and that's where we cut to the central Middle Ages sequence.

The Hawks and the Sparrows employs a lot of speeded-up footage – more than any other Pasolini movie. The device comes from silent movies, but there's so much it smacks of desperation. When scenes slow down too much, editor Nino Baragli orders up another fast film sequence.

Death is another issue that *The Hawks and the Sparrows* confronts. Early on the father and the son stumble upon a bunch of rubber-neckers watching the emergency services carrying some bodies out of a home where a domestic murder (or something like it) occurred (or so it seems). They stand and watch because, well, that's what you do, isn't it, when there's a crowd?[16]

□

There's no doubt that some sections of the films directed by Pier Paolo Pasolini are patchy and even downright amateur and feeble – you find weak sequences in *Mamma Roma, The Hawks and the Sparrows,*

---

12 That scene seems Godardian.
13 The animal wrangler was Pino Serpe.
14 Filming the crow was 'an enormous struggle', 'the toughest fight of my life', 'a terrible ordeal', Pasolini recalled (PP, 101).
15 There's a phrase in *The Hawks and the Sparrows* which everyone thought was by Karl Marx, but was in fact by Pope Paul VI.
16 Later in *The Hawks and the Sparrows,* there is a lengthy series of images filmed at the public funeral of Palmiro Togliatti, the leader of the Italian Communist Party (he is also referenced in the dialogue).

Pigsty, and the 'trilogy of life' films. Maybe they don't harm the overall impact of Pasolini's cinema, but there are times when you wish Nino Baragli and the film editors had been fiercer with their scissors. (Certainly, perfectionist film directors, such as Akira Kurosawa or Andrei Tarkovsky, would never allow such sequences to remain in the final cut). Pasolini later admitted that *The Hawks and the Sparrows* had been too heavy-handed with its ideology, and hadn't quite turned out as poetic and mysterious as he had hoped (PP, 113).

The Hawks and the Sparrows is indulgent, too: it has the feel of a movie where the filmmakers were allowed to get away with whatever they liked (provided they were on schedule and on budget). Nobody is standing behind Pasolini and pointing out that, no, this scene isn't funny (*viz.*, Totò putting cream on his feet to soothe them and finding out that it's contraceptive cream. Was that amusing in 1966?).

You could say that *The Hawks and the Sparrows* is orchestrating many of Pier Paolo Pasolini's recurring concerns – religion, Catholicism, prayer, worship, politics, Marxism, education, Rome, the *borgate*, desire – but somehow the 1966 movie isn't strong enough or interesting enough to keep the exploration of those issues buoyant (and it doesn't find the images to support the thematic content, and it doesn't discover the dramatic means to illustrate or explore the issues and the themes).

The Hawks and the Sparrows is one of those films that's not as good as the stuff that's been written about it (as with the works of Lars Von Trier, Christopher Nolan, Derek Jarman or Quentin Tarantino). For example, Enzo Siciliano in his outstanding biography of Pier Paolo Pasolini, evokes the poetry, the pathos, the heart and the philosophy of this 1966 movie, but I can't see it. I mean, rather, I know it's there, but it's presented in such a casual, almost throwaway manner, it barely registers. (Seeing *Totò Versus the Martian Concubines* might be preferrable).

Meanwhile, Sam Rohdie in *The Passion of Pier Paolo Pasolini* reckons that *The Hawks and the Sparrows* is about 'the end of ideology and the end of commitment', it's about the eradication of the olde worlde that Pier Paolo Pasolini enshrined, a world in which the politics of revolution and committment were possible (136). *The Hawks and the Sparrows* is the swansong for that.

Again, the 1966 movie doesn't hold up to such assessments: it is simply too nonchalant, too diffuse, too casually incoherent (yet also too pedantic and preachy), to justify such a grand, ideological assessment. Or, put it like this, Pier Paolo Pasolini said everything he wanted to say in

The Hawks and the Sparrows far better in films such as *Salò* and *Theorem* and *Mamma Roma*. And in his poetry. (Maybe *The Hawks and the Sparrows* would fare better if it had been entitled *Notes For a Film Called The Hawks and the Sparrows*. It's a rambling, essay-ish film that just doesn't work).

Compare *The Hawks and the Sparrows* with *Weekend* (1967), the *tour-de-force*, apocalyptic extravaganza directed by without question the key European director of the 1960s, along with Ingmar Bergman – Jean-Luc Godard. *Weekend* is a scorching, *incredibly* furious, *astonishingly* angry movie which is also very funny, very silly, very over-the-top, and very enjoyable. *Weekend* makes pretty much all movies with similar targets and realms of operation (including Pasolini's own *Salò*) look weedy by comparison. *Weekend* takes on all of the *bête noires* of Pasolini's that appear in *The Hawks and the Sparrows*, but not only goes much further, it is infinitely more accomplished. (I guess I prefer Pasolini when he's on fire – *Accattone*, *Salò* or *The Gospel According To Matthew* – rather than puttering along like a 50cc moped that's running out of gas).[17]

☐

In a road movie or quest format, related in episodes, there are bound to be some sections that're weaker than others. The early scene where the travellers join the rubberneckers outside the murder house is poor, as is the skit where they meet a bunch of people pushing a Cadillac car, and witness a baby's birth (parts of the Cadillac scene are terrible, viewed in isolation).

The skit featuring a band of travelling players who have a huge American car (which's broken down), seems to be partly a pop at Federico Fellini's form of cinema (we know that Pier Paolo Pasolini and Fellini had fallen out badly over the fate of *Accattone*). The scene contains ingredients which don't add up – like the procession of people that isn't explained (they walk behind Totò and Ninetto), which evokes the penchant in Fellini's work to turn scenes into festivals or celebrations for no particular reason other than conjuring up colour, noise and movement. The inconsequential tone of this episode in *The Hawks and the Sparrows* seems to be sending up the Fellini Circus.

One skit in *The Hawks and the Sparrows* hits the dirt like a dead duck, and you wonder how it ever made it into the final cut. It features a poor mother struggling to feed her family by cooking birds' nests (they live in a hovel). Survival, food, poverty and eating are recurring motifs in

---

17 And so some sallow, Caravaggian youth has to push it back home to the tenements outside Roma.

Pasolini's work (like the hungry guy Stracci in *Curd Cheese* who overeats and dies, or the subproletariat fighting to survive in Rome's poor suburbs in *Accattone*).

But this skit is one of those scenes which not only hasn't aged well, it's desperately unamusing, and contains bits of business which perplex: like, the use of cod-Chinese music, and the derogatory references to Chinese people.

☐

Late in the 1966 piece some newsreel footage of the public funeral of the Italian Communist Party leader Palmiro Togliatti thru the streets of Rome plays; it is clumsily integrated into *The Hawks and the Sparrows* (as if father and son just happen to stumble across thousands of people thronging the streets, when they are obviously nowhere near, in time or space. And then they wander off and do something else!). What has this public event got to do with the rest of *The Hawks and the Sparrows*? Is it another Godardian device, turning *The Hawks and the Sparrows* into a film-essay? It's an awkward interval in the movie (but it lasts three minutes).

Similarly, one of the skits in this part of *The Hawks and the Sparrows* is a pop at the social world of ridiculous, pompous aristocrats and intellectuals, when father and son stumble into a posh *soirée*. The skit seems a send-up of the subjects taken up by directors such as Luchino Visconti (and the cast of eccentrics at the party inevitably evokes the films of Federico Fellini, and *La Dolce Vita* in particular).

The penultimate skit in *The Hawks and the Sparrows* is an erotic dalliance with a young woman called Luna (Femi Benussi[18]), who's waiting on the roadside near the Leonardo da Vinci airport in Fiumicino. Why this segment wasn't put much earlier, where you'd expect it, is a mystery. (Pier Paolo Pasolini explained the woman represents vitality, life, and the story starts up again after death and grief). Daddy and sonny take turns with the *donna* in a field.[19]

And then the heroes eat the crow (eating gods, the Roman Catholic Mass, etc,[20] where our heroes assimilate Marxism); and *The Hawks and the Sparrows* simply stutters to halt – with father and son walking off into the sunset – rather than finishing with a more satisfying close.

☐

There's no doubting the energy of Ninetto Davoli in *The Hawks and the Sparrows,* tho', or Totò delivering the comic timing and facial

---

[18] A star of Italian exploitation pictures.
[19] Nino's idea of a romantic line is to mention a hooker that he and the boys go with, who's, like, a 100, with no nose.
[20] A bit of cannibalism that looks forward to *Pigsty* and *Salò*.

expressions of the professional comedian (you can see why, for instance, Totò was a much-loved comic in Italy). As Enzo Siciliano put it:

> The film has an abstract and intangible plot; the adventures are flimsy and symbolical, but they are saved by Totò's irresistible performance and the unequivocal vitality of Ninetto. (297)

In later movies, Pier Paolo Pasolini would place an enormous amount of the impact of his movies on the performance of his lover Nino Davoli (which must've put some pressure on the actor). But it didn't always pay off, and Davoli wasn't always able to save the scenes (Davoli, at least in the way that Pasolini directs him, and using Pasolini's material, isn't wholly successful or satisfying as an actor or as a comic actor. But then, I reckon quite a few actors would've struggled with some of the things that Pasolini thought were amusing, or that he wanted actors to do in a scene). And Davoli, 18 at the time, is just too young and inexperienced at comedy to match Totò (that is, the straight man in a comic duo has to do some work, too – *viz.*, Laurel and Hardy or Bing Crosby and Bob Hope).

Am I being harsh about the 'comedy' in Pier Paolo Pasolini's movies? Yes! Comic geniuses like Woody Allen, Mel Brooks or the Zucker-Abrahams-Zucker team would have done one thing with Pasolini's material: cut-cut-CUT! Cut that scene with the Ninetto Davoli as Charlie Chaplin in *The Canterbury Tales*, or Davoli's goofing off in *The Hawks and the Sparrows*. Or at least trimmed the scenes down![21]

☐

OK, let's put aside comedy and humour, and look at the rest of *The Hawks and the Sparrows*. The wistful, nostalgic aspects of the duologues are entertaining, as if, as the father and the son walk along the new but unfinished freeways in the present day, they are lamenting the passing of the Olde Worlde, the Rome they knew in their youth. The ugliness of those concrete bridges and roads says it all – the image of how these modern constructions blast thru the Roman *campagna* is enough on its own. Capitalism, authority, the sacrifice of Old Europe for the New World following World War Two, it's all evoked here.

But the wistful longing for the Olde Worlde isn't successfully rendered in *The Hawks and the Sparrows*, either. Surely Totò, as Italy's beloved clown, would be able to bring a tear to the eye over Italy's vanishing culture?

---

21 But, using the approach of Brooks or Zucker-Abrahams-Zucker would mean that *The Hawks and the Sparrows* would be reduced to about ten minutes!

The Hawks and the Sparrows (1966).
This page and over.

The surprise comedy hit of the New York Film Festival.
"A FASCINATING FILM ...keen mocking humor."
— Bosley Crowther, N. Y. Times
"AMUSINGLY FRESH AND NICELY CRAZY ...endearing charm ...a wildly comic fable."
— Frances Herridge, N. Y. Post
"DELIGHTFUL ...the whole show is wonderfully fey."
— Time Magazine
AWARDS
TOTO
Special Prize Winner
CANNES FILM FESTIVAL
GOLDEN GLOBE AWARD
THE HAWKS AND THE SPARROWS
(UCCELLACCI E UCCELLINI)
Written and Directed by PIER PAOLO PASOLINI
Starring the inimitable TOTO
Also starring NINETTO DAVOLI AND THE WORLD'S ONLY TALKING CROW
Produced by ALFREDO BINI
Released by BRANDON FILMS, INC.

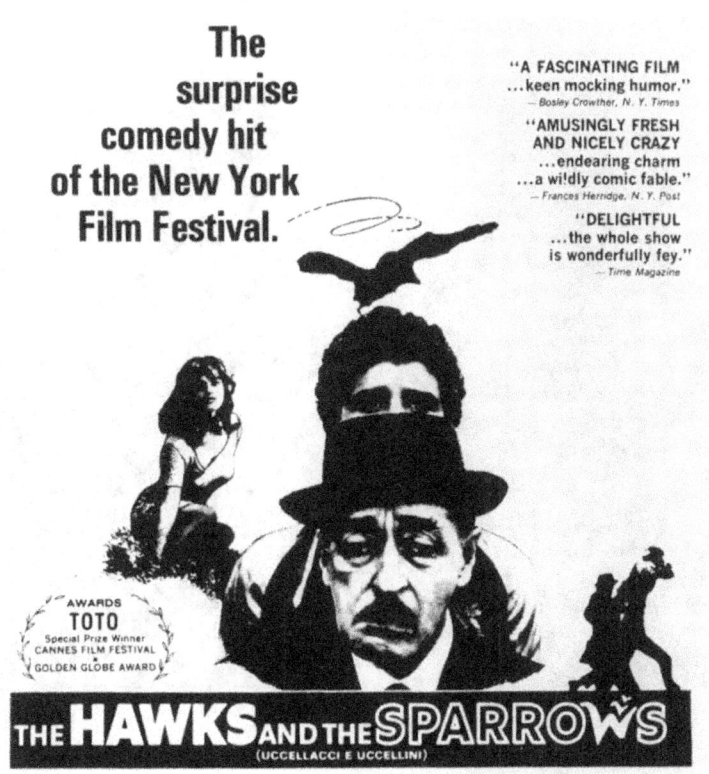

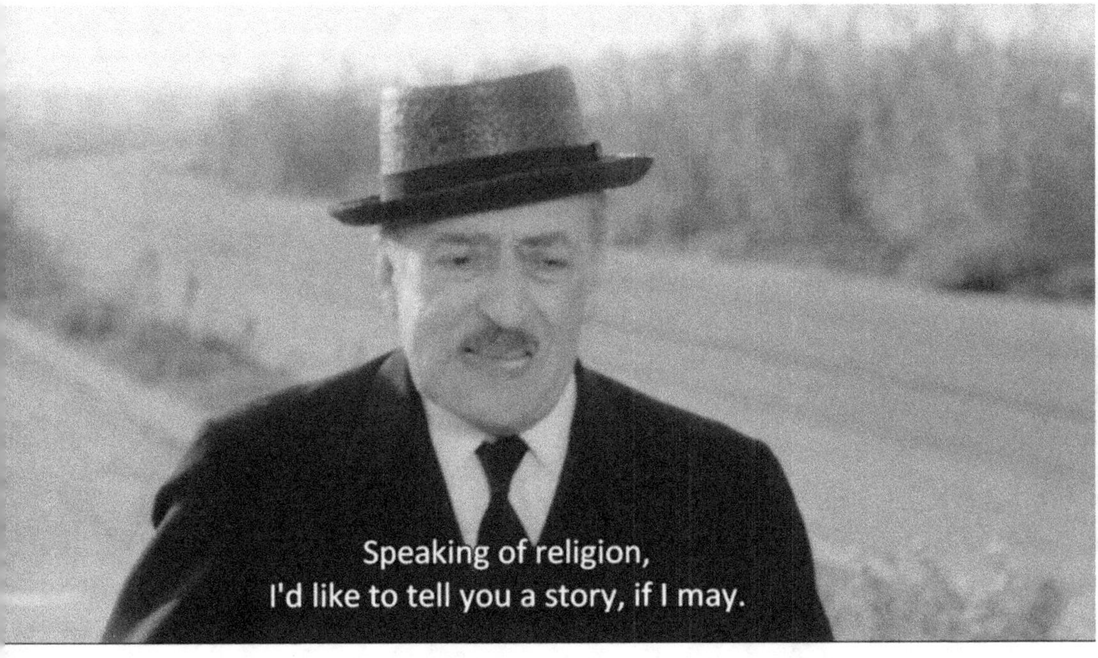
Speaking of religion,
I'd like to tell you a story, if I may.

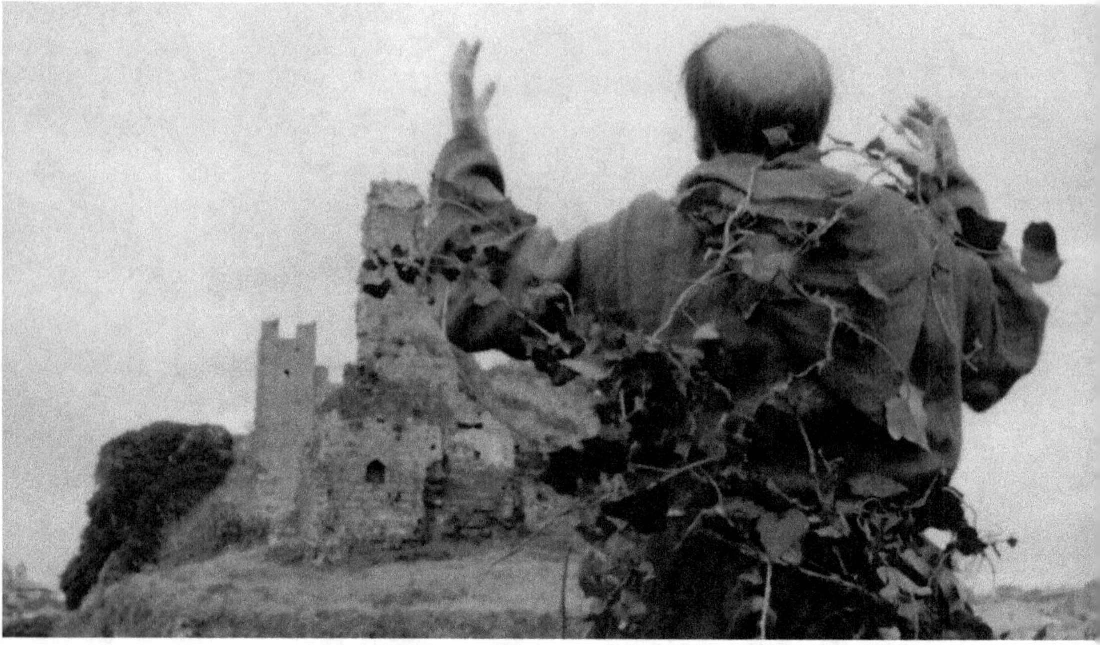

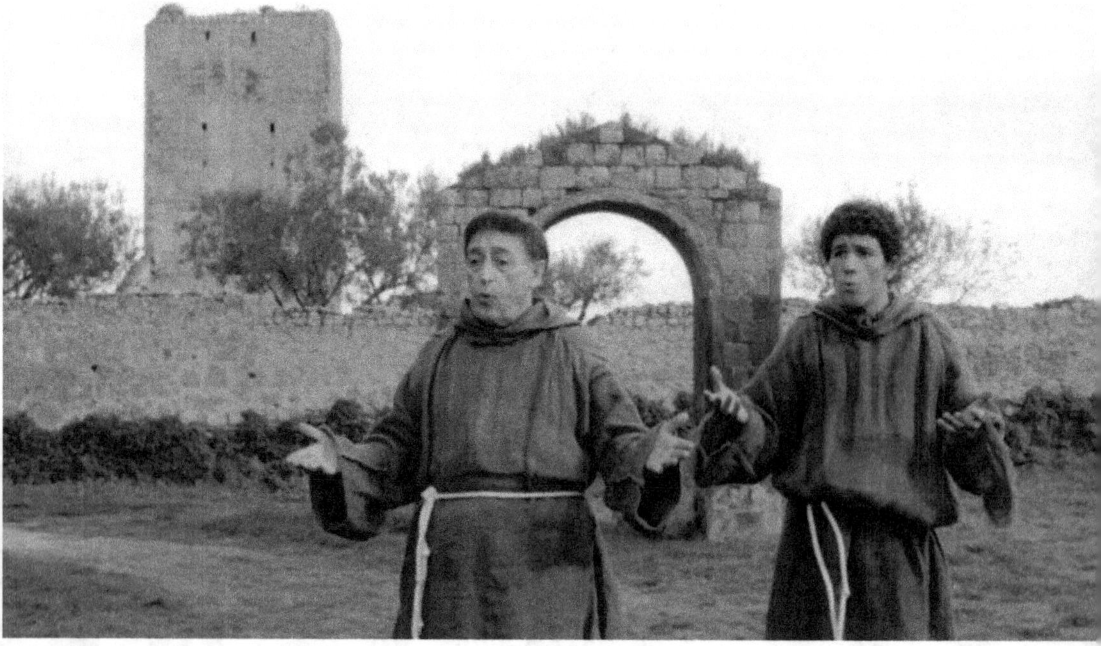

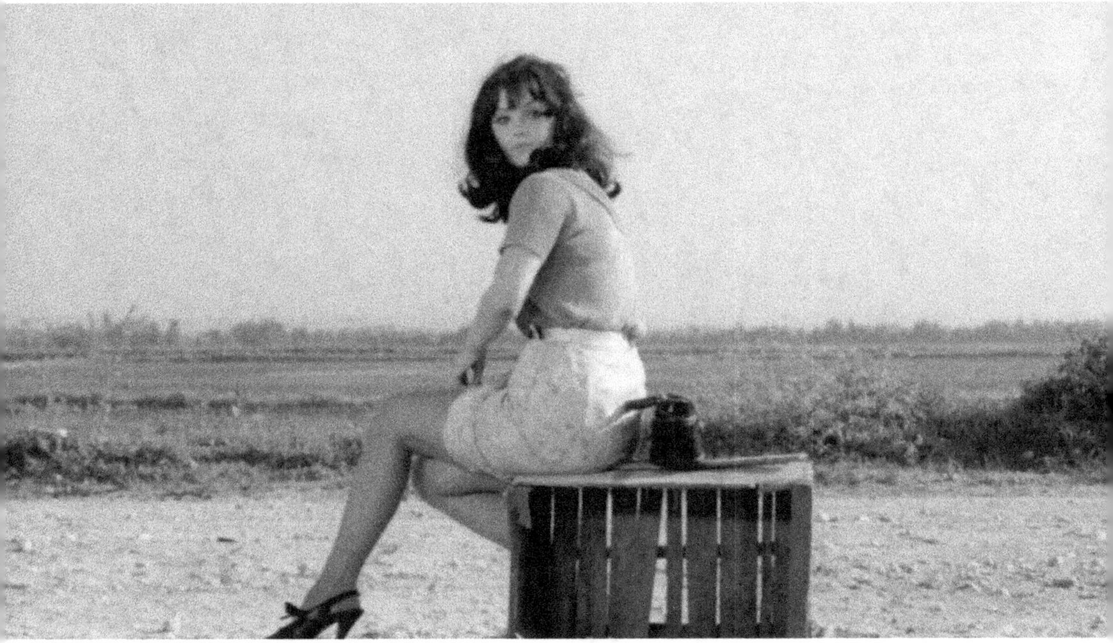

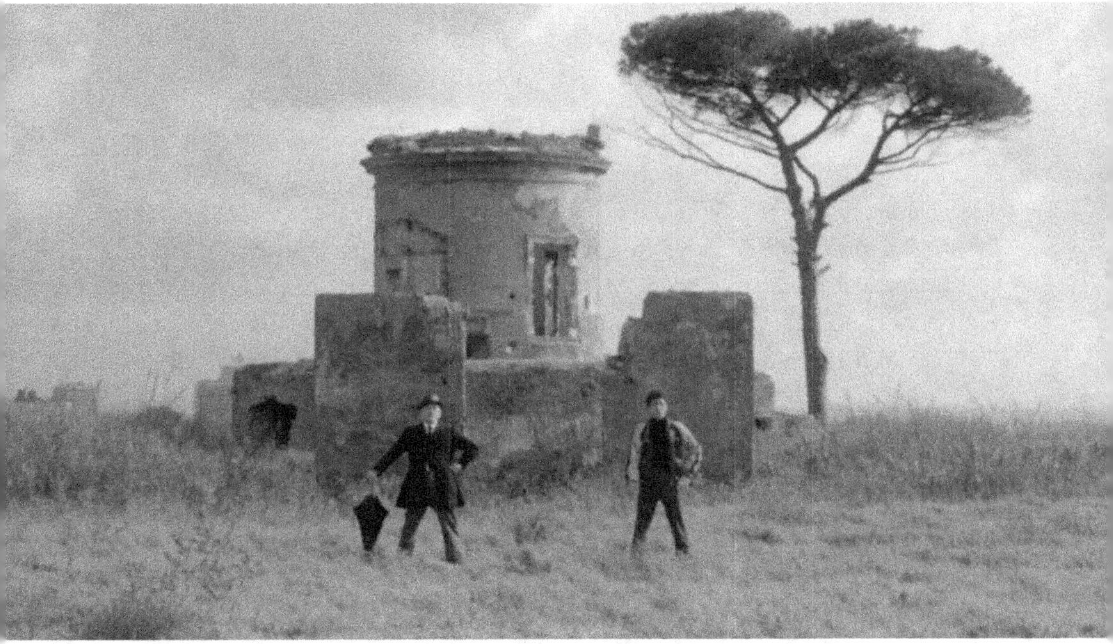

10

EDPIO RE

OEDIPUS REX

...But since I possess history,
it possesses me; I am illuminated by it:

but what good is the light?

Pier Paolo Pasolini, 'The Ashes of Gramsci'

INTRODUCTION.

The 1967 version of Sophocles' *Oedipus Rex* and *Oedipus at Colonus*[1] (a.k.a. *Edipo Re*), directed by Pier Paolo Pasolini is, like Pasolini's other films from ancient sources, a stark, sometimes brutal and uncompromising work. With their customary deftness and economy, Pasolini and the team conjure up a convincing and poignant depiction of an Ancient Mediterranean or Middle Eastern world.[2] It's a self-consciously multi-cultural production: an Italian cast and crew take a Greek story and film it in North Africa and Italy, backed with music from Eastern Europe and Japan. The familiar Pasolinian trademarks are here: the barren, dusty landscapes, the Middle Eastern locales, the peasants, the extras and actors drawn from local people, the wide range of human types and faces, the use of unusual folk music (in this case from Romania,[3] Indonesian and

---

[1] *Hercules Unchained* (Pietro Francisci, 1959), one of the early lucrative *Hercules* sequels, was based on *Oedipus At Colonus* by Sophocles.
[2] Locations included Bologna (San Petronio Basilica, Piazza Maggiore, and the Palazzo Communale); Emilia-Romagna; Lodigiano; Pisa; and Morocco.
[3] Pier Paolo Pasolini had scouted locations in Romania, but found it too modern. The Romanian songs come from the album *Anthology of Romanian Folk Music* on the Electrecord label.

Japan), mixed with Western, classical music (such as Wolfgang Amadeus Mozart's *Quartet in C Major, K. 475*, *Marcetta Bandistica* by Antonio Fuselli, and *In Santa Lucia* by Otto Stransky), the jump cuts, the sudden eruptions of violence, and the fantastic (and sometimes bizarre) costumes.

Alfredo Bini produced *Oedipus the King* (for Arco Film); Bini led the Pasolini Circus into the North African desert. The crew included Giuseppe Ruzzolini (DP), Luigi Scaccianoce (prod. des.),[4] Andrea Fantacci (set dec.), Danilo Donati (costumes), Giulio Natalucci and Goffredo Rocchetti (make-up), Ernesta Cesetti and Maria Teresa Corridoni (hair), Fausto Ancillai and Carlo Tarchi (sound), A.D.s: Jean-Claude Biette and Benoît Lamy, and Nino Baragli (editor). Pasolini translated the text. *Oedipus Rex* was premiered at the Venice Film Festival on Sept 3, 1967.[5] 104 minutes.

The cast of *Oedipus Rex* included: Silvana Mangano (Jocasta), Franco Citti[6] (Oedipus), movie icon Alida Valli (Queen Mereope), Carmelo Bene (Creon), Julian Beck[7] (Tiresias), Luciano Bartoli (Laio), Francesco Leonetti (herdsman), Ahmed Belhachmi (King Polybus/ Polibo), Giovanni Ivan Scratuglia (Sacerdote), Giandomenico Davoli (shepherd), Laura Betti (Jocasta's maid), and Ninetto Davoli (Angelo). The maestro has a cameo as a High Priest.[8] The cast includes a huge number of minor roles – for guards, handmaids, workers, etc.

There was a rival production to the 1967 film of *Oedipus Rex* (as occasionally occurs in cinema's marketplace)*: Oedipus the King* (Philip Saville, 1968) was a British project with a terrific actor – Christopher Plummer – in the title role. Another connection in this version to Pasolini was Orson Welles (playing Tiresais, inevitably); Lilli Palmer, Richard Johnson and Cyril Cussack also appeared. A solid if predictable rendering of Sophocles' play (a good flick for students who're revising for a test on Sophocles the next day, as Leonard Maltin[9] put it in his *Movie and Video Guide*), *Oedipus the King* didn't have the art cinema flourishes of the Italian version.[10]

□
SOPHOCLES.

Sophocles (496-406 B.C.) was born near Athens, in Colonus. Of the

---

[4] With Dante Ferretti as assistant.
[5] It was nominated for the Golden Lion Award.
[6] Citti is credited as being dubbed by Paolo Ferraro (his dub actor in *Accattone*). But why did Pasolini have Citti dubbed again, having said it was a mistake to replace Citti's voice in *Accattone*?
[7] Beck (1925-85) was an American theatre director.
[8] Tho' he too seems to be dubbed.
[9] But Maltin didn't go for the Pasolini version, calling it a 'pictorially arresting but dull, disappointing adaptation'.
[10] Incidentally, director Philip Saville went on to direct, aged 73, a big TV mini-series of the life of Christ, *The Gospel of John* (2003), which was a solid, convincing piece of work.

100+ plays that Sophocles is supposed to have created, seven tragedies have survived: *Ajax, Antigone, Electra, Philoctetes,* the *Trachiniæ, Oedipus the King* (written in 428 B.C.) and *Oedipus At Colonus.*

As *The Oxford Companion To the Theatre* notes:

> Few moments in drama are more poignant than Sophocles' tragic climaxes. His language, compared to that of Aeschylus, is clearer and more incisive, his characters are more fully rounded; but he inherited his predecessor's concern with questions of moral law, though he set those questions in a framework with which his audience could more immedately identify. (777)

There is an element of mystery and ambiguity in *Oedipus Rex*, the play: the events in the end seem to be unfair, and the Gods beyond comprehension. That Oedipus condemns himself, that he is revealed to be the murderer, that he has married his own mother, and killed his father, is one of the great storylines of all tragedy in literature. But there is also something about the suffering that Oedipus undergoes, and the way that he is condemned by the Gods, that seems beyond logic or understanding. As James Davidson noted in his study of homosexuality in Ancient Greece:

> Oedipus didn't know what he was doing, he has acted reasonably, heroically, responsibility; it is all so unfair. It is entirely possible that this mysterious sense of ultimate dissatisfaction was part of Sophocles' plan. (234)

The plays *Oedipus the King* and *Oedipus At Colonus* have proved themselves to be powerful enough without needing modern-day entry-points for the audience. The 1967 movie doesn't need the prologue or the epilogue. Pier Paolo Pasolini knew that, but he seems to have wanted the autobiographical resonances, to personalize this particular story to a striking degree. And he was very proud of the prologue, reckoning it was one of the best things he'd done. (Pasolini talked about trying to make *Oedipus Rex* a 'completely metaphoric – and therefore mythicized – autobiography' [PP, 120]).

☐

Oedipus the King employs many of the filmic devices that Pasolini and co. had already developed in films such as *The Gospel According To Matthew* and *Accattone*. Indeed, if *The Gospel According To Matthew* had been filmed in colour, it might've looked like *Oedipus Rex* (and *Medea*). We have the *tableau* approach, for example: a scene is staged in flat planes for the camera, which slowly pans across faces and bodies (maybe a quarter of the scenes in *The Gospel According To Matthew* were filmed like that).

Oedipus the King takes place simultaneously in a symbolic, mythic realm[11] and a recognizable, Middle Eastern world, of the 'Third World', people in peasant clothing, cattle and donkeys, and isolated settlements. In the midst of the earthy, dusty landscapes, part-desert and part-scrubland, which could be anywhere in the present day Middle East from the Maghreb to India (but is actually Morocco), the 1967 Italian movie places symbolic milestones bearing the insignia of the past ('Thebes' and 'Corinth').

As in films such as *Medea* and *The Gospel According To Matthew*, *Oedipus Rex* brilliantly fuses costumes from Mexico and the Maghreb, music from Japan and Romania, actors from the Roman *borgate* and extras from Morocco, accents from Sicily, Ancient Greek mythology and literature, and Freudian psychology (not every filmmaking team would be able to make this work, but Pier Paolo Pasolini's vision blends it all together, altho' Howard Hughes carps that the costumes look 'at once authentic and risibly bogus').[12]

Mixing the ancient world and the modern world was one of Pasolini's favourite cinematic devices – had he continued with his film plans after 1975, to produce his version of *St Paul* and other projects, we would have seen more scenes set in both the modern-day West (such as New York City) and the ancient world (Pasolini filming in Gotham is an enticing prospect. Surely Pasolini would've filmed New York like it had never been seen in movies before).

Oedipus the King again confirms Pier Paolo Pasolini as one of the great epic film directors, marshalling large crowd scenes, hundreds of costumes and props, all sorts of animals, and handling the complex logistics of working on location far from the studio. The assistant directors – Jean-Claude Biette and Benoît Lamy – were invaluable in organizing it all. (However, *Oedipus Rex* was not all filmed on location: there is studio work for some of the interiors, for example (such as the Thebes palace scenes).)

One of the stars of *Oedipus Rex* is definitely Giuseppe Ruzzolini: the cinematography is ravishing, a marvel of textures, and light of all kinds (unreal day-for-night scenes, a disturbing half-light, firelight, candlelight, and light splintering the lens). Ruzzolini's incredible camerawork also captures the unique costumes of Danilo Donati, bringing out their colour.

---

11 The central section of *Oedipus Rex* was meant to have the feeling of a dream, Pier Paolo Pasolini remarked. 'I wanted it to be a kind of æstheticizing dream' (PP, 122).
12 H. Hughes, 26.

(*Oedipus Rex* is a visual feast: alongside Donati and Ruzzolini were Luigi Scaccianoce as production designer, with Dane Ferretti as his assistant).

Franco Citti's Oedipus is stoic, determined, ruthless, and given to violent outbursts. His is the best performance in the 1967 movie – with Silvana Mangano's Jocasta – and it is probably a career high for the 29 year-old Citti (even more than Accattone). Giuseppe Ruzzolini's camera concentrates on Citti's handsome face in long, moving close-ups (especially in the final act); Pier Paolo Pasolini is clearly in love with (the look of) his leading man. (And yet, some have said that Citti is mis-cast; there is some truth in that – there are times when Citti struggles to circumnavigate the intricate layers and depths of this remarkable role in tragic theatre.[13] Oedipus is a very challenging role – it needs plenty of thought from an actor, and preferably a strong director, with a vision. The issue of being miscast for Citti, then, might apply to this particular version of *Oedipus Rex*, with its extreme stylization. There are certainly times when Citti seems to be fighting the heightened cinematic form).

Editor Nino Baragli employs the New Wave techniques of jump cuts and discontinuity, as after the visit to the Oracle, where shots of Oedipus surrounded by people and cattle are intercut with shots of Oedipus alone (and point-of-view shots, as Oedipus makes his way back through the crowd).[14] This is a lengthy sequence of shock and dismay for Oedipus, as he reels from the encounter with the Oracle (this forms the climax of act one).

Pier Paolo Pasolini's choice of settings is as sublime as usual in *Oedipus the King*. Pasolini again displays his præternatural ability to eke out the most unusual (as well as suitable) locations. The walled city of Ouarzazate was the primary town location in *Oedipus Rex*, and Giuseppe Ruzzolini's *macchina fotografica* pans back and forth along the long, red city walls many times.

Filming in Morocco has the 1967 Italian movie using Moorish and Islamic architecture as a correspondence for the Ancient Greek settings of Sophocles' play. It works (in the main), even tho' Ancient Greece never looked like this (where are the olive trees, the temples and columns, the dazzling ocean, the Attic costumes and faces?). Locations in Morocco included Zagora, Ait-Ben-Haddou and film favourites such as Ouarzazate (Ouarzazate was used in *Lawrence of Arabia, Gladiator, The Mummy, The Man Who Would Be King, The Living Daylights, Kingdom of Heaven, Game of Thrones,* etc), and numerous valleys, alleys, fields, out-

---

[13] The way he bites his hand, for example, seems a rather overly theatrical, silent movie gesture.
[14] Pasolini said he filmed the same scenes with Oedipus on his own, and also with the crowd (PP, 127)

buildings, gateways, walls, stairs and windows.

Who is the star of *Oedipus Rex*?

Sophocles?
Pier Paolo Pasolini?
Franco Citti?

I think it might be Morocco.[15]

Closely followed by Danilo Donati, whose costumes and designs steal the human-made parts of the show.

STYLE, STAGING, DESIGN, MUSIC.

Oedipus Rex is not naturalistic or literal; it employs disruptive editing;[16] professional actors and locals; handheld camerawork; looped dialogue and sound fx; and folk and classical music.

Dialogue is dispensed with in *Oedipus the King*: where Sophocles and his fellow Greeks Aeschylus and Euripides invented modern drama by having everything talked about (or sung by the chorus), the movie adaption of *Oedipus Rex* drops much of the text. But it also *doesn't* find visual or aural or other correlatives for the dialogue, or for the information contained in the dialogue. (Yet, perversely, *Oedipus Rex* does include captions which use selections from Sophocles' text. Perverse, because the dialogue could just as easily be delivered by the characters in the scenes. But the filmmakers have clearly decided *not* to do things the usual way!).[17]

The music in *Oedipus Rex* includes Japanese folk music (with a mournful, piercing whistle and ominous, thudding drums[18]), Romanian and Indonesian folk music, a string quartet, a Russian folk song (another of the revolutionary songs of the Resistance in WW2 which Pasolini was fond of), and choral music. The movie begins and ends in the 20th century Italian setting, which is accompanied by, appropriately, the cool, elegant sounds of Wolfgang Amadeus Mozart.

Altho' the selection of music in *Oedipus the King* is quirky, impressive and powerful, there are times when you miss something fixed closer to the content of the images. For example, the dancers in the 1967 movie are clearly not dancing to the music we hear, and neither are the musicians playing drums, woodwind and brass instruments on screen

---

15 *Oedipus Rex* is certainly one of the great movies of North Africa and Morocco.
16 Not all the time: the movie is actually conventionally edited.
17 Is this once again the influence of Jean-Luc Godard, without doubt the Dragon Emperor in all cinema of using captions and written text in movies.
18 Music that might accompany one of Akira Kurosawa's historical dramas.

making the music we hear (as often happens in movies). The picture might benefit from some direct sound, so that we can hear the goatskin hoop drums which the musicians are beating with their palms (drum groups like that make a terrific sound – if you've been in the middle of a gathering of drummers, you'll know what I mean!). But no, *Oedipus Rex*'s soundtrack replaces the Moroccan drummers with yet more pre-recorded folk music. And that simply doesn't match the vitality of the images, particularly with the Eastern European music, which isn't exotic enough to match these scenes. (Ah, yes, here I am *again* yearning for direct sound in an Italian movie of the 1960s! It ain't gonna happen!).

Oedipus the King might be one of the great 'hat' movies. I can't think of another film director who so fetishized hats. Danilo Donati was costume designer (who else could it be?!): he and his assistants were the ones who actually came up with that remarkable head gear.

It raises a laugh to even draw attention to hats! But in the cinema of Pier Paolo Pasolini, hats and headdresses are foregrounded to an extravagant degree.[19] (Piero Gherardi, who designed for Federico Fellini, was another hat lover, as was Piero Tosi, who designed *Medea* for Pasolini and many films for Luchino Visconti). *Oedipus Rex* is one of the best examples of the maestro's love of outlandish (or out-hattish) headdresses: the massive, wide-brimmed hat Oedipus wears; the giant hat with three eagle's wings on each side;[20] the soldier's metal helmets; the tall, blue headdresses of Oedipus's palace officials; the tall-as-a-tower gold crown of King Laius; the double-headed crown of the Oracle; and the giant, 'primitive' mask of the Sphinx.

SOME SCENES.

Let's have a look at some of the scenes in *Oedipus Rex*. It contains scenes of violence,[21] murder and sex: Oedipus tupping his mother, murdering his father and guards, and blinding himself. The most shocking scene is where Oedipus dispatches the four guards and King Laius.[22] It is played in a quasi-real time, in a strange, near-silent sequence, the silence broken by Oedipus's panting as he runs, his crazed screams as

---

[19] To the point that a costume designer working for Pier Paolo Pasolini has to be great with hats! They know that, if they're going on location, they'd better make a whole battery of hats, including multiples for hats that get damaged (which, filming in those tough, rocky locations, is going to happen!).
[20] What did Franco Citti think when Danilo Donati put this hat on him?!
[21] Sometimes the British cinema ratings system can appear illogical. Some films are given classifications which seem too low, while others receive ratings which are too high. Pier Paolo Pasolini's *Oedipus Rex* is classed as a '15' certificate in Britain, and contains scenes of violence, murder and sex: Oedipus taking his mother, killing his father and guards, and blinding himself. The sex and violence isn't as graphic as in contemporary '15' and '18' rated films (and would pass as 'PG-13'/ '12' today); compared with the relentless gore and brutality in *Braveheart* (Mel Gibson, 1995), for example.
[22] Killing the father, a recurring Pasolinian theme, is part of Pasolini's next film but one, *Pigsty*.

he attacks each guard, and the clank of sword-on-sword. Oedipus is shown running away from the King and company along a stony, desert road[23] (for a *long* time), then turning to face and attack each soldier.[24] The killing is swift and ignoble, and much more visceral than many Hollywood action movies with their special effects, animatronic limbs flying off, Dolby-enhanced slicings and groans and buckets of blood.

The filmmakers create a sense of the long, long road, in the middle of nowhere, inhabited by dust, sunlight and silence, then these eruptions of violence and death. Oedipus is often framed against the sun in the fights,[25] invoking tropes of divinity, kingship and power, but also his future blindness (even in the brilliant light, Oedipus still can't see who these people are). DP Giuseppe Ruzzolini allows the sun to shine directly into the lens several times, making use of the existing context, a favourite New Wave technique; Oedipus and his victims are composed against the low sun.

Oedipus's first act of violence has several disorientating aspects: it includes cowardly acts (he throws a rock at one of the guards then turns and flees). But rapidly it becomes senseless: there is no strong reason for Oedipus, in movie terms, as the movie presents it, to threaten the King's entourage, nor for the entourage to threaten him. Oedipus stands in the road, and the entourage demands he move aside to let them pass. He declines. (Is Oedipus having a bad day? Does he have a headache and decides to take it out on the people in his way? Is he simply being stubborn? No, let's be serious here: is he driven to fulfil the prophecy at Delphi, no matter what he does? Is he a doomed soul, a lost soul? Does he oppose the King and his bodyguards for thoroughly nihilistic reasons? Does he attack them precisely because it's senseless/ pointless/ affectless? Is he driven by the Furies, the divine powers that also rage through the *Medea* movie?).

As Oedipus explains later in the film (in the third act), he opposed King Laius and his entourage because the King hoped to dominate him, to subjugate him to his will. And Oedipus, as we see throughout the film, doesn't listen to anybody: the stubborn resistance or rebellion is given a very Pasolinian, Existential twist in *Oedipus Rex* (we saw the seeds of it in *Accattone*).

The Sphinx sequence is another scene in *Oedipus the King* where the

---

23 It's a harsh, empty setting.
24 One of the soldiers collapses in exhaustion after running half a mile (understandable in that heat. For the actors, this might be the 5th take).
25 When Oedipus brutally murders Laius's guards in the desert, and the camera is down on the ground, looking up at Oedipus, who's framed against the setting sun, moving back and forth against the light (it's far more powerful than the similar moment in the Steven Spielberg-directed *Empire of the Sun*, 1987).

conventions of filmic narration are put aside in favour of an almost documentary approach to presenting a series of movements and actions. It isn't, to put it politely, the most successful segment of *Oedipus Rex*. In fact, it has very little impact – it's probably the most *un*-mysterious Sphinx scene ever put on celluloid. This is a problem, because by killing the masked Sphinx Oedipus is supposedly ridding the kingdom of a spiritual blight. But none of that is dramatized – it's all carried in the hurried and somewhat garbled dialogue of Ninetto Davoli's Angelo (a messenger).[26]

The 1967 movie makes up for this poorly staged section of the Oedipus story by following it with a big, colourful scene full of extras as the victorious Oedipus is led (by Angelo) towards the city to be united with its bride, Jocasta. These scenes are amazing for their vibrancy and stylization – how the filmmakers continue with the *tableau* and frontal/planar approach to staging and photography even in the midst of a brilliant, Moroccan day.

Oedipus making love to his mother is also portrayed as a brutal act, with Oedipus frantically kissing Jocasta's neck and face before lying on top of her.[27] It's a rough, unlovely, loveless coupling, sex with every ounce of eroticism, tenderness or pleasure eviscerated. Silvana Mangano plays Jocasta in a restrained, passive manner, her face hieratic and pale like a Renaissance Madonna (out of Piero della Francesca, perhaps, or the more severe Trecento painters).

Silvana Mangano certainly has one of the most unusual faces in cinema, with her lack of eyebrows enhancing her already scorching, heavily kohled eyes. (Giulio Natalucci and Goffredo Rocchetti did the make-up, and Ernesta Cesetti and Maria Teresa Corridoni did the hair.) However, like Oedipus, we are always outside Jocasta, and we never know anything about her interior life. There is no hint that Jocasta knows who Oedipus is.

The scenes of lovemaking are filmed in a manner that echoes the staging in the framing story (the prologue), with Silvana Mangano playing the same role (thus, Oedipus is placed in the position of his father in the prologue).

The important scene where Tiresias confronts Oedipus, now King of Thebes, seems a little fudged. Here, Tiresias sums up the plot and lays out the themes, but the voice dubbing this time isn't convincing.

---

26 Ninetto Davoli plays Angelo, toothy grin and curly hair firmly in place. Angelo is the messenger (which's how Pier Paolo Pasolini saw Davoli), a bearer of news (and exposition), a fixer, an intermediary (like an angel, Angelo makes the noise of jangly bells as he goes). Angelo survives into the epilogue of *Oedipus Rex*, leading the now-blind and broken Oedipus around modern Italy.
27 Notice that Oedipus's father does the same in the prologue.

Although it is essentially a conversation between two people (the basic building block of all drama), the scene features *four* people – the two voice actors (Paolo Ferrari was one of them) are just as significant here as actors Franco Citti and Julian Beck.

ANTI-ART, ANTI-CINEMA.

Significantly, *Oedipus the King* doesn't provide (1) context, (2) psychology, (3) meaning, (4) value, or (5) mythology to the action in Sophocles' story.

1. There is no <u>context</u> for the acts: one incident follows on from another, but without the usual cause-and-effect progression of conventional narration. Events occur without explanation. Oedipus goes to the Oracle, but then appears to go insane as a result of the prophecy (we see him wandering in the desert,[28] we see him attending a wedding, or seeing people dancing, but with no connection to humanity). He then appears to act out the prophecy, as if he's driven by it: he murders the guards and King Laius apparently for no reason. The violence comes from nowhere, but it also *goes nowhere*. It achieves no goal whatsoever, and satisfies no craving (except, perhaps, to fulfil the prophecy of the Oracle. As if, once the Gods or Powers or Furies have decreed something, it must take place. Or as if one can never escape one's fate. Or as if Oedipus has no real agency or individuality anymore, he is merely a puppet of the Fates, and thus has no identity – he is a hollow man. Certainly, the movie spends quite some time depicting Oedipus weeping, distraught, following his visit to the Oracle. It's not even the Oracle's pronouncement that damns Oedipus, perhaps, but how Oedipus reacts to it. With a single sentence – *you will make love to your mother and kill your father* – the Oracle condemns Oedipus to a life of hell).

Or is this version of *Oedipus Rex* about faith and belief? That is, Oedipus's dead certainty that the Delphic Oracle speaks the truth imprisons him in a cage of his own making. He *believes*, and thus it takes place.[29]

2. *Oedipus Rex* avoids <u>psychology</u>. It doesn't psychologize the events, doesn't provide motives or goals, and doesn't get into why Oedipus is acting as he does. In conventional forms of drama, events are given explanations and contexts. And if an extraordinary event occurs (like the murder of five people in the King Laius scene), there will be aftermath scenes, explanation scenes, and *dénouement* scenes. In *Oedipus*

---

[28] Once again, the film uses too many second unit shots of Oedipus wanderin' and a-wanderin'.
[29] As Tiresias berates Oedipus: he has been told things that are of no use to him, and that knowledge won't help him.

Rex, nothing: Oedipus simply continues his wanderings. (The cinema of Pier Paolo Pasolini often refuses to psychologize or explain events: life simply happens. One thing after another. And yet, of course, *Oedipus Rex*, like other Pasolini movies, does follow a conventional dramatic progression, and it does follow the basic narrative outline of Sophocles' play). Pasolini said that 'instead of projecting the myth on to psychoanalysis', the film had 're-projected psychoanalysis on the myth' [PP, 120]).

Notice, for instance, how the 1967 Italian movie stays *outside* of Oedipus, even tho' he is in most of the scenes, even tho' it is *his* story we are following, and even tho' the camera plays across Franco Citti's sunburnt face sometimes in extreme close-ups (rare for Pier Paolo Pasolini's cinema). As with Michael Corleone in *The Godfather II* (which Citti also appeared in), we are never allowed inside Oedipus. Despite the use of subjective camera, which places us inside Oedipus's mindscreen, we don't feel we are with him or inside him at all (that blankness recalls the way actors are told to act in the cinema of Robert Bresson and Carl-Theodor Dreyer, or like Martine Carol in *Lola Montes*: *do nothing*).

However, by keeping an audience permanently *outside* a character, you risk alienating them. Of course, that might be your goal. But if you've lost the audience, whatever you try is wasted anyway, because they're not there anymore. (This was part of Pier Paolo Pasolini's project, however, at this time: you can see him going even further in post-Brechtian alienation with his next movie, *Theorem*, which some found wilfully obscure, and part of that's due to the decision to stay outside the characters. The alienation technique continued in *Pigsty*, and the approach reached its apogee in Pasolini's final film, *Salò*, of course – a movie where *everything* is an alienation effect).

Altho' *Oedipus the King* is anti-psychoanalytic, it certainly employs elements of psychoanalytical theory. *Oedipus the King* is also one of Pasolini's anthropologically-informed movies: you can see where the filmmakers have drawn on the writings of anthropology[30] (such as, in the 1960s era, Claude Levi-Strauss and Gaston Bachelard. Pasolini would pursue the anthropological approach even deeper in *Medea*, and the psychoanalytical angle in *Pigsty*).

3. *Oedipus Rex* avoids fixing the <u>meaning</u> of any of the events. Not that it leaves it up to the audience to figure out what's happening. No. The movie is opaque. It's blank. It's a wall (a red, adobe, African wall). It's not that Oedipus reverts to the level of an animal, or a natural force,

---

[30] The 'world music' or 'ethnic music' also reflects the anthropological approach.

or the embodiment of an emotion or a trait – it's that he is nothing.[31] Wherever he comes from, he is nothing in himself.

The 1967 movie of *Oedipus Rex*, interestingly, presents Oedipus's decision to go visit the Oracle as something like a quest, a quest for (his) identity, for meaning, to find out who he is and what he is doing here on Planet Earth (reminiscent of fairy tales and myths of young heroes, where setting forth into the wide, wide world is the first step of an adventure). That apparently Existential or metaphysical or spiritual quest (for knowledge, for self-awareness) is rapidly scuppered, tho', when, on his knees before the Oracle, he learns that he will murder his father and marry his mother. Instead of laughing[32] at the hilarity of such a ridiculous pronouncement (the Oracle laughs heartily and scornfully), Oedipus goes something close to insane.

We see Oedipus wandering aimlessly in the desert, as if his identity, his self, his soul, has been ripped to pieces (in which case, hell, it must've been pretty shaky to begin with!). We see him stumbling away from the Oracle at once in the real world (full of the crowds come to see the Oracle) and, in match cuts, lost in an unreality where he's the only person left in the entire world, vividly expressing his complete isolation from everybody else – there is nobody to call on for help. He is truly alone. (So you can't survive getting too close to the Gods – they will tear you to pieces. *Oedipus Rex* is certainly highly accomplished at evoking the primal, visceral forces at work in the ancient world. Despite its radical stylization, *Oedipus Rex* conjures a convincingly tough, earthy realm where the hysterical laughter of the Gods is heard one moment, and the next moment you're alone in a harsh, near-inhospitable world of dust, sun and heat, abandoned by all).

4. The Italian movie version of *Oedipus the King* empties the events of Sophocles' story of <u>value</u>. When five people are killed for no decent reason, life has lost its value (life becomes as meaningless as a holocaust). And the values which movie audiences expect to find in a film are also left out. Issues such as consequences, reactions, discussions and the like are expected after calamitous events, but they simply aren't included in this version of *Oedipus the King* (in a way, this is an anti-literary, anti-psychological, anti-dramatic version of Sophocles' tragedy. This is not a movie you'd use for students writing an essay about *Oedipus the King*![33] Except, maybe, to demonstrate that not every adaptation of a play

---

31 Samuel Beckett's later texts (including his 'fizzles', short texts of the 1960s), which emphasize nothingness and emptiness, might be a reference here.
32 The first reaction shot of Franco Citti when he hears the pronouncement suggests that he's going to laugh at the idea.
33 The version of the tragedy released the following year is a good one, though.

from the ancient world needs to be contextualized, psychologized – or, in short, normalized).

5. The elements of mythology, where events are mythologized and aggrandized, where action becomes legend, are also dispensed with in the 1967 *Oedipus Rex*. As in the later Westerns of Sam Peckinpah or Howard Hawks, the grandeur of the desert scenery is actually completely beside the point in *Oedipus Rex*. This is not a movie about the desert! Or about nature! Or about humans in relation to the landscape, or to the elemental forces.

Oedipus the King is a conscious (and, in a way, quite radical) effort at demythologizing Sophocles' play, and also the concept of literary evocations of tragedy. It's an anti-play, an anti-tragedy. It's directed by a poet who's of course steeped in the great literature of the Western world, yet it's as if Pier Paolo Pasolini has decided to go *against* all he knows, all he reveres in Western literature (we know that Pasolini has a tendency to rush from one extreme to another!). Not to 'deconstruct' literature and tragic forms, not to 'analyze' them, or 'psychoanalyze' them, not to take them apart and reconstruct them in his own fashion, but simply to *avoid them* altogether.

Oedipus Rex is a multi-level movie which destroys itself even as it presents the famous story of Oedipus pretty accurately. This doesn't always work, this simultaneous celebration and demolition (many have tried it). This 1967 adaptation succeeds (on the whole), partly because it does all of the things mentioned above, by avoiding or repudiating value, meaning, context, psychology, mythology, spirituality, purpose, goals, motives, etc etc etc.

THE FRAMING STORY.

The beginning and ending of *Oedipus Rex* takes place in a modern, Italian setting;[34] the first days of the infant Oedipus's life occur in a rural, Italian world. The delivery of the child (glimpsed from a respectful distance, from the window). Long shots of giggling, laughing women and the baby in the fields[35] during a picnic. The narrative returns to the same fields at the end of the film, with the same subjective, handheld shots of the tops of the trees, and the same pan and tilt down from the trees to a large field. (In the ten minute prologue, however, we are in the early part of the 20th century, but in the epilogue we have shifted to the present day of the film (i.e., 1967). In other words, the prologue and

---

[34] The next film dir. by the maestro, *Theorem*, was set in the same *milieu*.
[35] 'This field is almost exactly like the place where my mother took for walks when I was a child', Pasolini explained in 1970.

epilogue reflect the life of the director, from childhood to the present day).

The 1967 *Oedipus Rex* emphasizes the link with Renaissance paintings of the Virgin Mary when the filmmakers shoot an early scene in the Italian countryside of Jocasta breastfeeding her baby in the frontal, adoring manner of a Renaissance master such as Giovanni Bellini in his painting *Madonna of the Meadow* in London.[36] (And Mangano has never looked more gorgeous in the warm sunlight – this is why you cast a star in a role like this, someone who can communicate a slew of emotions with her face. Mangano smiles, evoking maternal bliss, but after a moment she frowns, as if troubled by visions of the future, and what her child will undergo).

Before *Oedipus Rex* introduces the soldier father and the apartment, it evokes a perfect Summer's day and a picnic in a lyrical, heightened manner. The fields, the sunlight, the greenery, the sky, and the joy of the union between mother and child are some of the most serene scenes in the Pier Paolo Pasolini canon. It can't last, this being a major tragic play in the Western tradition, but the scene is vital. (Yes, there *was* a time of ecstasy, or union, or oneness, or at least peace for the hero – and that was, in the true, Freudian tradition, in the arms of Mamma[37]).

There is also a very lengthy pan shot along the tops of the trees in full leaf (which is a kind of subjective view for the child)[38] – the deep greens against the blue sky contrast vividly with the harsh mountainscape of stones and cliffs in the opening shot (another long, slow panning movement) of the ancient world section of the movie. The oppositions are typical ones in Pier Paolo Pasolini's cinema:

modern Italy	Ancient Greece
the modern world	the ancient world
Europe (Italy)	Africa[39] (Morocco)
the mother	the father
love	separation/ abandonment

Pier Paolo Pasolini said the early scenes of Oedipus's mother and father were autobiographical:

> In *Oedipus,* I am recounting the story of my own Oedipus complex... I am narrating my own life, mythologized of course, made more epic via

---

36 In the coda, Oedipus walks past a wayside, Catholic shrine.
37 It's the unity of the mother-child relationship, as described in the works of Julia Kristeva.
38 Godard is very fond of this sort of shot.
39 'Pasolini's films are self-centred. They are not about Africa or African consciousness, but about Pasolini and a poetic consciousness' (S. Rohdie, 97).

the legend of Oedipus.
[...]
I've stated various times that *Oedipus Rex* is an autobiography: my father who was an officer and my mother was more or less the woman played by Silvana Mangano. I live the Oedipus complex in a kind of laboratory fashion, in an almost elementary and schematic way. (1971)

Pier Paolo Pasolini makes the framing scenes of *Oedipus Rex* very much about himself, equating himself with Oedipus (and using an actor in the movie who is one of his alter egos on screen, Franco Citti). This turns *Oedipus Rex* into one of Pasolini's most personal movies – even the Northern Italian setting has personal resonances for Pasolini (tho' of course the scenes are also idealizations and stylizations). Similarly, Pasolini selected the Friuli-Venezia Giulia area in Northern Italy for the home of Jason in the follow-up to *Oedipus Rex*, *Medea*.

The filmmakers portray the emotional tensions between the parents and the child in the prologue of *Oedipus Rex* in a largely silent, visual manner; the point-of-view is mainly with the boy Oedipus. The primal scene, of the mother and father making love, is straight out of the psychoanalytical textbooks of Sigmund Freud. The child's resentment and bewilderment is embodied by devices such as the shock cut to a very loud firework display (with gunfire mixed in with the explosions in the sky). The parents have left him alone while they go to a local celebration (not great parenting, then!).

Oedipus Rex stays with the child's point-of-view in the main: he sees his parents dancing (and embracing) at the local dance, across the courtyard, for example (the 1967 film subtly evokes the accusations of neglect and guilt towards his parents which the child can't express). In *Oedipus Rex*, parents are destined to disappoint their children, just as children are born to let their parents down (and, this being an Ancient Greek tragic play, the disaffection is manifested in blood and violence).

A significant scene in the prologue of *Oedipus Rex* has the soldier father staring at the baby in the buggy. Just that – staring, contemptuously. No dialogue, no voiceover: instead, silent movie-style, there's a caption, which states: 'you are going to take her away from me' (the force of the father's contempt is all the more powerful for not being expressed in dialogue; similarly, the caption appears on the screen without music or a voiceover). This is where the soldier father plans to remove the child from the cosy domestic scene he has with Jocasta.

And it is when the father decides to get rid of the child that *Oedipus Rex* switches from 20th century Italy to Ancient Greece, introducing the Classical world with a long pan around the Moroccan desert. (This camera movement (a favourite with Pasolini) is reprised many times, including during the blood-and-death finale).

The 1967 film cuts from the father in 1920s Italy grabbing the feet of the child to shots of the weeping boy being carried on a pole by a man (presumably his father). The 1967 movie lays the blame on the father: it's the father who performs the inciting incident which sets the tragedy in motion, by abandoning the child. The film criticizes the mother mildly, for being neglectful of her child, but it is forceful in its accusation that it's the father who upsets the status quo of the family. (The movie portrays the Freudian primal scene, with the child displacing the father, engendering the resentment, but it also evokes the child being wounded when the father distracts the mother's attention. In this interpretation of *Oedipus Rex*, the mother is glamoured by the father, with affection, attention and lovemaking, leading her to disregard her child).

In considering the prologue of *Oedipus Rex*, let's keep in mind how Pier Paolo Pasolini viewed his father: 'overbearing, egoistic, egocentric, tyrannical and authoritarian' (PP, 13). Pasolini had a very troubled, ambiguous relationship with his father (to say the least), which coloured his whole life. Some of this psychosexual turmoil is evoked in the framing story of *Oedipus Rex*.

THE FINALE.

The finale of *Oedipus Rex* shifts gear into full-on tragic staging, with Franco Citti playing many of his scenes at high volume, yelling the dialogue (as if the movie has been saving up dialogue, and it is unleashed in torrents. But the decision to dub Citti – by Paolo Ferrari – weakens the dramaturgy. The double acts of Italian cinema – one actor on screen and another actor on the soundtrack – sometimes falter. And big, passionate scenes can be challenging to replicate months later in a studio).

The final act of *Oedipus Rex* is grim, deadly serious stuff (the 428 B.C. play is all about the pay-off, all about the final act), as Oedipus avoids, denounces, flees and beats down every threat to his kingship, his identity, his life. The ghosts of the past come back to haunt him one after another, and the prophecies and former acts bear fruit in spades.

The violence of the retribution, with no hope of redemption, is impossible to miss in *Oedipus Rex*. There is nowhere else to go in a tragic play in its final stages: you have to stay with it to the end: you are locked into a scenario where the walls are closing in, where the claustrophobia increases with every breath, where the decline and fall has the inexorable momentum of the tides of the ocean, or the Earth careening around the sun. Ain't nobody nowhere who can stop the trajectory of the story.

As the Fates, the Furies, the Titans and the Gods close in on Oedipus, demanding payment for past crimes, the interpretation of this 1967 Italian movie version unleashes levels of self-loathing and self-inflicted agony that threaten to consume the enterprise. It's scorching stuff, a toxic miasma that seems to add a layer of Italian, Catholic self-pity and self-flagellation to the already coruscating, Ancient Greek energy. (Ascetic Christianity on top of ascetic, Ancient Greek tragedy – that's going to suffocate anyone!).

Cinematically, the finale of *Oedipus Rex* makes a striking use of close-ups – the dialogue is sometimes cut up into single lines which accompany a handheld camera pushing in to an actor's face. Thus, every time we cut back to Oedipus and his interlocutor, a single sentence is delivered, and the camera moves two or three feet closer to the actor (a similar montage technique was employed in the Sermon on the Mount section of *The Gospel According To Matthew*). Both Mangano and Citti are marvellous at holding the viewer's attention in those lengthy, lingering close-up shots. (Mangano shines in the third act, when serious acting is required; up to this point, she has been in part an iconic presence, an idealization of motherhood. But in the third act, her role is fleshed out considerably).

□

THE CODA.

In the coda at the end of the 1967 Italian film, blind Oedipus is led through the streets of present-day Bologna by his friend Angelo, a modern vagabond who plays his recorder like a busker or beggar.[40] (Pier Paolo Pasolini called the epilogue Freudian sublimation [PP, 129]). Oedipus is depicted sitting on the steps of the Cathedral (San Petronio) in the main square (Piazza Maggiore) in Bologna,[41] a weary, burnt-out shell of a man who relies on Angelo to lead him. After the harsh, earthy lyricism of the mythological, desert settings, the return to modern-day Italy is very strange. When the movie cuts to long shots of ordinary folk walking around central Bologna, in the cafés, and entering the Cathedral, they seem like inhabitants of another planet (why Bologna? For autobiographical reasons, of course, mirroring the prologue – Pasolini was born in Bologna).

On the Cathedral steps, *Oedipus Rex* plays Oedipus haunted by his

---

[40] He plays a recorder, actually, but the soundtrack features a flute and a whistle as well as a recorder.
[41] Which Pier Paolo Pasolini has probably done many times.

murderous acts: he stares into the camera in close-up, exhausted and beaten and greying. He anxiously calls for Angelo and is led away (the motif is repeated). A brief interlude is next, when Angelo is playing soccer on a dusty street in a forgotten corner of the town (a return of the *milieu* of *Mamma Roma* and *Accattone*). Oedipus is again portrayed sitting off to one side, by himself. In a close-up, Franco Citti suggests a tortured soul unable to escape the past, and forever doomed by the past (he bites his hand in agony, a recurring gesture). He has learnt his lessons too late: 'the film is very pessimistic. By the time Oedipus gets to understand it's no use to him', as director Pasolini put it (PP, 124).[42] Finally, the narrative takes Oedipus and Angelo to the countryside of Oedipus's youth, past his childhood home.

The 1967 movie closes with an image of nature, the camera panning across the trees and fields (repeating the shots in the prologue). It seems to be the same eternally sunny afternoon, an impossible return to a half-remembered childhood. We end as we begun (as Oedipus notes).

---

[42] 'This is the thing in Sophocles that inspired me the most: the contrast between total innocence and the obligation to know' (PP, 124).

Oedipus Rex (1967).
This page and over.

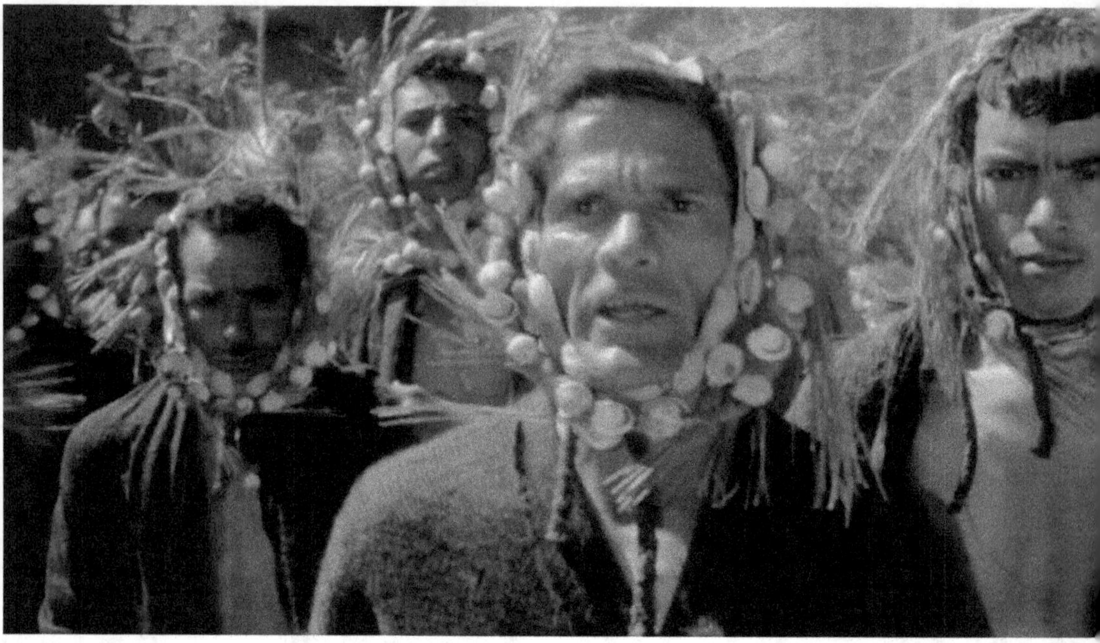

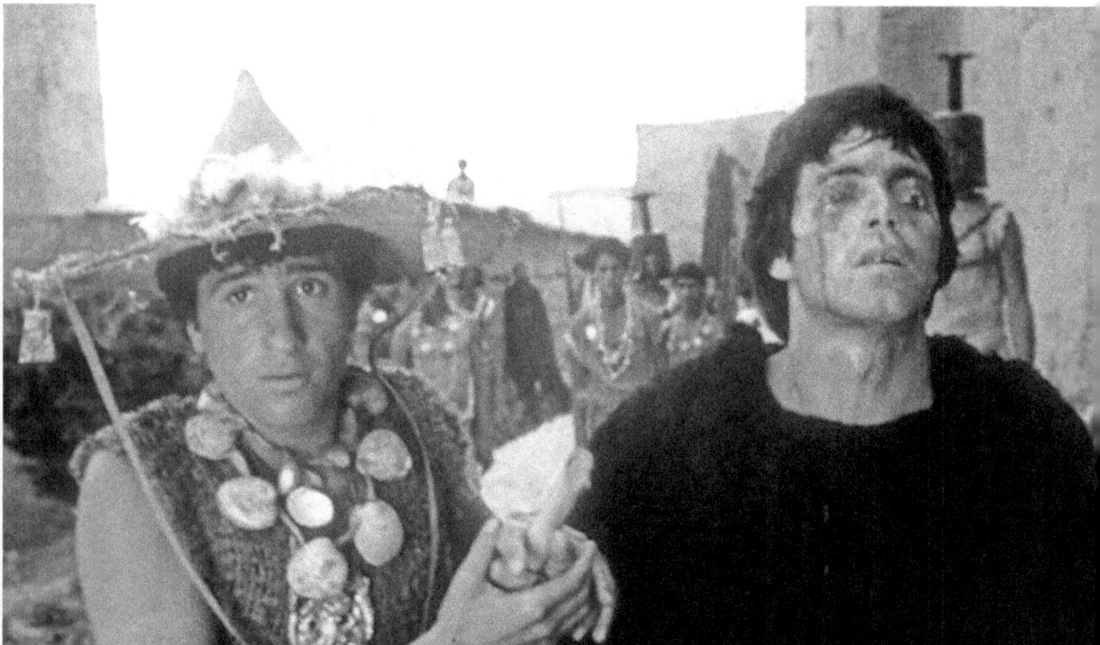

11

TEOREMA

THEOREM

Theorem (*Teorema*, 1968) featured many Pier Paolo Pasolini regulars, such as producer Franco Rossellini (Manolo Bolognini also produced, for Aetos Produzioni), DP Giuseppe Ruzzolini, music by Ennio Morricone and Ted Curson, A.D.s Sergio Citti and Luciano Puccini, and editor Nino Baragli. Costumes were by Roberto Capucci and Marcella De Marchis (not Danilo Donati this time[1]), make-up by Maria Teresa Corridoni, prod. des. by Luciano Puccini, and sound by Bernardino Fronzetti. Released Sept 7, 1968. 98 minutes.

Theorem began life as a play, part of a series of six verse tragedies, which Pier Paolo Pasolini wrote during an illness. They were characterized by troubled relations between fathers and sons (continuing the themes of *Oedipus Rex*), denunciations of consumer culture (looking forward to *Salò, or The 120 Days of Sodom*), and the utopias of youth (ES, 302).

Pier Paolo Pasolini said he felt it would be better if the bourgeois participants remained largely silent, and reworked the play as a film script (but *Theorem* was 'shot almost without a script at all', Pasolini remarked [PP, 133]). The novel of *Teorema* emerged at the same time. It was originally going to take place in Gotham,[2] but was transferred to Milano (i.e., the most bourgeois setting that Pasolini could find in Italia). It was filmed in Spring, 1968 (in Milan, at Giulia Maria Crespi's villa on the Ticino, and at Elios Studios). *Theorem* has been adapted as a play (2009)

---
1 So no outrageous hats!
2 One wonders how filming in the U.S.A. would've changed *Theorem*.

and an opera (by Giorgio Battistelli).

Theorem, as Pier Paolo Pasolini was keen to point out, was the first movie that he had directed that had been set in a bourgeois *milieu*, and featured bourgeois characters.3 It was a movie he seemed to feel he had to make (selfishly, I wish he'd gone straight from *Oedipus Rex* into his unmade *St Paul* movie, or perhaps the *Divine Comedy*).

As Pier Paolo Pasolini explained in 1968, *Theorem* was partly an attack on the bourgeoisie, whom he detested. The bourgeoisie were loathsome to Pasolini because of their hypocrisy, their vulgarity, and the mean attitude towards culture ('horrible conventions, horrible principles, horrible duties, horrible democratism, horrible fascism, horrible objectivity, horrible smiles').4

For Pier Paolo Pasolini, altho' the bourgeoisie in Italy were changing (which modulated Pasolini's views slightly), they were always wrong. No matter how sincere, profound and noble the bourgeoisie was, it was 'always on the wrong track'.

Pier Paolo Pasolini loathed the bourgeoisie with a passion that was total and beyond explanation. 'My hatred for the bourgeoisie is not documentable or arguable. It's just there and that's it' (PP, 26).5

That certainly comes across in *Theorem*: the detestation of the bourgeoisie turns *Theorem* into a cold, rather impersonal movie, too Godardian (*Weekend*), too Bergmanian (*Persona*), too Bressonian (*Balthazar*), and too Antonionian (*Red Desert*) for its own good.

That is, there is too much in *Theorem* that is apeing Bergman + Godard + Bresson + Antonioni (and several others). Pier Paolo Pasolini's cinema is at its weakest when it does that – when it hasn't got the strength and self-possession to withstand the influence of outside forces. You see it in *Pigsty* (Godard) and *The Hawks and the Sparrows* (Fellini, Rossellini, Neo-realism – even when it's documenting the 'death of Neo-realism').

Theorem concerned six main characters in a bourgeois family's household:

- the Visitor (Terence Stamp),
- Lucia, the mother (Silvana Mangano),
- Paolo,6 the father (Massimo Girotti),

---

3 Not totally true – the bourgeoisie appear in *The Hawks and the Sparrows*.
4 C. Cederna, "Tra le braccia dell'arcangelo", *L'Espresso*, Apl 21, 1968.
5 Making a film about the bourgeoisie, then, seems almost pointless, in a way. There's no exorcism/catharsis of loathing, and the movie attacks a target which's all too easy for filmmakers such as Pasolini or Jean-Luc Godard.
6 No need to note, but I will anyway, that Pasolini gives the two men in *Theorem* his names: Paolo and Pietro.

- Odetta, the daughter (Anne Wiazemsky),
- Pietro, the son (Andres Jose Cruz Soublette),
- and Emilia the maid (Laura Betti).

Also appearing were Pasolini's mom Susanna Colussi, Ninetto Davoli, Adele Cambria, Alfonso Gatto, and Cesare Garboli.

✦

The influence of Jean-Luc Godard is apparent in the later Pier Paolo Pasolini films of the 1960s in terms of casting: in *Porcile* and *Theorem* Godard's actors Anne Wiazemsky and Jean-Pierre Léaud appeared. The self-conscious politicization in terms of the on-screen discussions of the bourgeoisie and the workers at the beginning of *Theorem* seems particularly Godardian (though the Marxist debates over labour and factories are of course very much part of the era of the late 1960s – *Theorem* was released in 1968). Even the self-conscious quotation of Arthur Rimbaud is Godardian (Rimbaud's poesie formed a significant cultural layer *Pierrot le Fou* (1965), for example).

The first time I saw *Theorem*, the movie passed by without making much impression. It is a very different sort of movie from many of Pier Paolo Pasolini's works, and from most of his output up to that time: it lacks, for a start, the incredible and exotic imagery, the emphasis on texture and sensuality. It opens with a deliberately abstract and anti-narrational sequence of scenes. It eschews exposition, back-story, explanations, even characters' motivations and goals. (And not only because it self-consciously dispenses with dialogue).

Theorem was famous too for being a movie in which full male nudity was featured (by Terence Stamp and Andres Jose Cruz Soublette). However, it was sensitively handled (i.e., non-sexual) – brief glimpses, with the camera framing out the naughty bits. As Enzo Siciliano put it, *Theorem* was

> a combination of eros and religiosity – it was the first time that a completely nude male body, that of the protagonist Terence Stamp, had appeared on the screen in a film that disavowed pornography. (ES, 317)

The nudity, however, led to yet another run-in between Pier Paolo Pasolini and the authorities, with the maestro's almost supernatural talent for causing trouble: the confiscation of *Theorem* by Rome's public prosecution office in September, 1968. (The subsequent trial, in Venice in Nov, 1968, ended with the movie acquitted).

★

STYLE, LOOK, APPROACH.

Much of the music in *Theorem* comprises jazz by Ennio Morricone and Ted Curson (a rather mournful piece,[7] also heard over the credits, and not one of Morricone's best), and the *Requiem* by Wolfgang Amadeus Mozart. Compared to the staggeringly good soundtrack for the following year's *Medea*, or the incredible selection of music for *The Gospel According To Matthew*, the music for *Theorem* sounds thin, crudely mixed and not satisfyingly integrated into the piece.

Of course, Wolfie Mozart's unfinished *Requiem* is a huge and famous piece of music, utterly sublime, but it's mixed low often in *Theorem*, and it is artistically employed rather like background music – and *you just don't do that* with Mozart's *Requiem*! Not even if you're Pier Paolo Pasolini! The film allows the classical music to burble underneath scenes just like Hollywood cinema has done since the 1990s, turning music scoring into elevator music. It's included to stop audiences getting bored, or because producers think every scene needs music. It's a really disagreeable use of the greatest artform humans have created.

Unless, maybe, this is meant to be classical music as it is used by the bourgeoisie – as muzak, as merely a classy kind of background sound. Or it's an ironic, scornful use of classical music, turning it into a horrible, twittering, warbling noise – music which was deployed straight in *Accattone* and *The Gospel According To Matthew*. So that now, classical music is merely another weapon in the evocation of desperation and bitterness that is *Theorem*. (Similarly, the jazz music in the scene of Emilia's burial simply doesn't fit at all, has no link to the imagery or the drama, and grates on the ears like hell, as if Morricone was trying to make jazz even more unlistenable than John Coltrane's most out-there experiments in miserabilism. And the saxophone piece for the scenes after the Visitor's departure is tawdry).[8]

Thus, although *Theorem* is a movie with very little dialogue, and would seem to rely a lot on the soundtrack, the sound effects and the music, it is in the end a less-than-satisfying movie in terms of its sound.[9] (However, the swishing of cars, the piping of birds, heard in many scenes, does offer a sorrowful accompaniment to the evocation of modern *ennui*).

The family home in *Theorem* is a plush, roomy but bland dwelling: furnished in the minimal style of the 1960s, it is peculiarly empty of

---

[7] At times it seems downright dreadful.
[8] Meanwhile, the jazz music in the film *Notes Towards an African Oresteia* by Gato Barbieri and a band is abominable.
[9] However, the multi-ethnic approach of the soundtracks of movies such as *Medea* and *The Gospel According To Matthew* would be too distracting in this particular fable. Skirling Middle Eastern pipes wouldn't fit the restrained imagery of cool, Northern Italy.

personal touches (the bourgeoisie have money, but empty souls). Odetta's bedroom, for instance, is the polar opposite of a teenager's room in the 1960s, with nary a pop star poster or a record or a girls' magazine in sight (instead, Odetta has an old chest where she keeps childhood paraphernalia. She's like a Victorian child, pampered and old-fashioned). Meanwhile, the 1968 film often includes the sounds of cars whooshing by on the road outside those imposing gates (as if the outside world can't be shut out, even with lots of Lire). Much of the movie is so quiet there is only the sound of pigeons cooing. The Wintry season adds to the melancholy, detached, arid atmosphere, with bare trees and pale colours (however, the full sunshine[10] that illuminates scenes by the front door and in the garden isn't enough to add any real warmth to proceedings).

Theorem is structurally and narratively wilfully flat and unengaging:[11] the script tells a story, but it consciously jettisons many of the elements that conventional screenplays employ. For instance, there is no connection between each of the encounters between the Visitor and the family members: each encounter simply succeeds the other. Characters are not developed much, and aren't even characters (see below). The amount of dialogue in *Theorem* is tiny, but that's only one element in contributing towards the lack of interaction or affect amongst the characters.

Theorem is directed in a consciously flat style at times. The imagery has a chilly, distanced feel to it (it was filmed in early Spring, 1968, and the season coming out of Winter seems well-suited to the tale).[12] Cool colours, neat, clean interiors – the production design (by Luciano Puccini) is calm and middle-class, as are the costumes (by Roberto Capucci and Marcella De Marchis). There are few elements where the design indulges itself (the beds all have animal furs on them, for example).

Theorem partakes of a certain antagonism towards narrative and literature of the mid-to-late 1960s, as Enzo Siciliano points out (ES, 314). *Theorem* negated narrative in favour of an emphasis on the visual (the movies of Michelangelo Antonioni, and the more obscure ones of Jean-Luc Godard (particularly the Marxist diatribes he embarked upon from 1968 onwards with the Dziga Vertov Group), would be obvious examples of this anti-literary, anti-narrative tendency).

Like many another movie of ideas or metaphysical concerns, the characters in *Theorem* are not characters in the usual sense; they're not one-dimensional, and they're not puppets; rather, they are simply not

---

10 The sun that illuminates the father is linked to the sun-god in the movie, light and the sun being one of the primary motifs of the divine. A similar ploy was used in *Medea*.
11 Pier Paolo Pasolini said he planned to shoot *Theorem* in a different way, but it still ended up the same, with his particular style (PP, 99).
12 The Northern European setting of *Theorem* aligns it with the father, with the Law of the Father, in Pier Paolo Pasolini's universe (which meant towns like Bologna and Milan).

characters in the accepted manner. They embody aspects of the bourgeoisie, perhaps, but they're more like theatrical effects, Brechtian devices.

Or you could put it like this: in conventional script terms, there is no one to 'root for', no one to 'identify with' in *Theorem*, no one that the audience wants to spend time with, and no one who's going to tell us or show us anything of any interest. There's no passion, and very little emotion in the characters (despite, say, Emilia rushing into the kitchen to top herself in the gas oven, or Paolo feeling frustrated and taking it out on his wife, tho' he doesn't know why).

The blankness, the lassitude, the emptiness, and the lack of agency in the characters is part of the movie's (and Pier Paolo Pasolini's) denunciation of the bourgeois class, of course, but placed within the context of a 98-minute fictional movie, it doesn't quite work.

Further, using known faces/ stars also exacerbates the literary/ philosophical goals of the piece: it might've better to use unknowns (but this time not for the usual reasons in Pier Paolo Pasolini's cinema). However, *Theorem* does require real acting ability; a non-professional actor just being themselves wouldn't be enough.

★

Theorem opens with a vox pop-style interview at a factory somewhere in Italy about workers and the bourgeoisie. It's an unusual and scrappy prologue, almost as if it's been thrown in to deliberately irritate as well as to play to Marxists, radicals and other viewers desperate to be ideologically right-on. (It flatters them but also sends them up).

The filming style of the factory interviews in *Theorem* comes from Pasolini's documentaries: he liked to gather a group of people on the street and place an interviewer (usually himself) in their midst, firing questions at them. *Theorem* includes the device of having the interviewer asking loaded questions which are full of political views – i.e., the interviewer has already decided on the context and even the content of the interviews. And the interviewees can barely get a word in edgeways (they are expected to do is say, 'yes'). Pasolini was a fascinating interviewer, but also a dominating and very opinionated one.

Thus, a Pasolini interview was really another political/ ideological rant, using the general public as a sounding-board and the television interview format as a pretext for Pasolini to say whatever he fancied saying.

Following the prologue, *Theorem* shifts into silent movie narration – music and images. The film travels in the slice of the editor's razor on the Movieola to the volcanic setting of Mount Etna, which by then Pier

Paolo Pasolini had employed a number of times (and would do so in later films)[13] – most notably in *The Gospel According To Matthew*, in the Christ in the Wilderness sequence (thus, the images of the black sand and hillsides and clouds evoke the religious elements of that 1964 movie, which, coupled with the voiceover, lends *Theorem* an explicitly religious flavour).[14] *Teorema*'s credits occur here.

Sepia-and-white photography follows (for no apparent reason). There are no characters, no dialogue, no exposition – instead, abstract images of empty factory premises, a Mercedes moving thru the gates, and the main characters, introduced in deliberately mundane vignettes. (The daughter is depicted exiting a university;[15] she meets a boyfriend; the son is joshing about with his friends on the street; he too is shown with a lover; the maid is doing chores around the house; the mother is seen on the couch reading *Bourgeois Housewife Weekly* (just kidding); and the father is evoked as a factory manager).

Finally, with the scene of a bourgeois party at a bourgeois mansion, and an abrupt re-introduction into full colour,[16] the 1968 movie shifts into regular narration, and the Visitor (Terence Stamp) soon appears for the first time.[17] (So far, so *very* Godardian – hell, maybe Pasolini should've given the *Theorem* script and the budget to Godard! And we know what Godard would've done: placed the script in a bottom drawer, spent 90% of the budget on cigarettes and wine and a new Alfa Romeo, scribbled his own script on the back of a *Tel Quel* subscription form, phoned up his regular crew and filmed his own '*Theorem*' which would bear no relation[18] to Pasolini's script at all apart from the title!).[19]

Theorem is a perfect movie for college students, film critics, philosophy course majors and bored artists who want to whinge about something. Because *Theorem* is another of those multi-purpose movies which can be decoded any way you like – if you can be bothered. But *Theorem* itself can't be bothered – *Theorem* seems bored to death with itself, but it will go thru the motions anyway. *Theorem* is a movie collapsing on itself into a black hole of nothingness, but if you want to keep it alive for the few seconds it takes to prod it and analyze it, you are welcome to do so.

Thus, *Theorem* can be interpreted as:
• a Marxist deconstruction of the bourgeoisie.

---

13 In *Porcile*, for instance.
14 There are quotations from *Exodus* and *Jeremiah* in the narration over the Mount Etna images.
15 Notice the church prominent in the scenes.
16 Even the colour film stock itself is bourgeois. Just kidding.
17 He sends a telegram, as all polite aliens or angels should.
18 And Godard would dare anyone to complain!
19 And some shots of empty factories.

- an exploration of Existential philosophy.
- an attack on industrialization and consumerism (and what it's doing to modern Italia).
- a Christian fable.
- a post-Christian fable.
- a post-religious deconstruction of the religious impulse (and the religious movie genre).

CASTING.

As to casting, *Theorem* has an ensemble of strong performers. Massimo Girotti as the father looks like an older Pier Paolo Pasolini – the same suave looks, tall, slim, aristocratic, and restrained (Girotti played King Creon in the following year's *Medea*, and was well-known in Italian cinema). Pasolini said he had tried very hard to secure Orson Welles for *Theorem* (but getting the Great Welles to strip naked in Milan railroad station?! I don't think so! Welles wouldn't do a nude scene even if you promised him the entire Solar System!). Laura Betti[20] (Pasolini's long-time friend) was the maid Emilia. Andres Jose Cruz Soublette was the son Pietro. British actor Terence Stamp was the Visitor; he has exactly the beauty, aloofness, charm and mystery for the role (see below).

French actress Anne Wiazemsky was Odetta; she had appeared in Robert Bresson's film *Au Hasard, Balthazar* (1966), where she met and fell in love with Jean-Luc Godard – she was only 18 (and was 20 when she filmed *Theorem*). Wiazemsky appeared in Godard's films (such as *La Chinoise, Weekend,* and *Tout Va Bien*).[21] Wiazemsky also in the cast of *Pigsty* two years after *Theorem*, in the same sort of roles she did for Godard, particularly *La Chinoise*. (The name Odetta is probably a reference to the famous blues singer Odetta (d. 2008), whose rendering of "Sometimes I feel like a motherless child" was so memorable in *The Gospel According To Matthew*).

Meanwhile Silvana Mangano was an icon of Italian cinema; Mangano had been cast as the mother in *Oedipus Rex* (a role which has affinities with *Theorem*), appeared in the skit in *The Witches,* and as the Virgin

---

[20] This is Betti with a no make-up look, the opposite of the glamorous Betti we've seen in previous Pasolini movies.

[21] Jean-Luc Godard married Anne Wiazemsky, in 1967 (they later divorced). Godard hadn't wanted Wiazemsky to take up acting. Wiazemsky (b. May 14, 1947), was the granddaughter of the novelist François Mauriac (and Polish aristocracy on her father's side). Wiazemsky had written a fan letter to Godard after seeing *Masculin Féminin* and *Pierrot le Fou* (*Pierrot le Fou* 'struck me like an artistic thunderbolt', Wiazemsky said in 2003). It was really a love letter – 'one of the craziest things that I've ever done', admitted Wiazemsky, who up until then had been 'very prudent and shy'.

Godard was 36, Wiazemsky was 20; like Woody Allen, Godard has a penchant for young women. During their courtship in the Fall of 1966, they would go and see a film at 6 o'clock, have some food at 8 o'clock, and see another movie at 10 o'clock (the perfect Godard courtship; Wiazemsky and Godard split up because of Godard's intense jealousy, she says; there was also the age difference.

Mary in *The Decameron*. (Mangano got the concept straight away, Pier Paolo Pasolini recalled, without needing any discussion. Which is Pasolini's favourite kind of actor – no chat, no worried questions, no 'but I won't do that bit', they just get it, and they'll do it).

Also appearing in *Theorem* were Pier Paolo Pasolini's mother, Susanna Colussi (in the Emilia-as-a-saint sequence), and some actors from *The Gospel According To Matthew* (Luigi Barbini, who was James, as the young man that Paolo flirts with in Milan's train station, and Alfonso Gatto, who was Andrew, playing, suitably enough, a doctor).

TERENCE STAMP.

Terence Stamp (b. 1940[22]) has spoken at length about working on *Theorem* and with Pier Paolo Pasolini in a DVD interview. Although Pasolini might have been left-wing and a Communist, in theory at least, Stamp said that there was no holding back when it came to ensuring the finances for the movie were controlled. Stamp said he didn't receive a penny from *Theorem*, and was persuaded during production to sign away his points (the producers were Franco Rossellini and Manolo Bolognini). It's odd to see movies like this being analyzed at length by journalists and eggheads when the star wasn't even paid! (And when the producers acted shadily).

When Terence Stamp was cast in *Theorem*, Pier Paolo Pasolini altered his conception of the personality of the Visitor. Originally, he was going to be one of the old gods, a sun god, or God of the *Bible*, the Father. With Stamp on board, the Visitor became a more generic, metaphysical apparition, Pasolini explained, who might be the Devil or God, or a mixture of the two: 'the important thing is that he is something authentic and unstoppable' (PP, 157).

Terence Stamp recalled that Pier Paolo Pasolini didn't talk to him at all during the shooting. Instead, he talked to everyone else. It was presumably part of Pasolini's psychological strategy, which's been employed by many film directors (isolating an actor, or treating an actor differently, or keeping them apart from the rest of the cast, or having them stay in a different hotel). Laura Betti instead was the go-between for the director and the actor. (Pasolini didn't want to get into lengthy discussions about the roles. Working with a North American Method actor would be loathsome to Pasolini. Indeed, he acknowledged that he removed some of the basic elements of the actor's craft, such as miming naturalness, because 'I hate nuances and I hate naturalism' in actors [PP,

---

22 Some sources say 1938.

133]).

Terence Stamp said he aimed for a kind of non-acting or non-reaction in performing the Visitor. Being instead of doing. And not judging – not casting judgements on any of the characters (Stamp related his approach to the cultural atmosphere of the time, the late 1960s, and to his meeting with Jiddu Krishnamurti). For much of the film, Stamp's Visitor sits, walks and stands calmly, sometimes mildly amused by the people around him. With each character he's a different person – the youthful lad among the *ragazzi* when he's with Pietro (running off to play soccer, as Pasolini himself might do), or the attentive listener when he's with Lucia.

The blank or restrained approach to acting allows the audience to fill in everything else (and they can do it better than the filmmakers). The dramatic device is often employed with villains or powerful characters like kings or moguls – instead of them emoting, the context, the storytelling, the costumes and everything does the talking.

It was going to Italy to meet Federico Fellini (to appear in *Toby Dammit,* an episode in the anthology film *Histoires Extraordinares,* 1968, a.k.a. *Spirits of the Dead, Force of Evil/ Tales of Mystery and Imagination*), Terence Stamp recalled, that led him to being cast in *Theorem. Spirits of the Dead* was based (loosely) on the fiction of Edgar Allen Poe, and directed by Fellini (Peter O'Toole, Richard Burton and James Fox had been considered or offered the part).

At the time, Terence Stamp was one of the hotter actors in England (alongside David Hemmings, Alan Bates, James Fox and Albert Finney), having appeared in flicks such as *Far From the Madding Crowd, Modesty Blaise,* and *Billy Budd.* He was cast in the Fellini film (and Hemmings appeared in *Blow Up* – taking over the role from Stamp).

After *Theorem,* Terence Stamp's life changed radically, when in 1969 his career was in trouble, and he couldn't get arrested, he said. He went to India, leaving acting for spiritual pursuits, until his comeback in 1978 in the *Superman* movies. (A similar thing happened to James Fox, who abandoned acting after 1970's *Performance*).[23] More recently, Stamp has appeared in the *Star Wars* prequels and a Tim Burton film (*Miss Peregrine's Home For Peculiar Children*).

---

23 For part of this troubled period, James Fox took up Christianity. Fox joined the religious sect the Navigators after visiting South America for months after the *Performance* shoot. But he kept in contact with the entertainment world. Fox has always maintained that his mind was 'screwed up in lots of different ways prior to *Performance*' and that, ironically, he felt more in control when he was playing the character of the gangster Chas, because of the disciplines of making art (in M. Brown, *Performance*, Bloomsbury, London, 1999, 204).

THE VISITOR.

The Visitor may be God, or a god, or the Devil, or he's something transcendent, or an alien, or he's the religious impulse. Whatever... what's certain is that each encounter with the members of the household has some striking effect on them. Thus, the Visitor is dramatically a catalyst, an object of lust and affection, a figure of fascination and mystery, but he is also implacable, uncommunicating, distanced and aloof (like life itself)... He's a nobody, a somebody that was never anybody. He's just *there*, but he could be anyone. His physical attractiveness (Terence Stamp is a fine-looking guy, you have to admit!), is merely a function of the plot and the theme.

There is nothing *intrinsic* or *fundamental* in the Visitor. If he is divine, or if he has holy attributes, in the end that doesn't matter. Religion, you might say, is only *one* of many interpretations of *Theorem*.

The angelic, alien messenger in *Theorem* brings eros, spirituality, purity, but he doesn't have the desired effect on the affluent, bourgeois world.

Before the arrival of the Visitor in *Theorem*, the family members are barely alive. Or at least, they are solemn, alienated, separate, self-involved, and bored (remember how much Pier Paolo Pasolini loathes the bourgeoisie!). Lucia expresses some of this to the Visitor who, as ever, merely listens (it's enough to sit and listen to the bourgeoisie as they unburden their problems. Indeed, some films of this late 1960s/ Marxist/ 'revolutionary' period do just that – they listen to middle-class people whingeing and wittering. Hold on! – movies are *still* doing that today!).

At this level, *Theorem* is certainly an attack on the bourgeoisie, on their comfortable lifestyles which are empty of all life ('the whole of mankind is becoming petit bourgeois' [PP, 157]). They have *everything* but they have *nothing*. They have everything but they *are* nothing. They are members of the ruling class (running factories which employ 100s of souls), but their lives are barren and unfulfilled.

Yes, but the European bourgeoisie of this period are far too easy a target for a filmmaker like Pier Paolo Pasolini, as with Jean-Luc Godard or Ingmar Bergman. These filmmakers are so powerful and talented they are like gods who can destroy the middle-classes with a mere flick of the pen and the camera and the editor's cut (which they have done in movies). Such an easy target, why even bother to destroy the bourgeoisie?

The Visitor in *Theorem* is also a classic drifter figure in cinema, just anybody, right down to the copy of Arthur Rimbaud's poems he reads. Rimbaud! How cute! He's a bohemian, a wanderer, an out-of-towner, an

Existential, mid-20th century, Middle European outsider, right out of the fictions of André Gide, Jean-Paul Sartre, Albert Camus, Franz Kafka, Knut Hamsun *et al.* In short, he's a *poet*. The use of Rimbaud in *Theorem* is heavy-handed in the extreme – well, if you've written books about Rimbaud and many other poets, like me, it does seem like being whacked over the head with a mallet.[24]

And, being a poet and an artist, it's fitting that the Visitor is shown doing bugger all in *Theorem* except reading a book! Yes, *of course*, artists always do nothing at all except sit around in the garden reading books, don't they? Hell, every artist I know loafs around reading books and seducing the people they're staying with! (This is the Visitor as a hippy hobo, a drug dealer, one of those guys who comes to stay, hanging around, never cooks or buys food, never cleans, and sponges off his hosts, and does exactly nothing except sitting around reading, playing soccer with the family's son, etc. Rock and pop biographies are full of groupies, dealers and hangers-on like the Visitor).

One of the amusing aspects of *Theorem* is that it isn't really explained who the Visitor is or what he's doing at the house with the family (a lodger? A tourist from Detroit living with the family to improve his Italian? An insurance salesman who got lost and couldn't find his way back to Bologna?). The family's meal times are the most diverting scenes in *Theorem* in this regard (and a filmmaker with a flair for comedy would've extracted more juice from those scenes – imagine Mel Brooks with a scene like that!). But in *Theorem* it's all played pretty straight and solemn (except for the cameo from Ninetto Davoli as the messenger, who is, once again in a Pier Paolo Pasolini movie, allowed to goof around like a dimwit, flapping his arms like a toothy, mentally deficient angel. Pasolini has always indulged his lover Davoli to the max in his movies, as if Davoli's toothsome grin should be enough to satisfy any viewer. Trouble is, Davoli's messenger prances in from some other movie – it's one of the rare instances of a mistake of tone in Pasolini's cinema[25]).

Is *Theorem* designed to show that the bourgeoisie have nothing – but that when the Visitor leaves them they have even less? Is the Visitor's presence to reveal the absence and emptiness of the bourgeois class in Italy? That they are exiles to themselves? (Lucia sort of hints as much when she talks to the Visitor in the garden following his announcement that he has to leave).

Is it simply that, even if you think you've got nothing at all, to be

---

[24] Maybe young, wannabe Patti Smiths and Jim Morrisons thought, yeah, Rimbaud! So cool!
[25] Davoli performs the same idiotic routine in *Pigsty*.

alive is to have something or to be something – and that, whatever you are or have, when it's gone, that's when you miss it?

Being alive is enough.

What is life? is a question that *Theorem* asks. And one of the answers it suggests is: *not* as lived by the *bourgeoisie*! Pier Paolo Pasolini's cinema raises questions, for sure, and one of the questions is: would you want to live like this?

Thus: being alive is enough.

But: being bourgeois is *not* enough!

(The bourgeoisie are always wrong).

In his autobiography (highly recommended), Akira Kurosawa recounted this meeting:

> Once when I visited a farmer's house, he served me a vegetable dish with miso bean-paste sauce cooked in clamshells – a style called kaiyaki in this part of the country – and fish. While he drank saké over his meal, he said to me in thick dialect, 'You might wonder what could be interesting about living in a hovel like this and eating slop like this. Well, I tell you, it's interesting just to be alive.' (1983, 63)

In *Theorem*, the bourgeois class has everything, every modern amenity: food, a big house, a huge garden, nice clothes, the kids and wife don't need to work, a Mercedes car, even a maid, but it has nothing, it is not really alive – it is a non-life, a life you can't even call being alive. (So that contemporary capitalism and consumer culture, in the view of *Theorem* (and of Pasolini) is a dead-end).

SEX – OR NOT.

Many critics have commented upon the elements of sexuality in *Theorem* – how the Visitor has sexual relations with both men and women, for instance (three women and two men. Heterosexuality and homosexuality. Blah-blah-blah.) Yes, but sexuality is merely the *means* to a dramatic end (as often in all drama). *Theorem* is *not* 'about' sex, it couldn't give a *hoot* about sex. *Theorem* is *not* a movie, as some critics have insisted, about a nameless, holy Visitor (equivalent to Christ) who sexually enjoys a bunch of people in a bourgeois family in Northern Italy, including their maid.

Rather, sex in *Theorem* is an economical means or method of getting to a dramatic, ideological and philosophical place quickly and simply – the same way that sex is employed by many dramatists, writers and filmmakers (and by the advertizing and entertainment industries). Sex does a dramatic job in *Theorem*, in screenwriting terms – it cements (or expresses) the personal relationships, it evokes a relationship (between the Visitor and Odetta, say), but is not the essence of the relationship, the point of it, or what the relationship is 'about'.

An earlier scene in *Theorem* depicts the Visitor and Pietro looking at a book of paintings by Francis Bacon. The commentary here is multi-layered, as ever in Pasolinian cinema: Bacon (1909-92) was a famous, British, homosexual painter known for his images of bodies as bits of meat grappling with each other in solemn agony, in the familiar mid-20th century, Existential, Surrealist, modernist manner (Bacon's art was employed as an intertext in *Last Tango In Paris*, 1972). Beloved of the cognoscenti as a striking instance of modernist quasi-abtraction (though over-rated, I think), Bacon's work comments ironically on the gay sex between the Visitor and Pietro (and later between the Visitor and the father Paolo).

It's significant that the sexual encounters between the Visitor and the father *aren't* shown (again, one can draw autobiographical resonances with Pier Paolo Pasolini here).[26] In the other encounters, *Theorem* depicts Lucia the mother undressing in what appears to be the family summerhouse, while the Visitor plays with a dog by a lake; when he approaches her, she's naked, and they embrace. With Odetta, the maid and Pietro, the Visitor makes love to them on their beds in the family home (Odetta, a keen amateur photographer,[27] leads the Visitor into her bedroom and shows him her photo albums, sitting next to him by the bed). But with the father Paolo, the setting is an odd drive into the country (to Italy's lakeland again), where the cold, misty, colourless *mise-en-scène* and the dramatic tropes evoke an uneasy father-son relation. The Visitor lies down in the grass and, as usual, waits for the other to make the first move (when you're a god you can simply lie back and wait for the world to come to you. And it always does. The Visitor is a deity who doesn't need to lift a finger).

Each time the Visitor sexually takes a member of the family, the scenes are muted, enigmatic, detached – and not especially pleasurable or meaningful (the victims provide all of the meaning and value, not the Visitor, who remains implacable, inexpressive, affable but blank). Only the first moments of each encounter're shown (a more conventional film director might go further, for instance).[28]

It's not the encounters themselves that're important in *Theorem*, then, but what the encounters create or evoke or express in each person,

---

[26] Certainly, the Visitor, as embodied by Terence Stamp, is the sort of man that Pier Paolo Pasolini might be attracted to.
[27] A nod to *Blow-Up*, perhaps?
[28] But this film isn't about sex.

and how they add to the film's themes.[29] This's vividly portrayed in the way that each family member reacts to the Visitor's announcement that he has to leave. As soon as the Visitor says he's going, the foundation of each family member's life seems shaken, thrown into relief, or damaged.

Thus, the Visitor and his encounters with the Italian family and the maid in *Theorem* can be interpreted as being anything you like: he can be Christ, sure, but also life itself, or capitalism, or Communism, or Marxism, or society, or creativity, or art, or work, or whatever you want. He's a pretext, a narrative function of the film, but cleverly portrayed so that his presence can be interpreted in numerous ways.

In this all-purpose fable from 1968, the filmmakers have left enough ideological and philosophical room for everyone to leap in and carve their initials on the celluloid. (*Theorem* is a do-it-yourself essay kit: it supplies all the budding film student or film critic needs to write their own pieces about it. In *Salò, or The 120 Days of Sodom*, the companion piece to *Theorem,* Pasolini even provided his book sources on screen! In fact *Theorem* forms a kind of trilogy of films, with *Pigsty* and *Salò*).

But also in *Theorem* you can detect the self-disgust and self-doubt that would develop into a significant ingredient in Pier Paolo Pasolini's cinema (it staggers out from the swamp dripping blood and mucus and strangles *Pigsty*, the next film in the Great Pasolini Fresco Cycle). *Theorem* is thus also a commentary upon art and the artist, upon the filmmaker and this whole weird enterprise of making movies. Nothing is ever completely straightforward in the cinema of Pasolini – terms like 'complex' and 'complicated' are synonymous with Pasolini (as everybody who knew him attests, he was a complicated man).

And, like many artists, Pier Paolo Pasolini wants to have it both ways – to be idealistic and romantic but also cynical and pessimistic; to evoke something (whatever it is) at the same time as negating it or disavowing it; love and disgust simultaneously; spirituality and materialism; creation and destruction. (Part of Pasolini's personality is innately dualistic/ oppositional – rather like Jean-Luc Godard. If some person or some text or some institution suggests one thing, Pasolini, like Godard, will instantly – and automatically – veer to the opposite. And sometimes, like the smart-ass kid in school who always had a quick answer for everything, it seems as if Pasolini and Godard are being antagonistic for the sheer joy of rebellion. Pasolini and Godard know they are very clever – smarter than anybody who interviewed them. Godard was intimidating

---

29 *Theorem* doesn't seem to develop the images and set-pieces to express its theme or ideas. The drama doesn't support (carry) the text and subtext. It's a problem that occurs throughout Pier Paolo Pasolini's cinema.

because if an interviewer tried to be intellectual or daring, Godard could run rings around them. Pasolini was gentler and kinder, perhaps, than Godard as an interviewee, but there was no doubt who was dominant).

THE SECOND HALF.

The second half of *Theorem* is inaugurated when the angelic messenger-postman delivers a missive which calls the Visitor away (the Italian movie is structured in three acts, as usual, but with a turning-point halfway through).[30]

Theorem explores how each of the family members respond to what they interpret as a major crisis (it's not the Visitor leaving, as an event, that upsets their ontological equilibrium, but how they *react* to his departure. They all see it as a calamity).

Pietro is the artist who becomes inspired, ranting streams of quasi-intellectual garbage as he paints pseudo-Expressionist figures on sheets of glass[31] (following an anguished farewell speech delivered to the Visitor from his bed, the site of the first love scene in *Theorem*). So you could say that the Visitor has a positive and life-enhancing effect on the young son of the family (he's broken away from the suffocating bourgeois regime of the home and, crucially for Pasolini, from his parents). It's God and spirituality and art and creativity, all topics close to Pasolini's heart.

Poor Odetta, meanwhile, takes to flouncing about the family home and grounds: seemingly she's already lost (she was lost before, but didn't know it). She's depicted dancing and skipping in a self-absorbed moment, then, as memory kicks in, she's lingering in the garden, where she photographed the Visitor and her father, and she's back in her bedroom, looking at the photo album she created (longingly perusing the pictures of the Visitor). She paces out the garden, recalling exactly where the Visitor sat (her boyfriend, glimpsed in the opening scenes, is long forgotten).

And then Odetta sinks into a catatonia so deep she doesn't move, lying on the bed staring upwards, and is carted off to hospital. Pretty extreme! Is she too young? Too weak to withstand an encounter with a transcendent power?[32] Is she too passionate, like Jane Eyre? Was her life so shaky and empty before she met the Visitor, that she can't handle it

---

30 Actually, this moment corresponds fairly precisely to the mid-film turning-point in a conventional Hollywood movie. Although the script for *Theorem* sure isn't anything like a conventional Hollywood movie!
31 And, in desperation, he pisses on a canvas, a not-so-subtle satire of contemporary art in the 1960s (which was *much* weirder than anything in *Theorem*. Indeed, contempo art, performance art and 'happenings' in the Sixties make New Wave, Neo-realist and post-Neo-realist filmmakers look as exciting as wrinkled aunties knitting scarves.)
32 If the Visitor is the Devil, an innocent and yearning soul such as Odetta is easy pickings.

afterwards? Does he leave a hole in her soul so vast she crumples in on herself?

Is the sorry fate of Odetta in *Theorem* Pier Paolo Pasolini's mockery of the young heroine of romantic fiction, or the *shojo* (girl) of Japanese pop culture – from the 19th century, or from 1968? Those serious, demure, young women who faint away when their lovers announce they're leaving to fight against Napoleon, or when their suitors die in a duel with a cruel Count? Or is it a satire on the Victorian medical treatment of hysteria? (Once Odetta is plopped on a stretcher and hauled away, though, *Theorem* doesn't cut back to her story at all, altho' it still tracks the plotlines of Pietro, Lucia, Paolo and Emilia).

Next is Lucia, the beautiful, bored family matriarch: she resorts to driving in a white Mini car around Milano picking up young men who resemble the Visitor! And, this being a Pier Paolo Pasolini movie, of course when she enjoys them it's right next to a church![33] Oooh la la! And as there are multiple pick-ups, and as Lucia looks anguished and unhappy, we can guess that these stand-in guys are no substitute for the real thing, the Visitor. (There is a patronizing trivializing of Lucia's acts in *Theorem* – feminists would find it easy to demolish this movie).

No doubt biographers of Pier Paolo Pasolini could make cheap quips that what Lucia does – picking up young guys in her car – is what Pasolini was known for, too (including, according to the rumour of the Pasolini Legend, on that final fateful night in November, 1975). There is also a Pasolinian evocation of homosexual cruising in the Paolo scenes in Milan railroad station.

Silvana Mangano is superbly expressive in this sequence in *Theorem* – she is the sort of actor that Tim Burton raves about, a silent movie actor, who can emote without dialogue. Mangano's eyes are truly remarkable – so dark that even the lamps providing the eye-lights from Giuseppe Ruzzolini's lighting crew can't illuminate their depths. Torrents of feelings are flowing behind those eyes, but exactly what they are, we never quite know for sure. (Her anguish, however, is clearly expressed – and then instantly suppressed, as Lucia remembers herself. Has her life been reduced to this hollow existence?).

And how about her husband, the patriarch of the family? Well, Paolo too has a life-changing crisis: he gives away his factory to the workers (*Theorem* returns to the images of the factory at the beginning of the film, finally putting them into context). Easy pickings for Marxists and materialists and socialists in 1968 to dissect that particular move. Certainly

---

33 And she cruises them beside a church, too. And when she drops them off, she looks up, and there's a statue of Christ on a roof admonishing her even further.

Paolo's the figure who coalesces the familiar late 1960s themes of the bourgeoisie, ownership, labour, workers and industry within the capitalist system in *Theorem*. He is the stern patriarch, the factory boss who lives in splendour in his town villa in Milan (and summerhouse in the Po Valley).

Paolo undergoes a kind of mid-life crisis – he ends up right in the middle of Milan, at the main railroad terminus. A lengthy, lateral, Godardian tracking shot charts Paolo's Dark Night of the Soul. There is another evocation of homosexual desire here, with Paolo making eye contact with a young man (played by Luigi Barbini, who was James in *The Gospel According To Matthew*) – who then wanders into the station restroom!

But there are no more empty homosexual encounters for Paolo: instead, he undresses down to nudity on the main concourse of Milan's railroad station! And then he's suddenly transported to the black, gritty soil of Mount Etna, the setting for symbolic/ metaphysical scenes in Pier Paolo Pasolini's cinema, where he wanders in the nude and right at the end of the movie's 98 minutes, he screams incoherently, over the end title, 'FINE'.[34]

The notion of stripping down everything, and rejecting all of the trappings of modern, capitalist life, and being reduced to nothing but a naked body, is very much an ideology of its time, the late 1960s (it echoes the philosophy of the Surrealists and the *avant garde:* 'everything must go'). It is also an attractive theoretical manœuvre, compelling in its simplicity. But it's an impossible approach to existence: there is never absolutely nothing in life, and nothingness does not exist if you are still part of the so-called real world.

Lastly, Emilia the maid has a much more interesting reaction to the Visitor's departure: first, she leaves too. Bus journeys into rural regions: she winds up presumably in her homeland (where she is known by the locals). *Theorem* does an intriguing thing with Emilia now: she sits on a bench. Just *sits* there. For a *long* time, staring straight ahead. Of all the things that *Theorem* could have done with its protagonists, this is unexpected. But it works: because here comes the revival of the spiritual feeling of *The Gospel According To Matthew* and *La Ricotta*, as Emilia is transfigured into a saint (the subject fascinated Pier Paolo Pasolini – he had several projects about saints in mind, including his *St Paul*).

First off, she heals a young boy suffering from pox on his face. The shot-reverse-shot miracle revives the simple technique of *The Gospel*

---

[34] An early instance of Primal Scream Therapy in movies? – which was used by, among others, John Lennon around this time.

According To Matthew.[35] Big smiles all round. Adulation and awe from the crowd, who duly kneel (Pier Paolo Pasolini's mom, Susanna Colussi, is prominent in the Emilia-becoming-a-saint scenes. Mamma brings Emilia a tray of food, for instance, which Colussi must've done for Pasolini many times. Emilia declines the food – instead, she asks for stinging nettles! Oh yes, it has to be nettles for a Catholic saint-in-the-making, where suffering and masochism are deemed essential for spiritual transformation[36]).

A woman in the Christian tradition with miraculous powers as portrayed in cinema is somehow far more mysterious than a man – we have seen Christ at work in numerous Biblical movies (including *The Gospel According To Matthew*). And movies of the *Old Testament* in the main concern men (all those bearded patriarchs, Moses, Abraham, David, etc). But a female saint with spiritual powers is more unusual (Emilia's not a nun, for instance, the default position for women in the Christian, religious movie genre).[37]

The most suggestive aspect of Emilia's story, which the movie begins with but doesn't pursue, is that she just sits there. It's all of the onlookers who observe her who turn her into a saint. Emilia might be just anybody sitting on a bench, but her sainthood is created by the populace. However, when Emilia performs genuine acts of saintdom (or seems to perform them – which's the same thing for people who want to believe), like healing the child, *Theorem* moves into a more conventional form of narration, and it conforms to the religious stereotype.

Most inspired of all is the portrayal of Emilia transfigured and floating in the sky above the buildings. It's an impressive visual trick, flamboyant but in keeping with the movie and its theme (well, hey, this *is* an Italian movie about religion!), down to the detail of Emilia having her arms raised and outstretched, right out of Italian Renaissance paintings.[38]

The closing moments of Emilia's story are unusual, too: accompanied by the film director's mother Susanna Colussi, she finally shifts from her favourite spot on the bench, and walks to a building site and buries herself (both women are clad in Biblical black). Mamma wields a shovel, and gives Emilia an Edgar Allan Poe-style burial, while Emilia

---

[35] Remember Pier Paolo Pasolini complaining that he thought the miracles in *The Gospel* were cheesy and too obvious? But he does the same thing here!
[36] Does she eat them? Or whip herself with them?
[37] Tho' some nuns are seen observing her.
[38] Cleverly, *Theorem* stays back and below, with the viewpoint on the ground, and does not offer a close-up of Emilia: it's the effect her levitation has on the locals that's important, not how it feels to Emilia.

insists that it's not death or burial – she is there to weep.[39] Like the ending of Paolo's story, and the end of *Theorem* itself, it's not a satisfying close for the Emilia story.

If some aspects of the second half of *Theorem* are not wholly convincing or effective, including the Paolo-going-naked-in-the-middle-of-Milan sequence,[40] there's no point complaining now – *Theorem* is simply not a movie in which you can apply the conventional criteria of movie-going.

The final scene of *Theorem* depicts the father seemingly bereft of everything he hung onto, according to Bruce Kawin and Gerald Mast in *A Short History of the Movies*:

> no clothes, no sense of direction, no civilization, no concrete location, no purpose, a total moral and social leper.

Mast and Kawin insist that sexual identity is the basis for this stripping-away:

> The theorem that underlies this stripping process is, quite simply, that sexual passion knows no moral or social boundaries and that those who least know this truth – the grandest, *hautest* bourgeoisie – are most easily and completely overwhelmed by the discovery of the flimsy assumptions on which their entire lives are based. (338)

★

Variety gushed thus about *Theorem*: 'the most talked about foreign film of the year! Truly amazing in its decidedly homoerotic bias and extraordinary groin-oriented camera set-ups' (true – *Theorem* is a film for people who really fancy seeing numerous shots of Terence Stamp's crotch).

As Manny Farber puts it in *Negative Space*:

> Pasolini, in *Teorema*, places the figure as though it were sculpture in deep space. His movie becomes an ecstatic, mystical, hortatory use of mid-anatomy: Terence Stamp, languid silence and superior smile, his crotch exposed in tight, spiffy jeans, exuding compassion for all the flipping-out individuals around him.

Theorem annoyed Pierre Leprohon (in *The Italian Cinema*) with its 'concoction of half-baked symbolism and the least justifiable form of realistic emphasis', and Pier Paolo Pasolini's 'clever yet questionable ambivalence' (208).

Theorem does nothing to invite you in, it doesn't acknowledge you,

---

[39] There's a pool of tears next to her head.
[40] The nudity is cheated – Massimo Girotti is not wholly nude in Milan's train station. And when he walks, the camera lingers on his legs, in a different setting.

it doesn't care if you watch it or not. *Salò* is a tough movie to watch for some viewers, but even that film has plenty of showy moments, of let's-put-on-a-show moments, of storytelling moments. *Theorem* is so icy cold you're frozen out within minutes.

Theorem, you could say, is truly a vampiric movie – because it sucks the life out of you and gives nothing back. It's not a 'waste of time' watching it, it's not 'boring', it's not 'badly made'… but the 'worth' or the 'value' of it are very questionable.

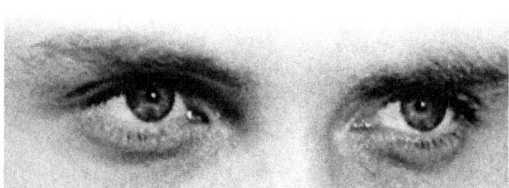

Theorem (1968).
This page and over.

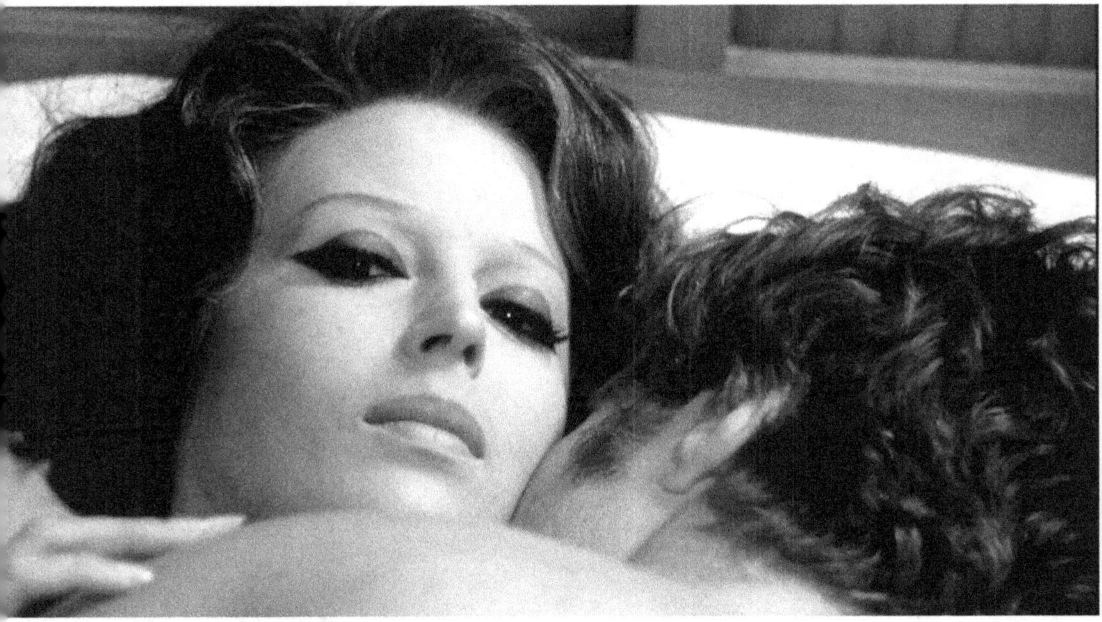

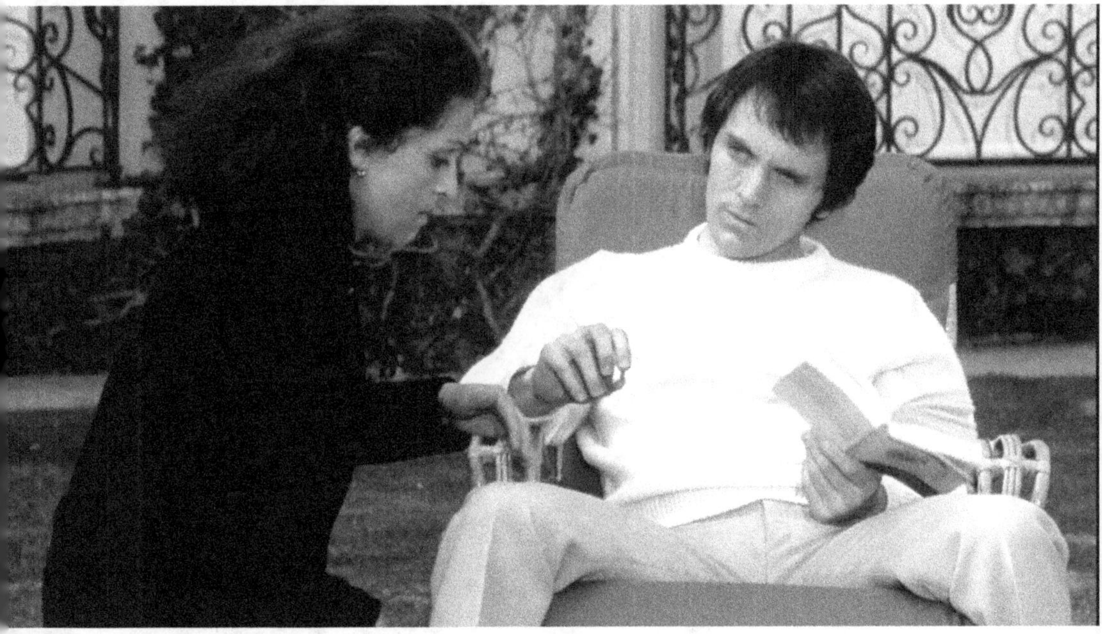

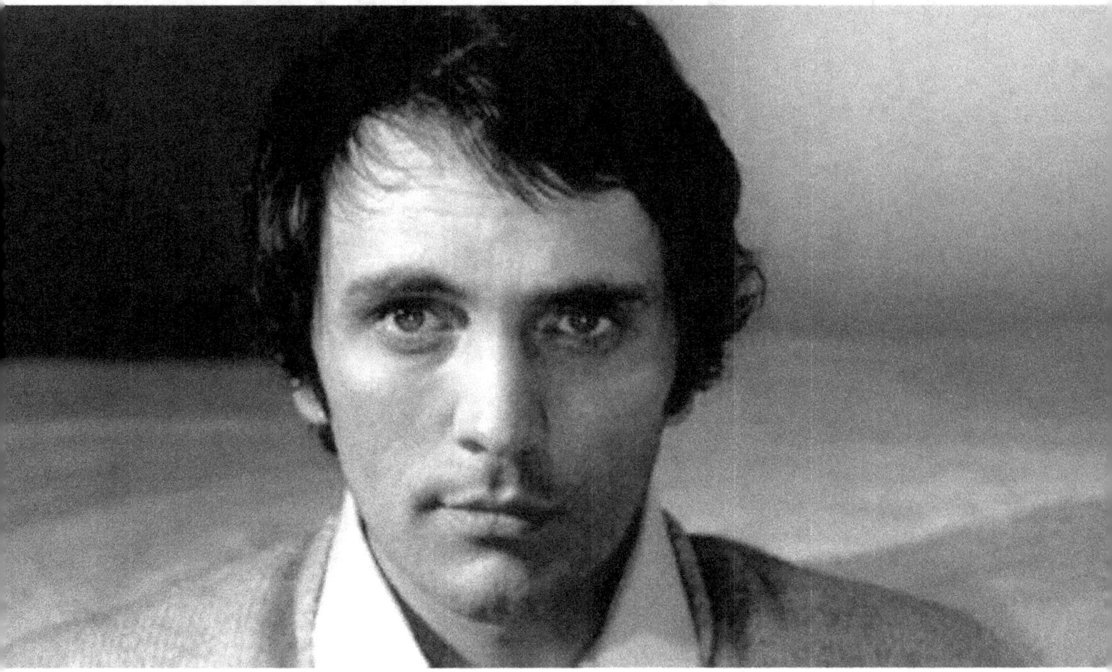

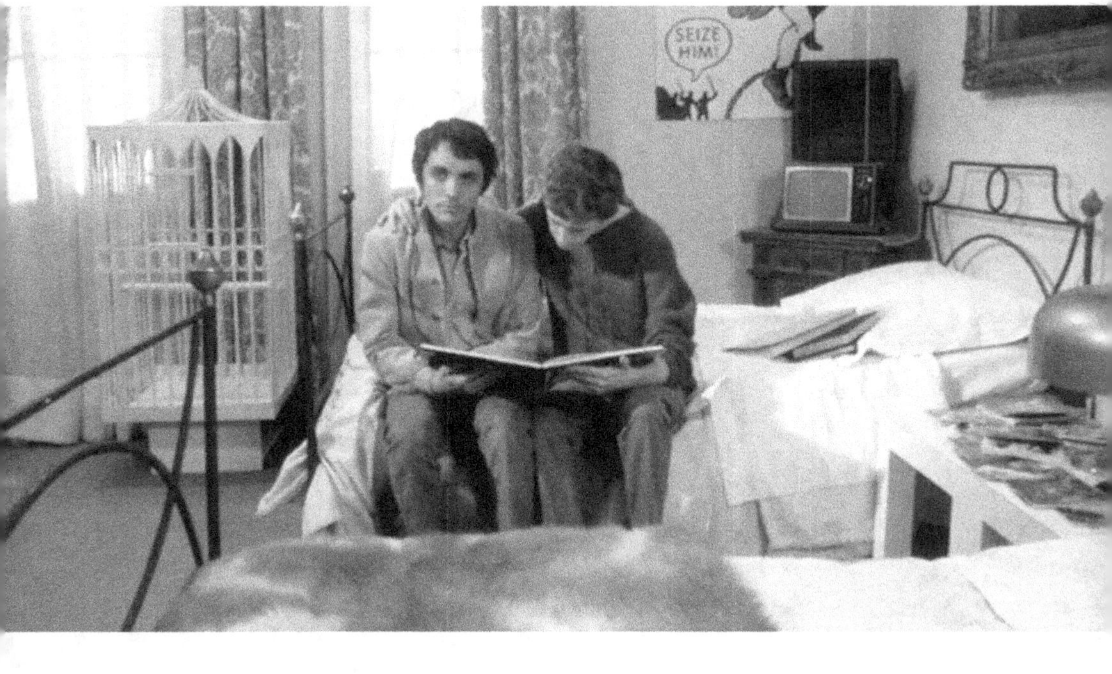
SEIZE HIM!

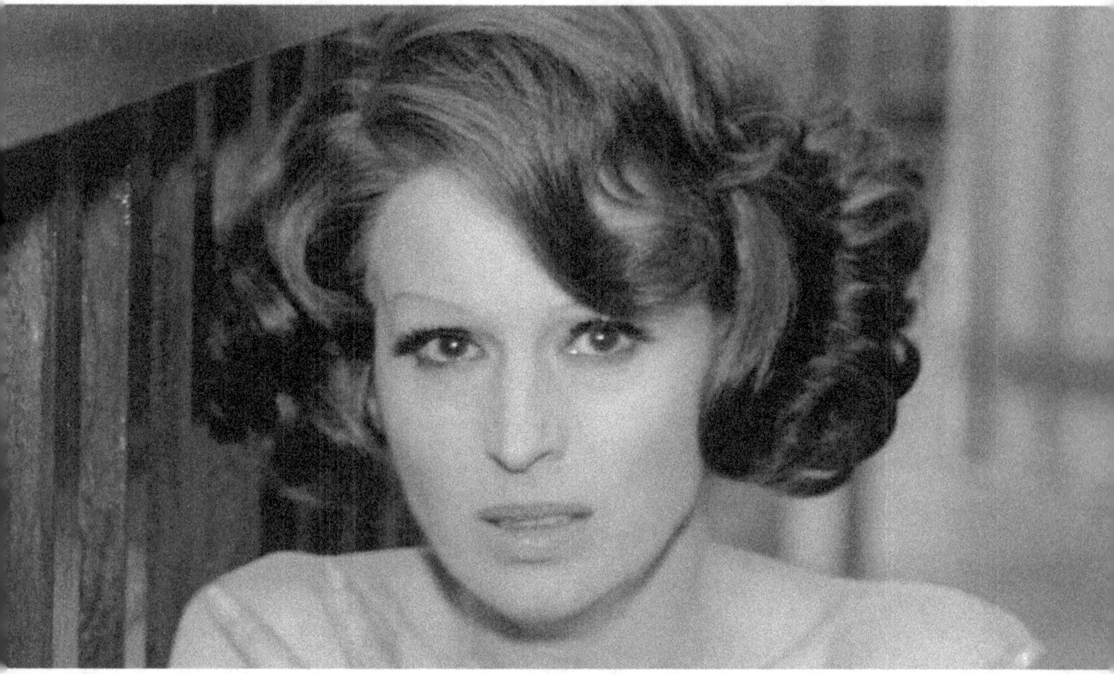

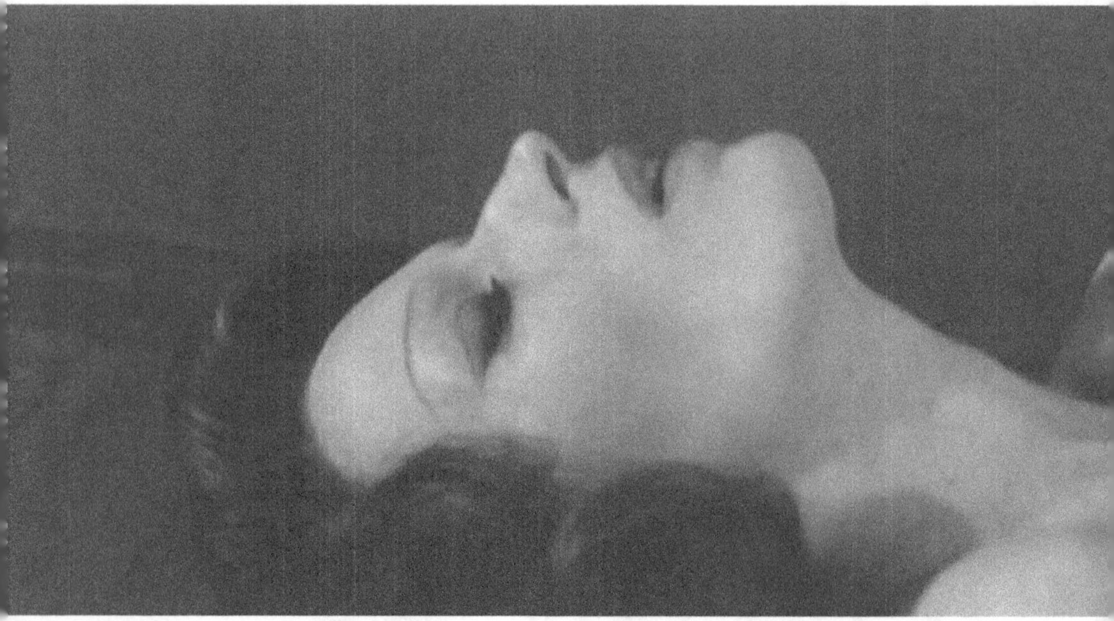

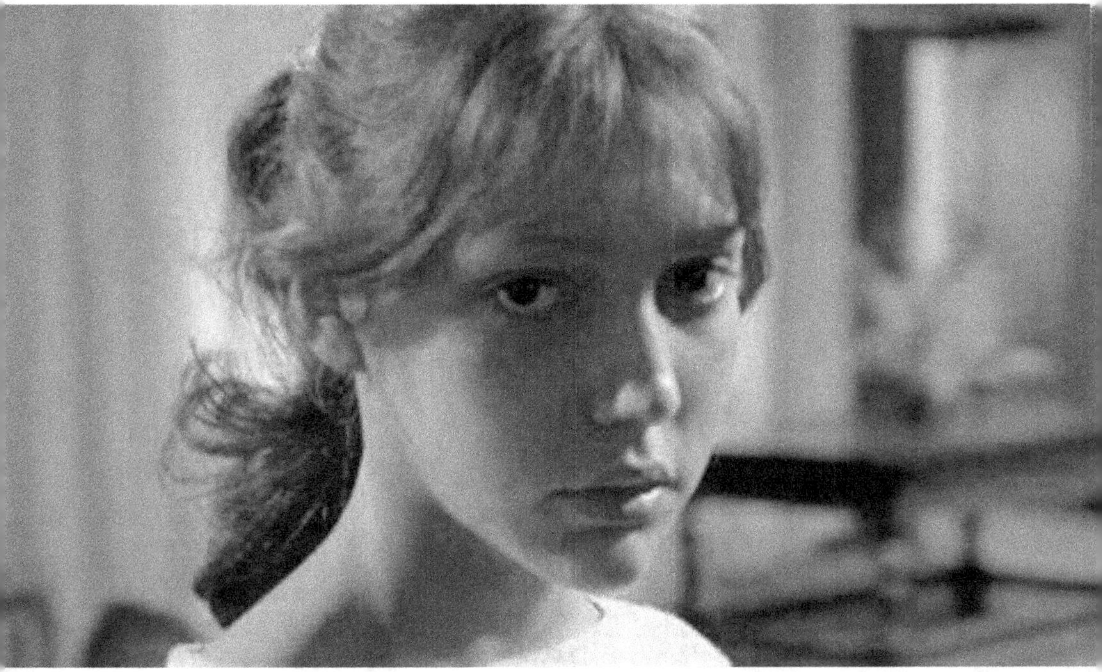

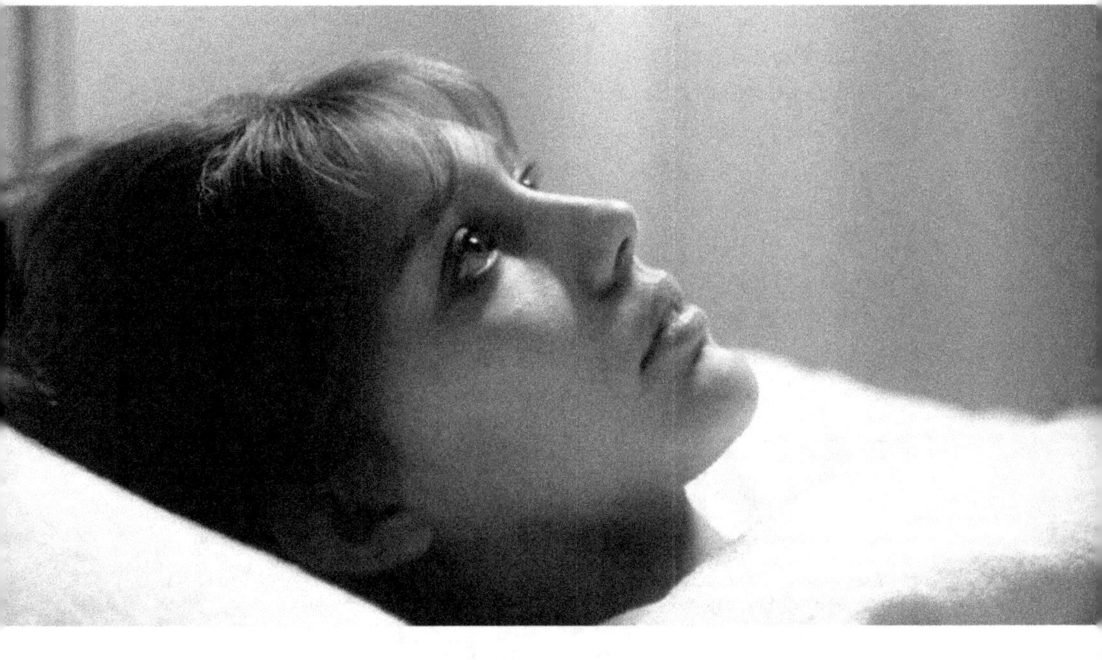

12

PORCILE

PIGSTY

Porcile (*Pigsty*, 1969) was filmed with the regular Pier Paolo Pasolini team (tho' with four cinematographers – Pasolini regulars Giuseppe Ruzzolini and Tonino Delli Colli, plus Stephen Burum[1] and Armando Nannuzzi). Gian Vitorio Baldi, Gianni Barcelloni, Paul Claudon and Macha Méril produced for Film Dell'orso/ Idi Cinematografica/ I.N.-D.I.E.F. (Rome)/ C.A.P.A.C. (Paris),[2] Benedetto Ghiglia composed the music, Danilo Donati designed the costumes, make-up: Piero Mecacci, sound by Alberto Salvatori, Nino Baragli edited, Sergio Citti, Fabio Garriba and Sergio Elia were A.D.s, and the cast included Pasolini regulars Ninetto Davoli and Franco Citti, plus Pierre Clémenti, Alberto Lionello, Margherita Lozano, Ugo Tognazzi and fellow Italian director Marco Ferreri. Chief among the actors were Anne Wiazemsky, wife of Jean-Luc Godard, and Jean-Pierre Léaud. Released: Aug 31, 1969. 99 minutes.

Pigsty combines two stories about cannibalism – one set in the 15th century, featuring Spanish soldiers, and the other in present day Germany, in a bourgeois family.

Leading the charge in *Porcile* is Pier Paolo Pasolini: he's the general who's guiding his circus of filmmakers up, up, up to the summit of the

---

[1] Stephen Burum was one of Francis Coppola's cronies at U.C.L.A. He went on become a regular DP for Coppola (*Apocalypse Now*, *Rumble Fish*, *The Black Stallion*, *The Outsiders*, etc).
[2] New Line Cinema distributed *Pigsty* in the U.S.A. In the 1970s, New Line Cinema's fare was mainly distribution deals and pick-ups on sexploitation films, 'freak' films, gay films, rockumentaries, 'midnight specials' and art films. 'Freak' films included *Reefer Madness*, *The Texas Chainsaw Massacre* (the low budget screamfest) and *Pink Flamingoes* (John Waters and Divine at their campest). Art films included *The Seduction of Mimi* (1974), and *Wedding In Blood* (1973). This was years b4 New Line Cinema became a Hollywood player with the *Lord of the Rings* movies.

volcano, Mount Etna. The old, Italian regulars in the production crew knew what they were letting themselves in for with this new Pasolinian venture, but the newbies must've wondered to each other: 'what are we doing all the way up here, on an active volcano?!' And one of the grizzled Italians in the crew might've replied, 'we're filming a 15th century tale of cannibalism'. And the newbies might've thought, 'Hell, we climbed 6,000 feet for *this*?! I thought we were filming an Akira Kurosawa samurai epic!' (And I bet some of them cursed the film director when they had to climb Mount Etna every day for two weeks).

When European art filmmakers get hold of an extreme topic such as cannibalism, they tend to over-intellectualize it, often turning it into too-obvious social and political rants. Peter Greenaway and Marco Ferreri are guilty, and *Pigsty* is, too. *Pigsty* is a rant employing Freudian-Marxist theory in the form of a chilly fable.

It takes the world of low-budget horror and comedy cinema to bring out the subject of cannibalism in all its splendour and terror. Mega-prolific Chinese film director Tsui Hark directed the marvellous horror-comedy *We're Going To Eat You* in 1980: it makes all of the same points about exploitation and consumption that arty, intellectual cinema does (including digs at oppressive regimes – referring to the People's Republic of China). But *We're Going To Eat You* is, unlike *Pigsty,* a masterful piece of political polemic delivered within a blackly comical satire.

Anyway, this particular 99-minute movie of 1969 was filmed in Italian. Unfortunately, *tra-la-la,* a substantial mistake in *Porcile* has both Anne Wiazemsky and Jean-Pierre Léaud being dubbed[3] by Italian actors.[4] If you know and love Léaud (and who doesn't?!), you'll appreciate that this fabulously charismatic, very funny,[5] and completely original actor delivers amazing performances that absolutely demand we hear his own voice! Dubbing Léaud is like dubbing Orson Welles or Woody Allen – you just don't do it, *tra-la-la*! (The Italian voices of Léaud and Wiazemsky contribute so much to the film, it's really a double act, as with Enrique Irazoqui and Enrico Maria Salerno who together performed Christ in *The Gospel According To Matthew*).

Not long before *Pigsty,* J.P. Léaud and A. Wiazemsky had been an

---

3 They are French actors playing Germans and dubbed by Italians.
4 Margherita Lozano was also dubbed – by Pasolini regular Laura Betti.
5 In some scenes, you can see Wiazemsky trying not to laugh as she acts with Léaud – he has an impish way and can be very amusing.

entertaining couple in *La Chinoise* (1967),[6] a film partly about a bunch of five young people who are sort of playing at being political radicals and even terrorists (in *Pigsty*, Wiazemsky's characterization is a continuation of/ commentary on her role as 'La Chinoise' in *La Chinoise*, and Eva in *One Plus One* (1968), the pseudo-documentary/ film essay partly about the Rolling Stones). All of the five actors among the student group are excellent in *La Chinoise*, but Jean-Pierre Léaud is absolutely brilliant (*La Chinoise*, with *Masculine/ Feminine*, is the key movie of the Godard-Léaud partnership). *Pigsty* sadly doesn't exploit what Léaud can do with the right script and the right context.

While for some the image of the Beatles or the Rolling Stones may embody the Sixties, for me the young Jean-Pierre Léaud encapsulates much of that era. The Léaud of the films of Jean-Luc Godard and François Truffaut, dressed in a jacket and sweater (or sometimes a tie), constantly flicking cigarettes into his mouth, slouching against walls, riding the Metro, sitting around in cafés, spraying anti-Vietnam War slogans on walls, looking longingly at (forever unattainable) girls, earnestly discussing Existential philosophy, and spouting polemical, political views. Léaud, the alter ego of Truffaut and Godard in many films, embodies certain aspects of the Sixties: youth, intensity, high-blown idealism, vulnerability, lust, political activism, Existential angst, melancholy and lassitude. As well as a certain, Gallic cool.

Best known for playing Antoine Doinel in Francois Truffaut's movies, beginning with *The 400 Blows,* Jean-Pierre Léaud also worked for both Truffaut and Jean-Luc Godard (the two fathers of the French New Wave) as an assistant, when acting jobs were not forthcoming (particularly in the first half of the 1960s). Godard employed Léaud as an assistant on *A Married Woman, Alphaville, Pierrot le Fou* and *Weekend.*

If ever there was an actor born to play the anti-heroes of the novels of André Gide, Albert Camus, J.-K. Huysmans and Jean-Paul Sartre, it was Jean-Pierre Léaud. The 'faces' of the Sixties in cinema are usually thought to be, in Anglo-American terms, Jane Fonda, Warren Beatty, Terence Stamp, Peter Fonda, Jeffrey Hunter, Dirk Bogarde, David Hemmings, Julie Christie, Alan Bates *et al*, but one should not forget the European stars, such as: Léaud, Jean-Paul Belmondo, Jeanne Moreau, Alain Delon, Marcello Mastroianni, Monica Vitti, Franco Citti, Brigitte Bardot, Catherine Deneuve, Romy Schneider and Sophia Loren.

---

[6] Shot in March and April, 1967, in Paris and Nanterre, and based on *The Possessed* (1872) by Fyodor Dostoievsky, *La Chinoise* was produced by the usual Jean-Luc Godard crew for Productions de la Guéville, Parc Films, Simar Films, Anouchka Films and Athos Films. Released: Aug 30, 1967. *La Chinoise* was Godard's biggest hit in the U.S.A. since *Breathless*. And yet *La Chinoise* is one of Godard's most violently anti-American films. Maybe it chimed with the anti-government, anti-Vietnam War feelings of the era. (Certainly, observers noted how prescient it was of May, 1968).

★

Both stories in *Pigsty* are fables, with fantastical, mythological and allegorical underpinnings. There isn't an ounce of 'reality' in either of them. This is ideological cinema, political-deconstruction cinema, cinema in quotation marks, happily displaying its cultural references (it opens, after all, with images of the voiceover inscribed on some carved stone tablets, followed by second unit images of pigs in a pig-pen, over which the titles play).

The usual Pasolinian philosophical oppositions are at work in *Porcile:*

the past	the present
Marxism	capitalism
Communism	consumerism
life	death
culture	nature
sons	fathers

The two tales *in Pigsty* don't stretch to a 99-minute flick, so they are combined: the decision to cut the two tales into bite-size chunks has pluses and minuses: on the minus side, you follow one story only to be dragged off to the other one at what seem at times like random points. You have to spend longer with both tales to develop the exposition. Dramatic progression and rising action are inevitably scuppered as you jump from one to t'other.

On the plus side, the editing by Nino Baragli does keep the pacing of the 1969 movie sprightly (but the integration of the stories, editorially, is uneven). There are plenty of visual and stylistic contrasts between the two stories. As one takes place high up on Mount Etna (and in the distant past), there's never any doubt which story you're following.

Curiously, one ingredient of cutting two stories together so tightly wasn't employed by Nino Baragli and the filmmakers: the opportunity to have one story directly and continuously comment upon and modify the other story. Oh, of course, they do chime at several thematic levels, but nowt is made of ironic contrasts (an image of Ida and Julian, say, picking at a feast, bored, intercut with the soldier grubbing for food in a volcanic wilderness). Instead, the big, thematic contrasts and connections are made as the stories unfold, and particularly towards the end.

★

Pier Paolo Pasolini called the second tale *Orgy* (*Orgia*) – he had written it originally (at the bidding of producer Vitorio Baldi) as a companion piece to *Simon of the Desert*, the marvellous Luis Buñuel picture of 1965.[7] So *Orgy* was conceived as a 40-50 minute piece to go with another movie.

Much of the second, 15th century tale in *Pigsty* comprises Pierre Clémenti as a hapless, hungry, lost (and apparently Spanish) soldier wandering around the black wastelands of Mount Etna, while the weather changes in every frame from bright, blue, wind-whipped skies to mist-filled cloudscapes *à la* Chinese landscape painting. As in *The Gospel According To Matthew*, everywhere you point the camera you get a sensational image. But for what purpose?

So Pierre Clémenti runs and runs (there are a *lot* of images of actors running hither and thither in this part of *Pigsty*), and... and... Well, there *is* a story, there *are* things that happen, there are issues raised, and questions asked, and themes sort of explored – but there are also times when you wonder to yourself, is this *really* the work of a major film director, a world-class film director? If this *really* a movie by the guy who directed *Accattone, Oedipus Rex* and *The Gospel According To Matthew*? (I have viewed *Pigsty* several times, but there's no benefit from doing that: *Pigsty* is not a movie that improves with time or further viewings. It's like a heap of garbage: once you've picked out all the stuff worth saving, that's it; there's no point going back to the trash hoping for more treasure).

Soldiers and processions are viewed from afar, while the cannibal hides from them. Then he runs some more. There's a sword duel with a rival soldier (played by Luigi Barbini, who was James in *The Gospel According To Matthew*). The soldier kills the guy and eats him.[8] (Yum! Human! My favourite – pass the seasoning).

And there are encounters with other soldiers (Franco Citti plays the second cannibal, who teams up with the first one, Pierre Clémenti). A party of females roped together on a cart and their guards is intercepted. The second cannibal rapes one of the women.[9] Later, a woman is pulled from a donkey (a reference to Mary and Joseph travelling to Egypt by donkey, often portrayed in Renaissance art), and beheaded, while her partner watches in horror (he scurries to town to warn the authorities, as you do).

(The 15th century narrative in *Piggysty* is allegorical/ mythical,

---

[7] *Simón del Desierto* (1965, *Simon of the Desert*), is a truly strange film: the lead character, the saint, Simon Stylites, spends most of the film on top of a pillar (it's about early Christian religious fanaticism). At the end, he is taken from the ancient world to modern-day New York City (Pasolini used similar transportations from the past to the present – such as bringing Oedipus into modern Italy). And he would've continued with that concept if he'd lived to make his *St Paul* script.
[8] After trying a butterfly and a snake.
[9] Made even more uncomfortable for the actors by taking place on sharp, jagged lava.

remember, so none of this makes 'sense' in the usual manner: for ex, what the woman on a donkey and the man are doing travelling on a barren volcano 10,000 feet high isn't clear (Mount Etna doesn't 'go' anywhere, and isn't a mountain range you need to traverse). Maybe they were heading for Egypt (during the Flight To Egypt part of the *New Testament*), and took a wrong turning? Joseph, being a stubborn, know-it-all man, would refuse to turn back or consult the map! Anyway, the woman is decapitated (her head is thrown into the Pit of Hell). This is a bitter satire of *The Gospel According To Matthew*, you could say, with *Pigsty* taking up religious iconography only to attack it.

Nor are the reasons clear for the cartload of women – are they the spoils of war? We know, as soon as they appear, that they will soon be victims – not of rape, but cannibalism! Actually, the four women survive – the second cannibal soldier (Citti) immediately launches himself at one of the women, while everybody else looks on blankly and glumly).

Maybe I've seen too many movies, maybe if I'd seen *Pigs Fried* in 1969 it might possess more *oomph* (however, weird, Euro-art movies didn't reach my desert island in 1969)... But the 15th century tale of cannibalism on a windswept volcano is, let's admit, intriguing, occasionally interesting, but lacks any ideological, political or cultural zest (let alone social or psychological impact).[10]

Pigsty's 15th century cannibalism tale also feels stretched, scraped of all its potential like meat on the bone, so there's nothing left. No heat, no juice. One single image hits home (apart from the super-spectacular setting of Mt Etna itself), and that's the delightful and archaic superstition of beheading a victim and chucking the skull into a smoking, volcanic fissure. That act has the authentic whiff and thrill of the ancient world. (Like the decision to film the 15th century cannibal story wordless, it works: besides, what dialogue would you include? – '*Uggg, urrr*, me eat you now!'.)

The obvious questions and answers don't need to be included, in *Pigs Try* and the occasional cry of agony or grunt of satisfaction or exertion are enough. The only words in this tale in *Pigsty* are the ones the first cannibal speaks, confessing that he killed his father (he repeats like a mantra: 'I killed my father... I ate human flesh... I experienced great joy'. Meanwhile, the accusations that the authorities read out against the cannibals when they're captured are ironically drowned by the sound of a

---

10 All notions of 'realism' are jettisoned: if you were starving on a mountain but could still walk, and could plainly see the countryside below, you know you could hike down the volcano in less than a day. But the soldier is forced to stay on the volcano, because he's appearing in a Italo-Marxo-Freudo-Sado movie.

tolling bell in a tower).[11]

Adam and Eve appear in the 15th century tale, tho' their appearance – as shy nudes depicted in long shots on the black, volcanic soil – is given no context, and the viewer is free to interpret them anyhow they like. A return to purity? The corruption of innocence? Paradise lost or found? Really, by this time I would imagine many viewers have *ceased to care*.

In the 15th century story, *Pigs Lie* introduces an observer figure halfway through, in the form of Ninetto Davoli. He's first seen cavorting and dancing in a bell-tower with a chum tooting on a recorder (Davoli's blue costume includes an anachronistic Charlie Chaplin hat – which Davoli also wears in the 'trilogy of life' films). Davoli's characterization – as Maracchione[12] – does not fit in the world of *Pigsty* at all. But what Pasolini says, goes.

I can't be the only archangel on the planet who does *not* want to see Ninetto Davoli prancing like an idiot through another Pier Paolo Pasolini movie! Alas, after this film – of 1969 – Davoli frolics several more times from one end of Pasolini's movies to the other (including the short pieces). Didn't anybody dare to inform the maestro that perhaps Davoli's capering was not at the humorous level of Charlie Chaplin, or even a run-of-the-mill mediæval jester?).

★

World War Two casts a long shadow over *Pigs Fly* (and over Pier Paolo Pasolini's life, his life-philosophy and his career),[13] as the 1969 movie explores more crimes in the long list of the 'Sins of the Fathers'. As in *Salò, or The 120 Days of Sodom*, there are evocations of decadent ex-fascists, of what the aged patriarchs in the country house did in the war, and of the Nazis' treatment of the Jews (there are references to the Holocaust, and repulsive analogies made between Jews and pigs). Klotz is delighted, in a childish, giggling way, to discover that he has the dirty on his rival with his Nazi war record and treatment of Jews.[14]

Pigs and fascism, pigs and sexuality, pigs and humans – humans as pigs, Jews as pigs, sex as base and animal and piggish, a youth (Julian) who has perverted relations with pigs... *Pigsty* is like a naïve, reductionist, overly-simplistic student essay on the relationships between the writings of Sigmund Freud and the Marquis de Sade and contemporary radical politics (including the materialist branch of Bolognan Marxism),

---

11 And there're sections in the 15th century tale where soldiers're sent up onto the volcano to deal with the cannibals.
12 The name 'Maracchione' means 'Frizzy-Haired Youth With Goofy Grin'.
13 He thought of himself as a child of the Resistance.
14 Pier Paolo Pasolini classified them as 'the neo-capitalists with the Nazi past and the more cultured paleo-capitalist' (PP, 142).

World War Two and the rise of fascism. (In Pasolini's cinema, fascism and his own father, Carlo Alberto Pasolini, are linked: the cool, geometric images in *Pigsty* echo the framing story of *Oedipus Rex*, and also look forward to *Salò, or The 120 Days of Sodom*).

★

So in the contemporary-set movie tale of *Pigsty* (set in 1967), we are in the world of the German, industrial bourgeoisie (set in Godesberg, near Cologne), where two bourgeois, German kids, Ida and Julian (Anne Wiazemsky and Jean-Pierre Léaud) embark on a series of discussions.[15] Filmed in Villa Pisani, Stra, Venice, using a classical approach (with the usual 50 mil lens), it has a stagey, static look which sometimes resembles the smart-ass but vacuous films of Peter Greenaway. (The camera is on a tripod, the framing employs vertical symmetry, centred framing, with clean, cool compositions. This blank, matter-of-fact form of cinematography enhances the sterile world of the bourgeois family: they possess a vast place to live in but it's cold and lifeless, with rooms too big and with few personal effects. The bourgeois characters seem to be alive but they're dead, and they don't realize it (yes, folks, it's *Theorem* all over again). Notice how little movement there is in the shots, as the characters face each other and talk at each other).

For costumes, Danilo Donati is relatively held back, compared to many of his films for Pier Paolo Pasolini. It's penitents' grey robes and peasants' rags for the 15th century story, tho' Donati allows himself a very ostentatious hue for all of the soldiers's costumes – lilac (and padded, too – Donati was fond of bulking up scrawny extras with padding[16]). In the modern tale, all is formal men's suits, as befitting the ruling classes of West Germany.

The dialogue in *Pigs Cry* is wry, fey, self-conscious, would-be clever-clever (but not funny in the slightest – even with the addition of the kids saying *tra-la-la* at the end of their sentences). It's as if Pier Paolo Pasolini is doing Jean-Luc Godard by way of Luchino Visconti, with generous doses of Freudian psychoanalysis and Frazerian anthropology, while Bertholt Brecht[17] and Karl Marx are waiting in the wings to add their stodgy dollops of warmed-over, post-Communist remains.

Ida talks about going to the Berlin Wall to piss on it with a bunch of radical friends, *tra-la-la* (*Pigsty* is *very* 1968, at least in spirit if not in actuality – the movie is more 1768 than 1968. We know that Pasolini in a poem famously regarded hippy radicals in the counter-culture of the late

---

[15] Julian and Ida are betrothed – but they also act like brother and sister, adding the theme of incest to bestiality.
[16] This is a standard device in costuming.
[17] Brecht and Grosz are cited in the dialogue.

1960s as bourgeois,[18] and that his political sympathies were with the cops, because they were working class. But Pasolini was also sceptical of the Italian government, its laws and the enforcers of those laws, the *carabinieri*. And he was sympathetic to some of the aims of the counter-culture, altho' he wouldn't want love and peace and revolution if it was created by bourgeois radicals).

Meanwhile, Julian is non-committal: he wears Jean-Pierre Léaud's impish, nonchalant, Gallic smile as a response to everything that Ida proposes. (He insists that he wants to stay home to do stuff. What stuff, *tra-la-la*? Ida wants to know – only later do we find out that it's stuff with pigs, *tra-la-la*.).[19] Ida's fate is to be fascinated by Julian and rejected by him.

Thus, *Pigsty* is a satire (feeble, though) of trendy, Sixties films where youths ache to be rebels – they come from an ultra-bouorgeois background (they are first seen in the vast mansion), but they hanker after taking a leak on the Berlin Wall like a cool revolutionary. Well, *Ida* does – Julian would rather stay at home and fondle pigs (that, too, is a send-up of the Godardian, romantic, radical couple – instead of spray-painting 'PEACE IN VIETNAM' on the side of the American ambassador's car (as in *Masculine/Feminine*),[20] Julian slopes off to the pig-farm).

The attack on the bourgeoisie in *Pigsty* – which is as easy and natural (and automatic) for Pier Paolo Pasolini as it is for J.-L. Godard – develops from *Theorem*, and finds its grandest and bitterest expression in *Salò, or The 120 Days of Sodom*. (That both Pasolini and Godard grew up in very bourgeois households is part of the aversion and the irony).

World War Two, West Germany, the Nazis, fascism,[21] postwar industrialization, capitalist business, the Cold War, the Holocaust, student protest, radicalism... *Pigsty* evokes a whole battery of Serious Topics only to: (A) dismiss them, or (B) demean them, or (C) score cheap jokes off them.

Julian is a curious characterization in the cinema of Pier Paolo Pasolini: in terms of drama, he is a character who says 'no' to everything. But not in the sense of being an Existential, Bohemian rebel who counters authority and society ('a rebel is someone who says no', as

---

18 But Pasolini did talk about love this period. Love is necessary for life, Pasolini acknowledged in 1970: 'without love, people die, they suffocate. It is depression, death'. But capitalist societies have no use for love because it doesn't lead to production: 'all societies are sexually repressive, because the energy that man consumes to make love fails to profit capital' (1970).
19 Thus, the opening images of *Pigsty* depict Julian's harem, perhaps!
20 Léaud and his chum do that in *Masculine/Feminine* (1966). Léaud takes to declaiming on politics, and indulging in the occasional act of political subversion: spray painting walls with slogans, or the side of a car (the side of a Ford limo used by some Americans is daubed with 'PAUX AU VIETNAM' and the two lads yell 'U.S. go home!). The graffiti-mad tendency would be continued by Anne Wiazemsky in *One Plus One*.
21 Mr Klotz looks like both Adolf Hitler and Benito Mussolini.

Albert Camus put it). Rather, Julian is empty, devoid of pretty much anything. Whatever Ida suggests, Julian negates it: he's not vindictive, or sarcastic, or hostile (well, he's a little hostile), he's just... empty.

Julian is a portrait of a late 1960s youth who seems to have everything (he's from a well-off family, doesn't have to work, has everything he needs, and has a pretty fiancée in the form of Ida), but actually has nothing. Or he himself *is* nothing (which was how Pier Paolo Pasolini seemed to view the bourgeoisie: they were leaders of society but had no idea how to lead, or where to go). It's typical of Pasolini to push the nihilism really far – it would develop in intensity up to *Salò, or The 120 Days of Sodom*.

Julian shares affinities with the mysterious Visitor in *Theorem* – these are seemingly attractive youths, apparently people with charisma and talent, but they don't know what to do with their lives. It's the spiritual emptiness of advanced capitalist society: following World War II, when Europe rebuilt itself and developed the affluence and materialism of the 1960s, life seemed better than it had ever been. It's the evocation of the upper echelons of society, where there's no need to work, and the struggle to survive has been eradicated by wealth and technology.

But for Pier Paolo Pasolini this section of society is not really alive. The bourgeoisie lack the joy of being alive, or all of the things that make life worth living. Notice how Ida, even though her political activity and her right-on friends are superficial and bourgeois, is at least engaging in life head-on. Not Julian, who at 25 years-old seems to have withdrawn from life completely. Whatever Ida suggests they do, Julian declines – he only wants to be left alone so that he can spend his hours in his own way (which means visiting the pig-pens).

Thus, the portrait of Julian by Pier Paolo Pasolini is a send-up of the Existential, outsider figure of European literature in the mid-20th century, the bourgeois, alienated youth who inhabits the fictions of Huysmans, Hamsun, Gide, Sartre, Durrell, Huxley *et al.* He's someone who can't connect, who refuses to be part of active society, who distances himself from everybody (later, in the 21st century, these people were dubbed 'shut-ins' or *otaku*, teenagers who preferred to stay indoors, to play with their cel phones and video games, and never venturing out).

Julian teases Ida about what he does with his time, but never lets her know what it is. He talks in mock-poetic terms – about a door, a floating leaf, and a grunt. This *haiku* could be anything, but later we're told that it relates to Julian hanging out with pigs.

If she really knew, Julian smarmily suggests, she would be shocked.

Julian is supercilious, arrogant – to mask his mental instability. Giving Julian such a grotesque hobby – bestiality – is typical of Pier Paolo Pasolini's black humour (tho' it's also not entirely successful. Pasolini's form of humour often masks a suppressed hostility towards all sorts of social targets, which you find in many comedians – along with manic depression and self-loathing. But many stand-up comics are actually very funny, using all of that angst and anger to create jokes, and Pasolini – let's face it – is not funny[22]).

One could take a biographical approach to the material in *Pigsty*, and relate it to Pasolini's life. The film evokes a sexual perversion which contravenes social norms, which can't be mentioned in polite society (and ends in d*e*a*t*h). Homosexuality might be inferred here.

★

Porky-Porcile is a series of conversations that go nowhere, that amount to nothing. The pointlessness of it all is one supposes part of the point. In one tale all is would-be witty repartee (usually between two actors framed on either side of the screen, facing each other, unmoving, like stuffed parrots on a stage); in the other story, no dialogue whatsoever, only the occasional grunt or effort noise, as actors run, run, run across black, volcanic dust and stones (i.e., action as opposed to stasis and sitting and lying down, but it's action as stasis, action that's empty of, well, anything[23]).

Some of the conversations in *The Gospel of Porky's According To Pasolini* are nigh-on interminable. Like the two-hander scenes between Mr Klotz (Alberto Lionello) and Hans Gunther (Marco Ferreri), and then between Mr Klotz and Mr Herdhitze (Ugo Tognazzi), his old friend and business rival from b4 the war, filmed against airy, Baroque paintings, as Mr Herdhitze relates a tale of Mr Klotz's son Julian, back in 1959, when he was in the countryside and started to visit the pigs every day (so he would've been 15. Some boys chase girls, this one chased pigs!). The tale goes on and on, with no end in sight, and, ultimately, closes with hints of bestiality. (Klotz doesn't want to hear this, of course – but Herdhitze gloats a little as he hints at his son's depravity). Pier Paolo Pasolini had snickered at Federico Fellini going off the deep end when he visited the set of *Juliet of the Spirits* (1965), but here in *Pigsty,* Pasolini stumbles and falls (into a volcanic chasm)

Klotz and Herdhitze are old business rivals: they are ultra-capitalists who are ruling over industrial empires in West Germany as it surges towards dominance in postwar Europe. Essentially, they are the kings of

---

22 Charlie Chaplin is cited in *Pigsty* – a filmmaker who would never attempt a satire of this kind!
23 The action doesn't take the characters anywhere, except to More Of The Same.

the New Europa – and as bosses and employers, they are the kind of people loathed by Marxists even more than bourgeois students (and in late 1960s films helmed by Pasolini, some of that hatred was vividly expressed).

Their encounter is filmed in a stagey manner as two wily businessmen pretending to be polite: the focus is on the exchange of dialogue and the undercurrent of animosity between them. Herdhitze has come to destroy Klotz, he tells him, with his long tale about Klotz's very unusual son, Julian the Pig-Boy. Herdhitze's notion is that the public revelation of Julian's perversions will topple his adversary, enabling him to take control of his business interests (it's capitalism's form of eating your enemy).

Pier Paolo Pasolini's well-known denunciations of consumerism in advanced capitalism, which he thought was undermining the way of life in Europe, are part of the context of the encounter between the business rivals (there are sarcastic swipes at Germany producing cheese and buttons).

Pigsty is a movie in search of the images and events needed to tell its two stories. Or it's two stories in search of faces, acts, gestures and images. *Pigsty* doesn't find the dramatics required to illustrate what are really two (not that compelling) rants. *Pigsty* is more like 'notes for a film', in the manner of Pier Paolo Pasolini's *Oresteia* documentary (or the 'notes for films' which Jean-Luc Godard produced).

In sum, *Pigsty* might be better served if was abandoned. Instead, I would suggest:

1. Pier Paolo Pasolini telling the audience the two stories, reading the script to-camera, in close-up, and commenting upon it.

2. An interview with Pasolini, in which director explains what he'd like to do in *Pigsty*.

3. A radio interview or an audiobook, on tape/ CD/ DVD/ MP3, etc.

4. A filmed rehearsal with Pasolini directing his actors (now *that* I would love to see! Any of the footage of Pasolini at work, even scrappy, image-only footage, is more compelling than this).

Because, in truth, Pier Paolo Pasolini *himself* is far more interesting than anything or anyone in *Pigsty*.[24] I would much rather watch and listen to Pasolini talking about the kind of movie he'd like to make with this material (and ditto with some of his other films). And then he wouldn't need to make it. And we wouldn't have to watch it. It would exist only

---

[24] Again, the biggest name in *Pigsty* is Pier Paolo Pasolini.

as talk, conjecture, musings.

Because, let's face it, what is *Pigs Buy* but a series of boring conversations filmed in a boring manner with boring actors in boring settings (yes, hard to believe, but *Pigsty* renders even the divine Jean-Pierre Léaud boring! And halfway through, it confines him to bed in a catatonic state! (This is a reprise of Wiazemsky's fate in *Theorem*). Well, that's not how to use a white-hot performer like Léaud!).

Meanwhile, the 15th century tale in *Pigsty* is a series of boring shots of boring actors performing boring actions (running, looking, standing, running) in a spectacular location. (And the theme/ issue/ motif/ metaphor of cannibalism is bloodless, as dry and barren as the black lava of Mount Etna).

There's no question that in *Medea, Oedipus Rex* and *Salò, or The 120 Days of Sodom*, Pier Paolo Pasolini and the filmmaking team came up with imagery and scenes and costumes and gestures and all the rest that were worthy of and expressive of and locked into the material. But not in *Pigsty*.

But as Pasolini said in 1973:

> I avoid fiction in my films. I do nothing to console, nothing to embellish reality, nothing to sell the goods.

★

Pigsty is one of those movies where dissatisfied audiences come out of the theatre and go:

A: 'What the hell was that?! What did we just see?'

B: 'Uhh, that was a Marxist-Freudian deconstruction of late 20th century (European) society, war/ fascism and culture by way of the Marquis de Sade and Georges Bataille.'

A: 'But there wasn't a single laugh in it! It was garbage!' [25]

B: 'Indeed, *garbage* is right, *caro mio*: refuse and excrement, like pigs and offal, and the body and sex, were one of Passie's key semiotic-semantic-pedantic motifs.'

A: 'I mean, it was *awful!* Why didn't Herr Pazzoleeny publish the script as an essay in *Diacritics*?! Why make audiences sit thru that junk?!'

Yes: because we *have* seen this kind of post-Freudian, post-Marxist deconstruction of the oral-anal elements in late capitalist society before. I mean, Pier Paolo Pasolini and *Pigsty* are *not* the only ones to have made those connections between money = gold = shit = offal = food = pigs =

---

25 'And *I* paid for our tickets!'

humans = bodies = sex = death = spirit = religion = God = fathers = sons, etc etc etc.

★

Back to the movie and to Adam and Eva – it seems as if the two nude people have been placed on the mountainside by the authorities to lure out the cannibals![26] Maybe it's the appeal of fresh, new bodies to cut up – they've already eaten the Virgin Mary, now they get to chomp Adam and Eva!

So symbolically the Garden of Eden becomes a charnel-house. Or something. Or it's the Catholic Mass, or it's eating gods. As the soldiers round up the cannibal gang, the first soldier disrobes. He and his cohorts are captured, in yet another anti-dramatic,, anti-action, anti-art scene. (This is the polar opposite of Hollywood movies when, in a cowboy flick, a posse chases down and captures a gang of hoodlums).

Thus, Adam and Eve appear as an admonishment, a warning from the local authorities: this is how you're supposed to behave, they suggest, by lying about on the ground, or just *being*, rather than running around like savages, kidnapping passers-by and killing them and eating them. (What the local administrators want is passive, compliant, meek citizens, like good Adam and Eve, rather than naughty brigands).

The Middle Ages tale in *Pigsty* ends with the cannibals caught and put on trial: their punishment is to be taken back up Mount Etna,[27] staked out on the hard, black lava and left for the wild dogs. So it's the themes of eating and being eaten, again (mirroring the ending of the modern-day story). Tied to wooden stakes on the ground is another twist on the Crucifixion, of course (during the trial and the punishment, the second soldier (Citti) is trembling and weeping, full of remorse, and kissing the Priest's cross[28]).

Meanwhile, during the carrying out of the punishment on the mountainside, the first soldier (Pierre Clémenti) works up to a confession, in a dazed, melancholic state: 'I killed my father... I ate human flesh... I experienced great joy'. In this post-Stoic tale of Existential nihilism, a confession like that amounts to absolutely nothing and doesn't halt his death penalty (as Julian tells Ida in the other story, he is completely indifferent).

You know that the endings of the two stories in *Pigsty* are going to be, well, underwhelming. I mean, there isn't going be a Big Finish, seeing as how the rest of the picture is less than stellar (no grand

---

[26] Yet the cannibal gang already has four women.
[27] Don't make us go back to Mount Etna! Couldn't we be staked out to die on the beach at Capri, perhaps? After a sauna and a final meal (lobster and white wine, followed by lemon sorbet ice cream)?
[28] Looking forward to how Citti confessed on his death-bed in *The Decameron*.

beginning, no riveting set-pieces in the middle, etc). *Pig's Eye* is an essay masquerading as a movie (nothing wrong with that), but it's a stuffy, secondhand essay, an essay submitted by a third-rate, rather dim student on a literature course which would be rejected by any cultural journal. It just doesn't stand up.

Worse: it pulls its punches. Just when it warms up to approaching something face-on, it dithers and backs away. It glories in its *un*dramatic qualities (then expects the audience to enjoy its restraint, its 'complete indifference'!).

Needless to say, the endings of both of the plots in *Pigsty* is the age-old formula of d-e-a-t-h. Pasolini had used it before, and he would use it again. Julian wakes from his coma (or was it an adolescent huff, rebellion as staying in bed and refusing to come out of his room?). He eats. Ida flounces in (sporting a mandatory Big Sixties Hat – this was 1969), announcing that she's getting married.

The duologue between Julian and Ida continues the waspish, nerdy, quasi-intellectual cat-fighting between the two, with Julian insisting on playing the too-cool, Existential rebel (though Léaud also performs one of his signature gestures – whistling – *tra-la-la*!).

We were told earlier that Julian sank into unconscious despair as soon as Ida left (to play political radicals in the German capital) – he never confesses to her how much she means to him (he's a youth who never uses the word 'love', and if he does, it's always sarcastically). So it's dramatically logical that when Ida leaves to get married, Julian should seem to walk to the pigsty to his doom, a kind of suicide.

So as *Piggysty* trundles towards its double endings, we wait – like an audience at a pompous lecture waiting impatiently for like the summing-up from the tweed-suited professor on the dais – and we know it can't be good. It isn't. Poor Jean-Pierre Léaud wanders over to the pig-pens (and we glimpse Ninetto Davoli in his blue outfit – he appears in both tales, and if anybody's going to pop up, it's got to be Davoli! Now he's one of the labourers on the Klotz estate, working in the garden[29]).

This is the scene where Julian gets eaten by the pigs! Wow! At last, some action! Some drama! Or, at least, something to vomit over! No such luck. *Pigstyle* does *not* dramatize this. We *don't* see Jean-Pierre Léaud being eaten by fat, muddy, grunting pigs! (At least Walerian Borowczyk in *The Beast* and *Three Immoral Women* depicted sex with animals. Mad, yes, but it paid off the premise and delivered on its promise). But poor, shy *Pig Poke* instead has it all back-announced,

---
[29] A reprise of Davoli as the shepherd in *The Gospel*.

discussed, talked about, in yet another dully directed, talky scene. (Likewise, the scenes where Julian apparently does naughty things with the porkers wasn't shown either. Instead, there are shots of pigs, as Julian drifts over to the pig-farm while the champagne and frivolity merger party is underway in the main house).

A bunch of shuffling, embarrassed, downcast locals turn up at the celebration, when Klotz and Herdhitze have buried the fascist hatchet, and joined businesses (it's the proletariat meeting the bourgeoisie, with an uncomfortable attitude of disdain on both sides).

And who does Pier Paolo Pasolini chose to be the spokesman of the locals who've come to report Julian's demise? Ninetto Davoli yet again! And why is the scene curiously staged, without anybody rushing to find the Klotzes? Why is it Herdhitze not Klotz who hears the news? Because of the merger, and now Herdhitze doesn't want to demolish his rival. So he asks the working class visitors to keep silent about it, once it's established that there is nothing left of Julian, no scrap of cloth, no button, nothing.

Yes, you could argue that Pier Paolo Pasolini had a powerful hi-faltuin' (ideological, political, poetic, psychological, philosophical and religious) reason for not depicting sex (or death) with pigs (on top of the usual film censorship. But I don't buy it. However, I don't *demand* to see it, either. I don't care either way (I'm 'completely indifferent', like Julian); I just think that the dramatic and cinematic solutions that *Pigsty* came up with for the resolving of the modern-day story were hopeless.

It's rather like Jean-Luc Godard *not* showing the car crash in *Contempt* (1963) where Jack Palance and Brigitte Bardot die. Two big stars expire in a car crash! Fritz Lang (who also appeared in the French-Italian movie), couldn't believe that Godard de-dramatized the event, and didn't show it.[30]

Ah, but that's Jean-Luc Godard! – wilful, strange, eccentric, unique, and especially perverse when it came to staging big action scenes (look at *any* of his movies – Godard simply *could not be bothered!*). Yet *Le Mépris* is still a masterpiece of cinema, whereas *Porcile* – perhaps Pier Paolo Pasolini's most 'Godardian' outing[31] – isn't worthy of cleaning the pig-*merde* off the tyres of Jack Palance's red sports car.

★

---

30 After the car crash (with a petrol tanker, of course!), *Contempt* literally falls to pieces, there's nowhere else for it to go, the juice and the heat have left the movie, and the characters disperse with mumbled goodbyes.
31 With competition from *Theorem*.

PIGSTY AND *WEEKEND*.

Part of *Pigsty* is a black comedy, but as a black comedy, it's a lame duck. *Pigsty* clearly draws on the work of Jean-Luc Godard, in particular his angrier works of the later Sixties, such as *La Chinoise, Made In U.S.A., One Plus One, Pierrot le Fou* and of course *Weekend*.[32]

Weekend is a forerunner of *Pigsty* in several respects: the political and ideological issues, Marxist deconstructions of postwar Europe, cannibalism (including references to pigs), and a black comedy approach.

Weekend, filmed in September and October, 1967, is an apocalyptic, hallucinatory, satirical, savage, spectacular, stupid, and very over-the-top movie. In my book on Jean-Luc Godard, I described *Weekend* as:

A refusal of co-optation.

A series of obscenities to uncover obscenity.

A Brechtian road movie.

Brecht meets Mao Zedong to discuss the Shell oil company while a French New Wave performance artist stages a series of road accidents behind them.

Weekend is one of Jean-Luc Godard's more politicized films (though nearly all of Godard's films have a distinctive, idiosyncratic ideological or political slant or agenda). In *Weekend*, though, Godard does not bother to hide his political or social targets. This is high octane satire, a petrol-driven savaging of the bourgeoisie, of contemporary France, and of Western capitalism. As one of the cannibal activists (Kalifon – Jean-Pierre Kalifon) at the end put it: 'the horror of the bourgeoisie can only be overcome by more horror'. Pier Paolo Pasolini attempts a similar tactic in the 15th century story in *Pigsty* (tho' *Salò, or The 120 Days of Sodom* was a more accomplished run at similar subject matter).

Weekend's mise-en-scène is unforgettable: once you've seen *Weekend*, you never forget it.[33] Jean-Luc Godard's image-making is superlative: it's an increasingly hellish landscape of smashed and burning cars, endless traffic jams, car crashes, hijacks, crazed terrorists, barroom philosophers and characters out of pop culture, including: Emily Brontë[34] (Blandine Jeanson) dressed as Alice in Wonderland, Tom Thumb (Yves Afonso), and Jean-Pierre Léaud, wonderful as Louis Antoine Léon de St Just, a

---

32 Enzo Siciliano cites two inspirations for *Porcile*: Jean-Marie Straub and Kenji Mizoguchi (ES, 331). One a Brechtian, polemical French filmmaker (who has worked mainly in Germany and Italy), the other one of the grand masters of Japanese cinema.

33 Pauline Kael loved *Weekend*, calling it 'a great, original work', 'the most powerful mystical movie since *The Seventh Seal* and *Fires On the Plain* and passages of Kurosawa' (1971, 167-8). Kael acknowledged the flaws in *Weekend*, but the movie was 'so surreally powerful' it went beyond its flaws: it was a vision of Hell to rank with the greatest (Bosch or Grünewald): 'the nightmarish anger that seems to cry out for a revolution of total destruction and the visionary lyricism are so strong they hold the movie together; they transcend the perfectly achieved satire' (ib., 171-2).

34 Lautréamont is quoted in the hippies scene.

figure from the French Revolution, declaiming about freedom and violence in a field in 18th century costume ('freedom, like crime, is born of violence'), and as a man in a phone booth who gets into a fight with Roland (Jean Yanne).[35]

Weekend sees the film director working at full power: this is Jean-Luc Godard firing on all cylinders, this time with material which is wholly in tune with his sensibilities and skills. *Weekend* is an *incredibly* angry movie – the bitterness in *Weekend* leaves all of Godard's disciples and imitators far behind (Bertolucci, Fassbinder, Stone, Tarantino – even Pasolini). It took until *Salò, or The 120 Days of Sodom* for Pasolini to put a similar sort of rage into a movie (even then, Godard at his fiercest is more nihilistic than pretty much any comparable filmmaker).

To achieve his assault on Western civilization, Jean-Luc Godard musters an impressive array of Godardian, Brechtian, modernist effects and techniques – the full arsenal, in fact (this is a kitchen sink film – it's all thrown in): graphic intertitles (mainly in red and blue), jump cuts, lengthy takes, endless tracking shots, half-naked women talking about group sex, sudden eruptions into violence, filmic references, characters delivering pieces to camera, characters reading aloud from books, allegorical characters, diatribes on North Amerika, the West, revolution, the French Revolution, Marxism, the proletariat, and so on.

As Jean-Luc Godard's movies provide forerunners of *Pigsty* (there are others, such as Pier Paolo Pasolini's own shambling 'comedies' like *The Hawks and the Sparrows* and *The Witches*), so *Pigsty* is itself a forerunner of *Salò, or The 120 Days of Sodom*. It's not too big a step from the icy, frozen aristocrats in their palatial and utterly frigid mansion in *Porcile* to the lakeland palazzos of *Salò*. (There is the same emphasis on archaic ritual and untameable violence: in Pasolini's world, the Furies of Greek mythology were never wholly assimilated into civilization, and civilized people always retain vestiges of aggression which never die).

---

[35] And it's all very *French* – it's a surreal, vicious view of France and the French, but it's also instantly recognizable as France and the French.

Pigsty (1969).
This page and over.

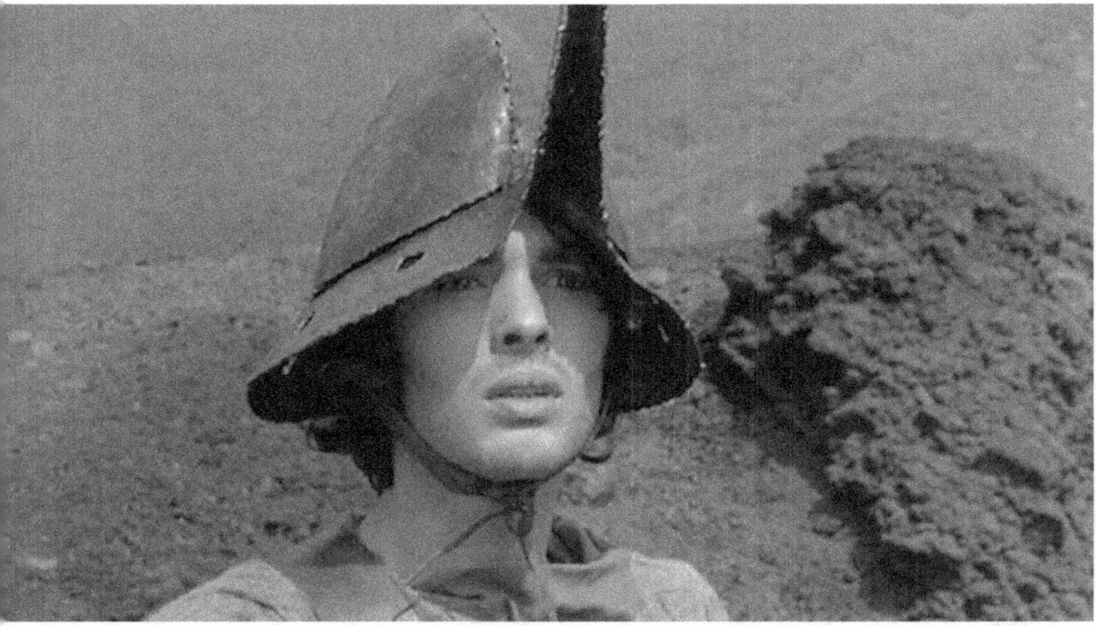

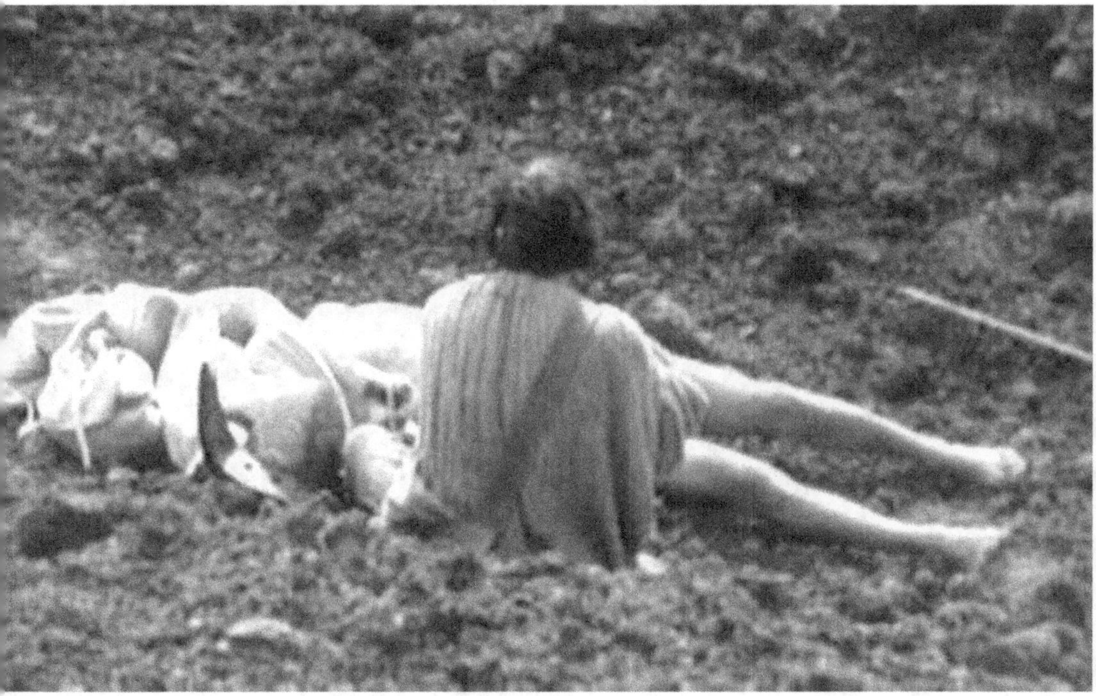

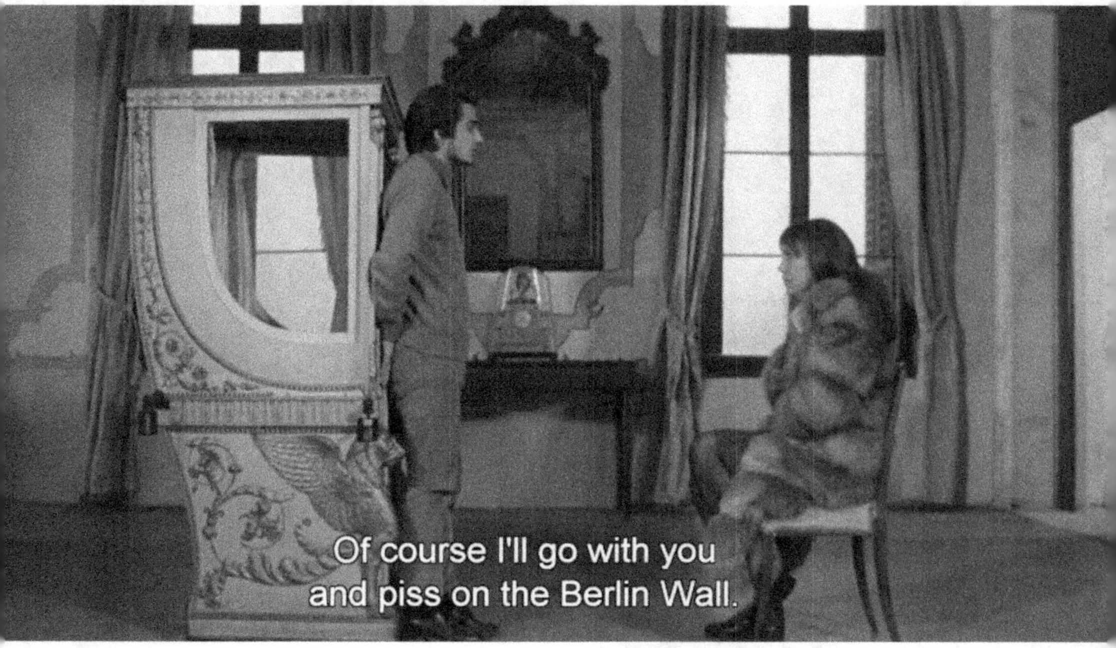
Of course I'll go with you
and piss on the Berlin Wall.

PORCILE

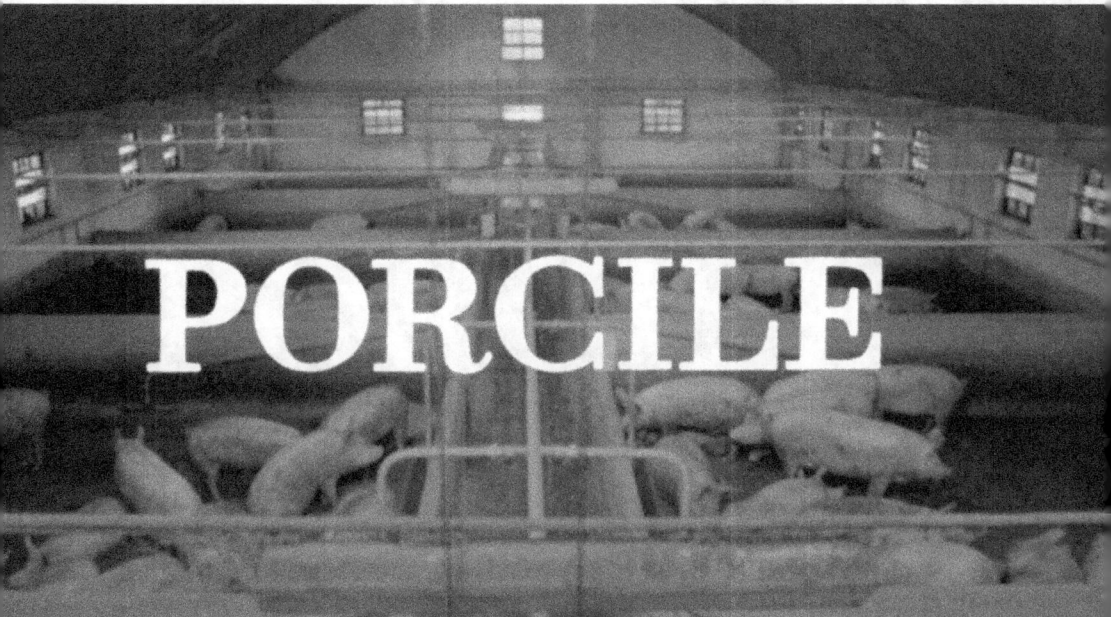

13

MEDEA

MEDEA

Whom God wishes to destroy, he first makes mad.

Euripides

This film can be summed up thus: Pier Paolo Pasolini directs Maria Callas in *Medea*. Working on *Medea* (1969) were many of Pasolini's regular team, including Dante Ferretti, Nino Baragli, Sergio Citti, Elsa Morante, and Franco Rossellini.

Medea was produced by Franco Rossellini and Marina Cicogna; Klaus Hellwig and Pierre Kalfon were associate producers; Ennio Guarnieri was DP; Nina Baragli was editor; Carlo Caruchio and Sergio Citti were A.D.s; sound by Carlo Tarchi; hair by Maria Teresa Corridoni and Marcella De Marzi; wigs by Goffredo Rocchetti; make-up by Romolo Sensoli; music was selected by Elsa Morante and Pasolini; Dante Ferretti was production designer (one of his first gigs for the maestro as department head, altho' he had worked before as an assistant). Released Dec 28, 1969. 106 minutes.

The cast included Maria Callas, Giuseppe Gentile, Laurent Terzieff, Massimo Girotti, Margareth Clémenti, Sergio Tramonti, Luigi Barbini, Gian Paolo Durgar, Luigi Masironi, and Paul Jabara. Filming ran from May to Aug, 1969 (a busy year for Pasolini, when he had two movies released – the other was *Pigsty*).

EURIPIDES. *Medea* was scripted by the maestro from Euripides'

---
1 Carl Dreyer had considered filming *Medea* in 1959, with backing from Kay Harrison. This would have been in colour (Harrison was the president of Technicolor in Europe).

play. Euripides (484-406 B.C.) was one of the celebrated Greek playwrights and poets, 'the most tragic of the poets', according to Aristotle. Euripides lived in the great era of Ancient Greek culture, that period in world history when the Ancient Greeks did *everything* (and then some), so that the whole of Western culture that followed feels like a mere footnote (including cinema!).

Euripides wrote 92 plays, according to contemporary accounts, but only 16 tragedies have survived, plus a satyr-drama, a comedy version of Odysseus' adventures, and fragments. Among Euripides' plays are *Hecuba*, the *Trojan Women*, *Orestes*, *Ion*, *Electra*, *Alcestis*, *Hippolytus*, *Helen* and the *Phoenician Women*. *Medea* was written in 431 B.C. (Euripides was a significant playwright for Pier Paolo Pasolini: he had contemplated filming a version of *Orestes* set in Africa, as explained in the 1970 documentary *Notes Towards an African Oresteia* – see below).

According to *The Oxford Companion To the Theatre*, Euripides was, compared to Sophocles,

> critical, sceptical, interested less in the community than in the individual, dealing less with the broad questions of morality and religion than with personal emotions and passions – love, hate, revenge – and with specific social questions like the suffering of the individual in war. (264)

Pier Paolo Pasolini's ancient world movies explore the world of the Furies – archaic figures of horror, cruelty, terror, and the irrational – and how the Furies are civilized/ humanized, divinities that still retain their 'irrational archaic' powers, but now preside over 'works of poetry, of fantasy, of feeling'. (*Medea*, about the mother, was the companion tragedy to *Oedipus Rex*, about the father.)

MARIA CALLAS. Starring as Medea was Maria Callas (1923-77, born in the U.S.A., but of Greek descent): this was a true superstar, an opera diva appearing in one of her only film roles. Callas, born in Gotham (on Dec 2, 1923), went to Greece aged 13 to study at the Athens Conservatory (her early studies and career were all in Europe). She spoke Italian and French. She was a strong singer with a powerful stage presence and brilliant technique. She debuted in Italia in 1947, as Gioconda (in Verona), and made her professional debut in 1941 in Athens, in Giacomo Puccini's *Tosca*. Callas appeared at La Scala, Covent Garden, the Met in New York, Chicago, etc, playing roles such as Lady Macbeth, Aida, Tosca, Imogene, Elvira, Amina, Isolde, Brunhilde, Lucia, Anna Bolena and Violetta (in works by Verdi, Spontini, Wagner, Donizetti, Bellini, etc). The word 'diva' might've been invented for Callas.

In the later part of her career, Maria Callas became over-worked and exhausted, and withdrew from performing opera, recuperating in an apartment in Paris. She made a comeback, but not in full-scale operas. On stage, Calas came across as a powerful personality, but she insisted that she was a woman, with frailties.

Maria Callas had already played Medea (at La Scala in 1953, in Luigi Cherubini's 1797 opera *Médée*), and as a music world diva has all of the regality, screen presence, charisma and marquee value to play the sorceress of the ancient realm. The camera loves her, and dwells on her face in close-ups – especially those dark, hypnotic eyes. (Alas, Callas doesn't sing[2] in *Medea* (and she was dubbed – by Rita Savagnone), tho' one can imagine Pasolini enjoying an alternative career directing opera, as several film directors have done – Ken Russell, Andrei Tarkovsky, Robert Altman, etc. Luchino Visconti directed Callas in several operas (including *La Traviatra, La Vestale* and *La Sonnambula*). But no, Pasolini hated opera! It was bourgeois rubbish for him. Federico Fellini also didn't like opera, though he changed his tune a little in the late 1980s).

Off-screen, Maria Callas was very well-known – not least as a celebrity (she had an affair, for instance, with Aristotle Onassis, and married G.B. Meneghini, an Italian industrialist, in 1949). Callas had been suggested as Medea by the film's producer Franco Rossellini (they were dating). She and Pier Paolo Pasolini struck up a friendship – she visited him in Rome, he saw her in Paris and Greece. And the newspapers gossiped about romance.

According to Maria Callas, she had received several film offers, but *Medea* was the first one that really appealed to her. In interviews on set, Callas said it was as if she was starting at the top, with a spectacular, difficult role.[3]

Pasolini on Callas:

> Maria Callas is an extraordinary tragic actress. She is the only actress who can express, even without acting and without saying a word, spiritual catastrophe.(1970)

Ken Russell planned a biopic of Maria Callas (it was announced by *Variety* in October, 1982). Russell recounted in his memoirs how he took a location trip through Italy (visiting Venice, Rome and Milan), and visited the star, Sophia Loren, and her husband, the Italian producer Carlo Ponti. However, as Russell recounted wryly, Loren wanted a number of

---

[2] A pity, perhaps, in a movie stuffed with music from everywhere.
[3] A superb documentary on Callas – *Maria By Callas* (2018) – includes footage of Callas and Pasolini making *Medea*.

changes to the script and the characterization of Callas that Russell and his co-writer and wife, Vivian Jolly, had created (including intimate details of Callas's marriage with G.B. Meneghini, with an accusation from Callas that Meneghini 'couldn't get it up'). When they couldn't agree, the project foundered: 'bang goes another year's hard labour', as Russell put it (1989, 211).

Unfortunately, the actor cast to play opposite Maria Callas in *Medea*, Giuseppe Gentile, is rather bland and he's mis-cast: he has the nondescript looks of a cheesecake model who might've walked onto the set from a commercial for shaving razors (Gentile was a sportsman). Gentile certainly doesn't have the screen presence of Franco Citti, who was so impressive in *Oedipus Rex*, and he's a weak figure beside Maria Callas (Gentile was – by Pino Colizzi). But then, Pier Paolo Pasolini directs Gentile like a Robert Bresson actor: unexpressive, unemotive, as if he's keen to make Jason as unheroic as possible. (And, besides, a superstar such as Callas is going to out-shine almost any co-star, so a non-actor such as Gentile doesn't stand a chance).

The dialogue for both Medea and Jason is drastically reduced in the 1969 Euripides adaptation: the filmmakers decided that Maria Callas's screen presence could carry much of the movie (plus the super-exotic locales and the ethnic music), and that they wouldn't try to get inside either Jason or Medea psychologically. Thus, *Medea* is a relatively rare instance of a film adaptation of a play opting for a primarily visual interpretation.

Indeed, Pier Paolo Pasolini took the same approach with *Oedipus Rex*: these are free adaptations of Classical Greek plays created specifically for the cinema, and for *his* form of cinema (which is very different from the conventional form of cinema). Pasolini hasn't adapted the plays in the usual manner of film versions, or translations of theatrical plays into movies. Pasolini's approach reworks Euripides' play for his own ends, to be produced in his own, highly idiosyncratic fashion.

Also, Pasolini likely reworked his adaptation even further with the casting of Maria Callas, and knowing that he would dub her voice (with her agreement). Callas is not a classical theatrical actress, and brought a different approach to acting (however, not all classically trained actors or chiefly theatrical actors are best suited to acting in movies, as film history has shown many times). Silvana Mangano would have made a terrific Medea, but she had already appeared recently in *Oedipus Rex* and *Theorem*.

Thus, not only is the dialogue reduced, whole chunks of Euripides'

Medea were left out (including some of the subplots); the structure of the play was altered; the ending was changed; many incidents throughout the play were re-jigged, and so on. (With a running time of 1h 46m, *Medea* is inevitably a cut-down version of the play anyway. On stage it typically runs longer).

★

It's easy to see why some critics exalt *Medea*, and other critics dislike it. There are parts of *Medea* where it can seem as if the maestro was conscious that the movie he was directing was going to be irritating and confusing to sections of the audience. And he loved it! Were Pier Paolo Pasolini and his entourage chuckling to themselves as they drove back to the hotel after filming bewildering scenes of arcana and ritual in some exotic, dusty locale in Syria or Turkey? Movies such as *The Gospel According To Matthew* and *Oedipus Rex* perhaps have more impact for some viewers than *Medea*, because the stories of Christ and Oedipus are better-known (and a film like *The Gospel* embraces the audience tenderly, while *Medea* is much more aloof and instructable).

The Marxist project in *Medea* is written in simplified, cartoony colours: the movie conjures the familiar oppositions in Pasolini's mythopœia of:

North vs. South,
Europe vs. Africa,
new vs. old,
modern world vs. ancient world,
horror/ terror/ irrationality vs. civilization/ rationality,
the West vs. the Third World.

For Pier Paolo Pasolini, the *Oresteia* is an analogy for modern Africa (S. Rohdie, 87). As Pasolini put it, 'the *Oresteia* synthesizes the history of Africa over these last one hundred years'.

Medea's quirky *tableau* and silent movie approach to an Ancient Greek play probably frustrates some viewers:

Isn't someone going to tell the story here? No.
Isn't somebody going to act it out for us? No.
OK, isn't someone going to narrate it? No.

The only contextualization and preamble comes from the Centaur Chiron at the top of the show, but, in typically idiosyncratic, Pasolinian style, it's not an explanation of the plot and the characters, or even some hints about what you're going to see. Instead, it's an overly-intellectualized rumination on issues such as the ancient world vs. the modern world. (After that, the movie says, you're on your own!).

In its staginess and overt theatricality (despite its actorly restraint, passivity and *tableau* approach), *Medea* is probably what a Pasolini play would look like in the theatre.

The music in *Medea* is incredibly powerful (Pier Paolo Pasolini and his friend, the novelist Elsa Morante, are credited with selecting it).[4] Indeed, *Medea* features one of the finest soundtracks in Pasolini's *œuvre*, and a rival to *The Gospel According To Matthew*. The music (which is all from existing, recorded sources) includes the skirling pipes of the Middle East, Persian *santur* music, Tibetan chants, choirs, plangent vocals accompanied by *ouds*, Japanese *Noh* music, Native American pow-wows, and Eastern European female choirs. (At times, tho', *Medea* does feel a little over-stuffed with music, amazing as it is).

Some of the strongest pieces of music are not African or European, but Asian: the clanging percussion, the wailing pipes and the rasping of the famous brass instruments come from Tibet. In almost any context, traditional, Tibetan music sounds other-worldly, and certainly enhances the first act of *Medea*.

The costume design in *Medea* – by Piero Tosi – is simply stupendous: what a feast of textures, of colours, of materials, of weave, of additions, of jewellery, of masks. Of hats! And headdresses! Some of the extras are wearing giant, wide sacks (ceremonial but silly). Every costume is thick with texture and weave, as if the thread and the fabric was nothing less than a quarter of an inch thick.[5] Wild, wild costumes – it's like seeing the exhibits of a natural history and ethnographic music being displayed for a travelling show. (Even so, these are not historical or factual costumes of the ancient world – they are based on Eastern European Mummers).

Piero Tosi and his team worked very much in the Danilo Donati mode in their approach to portraying Ancient Greece. Tosi (1927-2019) was Luchino Visconti's regular costume designer – *The Leopard, Senso, Death In Venice, Rocco and His Brothers, Ludwig*, etc (each of those movies is a masterpiece of costume design). Tosi also designed *The Night Porter, Le Notti Blanche, The Stranger, Beyond Good and Evil, La Traviata* and many others. For Pasolini Tosi designed some of the short films, such as *The Witches*.

Medea was filmed in Turkey (Cappadocia and Göreme), and early Christian religious buildings (such as monastic cells decorated with

---

[4] Morante had also helped with the music for *The Gospel According To Matthew*.
[5] As if Piero Tosi and co. were going for something that *didn't* flow (that remained solid and unbending), that *wasn't* loose in the heat, to allow air to move around.

Byzantine frescoes);[6] Aleppo in Syria (the fortress); Pisa (Piazza Dei Miracoli); Grado (island), Gorizia and Lido Marechiaro (back in Pasolini's beloved Friuli in N.E. Italia); Anzio stood in for Corinth; Viterbo.[7] The films of Pier Paolo Pasolini and his teams have a knack for employing historically anachronistic but culturally equivalent settings: thus, the cool, elegant architecture of Renaissance Italy formed a good match for the civilization of Corinth,[8] and the temple of the Golden Fleece is decorated in an early Christian manner (so that the pagan ancient world is surrounded by Christian saints – exchanging one form of magic for another, and reminding us that religion and magic stem from the same sources).

Not all of *Medea* was filmed in exotic, far-off locales: some scenes were recreated in the Cinecittà Studios in Rome. Also, many scenes were filmed in Italy (including the coastal scenes, not too far from Venice).

Sometimes the choice of locations in *Medea* jars: in the final third of the film, the sorceress and her entourage are housed in a Middle Eastern structure below a town wall, beneath brilliant blue skies (a fortress in Aleppo, Syria). Meanwhile, King Creon and co. are inside the town – but this is filmed in Pisa[9] in Italy, with its distinctive and very Italian Renaissance buildings. The characters move from one realm to the other: from the civilized society of King Creon and Corinth (i.e., Europe), to Medea and co. in the Middle East (i.e., Syria). They remain 'barbarians'.

There are no other movies in the history of cinema quite like this – like *Medea* or *The Arabian Nights* or *The Gospel According To Matthew*. Pier Paolo Pasolini is about the only filmmaker I know who possesses the ability to make this planet *really* look like another world. Not the other worlds of science fiction cinema or North American visual effects movies (which tend to look hokey), but the ability to find locations and film them and put them on screen and show you something you've never seen before. (Werner Herzog would be another film director with this ability – Herzog revels in the other-worldiness of this world. You can see it in his early film made in North Africa, *Fata Morgana* (1971), and in his many documentaries.)

In 1969's *Medea*, before you get to the story and the characters and the themes and the politics and all the rest of it, you are assailed by

---

[6] These were at the Open Air Museum in Göreme.
[7] *Medea* exploits an in-between zone, the place between two realms, where Medea resides, and where King Creon holds court in Corinth. Several scenes are staged on the steps in the hill between Medea's chambers and the walls of Corinth.
[8] In the Corinth scenes, Pier Paolo Pasolini once again deploys the cinematic parallels with Early Renaissance art, composing shots that consciously echo the painters Piero della Francesca, Masaccio and Giotto. Actors are set within alcoves, underneath arches, and in *tableaux*, as if they're appearing in recreations of a Piero or Fra Angelico painting.
[9] The Pasolini Circus also filmed part of *Oedipus Rex* in Pisa.

extraordinary *places*, and extraordinary *faces* and *bodies*, and extraordinary *costumes* and *props*, and extraordinary *images*. It really is a magical form of cinema, in which storytelling is only one ingredient, which's sometimes thrust aside by the boldness of the imagery or the costumes or the settings or the music (*Medea* boasts a startlingly eccentric and effective soundtrack).

It's not a travelogue, however, or a documentary: the way that landscapes're filmed in a Pier Paolo Pasolini movie is unique – sometimes there are static shots which encourage the audience to drink in the settings; yet at other times, the places are filmed as casually as a home movie, with no regard for integrating them into the narrative or the themes. The throwaway aspect to Pasolini's cinema is sometimes startling: he simply does not make much of elements which other directors do (*Medea* includes shots which many filmmakers would automatically reject as being technically inferior, including the tail end of shots where the camera wobbles madly). And there are dramatically empty shots, too (even boring shots) – like Absyrtus walking and walking. Other filmmakers would simply cut from one location to another, but Pasolini's films include the in-between bits, the schlepping between places (according to Pasolini, there was a lot of schlepping in the ancient world).

Of course, with a genius like Dante Ferretti designing the movie, these already extraordinary places were not used straight, but were adapted in numerous ways. Ferretti and his teams are especially adept at fusing existing buildings with imaginative and highly stylized art direction for the movies of Pier Paolo Pasolini. Ferretti and co. can take a beautiful but empty stone interior with one or two windows and transform it into something stately and elegant with their marvellous inventions and additions, such as the gold tower above King Pelias's palace.[10] (The literary adaptations of Pasolini should be mandatory viewing for courses on theatre studies and production design).[11]

There's a miraculous quality to the historical movies directed by Pier Paolo Pasolini, especially the ancient world and mediæval movies. With design teams headed by the incomparable Dante Ferretti and Danilo Donati, Pasolini's pictures deliver a vision of the ancient world and the mediæval world which's at once highly stylized and down-to-earth, at once imaginative and naturalistic, at once completely over-the-top and completely convincing. It is an ancient and Middle Ages world of the imagination, yes – but where else do the ancient and mediæval realms exist primarily now except in the imagination?

---

10 Add a bit of gold, and, *voilà*, you have a palace. However, the interior is back in the studio.
11 Certainly some historical pictures produced since Pier Paolo Pasolini's era do bear their influence.

Yes, these are *movies*, confections of the 1960s and 1970s filmed on 35mm celluloid by Italian film crews, they are so very much of their time, yet the worlds they portrayed seem also timeless and forever there.

What did audiences in the 1960s make of the ancient world movies of Pier Paolo Pasolini? One wonders... Because sword-and-sandal flicks were very popular in the 1950s and 1960s (and many were produced in Italia. And today audiences still enjoy *peplum* movies). But Pasolini delivered Biblical and Ancient Greek films so very different from those of Hollywood, Italy and the imitators: no grand voiceover from Orson Welles or Charlton Heston, no easy listening orchestral score or warbling choirs, no Hollywood stars (or Euro beefcakes and babes) in the lead roles, no A-B-C storytelling, no regular dialogue or conventionally dramatic scenes...

What was Pier Paolo Pasolini thinking?! Was he really going to try to make an Ancient Greek tragedy look and sound like it might've done two thousand years ago?! (Using analogous music, for instance – music with the same 'primitive' power and lyricism that might've been heard in the amphitheatres of Attica).

★

In *Medea*, and many of his historical movies, Pier Paolo Pasolini doesn't let the audience inside the principal characters. But the effect is not what Jean-Luc Godard[12] observed – that, in order to evoke the *inside*, you stay resolutely *outside*. No – in Pasolini's cinema, you always remain outside. Except with a movie like *The Gospel According To Matthew*, which does invite the audience into the internal realm of its protagonist. And this is a key reason why *The Gospel According To Matthew* is so successful dramatically, as well as so appealing.

But in *Medea*, no, the audience isn't given any windows into the world or souls of Jason or Medea. They are not characters in the usual sense, but they are not carriers of an author's concerns, either (which's common, especially in art cinema), or even functions of the plot (which many characters turn out to be), or even placed in scenes to give some focus to the shots (actors sometimes complain that directors are more concerned with visuals).[13]

With *Medea*, one can imagine the filmmakers being quite happy to make the movie without any principal characters at all. A movie of only extras. Or not even that – a movie of spaces and architecture. A travelogue, perhaps, of the ancient world. Or notes for a movie of *Medea* (like

---
12 *Medea* is quoted by Godard in his film *Socialism* (2010).
13 I was just there to give some focus to the scenes that Ridley Scott insisted on creating, complained Harrison Ford about *Blade Runner*.

Pier Paolo Pasolini produced documentaries or film essays in preparation for making a narrative film, including his planned adaptation of *Oresteia*).

Or perhaps what *Medea* really needs is a separate audio track in which Pier Paolo Pasolini can do what he loves to do – explain at length about what he is attempting in his film. Thus, as with his notes on *Oresteia* documentary, Pasolini could provide an audio description of *Medea* as it plays. You watch it once with the explanatory track, then again without it. (Pasolini would be a gift to the world of audio commentaries on DVD and home releases).

★

You may know *Jason and the Argonauts* (Don Chaffey, 1963), a Ray Harryhausen action-adventure movie, one of the most gloriously enjoyable pictures of its kind (filmed in Rome and around Italy, as so many similar movies were at that time). Greek mythology, monsters, gods, battles, voyages, storms, a quest for the Golden Fleece, and a sword fight between heroes and skeletons spawned from the teeth of the Hydra which for many is the greatest visual effects sequence put on celluloid. As Ken Von Gunden rightly pointed out in *Fantasy Films*, the scene 'has never been equaled'.[14]

Well, 1969's *Medea* is about as far from *Jason and the Argonauts* and Ray Harryhausen's form of cinema as pure fun as you can get! Sure, there's the hero Jason (Giuseppe Gentile) and his merry men, and there's a quest from King Pelias (Paul Jabara) for the Golden Fleece, and there are scenes aboard a raft in the ocean (filmed on the beach at Tor Caldara). But *Medea* is the polar opposite of an action-adventure picture like *Jason and the Argonauts*: for instance, obtaining the Golden Fleece turns out to be of little value in the end – a narrative non-event when it's finally handed over to King Pelias[15] (it's an anti-quest quest film). Meanwhile Jason's men are not individualized in the slightest (they could be anyone).[16] Even the attempts at macho horsing around among the band of brothers seem indifferent and beside the point. And they are also portrayed as bandits who steal rather than as noble Greek warriors. The 1969 film focusses on Jason in the scenes with his entourage, and on Jason and Medea when the witch joins them. But any potential for interaction among in group of adventurers is negated.

---

14 K. van Gunden, *Fantasy Films*, McFarland, Jefferson, N.C., 1989, 87.
15 The fleece may not be as powerful here as is in its original setting it's suggested, then the fleece is tossed aside.
16 Some of them are cast from actors that have appeared before in the Pasolini Cinematic Circus Maximus.

The *tableau* approach to filmmaking and storytelling which Pier Paolo Pasolini favours has been used by Sergei Paradjanov to amazing effect, and also by Werner Herzog, Theo Angelopoulos, Andrei Tarkovsky, Walerian Borowczyk, Carl-Theodor Dreyer, Jean-Luc Godard and Peter Greenaway. To have actors in extravagant costumes just standing there can misfire, but, combined with the right music, it can create striking results. The flattened, frontal space and the emphasis on decorative and pictorial effects apes painting, of course, and negates conventional dramaturgy. It's about subsuming everything to the camera and the soundtrack (to a 'vision'), disposing with naturalism, and emphasizing self-consciousness and the visual.

For audiences expecting conventional dramaturgy (and the dramaturgy associated with Ancient Greek tragic plays), the *tableau* approach can be too stylized for its own good, too reliant on the viewer already knowing the story (the audience has to supply the commentary on this commentary on the story – we are several layers or levels away from the original text by Euripides here).

Because if you *don't* know your Ancient Greek mythology and your Euripides, you may find *Medea* a tad confusing – or unengaging. The lengthy exposition at the top of the movie by the Centaur isn't fully satisfying (captions were added to some prints). If cinema is storytelling, *Medea* subverts that, and doesn't deliver it (or at least, not storytelling in the usual manner). Rather, it's in part a commentary on a story, but it's not a regular commentary or analysis; for example, it doesn't condense the analysis or commentary into dialogue or narration.

And, at times, one imagines that P.P. Pasolini couldn't care about that: if the viewer is floundering, tough, they are not *his* viewer, and don't deserve to be watching this film! (Or maybe there should be a sign nailed above the cinema door which would read: 'FOR POETS AND INTELLECTUALS ONLY'. And don't you dare to enter if you ain't one or the other – or, preferably, both![17]). We've all seen arty films where the snooty, overeducated filmmakers seem to be saying, *what?*, you *haven't* read Karl Marx or Mao Zedong?! Or – *eh?*, you *don't* know the difference between Lacan and Lukacs?!

And, it has to be admitted, the anti-art, anti-drama approach to Euripides' *Medea* produces a somewhat flat and unengaging movie experience at times. Despite the extraordinary visuals, parts of the '69 *Medea* are not especially enjoyable or effective. Impressive, yes, mysterious, yes, clever, yes, but not entertaining or emotional. A narrative flow

---

17 Pasolini is both – why aren't you both?

isn't developed, so that for much of the second act Maria Callas is filmed walking around her queendom, without any tension in the shots.

One of the biggest mistakes that amateur filmmakers and student filmmakers make is to have actors simply walking from A to B. Unfortunately, parts of *Medea* come across like that: there are scenes, for instance, where Maria Callas is filmed in close-up from the front, now from the side, and then walking thru rocky, dusty terrain. While it's true that Callas does have lens-melting eyes and a haughty, striking visage that might've stepped from a fresco in Ancient Crete or Thebes, there are simply too many similar shots.[18] A little voiceover might help, or a caption or two, because the acting style is so damped down and unemotive, exactly which part of Euripides' play is being portrayed here or there isn't clear. (In other words, *Medea* isn't entirely successful, as Pasolini hoped, in finding a cinematic and performative equivalent for Euripides' play, or for the play as performed theatrically. Pasolini has cinematized the play, so to speak, by translating it into *his* form of cinema, but the final result isn't completely convincing).

When Medea murders Absyrtus (Sergio Tramonti), for example, the 1969 movie steps back to capture the brutal act in long shot: time and again, Pier Paolo Pasolini can't resist denying what is expected, and rebelling against conventional dramaturgy. Instead of the tragic murder, we have a static *tableau* of men on horses watching something, *à la* the Renaissance master of horse scenes, Paolo Uccello. (The complete indifference of the Argonauts is intriguing, however, as they look at Medea chopping her brother up with an axe. Nobody intercedes, says anything, or reacts: it's not their business what Medea may or may not do. Possibly some of the Argonauts are thinking, *OK, I mustn't go near Medea when she's in a bad mood!*).

There are trade-offs with this distanced, Brechtian, Bressonian approach, of course, as well as dividends. What *Medea* gains in mystery and strangeness, in being aloof and implacable and primitive, it loses in drama and psychology and emotion. This *Medea* is profoundly anti-psychological, and anti-emotional (as if the filmmakers have realized that the Freudian psychoanalyzing in *Oedipus Rex*, from another Ancient Greek text, was too obvious, too expected, too intellectual, and too 20th century). And yet *Medea* also imparts a Freudian, psychological interpretation.

★

Again, sections of *Medea* are presented as anti-drama, anti-character,

---

18 Maria Callas looks as if she has been directed like a model in a TV commercial: 'look this way, now look that way... now look a little sadder'.

anti-art. Shot follows shot but no tension or forward narrative movement is generated: the cause-and-effect progression of drama is jettisoned for long stretches. No narrative linkage between shots or scenes, and thus no momentum. There are few shot-reverse-shot set-ups, few reverse angles which elucidate scenes. Everything becomes frontal, a *tableau*, a painting, with very little movement from the actors within each shot.[19] The music might add aspects of atmosphere, but often the music is coming from a (literally) wholly other world (often there's no attempt to position the music *within* a scene – what the Bay Area sound designers call 'world-izing', where sounds are re-recorded in settings which approximate to the filmic space). No – in a Pasolini movie, the audio tapes and vinyl records used as sources for a piece of music from Tibet or Turkey are simply cut into the soundtrack straight, without any electronic or acoustic treatment (and sometimes you can hear the scratches on the vinyl).

(Sometimes, the use of music in *Medea* smashes into a wall: in the final scenes, for example, music from Japanese *Noh* theatre is employed for the scene where Jason's sons play music in a room at night. There is some attempt by the editors and the sound editors to mickey mouse the performances of the children on screen with the singing,[20] but the idea that these kids could be producing something like Japanese *Noh* music is utterly ridiculous! The *idea* might be intriguing – using contemporary music that sounds suitably 'exotic' to modern ears to suggest the archaic music that might've been played in the ancient world, or that these characters might play in this moment, but it doesn't work).

★

Medea opens in a truly idiosyncratic manner with a six or seven minute continuous monologue – unusual for Pier Paolo Pasolini, and unusual for most movies. Especially when the guy rattling thru 20 pages of dialogue is a centaur! He's Chiron (played by Laurent Terzieff –who had appeared in the 1959 adaptation of *Ragazzi di vita*, *The Big Night*).[21] In *Medea*, he's talking[22] non-stop to a naked boy, who sits on the floor and listens (who we later learn is the young Jason[23] – the first shot of *Medea*, in typical provocative, Pasolinian fashion, is a medium close-up of a nude, 7 year-old child. At the end of the movie, two young boys are shown bathing naked). So it's another father and son scene. If the

---

[19] When the Nurse and the female Chorus follow Medea pacing and forth in her chambers, it seems too artificial, too theatrical.
[20] As they attempted earlier, when the Argonauts sing around a fire.
[21] Laurent Terzieff was a European character actor who appeared in many movies, including some by Jean-Luc Godard (indeed, Terzieff was considered by Godard for the iconic role in *Breathless*).
[22] Terzieff was dubbed – by Enrico Maria Salerno – who voiced Jesus in *The Gospel According To Matthew*.
[23] We see Jason at 7 years-old, then thirteen years-old, then full-grown.

Renaissance painter Michelangelo Merisi da Caravaggio were making movies, this is what they might look like! There are even the smiley urchins that Caravaggio liked to paint in *Medea*.

Ten tons of mythological exposition's included in the opening scene of *Medea* (far, far too much!), and no one's going to absorb it all on the first viewing (how about breaking up this indigestible hunk of speech into smaller pieces? Maybe the filmmakers thought, *si, si*, let's get it *all* out of the way in one go!). Handily, there are some amazing images to go with the monologue: a coast scene, by a lake or an ocean, some huts, tiny islands amongst water, and ravishing afternoon and magic hour sunlight.[24] (As well as exposition, there's some spiritual teaching, too: 'all is holy, all is holy, all is holy', Chiron tells the young Jason, adding the usual Pasolinian gloss of ambiguity and uncertainty. All may be sacred, but Chiron doesn't seem convinced by his own philosophizing. Chiron also draws attention to the artificiality of the natural world; what appears to be natural, isn't, he reckons. This is Pasolini talking to his audience, offering them slices of Pasolinian life-philosophy).[25]

But then *Medea* switches to the non-dialogue, image-based and music-based form of narration which's one of the favourite modes for Pier Paolo Pasolini and his teams, and for many filmmakers (as if to overcompensate for the overly talky first 7 minutes). Streams of music accompanied by incredible images: the production is fully in control of this panoply of colour and light, and the direction by Pasolini is totally confident and muscular.

Only Pier Paolo Pasolini would ask his producers (Franco Rossellini and Marina Cicogna) to hire a hundred extras and horses[26] (and very elaborate costumes), and have them do nothing but just *stand there*, all looking in one direction (no one except perhaps Sergei Paradjanov, who was making his highly charged and heart-breakingly beautiful movies around the same time in the late Sixties, where actors in elaborate costumes just stand there. Had Pasolini seen Paradjanov's films by this time? We know that Paradjanov was a huge fan of Pasolini's cinema).[27]

The locals in Colchis are assembling and waiting – and waiting and waiting – for something to happen at the ritual. Rituals are really like this, though (having been to a quite a few rituals myself, yes, this is what they're like!): like filmmaking, rituals require a lot of standing around,

---

[24] Filmed in Grado, in the Friuli-Venezia Giulia area.
[25] Laurent Eterzieff even looks like Pasolini, when he appears later without the stick-on beard.
[26] There are *a lot* of horses in *Medea*.
[27] The truly remarkable 1960s films of Sergei Paradjanov – such as *The Color of Pomegranates* and *Shadows of Our Forgotten Ancestors* – share with Pasolini's historical films the feeling for ancient rituals and arcania, for the life of peasants and communities who live on the land, for colour, costume and texture, and a similar passion for drawing on studies in ethnography and history.

and sitting around (tho' it's often colder than it looks in this desert!).

Which's what *Medea* depicts: the staging is static, and the cinematography is static. Many of the shots linger over the figures as if they're lining up for the production's stills photographer to come by and take a publicity picture of them in their costumes and hats. One image after another shows off the inventive and outrageous costumes by Piero Tosi – plus of course the mandatory bizarre headdresses in a Pasolini movie (and not forgetting several masks).

As the ceremonial sequence in *Medea* continues, a story emerges out of the stylization and stasis: this is a rebirthing ritual of sacrifice, in which a handsome youth (decorated with plants) is sacrificed to the gods and to the crops. It is very much like watching a chapter from *The Golden Bough* by J.G. Frazer or an article in an anthropology journal being acted out. This is Pier Paolo Pasolini in his scholarly mode, showing off his ethnographic research, and delivering, for the second sequence in *Medea*, a mini-documentary on primitive rites among Ancient Greek and Near East cultures.[28]

Yes, it's all here: the grand preparation, the people of the community of Colchis standing about in respectful witness, and the rites being overseen by the rulers and orchestrated by the priests. The victim is killed and cut up,[29] and the locals hurry in to take bowls of blood out to the crops. There are dancing scenes, too (to drumming). It's somewhat hokey, and silly, but maybe the extreme stylization captures some of the visceral roughness of prehistoric magic.[30] (There isn't a voiceover from Pier Paolo Pasolini explaining everything in detail, as he did in his documentaries, and in his filmed notes for an adaptation of *Oresteia*. Instead, the sound editors include several pieces of music, including a thrillingly jangly, excited piece for the moment of cathartic release, when the victim is slain and butchered).

It's *Anthropology 101*. The ritual in the first act of *Medea* can also come over as charmingly simplistic, as if this isn't the work of a 47 year-old, European intellectual who's already directed seven celebrated feature films, but an eager, 16 year-old anthropology student from the University of Bologna who's trying to impress his professor after spending all night reading Claude Lévi-Strauss, J.G. Frazer, Robert Briffault, Mircea Eliade,

---

[28] You won't be surprised if the end titles flash up a list of sources – Claude Lévi-Strauss, Géza Roheim, Robert Briffault, etc.
[29] With conscious nods to crucifixions – the lad's tied to a wooden structure resembling a cross.
[30] *Medea* includes mysterious scenes where the sorceress converses with the sun god Helios (seen in a golden sunset from the window of her chambers). Like scenes with the oracle in *Oedipus Rex* or the Angel in *The Gospel According To Matthew*, these are Pasolini's unusual, poetic solutions to the problem of portraying a divine presence on celluloid.

Géza Roheim *et al*. Or maybe it was *The White Goddess*[31] by Robert Graves, very popular in the 1960s (Orson Welles was a big fan).

★

The second section of *Medea* explores Medea's realm, and the production manager (Fernando Franchi) has come up trumps with a remarkable location (Goreme in Turkey) with deserts, green fields, and dwellings carved from stone outcrops like witches' hats.

It is some 12 minutes before we see the star of *Medea*, Maria Callas, and some 21 minutes before she speaks or does anything significant (presiding over the agricultural ritual). At this point in *Medea*, all that Callas does is stand there and look regal (which Callas can do fairly successfully, and which she does a lot of in the 1969 picture. Callas has 'Queen' and 'Regal' written all over her. There's no need for a retinue of submissive servants, either, because Callas gives the impression 100% that she is royalty[32]).

Medea is another case of Pier Paolo Pasolini opting for non-acting as much as possible: just be yourself, just stand there, he and his assistant directors (Sergio Citti *et al*) seem to have told the cast and the extras. Pasolini relied on the camera, on the editing, on the music and on the movie itself to do the storytelling. In Pasolini's films, people are encouraged to simply be people, not characters, not dramatic, and not storytellers.

Quite a bit of the second section of *Medea* comprises music: that is, images and music, but with music so powerful it seems as if we are really listening to music rather than watching a movie. You can't ignore this music: it asserts itself with total authority.

The first act of *Medea* climaxes with Medea and Jason meeting – in the temple of the Golden Fleece. It is one of the more mysterious scenes in an already mysterioso movie. When the Fleece is taken, Medea is aided by her brother Absyrtus, and Jason and his crew. Again, the sequence is anti-dramatic, even tho' it includes movie-spectacle scenes of horses riding thru rocky deserts (with rock formations that resemble Zabriskie Point in California). It's here that the sorceress butchers her brother Absyrtus.

In a bizarre sequence, the retinue sent from Colchis to pursue the Argonaut thieves of the golden fleece find the head of Absyrtus, and then parts of his body, which've been flung on the road at intervals. King Pelias and the posse duly halt their horses, and descend to pick up an arm

---

31 *The White Goddess* is full of material about ancient rites like sacrifice and the death of the king and the resurrection of the land. Graves, however, linked the rituals to the poet dying and being reborn for his Muse, the Goddess.
32 And in the opera world, Callas was certainly royalty.

or an organ. It's all played deadly seriously – you sort of wish that Harpo Marx or Woody Allen was around to add some slapstick or a quip or two to lighten this solemn (and rather leaden) filmmaking (it's another rather literal interpretation of the famous anthropological theories popular in the 1960s).

Medea features several instances of delayed reaction from actors: something terrible has happened or is about to happen, and the movie holds and holds on the actors, until finally they explode. For instance, when Glauce (Margareth Clémenti) has the gift dress and jewellery put on by her handmaids, she stands there patiently (and not seeming to enjoy any part of it), until she screams in agony.[33] In a connected scene, Medea enters her apartments in shock, at her lowest point. Her maids watch anxiously; the film holds on a shot of the sorceress for some moments before she collapses to the floor.

Medea at times seems unsure of what to do or show with the character of Medea. The *tableau* and anti-art, anti-psychological, non-literal approach means that the audience has to supply some of the dramatic juice: that's fine, but sometimes *Medea* stumbles. It's awkward, it doesn't always find the images to express or manifest what it wants to be or to say. But then, Pasolini considered movies as ways of raising questions, to be poetry; they didn't necessarily have to make 'sense'.

For instance, can an actor just stand there and emote? Can they just 'be' on film? (In the Bressonian manner). Do they need to speak, to relate to other characters? To build drama via interactions? The dramaturgical solutions provided by *Medea* aren't always effective. The 1969 film resorts, for instance, to having Medea confer with her servants (the Chorus): Medea has several scenes with the Nurse (Annamaria Chio), one of the few who dares to disagree with the sorceress (and also acts as a go-between). Euripides' play, of course, has plenty more for the Nurse and the Chorus.

★

In the third act, the narrative of *Medea* loses its way somewhat. By this time – one hour twenty or so minutes into the narrative – the 1969 Italian movie has made most of the points it wants to make, and created most of its exotic *tableaux* (and nothing new, as in most movies, is introduced at this late stage).

A daring dramatic device is employed: showing the same action twice, as Medea wields her sorcery to attack Glauce, the daughter of King Creon. So we see the same sequence twice, as Medea takes up the dark

---

[33] The film cuts repeatedly to the mirror, emphasizing the vanity, the vanity, of all existence.

dress and jewellery and hands it to Jason and two children who innocently deliver it to Glauce[34] (the second time is filmed differently, with the characters more serious). Both times the dress and the jewels[35] kill Glauce – once in setting her on fire: she rushes out onto the hillside below the city walls and perishes, and Creon does too, trying to put out the flames. Then it happens again, this time with Glauce tumbling from a building to her death, and Creon following her down.

Dramatic sequences of this kind are risky because they can alienate the audience. They are a favourite trick of the time travel movie, or the multiple viewpoint movie, where the same actions are seen from different points-of-view. In *Medea*, I'm not sure it works, even if it does play into the first sequence being Medea's desire, or her dream, or her imagination, or her threat.[36] (Unusual cinematic devices in Pier Paolo Pasolini's work, such as lingering superimpositions, are employed. Pasolini rarely took up editing or optical tricks, preferring the simple cut. No step-motion or slow motion for him, which's everywhere these days).

There is another break in the flow of dramatic time or a pause when, after the second demise of the Princess and her father the King, there are no reprisals or consequences. Instead, Medea is able to continue her infernal schemes in her apartments – bathing the children and then killing them.

'All is sacred', the Centaur tells Jason at the top of the 1969 picture, but the ending of *Medea* is the opposite of that tranquil teacher-pupil scene on the sunny coast: a conflagration cooked up by the sorceress with Jason's children stabbed and burning inside her chambers. *Medea* closes with the memorable image of Medea glaring at Jason from on top of the house, berating him, while flames flicker in front of her. (The fire adds a suitably apocalyptic flavour to the final scenes of *Medea*, filmic correspondences for the sun god's chariot).

Medea is certainly one of the most unusual adaptations of an Ancient Greek play; it was always guaranteed finding an audience due to the casting of music superstar Maria Callas.

---

[34] Glauce's maid (Graziella Chiarcossi) warns her not to accept the gift.
[35] There's a lengthy scene where Glauce's maids dress her.
[36] Following the sequence, the movie cuts back to Medea in her chambers, revealing that this has been her dream or her intent.

14

APPUNTI PER UN'ORESTIADE AFRICANA

NOTES TOWARDS AN AFRICAN ORESTEIA

Appunti per un'Orestiade Africana (*Notes Towards an African Oresteia*, 1970) is for diehard Pasolinian fans only (I wouldn't recommend it unless you are an obsessive completist who simply *must* see everything by the maestro). It exhibits most of the faults in the cinema of Pier Paolo Pasolini, so it's instructive to look at for that reason.

Flaws include:
- it's ideologically dubious (both within the piece, as a concept, and externally, as a production);
- it's patronizing and imperialistic;
- it's bitty, uneven, and doesn't fit together structurally;
- it is unengaging, and doesn't deliver on its promise;
- it's tough to sit through.
- shoddy technical quality;
- awful camerawork;[37]
- terrible sound, including an appalling sound mix.

And *Notes Towards an African Oresteia* features some of the most revolting music ever used in a film soundtrack.

In 1970, Pier Paolo Pasolini visited Tanzania and Uganda with an

---
[37] The camerawork in *Notes Towards an African Oresteia* is just terrible. My kids when they were sixteen could do better! Can't anybody in an Italian film crew hold a camera steadily? It's not impossible if it's a lightweight 16mm camera!

Italian film crew to explore the possibilities of making a version of Aeschylus' *Oresteia* in Africa. The visit was filmed for *Appunti per un'Orestiade Africana* – notes for a film for an African *Oresteia* (a documentary that comprised notes for a movie is something that Jean-Luc Godard was a master of, a film that gives birth to another film, yet in this case, that other film wasn't made). Giorgio Pelloni, Mario Bagnato and Emore Galeassi were DPs, Cleofe Conersi was editor, music was by Gato Barbieri, and Angelo Romano produced. 63 mins.

So *Appunti per un'Orestiade Africana* was another exploration of recurring Pasolinian concerns: of Africa (one of his favourite places to visit), of the 'Third World', of the ancient world, of finding the ancient world in places like the 'Third World', of finding the past in the present day, but outside Europe (or in Southern Italy, which still, for Pier Paolo Pasolini, contained elements of the ancient world).

The adaptation of the *Oresteia* by Aeschylus would've been the third of Pier Paolo Pasolini's versions of Classical Greek texts, to accompany *Medea* by Euripides and *Oedipus Rex* and *Oedipus at Colonus* by Sophocles. (However, Pasolini did create an ancient world trilogy, if you include *The Gospel According To Matthew*).

It's significant that, of all the plays of the ancient world to adapt, Pier Paolo Pasolini should've chosen three Greek plays, and three tragedies. (Pasolini didn't seem interested in adapting Ancient Roman texts, for instance – Petronius, Ovid, Cicero, Seneca, Catullus, etc, as if Pasolini's view of the ancient world was anti-Roman, or non-Roman, or at any rate, *not* Italian[38]).

Aeschylus (525/4-456 B.C.) is one of the great playwrights of Ancient Greece, along with Euripides and Sophocles. He wrote 90 plays, according to legend, tho' only 7 have survived. The *Oresteia* of 458 B.C. is itself a trilogy of plays: the *Agamemnon*, the *Choephori* or *Libation Bearers*, and the *Eumenides*. Aeschylus' other plays are *Prometheus Bound*, the *Seven Against Thebes*, the *Persians*, and the *Suppliant Women*. According to *The Oxford Companion To the Theatre*, Aeschylus was 'his own director, chief actor, designer, composer, and choreographer' (a Renaissance Man quality which would appeal to Pier Paolo Pasolini). *The Oxford Companion To the Theatre* continues:

> The grandeur of his conception was matched by bold dramatic technique, immense concentration, a wonderful sense of structure, and magnificent poetry. He made the utmost use of spectacle and colour; and by virtue of the beauty and strength of his choral odes he might well be regarded as

---

[38] Federico Fellini and co. had produced an adaptation of Petronius the year before: *Satyricon* (1969).

one of the greatest of dramatists. (11)

✳

Some of Pier Paolo Pasolini's ideas for his African *Oresteia* are pretty bizarre. For instance, for the Furies he will use trees. Yes, images of big trees (!). Or maybe a lion (better). And for the Temple of Apollo… a modern university. Indeed, as *Notes Towards an African Oresteia* progresses, you realize that the final movie, if it ever gets made, will need a voiceover explaining it all, plus footnotes and bibliography (on insert screens). It will also require that the audience knows Aeschylus's plays very well. And it will be a *very* strange film, even by Pasolini's standards.

Incredibly, *Notes Towards an African Oresteia* really does attempt to use *trees* to act as the Furies pursuing Orestes. The Walt Disney Studios could do it, Japanese animators could certainly do it,[39] but shots of trees waving in a gale falls far short (even with the disgusting, wailing music turned up full).

In a section near the end of *Notes Towards an African Oresteia*, Pier Paolo Pasolini films a scene from the *Oresteia* as if it's a dry-run for the final movie. Unfortunately, it's not engaging at all: so-and-so walks over there, looks this way, then walks over here (this kind of direction – which Pasolini used *a lot* – is a sure sign of a director who's out of ideas. It's also one of the things that film students do when they get hold of a camera: they have their non-professional actors (.i.e., their friends) walking, or looking off into space, having no clue about storytelling or dramatizing a theme or an issue). Or put it like this: on the basis of viewing *Notes Towards an African Oresteia*, would any sane film producer hand Pasolini $2 million to make the feature-length verson? No (not even $20,000).

Someone walking over there is not a convincing or compelling dramatization of an Ancient Greek tragedy, until it has Pasolini's voice-over *explaining* what's happening.

✳

Back in Roma, Pasolini and co. gathered a group of African students[40] studying in the Italian capital and asked their views on the notion of filming an Ancient Greek tragic play in modern-day Africa. Thankfully, some the students are confident enough to contradict the formidable, Italian film director interviewing them: they point out that Africa is a vast continent, and talking about 'Africans' is too generalized; they object to the idea of equating Ancient Greece with modern Africa

---

39 Both Disney and *animé* have animated trees many times.
40 They are all male, in their 20s and 30s. Why?

(with its suggestion that Africa is still backward enough to stand-in for the ancient world); and one of them asserts that the emphasis on tribespeople in Africa is a European construct (a relic of colonial ideology). Talk about Nigerians, instead of concentrating on Biafrans, the guy insists; do you talk about Bretons when talking about the French?

The newsreel footage of Biafra cut into *Notes Towards an African Oresteia* is shocking and Pier Paolo Pasolini, usually never at a loss for words, can't find any words to say over the imagery, so he shuts up. Even this seems a little patronizing – the inclusion of recent news footage which Pasolini bends and pushes into the context of war in the ancient world. But the Biafran conflict footage seems inserted in the documentary chiefly to add the drama that the documentary plainly lacks. (Parts of *Notes Towards an African Oresteia* are thus not filmed by Pasolini, and ten or more minutes are taken up with the disastrous 'sung' version of *Oresteia*).

Meanwhile, *Notes Towards an African Oresteia* omits any mention of the cinema of Africa and African nations, which by 1970 had already produced many classic films. As well as fiction films, Africa had a strong tradition of documentaries, and of politically-conscious works. Algeria, Morocco, Tunisia, Egypt, Senegal, Nigeria and others had – and have – important film cultures.

★

Halfway thru *Notes Towards an African Oresteia*, the director announces a change of tactic: now he will produce his version of Aeschylus' play as a musical and sung piece (music, odes and choruses are a key element in Ancient Greek drama. However, on the basis of what we've seen so far, don't expect too much).

So, the scene shifts to modern Italy (to 'a Western city'): now the maestro tells us he's going to use modern jazz music (i.e., an American, and black American, and African American musical form). And he will use African Americans to do the singing, and an African American band (but then, when the music starts up, the first person we see is a white guy! It's saxophonist Gato Barbieri, best known as the sax player in *Last Tango In Paris*).

Well, we know that Pier Paolo Pasolini is a world-class film director, and many of his movies are wonderful, but OMG, this is just appalling! Gato Barbieri and his band deliver a truly abysmal simulacrum of the *avant garde* jazz music of John Coltrane, Cecil Taylor and Ornette Coleman. This is an offensively dreadful pastiche of Coltrania. You can't believe the terrible noise that's produced by the drummer, the double bassist and the saxophonist!

Meanwhile, whichever sound engineer came up with the recording set-up should be shot: two vocalists (Yvonne Murray and Archie Savage) are standing right in front of the sax player, next to the mics! It's terrible. So these poor vocalists attempt to sing the poetry of Aeschylus (in English),[41] while Gato Barbieri blasts away incredibly badly two feet away!

All in all, this would be my pick for the shoddiest scene in the Pasolini canon, where our resident Radical-Marxist-Genius-Poet-Iconoclast crashes and burns (and this torture scene runs on *and on*).

✻

Back in Africa, the camera (operated by Giorgio Pelloni, Mario Bagnato, Emore Galeassi and Pier Paolo Pasolini) is pointed at all sorts of people on the streets of Uganda and Tanzania, while the maestro rattles off his ideas about Aeschylus and Africa on the soundtrack (once again, Pasolini doesn't appear much on screen in *Notes Towards an African Oresteia*, except for one or two glimpses. He prefers to remain the controlling power behind it all, and to add his voice months later back in the Eternal City).

Notes Towards an African Oresteia relies heavily on Pasolini's eccentric artistic approach to using 'real' people: just filming them is enough. No acting required. No dialogue. No interaction with other actors or 'real' people. Just stand there and accept having a camera pointed at you.

It's a kind of home movie approach to filmmaking – you film whatever is front of you on your travels. It's a method that hopes to turn tourist-style footage of people into drama and fiction. For Pasolini, the human face is enough on its own – it is poetry, it is reality, it is already drama and tragedy.[42]

The narration in *Notes Towards an African Oresteia* suggests that some of the people the camera films could be characters in the *Oresteia* (this could be Agamemnon, Pier Paolo Pasolini muses, over an image of a middle-aged man, and here's a modern, Electra girl in a headscarf). The idea of going to Africa and using local non-professionals to play famous characters from a Classical Greek play is ambitious,[43] but also politically

---

41 The text is from Cassandra's dream in Aeschylus.
42 One wonders if Pasolini contemplated still photography, pursuing his notion of the sacrality of the human face and body, like the great photographers of the 20th century (such as Paul Strand, Dorothea Lange, Edward Weston, Robert Doisneau, and the most Pasolinian photographer, Robert Mapplethorpe).
43 *The Oxford Companion To the Theatre* notes that the characters in the plays of Aeschylus tend to be 'normally removed from the realm of the everyday, and are depicted as gods, demi-gods, or heroic supermen' (11).

dubious. (Why not, for example, adapt some African literature, including Ancient African mythology, which would make the same philosophical/ social/ political statements, instead of imposing European/ Greek mythologies onto Africa?).

However, the *idea* of the documentary film as notes for an adaptation in Africa of the *Oresteia* may be actually more intriguing than the documentary itself. Because parts of the 63 minutes of *Notes Towards an African Oresteia* are unengaging, somewhat clumsy, and ideologically shaky.

At times, *Appunti per un'Orestiade Africana* is patronizing in the post-colonialist manner which Pier Paolo Pasolini was so critical of (not even a filmmaker as acutely politically aware as Pasolini can avoid the fact that a white, European film crew is visiting parts of the so-called 'Third World' in order to follow its own fantasies, and in order to impose its own views on the place. And self-consciously focussing on the 'tribal' or 'primitive' aspects of Africa).

The ideological resistance to the white, European view of Africa, tho', is included in *Notes Towards an African Oresteia*, when some of the students in the panel discussion scene (filmed in Rome) note that: (1) Africa can't be summed up as a single place/ country/ continent; that (2) the Westerners' view of Africa as a bundle of 'tribes' is out-dated and inaccurate; and that (3) the idea of recreating Ancient Greece in modern Africa is dubious.

One can't escape the feeling that Pier Paolo Pasolini in *Notes Towards an African Oresteia* is once again idealizing: (1) Africa, (2) the ancient world, (3) the peasant/ working class, and (4) otherness. All for the sake of it, for the romance of it. Is Africa fascinating to Pasolini simply because it's *different*? Or perhaps because Africa is *not* Europe?

The issue of *time* is fundamental: Pier Paolo Pasolini thought that modern Europe was rapidly being corrupted and ruined by neo-capitalism. This isn't *Marxism*, it's *anti-capitalism*. Pasolini had a nostalgic veneration for a way of life (among the peasants and the proletariat), of Europe, of Africa, of India, that probably never existed in the first place. But he *thought* it did (and that's what mattered, to him). Pasolini took the nostalgic enshrinement of the proletariat of old lefties and turned it into something eccentric and wilful – that is, he poeticized it, he Pasolinified it.

Thus, flying to Africa was a way of stepping into the past. It could've been anywhere, it was the travelling back in time that fascinated Pier Paolo Pasolini. The way of life in the African villages was perceived as analogous to the ancient world, even tho' the social structures are clearly very different and, as several of the African student interviewees in Roma point out, only a small percentage of Africans live like that now. Indeed, the African students in the panel discussion in *Notes Towards an African Oresteia* reject Pasolini's idealizing and totalizing view of Africa as an equivalent for Ancient Greece. (But Pasolini wants his sentimental, nostalgic view of tribal Africa, so that's what he pursues).

Soviet Union workers' songs and revolutionary songs (dour male choirs) are warbling underneath the images: this seems like another riff on the Marxist cinema of Jean-Luc Godard (which Godard was heavily into in the late 1960s, with Jean-Pierre Gorin and the Dziga Vertov Group). As well as the horrible jazz music, Russian Communist songs seem especially patronizing when combined with the images of Africans.[44] (Another link might be the Marxist and Communist politics foregrounded in African cinema, and to the presence of Soviet ideology in African societies).

---

[44] Maybe it's meant to be an ironic commentary on the impact of the Soviet Union in Africa.

Medea (1969), this page and over.

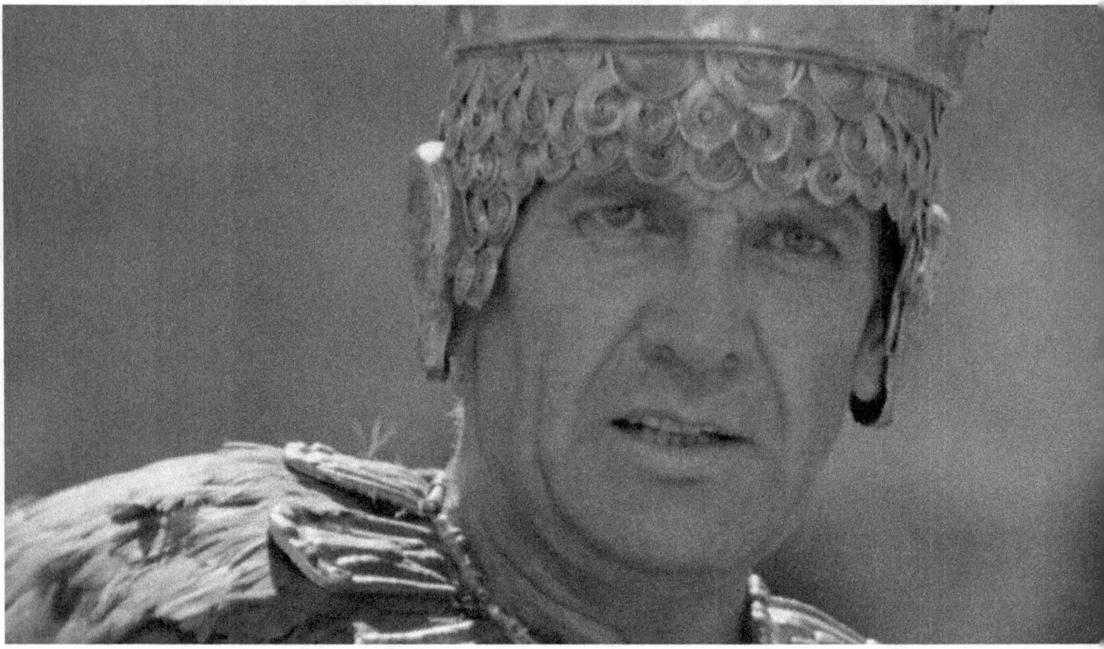

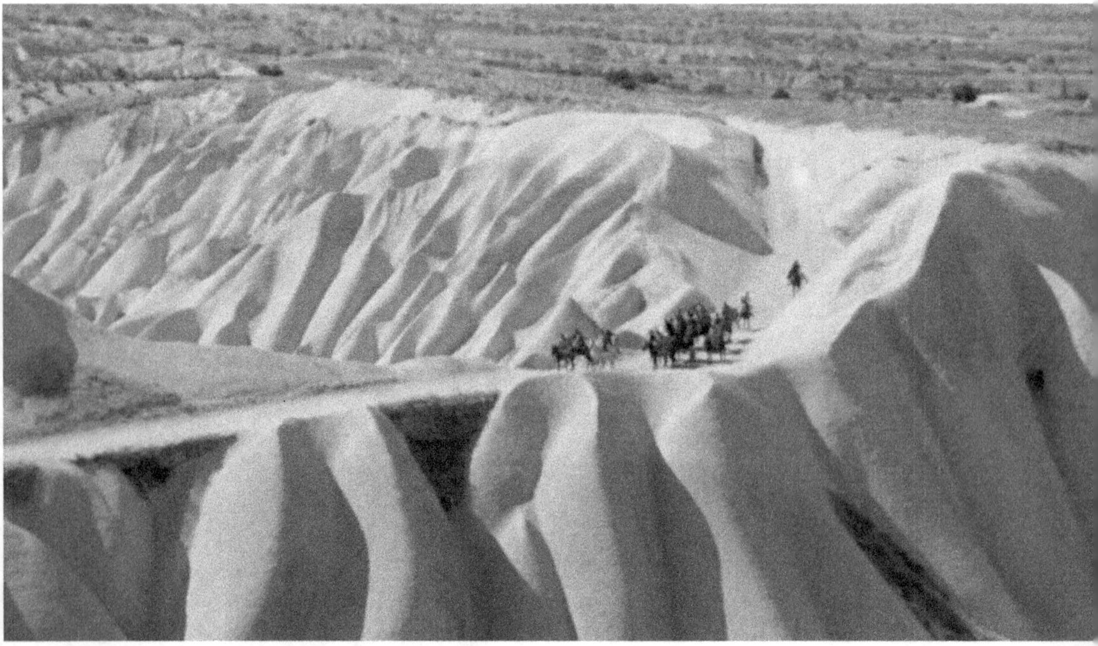

Notes Towards an African Oresteia (1970).

15

IL DECAMERONE

THE DECAMERON

INTRODUCTION.

The 'trilogy of life'/ 'trilogia di vita'/ 'mediæval trilogy' movies of 1971/ 1972/ 1974 were produced at a very particular time in film history: they were part of a group of European art movies of the early-to-mid-1970s which explored the boundaries of 'taste', 'decency', morality and a relaxation of film classification: *Last Tango in Paris, Ai No Corrida, I Am Curious, Yellow, The Music Lovers, Blow Out, The Beast* and *Immoral Tales* (and related porn films, such as *Deep Throat* and *Emmanuelle*). It was a period when porn/ erotica became lucrative, when a movie such as *Emmanuelle* could play in a Paris theatre for eons. This was also the period of the 'New Hollywood' cinema, for some the finest moment in recent North American film history.

Inevitably, each of the 'trilogy of life' movies kicked up controversy upon their releases. In Italia, *The Canterbury Tales* was confiscated (10.7.1972), then released (1.9.1973), then confiscated again (3.19.1973), then released again (4.2.1973), then confiscated two days later. A complaint was raised against *The Arabian Nights* (6.27.1974), then annulled (8.5.1974). As for *The Decameron*, over 30 complaints were filed against it in Sept-Nov, 1971. It was seized in Ancona and Sulmona.

GIOVANNI BOCCACCIO AND *THE DECAMERON*.

Italy has one of the richest and most important histories of fantasy and fairy tale literature in the world. For instance, *Lo Cunto de li cunti* (*The Tale of Tales,* a.k.a. the *Pentamerone,* 1634-36) by Giambattista Basile (1575-1632), is one of the great collections of fairy tales in all Europe. Add to that Giovanni Boccaccio, *Pinocchio,* Carlo Gozzi, Italo Calvino, Luigi Capuana, and the fantastical parts of *The Divine Comedy,* etc.

Il Decamerone (= 'ten days') is one of the great poems of mediæval Italy, alongside Dante Alighieri's *Divine Comedy* and *Vita Nuova* (though far bawdier than anything in Dante's poetry). It is historically linked with *The Canterbury Tales* (which appeared to be influenced by it).

There is a huge amount of material and research on Giovanni Boccaccio (1313-75) and *The Decameron*, if one wants to explore the cultural and historical background of the 1971 movie further (there isn't space here – it would require several books). There have been film versions of *The Decameron* in 1953[1] and 2007 (the latter was produced by Dino de Laurentiis).

Boccaccio '70 (1961) was a precursor of *The Decameron*, produced by Carlo Ponti: four Italian directors took on risqué topics:[2] Federico Fellini, Luchino Visconti, Vittorio de Sica and Mario Monicelli (some of the crew of *Boccaccio '70* later worked for Pasolini).

The Decameron (1349-50) is a central text in Italian culture, like *The Divine Comedy* by Italy's national poet, or the *Rime Sparse* by Francesco Petrarch. As with Petrarch and Dante, Boccaccio straddles the mediæval and early Renaissance eras, the shift from the feudal/ chivalric age and the era of the emerging bourgeoisie, the mercantile class and colonialism. *The Decameron* drew on Classical mythology, *The Divine Comedy, chansons de geste,* mediæval *fabliaux, lais,* and other popular tales. The Black Plague (1346-53) was a key event. Geoffrey Chaucer used some of the same sources in *The Canterbury Tales.*

The title *The Decameron* means 'ten-day event' – it takes ten days for the frame story to be told. The sub-title, *Prince Galehaut,* refers to a character in the Arthurian legends, Arthur's enemy, and friend of Lancelot.

An extract from Boccaccio's text (the 'Proem') illustrates the prose style of *The Decameron*:

---

[1] The 1953 Hollywood version of Giovanni Boccaccio (*Decameron Nights*) starred Louis Jordan and Joan Fontaine, and was directed by Hugo Fregonese.
[2] In the end, there was only a minor link to Boccaccio's famous text.

Who will deny, that it should be given, for all that it may be worth, to gentle ladies much rather than to men? Within their soft bosoms, betwixt fear and shame, they harbour secret fires of love, and how much of strength concealment adds to those fires, they know who have proved it. Moreover, restrained by the will, the caprice, the commandment of fathers, mothers, brothers, and husbands, confined most part of their time within the narrow compass of their chambers, they live, so to say, a life of vacant ease, and, yearning and renouncing in the same moment, meditate divers matters which cannot all be cheerful.

The Decameron has been taken up by authors such as William Shakespeare, John Keats, George Eliot, Edgar Allan Poe, Molière, Jonathan Swift, H.W. Longfellow, Percy B. Shelley, and Thomas Middleton.

It's worth noting the Orientialization of *The Decameron* here: as Jack Zipes remarked in 2012's *The Irresistible Fairy Tale*, and Bartolomeo Rossetti in his 1966 introduction to Giovan Francesco Straparola's *Le Piacevoli notti*,[3] Boccaccio drew heavily upon Oriental fairy tales, especially those that had percolated thru Italy's ports (and Venice in particular). Some of the stories are very old, going back to the ancient world. Pasolini would explore tales of the Orient in the last film in the 'trilogy of life' series, *The Arabian Nights*.

PRODUCTION

The Decameron (*Il Decamerone*, 1971), Pier Paolo Pasolini's take on Giovanni Boccaccio's poem, was produced by Alberto Grimaldi and Franco Rossellini, lit by Tonino Delli Colli, designed by Dante Ferretti, set dressed by Andrea Fantacci, edited by Nino Baragli and Tatiana Casini Morigi, with hair and make-up by Jole Cecchini and Alessandro Jacoponi, costumes by Danilo Donati, casting by Alberto di Stefanis, sound by Gianni D'Amico, Mario Morigi and Pietro Spadoni, the A.D.s were Umberto Angelucci, Paolo Andrea Mettel and Peter Shepherd, with music by Ennio Morricone[4] (who scored all three of the 'life' films).

Released Dec 12, 1971 (in the U.S.A., by United Artists). Worldwide gross was $6.5 million. 106 minutes.[5]

In Italy, *The Decameron* enjoyed 'colossal success' (according to Howard Hughes in his history of Italian film, p. 140), with some 11 million tickets sold (an enormous number), and over 4 billion Lire. A side effect of the success saw other film producers swiftly cashing in with

---

3 Pier Paolo Pasolini would've known Straparola well.
4 The film drew on an album of folk music from Italy (*Italian Folk Music, Volume 5*, Folkways Records). The choral music included *Veni Sancte Spiritus*, and the *Tournai Mass*.
5 In the credits of *The Decameron* there are actors listed who appeared in scenes that were deleted: Patrizia Capparelli as Alibech and Jovan Jovanovic as Rustico. Indeed – the story about Alibech the Tunisian princess (filmed in Tunisia, Yemen and Mt Vesuvius) was cut from the movie before the premiere. Another dropped scene featured a trip to Paris for Girolamo and Salvestra.

flicks such as *Decameroticus, Hot Nights of Decameron, The Decameron 2, Last Decameron, The Warm Nights of the Decamoeron, Sexy Sinners (Decameron Proibitissimo), Boccaccio caccio mio statti zitto*, and *Decameron's Sexy Kittens* (most appeared in 1972). Pasolini was irked by these rip-off movies (altho' it also proved that his films were hitting the big time. Nobody cashed in on, say, *Mamma Roma*).

In the cast of *The Decameron* were: Franco Citti, Ninetto Davoli, Jovan Jovanovic, Vincenzo Amato, Angela Luce, Giuseppe Zigaina, Maria Gabriella Maione, Vincenzo Ferrigno, Vittorio Vittori, Gianni Rizzo and Monique van Vooren.

The Decameron is a gorgeously *Italian* movie, unapologetic in its *Italianness*, its evocations of Italian institutions, *mœurs* and locales. It *is* a panoply of life, to a degree: you've got sex, marriage, art, family, the Church, Catholicism, crime, politics, work, nature, community, festivals, funerals and other institutions.

The locations in *The Decameron* are unlike any other Italian movie or movie set in Italy in the history of cinema (including Pier Paolo Pasolini's own movies). The poem had been set in Florence, but Pasolini moved the production to Naples,[6] in keeping with his preferences (particularly for Southern Italy, and his love of Napoli and Neapolitan culture). The 1971 movie seeks out marvellous, sun-lit corners and secret, shadowy back alleys of Italy that dazzle and charm the viewer. Catacombs, churches, chapels, squares, back streets, villas, towers, mansions, mills, monasteries, and vineyards (numerous scenes are set in over-grown vineyards).

Locations included: Mount Vesuvius; Naples; Amalfi, Salerno; Ravello, Salerno; Bressanone, and Bolzano, Trentino-Alto Adige; Nepi, Viterbo; Caserta Vecchia, Caserta, Campania; Rome; Safa-Palatino, Rome; Sorrento; Paris; Sana'a,[7] Yemen; Gafsa, Tunisia; and the Loire Valley.

SOME EPISODES.

The Decameron illustrated a series of bawdy clichés and stereotypes:

• a goofy youth (Andreuccio of Perugia[8] – played of course by Pasolini regular Ninetto Davoli the Hapless) – who's taken for a ride by a woman;

• later, young Andreuccio helps a couple of old coots rob the tomb of a recently-deceased Archbishop in a church;

---

[6] And it was played in a Neapolitan accent.
[7] *The Walls of Sana'a* was also made in 1971.
[8] Taken from the 'Andreuccio of Perugia' tale, 2.5. (This story goes back to 2nd century Ephesus).

• the simple-minded, cuckolded husband and his clever, adulterous wife;[9]

• the young lovers, discovered naked in bed on a balcony after a night of sex by their parents (who, instead of scolding their daughter Caterina, congratulate the lovers and persuade them to wed);

• a youth pretending to be deaf and dumb is enrolled as a gardener in a convent, and ends up servicing the inquisitive nuns one by one in an out-house;

• a woman's labourer lover's killed by her jealous brothers; she decapitates the corpse and keeps the head in a plant pot in her bedroom (as you do);

• the pious man whose dead brother appears to tell him that lovemaking isn't a sin after all.

NOTES FOR A FILM OF *THE DECAMERON*.

The Decameron sees Pier Paolo Pasolini the film director in his earthy, bawdy element. *The Decameron* might be seen as a reaction against the seriousness of some of Pasolini's works preceeding it – *Medea, Pigsty, Theorem*, etc. *The Decameron* is a return to the light-hearted approach of *The Hawks and the Sparrows* and *La Ricotta*.

While *The Decameron* is sensuously cinematic, there are scenes where the direction seems uninspired, and scenes boil down to dull shot-reverse shot patterns, and sections that are just too talky and static (often a sure sign that a director's lacking inspiration, or that the script is over-written and/ or indulgent, or that the editing isn't pacey enough).

The Decameron is a comedy throughout – there are pranks (some with an undercurrent of real aggression), the sex is never sexy, but always interrupted, as in all comedy, and some of the situations come across as an art movie version of a *Carry On* film (except not as funny[10] – as even a *bad Carry On* movie!). It does appear occasionally as if Grimaldi, Pasolini, Rossellini, Delli Colli, Ferretti, Donati and the rest of the team working on *The Decameron* have taken up a mediæval sex comedy script and done it over as an Italian art movie romp.

Sure, the big political themes of Pier Paolo Pasolini's cinema – of Marxism and materialism, of the peasant class, of power relations in societies, of the exploitation of the lower class – are all there in *The Decameron*, if the academic critic in you wants to find them; but just as prominent are silly scenes of wives being interrupted giving blowjobs by

---
9 From the tale 'Giletta of Nerbona', 3.9.
10 But Raymond Murray noted in *Images In the Dark: An Encyclopedia of Gay and Lesbian Film and Video* that *The Decameron* was 'perhaps Pasolini's funniest film and certainly one of his best' (107).

husbands getting home too early, or botched robberies, or lusty youths falling into cisterns of doo-doo.

In fact, quite a bit of *The Decameron* comes across as lazy, uninspired and just plain *bad* filmmaking. Can this really be the director who helmed *The Gospel According To Matthew* and *Accattone*? Well, yes, but... They say that no one *deliberately* sets out to make a bad movie (!),[11] but with filmmakers like Pier Paolo Pasolini (and Jean-Luc Godard), sometimes you have to wonder. Because you can't believe that the phenomenally talented and incredibly smart Pasolini could've staged and filmed some of the scenes in *The Decameron* (and ditto with *The Canterbury Tales, The Arabian Nights, Pigsty* and *The Hawks and the Sparrows*).

✦

Like Jean-Luc Godard, Pier Paolo Pasolini liked to produce notes for films (such as in his *Notes For an African Oresteia* or *Notes For a Film In India*). Not a finished film, but a film essay in which the filmmaker ponders on producing the film. Indeed, some of Uncle Godard's most satisfying works are preparations for movies – as such his *Scenario For Passion, Scenario For Every Man For Himself* and *Petites Notes à propos du film Je vous salue, Marie*. In those short pieces, Godard talks, as only Godard can. Boy, that guy can talk! And so can Pasolini: at the beginning of *Notes For an African Oresteia*, for instance, Pasolini is yakking at length about *Oresteia* and Aeschylus, and it sounds un-scripted, as if Pasolini is simply talking over the images.

Maybe *The Decameron* can be thought of like that – not as a finished, slick 35mm movie, but more as a 16 millimetre, *cinéma vérité* preparation for the movie, much as some filmmakers (like Francis Coppola) have filmed rehearsals on video, and cut them together with production material (part of his concept of 'electronic cinema'), or like filmmakers heavily into visual effects will pre-visualize a movie in storyboard form or in digital, animatic form, adding temp music and sound effects and voices.

THE COMEDY AND THE FLAWS.

Again, the sound and dubbing (by Gianni D'Amico, Mario Morigi and Pietro Spadoni) lets down *The Decameron*, as with too many of the movies that Pier Paolo Pasolini directed. Sometimes it appears as if every movie in Italy after WW2 was dubbed in the same place (often at

---

11 And nobody deliberately pays to see a bad movie.

Cinecittà[12]), and by the same sound team – and they couldn't care less.[13] The sound in too many Italian movies is crude and dodgy like the first sound films in Hollywood *circa* 1929 and 1930. And it's such a pity, because we are talking about some truly magnificent masterpieces of cinema here.

In consequence, *The Decameron* loses some of its power to entrance and move an audience. And sometimes it appears as if the film was shot with the same casual, can't-really-be-bothered attitude. There's a point when loose, handheld camerawork becomes grating, and starts to detract not add to the proceedings. However, the camera is on a tripod in the main, dispensing with the irritatingly shaky handheld camera of other Pasolini movies.

And the sound in *The Decameron*, as in many of Pier Paolo Pasolini's other pictures, just appears clumsy and awkward where it should be punchy and convincing. In short, Pasolini's films would not be classed among the great sound movies. In the use of dialogue and sound effects, Pasolini is no Francis Coppola or Orson Welles or Jean-Luc Godard. In terms of *music*, however, Pasolini's films can be astonishing – topped off by the incomparable soundtrack to *Il Vangelo Secondo Matteo*.

It always strikes me as odd – when *so much effort* is put into the costumes or the production design or the casting and dressing of the extras in Pier Paolo Pasolini's cinema, that the soundtrack and looping should be so casually slapped onto the movies (but, once again, it's also due to the way the Italian film industry works. It's also true that after WWII the Italian film industry, as with other European countries, wasn't as well equipped as its North American counterparts). For designs, sets and costumes, weeks might've been spent (and weeks of location scouting); but for sound dubbing and mixing – it looks like a day at most (with a three-hour break for lunch and a siesta).

But that's typical of the film business: crews work incredibly hard on scenes only to have them cut. Sets are built but not used. Costumes are designed and made (sometimes 100s), but the production is cancelled. It goes with the territory. At least many of Pasolini's movies found an audience, so all of that effort wasn't wasted.

(Sets[14] were built for Federico Fellini's grand project *The Journey of G. Mastorna* in the mid-1960s (at Dinocittà outside Roma), but it was

---

12 Tho' here it was at the offices of Grimaldi's company.
13 They were probably under-paid, and clocked in and out of work as in a factory. Right after mixing the sound for *The Decameron* they might've done a TV commercial for electric shavers and then the Italian dub for an episode of *Columbo*.
14 Including an airliner, a motel and a Cathedral.

abandoned. 22,000 costumes were made for a mid-1990s movie, *Crusade*, starring Arnold Schwarzenegger, but Carolco cancelled it when the budget approached $120 million).[15]

Quite a bit of *The Decameron* appears as if the filmmakers were going thru the motions and couldn't be bothered with it. The luxury of some of the components (the settings, the costumes, the props, the large-scale scenes with extras), are negated by the sorry state of the inept acting, blocking, camerawork, editing, sound and pacing.

And sometimes in *The Decameron* and other Pier Paolo Pasolini movies, like *The Canterbury Tales* or *Arabian Nights*, it appears as if the filmmakers were trying to get by with simply relying on the bizarre faces they'd found from open casting calls in Naples or Rome. The faces *are* extraordinary, and the camera lovingly lingers on them – and, yes, there is nothing so wondrous as the human face. But... sometimes you wish for a little more... In *The Gospel According To Matthew* it worked like gangbusters: the combination of those amazing faces of ordinary folk from Southern Italy and the unusual music, and set within the context of a religious epic, was deeply moving. (This is partly because the narrative framework of the *Gospel* movie – the Christian story – is absolutely enormous, containing a grandeur, a drama, a lyricism that few other stories in the Western world boast).

But in a fundamentally comical/ farce genre, like the 'trilogy of life' movies – which are *comedies*, though heightened and stylized comedies – lingering over faces at length just isn't enough. Close-ups of faces, done like this, isn't comedy. A close-up of the wonderful Totò, yes, but not amateur actors. (One has to admit, too, that the film editing by Nino Baragli and Tatiana Casini Morigi is simply not great comedy film editing in the 'trilogy of life' movie series. The finest screen comedies need absolutely ruthless control over the editing. As Woody Allen explained, in working with his editor Ralph Rosenblum, anything that wasn't funny was out, *out*, <u>out</u> – anything that didn't get laughs was dropped instantly. *The Decameron* is shoddily edited, in terms of exploiting the humour. However, I haven't seen the movie with an Italian audience in a theatre, and you can bet there are ingredients that go over much better with a home audience (it was Pasolini's biggest hit, remember, selling 11,000,000-plus tickets).[16] Comedy is notoriously difficult to carry over cultural and national borders. Also, time is tough

---

[15] The *Crusade* project eventually turned up in 2005, helmed by Ridley Scott. But, oh how woeful was *Kingdom of Heaven*! Sure, the battles and the action were terrific, but Orlando Bloom in the lead role had the charisma of a soggy cardboard box.

[16] There is also the novelty factor – films with so much nudity and sex were still relatively new in 1971.

on film comedies, isn't it? Somehow, comedy movies have to be much more resilient to stand the test of time, compared with, say, dramas).

One would have to admit that, as with Steven Spielberg, Ridley Scott, James Cameron, Michael Cimino, Bernardo Bertolucci and 1,000s of others, comedy is not one of Pier Paolo Pasolini's strongest points, as a filmmaker. He would like it to be, and there is certainly a smug assurance that the 'trilogy of life' movies *are* funny. But they are not especially amusing. Pasolini is brilliant at irony (sometimes savage, as in *Salò, or 120 Days of Laughing*), and one or two knockabout gags.

Of course, many of the celebrated art movie filmmakers never tried to make comedies – Carl-Theodor Dreyer, Andrei Tarkovsky,[17] Stan Brakhage, and Robert Bresson (and some of the ones that did try to do comedies – Ingmar Bergman being the obvious example – were not wholly successful, as 100s of film critics attest). But Pier Paolo Pasolini is definitely trying for broad laughs in his 'mediæval trilogy' films.

And failing.

If a movie fails as a comedy the first place to look – and this applies to any genre, or any type of film – is the script (scripts are worked over and over and *over* in the best comedy films). Unfortunately, in the 'trilogy of life' flicks shaky scripts are further let down by shaky direction and performances and casting.

Take the scene in *The Decameron* where Andreuccio is persuaded by the sly, manipulative robbers to enter the tomb of the recently deceased Archbishop. It's a classic black humour comedy situation of corpses, thieves, nighttime, creeping about, a church. Ninetto Davoli isn't a bad comic actor, but the direction, the performances, and the script itself don't exploit the situation. Imagine one of cinema's comedy geniuses tackling the same scene, and you can see how far short Pier Paolo Pasolini and the team fall. However, there's some genuine comedy between the two brothers Meuccio and Tingoccio near the end of the movie.

Let's have a look at some of the stories in *The Decameron*:

CIAPELLETTO.

Franco Citti makes his customary appearance in a Pier Paolo Pasolini movie as an atheistic, violent, morally corrupt heavy, Ciappelletto (i.e., it continues his characterization in *Accattone*), a proto-gangster who'd be quite at home in the world of 20th century Sicily or *The Godfather* (Citti duly appeared in two *Godfather* films). Citti is another of Pasolini's rough-and-ready men of the streets: in an early scene in *The Decameron*,

---

[17] An Andrei Tarkovsky comedy?!

Ciappelletto preys upon a teenage boy, offering him money for sex (touching him near the groin – like the other two 'trilogy of life' movies, actors are often photographed to emphasize the crotch. Pasolini never got tired of filming shots of men's crotches (it began with *Theorem*), and *The Decameron* and the other 'trilogy of life' films contain plenty of them. Once Pasolini realized he was allowed to film crotches, they appear in most of his subsequent films).

Indeed, *The Decameron* opens in a very unusual manner, which seems to come from a different movie: in medium close-up, Franco Citti beats an unseen victim to death (finishing off the task by hefting a large stone). Then Ciappelletto carries the corpse in a sack at dusk up and down steps, and tips it down a slope. This is the first of many, many walking scenes in all three of the mediæval movies. (The scene wrong-foots the audience, but not in a good way).

Only after this sequence does the 1971 movie shift into a more familiar form of narration, with a big, crowd scene in daytime (it's a market, as at the start of *The Canterbury Tales*). It's a mandatory scene in any historical movie, where the production values are shown off[18] (this leads to the start of the first tale).

But why did the filmmakers choose to open *The Decameron* with this very violent scene? It's a murder (killed by death!) in the very first shot! It's played straight, and powerfully. It doesn't fully represent the rest of the movie (tho' there are murders, such as of Lorenzo, Isabella's lover). And there's no build-up, no establishment of dramatic suspense: the film cuts right into the murder as it's happening: we don't meet the victim first, and Ciappelletto stalking him (we only hear some off-screen pleas. After that, the sorry soul is a bundle of meat in a sack).

Is it to put the audience off-balance? To encourage them to expect a particular sort of movie? To understand that this will not solely be a mediæval comedy? (The more obvious opening scene for *The Decameron* would be the following one, depicting Ninetto Davoli as Andreuccio in the big, bustling market scene).

But the scene does establish Ciappelletto's character in broadstrokes, so that when he pops up in the crowd listening to the old storyteller, we already know something of who he is.

The Ciappelletto sub-plot is spread throughout the 1971 film, so that we return to it at several points (thus providing a loose dramatic structure). Sent to collect a debt in Northern Italy,[19] Ciappelletto finds

---

18 Look, we hired lots of extras and dressed them and gave them wigs and provided them with props and animals and all!
19 Or is it France?

himself out-matched by a pair of wily, old debtors, and ends up dying – or seeming to die (punishment, once again, for 'sins', non-belief, and Doing Bad Things). But not before a *very* lengthy confession scene (yet Ciappelletto barely confesses to anything, telling a bunch of lies instead – his final admission, in keeping with the key themes of a Pier Paolo Pasolini movie, is about his mother, who carried him in her womb for nine months, night and day, and whom he cursed as a youth. It's a continuation, in part, of the characterization of Accarttone).

The priest ministering last rites buys it all, and Ciappelletto is instantly celebrated as a Catholic martyr. In a subsequent scene, which is pure Pasolini, Ciappelletto's corpse is carried into a sepulchre, where a solemn crowd venerates him as a saint (reaching out to touch his body on a raised platform). This is Pasolini the religious anthropologist, fascinated by how (and why) certain individuals are sanctified and worshipped, even if they are thoroughly venal. Even a murderer can become a saint. (This scene ends the first part of *The Decameron*[20]).

ANDREUCCIO.

Back to Ninetto Davoli, playing his usual goofy, well-meaning but simple-minded youth in *The Decameron*, complete with ridiculous frizzy perm (second day – fifth tale in Giovanni Boccaccio's tome) – and the 1971 movie enjoys punishing him for, in this case, simply existing (if you're dumb enough to wander into a Big, Bad City like Napoli without being hard as nails, tough luck!). Davoli's Andreuccio di Pietro is a preening, gullible twerp (when we meet him, he's a vain, strutting guy trying to buy some horses at the Napoli market). He's an easy mark, and the Lady, the Sicilian woman and her whole household connive in fleecing him of his dough (which he foolishly waves about). Yes, Naples was the Babylon of the Middle Ages – when Andreuccio is soundly pranked, everybody is leaning out of their windows, berating Andreuccio loudly, yelling at him to, 'Via! Via!'

This is from Boccaccio in the horse market scene:

> While [Andreuccio] was thus chaffering, and after he had shewn his purse, there chanced to come by a Sicilian girl, fair as fair could be, but ready to pleasure any man for a small consideration. He did not see her, but she saw him and his purse, and forthwith said to herself: – "Who would be in better luck than I if all those florins were mine?" and so she passed on. With the girl was an old woman, also a Sicilian, who, when she saw Andreuccio, dropped behind the girl, and ran towards him, making as if she would tenderly embrace him. The girl observing this said nothing, but stopped and waited a little way off for the old woman to rejoin her.

---

20 That's your cue to buy ice cream and popcorn in the foyer.

Andreuccio turned as the old woman came up, recognised her, and greeted her very cordially; but time and place not permitting much converse, she left him, promising to visit him at his inn; and he resumed his chaffering, but bought nothing that morning.

So the Lady invites Andreuccio to her house then robs him, aided by the Sicilian woman (after he's tumbled into a toilet that's been rigged, and climbed out of a window covered in filth).[21] Everybody is in on the jape, and the hapless Andreuccio doesn't stand a chance against these mean locals. The episode introduces the elements of bawdy comedy and farcical (often crude) scenarios which the 'trilogy of life' movies explore at length.

Andreuccio only triumphs in the second episode (the tomb robbing) because there's a second band of looters even more inept than he is: he scares them off (after being trapped in the tomb by the first bunch of thieves), and gets to keep the bishop's shiny, ruby ring from the sepulchre. So Andreuccio dances off into the night out of the chapel – and, yes, Ninetto Davoli really does caper and skip with joy like a Disney bunny rabbit (every Pasolini film from *The Hawks and the Sparrows* onwards had a clause in the film director's contract that a scene of Nino Davoli prancing about must be included: [Clause 21.4.B] *Lo, there will be prancing, and the prancing will be done by Davoli. Amen*).

PERONELLA AND THE CUCKOLD.

The episode (from the seventh day – second tale) featuring the shrewish wife Peronella (Angela Luce)[22] and her gormless, grinning fool of a husband, Giannello (Vincenzo Ferringo), is delightfully (or painfully) idiotic. The script wouldn't survive the first five minutes of any meeting of TV or film writers, but it is obediently acted, dressed, lit and filmed here (when your director is Pier Paolo Pasolini, he is King On The Set, and you just do what he says).

So, after being interrupted mid-tup by the unexpected return home of her useless hubby, Peronella orders the toothy, grinning spouse[23] to climb inside a giant jar to scrub it (it's up for sale, and a shifty guy is hanging around hoping to buy it – she claims), while the lusty wife is taken from the rear by her lover and calls out encouragements to both men – 'higher... lower... that's the spot'.

The Petronella episode is a lame, French farce with some nudity, featuring humour at the level of a saucy newspaper strip. Can this really

---

21 The film re-uses this location for part of Petronella's house.
22 The most memorable aspect of the Petronella skit in *The Decameron* is the shrill violence with which Angela Luce (or whoever dubbed her voice) attacks her husband.
23 Such a dimwit deserves to be cuckolded.

be the same movie director who made *Oedipus Rex* and *Accattone?* This is Pier Paolo Pasolini the poetical-political firebrand of Italian contemporary culture cutting loose, proving that he's not scarily earnest all of the time, that he can put aside his Communist, anti-capitalist rhetoric and do something different from his rants about the decline of Italian society.

A GARDENER AND SOME NUNS.

There's an amusing episode in *The Decameron* (third day – first tale) set in a convent by the sea (what a location!),[24] with an attractive youth, Masetto da Lamporecchio (played by Vincenzo Amato) satisfying the itches of a bunch of nuns (the actor spends much of the time wearing only a ragged shirt and nothing else, plus some cute shorts that Danilo Donati has created). Da Lamporecchio pretends to be deaf and dumb (and simple), and offers himself to the convent as a gardener. It's pure male fantasy, right out of adolescent porn, and quite offensive if considered in the light of (second wave) feminism or political correctness (for instance, of course, it's the *nuns* who seduce the gardener, not the other way around. The instigator is a curious nun (Patrizia de Clara) who contemplates in a lengthy dialogue scene the possibilities of communion with her cohort. Meanwhile, da Lamporecchio works up a ladder, in a tree, allowing the sisters to contemplate his groin). At the end of the episode, the Mother Superior opts to sample the gardener's meat and veg too, declaring it a miracle when the guy starts to talk.[25] The scene of the two nuns in the hut with the mute gardener runs thus in Boccaccioi's *Decameron*:

> And then she led him into the hut, where he needed no pressing to do what she desired of him. Which done, she changed places with the other, as loyal comradeship required; and Masetto, still keeping up the pretence of simplicity, did their pleasure. Wherefore before they left, each must needs make another assay of the mute's powers of riding; and afterwards, talking the matter over many times, they agreed that it was in truth not less but even more delightful than they had been given to understand; and so, as they found convenient opportunity, they continued to go and disport themselves with the mute.

The best moment in *Nuns 'R Us* has the Brides of Christ lined up outside their cells, as Mr Weenie works his way from room to room, servicing each one. It might be a Ken Russell or Walerian Borowczyk movie from the Seventies. Except Borowczyk has done this scenario of nuns and sex so much sprightlier and wittier – in *Behind Convent Walls*

---

24 The white-washed walls and tiny cells evoke monasteries in Greece.
25 She disregards the fact that he has violently berated them.

(1977),26 for instance, which's a truly wild movie, or the *Thérèse Philosophe* episode from *Immoral Tales* (1974), where God teaches a young woman locked in her room for misbehaving how to masturbate.

Once again, it seems as if this episode, like some others in *The Decameron*, is being treated ironically and cynically by the movie as well as being played straight, *and* for comedy. *The Decameron* seems unsure about how it really feels about the stories and the characters it's presenting, and as if it secretly realizes that this whole movie is total rubbish. But someone's getting paid, someone needs the money on this production, so – what the hell – the filmmakers soldier on.

CATERINA AND RICCARDO.

The lovely Elisabetta Genovese, with her incredible, radiant smile, has her biggest role in a Pier Paolo Pasolini movie as Caterina, the daughter of the merchant Musciatto (Guido Alberti). Clearly not a professional actress,27 Genovese charms the audience with her performance as a loving young woman who arranges a tryst with her beloved Riccardo on the rooftop of the family home (fifth day – fourth tale). She tells her mom she can't sleep because it's too hot. They make love, of course.

Once again the 'trilogy of life' movies depict young love and first love and virginal love (usually at the same time) – the 1971-1972-1974 films seem to promise the possibility of new beginnings and of rebirth. For all the obvious reasons, the 'trilogy of life' pictures keep coming back to new love.

The capper of this episode has Caterina's folks appear on the rooftop in the early morning, discovering the lovers lying naked beside each other (Caterina has her hand possessively on Riccardo's penis – 'this is mine now'). Mom and dad consider the possibilities: death or money. The economic basis of marriage is evoked when the parents decide that the kids' union might increase their wealth.

The Caterina/ Riccardo episode in *The Decameron* is disarmingly simple and charming. It's the closest that Pier Paolo Pasolini's cinema gets to the unapologetic innocence of a Hollywood musical movie, where the entire machinery of film production, which's so expensive, so complicated, and so cynical, is orchestrated by veteran producers to create something as simple and sweet as a teenage love story.

There are no Disney doves optically printed into this episode, there's

---

26 *Behind Convent Walls* (1977, a.k.a. *Interieur d'un Convent, Sex Life in a Convent* and *Within a Cloister*) was shot in Italy, and starred Walerian Borowczyk's wife, Ligia Branice and the future star of his later films, Marina Pierro (as Sister Veronica). It was based on Stendhal's *Roman Walks* (I haven't read *Roman Walks*, but somehow I bet Stendhal wouldn't have thought it would be adapted someday into a story with nuns masturbating with dildoes.)
27 She struggles with her dialogue.

achieved. Well, at least the episode expressed the corrosive sexism of the period, and portrayed masculinity at its most disagreeable: arrogant, ignorant, stupid, hypocritical,[28] controlling and violent[29] (it portrays the worst aspects of mediæval, European men and patriarchy – but that behaviour and those attitudes can still be found in Europe, and Italy).

Only at the end of this episode did something vaguely intriguing occur, when the lover Isabella decides to uncover the grave of her slain boyfriend Lorenzo (he's seen in a dream, visiting Isabella as she sleeps, like the vision of the dead man later on). So Bella goes into the vineyards with her woman-in-waiting, scrabbles in the dirt, finds the corpse, and chops off her beloved's head (as you do).[30] She takes the head home, cleans it and plants it in a pot. Well, that's not something you see everyday in a movie, a young woman decapitating her lover.

The tale of the pot of basil ends thus in *The Decameron* by Boccaccio:

> Whereat the young men, marvelling mightily, resolved to see what the pot might contain; and having removed the earth they espied the cloth, and therein the head, which was not yet so decayed, but that by the curled locks they knew it for Lorenzo's head. Passing strange they found it, and fearing lest it should be bruited abroad, they buried the head, and, with as little said as might be, took order for their privy departure from Messina, and hied them thence to Naples. The girl ceased not to weep and crave her pot, and, so weeping, died. Such was the end of her disastrous love.

GIOTTO AND PAINTING.

The Decameron included a cameo from the director himself as Giotto di Bondone (*c.* 1267-1337), Italy's greatest painter of the 14th century, who, according to Dante Alighieri, out-shone Cimabue. (Sometimes Pier Paolo Pasolini is described in the subtitles as playing a disciple of Giotto). This enabled Pasolini to address directly his passion for painting and for Early Renaissance art and pre-High Renaissance art, with its Renaissance space (the frontal, flattened perspectives of Giotto, Duccio Buoninsegna, Masaccio and Piero della Francesca), and religious subjects. The teeming crowd scenes of Pieter Brueghel were also inspirations. (*Not* Mannerist or Baroque, then, as Italian filmmakers such as Pasolini are often dubbed, along with Bernardo Bertolucci, Luchino Visconti and Federico Fellini).

Playing Giotto (from the sixth day, fifth tale of Giovanni Boccaccio's text) offered a portrait of Pier Paolo Pasolini the *auteur*,

---

[28] One of the brothers is seen tupping a woman, but in the double standards of the era, it doesn't matter.
[29] One of the other brothers goes scarily apoplectic when he hears their sister is having an affair.
[30] But she simply walks away from the rest of his body! – she doesn't even cover it up.

no cooing, Hollywood choir, and no colourful, lavish M.G.M. sets and props, but the Caterina/ Riccardo segment of *The Decameron* is just as sentimental and cheesy as M.G.M., Disney and Hollywood.

Part of the Caterina/ Riccardo episode is intercut with the Giotto Painting The Church episode – an unusual instance where two of the stories in *The Decameron* are edited in parallel. For example, we see Giotto on the street in the busy marketplace spotting Caterina and her folks (Pasolini as Giotto frames them with his fingers over his eyes, lining up a shot movie director-style). The encounter in the bazaar also suggests how the artist finds his inspiration on the streets, and how a beautiful creature like Caterina might inspire Giotto's version of the Virgin Mary.

✦

Many episodes in the three mediæval movies are actually love poems – poems to love, poems about love, poems made with love. Altho' Pier Paolo Pasolini is portrayed in the media as the super-intelligent, politically radical rebel of Italian cinema, much of the 'trilogy of life' series is actually a straightforward exaltation of love and sex and passion. There are scenes of lovers trysting, of lovers rushing to each other, of lovers mistaking each other, of lovers worshipping each other from afar – all of these are staples of mediæval literature, found in 100s of courtly love poems.

THE DEAD LOVER.

Among the least convincing and shoddiest episodes in *The Decameron* (fourth day – fifth tale) concerned a Sicilian labourer, Lorenzo (Giuseppe Arrigio) who's caught tupping a merchant's daughter, Isabella: her three brothers decide they're going to dispatch Lorenzo (well, this *is* the Middle Ages, and it's Italy, where erasing people who get in the way or who disrupt society is an accepted activity). This was also the source of the famous poem 'Isabella, or The Pot of Basil' by John Keats, and illustrated in Pre-Raphaelite art.

The Isabella episode involved some of the dullest evocations of Italian *braggadocio* and machismo in movies, as the *ragazzi* lure the hapless youth to the family vineyards (but the murder itself occurs off-screen – with a Godardian nonchalance. Just as the brothers hurtle after Lorenzo, with their daggers drawn, the film cuts to Isabella in her chambers).

The episode's reminiscent of the Romeo-Mercutio-Tybalt brawls in William Shakespeare's *Romeo and Juliet*, but crudely and shabbily surrounded by assistants, the centre of attention, the only one who could add the magic touch and vision of the artist, who can be called 'Master' by his workers (and he played Geoffrey Chaucer, England's great poet, in the next 'trilogy of life' film, *The Canterbury Tales*). Pasolini's Giotto was shown carrying out a major commission in a large Cathedral (evoking Giotto's famous frescoes at Padua; and also Assisi), to paint frescoes on a massive, bare wall in the nave, orchestrating his minions who mixed paint, prepared materials, painted the ground for the frescoes, set up the wooden scaffold, etc (Giotto is visiting from the North, as the film production was).

The painter was depicted as a heroic figure, standing in the centre of the frame while his lackeys pushed the two storey scaffold into place. There were cuts from the frescoes to Pasolini as the painter looking suitably serious and intent in the midst of his work. (Pasolini gave himself very little dialogue, however, as if to preserve the persona of the artist-as-enigma – he yells at his team at one point, hurrying them to work, and apologizes at lunch for leaving early,[31] but not much more[32]).

In the episode, Giotto di Bondone was depicted as an artist so consumed by his work he dreams about it at night (this is where the vision of the Virgin Mary and the angels appears), observes people in the market square outside, and rushes eating his grub so he can get back to work when inspiration strikes him. This is the artist as mirror of life, taking real people as his inspiration (plus some of his visions). It was surprisingly conventional in its view of art and artists, perhaps, considering that it came from Pier Paolo Pasolini, a poet who has a highly developed conception of creative issues.

Narratively, the Painting of the Fresco episode amounted to nothing really. It contained no drama, conflicts, goals, resolutions, or propulsion (well, there *are* some ruminations on the relationship between art and life). It was a parable, in essence, a simple story: *And lo, a Painter named Giotto, praised by Boccaccio and Dante, came to a Church in Southern Italy and painted a fresco, and, behold!, it was mighty handsome and good...* So a painter comes to a Cathedral and paints a fresco with a bunch of gnarly, rough-and-ready assistants (plus some Caravaggesque *ragazzi*, of course). That's all there was to this section of 1971's *Il Decamerone*: yes, and at the end of the episode, when the fresco is completed, wine is passed round the workers as they celebrate a job well-done (a kind of wrap party for the movie on screen). Pasolini has the last line in *The Decameron* – looking at his frescoes, he muses if it's

---

[31] Because he's suddenly inspired.
[32] Here, the assistants scurry about with speeded-up film, another silent cinema motif.

better to dream about an artwork rather than making it (maybe it is – but Pasolini didn't take that advice – he never stopped making poetry and art).

However, the Giotto sequence opens Part Two of *The Decameron* (i.e., it's put in a significant place in the movie's structure), and it's intercut with the Caterina/ Riccardo episode, suggesting that Giotto is being inspired by the tale of simple, teenage romance (he uses Caterina as an inspiration for the Madonna). The intercutting (which occurs in the subsequent tales), also gives the Giotto sequence an aspect of a narrative frame, as with the Ciappelletto sequence in Part One of *The Decameron* (which was also intercut at intervals in between the episodes). The Giotto sequence also closes the 1971 picture (another important spot), with the celebration scene in the Cathedral.

I wonder if *Andrei Roublyov* was an influence in this section of *The Decameron*: the 1966 Mosfilm production, directed by Andrei Tarkovsky and co-written with Andrei Mikhalkov-Konchalovsky, is a remarkable recreation of 15th century Russia. Tarkovsky and Mikhalkov-Konchalovsky took up the scenario of an itinerant artist travelling to churches to fulfil commissions to paint frescoes and turned it into a disquisition on the poetry of art and the poetry of cinema. The scene where Giotto, da Rabatta and the boys are caught in a rainstorm in the countryside in *The Decameron* seems to be an *hommage* to the similar scene at the beginning of *Andrei Roublyov*, which, in turn, was likely inspired by Akira Kurosawa and *Rashomon* (1950) and its famous rain scenes. (Meanwhile, Walerian Borowczyk staged a delightful recreation of the Renaissance artists Raphael and Michelangelo Buonarroti painting the Vatican in his amazing 1979 movie *Three Immoral Women*).[33]

THE PRIEST AND THE MARE.

One of the silliest episodes in *The Decameron* (in a film stuffed with dumb tales), concerns a self-important priest/ doctor, Don Giovanni (Vittorio Vittori) who attempts a ridiculous prank on two simple-minded peasants. When Don Giovanni discovers that the wife Gemmatta (Mirella Catanesi) of his attendant Pietro da Tresanti is young and attractive,[34] and as gullible as a two year-old child, he goes along with her request to be turned into a mare. While Gemmatta's gormless spouse da Tresanti looks on, befuddled and spluttering, the priest has Gemmatta undress, then he

---

[33] *Three Immoral Women* has all of the classic Walerian Borowczyk touches and obsessions: women in lead roles; tons of art on display; plenty of sex scenes and acres of nudity; floaty, white, see-through dresses; historical settings; period music; women bathing; still-lifes; animals; organ music; fabulous costumes and hats; and it's been art directed to perfection.

[34] Don't ask how this ugly, unkempt peasant landed himself a lovely, young wife.

fondles her and mounts her, all the while gushing over her body which'll make a very fine mare. And pinning on the tail of the mare is the trickiest part of the magical transformation! (It's a saucy version of the kids' party game of being blindfold and pinning the tail on the donkey).

The priest and the mare is a farcical riff on authority figures exploiting the peasant class – literally, by taking their women for themselves. Da Tresanti and his wife Gemmatta don't possess strong enough defences against the wiles of a bourgeois, educated priest, who finds them an easy mark. The scenario of power, class and exploitation was reprised later in the 'trilogy of life' films and of course taken to an extreme in *Salò, or The 120 Days of Sodom*.

THE VIRGIN MARY.

In an extraordinary, breathtaking sequence in *The Decameron*, in one of the last tales, the production team recreated an Early Renaissance painting of the Virgin Mary in glory, surrounded by angels, with a Last Judgement acted out underneath (a replay of *Curd Cheese*), as sinners are manhandled by devils into the depths. The scene, which's very brief (and a little clumsily filmed and edited),[35] was accompanied by choral music (*Veni Sancte Spiritus*). It was the nighttime vision of the painter Giotto waking up in bed.

The scene was presented in the flattened space of Renaissance art, against a pale, blue sky and a wall of grey soil (taken from a Giotto painting). The Madonna (played by – who else? – Silvana Mangano) sat on a throne, a gold *vesica piscis* enveloping her, with angels (choiring children out of Piero della Francesca) in white robes in rows either side, standing in front of gold, embossed haloes (plus nobles on thrones on either side). The lower half of the scene combined elements from Renaissance depictions of Adam and Eve being expelled from Paradise, the *Crucifixion*, and *The Last Judgment*.[36] (With the curious omission of Christ – the Cross is empty – Jesus is sitting on the Madonna's lap).

Giotto's dream is staged in the fake-theatrical-pictorial manner that seems to be the special province of Italian cinema, a cross between a puppet show at a religious festival, a procession of carnival floats in Venice, and theatrical-cinematic trickery (which became the approach of later Federico Fellini films such as *Casanova* and *City of Women*).

Certainly Pier Paolo Pasolini was at his finest and most overtly romantic as a film director when he and his teams were recreating Italian

---

[35] The dream vision is edited as flash cuts (and some longer pan shots), combined with reaction shots of Giotto in bed, looking slightly off-camera.
[36] Some of the bodies hanging are dummies; the Virgin in the wide shot is a dummy, too, to be in scale with Christ on her lap, played by a child.

Renaissance art – in *Curd Cheese*, *The Canterbury Tales* and *The Decameron*, Pasolini is deliciously self-indulgent. One could happily watch hours of this kind of filmmaking, with its joyous and uniroinic celebration of Italian Renaissance art (but if anybody can render Italian Renaissance art, it's probably best done by a bunch of Italian filmmakers who know it inside-out – it's in their blood[37]).

THE TWO BROTHERS.

In the tale of the two brothers (seventh day – tenth tale), the final story in *The Decameron*, we discover that lovemaking isn't a sin! Yay! *Si si*, we *really* needed to hear that in 1971, didn't we?! Or today!

So here're evocations of sex and repression once again, with sin and guilt as the ever-present moral threat/ punishment hovering over everything in the Catholic/ Christian world. So there's the pious brother (Meuccio) who tries to abstain from sex and the virile brother (Tingoccio) who's out carousing and swiving a lot. Meuccio and Tingoccio are humble merchants who have sweethearts among the stalls near them in the street market (outside the Cathedral, where Giotto is painting inside). Meuccio complains that Tingoccio is at it all the time (two, three, four – nine times a day!). Meuccio is the neurotic one, a 14th century Woody Allen, who worries about getting into Heaven (or, rather, trying to stay out of Hell). Tingoccio has girls as much as he likes, but pays for his actions with death (he's literally killed, it seems, by over-indulgence – the wages of sin).

There is some genuine comedy in the tale of the two brothers in *The Decameron* (both actors are terrific). The horny Tinogoccio comes back from the dead at night to let his brother Meuccio know what Hell is like (as they promised each other). When Tingoccio tells his brother Meuccio that the sin of sex doesn't count in Hell (or Purgatory), what does the pious brother do? He bursts out of bed in joy, rushes gleefully thru the nighttime streets to leap upon his naked beloved in her chamber, crying out, 'it's not a sin!'

The Decameron thus closes with two upbeat episodes: the black comedy of the two brothers, with the message that love isn't a crime, and the completion of the fresco in the Cathedral. The scenes close *The Decameron* with some positive statements: go and make love, folks, because it's not regarded as a sin in Hell... and maybe art is best left in the realm of dreams, where it can swim unfettered.

---

37 And who are steeped in it – in Rome.

The Decameron (1971).
This page and over.

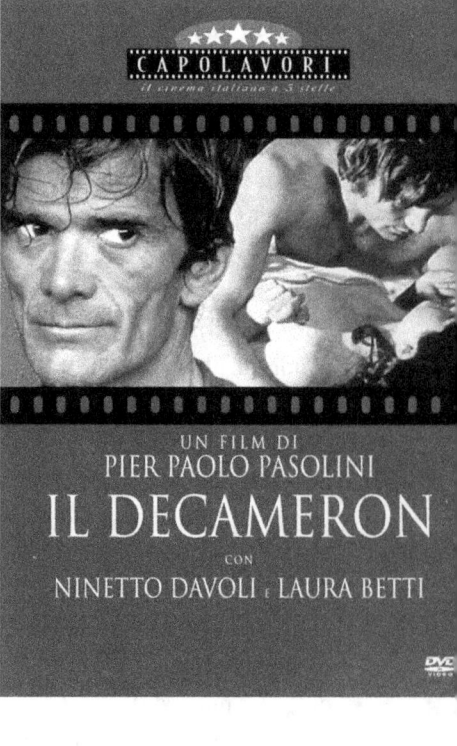

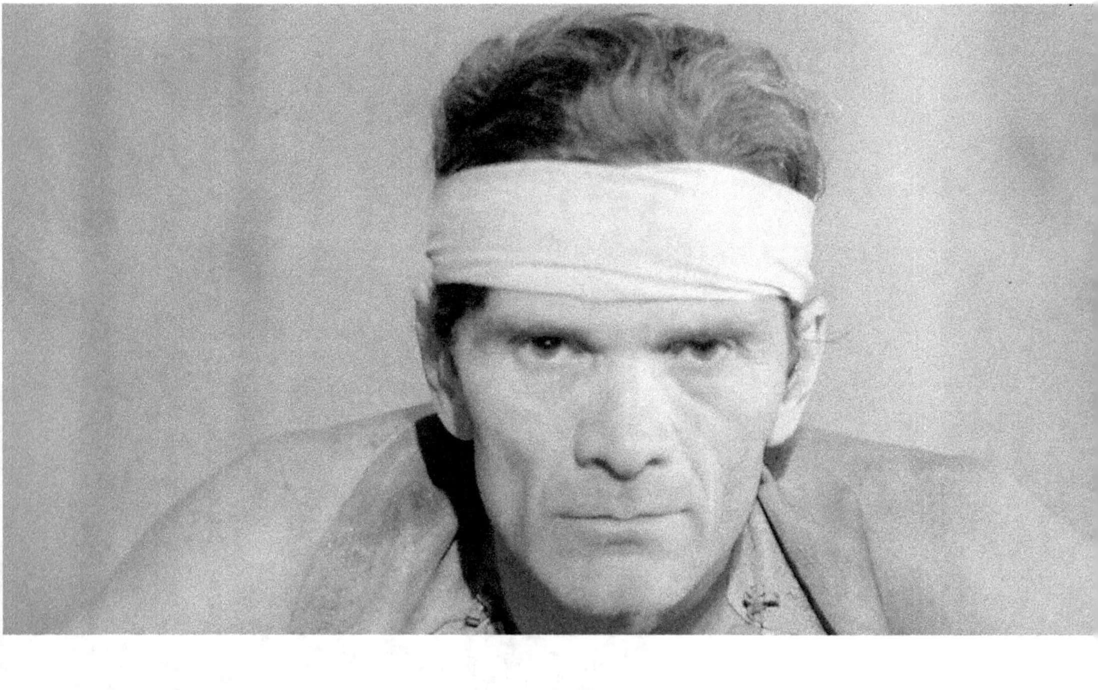

Pasolini's cameo in The Decameron.

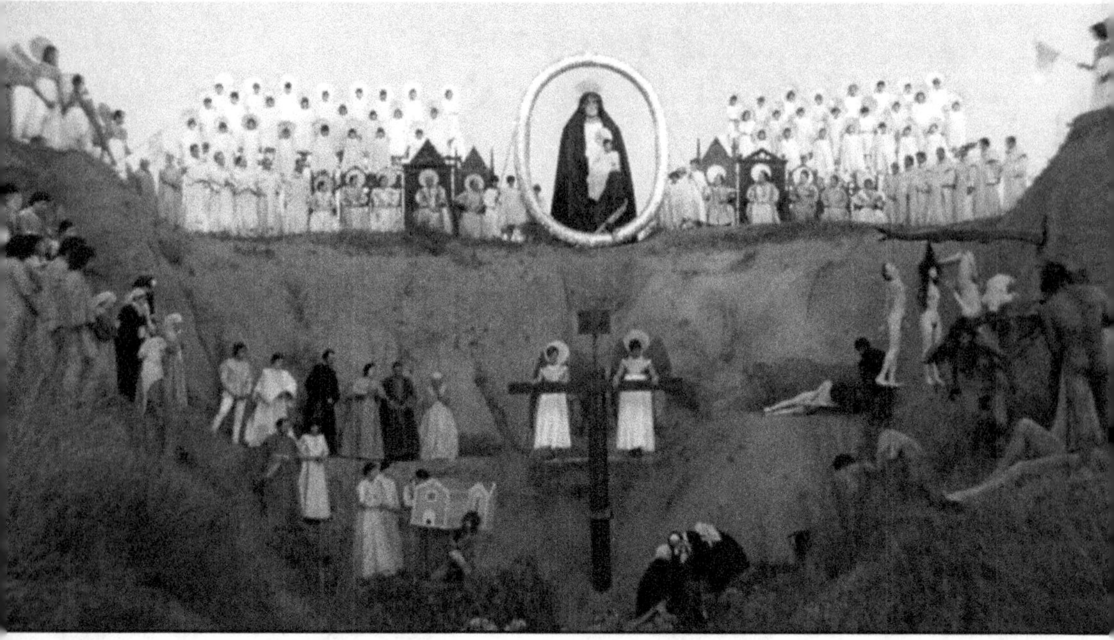

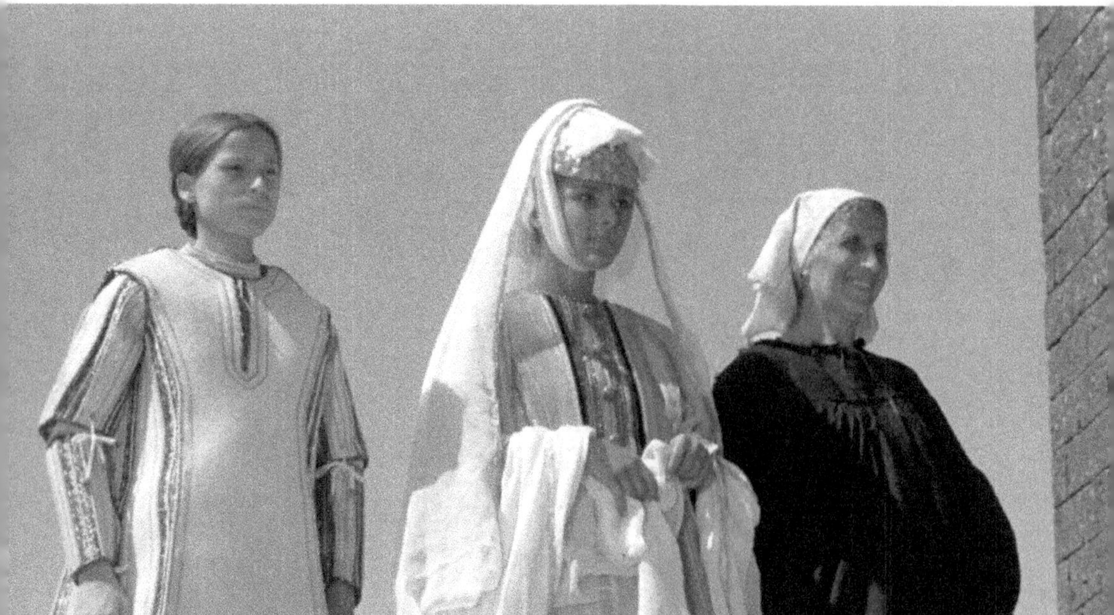

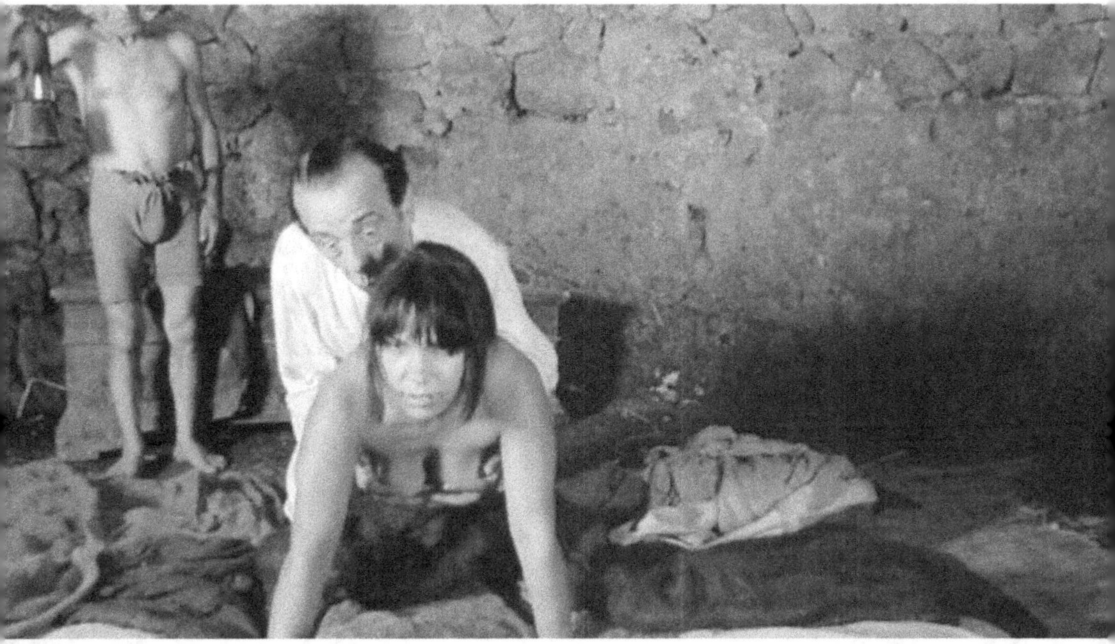

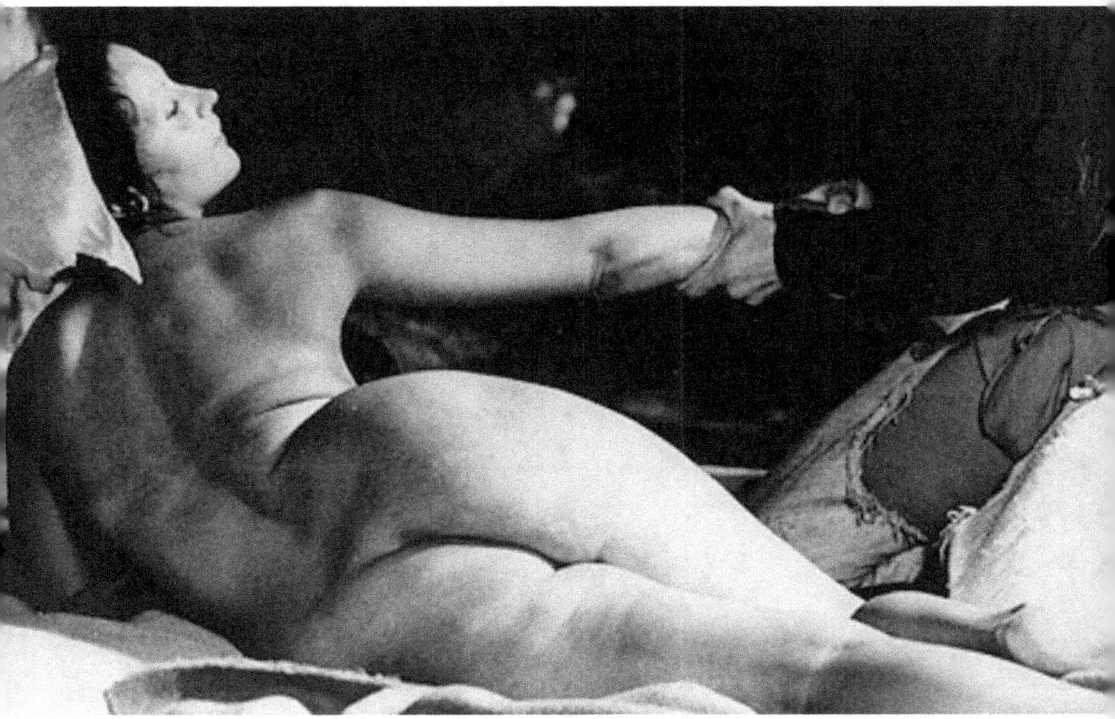

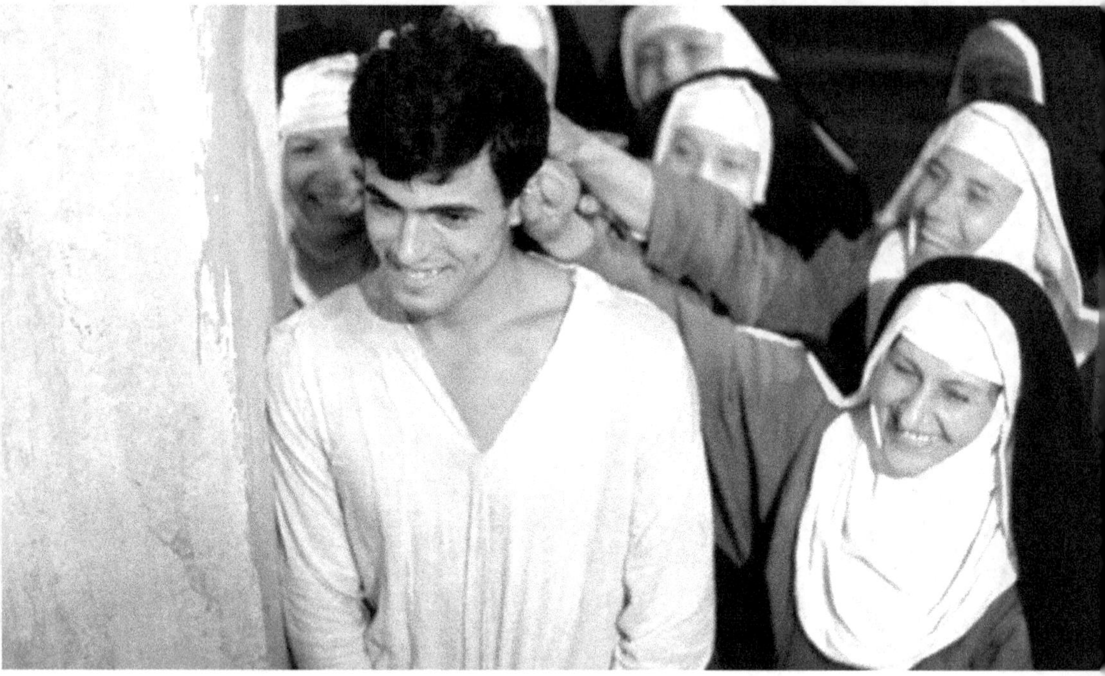

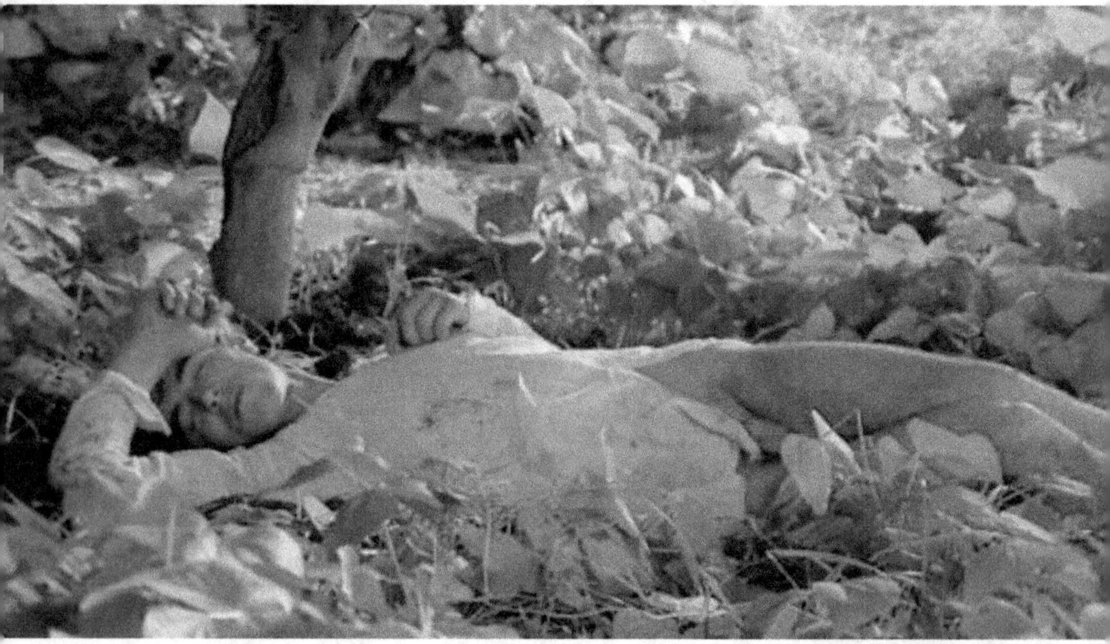

16

I RACCONTI DI CANTERBURY

THE CANTERBURY TALES

> This world nis but a thurghfare ful of wo,
> And we ben pilgrimes, passinge to and fro;
> Death is an ende of every worldly sore.
>
> Geoffrey Chaucer, *The Canterbury Tales*

PRODUCTION.
The Canterbury Tales (*I racconti di Canterbury,* 1972), Alberto Grimaldi's and Pier Paolo Pasolini's 1972 adaptation[1] of Geoffrey Chaucer's famous poem, was the second of the trilogy of mediæval or 'life' films.

Alberto Grimaldi was producer (for Les Productions Artistes Associés and Produzioni Europee Associate); Danilo Donati designed the costumes; Tonino Delli Colli was DP; Dante Ferretti was production designer; Carlo Agati was art director; Ennio Morricone composed the score; Giancarlo De Leonardis was hair stylist; Otello Sisi was make-up artist; the A.D.s were Sergio Citti, Umberto Angelucci and Peter Shepherd;[2] and sound was by Gianni D'Amico and Primimiano Muratore.

Released: Sept 2, 1972 (Italy). 122[3] minutes.

European rentals were $2 million (about half of the gross). *The Canterbury Tales* played well in France and Italy (its primary markets), and led to some cash-in movies – *The Lusty Wives of Canterbury, The*

---
1 The script for *The Canterbury Tales* was written in Romania (Pasolini had gone there to scout locales for *Oedipus Rex*).
2 The A.D.s should be admired (or pitied!) for marshalling this huge cast of unruly, ugly Brits.
3 A cut version runs 110m.

Other Canterbury Tales, The Forbidden Canterbury Taes and *More Sexy Tales From Canterbury* (all these were produced in 1972. And *The Sexbury Tales* pre-empted Alberto Grimaldi's movie, coming out in 1971). It won the Golden Bear at the Berlin Film Festival.

Just why Alberto Grimaldi took the production to England is a bit of a mystery. Because if Pier Paolo Pasolini and the team can film a Biblical movie in Italy, they can certainly stage a mediæval, European flick from anywhere in Europe back in Italy. And why the maestro selected Geoffrey Chaucer to adapt instead of another mediæval text is curious (*The Romance of the Rose, The Art of Love* and Chrétien de Troyes are obvious candidates, though *I racconti di Canterbury* features the crude humour that Pasolini was looking for).

The Canterbury Tales' cast is non-professionals plus some minor actors almost unknown outside of England, such as Tom Baker, Jenny Runacre, Phil Davis and Robin Askwith; Adrian Street, Alan Webb, Vernon Dobtcheff and Derek Deadman also appear. Some of the British actors're familiar from British TV and movies. Hugh Griffith is probably the biggest name in *The Canterbury Tales* among the Brits (he was in *Ben-Hur* and *Barbarella*), while Italians such as Franco Citti, Laura Betti and Ninetto Davoli make their mandatory appearance in a Pasolini production.

One or two other faces in *The Canterbury Tales* might be recognized by diehard film fans: Charlie Chaplin's daughter Josephine appears; and Jenny Runacre plays the old merchant's wife in one of the middle stories: she was in *Jubilee* (dir. Derek Jarman, 1978; as the Virgin Queen, of course!).

The other two movies in the 'trilogy of life' are marvellous (tho' with many flaws), but *The Canterbury Tales* is beset with failings. *The Arabian Nights* and *The Decameron* share much of the same production team, and much of the same comic-bawdy-satirical approach as *The Canterbury Tales*, but they are so much more successful. (Maybe I'm just put off by those spotty, freckly, ginger-haired English kids[4] horsing about in *The Canterbury Tales*. Those sideburns! That hair! That acne! Those horrible teeth! Didn't anybody shave or wash in Blighty in 1972? And then there's the curious, somewhat unsettling phenomenon of a bunch of ugly Brits being dubbed by Italians).

Presumably the production team would've advertised for local extras in newspapers and maybe on the radio in England. Along the lines of:

---

[4] The lads in *The Canterbury Tales* look like they should be on the football terraces of Arsenal and Man U.

'WANTED: Weird-looking old coots required for controversial movie from acclaimed Euro-art director, Mister Danger himself, Pier Paolo Pasolini. Bring your own food if you don't like spaghetti (!). Some nudity and jester-capering required. Pay? Don't expect-a much.'

✦

GEOFFREY CHAUCER.

Many of the elements in Geoffrey Chaucer's (*c.* 1340-1400) poems derive from European sources – the French troubadours, Pierre Ronsard, *The Art of Love*,[5] and the Italian *stil novisti* (Dante Alighieri, Guido Cavalcanti, Guido Guinicelli *et al*). It's all familiar stuff if you know the courtly love poetry tradition: young lovers trysting in secret, separated at dawn... cuckolded older husbands... lusty, old coots hankering for some young flesh... the young lover admiring an unattainable woman from afar (he's a servant, she's a lady)... guys having heart attacks while swiving...

This is a typical verse from the French courtly love poet Arnaut Daniel:

Del cors li fos, non de l'arma,
e cossentis m'a celat dinz sa cambra!
(Would that I might be hers with my body, not with my soul, and that she might admit me in secret to her room!)[6]

And this is from Beatrice, Countess of Die:

Ben volvia mon cavallier
tener un ser en mos'bratz nut.
(How I'd long to hold him pressed
naked in my arms one night)[7]

In the mediæval, courtly love tradition, this kind of fooling around between men and women is given the full-on, intellectual, philosophical and religious treatment, refined into ever-more exquisite verses composed for the delectation of highly-educated audiences in courts (many were composed as songs. These were the days with no cel phones, television, online games, etc). But in the earthy, bawdy side of poesie, the primal instincts and lustful impulses are encouraged to erupt (with troubadours slyly hiding bodily functions underneath elaborate rhyme schemes, witty puns and over-cooked symbolism).

The 'trilogy of life' movies are further installments in the comedy of life genre, thousands of years old, where sex, love, desire and death are recurring motifs. It's a style of storytelling that goes back to Ovid and

---

[5] This is cited in the film.
[6] G. Toja: *Arnaut Daniel's Canzoni,* Florence, 1960; and in L.T. Topsfleld, *Troubadours and Love,* Cambridge University Press, 1975 214.
[7] Quoted in Peter Dronke, *The Medieval Lyric,* Hutchinson, 1968, 106.

Catullus in Ancient Rome, and then further back. As soon as people started telling stories, you can bet that the earthy, bawdy side of love and romance was a regular feature.

> Love wol nat ben contreyned by maistrye;
> Whan maistrie comth, the god of love anon
> Beteth hise winges, and farewell! he is gon!
> (Geoffrey Chaucer, *The Canterbury Tales*)

The Canterbury Tales is one of the treasures of English literature, endlessly discussed in literary criticism, and thousands of people study it every year (to the point where many teenagers probably never want to hear someone trying to speak mediæval English ever again). *The Canterbury Tales* has been adapted many times, often for television.

Eight of the 24 tales in *The Canterbury Tales* were adapted in the 1972 picture: *The Friar's Tale, The Wife of Bath's Tale, The Cook's Tale, The Merchant's Tale, The Reeve's Tale, The Summoner's Tale, The Pardoner's Tale* and *The Miller's Tale*. The episodes were not captioned or announced, the film simply moves from one to another. (And there were few attempts at introducing each episode with its own style). There are many study guides published for students for *The Canterbury Tales*, of course – but the Italian movie simply assumes the audience can keep up.

Among the scenes filmed but subsequently deleted from *The Canterbury Tales* were more scenes at the Tabard Inn (including more of Geoffrey Chaucer talking with the guests at the Inn), more of *The Wife of Bath's Tale*, more of *The Summoner's Tale*, and more of *The Pardoner's Tale*. A whole tale was dropped – Sir Thopas (this was filmed at a favourite Pasolini location, Mount Etna). Perhaps the most significant deletion was scenes where characters introduce their tales. The focus thus shifts to Chaucer as the grand architect of the storytelling, rather than each of the travellers at the Tabard Inn telling their tales.

Geoffrey Chaucer's world of lords, ladies, priests, nuns, monks, peasants, millers, prostitutes and farm hands was depicted by Pier Paolo Pasolini and the team with the same irreverence and love of life as the Middle Ages author (of course, Pasolini himself played Chaucer, the lofty artificer of his mediæval fantasies, seen here in scholar's garb (nice cap, Pier Paolo!), dreaming up his stories at a wooden desk (or chuckling over a copy of *The Decameron*), in the short linking passages between the tales. The setting for Chaucer at work was based on Renaissance depictions of St Jerome, in particular the famous painting *St Jerome In His*

Study (1474) by Antonello da Messina, which portrays the scholar at his desk in an ecclesiastical setting).

✢

STYLE, DESIGN, COSTUMES.

The Canterbury Tales was a lavish production, with a very large cast, many extras, props, animals, locations, settings and costumes. Yet it was surprising how casually Pier Paolo Pasolini and the crew approached this production, how expensive crowd scenes would be covered with a shaky handheld camera and barely one or two shots. Pasolini and the team didn't seem bothered with capturing all of that time and effort and expense on screen just for the sake of pleasing people (like the producer (Alberto Grimaldi) and the backers). If the filmmakers caught it on camera, fine; if not, also fine. The loose, informal cinematic approach also applied to the dubbing (*The Canterbury Tales* was very poorly looped. I guess, with the primarily British cast, they acted in English and were dubbed back in Rome by others. Wherever Pasolini made his films, and whatever language the performers spoke, they were always dubbed in the Eternal City, in Italian). As so often with Italian films, at first it's irritating and disorientating, but then it enhances the experience (especially in a film with so many crazy, comical and grotesque things going on).

The attention to detail in *The Canterbury Tales* was startling; rarely has mediæval life been put up on screen in so rounded a fashion. This was Middle Ages existence as a grimy, earth-bound, and practical kind of life, a world away from the glossy, clean castles and palaces of the typical Hollywood, historical movie, with their starchy, ponderous dialogue and starchy, ponderous performances.

The costumes (by Danilo Donati) were beautiful, with some outrageous touches (in particular, as in *The Gospel According To Matthew*, the enormous hats, or the preposterous golden axes sported by Sir January's guards. May's huge white hat at the nuptials is more suited to a fashion show in Paris. Some of Donati's ideas for clothing are absolutely ridiculous, you have to admit, and would be more appropriate for the Venice Carnival. Altho' *The Canterbury Tales* presents an earthy, lived-in mediævalism, the colourful costumes – in scarlet, purple, blue, green – pop out self-consciously).

The Canterbury Tales filmed in Merrie Englande itself,[8] including the counties of Suffolk, Gloucestershire, Essex, Sussex, Kent and Avon. Provincial English towns such as Chipping Campden in Gloucestershire;

---

[8] You can visit the locations for *The Canterbury Tales* on the Pasolini Movie Tour (there are options for tourists to dress up in rags and have terrible teeth fitted).

Lavenham in Suffolk;9 Cambridge; Bath; Canterbury, St. Thomas a Becket Church, Fairfield and Maidstone in Kent; Rolvenden, Battle Abbey and Rye in Sussex; Layer Marney Tower, Tiptree, Grange Barn, Coggeshall and St Osyth in Essex. Sicily and Italy were also used (Mount Etna, Roma, etc). The cast and crew must've been driving all over the place in cars and buses, as usual for a Pasolini production.

The volume, variety and quality of locations was striking (the location scout, production designer Dante Ferretti and art director Carlo Agati did their jobs very well on *The Canterbury Tales*. The production team was Pasolini's regular one: Grimaldi, Delli Colli, Morricone, Ferretti and Baragli).

One of the odd things about *The Canterbury Tales* (for a British audience) was this: the Pasolini Carnival coming to England.

Because most of *The Canterbury Tales* was shot in locations in England, such as Canterbury, Chipping Camden, Bath, Battle, Maidstone, Rye and Wells. It was curious seeing a cool, radical, European *auteur* like Pier Paolo Pasolini, whose films are full of images of sun-kissed Southern Italy, or the *borgate* in Rome, or the Middle East, winding up in little, English streets under over-cast English skies. (You can see the cinematographer Tonino Delli Colli, his gaffer and his camera crew battling against the God-awful light in Britain many times – especially in the outdoor scenes. By the time they'd driven to a new location (down winding, too-narrow lanes), and got everybody in costume, make-up and in place, plus the animals, props and what-not, the light would be going. The light in the other two 'trilogy of life' flicks is far more appealing (of the Mediterranean and the Middle East).)

The English locations, plus the appearances of British TV and film actors (such as Tom Baker, Hugh Griffith and Robin Askwith), plus the bawdy humour, linked *The Canterbury Tales* to movie series of the same period such as the *Carry On* or *Confessions of...* series (camp, British sex comedies).

I challenge you to recall any of the music from the 'trilogy of life' movies. Although the composer is Italian screen legend Ennio Morricone, there isn't a single memorable melody from Morricone in the three Middle Ages flicks. There is plenty of music in the films, though much of it is recreations of Middle Ages music and traditional folk songs.10 As it plays alongside each movie, it is quite beautiful, but the soundtrack of

---

9 Also used in *Harry Potter and the Deathly Hallows* (2010), *Barry Lyndon* (1975) and *The Witchfinder General* (1968).
10 Many characters are whistling and singing (the movie opens with a M.C.U. of a guy singing). Perkin winds up in the stocks and sings his defiant, silly song. Curiously, some of the songs seem to be in English.

Canterbury is not a masterpiece like *The Gospel According To Matthew* (and *The Gospel* did not use much music specially composed for the movie).

There is an enormous amount of music in *The Canterbury Tales* – and altho' some of it is very fine (there are contemporary folk and 'world music' pieces, as well as recreations of mediæval music – part of the developing fashion for early music), it is mixed into the soundtrack (by Gianni D'Amico) with the customary casual, can't-be-bothered attitude of Italian sound editors of this 1960s/ 1970s period. So what could be really magical scenes fall flat.

Again, it appears as if the filmmakers reconvened at Cinecittà (or the Produzioni Europee Associate studios in Viale Oceano Pacifico) weeks or months after principal photography wrapped in England, and mixed the music for the movie in half a day, in between lengthy lunches or wine-tasting sessions in the commissary.

✦

THE COMEDY OF SEX.

The Canterbury Tales was a panoply of mediæval life, deliberately, self-consciously bawdy, lusty, gross and over-the-top. It was a film of people rutting, cursing, chasing, pissing, farting and dying – life in the Middle Ages as a ship of fools. Copulation seemed to be everywhere: gnarled, fat, old men groaning on top of nubile, young women (tho' only in the missionary position); sexual fantasies out of soft-core pornography (a wedding full of naked women); lovers trysting while the old man's away, etc. And it was all fairly healthy, straightforward stuff (no Marquis de Sade here, no S/M, bondage[11] or role-playing – that came later, in *Salò*. However, you can see the seeds of *Salò* here in the 'trilogy of life' films in the way that bodies are filmed).

✦

There's plenty of flesh on display in *The Canterbury Tales* – nude bodies are all over the place, but the movie's anti-erotic (it's about as erotic as a piece of rotting cheese injected with plutonium). The casting director has selected some pretty and unknown actors and actresses for the maestro to use in his movie for the nude scenes, but for all the fooling around, there's a striking lack of sensuality in *The Canterbury Tales*. (Instead, the sensuality is in the textures, the look, the *mise-en-scène*).

If you want earthy eroticism and extraordinary visual style and divine costumes (and maybe some kinky sex) in a mediæval (or Renaissance) setting, the 1970s films of Walerian Borowczyk are far superior to *The*

---

11 There is a brief scene of a woman whipping a man.

Canterbury Tales: *Immoral Tales*, *Blanche* and *Behind Convent Walls*.

Instead, *The Canterbury Tales* presents, like all of Pier Paolo Pasolini's movies, the *idea* of sex, sexuality as a discourse to be dissected, and links sexuality to Foucauldian issues like power and ideology (it's sex as 'desire', the term favoured in post-Lacanian theory). It's sex portrayed as one of the key ingredients in relationships between humans. A means to an end, a process by which power and influence are maintained. *The Canterbury Tales* is a series of notes for a possible movie which might be made at some point in the future about sexuality, power, class and relationships in the Middle Ages.

> Tragedie is to seyn a certeyn storie,
> As olde bokes maken us memorie,
> Of him that stood in greet prosperitee
> And is y-fallen out of heigh degree
> Into miserie, and endeth wrecchedly.
>
> Geoffrey Chaucer, *The Canterbury Tales*

SOME SCENES IN *THE CANTERBURY TALES*:

THE FRAMING STORY.
Let's away, then, ladies and gents, let's hie hence – let's put on our curly wigs and rotting teeth and silly hats and shabby rags and undertake a journey through some of the scenes in ye olde filme, *The Canterbury Tales*.

The 1972 movie opens with a messy recreation of a mediæval village, populated by a host of hideous, British extras (plus assorted farmyard animals, hay, wrestlers, priests, musicians, singers, and a market). It's here that Pier Paolo Pasolini makes his entrance as one of England's great poets, Geoffrey Chaucer (sporting a preposterous hat[12]). So it's assumed that Chaucer is there to write all of these stories down.

In the village scene comes the familiar exposition of the pilgrimage to Canterbury and the telling of the tales. The filmmakers hope that everyone knows the narrative set-up, because the indifferent direction and staging don't deliver it satisfactorily.

In fact, the narrative contract to tell stories isn't set up really – the film simply cuts to the first story, about Sir January the Pompous

---
[12] In the real England, you'd be lynched for looking like that.

Knight. Yet this is *one scene* that needed to be delivered fully and properly! It's as if the filmmakers spent so long dressing the set, gathering together the farmyard animals, and costuming (and feeding) the extras, they ran out of time for filming it all fully. (However, the notion of a group of travellers being encouraged to tell stories is announced by a guy on screen; as soon as he introduces the concept, the film shifts to the Sir January tale).

The village and farmyard scenes do, however, offer some clichéd images of life in the Middle Ages, where dogs, ducks, horses and chickens are running around, where kids are playing, where adults are drinking at an Inn, where hicks wrestle for a prize (a goat! a goat for the winner, good folk of Britain!), and where travelling players visit the Inn. (These scenes do have some appeal – that is, if watching a bunch of extras pretending to be mediæval peasants is your thing. *The Canterbury Tales* does come across as the home movie of a third-rate, historical re-enactment society – you know, those guys and gals who pretend to be Napoleonic troops or Civil War soldiers on Summer weekends).

The village sequence in *The Canterbury Tales* also does something that many films do in their opening scenes: it introduces some of the well-known performers early on in the piece (Pier Paolo Pasolini and Laura Betti). After this, they disappear for some time.

SIR JANUARY.

The first story[13] of *The Canterbury Tales* concerns the ageing patriarch Sir January (Hugh Griffith) taking a young wife[14] May (Josephine Chaplin,[15] b. 1949, daughter of Charlie Chaplin), while she tries to find ways of meeting her young lover, Damian (Oscar Fochetti, who moons about outside the palace, periodically clutching his crotch in desperation, as you do). The court's a joke, the courtiers ridiculous (Sir January's foppish brothers are satirized), the whole thing's played for laughs but somehow there aren't any laughs to be found anywhere (Griffith seems to recognize that this is a very silly movie, an attempt at a comedy, and based on a comical poem, but somehow not funny at all. With his trademark bulging eyes, grizzled beard and lascivious grin, Griffith[16] evokes Keith Moon in *Tommy* (as Uncle Ernie), but aged up to his sixties. A scary image indeed!).

In Sir January's secret garden[17] (a stand-in for Eden), two gods,

---

13 It was partly filmed in Wells, including the famous mediæval street and houses.
14 May is selected when her buttocks are exposed to Sir January as she kneels in the street. It's an early version of the ass contest in *Salò*.
15 Josephine Chaplin has appeared mainly in French films and TV.
16 Griffith is dubbed by the crustiest, hoarsest voice actor available in Rome.
17 The garden seems made up of several locations, and includes some anachronistic topiary.

Prosperine (Elisabetta Geneovese)[18] and Pluto (Giuseppe Arrigio),[19] wander, naked and garlanded with flowers. Sir January staggers about, now blind, with his sight being lifted by Pluto at the inopportune moment when his wife's in a tree (!) in a clinch with her *inamorato*, just about to do the nasty.

Sir January is a delightfully silly send-up of a lascivious but dim-witted king or lord: the sight of Hugh Griffith tottering about in ridiculously voluminous scarlet robes[20] (or an equally bulky white night-gown), his eyes rolling in lust, is certainly memorable. For about two minutes. Then you forget this episode entirely.

Again, there's an unfinished, clumsy quality to *The Canterbury Tales*, as with other Pier Paolo Pasolini movies. The maestro defended himself by saying that his films 'asked questions' rather than 'provided answers' or delivered something 'finished'. But, dear Pier Paolo, what possible 'questions' are being 'asked' in this bodged rendition of a clichéd, simplistic erotic triangle, and of a husband being cuckolded? It's one of the most well-used, oft-known scenarios in all drama, with no philosophy/ spirituality/ ideology/ politics/ morality in it that we haven't already seen a zillion times. *We know all of the answers! And we know all of the questions!* Come on, Pier Paolo, coming from a highly sophisticated, intellectual filmmaker such as yourself, this is puerile claptrap!

THE DEVIL, THE INQUISITOR AND HOMOSEXUALITY.

Homosexual scenes were depicted in *The Canterbury Tales* – in sequences where people spied on men fucking, hidden behind closed doors and informing on them (the Devil is the ultimate informer, spy, traitor). From this the 1972 movie shifted into witchhunt territory – with a gay man (David Hatton) being burnt to death (an older guy (Athol Coats) manages to bribe his way out of punishment by paying the authorities). Pretty brutal, grotesque stuff, and with all sorts of added resonances because Pier Paolo Pasolini was famously a gay filmmaker, and had been in trouble with the authorities several times for sexual acts, including with minors. (The sequence seems wholly contemporary – 1972 – in ambience).

The execution[21] was portrayed in the same manner as the trials in *Il*

---

18 Elisabetta Geneovese has a spectacular smile which lights up the screen – a close-up of her as Prosperine is used for the Blu-ray and DVD re-releases of *The Canterbury Tales*. Genovese also appeared in *The Decameron*, as the young lover Caterina who sleeps on the balcony in order to meet her beau. She is also in *The Arabian Nights* and *Bawdy Tales*).
19 He wass Lorzenzo in *The Decameron*.
20 The far-too-large clothes enhance the blustering vanity of the knight.
21 The trial isn't shown.

Vangelo Secondo Matteo – with a handheld camera from the sidelines, in amongst (and behind) the crowds, as well as in a *tableau*-style drawing on mediæval illuminations. Meanwhile, Satan lurks behind the crowd, selling food from a tray (in this film, even the Devil has to earn a living. It's a classic Italianism, where everybody is on the make).

The execution episode is a huge scene filled with extras, costumes, guards, spectator stands and dignitaries. It was filmed in the cloisters of Canterbury Cathedral. I bet the clergy in Kent hadn't seen anything like this in their precincts before: a semi-naked man being burnt to death. (Did the authorities of the famous Cathedral know that the crime was for homosexual sex? And that the sequence as a whole featured nudity and gay sex? The administrators of Canterbury Cathedral famously turned down the *Harry Potter* movies which wanted to film there – due, apparently, because they thought that *Harry Potter* promoted paganism or witchcraft).

Voyeurism is a staple of the courtly love poetry tradition (which Geoffrey Chaucer drew on) – lovers are forever being spied on by maids, night watchmen or such like (escaping prying eyes before dawn after a night of intimacy is a popular motif). So in this episode, there were two voyeurs: one's the informer, but the other is no less than Lucifer (only later in this episode does Franco Citti reveal himself as the Devil).

Having Franco Citti as Satan is an attempt at creating a recurring character in *I racconti di Canterbury* (along with Pasolini-as-Geoffrey-Chaucer), but it doesn't really work (*The Decameron* also used Citti as a recurring character – and a vicious one, too). Similarly, the framing device of Chaucer dipping his quill to compose the next scene at his desk or on some parchment during his travels, which duly cuts to the next episode, adds nothing to the piece. (The segment continues with Satan and the Inquisitor (credited as 'O.T') travelling together as tax collectors, to extract payment from an old woman at a remote windmill; she falls to her knees and begs the Inquisitor to send her troubles to the Devil. The Inquisitor makes a Faustian pact with Mr Sulphur).

THE COOK.

Ninetto Davoli makes his mandatory appearance in a Pier Paolo Pasolini movie by playing Perkin the Smirkin' Jerk, a Middle Ages Charlie Chaplin, a simpleton who larks about in the feeblest Chaplin skit you've ever seen. This is one of the low-points in Pasolini's cinema. The Cook (J.P. Van Dyne) leaves Perkin the Doofus in charge of his egg stall in a bazaar, and silent comedy slapstick ensues. Perkin's a soft-in-the-head thief who, like all of Davoli's characters in Pasolini's movies, goofs around and drifts in and out of the story like a lost child who has had a perpetual cheesy grin nailed onto his face by the curse of an evil witch. Davoli tries hard to make his former lover laugh, singing and skittering about, but it's desperate. (There's a pleasant enough wedding ceremony in *The Cook's Tale* of *The Canterbury Tales*, including a dance and a band of musicians, while the bride's father (Francis De Wolff) becomes irate. Later, Perkin fantasizes about dancing at the wedding, with the guests replaced entirely by nude women, as he shares a threesome in bed with a couple of uncomely Brits).

Charlie Chaplin was a favourite director for Pier Paolo Pasolini, and there are several Chaplinesque touches in *The Cook's Tale*: the father of the bride recalls the burly oaf played by Eric Campbell in Chaplin's movies; Perkin sports the signature bowler hat and cane (several other characters wear bowler hats); hunger, food and poverty[22] is a theme; and of course there are cops to chase Perkin.

THE WIFE OF BATH.

The Wife of Bath episode (which's the most well-known story in Geoffrey Chaucer's *Canterbury Tales*), was one of the more successful segments of the 1972 movie, partly because the concept and story is strong and clear (and Laura Betti's amusing performance as the fierce, domineering Wife of Bath helps).[23] Her new relationship – with the scholar, Jenkin (played by Tom Baker with his usual bug-eyed, Harpo Marxian eccentricity)[24] – is bizarre. It starts[25] off with some voyeurism – and, in an rare reversal of the male voyeur trope, two women watch the scholar bathing nude.

The Wife of Bath episode contains one of the biggest scenes in *The Canterbury Tales*, a festival populated by coachloads of extras (it looks like the Glastonbury Fayre in 1971), as the denizens of dear, old Blighty perform a *Wicker Man*-style ritual burning of a wicker man figure (because when they're at a loose end – when there's nothing on TV and it's raining again and football's cancelled, and there's nothing else to do, the jolly, rosy-cheeked bumpkins of Britain were always burning wicker men in the early Seventies).

In midst of the outdoor jamboree, the Wife of Bath nonchalantly gives the scholar a handjob while he casually reads a book. They discuss

---

22 Perkin queues up with some other hopefuls in a scene out of the musical *Olivier!* (He carries an out-size bowl).
23 Aided by her plump chum Isolde.
24 In this period Tom Baker played Dr Who on TV.
25 Actually, the first shot of the *Wife of Bath* episode is lovemaking between the Wife and Giannozzo.

marriage. The Wife of Bath soon becomes unenamoured of her new husband, having also worn out the last one, Giannozzo (Reg Stuart), with too much fooling around. Jenkin would rather read a book than do his duty as a husband. (He insults her, they fight, she falls, and asks for a final kiss.; then she bites his nose).

THE YOUNG SCHOLAR.

One of the longer tales[26] in *The Canterbury Tales* is a meandering piece of fluff concerning a scholarly youth's seduction of an older man's wife, Alison (Jenny Runacre). The youth Nicholas (Dan Thomas), who looks like he's wandered in from presenting a groovy, early Seventies kids' TV show, loons and moons about in his rooms, praying (and nursing his weiner). The boy eventually concocts the truly bizarre ruse (with some fire and brimstone religious nonsense) of persuading the old coot John (Michael Balfour) to save himself from the oncoming Biblical Flood and Apocalypse by sheltering in some wooden tubs hanging high up from ropes under the roof.[27] While the old geezer snoozes, the lovers creep out of their tubs and get freaky, as expected. It's one of the strangest sequences in a Pasolini movie.

There's some protracted business with another hapless suitor, Absalom[28] (Peter Cain) calling at night at Alison's home to beg for a kiss, and having Alison stick her ass outside the window in his face and fart. But when the scholar Nicholas does the same a while later, the resourceful Absalom's already run off to a nearby blacksmith to borrow a red-hot poker, which he shoves up the scholar's butt.

Oh boy, they are rolling in the aisles at this nonsense. It's lame. It's comedy in the style of *Tom and Jerry* or Laurel and Hardy but performed by a bunch of tenth grade school kids let loose with a 35mm camera and a canvas sack of Middle Ages costumes.

Meanwhile, back in Rome, someone has edited all of this garbage, someone has organized actors and dubbing stages, actors have looped the dialogue, Ennio Morricone and his team have added music, and it all goes nowhere and does nothing. *The Canterbury Tales* is not a movie that gets better, richer, deeper with each viewing. The opposite, in fact.

THE MILLER.

A windmill[29] and a small holding owned by Miller Simkin (Tiziano

---

[26] Filmed in Wells.
[27] This scene might be a send-up of *The Bible*, the giant Dino di Laurentiis Italian-American production filmed in Rome.
[28] Absalom's chum Martin (Martin Philips) is another goofy youth (and apparently gay).
[29] Filmed at Rolvenden in Sussex.

Longo) is the location for one of the later stories in *The Canterbury Tales*, in which our heroes (two young, Pasolinian *ragazzi* – Alan (Patrick Duffett) and John (Eamann Howell)), scholars from Cambridge – get the best of him and manage to seduce his wife (Eileen King) and daughter Molly (Heather Johnson). It's played out as broad farce with a nighttime game of can't-see-a-thing switching of beds and partners, complete with the expected misunderstandings (the lads take the women, only to be found out by the Miller when one of them climbs into the wrong bed, and the Miller wakes and explodes. The lads flee after beating the Miller). Again the s-l-o-w cutting and the laborious staging takes the pizzazz out of the potential for humour. This kind of pacing might work in the theatre, but it is too lethargic for comedy.

THE BROTHEL.

The section of *The Canterbury Tales* set in a brothel[30] livens up the narrative of the 1972 Italian flick with some sexual *tableaux* (a couple of blowjobs, sex from the rear, and a naked woman whipping a naked man – no historical sex comedy set in Britain is complete without some corporal punishment! Brits love it).

The brothel sequence culminates with Robin Askwith[31] (as Rufus) urinating over everyone in the inn below from a balcony while he rants in mock, Biblical tones (perhaps Askwith's finest hour outside of the *Confessions* sex comedy movies). Would a bunch of peasants sit and laugh while someone pisses on them? And collect the liquid in bowls? In this movie, yes!

DEATH PAYS A VISIT.

The second section of this episode of *The Canterbury Tales* is one of the poorest outings in Pier Paolo Pasolini's cinema – a waste of your time, my time, and everybody else's time. It looks like Pasolini handed it over entirely to a second unit director (but not a *good* second unit director!).[32]

It involves yet another brotherhood of young, Pasolinian, pseudo-Caravaggian *ragazzi:* Dick the Sparrow (Edward Montieth), Jack the Justice (Martin Whelar), and Johnny the Grace (John McLaren). This time the lads are planning to kill Death Himself and steal some shiny loot (the Grim Reaper has cut down one of their number from the bordello in the

---

[30] Filmed in St Osyth in Essex and Chipping Camden.
[31] Askwith has dined out on his anecdotes of meeting Pier Paolo Pasolini, filming *The Canterbury Tales*, etc.
[32] The location is the outskirts of Rye, one of the haunting, atmospheric parts of England. There's a big market day scene with an English street that's been filled with mud and straw to hide the road markings.

previous scene – the results of too much whoring, the usual mediæval, Christian moralizing about debauchery). Betrayal, knifing and poisoning swiftly follow (as in the pirate genre), as they squabble over the booty, but the sequence is extraordinarily clumsily staged and shot (and the script is, well, just weedy).

The characters are dull, the scenario is dull, the 'acting' is dreadful (here is where using amateurs completely backfires), the sound mix is bad, the dubbing comes from another movie, and the sequence contains the barest minimum of camera angles and shots to cover the action (one of several indications that the filmmakers were utterly unengaged with the material).

LET'S GO TO HELL.

Towards the end, like thousands of movies before it and thousands of movies after it, *The Canterbury Tales* throws everything at the viewer, with a truly Out-There sequence set in Hell (which looks suspiciously like the waste ground of Pigneto outside Roma where *La Ricotta* was filmed). A greedy friar (John Francis Lane) is taken there (by an angel, Settimo Castagna) after trying to steal from a dying rich man. Colourful demons in full body make-up (red, blue, green), with bat-wings and fabulous masks torture the sinners (torturing some, and taking others from the rear).[33] Chaos reigns, presided over by a giant, red Satan, who bends over, lifts his tail, and farts out friars. They fly through the air out of a full-size, scarlet butt, accompanied by loud, rasping farts.

Yes, it's truly silly, a *Monty Python*-style skit – but with more money, staged on some waste land. It's a case of filmmakers trying to out-do themselves and everyone else. It's delivered as a mighty joke (except it's not very funny).

This's underlined when the 1972 movie cuts back to Geoffrey Chaucer at his writing desk (wearing another preposterous hat), grinning broadly as he dreams up this schoolboyish, anal-oral nonsense. Maybe Chaucer-Pasolini is simply enjoying the total chaos of filmmaking. Maybe he's thinking, 'hell, someone gave me $2 million to shoot this farce!' Maybe he's chuckling because he knows that this sequence will *really* irritate some sections of the audience (and it did). The 1972 film might just as well have cut to a shot of Pier Paolo Pasolini and the crew standing behind the camera, giggling at the crazy stuff they've cooked up. Oh, what fun and jolly japes it is to be a European art filmmaker in the

---

33 Being buggered by a demon for years on end would some perv's idea of Heaven!

1970s![34]

The Canterbury Tales ends swiftly following the visit to Hell: we finally reach Canterbury at the end of Pilgrims' Way. There's the briefest of shots of the Cathedral and a religious ceremony, and then the movie stumbles to a clumsy halt.

It's not a satisfying close to a movie of this kind by any means – *The Canterbury Tales* might have been episodic, like a road movie, but it's not a quest film, or a road movie film in structure. It dispenses with the dramatic structure of a quest and a journey, and focusses on individual episodes. Meanwhile, the sequence in Hell comes from another movie, and jars with the rest of the piece with its outrageous imagery. Nothing can follow that, and the movie seems to acknowledge this, by simply juddering towards a feeble ending. (However, if all of *The Canterbury Tales* had been filmed with the manic intensity and crudity of the Visit To Hell episode, maybe it would have been a much greater work).

HOW BAD IS *THE CANTERBURY TALES*?

You have to see *The Canterbury Tales* for the sheer zaniness of the imagery and scenes. Even if so much of the movie is handled with an amateurish, throwaway quality, as if Pier Paolo Pasolini and the crew are just playing at being filmmakers, as if they're pretending they're not professionals, there is certainly plenty going on. And plenty of it is quite bonkers.

There's enough fumbling around with bawdy comedy and nudity in *Carry On In the Middle Ages* to keep the viewer amused, if only for the time that elapses as the movie unfolds (after that, after the final, much-longed-for 'FINE', everything is swiftly forgotten, consigned to the oblivion of a billion other movies).

Oh, some of *The Canterbury Tales* is woefully bad.[35] It's bad on the level of direction. It's bad on the level of conception and screenwriting. It's bad on the level of performance. It's bad on the level of camerawork and sound quality. It's bad on the level of casting (so many really grisly,

---

34 Indeed, *The Canterbury Tales* closes with a close-up of Mr Pasolini as British poet Geoffrey Chaucer, smiling to himself, all too smugly, at the crazy visions he's just conjured up with a team of artisans (courtesy of Chaucer) back in the final segment of the movie, the Visit To Hell.

35 Some scenes are simply thrown away in *The Canterbury Tales* – such as when Satan, skulking thru a Cathedral, stops for a funeral procession (a corpse's carried on a bier with candles flaming above it).

English extras! None of whom can act! They are non-professional actors for a good reason! They stink!).

Sorry to say, but too much of *The Canterbury Tales* comes across as a not very good *Carry On* flick or a *Confessions of* flick or an *Emmanuelle* movie (which were being churned out at the time or not long afterwards). And too often *The Canterbury Tales* is *not* one of those films that are 'so bad they're good'. No. It's just *bad*.

How can this be? This is directed by the man who helmed *Medea* and *Oedipus Rex* and *Il Vangelo Secondo Matteo*! Oh boy. (But did Pier Paolo Pasolini *really* direct *The Canterbury Tales*? Sometimes I wonder if he stayed behind in Rome and let someone else direct this turkey).

Take the humour in *The Canterbury Tales*: it *should* be bawdy, broad and above all it should be *funny*. But it's *not*. At the level of comedy, *The Canterbury Tales* is outrageous and over-the-top, but, darn, it's *not amusing*.

And *The Canterbury Tales* is trying *really hard*. But, let's face it, humour just isn't one of Pier Paolo Pasolini's strengths. Even the grinning, energetic, winsome Ninetto Davoli, playing the foolish Jerkin-Perkin, can't save his section of the piece (instead, he murders it).

When a master of modern European cinema is directing his favourite actor in the guise of an icon of cinema (Charlie Chaplin) in a mediæval romp (in *The Cook's Tale*), you'd expect something better than this. There's some messing about with eggs, some loafing around with games, a gag with an over-size bowl (to receive alms from the Church), and a wedding feast.[36]

Have a look at the first episode of *Everything You Wanted To Know About Sex But Were Too Afraid To Ask*, produced around the same time (1972), to see a really good send-up of the mediæval genre, with all the usual jokes about lusty lovers and royal feasts and courtly life. (Woody Allen's spoof on mediæval courtly lingo has never been done better – and he includes a send-up of arty, would-be cool Italian movies, too![37]).

Woody Allen nails the Middle Ages, and in just a few minutes. *The Simpsons* have also delivered skits on the Middle Ages infinitely superior to *The Canterbury Tales*.

Or have a look at two other films of the same period: *Jabberwocky*

---

[36] This part of the Chaplin skit was the most successful – particularly in Perkin's night dream of the wedding feast, but populated wholly by young, naked women.
[37] In "Why Do Some Women Have Trouble Reaching an Orgasm?", the filmmakers send up modern, European cinema, in particular the more pretentious efforts of directors like Michelangelo Antonioni and Federico Fellini.

(1977) and *Monty Python and the Holy Grail* (1974),[38] which are genuinely amusing, and also depict elements of the mediæval genre beautifully.

FURTHER VIEWINGS.

The notes above were written before I'd seen the movie again: on further viewings, *I racconti di Canterbury* still comes across as bloody awful at times: the direction is often inept, the acting ranges from mediocre to terrible, and the script is really poor.

If *The Canterbury Tales* had been produced for a Hollywood studio (impossible, I know!), the head of production would've ordered Pier Paolo Pasolini to go back and start everything again as soon as they saw the first of the rushes.

Put it this way, if *The Canterbury Tales* was the first film directed by Pier Paolo Pasolini you saw, many people would *not* come back for more. And if you knew that this was directed by a guy who's supposed to be one of the great, postwar European *auteurs*, you wouldn't believe it!

Because too much of *The Canterbury Tales* is so amateurish it's not true. Or is it just that the 1972 movie hopes to give the *impression* of a freewheeling, laid-back style, when it's really controlled by a rod of iron by the filmmakers? Is Pier Paolo Pasolini and the team producing a *deliberately* bad movie? No, I don't think so.

The terrible looping doesn't help. This is a film set in England, filmed (mainly) in England, based on an English poem, performed by a mainly English cast, and also acted in English, but dubbed into Italian, and with an Italian crew (at least in the heads of department jobs). And yet the text of Geoffrey Chaucer was updated from mediæval English to modern English, and then an Italian translation would've been used by the filmmakers.

So it's an odd hybrid. It's even odder if you know those locations in Britain very well (as I do), and recognize some of the actors (though I'm sure international audiences wouldn't be familiar with a single actor in *The Canterbury Tales* with the exception of Hugh Griffith, maybe, and Pier Paolo Pasolini's two starring regulars, Ninetto Davoli and Franco Citti).

Part of the time I'm just looking at the beautiful locations in *The Canterbury Tales*, and I'm reminded: isn't England so gorgeous? Aren't there some lovely buildings in Deare Olde Englande?

I wonder what the British extras from towns like Rye and Bath and

---

[38] The Monty Python team spoofed *The Devils* in their King Arthur movie, and also Pier Paolo Pasolini, Ingmar Bergman (*The Seventh Seal*), *Throne of Blood* (Akira Kurosawa), and the films of Walerian Borowczyk (*Goto: Island of Love* and *Blanche*).

Wells thought of this Italian production wheeling into town, and what the members of the British crew thought. I wouldn't be surprised if some of the actors and crew reckoned Pier Paolo Pasolini was nuts![39] You only have to look at some of the big scenes, and see what the assistant directors (Sergio Citti, Umberto Angelucci and Peter Shepherd) have got the crowds doing, to see that this was an unusual historical picture.[40] It was no quaint British Broadcasting Corporation TV adaptation aiimed at a family, early evening audience!

Yet *The Canterbury Tales* was so much more effective in evoking the mediæval period than your average television adaptation or movie: the way that Dante Ferretti and Carlo Agati transformed the existing buildings and streets of England was a lesson to all the British TV (British Broadcasting Corporation and Independent Television) and international television historical productions. This was production design as a fine art. And the look and locations are the finest elements in *The Canterbury Tales*.

---

[39] However, some of the actors making *Star Wars* in 1977 thought the movie was just silly sci-fi.
[40] They look at the camera with puzzled expressions. The older actors just get on with it and do what they're told.

17

IL FIORE DELLE MILLE E UNA NOTTE

THE ARABIAN NIGHTS

INTRODUCTION.

Co-written by Dacia Maraini[41] and Pier Paolo Pasolini from *The 1001 Nights*, *The Arabian Nights* (1974, a.k.a. *Il Fiore Delle Mille e Una Notte*), was produced by Alberto Grimaldi, and distributed by United Artists.[42] It won the Grand Prix Special Prize at Cannes in 1974.[43]

Worldwide gross was $4.5 million. Released: June 20, 1974. It is 129[44] minutes long.[45]

The production team working on *Il Fiore Delle Mille e Una Notte* included Pasolini regulars such as Nino Baragli (editor – with Tatiana Casini Morigi), Ennio Morricone (music), Dante Ferretti (production design), Danilo Donati (costumes) and Giuseppe Ruzzolini (camera). Iole Cecchini handled the hair, with make-up by Massimo Giustini. Fausto Ancillai was sound mixer, and Luciano Wellisch did the sound. Umberto Angelucci, Paolo Andrea Mettel and Peter Shepherd were A.D.s. Once again, Pasolini was working some of the giant talents of the Italian film industry, including Ferretti, Donati and Morricone.

The cast of *The Arabian Nights* included Ninetto Davoli, Franco

---
[41] The script was written in August, 1973, in Sabaudia.
[42] So Leo the Lion roars out of the M.G.M. logo at the start of this most un-American movie!
[43] The combination of fantasy, exoticism (Orientalism) and eroticism in *The Arabian Nights* is tailor-made for the arty/ boho sections of the international movie crowd in the South of France in Cannes.
[44] An early cut was 155 minutes.
[45] There's a couple of deleted scenes on the DVD of *The Arabian Nights*. One involves Zumurrud as the King having a lengthy, badly staged sword fight on some cliffs. Another scene depicts Nuredin quarrelling with his father.

Citti, Franco Merli, Margareth Clémenti, and Ines Pellegrini, plus a host of unknowns: Tessa Bouché, Zeudi Biasolo, Luigina Rocchi, Alberto Argentino, Salvatore Sapienza, Elisabetta Genovese, Barbara Grandi, Francesco Paolo Governale, Francelise Noel, Ali Abdulla, Jeanne Gauffin Mathieu, Mohamed Ali Zedi, Gioacchino Castellini, Abadit Ghidei, Christian Aligny and Salvatore Verdetti (one or two of these – such as Elisabetta Genovese and Margareth Clémenti – appeared in other Pasolini movies). Notice that altho' *The Arabian Nights* draws on numerous local extras hired in Yemen, Iran and Nepal, most of the key roles are played by Italians (it was the same with other Pasolini productions, whether they were set in Ancient Greece or Ancient Palestine. So the films were not wholly enshrining a poetic vision of the 'Third World').

1001 NIGHTS IN POPULAR CULTURE.

The Thousand and One Nights (*Alf laila wa-laila* in Arabic), a.k.a. *The Arabian Nights*, dates from around the 15th century in its earliest form in manuscripts. There are around 270 core tales, drawing on Persian, Indian and Arabic cultures which stretch back to hundreds of years before the tales were written down between the 9th and 15th centuries.[46] The tales were collated in three important editions: (1) Persian stories with some Indian ingredients which were translated into Arabic by the tenth century; (2) stories collected in Baghdad between the 10th and 12th centuries; and (3) tales collated in Egypt between the 11th and 14th centuries. As Jack Zipes explained in *The Enchanted Screen*:

> No other work of Oriental literature has had such a profound influence on the western world as *The Thousand and One Nights*. Translated first into French between 1704 and 1717 by Antoine Galland, a gifted Orientalist, the *Nights* spread quickly in French and other translations throughout Europe and then to North America. (84)

In the Western world, key translations included that of 1883-86, by Richard Burton (as *The Book of the Thousand Nights and a Night*).[47] (When I was in Egypt in 1994, people there insisted that *The Arabian Nights* was very much about Cairo, not Baghdad. Certainly, in parts of Cairo you feel like you are in a living *Arabian Nights*).

Pretty much every serious author in Europe attempted a version of *The Arabian Nights*. As *The Oxford Companion To Fairy Tales* put it, 'the magic elements in the *Nights* combined with the explicit and

---

46 See J. Zipes, 2002, 22.
47 In Arabic, the key collections were *Calcutta I* (1814-18), a.k.a. *Shirwanee Edition*; *Bulak*, 1835, a.k.a. the *Cairo Edition*; *Calcutta II*, 1839, a.k.a. the *W.H. Macnaughton Edition*; and *Breslau*, 1825-38.

unpretentious representation of sexuality created a powerful inspiration for the European imagination' (372).

James Joyce, Marcel Proust, Jorge Luis Borges, Joseph Addison, Edgar Allan Poe, Samuel Coleridge, Samuel Johnson and Washington Irving are among the many authors who took on the *1001 Nights*.

The Thousand and One Nights has influenced artists and writers (and filmmakers), including Denis Diderot, Voltaire, Thomas De Quincey, George Meredith, Robert Louis Stevenson, Friedrich Schiller, Hermann Melville, John Barth, Robert Southey, Horace Walpole, Charles Dickens, William Thackeray, Alexander Dumas, Stendhal, Walter Scott, Johann Wolfgang von Goethe, Leo Tolstoy, E.T.A. Hoffmann, Alexander Pushkin, etc.

The framing story of *The Thousand and One Nights* concerns clever Scheherazade, daughter of the Grand-Vizier, who placates the murderous Sultan Shahryar (he kills a new woman every morning), by telling him stories (staving off nasty events in the framing story is reflected in the tales themselves – the framing story itself begets a series of tales). Some of the aspects of Scheherazade are found in the personality of Zumurrud in the 1974 movie.

In *The Thousand and One Nights*, stories intertwine complexly: stories create further stories, and stories reflect or re-play earlier stories. (The 1974 movie takes up only parts of this concept, tho' it does perform the appealing trick of one story tumbling into another, which helps to give the piece a hypnotic momentum).

The *Thousand and One Nights* tales have provided motifs and characters which've become as well-known as Cinderella or Snow White: Sinbad, Aladdin, Ali Baba, magic lamps and genies, princes, princesses, thieves, merchants, palaces, evil viziers, and so on.

In *The Arabian Nights*, the stories with fairy tale components can be put into categories such as: talisman stories (about magical objects); powerful demon stories; quest stories; transformation stories; and demons under restraint tales.[48] The *Arabian Nights* film uses all of those story types.

The 1974 *Arabian Nights* wasn't the only movie of the *1001 Nights* of the era: Rankin and Bass, for instance, produced a cartoon, *Arabian Nights*, in 1972; plus *The Thousand and One Nights* (Eiichi Yamamoto, 1969), *The Thousand and One Nights* (Karel Zeman, 1974), and a TV series in 1975 (*Arabian Nights*, dir. Fumio Kurokawa and Kunihiko Okazaki). And the *1001 Nights* has been filmed many times since.

---

[48] See Mia Gerhardt, *The Art of Story-Telling*, 1963.

Italian cinema had taken up the *1001 Nights* before, of course: there was a mini-cycle in the early 1960s, for instance: *The Conqueror of the Orient* (1960), a Steve Reeves[49] version of *The Thief of Baghdad* (1961), *The Wonder of Aladdin* (1961 – photographed by Pier Paolo Pasolini's chief DP, Tonino Delli Colli), *The Thousand and One Nights* in 1961 (dir. Mario Bava and Henry Levin), *The Golden Arrow* (1962), *Anthar the Invincible* (1964) and *Ali Baba and the Seven Saracens* (1964).

Géorges Méliès had pioneered adaptations of *The Arabian Nights* way back in 1905 (just as Méliès got there first with pretty much every famous folk tale, fairy tale and myth).

Films and TV series of the *1001 Nights* appeared in 1920, 1921, 1927, 1940, 1942, 1958, 1959, 1962, 1964, 1968, 1979, 1990, 1991, 1994, 1996, 1999, 2000, etc.

Thus, there are literally 100s of movies based on the *Thousand and One Nights* tales. Many are animated films, and many are made for children and families. Western cinema and TV has taken up *The Arabian Nights* numerous times, from famous Hollywood versions like *The Thief of Bagdad* (1924 and 1940), to many television mini-series (a Tim Burton version for Shelley Duvall's *Faerie Tale Theater*, for ex), and cartoons from Disney (*Aladdin*, 1992) and DreamWorks (*Sinbad*, 2003).

But viewers hoping for a fantasy extravaganza from *The Arabian Nights* like a Disney *Aladdin* or a Ray Harryhausen *Sinbad* will be *very* disappointed! No – the 1974 *Arabian Nights* is *1001 Nights* Euro-art movie style, and this version is definitely *not* for children or families!

THE ARABIAN NIGHTS AS FANTASY.

In *The Arabian Nights*, Pier Paolo Pasolini and his regular cast and crew return to the world of mediæval mythology (for the last time – a pity, because Pasolini could've worked his way thru every classic of Middle Ages literature had he lived longer: Rabelais was discussed in the early 1970s, and *The Divine Comedy* would surely have been high on the list of possible projects, altho' elements of the *Divina Commedia* crop up in many of Pasolini's films).

The Arabian Nights is like no other movie you've seen. On almost every level, it is extraordinary. It is not your conventional movie. Of course, films have been made from the classic, Arabian tales many times – such as the versions of *The Thief of Baghdad*, or Walt Disney's *Aladdin*, or numerous pantomimes and theatre shows (*Aladdin* is a regular Christmas panto). But there's no interpretation of *A Thousand*

---

[49] Steve Reeves seems to have starred in everything in the early 1960s, following the huge success of *Hercules*.

and One Nights like this 1974 Italian movie. (It's significant that the most successful artistically of the three Middle Ages movies in Pier Paolo Pasolini's cinema should be the non-European one, the Oriental/ Middle Eastern one).

Occasionally, you'll be watching *The Arabian Nights* and wondering what the hell you're looking at. *The Arabian Nights* is so dreamy and hypnotizing, the images and scenes flicker past with a languour and sensuality like a Symbolist painting by Gustave Moreau or a Decadent poem by Paul Verlaine. This is certainly Pasolini's most fantastical movie, a piece which actively pursues fantasy. (The movie opens with a quote about dreams from *1001 Nights* – 'truth lies not in one dream, but in many dreams'[50] – in this movie, dreams beget dreams as stories beget stories. But cinema is, as Pasolini knew well, already poetic and dream-like).

Just to define exactly what is going on in a movie like *Il Fiore Delle Mille e Una Notte* takes some time and effort. Let's start with the *mise-en-scène* of *The Arabian Nights*: it has an extraordinary sense of place, space, texture, colour and light. There is so much going on in Pier Paolo Pasolini's films, that one forgets how visually stunning they are. There are very few film directors with such an acute sense of space and place. Pasolini is up there with Orson Welles, Sergei Paradjanov or Ken Russell[51] in his incredible ability to seek out amazing buildings, squares, walls, doorways, gateways, alleys, covered markets, churches, temples, castles, palaces, arches, fountains and rooms. *The Arabian Nights* contains spaces and places that are so beautiful and unusual – it's a very rare gift in a world smothered with thousands of films and millions of images to find so many sites that can astound the spectator. (However, the *action* that's staged within these amazing spaces is often very boring – a character walks or runs thru a square, or leans on a wall, or sits on a stone step. And that's all. Sometimes the staging in Pasolini's cinema is frustratingly static and almost deliberately unengaging and unimaginative).

The look and feel of *The Arabian Nights* is intoxicating in the extreme – simply on the level of *locations* – of the buildings and the towns and the hillsides – *The Arabian Nights* is incredible (I adore Africa and the desert, so I am already converted!). It was filmed in locations such as Ethiopia and Erithrea in Africa, the Red Sea, Shibam, Ta'izz, Seiyun, Wadi Dhar, Zabid and Sana'a in Yemen, Bhaktapur, Kathmandu,

---

50 The line is quoted late in the film.
51 Ken Russell's astonishing *The Devils*, produced a year before *The Canterbury Tales* (and filmed on the backlot at Pinewood Studios), is a textbook example of how to stage a historical piece.

and Patan in Nepal, India, and Esfahan in Iran (the Mesjed-e-Imam, Ali Qapu Palace, Masjed-e Jomeh and Chehel Sotoun Palace). Studio scenes were filmed in Rome (at Laparo Film Studios).

Some of the interiors are stupendous in *The Arabian Nights*. Some are real places; the location scout and the location manager deserve every credit (this 1974 production is the result of the team driving hundreds of miles to find those places). If you said, find me the most exotic, richly historical, palatial Islamic interiors possible in Africa or the Middle East, you might come up with something like this. Two interiors are outstanding: the mirrored room in which the crossdressing King Zumurrud has her bedroom (filmed in Chehel Sotoun in Esfahan), and the underground palaces (filmed in Ali Qapu and Chehel Sotoun,[52] not to mention the nearby baths, also filmed in Ali Qapu and Chehel Sotoun). Then there's the whitewashed chamber in the Aziz and Aziza story, with its modernist (anachronistic) stained glass. And bedouin tents. And the strikingly exotic interiors of the Esfahan mosque (Mesjed-e Imam), one of those locations where you can point a camera anywhere and get a great image.

The Islamic architecture, so distinctive and atmospheric, with its abstractions and elegant patterns, and its intense feeling for decoration over flat planes, gives *The Arabian Nights* a group of perfect settings. Much of it is built from dusty, crumbly stonework, but even when Pier Paolo Pasolini and the location manager[53] select modern, Islamic buildings, it still works beautifully.[54] (It's startling that *The Arabian Nights* can employ modern apartment blocks in many scenes, and can pan the *macchina fotografica* repeatedly across modern cities in the Near East, and yet it still feels like Middle Ages Arabia (with the judicious use of a few camels, some wicker baskets strewn about, and extras in colourful costumes). There are several scenes on top of the roofs overlooking the town of Sana'a in the Middle East (in the Aziz and Aziza story) which looks completely mediæval (no forests of TV aerials to take down, as some film productions have done in other towns). Maybe it's because the views are carefully selected to include a backdrop of mountains and palm trees, instead of the freeways and cars you might see from the other direction. Maybe it's because modern, Islamic architecture simply looks exotic and different to the Western viewer, or maybe because the beauty of even simple, external decoration in plaster using Islamic designs is so evocative of ancient Arabia, or maybe it's because modern towns in the

---

52 The scenes where characters descend rope ladders from a beach into underground chambers are wonderful (the narrative device is repeated). And Nuredin is winched up from street level in a basket.
53 The production managers were: Giuseppe Banchelli, Mario Di Biase and Alessandro Mattei.
54 The wedding, for instance, was filmed in the Mesjed-e Imam, built in 1638, in Esfahan, Iran.

Maghreb or Middle East have mosques and towers which are built along mediæval lines, or maybe it's because the movie has already persuaded us to buy into it all. But you couldn't do that in a movie made in a Western city, where modern apartment blocks cannot be passed off as mediæval, and filming a wide shot of a city from a roof in the West reveals 100s of modern buildings, with power and telephone cables everywhere, plus jets, helicopters, and ten million lights).

Il Fiore Delle Mille e Una Notte is a magic carpet ride to quite a large degree, and as such the settings are vital in conjuring up the necessary sense of wonder. And then there's the costumes – designed by legend Danilo Donati, a genius among costume designers.

What costumes! The *Arabian Nights milieu* allows the wardrobe dept to indulge itself in gold and embroidered extravagance. Bright red and blue costumes for the nobles, waiters in scarlet Sinbad pants, and extras clad as peasants out of Biblical tales. Oh, and giant, elaborate headdresses, of course – all of Pier Paolo Pasolini's movies set in the past (which's most of his movies in fact) feature OTT head gear (for instance, the fancy, white felt hats the forty thieves wear, or Nuredin's white and gold turban, or the extraordinary helmet, mask and gold beard combo that crossdressing King Zumurrud sports).

And the props and production design – the incomparable Dante Ferretti creates some jaw-droppingly wonderful settings and props and furniture for this journey into Arabic mythopœia (only a few designers anywhere could've pulled this off (and on this budget), and Ferretti has a look wholly his own). As Ferretti has explained in interviews, sometimes they would dress existing locations quite simply, but sometimes extensively. The mirror room of the Chehel Sotoun Palace in Esfahan, for example, is already an exotic space, but it is still dressed by the art department to stand in for the King's bedchamber.

As a collection of settings, props, locations and architecture within a movie, *The Arabian Nights* has few peers as a Western interpretation of Islamic and Arabic culture and design. Western cinema has been dining out on recreating Middle Eastern culture since the early excursions into Oriental exotica of pioneers like Géorges Méliès, but *The Arabian Nights* has to be one of the finest and most extravagant in film history.

So all of that – the look, the texture, the locations, the costumes, the make-up, the hair, the lighting (by DP Giuseppe Ruzzolini), etcetera – dazzles the viewer in *The Arabian Nights*, and consumes much of their attention. Even before you reach aspects such as performances or narrative or sound or music, the *mise-en-scène* of *The Arabian Nights* is staggering.

CHARACTERS.

The characters in *The Arabian Nights* are types, and they are interchangeable: the eager, immature lover, the enigmatic, attractive object of his desire, the wily, old pederast or predator, the stern king... You will notice that many character types are *not* represented much at all: older women, grandmothers, wives and queens (the female characters tend to be young women or princesses). Despite the crossdressing and a few role reversals, the *Arabian Nights* movie reflects the very patriarchal, male chauvinist and masculinist slant of the original Arabic tales (most of the sexual relations here are heterosexual, tho' there are depictions of homosexuality – discussed below).

This might be a fantasy version of Pier Paolo Pasolini's beloved ancient world and 'Third World', in which white, bourgeois Europe and the West is superseded and replaced by a dream-cast version of the Middle East, but it is as thoroughly patriarchal as any society in the history of humanity. Women have their place, and they are expected to stay in it. It's men who have agency, who travel, who act (even the kids out on the streets of the Arabia in this film are all boys).

Thus, another reason that Pier Paolo Pasolini later rejected the 'trilogy of life' films might be because the three films valorize societies and cultures which are very regressive, very conservative, very traditional, and very hierarchical. There is no social mobility: every character has their place in the hierarchy of the community and is expected to stay there. Kings and rulers are at the top (i.e., the fascists).

CINEMATIC ASPECTS OF *ARABIAN NIGHTS*.

For some of *The Arabian Nights*, Ennio Morricone provides a dreamy score, which you might not notice on first viewings, because there's so much else going on. However, quite a bit of *The Arabian Nights* is taken up with rather non-descript (European) string quartet (and choral) music (including Wolfgang Mozart's *String Quartet No. 15*). There isn't the dynamic relationship between the images and the music that characterizes the best of Pier Paolo Pasolini's cinematic work. Instead, the music tends to dribble and putter underneath scenes for a long time, without variation, and without much connection to what's happening (so that even Mozart is reduced to the level of muzak, And that is just not right. This is white, bourgeois, European music, too, of the classical era, which jars with the exotic, Middle Eastern *milieu* and characters).

The music in *The Arabian Nights* recalls the tendency in modern, Hollywood movies for filling a film with tons of background music, music which doesn't add much to anything except to be just another sound; music as muzak. (Hollywood producers and studios get uneasy when there isn't any music for some time in a movie, and movies have been re-scored just to fill them out with music. A typical Hollywood movie these days is scored almost throughout its entire running time, adding even more pressure on composers to come up with hours of music).

In *The Arabian Nights*, it looks as if the sound editors (Fausto Ancillai was sound mixer, Luciano Wellisch did the sound, and Nino Baragli was editor), found some temp music of string quartets from a film music library and plastered it underneath the movie in a slipshod manner. After some viewings, you will notice this aspect of the music, and it isn't the finest hour for Pier Paolo Pasolini or Ennio Morricone. You can see what I mean when the movie uses a proper music cue (and properly mixed), and as a result suddenly shifts up a few gears. Similarly, the music that is meant to be played by the actors on screen, but clearly isn't (such as in several of the celebratory scenes), is clumsily incorporated into the flow. (It's a lost opportunity – African and Middle Eastern music is some of the richest and most vibrant in the world. What a pity the sound team didn't record some local musicians while they were on location, or at least buy some audio tapes from local musicians, which anyone can do when travelling in those regions. Stalls selling music cassettes were common in the 1970s).

✦

As to performances – well, the actors and non-professionals are engaging as ever in a Pier Paolo Pasolini picture, but you wouldn't place *The Arabian Nights* in a list of Great Screen Performances. There are the usual Pasolinian faces – such as toothy, curly-haired Ninetto Davoli and suave, dangerous Franco Citti (despite the ginger wig!) – and the film is clearly enamoured of the grinning, fresh-faced teenager Franco Merli, and his *inamorata*, Zumurrud (played by 20 year-old Ines Pellegrini). Merli and Pellegrini are the magical couple at the heart of this wilfully eccentric confection of a movie. Merli is another of the rough *ragazzi* that Pasolini loved to put in his movies – eager and winsome like a puppy, lovelorn and wan like a doll, weepy like an abandoned tot, and so very young. (It's a role that Ninetto Davoli would no doubt have played had he been younger).

The maestro had found 16 year-old Franco Merli (b. 1956) working at a gas station, according to Ninetto Davoli (that does sound like Pier Paolo Pasolini), and decided to cast him as the lead in *The Arabian Nights* (and as one of the principal victims in *Salò* a year later). Merli embodies the spirit of youth, of innocence, of possibility, of yearning – of love – and his Nuredin (Nur-el-Din) character remains uncorrupted throughout the movie (which's remarkable considering his many adventures and trials). The first shot of *The Arabian Nights* is of Nuredin walking through the market where Zumurrud is sold, and the last shot is a close-up of Nuredin, joyful now he's found his long-lost lover Zumurrud.

Like so many actors in Pier Paolo Pasolini's movies, Franco Merli acted in one or two other movies, but not much after that. Indeed, many of the actors in Pasolini's movies only appeared in his films (it's the same with the unknown actors in the films of Walerian Borowczyk or Jean-Luc Godard). In some cases, that's a pity: Ines Pellegrini, for example, is wonderful, but she has only appeared in the 'trilogy of life' movies and *Salò*, and Luigina Rocchi, who played Fatima (Budur) in *The Arabian Nights*, is beautiful, and Merli has a winsome charm.

But there's no *acting* in the usual sense in *Il Fiore Delle Mille e Una Notte*. No. The performances have the naturalistic appearance of just happening in front of the camera, but not in the sense of actors who're professionally trained, and who've rehearsed a lot, to make scenes look as if they were improvized.

Improvization is a much mis-understood and mis-used term. Scenes in *any movie* are *very* rarely improvized in the way that critics and viewers mean. What usually happens is that spectators and critics are fooled into thinking that the stuff that's happening on screen looks as if it just took place spontaneously.

It doesn't (visit a film set and you'll see why instantly). But in *The Arabian Nights*, for once, it does seem as if the actors have been given some rudimentary direction and then been filmed in one or two takes. (The movie encourages the actors not to act, but to be themselves (as the maestro preferred). Impossible perhaps in the very artificial and strange setting of a movie set or a location surrounded by twenty or thirty people in the crew). And besides, the footage of Pier Paolo Pasolini at work filming *Salò, or The 120 Days of Sodom* reveals that he *would* ask for repeated takes, until everyone was satisfied. It also showed that Pasolini was coaxing the actors along with verbal instructions, including throughout shots.

As to acting compared to conventional movies – well, you just can't compare *The Arabian Nights* or the other 'trilogia di vita' pieces to the traditional manner of performance in Western movies. Pier Paolo Pasolini and the team employ a contrived *tableau* approach to some scenes, and many scenes are duly blocked in the static manner of formal/ classical paintings. And in other scenes, actors are given simple directions – run down this path and round the corner – and the scenes are filmed in a loose, casual manner. Quite a bit of *The Arabian Nights* exhibits the carefree, informal attitude of a home movie – no need for a tripod, the camera is switched on, focussed, framed and the exposure's set quickly, and catches an actor running down an alley. (Much of *The Arabian Nights* has the camera handheld or on a tripod – there are very few tracking shots, and no crane shots). However, there *are* more formal shots, and many duologue scenes are filmed with a tripod and tight close-ups, plus there are some optical/ process shots, and even miniature shots.

✢

The Arabian Nights is another huge undertaking in terms of actors and extras. *The Arabian Nights* marshalls a massive amount of characters on screen, from clusters of running, jeering children to solemn, middle-aged men who sit around palatial feasts, to the usual Pasolinian retinue of crones and old coots. So the assistant directors – Umberto Angelucci, Paolo Andrea Mettel and Peter Shepherd – should take much of the credit here: there are so many big scenes in *The Arabian Nights*, for instance, involving many extras and animals.[55] Just to organize the people and camels and horses in those scenes takes a lot of planning and effort. Some of Pasolini's later movies really are *big films*, on the scale of the Hollywood Biblical epics, though they are usually thought of as a smaller-scale, European art films.

The cast of *Il Fiore Delle Mille e Una Notte* is far from the plastic actors of a Hollywood movie, with their hard, toned, tanned bodies and surgically-enhanced faces. In *The Arabian Nights*, everything is allowed to spill out, and terms such as 'ugly' or 'unshaven' or 'bad teeth' or 'bad hair' don't exist. In a Pier Paolo Pasolini movie, everyone, including the lead actors, looks as if they've walked on set straight from the bus or the hotel. No showers, no make-up trailers, no on-set hair and make-up people fussing around the actors seconds before a take begins. (Of course that's not quite true, and Pasolini's movies, just like most movies, are very particular about how the main performers look, and all of the leads are in make-up. And you can't imagine divas like Silvana Mangano or Maria Callas being happy to slum it along with the extras (they'd have

---

[55] *The Arabian Nights* is full of animals – doves, horses, chickens, and of course camels. Plus a star role for a chimp!

hair and make-up artists fussing over them). Hair on *The Arabian Nights* was by Iole Cecchini, and make-up by Massimo Giustini – plus an army of assistants on the Big Scene Days).

And *The Arabian Nights* includes a slew of non-European actors, including many black and African actors. One of the main characters, Zumurrud, is played by a 20 year-old, black woman, Ines Pellegrini (b. 1954). She's terrific, hitting just the right note of naïvety and enthusiasm for a Pier Paolo Pasolini film. Abadit Ghidei and other key actors are also black.

In the scenes in the deep desert, we are far, far away from Cinecittà and anything European – or even anything to do with the usual interpretations of the Arabian tales of the *1001 Nights*. It's a case of Pier Paolo Pasolini wanting to use modern Africa and the Middle East for the ancient or mediæval world, and it's about Pasolini's love for Africa and the 'Third World' (and his insistence on moving away not only from Hollywood, but from the cinema of Rome and Italian cities, too – he preferred to venture into the lesser-known regions of Italy[56]). In the scenes of the poet Sium picking up three guys for sex, for example, towards the beginning of *The Arabian Nights*, everyone appears to be a black, African actor, and the village setting is a place with round huts with straw roofs (this was filmed in Ethiopia).

The Arabian Nights has the appearance, in parts, of a Giant Home Movie – as if Pier Paolo Pasolini had somehow persuaded a bunch of filmmakers (who would *not* be highly paid, one imagines), to trudge to far-flung locations (where decent hotels were thin on the ground, and the food was terrible), and to enact his wildly unusual interpretations of Arabic fairy tales (which nobody else understood, least of all the actors).

Thus, when Orson Welles described Pier Paolo Pasolini as a great leader, he was identifying a key requirement for a film director: leadership. Pasolini was one of those mavericks, one of those unusual and highly talented individuals who could (like Welles) somehow induce film crews and casts to go pretty far – physically, emotionally, psychologically.

✦

As with *Il Decamerone* and the decoration by Giotto di Bondone of a church, there is a painting scene[57] in *The Arabian Nights*: this time it's the decoration of a chamber by the suitor Prince Tagi (Francesco Paolo Governale) to charm the red silk sari off a beautiful, young woman

---
[56] Yet most of the lead roles in *The Arabian Nights* are played by Italians, as in nearly all of Pasolini's other movies.
[57] Also, Aziza paints a scroll for her lover.

(Princess Dunya (Abadit Ghidei), the woman who has the disturbing dreams of trapped birds). The art department provides a lavish recreation of mediæval tiles and stained glass, and the two artisans in turn relate (and star in) the later stories of the 1974 movie.

✦

There are visual effects a-plenty in *The Arabian Nights*, too. Now, Pier Paolo Pasolini has always used special effects, which are also known as practical effects, such as effects like fire and smoke, or the special make-up in *Il Vangelo Secondo Matteo*. But in *The Arabian Nights* the filmmakers employ those effects (like models and optical effects) that critics tend to think of when they talk about 'visual' or 'special' effects' (i.e., visual effects created in post-production).

The visual effects in *The Arabian Nights* are ropey – the scene where the Devil takes the Prince for a flying ride, for instance, which combines aerial photography with the actors optically superimposed on top. *Superman* or *Star Wars* this ain't; nor is it anywhere near *The Thief of Baghdad* or one of Ray Harryhausen's marvellous *Sinbad* pictures. But it doesn't matter a jot. (However, the model shots of the boat hitting the cliffs and the sinking of the island are terrible – reminiscent of Ed Wood, but even worse than Wood, if they are meant to be serious).

✦

One of the motifs of *The Arabian Nights* is not wholly worked-out or quite as satisfying narratively as it should be: that is the rhyming of visuals, of places, of rooms, of characters, and of events. There are two upper chambers, for instance: one where Aziz and Aziza meet, and one where Princess Dunya's romanced by Prince Tagi. There are two visits to mysterious underground palaces. Two scenes where youths lie face-down on beds with their clothes pulled down. There are two scenes where Zumurrud in her mirrored bedroom as the King undresses to reveal she's a woman. These poetic doubles and rhymes don't quite play out as richly as the material deserves. (The films of Pasolini tend to avoid really milking cinematic devices such as visual rhymes).

What *does* work, however, is the interlinking of the stories, how one story can engender another, how a meeting with a new character means the relating of a new story. So the stories form a spiral, a cycle, a flow – of one story into another – the ending of one story leads directly into the beginning of another story. And the tales are dreams-within-dreams, creating an infinity of dreams, a labyrinth of interconnecting tales. (A good example occurs when Aziz meets Prince Tagi in the desert and relates the long story of his courtship of Fatima and marriage to Aziza, which takes up much of the middle section of *The Arabian Nights*: when he has finished his story, Aziz and Tagi venture into another town, where another story starts up, when they meet the brothers that Tagi hires to decorate the chamber).

The Arabian Nights is of course a *hommage* to stories and to storytelling – to the magic of storytelling, the romance of it, the seduction of it, and the *necessity* of it. *The Arabian Nights* is one of numerous movies which remind audiences of the importance and value of stories and storytelling (good examples would include *The Princess Bride* and *Big Fish*).

BAD SOUND.

Where *The Arabian Nights* is let-down, for me, is on the level of sound and dubbing and music. Pier Paolo Pasolini's movies seem to have been staged in a variety of far-flung locations with a large group of people over months. But for the post-production, it appears that they have been dubbed and edited months or even years after the shooting, and the dubbing and cutting would be produced by a small group of people, probably in Rome. And some of those people maybe had nothing to do with the shooting of the movie (i.e., they have no investment in it), so there appears to be a disconnection between the images and the soundtrack. And it seems to have been done too quickly. (Certainly, many of the voice actors are *long ways* from the faces and personalities of the performers on screen).

What I mean is that there's a clumsy, awkward feeling to the sound in a Pier Paolo Pasolini movie, a wilful negligence in the post-production process. As if the voice dubbing was crammed into two days, and the mixing and dubbing into one day.

I don't know the circumstances here – because in the Hollywood system, movies are sometimes taken away from the filmmakers, and very few film directors have *true* final cut (they say they do, but studios still have the *real* final say – not least because studios legally own movies – and they pay for them).

I wouldn't imagine that Pier Paolo Pasolini had movies taken away from him, or that producer Alberto Grimaldi fell out big time and had the films cut in his own way (because, how the hell are you going to re-edit a Pasolini movie without the maestro's input?! Who the hell else can make sense of all that crazy footage?!). It's partly the Italian film industry's standard procedure, of course, of dubbing everything, and not shooting sync sound (there's not much live sound in many of Pasolini's movies, and the maestro wasn't a fan of it anyway). And, clearly, few if any of those extras and actors employed by the production in locations in Africa or Asia were invited to Rome and were present on the dubbing stage (even many of the lead actors, too, are not voicing their own roles – standard practice in the Italian film business even for starring roles). Instead, it's probably the usual bunch of Italian actors who dubbed most every big film that came through Rome. (Ditto with the foley work and the sound effects – in *The Arabian Nights*, they are patchy and inept. Crowd scenes have generic (and inconsistent) 'crowd sounds' (often for the market scenes),[58] music isn't in sync with the performers on-screen (and is clearly nothing like the music being played by the musicians), and the extras are shoddily represented. In short, 70% of the soundtrack of *The Arabian Nights* doesn't fit).

The issue, though, is not live sound vs. looped dialogue, it's that the sound in so many of Pier Paolo Pasolini's movies appears rushed and clunky. Sometimes I wonder that if Pasolini's movies had been dubbed and cut to a much higher standard, along with other technical aspects, Pasolini would now be regarded as a truly major filmmaker like Ingmar Bergman or Akira Kurosawa. For some critics, and for me, he is in that league, but not for many critics and viewers.

WEST MEETS EAST.

When you consider the individual scenes or images in *The Arabian Nights*, there is so much that is striking. Much of the imagery is very beautiful – the *light* of the whole film is absolutely haunting. This is the light of Africa, of North Africa, of Yemen and Iran, and of Asia. I for one *adore* those places, and can watch hours of this kind of footage. *The Arabian Nights*, for instance, is a terrific *desert* film, in the same class as *Lawrence of Arabia* or a John Ford Western.

However, *The Arabian Nights* is plenty more than a mere travelogue of pretty and exotic places. It's got the *A Thousand and One Nights milieu* down to a 'T' – including the princes and nobles in red and blue silk pants at festivals, bustling market scenes (including gorgeous, covered *souks*), dusty squares and alleys, elaborate mosques and towers, voyages in creaky, wooden boats, and caravans of camels and merchants moving across the desert. *The Arabian Nights* is unashamed in its evocation of classic movie clichés, and of Westerners' enshrinement of the exotic Middle East. *The Arabian Nights* is 'orientalizing' the East, in Edward Said's term, just as much as *Lawrence of Arabia* or the *Indiana*

---

[58] And the background and atmos sounds (of crowds in the markets, for ex), don't match the scenes, either.

Jones franchise or *55 Days At Peking*. *The Arabian Nights* is still a European film production taking on the Arabic tales of the mediæval era, and despite Pasolini's (Marxist) politics (always remarked upon in any appraisal of Pasolini's cinema, and, as Pasolini admitted, not that significant in his cinema after all), *The Arabian Nights* is *still* West Meets East, the West exploiting the East, the West using the East for its own ends.[59] (For ex, many European (mostly Italian) actors take the lead roles in each of the stories).

The filmmakers want it both ways (as filmmakers – and all artists – always do): they want to produce a different kind of Middle Eastern movie, a different slant on the usual *1001 Nights*/ fairy tale/ fantasy movie, an *Arabian Nights* using archaic (yet contemporary) Africa instead of the usual 'historical' views of the Levant. But they also want to reproduce the familiar West-meets-East exoticism, and romance, and fantasy. (And they want to have Italians playing most of the lead roles).

SEXUALITY.
And there's sex.
Yes, *The Arabian Nights* contains plenty of tupping and nudity.[60] And men as much as women disrobe in this movie. As erotic as it is (it is probably Pier Paolo Pasolini's most conventionally erotic movie), *The Arabian Nights* departs from your usual picture in its portrayal of sex and nudity. The distanced, Brechtian, *tableau* approach to the performances and the narrative in *The Arabian Nights* means that the sex, like the drama or the characters or other narrative elements, is not treated in conventional terms.

In short, *The Arabian Nights* simply does not tell a traditional story in a traditional manner (even tho' it's dealing with probably the greatest set of stories in human history). It does not use the usual elements of dramaturgy – such as rising action, or cause and effect, or motives, or backstory, or goals. Yes, (some of) those elements *are* present, but they are not integrated into the fabric of the movie in the customary way. (But all you need to know in *The Arabian Nights* is that *desire* is all-pervading, and informs everything the characters do: they desire, desire, desire. And the desire is always for romance and love and sex. Which might be another way of pinpointing the desire for fulfilment. Or transcendence).

---

[59] I bet, for example, that Alberto Grimaldi's film production team didn't pay the local extras in the Maghreb the going rate they'd get in Cinecittà, and certainly not the union fee for Burbank.
[60] For Sam Rohdie, *The Arabian Nights* is a 'myth about eroticism', but it's not 'a film about sexuality which the film converts to myth, but a film about the cinema which presents a myth of a lost sexuality' (54-55).

It's one of the aspects of Pier Paolo Pasolini's cinema that takes a little getting used to – the viewer has to shift into a different way of looking at movies. The filmmakers are not going to provide dramaturgy in the usual manner, so don't expect dramatic devices such as rising action, or one scene providing the energy or tension or dialogue cue for the next scene (known as the 'hook'), or for dramatic climaxes (or for dramatic highpoints at the end of scenes). Indeed, the *lack* of narrative climaxes in movies like *The Arabian Nights* is one of the chief characteristics of Pasolini's cinema. A film such as *The Arabian Nights* is certainly telling a story (and is of course a story about stories, about how stories are created, and how one story suggests or gives birth to another, and how stories are dreams which intersect/ multiply), but it *does not* punch home its dramatic highpoints, like a conventional North American or European or Indian or Japanese or Chinese movie.

Oh, there *are* conflicts between characters in *The Arabian Nights*, and scenes where characters argue (with attempts to resolve issues), but the movie is simply not interested in staging conflicts or the resolutions to conflicts in a conventional manner. Consequently, there are no moral messages, no summaries of narrative or theme, no plot devices to update audiences, etc. (The framing story of the *1001 Nights*, for example, is dispensed with – where Scheherazade tries to appease the Sultan Shahryar).

In your typical contemporary, Hollywood flick, relationships and characters and situations are so highly wrought that everything is played at the maximum of emotion and conflict. In those high octane narratives created by M.B.A.s and executives and their writer-slaves in Culver City or Burbank, nobody is happy, everyone has a wise-ass quip about everyone else, and the world is always about to end.

By contrast with contemporary, Hollywood cinema, *The Arabian Nights* is fabulously laid-back and free-wheeling, loose and sensual. However, there *are* some resolutions to conflicts, and some moral outcomes: for instance, some of the villains are punished (like the 'blue-eyed Christian', Barsum, who kidnaps Nuredin's beloved Zumurrud). Aziz is chastized for his abominable treatment of women (with castration). And there *is* a moral pattern established at the end of each episode. (And, yes, some of the characters, such as Nuredin and Aziz, are played at hysterical levels, with their weeping and gnashing of teeth over lost lovers. In many scenes actors've had glycerine applied to simulate tears. Well, hell, this *is* a movie made by Italians! Where weepy men litter the floor! Men weep in three-quarters of Pasolini's movies).

And for some critics, *The Arabian Nights* may come across as self-indulgent and a-political: for the intellectuals and politicos who hanker after Pier Paolo Pasolini-the-Marxist-Revolutionary, *The Arabian Nights* is probably decadent tripe in which a former firebrand of Communist ideology and the left-wing has descended into children's tales of the exotic Levant coupled with travelogue photography and some titillating, soft-core porn sex.

Sure. *The Arabian Nights* is not everyone's cup of champagne. I'd say, tho': how can you *not* enjoy *The Arabian Nights*? It has so much going for it! And it's clear that Pier Paolo Pasolini and the team are exploring the same themes and issues in *The Arabian Nights* that they have always explored. But in *The Arabian Nights*, the trappings and the gift-wrapping are so spectacular and entrancing, it can be very distracting.

And one should always remember with Pier Paolo Pasolini that while his cinema is about poetry and ideology and narrative and ideas and all those elements that critics and intellectuals solemnly discuss and deconstruct, he is also a *filmmaker*, someone who is very concerned with staging and characters and colours and light and music. Pasolini's movies are not essays published in *Diacritics* or *Yale Po-Faced Studies*. They are movies, folks, and even though they are often categorized as European art films, they are also *movies*, just as much as entertainment movies such as *Singin' In the Rain, Grease* or *Avatar*.

✦

Although it is unconventional narratively, and although it contains a lot of nudity and sex, *The Arabian Nights* is totally conservative and even regressive, if you consider it politically in relation to some of Pier Paolo Pasolini's other movies. *The Arabian Nights* enshrines love and sex and romance and the heterosexual couple through and through (just as the original tales did). Even the gender-bending and portrayals of homosexuality are very mild (compared to what we might expect from Pasolini) The crossdressing, for instance, occurs wholly within conventional narrative forms. People having sex and falling in love is always going to be conservative and traditional (tho' the portrayals in art and cinema might not be). Not right-wing and reactionary, or left-wing and Communist or socialist, because love and sex don't have anything to do with that kind of politics in this movie.

Maybe you can find some left-wing or Marxist or right-wing and fascistic politics outside the 1974 movie, or inferred from inside the movie, but if you consider the levels of narrative and characters and themes and images, this is an a-political movie which enshrines love and sex and marriage and the family. (Again, this ardent pursuit of a-politics or non-politics might feed into Pier Paolo Pasolini's artistic reversal about his 'trilogy of life' pictures).

In the Aziz and Aziza story, for instance, there are numerous scenes of Ninetto Davoli running back and forth between his spurned bride Aziza and his beloved Fatima. And that's all it is, for thirty minutes, the sequence goes on and on and on – a man hurrying between two women, with some weedy *Carry On* comedy, and some exotic settings.

Is it bourgeois? Fascist? Totalitarian? Marxist? Communist? Radical? Separatist? Terrorist? It doesn't matter.

And *The Arabian Nights* is episodic in structure, knitted together by the running story of – what? Of a man looking for a woman. Yes folks, the linking narrative in *1001 Nights* is just that: a boy (Nuredin) searching for a girl (Zumurrud), a lover looking for his beloved (which is as conservative and traditional as possible).

HOMOSEXUALITY.

Some critics drew attention to the heterosexual nature of the sexual relations on display in *The Arabian Nights*, but there are many references to (and portrayals of) homosexual identity and gay sex.[61] And there's just as much male nudity as female nudity (all of the actors working for Pier Paolo Pasolini would likely have known by this point in his career that he was a famous gay film director). And not only male nudity, but male bodies filmed with a painter's eye for beauty: if you like young men's butts, there are plenty on show in *The Arabian Nights* (as well, of course, as everything else in the male body).

The Arabian Nights might be P.P. Pasolini's version of the modern art of famous gay artists like Tom of Finland or Robert Mapplethorpe (Mapplethorpe was photographing beautiful, young men in Gotham in a very similar manner as *The Arabian Nights* around this time – the mid-Seventies). And, with the young actors framed in settings such as Byzantine or Early Renaissance chapels, you might be looking at updated versions of the paintings of the two Michelangelos (Buonarroti and Caravaggio).

The scene where a merchant poet (Sium) picks up three youths in a rural (African) village is one of the most obvious (and clichéd) homosexual encounters in Pier Paolo Pasolini's *œuvre* (it's the second sequence in *The Arabian Nights*, so it introduces a homosexual theme early on. It's a scene of full nudity that Pasolini might've filmed in the early

---

[61] There are jokes about some men preferring bananas to figs.

1960s, if the social climate would have allowed it). It's the archaic, stereotypical tale of an old pederast with three pretty boys (a scenario in fiction at least 3,500 years-old): the filmmakers make the gay eroticism of the scene explicit, by having the three black *ragazzi* fully naked, lined up for the fully-clothed poet Sium to inspect and joke with and fondle their genitals. (The scene seems tailor-made for those critics who persist in taking the biographical approach to the cinema of Pasolini – for them, this scene is probably a barely concealed self-portrait of Pasolini the predatory gay man, preying upon comely, young boys).[62]

When Prince Yunan (Salvatore Sapienza) climbs down into the underground palace, late in the movie, there's a frightened youth who's just turned fifteen. Yunan is naked for quite a lot of this episode of *The Arabian Nights* (this is tough acting for Sapienza: he has to swim, clamber over rocks, run around mountains, beaches, climb down rope ladders in the palace, etc, and much of the time fully naked).

The sex acts between Yunan and the 15 year-old kid aren't depicted. Instead, there's a classic evocation of homoerotic bonding – they horse around in a big bath (in some extraordinary catacombs. You can see a similar scene in the restored *Spartacus*, 1960). There is nudity from both actors, and they sleep in the same bed. (Getting that scene with nude, under-age actors filmed today might be tricky even for a revered *auteur* like Pier Paolo Pasolini.)[63]

The dreamy idyll in the subterranean palace between Prince Yunan and the 15 year-old boy is thoroughly gay-inflected (and the camera dwells lovingly on actor Salvatore Sapienza's form. No one can miss that he also resembles a young Pasolini). When Yunan stabs the boy with a knife (as has been foretold), he pulls down the lad's clothes, for no particular reason, exposing his bare rear (as he lies face-down on the bed). The knife, the blood, the wound, the nudity, the bed, the under-age boy – there are numerous signifiers of sodomy, murder and gay sex (which Pasolini would explore even further in his following film as director, *Saló, or The 120 Days of Sodom*).

There's also a gay theme to the final scene of *The Arabian Nights*, where Nuredin and Zumurrud are re-united, and some of the male guests at the wedding feast quip that they wouldn't mind having Nuredin themselves (it's those big, cute eyes!).

---

62 And, yes, some film critics have made that connection.
63 The tabloid press, plus the authorities, would probably seize upon a gay film director with criminal convictions of predation filming under-age actors in sex scenes with relish.

ZUMURRUD AND NUREDIN.

Let's slip on our scarlet, Aladdin pants and rim our eyes with kohl and take a look at some of the episodes in more detail in the 1974 film:

The Arabian Nights opens with a scene designed to turn the tables on the conventions of *1001 Nights* adaptations, with some gender-swopping play: the slave Zumurrud, a woman in amongst a group of men at a slave market, loudly and jokily denounces some of the guys around her, in sexual terms (deriding their manhood). This scene leads to the unlikely formation of the central couple of *The Arabian Nights*, Zumurrud and Nuredin, when Zumurrud announces that she will only be sold to Nuredin, having spotted him in the crowd (and despite some of the buyers coveting her, such as Barsum (Salvatore Verdetti) and his pay master Ali – Ali Abdulla). The seduction by a woman of a man, and a woman who will later become a king (and a black woman, too), sets up the themes of playing around with gender (and race), and a proto-feminism (which isn't really present in the original mediæval *1001 Nights* tales).

Thus, after the customary two minutes of opening credits (in black lettering on white) of a Pier Paolo Pasolini picture, *The Arabian Nights* dives straight into a lively *souk* scene, delivering the cliché of the *Thousand and One Nights* (a bustling, Middle Eastern setting, and Nuredin as the hapless, grinning youth). And, true to form, the 1974 movie also hurries right into a full frontal sex scene, as Zumurrud and Nuredin get freaky (with Zumurrud initiating the virginal and clumsy Nuredin). Thus, the first erotic scene in *The Arabian Nights* is happy, consensual and loving – as if the 'happy ever after' occurs at the top of the movie, and everything disintegrates into disconnection, separation and liminality (or, more bluntly, before it all goes cock-eyed). So the movie begins with consensual lovemaking, and it ends with our lovers re-united, and the re-affirmation of love – heartfelt, romantic union (it's the sappiest ending to a Pasolini film[64]).

The idyll of love cannot last long, because the insulted men at the slave auction take their revenge: the 'blue-eyed Christian' Barsum kidnaps Zumurrud and has her carried by basket to Ali, who whips her for deriding him in front of everybody in the bazaar.[65] Thus begins the lengthy narrative device of the separation of the lovers, which is sustained throughout *The Arabian Nights*, right up until the reunion of the soulmates in the very final frames (thirty seconds before the caption

---

64 No death here, then – both characters make it to the end of the show in one piece.
65 There is less rape and abuse than one might expect in this interpretation of the *1001 Nights* by Pier Paolo Pasolini and the team – and also in the other 'trilogy of life' movies.

'FINE' comes up).

Barsum and his cohorts (such as the leader of the forty thieves) get their just desserts, with the running gag of guests at the wedding feast taking food without being invited, and being carted off to be crucified[66] (cut to images of crucifixions at sunset outside the city walls. It's a hefty sentence for grabbing a handful of rice, but this is a fairy tale, after all, and it doesn't matter what the taboo is). All of Pasolini's historical movies feature scenes of punishment (sometimes conceived along ritualistic, mythic lines, as in *Medea*).

Poor Nuredin has a pretty tough time of it, wandering thru the whole 1974 movie looking for his lost love Zumurrud (in some scenes he's running like mad, and being chased by a group of yelling kids).

In one of the more bizarre sequences in *The Arabian Nights*, he has an encounter with a magical lion in the desert (who leads him, via the trickery of optical process imagery, to Zumurrud's city).[67] This is where Nuredin is at his lowest point, in the midst of an uninhabited desert: from this lowest ebb, Nuredin's fortunes bounce all the way up the ecstasy (i.e., it's a conventional reversal of fortune, pushing a hero down to the lowest point), when he is led to the city where Zumurrud is King.

However, it's not all bad for Nuredin during his journey: in one scene, he's literally hauled up off the street (in a basket on ropes), and undressed and seduced by three women in an inner courtyard. In another scene, he's bathing naked in a pool surrounded by colourful fruit and flowers with three naked maidens (one of them is Elisabetta Genovese as Munis), where they play the 'Guess the Name For the Genitals' game, teasing Nuredin and kissing him.[68] (Jean-Luc Godard has employed this game in at least three movies – Godard has characters coming up with different words for the buttocks in *Masculine Feminine* (1966), for example, as they lie in bed, and even has the young Jesus hiding under the Virgin Mary's dress in *Hail Mary* (1985), and talking about her breasts and mound).

Nuredin is the embodiment of love pure and total – he never gives up on Zumurrud,[69] and is seeking her to the end (after the scene with the bathing beauties, Nuredin is soon waking, and hurrying away, crying, 'Zumurrud!', which's his mantra throughout *The Arabian Nights* – '*Zumurrud! Zumurrud!*'). Nuredin isn't portrayed as a psychologized (or psychologizing) character – he's no Hamlet or modern, Western character

---
[66] The actor who plays Barsum (Salvatore Verdetti), with his blue eyes, might be cast as Christ.
[67] Both the lion and actor Franco Merli are optically composited into the desert landscapes featuring drifting clouds.
[68] The poetic names for genitals are right out of Oriental erotic tales (such as in *The Perfumed Garden* and the *Kama Sutra*).
[69] Never giving up is one of the hallmarks of a hero.

analyzing everything. *The Arabian Nights* seems to draw on (Freudian) psychology, like other Pasolini pictures, but it presents its figures as more archaic, more primitive, and more fundamental than something that modern psychoanalysis can grasp. The characters in *The Arabian Nights* seem anti-psychological, anti-intellectualized – anti-Western. Certainly anti-modern or pre-modern, and anti-capitalist or pre-capitalist.

CARAVAN OF DREAMS.

The caravan of dreams sequence depicts the cliché of Ancient Arabian folk tales, a caravan of camels, horses, kids, animals and merchants in the desert. It's Pier Paolo Pasolini's little piece of *Lawrence of Arabia* – and it's presented, amazingly, without the usual veneers of irony/ politics/ ideology. As if Pasolini, a white, bourgeois, European man really can fly loose of his uptight, intellectual background and stage an Oriental fairy tale with all the trimmings.

Two merchants pick up two fifteen year-old kids, and use them for a quaint, naïve scene exploring the origins of love in the form of a private test. Charm and innocence disguise the elements of exploitation and slavery: Zuedi (Zuedi Biasolo) and Sium the poet watch the teens waking up and making love in a tent from a perch above, like gods. The boy, Berhame (Fessazion Gherentiel), wakes,[70] sees the girl, moves over to her bed, and makes love to her, and then vice versa. It's as if love (sex) transcends all.

Maybe Pier Paolo Pasolini disapproved of his 'trilogy of life' films in his famous reversal ("Repudiation of the *Trilogy of Life*", June 1975) because there's too little of the cynicism and irony that seems mandatory in any Euro-art flick. Delivering so many love stories straight, without the usual levels of self-consciousness and self-criticism, was not the done thing. *The Arabian Nights* is certainly a love letter to *love* as well as to the 'Third World', to Africa, and to the Middle East, and to, of course, the past, the ancient world, and the utopia/ paradise that never existed. (It's the world that Pasolini wished Italy still was, which he pined for).

AZIZ AND FATIMA.

Among the most successful episodes in *The Arabian Nights* is the central section, where Aziz (played by Ninetto Davoli) trysts with Fatima (also known as Budur, played by Luigina Rocchi[71]), in one of the story-within-a-story sections (yes, Davoli and his cheesy grin duly turns up in *The Arabian Nights* – 45 minutes into the show. However, this is

---
70 Prodded awake by the onlookers.
71 Again, the performers in this episode are Italian and French.

Davoli's finest role in Pasolini movie).

Aziz and Fatima meet in a beautifully-designed, orange-red fairy tale tent in a desert garden, and make love. This section includes one of the iconic images of Pier Paolo Pasolini's cinema, framed like an illustration from a mediæval manuscript: the nude couple facing each other, Fatima with her legs open, and Aziz brandishing a golden bow and arrow, with a gold cock and balls at the end of it,[72] which he fires into Fatima's holy of holies.

It's a long episode, filmed in the palm trees and greenery in the desert of Iran, and involves a back-and-forth romantic plot in the manner of *Cyrano de Bergerac*. Aziz is another of Pier Paolo Pasolini's and Ninetto Davoli's dopes, a lusty but very dim youth who falls in love at the drop of a hat with a woman glimpsed for an instant from an upper window, even tho' he's in the midst of marrying Aziza (Teresa Bouché). Poor Aziza becomes the Roxanne for Aziz, feeding the hapless Aziz with lines of romantic verse to say to Fatima, and translating her enigmatic sayings and gestures back for him when he returns. In the end, Aziz betrays both women. (Aziz's mother (Pasolini regular Margareth Clémenti) castigates him for his failings – but not as much as an Italian mother would!).

The Aziz-Fatima episode's strung out for too long and is rather shabbily edited (by Nino Baragli and Tatiana Morigi), but plenty of elements make it one of the more engaging and narratively satisfying sections of the 'trilogy of life' movies (such as the beauty and texture of the imagery, the appeal of the actors (Luigina Rocchi is lovely), the innocence of the lovemaking,[73] and the naïvety of it all, the cuteness,[74] the fact that one could switch Ninetto Davoli and Teresa Bouché and Luigina Rocchi for Disney cartoon animals, and it would still be entertaining[75]).

Indeed, the appeal of *The Arabian Nights* is precisely that the stories themselves are so simple – or, rather, uncomplicated. A man visits a woman, but sees another woman he likes more on the way. That's all it is. The narrative component of *The Arabian Nights* is thus only one ingredient of this shimmering, beautiful movie. It's a little like a Hollywood musical film or a Hong Kong martial arts movie, where the story is

---

72 You can bet that this prop was swiftly stolen from the set. Indeed, if you were turning *The Arabian Nights* into merchandizing for movie fans with money to waste, the golden genitals would be ideal. Pasolini's movies are full of silly props like this which might be sold in a sex toys store.
73 There are scenes of Fatima licking wine off Aziz's body, for instance.
74 Wait, did I just say 'cute' about a Pier Paolo Pasolini movie?!
75 Altho' Disney's Bambi and Thumper never got up to this level of naughtiness.

often simple[76] and just an excuse for the filmmakers to stage a whole bunch of extravagant set-pieces (thus, insisting on fully developed characters, themes and plots completely misses the point). *The Arabian Nights* might be the closest Pasolini came to making a musical movie (but of all the European New Wave *auteurs*, you just can't imagine Pasolini directing a musical! However, Jean-Luc Godard did – *A Woman Is a Woman* (1961). And other Godard pictures, like *Pierrot le Fou* and *Band of Outsiders,* have musical and dance interludes.[77] And even Ingmar Bergman, for some critics *the* arch miserablist of world cinema, made a few musical and theatrical movies).

But no, no one dances in a Pier Paolo Pasolini movie (except Salomé in *The Gospel According To Matthew*). In the 'trilogy of life' movies, Pasolini got close – he had Ninetto Davoli do a Charlie Chaplin skit, for instance, in *The Canterbury Tales* (though it was awful). And there *are* dances in the 'mediæval trilogy' – but they seem to occur only at weddings – the peasants dance in *The Decameron*, and Perkin dances at a wedding in *The Canterbury Tales*.

The luxuriously staged wedding in *The Arabian Nights*, between Zumurrud and her/ his bride Hayat, cries out for some choreography (but even the music in that scene, which should be as delightful as the colourful costumes and food, is fudged. (If this was a Bollywood musical, the entire ensemble would be dancing across the screen, and Zumurrud would certainly belt out a love song).

Anyway, back to Aziz and Fatima: what happens to Aziz? He is castrated (!) – rather spectacularly, too: he turns up at Princess Fatima's fancy tent in the garden after a year, having married (a third woman) and had a child, and is rightly set upon by a group of harpies at Fatima's behest. That he isn't slaughtered on the spot is amazing – poor Fatima's been waiting a year perched on the same patch of dust outside her tent, without food or water! (Or so she claims). Instead, there's a graphic castration scene, in which Aziz's genitals're tied up with twine in giant close-up. Ouch! (So he becomes a castrated, feminized man. Is this Pasolini's cinematic response to his former lover Davoli getting married? Pasolini was apparently distraught when he heard the news about Davoli, in January, 1973, during the filming of *The Canterbury Tales*. Some observers have thought so. The very long Aziz and Aziza sequence in *The Arabian Nights* is, after all, all about fidelity and infidelity, and for his betrayal of both women, Aziz is severely punished. It looks forward to

---

[76] Actually, the plots are seldom 'simple', but intricate. The over-arching concept may be 'simple', but the way it is plotted isn't.
[77] Some of these were to please his wife, Anna Karina.

Salò).[78]

DUNYA AND TAGI.

The Arabian Nights also enters dreamland, moving into a character's dreams, though not as often as one might imagine – because the entire movie is so dream-like (and films are already dreams, as Pasolini pointed out). It's Princess Dunya's (Abadit Ghidei) dream of birds, of birds being trapped under nets, and breaking free (it's this dream that becomes the basis of the decoration of the upper chamber by Prince Tagi, in order to woo her. How romantic!). When Dunya sees this, of course she breaks into tears (which's how every lover responds to anything in *The Arabian Nights* – the movie is full of young people weeping from love's cruelty). Tagi and Dunya make love (she kneels down to worship the male organ in the D.H. Lawrencean manner), then they continue on the floor (with Dunya covering up Tagi so he can't look at her as she services him).

There is also a reprise of the caravan of camels and travellers out of Middle Eastern fairy tales in this sequence, when it's attacked by bandits (and the Prince survives by smearing himself with blood and pretending to be dead). The way that the bandits are introduced calls back to the Massacre of the Innocents section of *The Gospel According To Matthew*: a montage of close-ups of the robbers looking off-screen is followed by a sudden burst into movement accompanied by music.

THE ENDING.

Towards the end of *The Arabian Nights*, the film seems to be running out of steam somewhat. It's a long movie – or it *feels* like a long movie (it's two hours and ten minutes long, with a lost, early cut running 2h 35m). But not in a bad way – I for one could watch this kind of movie for hours and hours. But by the one hour and thirty minute mark, the filmmaking team have clearly said pretty much what they wanted to say and staged pretty much what they wanted to stage (here's where really expert editors and screenwriters make their mark, by reviving a flagging audience and revving them up for the last act). When you look at a lot of movies that run over two hours, you often find that between 1h 20m and 1h 30m is a danger point (*The Arabian Nights* doesn't have an intermission, as *The Decameron* did, and as very lengthy movies sometimes did in this period).

Although a running time of 2h 10m always means a four-act movie

---

[78] Pursuing the biographical approach further, Ninetto Davoli is sexually objectified in a striking manner; there are several close-ups of his weiner and buttocks, for instance. And to punish his former lover, Pier Paolo Pasolini has his genitals tied up and tortured on film!

in terms of narrative structure, *The Arabian Nights* is a very rare fiction/ feature film because it isn't composed in act form. Instead, it is fashioned in episode form.

And, no, there isn't going to be a big action climax to this kind of movie. Oh no. But *The Arabian Nights* does reach some interesting places, with sea voyages in old, wooden boats, encounters with magical lions in the desert, islands that collapse into the ocean like mythical Atlantis, and descents into underground palaces.

Franco Citti appears in these scenes in a brief cameo as a demon (a *djinn* = genie): he has a bizarre look, with an orange-red fright wig and Aladdin pants (and he's topless, and also sports a text around his neck).[79] Time for a little bit of Italian horror out of Dario Argento, Mario Bava, and *gialli* cheapies, too, when the demon chops off the hands and feet of Prince Shahzmah's lover, then her head (that she doesn't make a sound, but keeps looking fondly at Yunan is a great touch).

This particular story in *The Arabian Nights* goes further into *ciné fantastique* territory when it has the demon turning Prince Shahzmah (Alberto Argentino) into a chimpanzee. Yes, folks, Pier Paolo Pasolini has made a movie where a clever chimp is carried on a litter like a king by slaves, and writes in an elegant, Arabic script! But this isn't a Disney TV special, or *The Jungle Book*, or another re-telling of the Chinese epic *Journey To the West* – it's a tale where the Prince is having A Very Bad Week. As if seeing his beloved having her limbs chopped off, followed by her head, isn't enough, he's turned into a monkey, and is kept as a pet by a laughing sailor.

Filming in India and Nepal paid off in *The Arabian Nights* with some of the most dream-like sequences in the Pier Paolo Pasolini cinematic *œuvre*: as the monkey-king is carried thru a town, bells are rung by onlookers. And then more bells, and more bells – with the sound editors in Rome coming up with something suitably imaginative on the soundtrack (instead of the usual mundane sounds). The staging is uninspired, the acting is low-key, and the action doesn't convince (or move us), but the India and Nepal episode in *The Arabian Nights* is lifted by another set of extraordinary spaces. It's a whole world away from the deserts of Yemen and Iran. (Pasolini might've been the greatest documentary filmmaker of exotic places in recent times had he been inclined. Some filmmakers pride themselves on shooting in remote or dangerous spots – Werner Herzog comes to mind – but Pasolini has a magical ability (a poet's nose) for seeking out the strange and the poetic everywhere he

---

79 It's definitely Citti's oddest outfit for a Pasolini movie.

goes. Pasolini could visit a town or city you are very familiar with, where you've lived for years, and he would uncover something you'd never seen before).

The episodic nature of *The Arabian Nights*, and each of the 'trilogy of life-and-death' movies, means that the rising action device and the cause-and-effect mechanisms of the conventional movie aren't going to work. However, the film has employed the running motif of stories-within-stories, which has recurring characters like Zumurrud and Nuredin cropping up: the search for love provides the narrative glue that cements the 1974 movie together at the close (*The Arabian Nights* embodies Pasolini's tenet of art as 'a search for magic').

✦

And how about the ending of *The Arabian Nights*? Outside of *The Gospel According To Matthew*, it's the all-out happiest ending in Pier Paolo Pasolini's cinema. What does the ending consist of? The union of the two lovers (Nuredin and Zumurrud) separated in act one, of course. Cue the music! Cue the kissing! Pure fairy tale, pure Hollywood. The most conservative ending possible. Love – sex – romance – it always works.

But even that ending of *The Arabian Nights* has a kinky twist, as Zumurrud, for no particular reason (except maybe she's getting fond of being King), teases poor Nuredin mercilessly by having him massage her feet, then lie on the bed, then turn over, with his pants pulled down over his behind (at this point, the always-innocent Nuredin thinks that the King is a man and he's been summoned to the King's chamber to be his sex slave). Only as she recites poetry does Zumurrud undress and finally reveal herself to Nuredin, who at that point still thinks he's going to be buggered by the man. She takes his hand and puts it between her legs. (The scene shifts from homosexual rape to heterosexual love).

The suggestion of sex games and S/M seems a little out of place, but you can trust Pier Paolo Pasolini and the team not to finish up this far-flung fantasy in wholly expected terms. But when the music swells up and the kissing starts, the world of heterosexual normality is rapidly re-instated (the final image of *The Arabian Nights* is a close-up of Franco Merli, lying on the bed, looking at Zumurrud, happy. Plus the glycerine tears, of course). It is as sappy, as simplistic, as dumb, and as unconvincing as any 'happy ending' in any movie in film history.

The Canterbury Tales (1972).
This page and over.

Pasolini's cameo in The Canterbury Tales

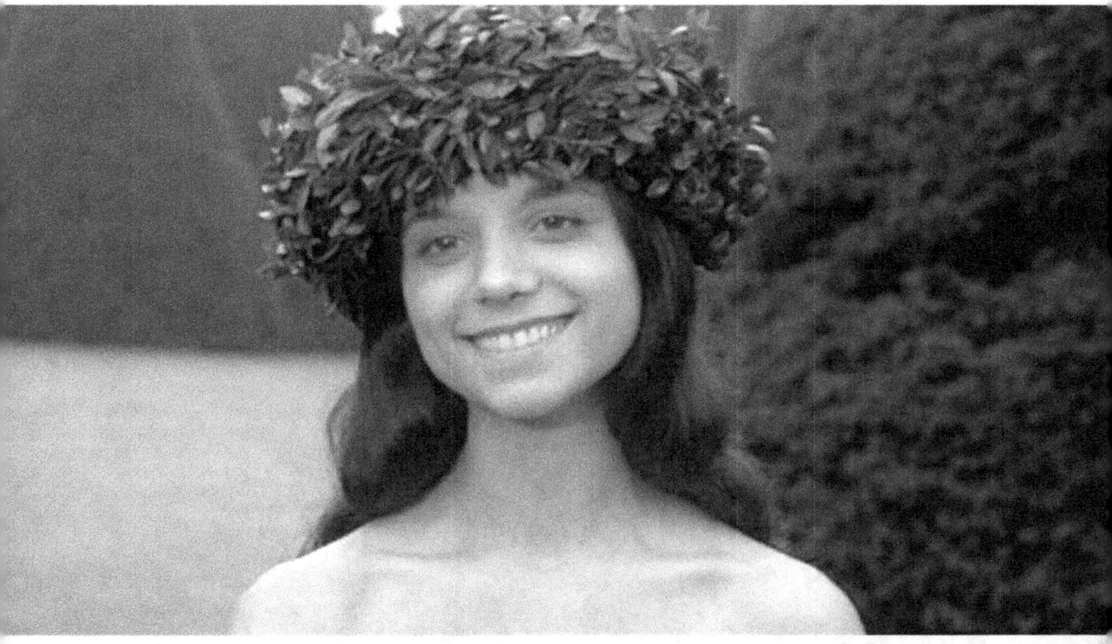

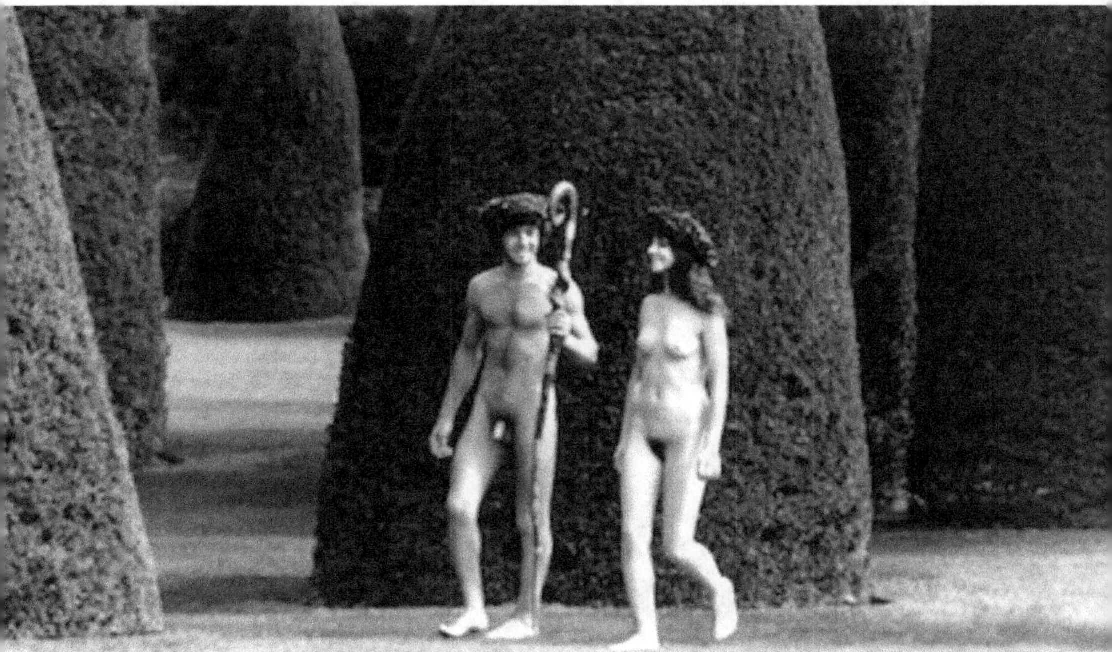

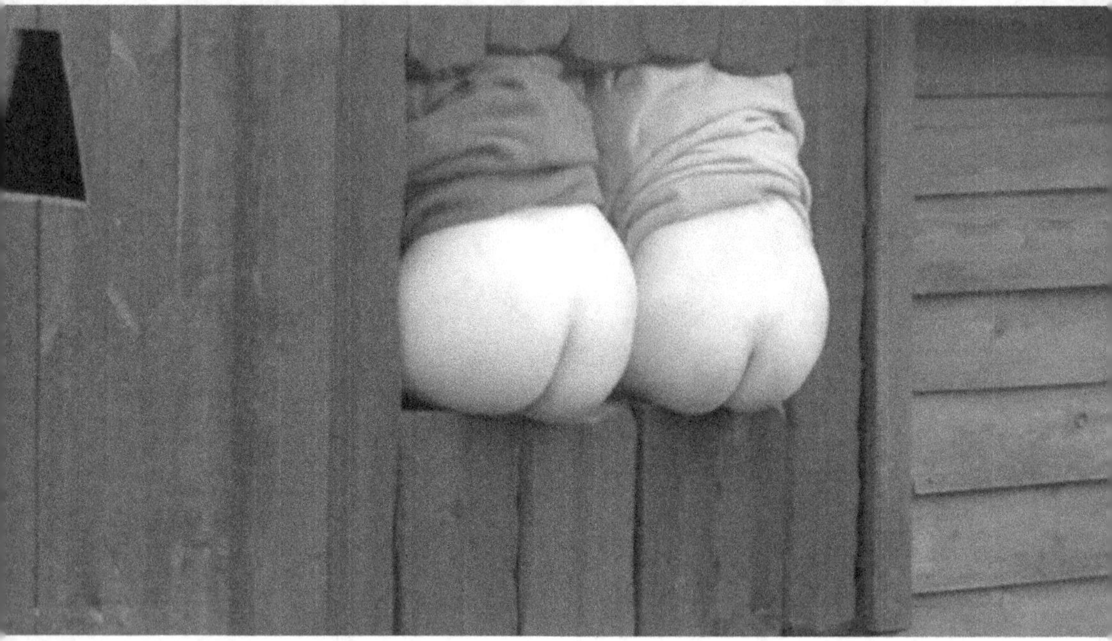

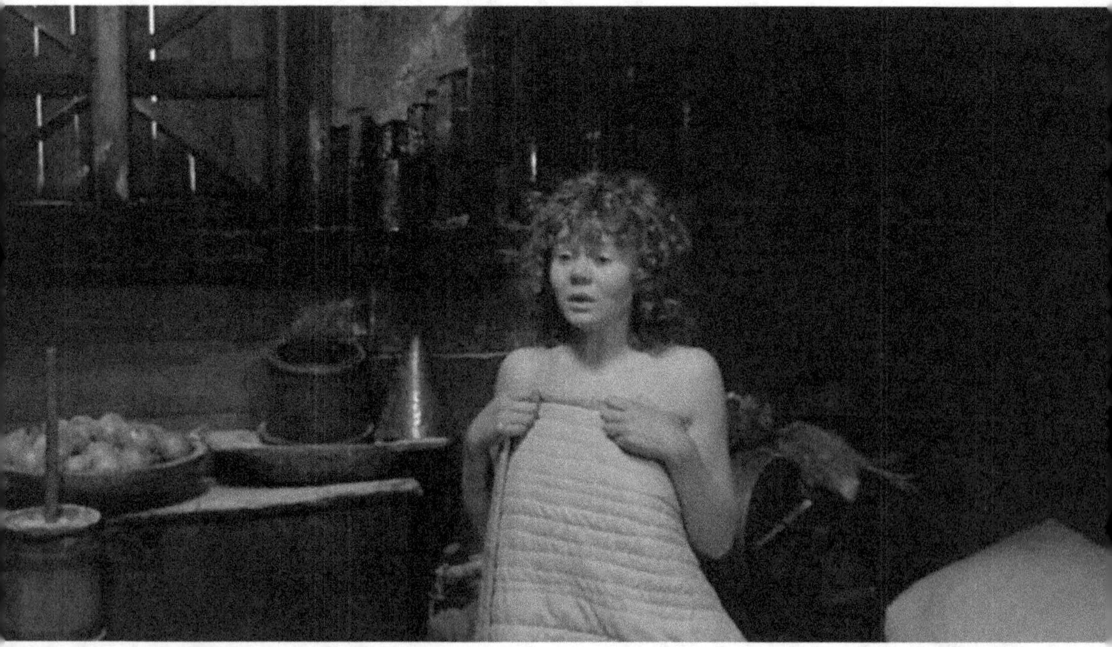

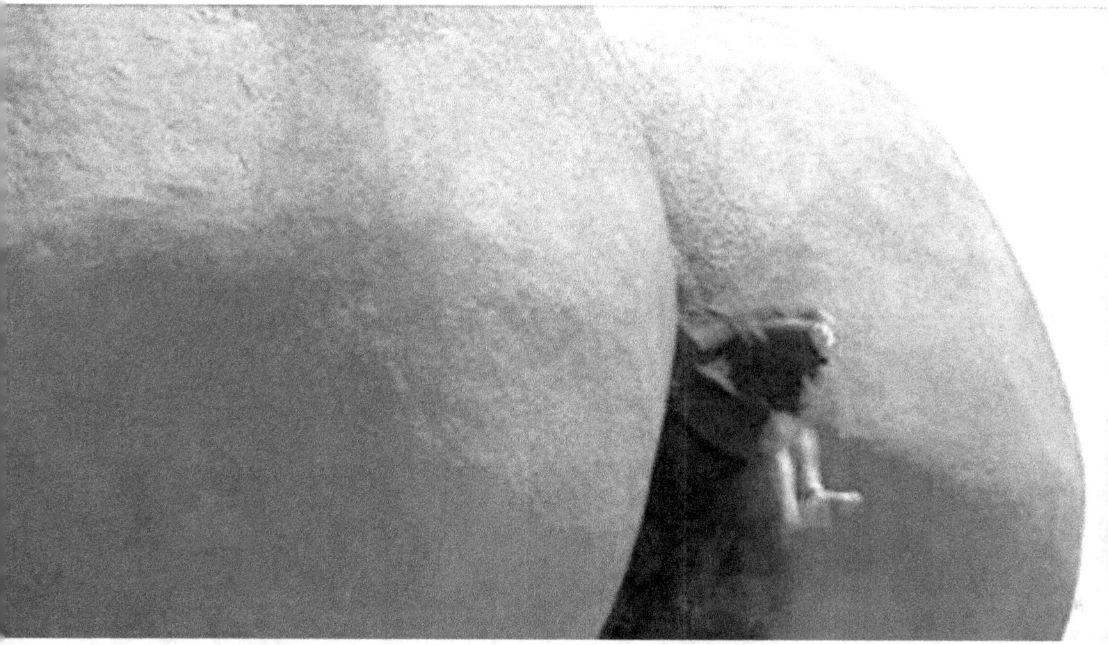

We are going to visit Hell.

The Arabian Nights (1974).
This page and over.

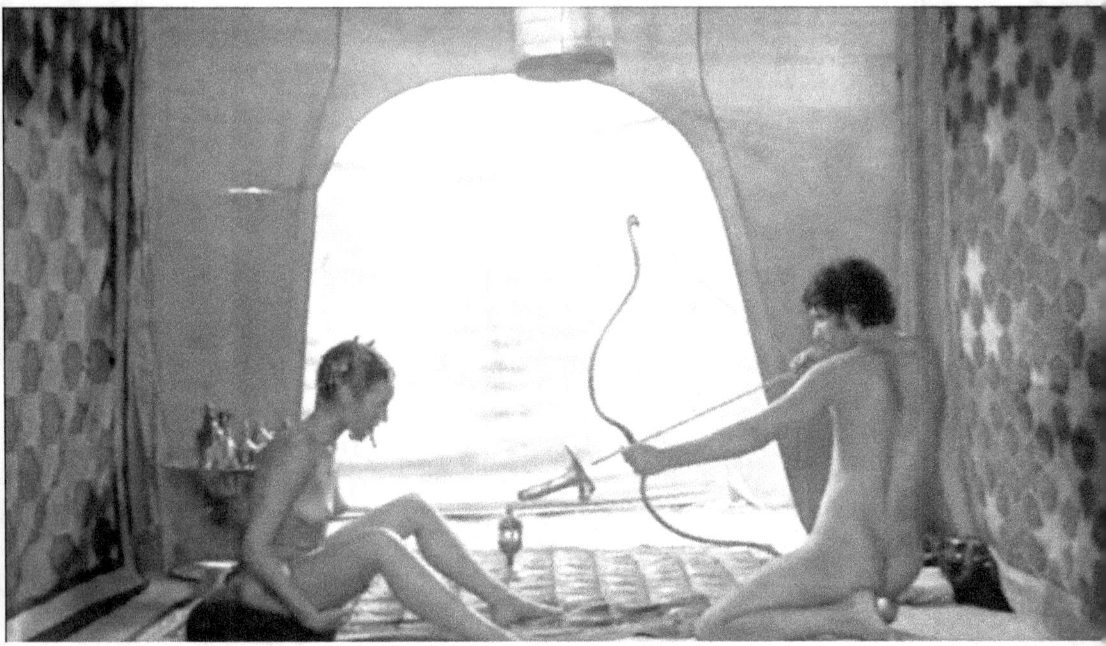

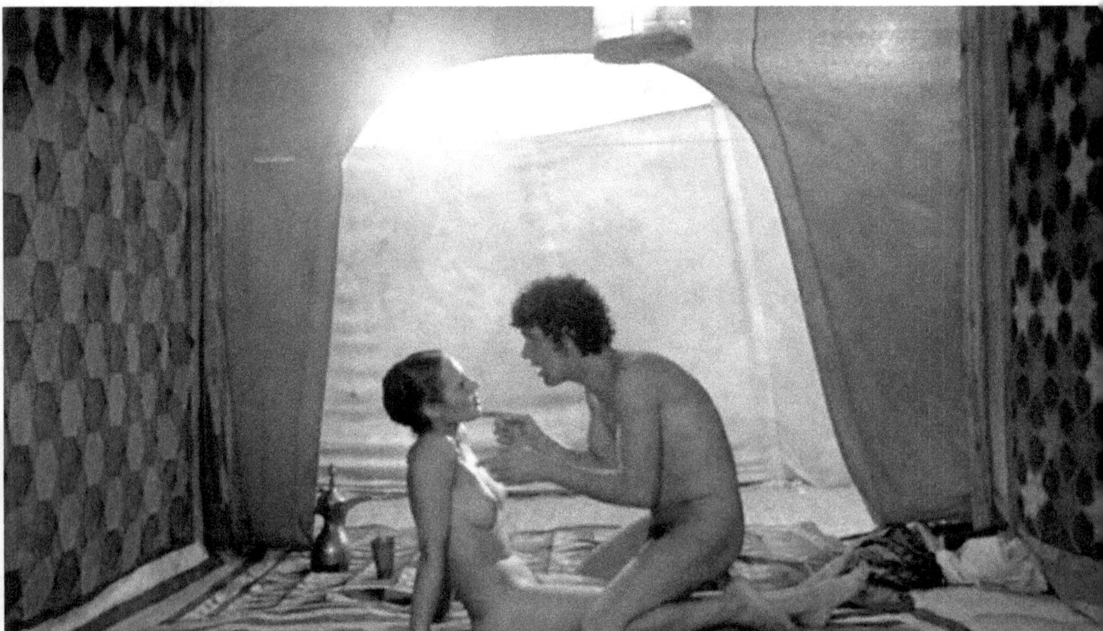

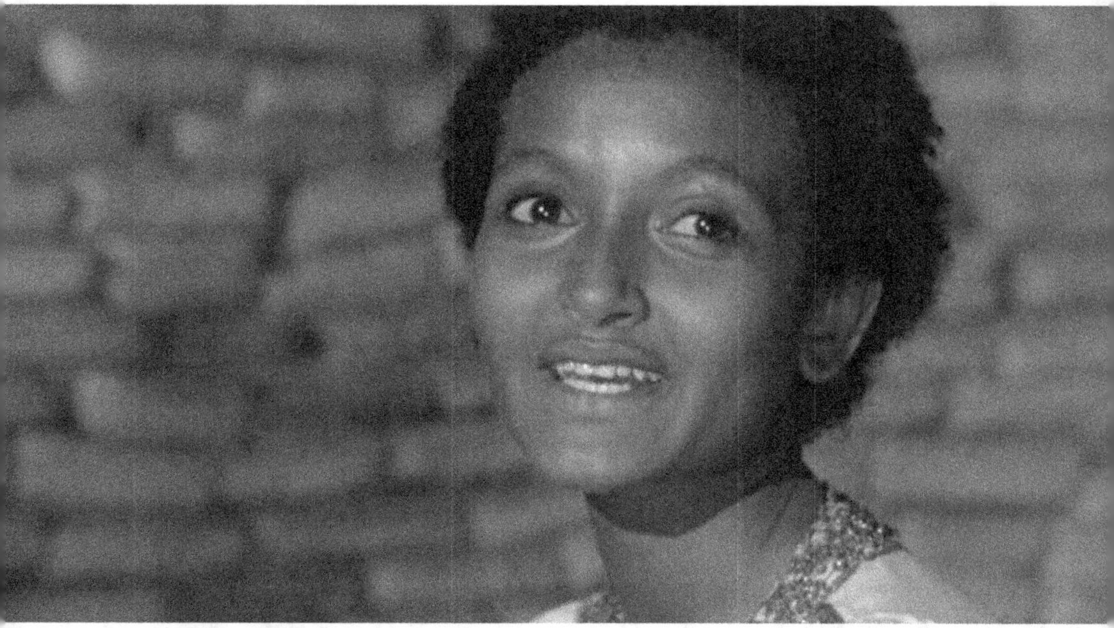

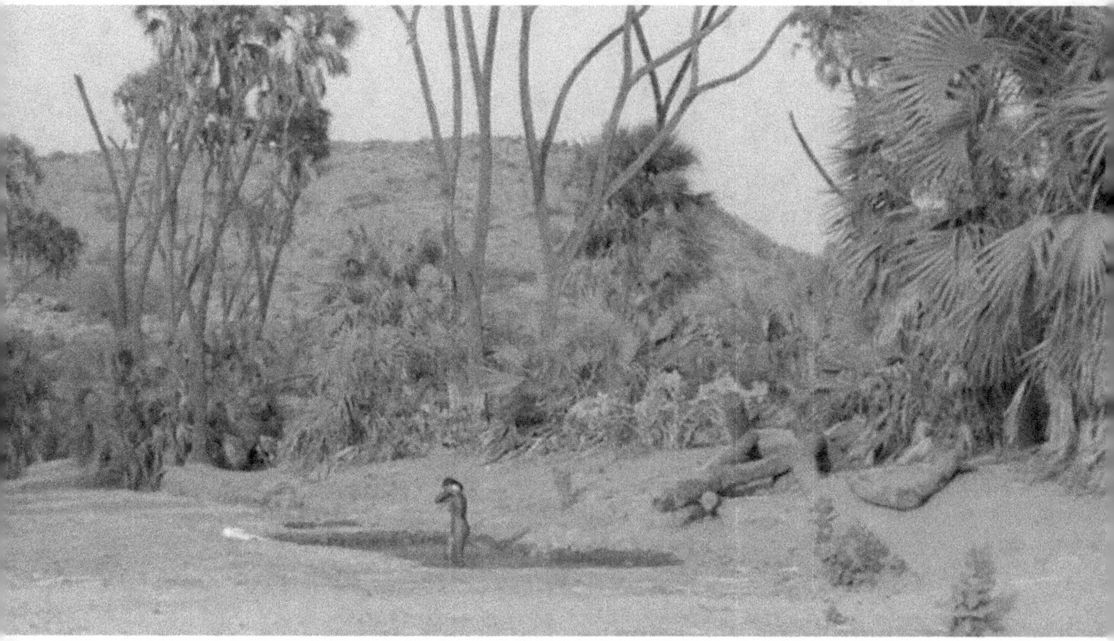

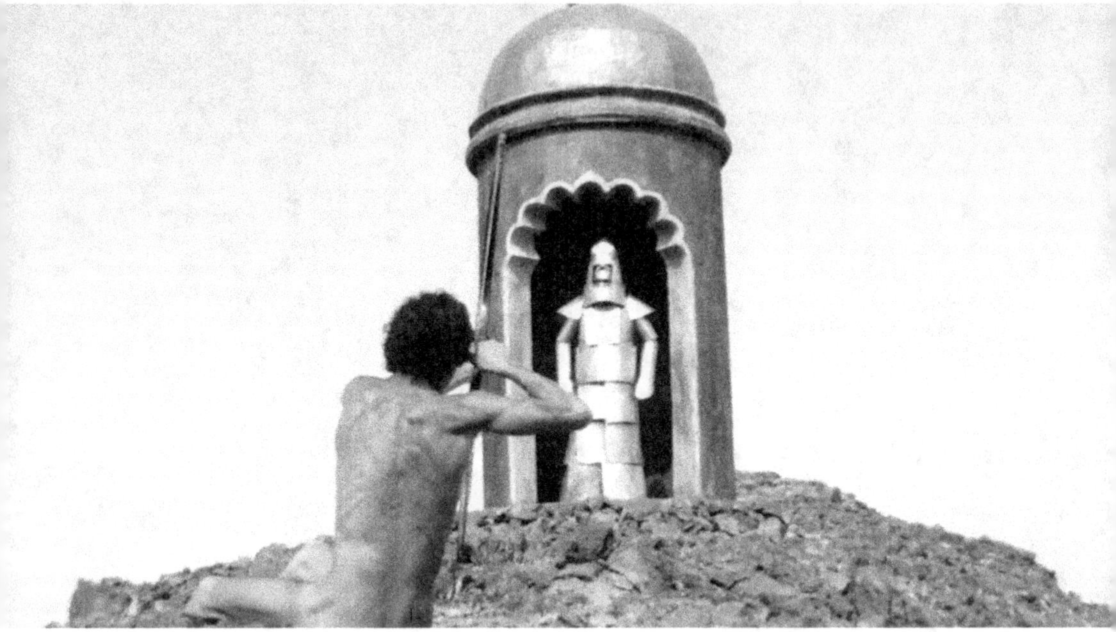

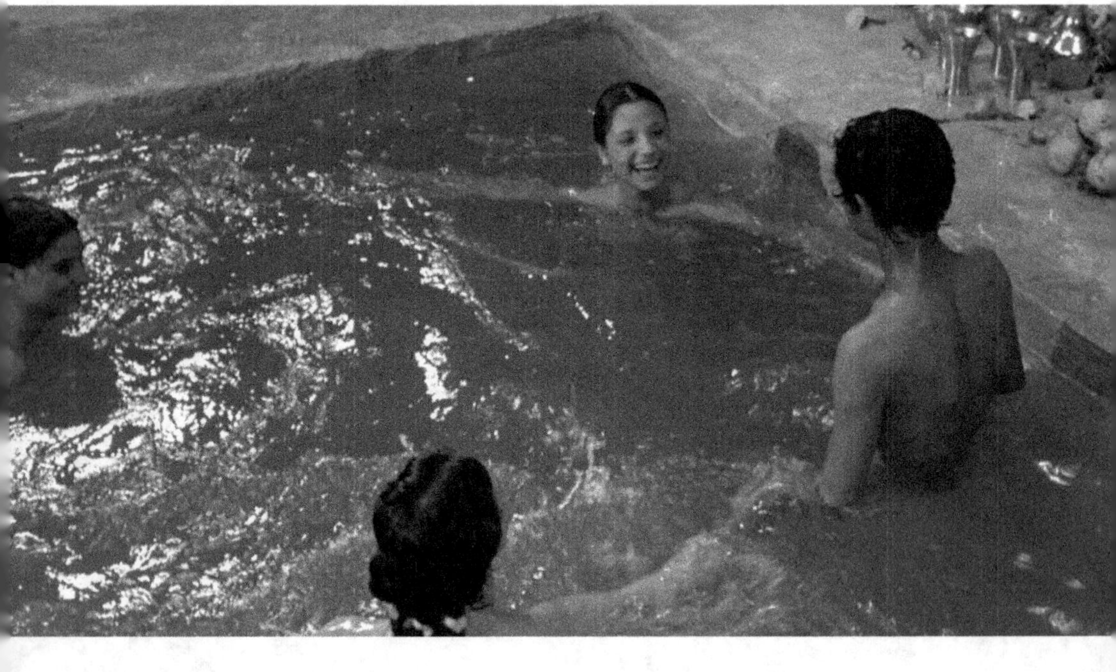

18

SALO, O LE 120 GIORANTE DI SODOMA

SALO, OR THE 120 DAYS OF SODOM

My friend, sensual pleasure was always the dearest of my possessions. I have worshipped it all my life and I wish to embrace it to my end.

Marquis de Sade, *Dialogue entre un Prêtre et un Moribond* (1782)

One should never hope for anything. Hope is a thing invented by politicians to keep the electorate happy.

Pier Paolo Pasolini (1975)

INTRO.

...A man lies on his back and forces a girl to piss over him...

...A man shits on the floor (in front of 30 people), then orders a girl to eat his fæces...

...A man fucks a young woman from behind while another guy in turn does him...

...A youth is staked to the ground and has his tongue cut out...

It can only be *Salò, o Le 120 Giornate di Sodoma*,[1] the last feature movie directed by Pier Paolo Pasolini.[2]

Salò, o Le 120 Giornate di Sodoma (= *Salò, or The 120 Days of Sodom*, 1975) had some high power credits: it was *un film scritto e*

---
[1] The film's title brings together Italy and France, fascism and de Sade.
[2] Before his death on the night of Nov 1-2, 1975.

diretto da Pier Paolo Pasolini from the Marquis de Sade's 1785 novel *The 120 Days of Sodom*, with assistance with the screenplay from Sergio Citti and Pupi Avati, produced by Alberto Grimaldi, Alberto De Stefanis and Antonio Girasante for Produzioni Europee Associate S.p.A. (Roma) and Les Productions Artistes Associés S.A. (Paris), Ennio Morricone was music advisor,[3] Dante Ferretti was production designer, Enzo Ocone was supervising editor, Nino Baragli was editor, Danilo Donati was costume designer (Vanni Castellani was wardrobe assistant, and Sartoria Farani created some costumes), make-up by Alfredo Tiberi, hair by Giuseppina Bovino, wigs and special make-up by Carboni-Roccohetti, special make-up by Sergio Chiusi, Umberto Angelucci was A.D., sound[4] was by Domenico Pasquadibisceglie and Giorgio Loviscek, and Tonino Delli Colli was DP (in short, a very strong and very talented group of film-makers, many of whom had worked with the maestro for years, and some of them right back to his first film, *Accattone*, in 1961).

Principal photography ended on May 16, 1975. *Salò* was completed by the end of October, 1975. The film is in the standard 35mm ratio of 1:1.85. Technicolor. (The movie, as usual in Italian cinema, was entirely looped). Released November 22, 1975 – it premiered in Paris (Italian release: Dec 23,[5] 1975). 118 minutes.[6]

The *Salò, or The 120 Days of Sodom* project did not originate with Pier Paolo Pasolini: Sergio Citti had developed the idea, and Pasolini helped him with the screenplay. Pasolini became more interested in the concept as they co-wrote it, while Citti lost interest and moved onto other projects (by this time, Citti was forging his own career as a film director; he had recently directed *Ostia*, 1970 and *Bawdy Tales*, 1973).

Among *Salò*'s cast it's likely you will not recognize a single actor, unless you have seen other Pier Paolo Pasolini movies, or other Italian movies and TV of the era. With many of his films, Pasolini cast at least one known face among the cast (such as Anna Magnani, Totò, Jean-Pierre Léaud and Terence Stamp) – possibly at the behest of his producers/backers. Here, none.[7] Instead, *Salò, or The 120 Days of Sodom* is sold with two names:

---

[3] The music in *Salò, or The 120 Days of Sodom* includes a piano version of 'These Foolish Things', Mikhail Glinka (*Nocturne In F Minor*), and Frédéric Chopin (*Prelude 28: 17* and *Valse* 34: 2). Pasolini had planned to use *Carmina Burana* by Carl Orff – 'typical fascist music', as he called the now very famous music.
[4] The sound mixes were in mono.
[5] Released at Yuletide, it's the Ultimate Non-Christmas or Anti-Christmas Movie!
[6] Running times on the home format releases range from 1h 51m to 1h 56m. (Some of the variations are due to the speed up of 4% for P.A.L. systems).
[7] One reason is probably the kind of things the cast are asked to do in *Salò:* Marlon Brando might bugger Maria Schneider in *Last Tango In Paris* (yes, while keeping his clothes on!), but would he want another guy kneeling over him and taking *him*? Well, 1,000s of actors and actresses wouldn't want to do that!

PASOLINI DE SADE

(Indeed, Pier Paolo Pasolini taking on de Sade would be enough to bring a few punters into a cinema in Italy in 1975).[8]

Salò, or The 120 Days of Sodom's cast included Paolo Bonacelli[9] (Blangis), Giorgio Cataldi (the Bishop), Umberto Palo Quintavalle (Curval), Aldo Valletti (Durcet), Caterina Boratto (Signora Castelli, the narrator), Elsa De Girgio (Signora Maggi) and Hélène Surgère (Signora Vaccari). However, there are two name actors in *Salò, o Le 120 Giornate di Sodoma* in the voice dubbing: Bonacelli was dubbed by Michel Piccoli and Laura Betti dubbed Hélène Surgère. In Italy, Giancarlo Vigorelli dubbed Bonacelli, Marco Bellocchio dubbed Aldo Vitlletti, Giorgio Caproni dubbed Giorgio Cataldi and Aurelio Roncaglia dubbed Umberto Quintavalle. Some of the actors were friends of the director (such as Valletti and Betti).

It's odd that Laura Betti, one of Pasolini's favourite actresses, wasn't cast as one of the four matriarchs in *Salò, o Le 120 Giornate di Sodoma*; however, she was appearing in *1900* (*Novenceto*, 1976), filmed at the same time, nearby. Betti did, tho', supply the voice of Hélène Surgère (playing Signora Vaccari – which she would've played had she appeared in *Salò*. Surgère tells several stories in the first half of *Salò*, so Betti's contribution as her voice was considerable). Franco Citti might've played one of the collaborators.

Other actors in *Salò, or The 120 Days of Sodom* included: Ezio Manni as the Collaborator; Inès Pellegrini as the Slave Girl; Sergio Fascetti; Bruno Musso as Carlo Porro; Antonio Orlando as Tonino; Claudio Cicchetti; Franco Merli; Umberto Chessari; Lamberto Book (Gobbi); Gaspare di Jenno as Rino; Giuliana Melis; Faridah Malik as Fatimah; Graziella Aniceto; Renata Moar; Dorit Henke; Antiniska Nemour; Benedetta Gaetani; and Olga Andreis as Eva. Some of the characters take their names from the actors playing them (such as Franco, Claudio and Sergio).

If you've seen the later Pier Paolo Pasolini movies, you will recognize Franco Merli and Ines Pellegrini in amongst the large cast – they were Nuredin and Zumurrud in *The Arabian Nights*. And for once Ninetto Davoli *isn't* cavorting thru this movie with his trademark

---
[8] Gideon Bachmann: 'The Marquis de Sade couldn't have found a better interpreter. Pasolini was making a film against fascism, maybe, but he was also making a film that showed how deeply anchored in our souls cruelty and destructiveness really are.'

[9] Paolo Bonacelli appeared in *Caligula* (1979), a film which seems partly inspired by the erotica of the 'trilogy of life' series. Incidentally, several others from Pasolini's team worked on *Caligula*, including Danilo Donati and Nino Baragli.

permanent, goofy grin! (Anyway, who would Davoli play in *Salò*? Not one of the victims, and seeing Davoli as one of the soldiers or collaborators would be uncomfortable[10]).

As to the locations of *Salò, or The 120 Days of Sodom*, the scene where the candidates are chosen is Villa Feltrinelli (the former home of Benito Mussolini – it's now a hotel); the bridge where prisoners try to escape is on Via Gardeletta, at Gardeletta. The main mansion is Villa Aldini, Via dell'Osservanza 35, Bologna (for the exteriors). Some interiors were filmed in the Villa Gonzaga-Zani in Villimpenta, and Villa Riesenfeld, Pontemerlano, near Mantua (it was abandoned, and adapted by the production). Villa Mirra at Cavriana, near Mantua, was also used. The round-up was staged in a public park near Bologna. The courtyard and interiors were filmed at Cinecittà Studios.

Salò, o Le 120 Giornate di Sodoma was not filmed in secret, miles from anywhere; it was produced at Cinecittà in Roma and on location in Mantua. And it had people photographing and filming it (U.S. journalist Gideon Bachmann[11] kept a diary of the production, and was also involved with a filmed record (some of the footage has appeared in documentaries about *Salò*. The documentary cameras covered the final week of photography, the torture scenes in the finale, filmed at Cinecittà).)

The film was dubbed at Alberto Grimaldi's Produzioni Europee Associate studios in Viale Oceano Pacifico in Rome (also the production office for the movie), during July, 1975.

Pier Paolo Pasolini was directly involved in the sound mixing for the French version of *Salò, or The 120 Days of Sodom* (he went to Paris to oversee the French dub in Oct, 1975). Apparently, Pasolini considered the French version to be the 'official' one.[12]

Several versions of the film exist. *Salò, or The 120 Days of Sodom* originally ran 145 minutes, but Pier Paolo Pasolini took out 25 minutes for story pacing reasons (some versions have been released by Gaumont/ Columbia, Criterion Collection, British Film Institute and others). There are slight differences of running times, the odd scene, and elements such as the quotation of a poem by Gottfried Benn lasting 25s.

*

Like *Apocalypse Now, Cleopatra, Heaven's Gate* and *Basic Instinct*, *Salò, o Le 120 Giornate di Sodoma* was one of those movies about which people have asked: just what went on during filming? Did actors

---

10 Apparently, Davoli was going to play one of the collaborators, Claudio.
11 Gideon Bachmann had been making a film about Pasolini during 1975; it was planned to be a biographical portrait as well as about artists and art. It remained unfinished, altho' interviews had been filmed, plus the last week of principal photography of *Salò, or The 120 Days of Sodom* at Cinecittà.
12 I'm not sure why.

really eat shit on film? Was the sex simulated or real? Did anybody get paid?

Salò is one of those films that will *never* be broadcast on a major television network in many parts of the world (even at four in the morning), unless maybe the Roman Empire or the Third Reich is resurrected. *Salò* is problematic in pretty much every way.

If there really was a Fascist, Sadeian Holiday Camp[13] as depicted in *Salò, or The 120 Days of Sodom* – let's call it Hotel Sodom or Hotel De Sade – where orgies were the first and the only item on the daily schedule, it would be popular with a certain section of the global population. (It would be built in Las Vegas, of course. In fact, the Fifth Level of Hell already has an outlet branch on the Vegas Strip – you take the elevators down from street level next to the M.G.M. Grand. More people than you'd think are willing to pay the high price of entry – your soul[14]).

Salò, or The 120 Days of Sodom doesn't come out of nowhere – this is Pier Paolo Pasolini we're talking about! Consider the tortures and horrors that're performed for the libertines in *Salò*. Well, Pasolini-sensei had already filmed similar scenes of archaic, violent rituals in movies such as *Medea* and *Porcile,* where victims're killed and eaten, or have their blood strewn over field crops. Pasolini's movies are fond of ceremonies conducted in a slow, arcane (and somewhat chilly) manner. If the rites feature sensational elements – like cannibalism or slaughter – all the better! (By the way, Italian cinema in the 1970s was still churning out horror and *gialli* movies, which contained plenty of graphic violence.)

Salò, or The 120 Days of Sodom isn't interested in staging grand scenes, or humanizing or characterizing the victims. It's anti-grand, anti-arty, anti-emotional, anti-operatic. (If it were turned into a Broadway theatre musical (!), *Salò, or The 120 Days of Sodom* – a sort of *Hair* meets *Sweeney Todd* meets Grand Guignol – it would be really boring, because all of the emo-psycho-spirito-socio ingredients and the amazing potential for theatrical wackola would be ditched by the Stern Schoolmistress of a Stage Director).

✻

Salò, or The 120 Days of Sodom is a film-text that can (and has) been interpreted in many ways: the sex-death-violence-nudity aspects are merely the flashy top level that grabs the attention. Power (the abuses of power) is a far more pertinent layer to *Salò* than sex or nudity. Con-

---
13 A Hogwarts boarding school for pervs and psychos.
14 But you do get two free drinks per soul – three if it's a party of ten.

sumerism, the degradation of neo-capitalism and commodification, are absolutely fundamental issues in this movie (as Pasolini explained in interviews). The violent treatment of the body in political systems is key, too. Another layer is the lament over the destruction of Ye Olde Italie.

Salò, or The 120 Days of Sodom is also an attack on the apparent 'freedom' of consumerism, the illusion of 'progression' of capitalism, and the over-reliance on the individual pursuing their own goals of a better standard of living (degrading the emphasis on community and the socialist projects of Communism). The 'me' society, the 'greed is good' society.

The script for *Salò, or The 120 Days of Sodom* was precisely worked out: Pier Paolo Pasolini wanted the actors to speak the lines as written, even though the entire movie was looped. It's customary for Italian movies to have dialogue changed during dubbing, or rewritten, but for *Salò, or The 120 Days of Sodom* the script was retained. Also, the screenplay was filmed as written, though inevitably some scenes were shot but cut out (and some footage was stolen in Oct, 1975).

THE MARQUIS DE SADE.

God of the Surrealists, of French intellectuals and bohemians, and Grand Vizier of pornographers, wannabe trendies and avant gardists, Donatien-Alphonse-François de Sade, a.k.a. the Marquis de Sade (1740-1814), is the controversial author of 4 novels, short stories, plays, dialogues, letters, journals and pamphlets (including *Justine, Philosophy of the Bedroom, The Story of Juliette* and *Les Cent Vingt Journés de Sodome*). De Sade's was a notorious life, leading to a number of spells in prison (prostitutes, attempts on his life, run-ins with the police, accused of poisoning Marseilles hookers, etc).[15] He apparently indulged in some of the sadomasochistic practices described in his fiction (some of which led to his imprisonment); that's part of the Sadeian myth and legend, of course.[16]

The Marquis de Sade has been exalted to the status of Major Philosopher for many Euro-intellectuals, taking his place alongside Friedrich Nietzsche, Sigmund Freud, Karl Marx and Jean-Paul Sartre.

And the Marquis de Sade himself has been the subject of many movies and famous plays, including the plays *Marat/ Sade, Sade, Divine Marquis, Lost Cherry Orchard* and *Quills,* horror flicks from Jess Franco

---

15 According to Gérard Zwang, 'it is because of excessive imprisonment and vindictive and cowardly censorship that Sade has been put on a pedestal and consecrated a martyr, great philosopher, major writer and specialist in eroticism' (quoted in B. Groult, 69).

16 We want to believe that notorious writers are *really* notorious! And not just like everybody else after all.

(*Justine, Eugenie*) and Hammer horror, such as *The Skull* (with the Marquis as a villain or monster), to lit'ry, arty fare such as *De Sade* (1969), *Justine de Sade* (1972), *Cruel Passion* (1977), and the play and film *Quills* (2000). Richard Matheson, Peter Brook, Tobe Hooper, Luis Buñuel, Philip Kaufman, Jan Svankmajer and others have taken on de Sade as a person or character, and he's been played by Klaus Kinski, Christopher Lee, Geoffrey Rush, Keir Dullea, Patrick Magee, Robert Englund and Daniel Auteuil.

The Marquis de Sade has been a high profile and much-loathed target for feminists. Andrea Dworkin decimated de Sade in her 1983 book *Pornography*. 'The commercialized sex movement's theoreticians have unearthed the Marquis de Sade and undertaken to deify him', noted Benoîte Groult in "Les Portiers de Nuit" (69).

Benoîte Groult summarizes the work of Georges Bataille, the Marquis de Sade and Henry Miller as 'monstrous selfishness, morbid scatology, and the most classic of sado-anal regressions'. It's grim stuff for Groult: 'there is not the slightest trace of a kiss in the works of these morticians, not the slightest tenderness'.[17]

The 120 Days of Sodom (*Les Cent Vingt Journés de Sodome*, 1785) was written in the Bastille prison. in Paris[18] It concerns four aristocrats (they are described as libertines/ perpetrators/ collaborators/ lusty fuckers) who form a cabal devoted to sexual pleasure; three of their wives join the inter-related group, as well as one of their daughters, and four women who procure their victims (as well as recount stories). There are also four decaying, elderly women. And eight boys and girls, all teenagers, and eight youths (16 victims), also described by de Sade as 'lusty fuckers'.[19] (In the film version, the four tycoons are representatives of modern, Italian society: a Duke, a Judge (magistrate), a Businessman and a Bishop.[20] They embody institutions such as wealth/ privilege, the bourgeoisie, capitalism, the law, and religion).

The victims are interchangeable, but so is everybody else. There are four categories of participants in *Salò, or The 120 Days of Sodom:* 1. libertines; 2. courtesans (and storytellers); 3. accomplices; and 4. victims. (It's a condensation of social roles rather like a mediæval tale, where you have kings/ queens, merchants, artisans, soldiers and peasants). The number four in the film also extended to the soldiers aiding the operation, the four daughters lined up for marriage, and so on.

---

17 As for giving pleasure, forget it! There's no mention of the clitoris, for instance, 'since the 'heroes' give no thought to wasting their time by arousing female pleasure'.
18 It was rediscovered in 1904. It had been rescued by a guard during the revolution.
19 See M. Crosland, 2000.
20 The libertines were not proletarian or peasant class, Pasolini explained, they were cultured, they could quote from French philosophers.

Incest is a much bigger issue in the Marquis de Sade's laugh riot novel of 1785 than in the 1975 movie (incest, like anal sex, seems to really titillate French pornographers). Thus, that each of the libertines has had sexual relations with their daughters is a given, but the film adaptation doesn't make much of that. (However, the aristos offer their daughters to each other in an early scene, which is a correspondence with de Sade's incest theme).

It is not only the sexual perversions explored in *Les Cent Vingt Journés de Sodome* that interested Pier Paolo Pasolini, but other aspects of the Marquis de Sade's story: for instance, that the four procuresses also tell tales (storytelling is an important ingredient in Pasolini's cinema – the 'trilogy of life' films had been founded on it, and even Jesus in *The Gospel According To Matthew* is a storyteller,[21] and the *Scriptures* themselves are also stories. Notice how the libertines demand imaginative tales with full details, and aren't satisfied unless their demands are met (the first story in *Salò, o Le 120 Giornate di Sodoma* is interrupted to make this clear): like film producers, they command the storytellers to deliver the goods, to arouse them. Porn must be titillating, and telling a good anecdote becomes more important than whatever the story is about – sex, adventures in distant galaxies, or lawnmowers).

The stories told by the ladies tend to be about under-age sex (to add to the shock value), and about lewd acts with old men, with an emphasis on anal sex, defecating, urination and the buttocks (however, they are heterosexual stories, although they're about child abuse).

According to the storytellers, the tales are actually memories, things that happened to them when they encountered pervy, old guys when they were pre-teens or teens. The stories are Sadeian skits, sketches told in the style of the Marquis de Sade's prose: the women remember being young girls who were preyed upon by old men; following defecation or the caressing of the all-important ass, the stories end with ejaculation. Thus, the tales adhere to the standard format of pornography: some scene-setting, the first meeting, the undressing, the foreplay and groping, intercourse and the orgasm.

The unreality and high fantasy of the scenario in the *120 Days of Sodom* novel by the Marquis de Sade – a group of aristos who cut themselves off from the rest of the world to indulge their desires – would also appeal to Pier Paolo Pasolini.[22] The aristocrats are like artists, but very rich, who have the funds and resources to recreate a world to their own liking (a position very few filmmakers have enjoyed!).

---

21 Philip Pullman describes Jesus as one of the greatest storytellers in history.
22 'Rendering Sade's decadent Salon as a sort of homicidal boarding school' (Gary Indiana, 56).

The 120 Days of Sodom was written while the Marquis de Sade was in prison. It is set shortly before 1715. As Margaret Crosland describes in her excellent *De Sade Reader*, *The 120 Days of Sodom* came directly out of de Sade's experience of being behind bars:

> If his physical life was empty, his head was full of ideas. He now began to write the blackest of his books; blackest because no ray of light, no memory of what might have been happy or 'good' ever gleams through it. Sade conceived and wrote it (part of it, at least) as though the 'normal' world did not exist, and he may well have thought that even if it did, he might never see it again. (2000, 31)

That Pier Paolo Pasolini would take on the Marquis de Sade seems somewhat inevitable – de Sade being a perfect author for Pasolini (and for filmmakers like Jean-Luc Godard, Rainer Maria Fassbinder, Walerian Borowczyk and Luis Buñuel). And that Pasolini would do so in his own highly unusual manner is also to be expected (following the 'trilogia di vita' movies, it was certain that Pasolini and the team would deliver a unique take on de Sade's text. And they did. From the comedy and conservatism of the 'trilogy of life' movies, Pasolini and co. bounce back in the other direction, just as they did after the earnest ambience of *Medea* and *Pigsty* into the comedy of *The Decameron*). That the author was very controversial, and spent a good deal of his life in prison, or living in notoriety, added to the spice for Pasolini (he feels an immediate empathy with the underdog, with masochists, with those who've been persecuted. An author set against society (like, say, Jean Genet or Arthur Rimbaud) is the ideal material for Pasolini to adapt (and yet Pasolini also adapted works from conservative, very traditional authors, such as Ancient Greek mythology, Sophocles, Giovanni Boccaccio, Geoffrey Chaucer and the *Bible*).

The Marquis de Sade also possessed the childish urge to shock society, which Pier Paolo Pasolini also never grew out of (nor did the Surrealists and so many other avant gardists – and a good many filmmakers, too!). There is undoubtedly an urge to upset audiences in the *Salò, or The 120 Days of Sodom* film, a conscious effort to find *something* that will angrify someone in the audience.

After the Marquis de Sade, the fiction of Henry Miller, Jean Genet,[23] Georges Bataille and even William Burroughs seems a mere postscript. This extract from *The 120 Days of Sodom* is typical:

> Curval, who had not been experiencing such an onslaught, blasphemed

---
[23] Bruce Kawin and Gerald Mast in *A Short History of the Movies* link the four pillars of society represented by the four fascists to themes in the plays of Jean Genet (338).

with joy. He quivered in excitement, opened his legs wide and prepared himself. At that moment the youthful sperm of the charming boy he was masturbating dripped down to the enormous tip of his frenzied instrument. This warm sperm which drenched him, the repeated shuddering of the duke who was beginning to discharge also, everything led him on, everything brought on his climax and floods of foaming sperm flooded Durcet's arse.[24]

We talk all the time about Pier Paolo Pasolini in relation to *Salò, or The 120 Days of Sodom*, but of course we have to remember that he co-wrote the picture with Pupi Avati and Sergio Citti (and in this movie, the script is the foundation of the entire enterprise). And also, it was Citti who developed the project initially, before handing it to Pasolini. In additon, it was the Divine Marquis, bless his twisted mind, that came up with the scenario: four aristos who gather a host of victims for 120 days of naughtiness and nastiness in a mansion.

Si, si – Salò, o Le 120 Giornate di Sodoma is the fiction of Marquis de Sade by way of Georges Bataille and Jean-Luc Godard, but if you know those authors, and also writers such as Arthur Rimbaud, William Burroughs and Henry Miller, you'll know that the movie *Salò* isn't a patch on any of them. Burroughs in *The Naked Lunch*, Miller in *Tropic of Cancer*, and Bataille in *The Story of O* had not only already explored the same territory of coercion, power, excess and extremism in terms of politics and sex (sexual politics and political sex),[25] they had also done it better, quicker, and *way* more radically and polemically.[26] (There is, however, an added jolt in *seeing* this kind of material on a movie screen, compared to reading it in a novel. One imagines that de Sade himself would be delighted).

PASOLINI ON SET.

There are several documentaries about *Salò, or The 120 Days of Sodom,* including *Fade To Black* (2001), with Mark Kermode, *Salò: Yesterday and Today* (2002), *Pasolini Prossimo Nostro* (2006, Italian), *Enfants de Salò* (2006, French) and *The End of Salò* (2008).

In the video documentaries, you can see the Italian maestro at work at Cinecittà Studios making the film (some of the footage was filmed by Gideon Bachmann and co.). The 2002 documentary (*Salò: Yesterday and Today*) contains among the fullest footage of Pasolini working on set of

---

[24] Quoted in M. Crosland, 2000, 37.
[25] *Salò, o Le 120 Giornate di Sodoma* is very much a film of the mid-1970s, when (second wave) feminists and intellectuals spoke of the 'politics of sex', and 'sexual politics', the era when the issues of gender, sex and eroticism were politicized.
[26] De Sade is one of the key forerunners of the 'no limits' modernist tradition: Henry Miller, Pauline Réage, Jean de Berg, Emmanuelle Arsan, Géorges Bataille, William Burroughs, D.H. Lawrence, Anaïs Nin, etc.

any of his productions as director. The 2006 documentary (*Pasolini Prossimo Nostro*), directed by Giuseppe Bertolucci, comprises mainly on-set photographs, plus some of the same footage as the 2002 documentary, and several audio-only interviews with Pasolini, plus extracts from a filmed interview at the time of *Salò*.

In the documentaries, Pier Paolo Pasolini is clearly the leader on set, and everybody defers to him (i.e., he's the director-as-king in the Italian system). He often operates the *macchina fotografica* himself (here is definitely where some of the shaky camerawork in Pasolini's cinema originates!). And he is constantly directing the actors during the takes (he implores them, more screaming!,[27] or move over there, or he cues them). Thus, the production (live) sound of a Pasolini movie would consist primarily of the director talking to the actors (that would be the same in silent cinema), plus camera noise, plus wind noise, plus the mandatory jets and cars (which always appear out of nowhere as soon as you turn on a camera. Try it: go outside with a camera and try to film a quiet, emotional scene, and World War Three will break out and the sky will be full of B52-H bombers so you can't hear a thing).

Altho' *Salò, o Le 120 Giornate di Sodoma* isn't a bunch of laughs, and altho' it comes across as a deadly serious work, the filming of *Salò*, as the actors attest, was often filled with laughter as one of the teenage cast made a joke. If you only consider the movie, you'd think that *Salò, or The 120 Days of Sodom* was wall-to-wall horror and boredom for everyone concerned. But it wasn't: the shooting was something else – there was rehearsal, plenty of discussion, and the atmosphere on set was informal.

Salò, o Le 120 Giornate di Sodoma was filmed mainly in the studio for obvious reasons. Material as tricky as this to stage (plus a young and amateur cast) required the controllable and more comfortable environment of Cinecittà, Pasolini's home-from-home, and the adapted buildings in Mantua.

Pier Paolo Pasolini wanted the actors to stick to the script in *Salò, or The 120 Days of Sodom*. He was after takes which repeated the action, so it meshed. It wasn't a question, this time, of shooting material until the filmmakers had enough to create a movie (Pasolini's usual method).

REFERENCES, ALLUSIONS.

Salò, or The 120 Days of Sodom is a movie in which a list of intellectual writers and philosophers are part of the opening credits[28]

---

[27] Alas, none of those screams make the final cut – they're all dubbed.
[28] Accompanied by some *ersatz* jazz composed by Ennio Morricone.

(predominantly French literati such as Simone de Beauvoir, Philippe Sollers, Roland Barthes, Pierre Klossowski and Maurice Blanchot). The references in the 'Essential Bibliography' to left-wing writers and intellectuals makes the movie feel like an essay, a PhD thesis, perhaps. (Did you bring your notebook? Start writing those names down! There will be a test in tomorrow's class!).

The 'Essential Bibliography' of *Salò* includes:
- Roland Barthes: "Sade, Fourier, Loyola",
- Maurice Blanchot: "Lautréamont et Sade",
- Simone de Beauvoir: "Faut-il-brûler Sade",
- Pierre Klossowski: "Sade mon prochain, le philosophe scélérat",
- Philippe Sollers: "L'écriture et l'experience des limites".

Wait a minute – a film which opens with a list of philosophers and intellectuals? Are you kidding!? Talk about pretentious! Except we know that Pier Paolo Pasolini wasn't 'pretending'. Oh no, Pasolini was the real deal: that list of Euro-eggheads isn't put there to raise a laugh! Pasolini means it, *man*. (But the film doesn't mean it, always – the citations and hi-falutin' allusions are also derided. And anyway, in a film this savage in its satire or comedy or whatever it is, nothing is to be taken straight).

There are allusions to poets and poetry in *Salò, or The 120 Days of Sodom*: Dante Alighieri, Italy's national poet, inevitably (the four sections of the movie are titled: 'Ante-Inferno', 'Circle of Manias' ('Girone delle Manie'), 'Circle of Shit' ('Girone della Merda') and 'Circle of Blood' ('Girone del Sangue')). Thus, *Salò* might be as close as Pasolini got to filming *The Divine Comedy*. Other references include Charles Baudelaire, St Paul and Gottfried Benn. Plus Friedrich Nietzsche and J.-K. Huysmans (of course). Many modernist paintings decorate the walls of the villa (some are in the Italian Futurist style, others are Cubist, including Fernand Léger).

There are religious/ Catholic allusions in *Salò, or The 120 Days of Sodom*, too – inevitably for a Pasolini project: the first young woman to be led into the interview room and stripped is of course called Eva (Olga Andreis). As they sit in a bathtub covered in fæces, one of the young women cries out, 'Lord, why hast thou forsaken us?' (As you do – I mean, that's what *you* would yell out if you were sitting in a tub covered in filth, wouldn't you?). The allusion to the Crucifixion, in this particular context, makes a striking contrast with Pasolini's most celebrated film, *The Gospel According To Matthew*.[29]

---

[29] Eve Tushnet called *Salò, or The 120 Days of Sodom* 'even more uncompromisingly Christian than Pasolini's 1964 *The Gospel According To Saint Matthew*. *Salò* depicts a world of Christian anthropology without Christian eschatology – a world where human beings are made in the image of God, and there's no hope' (*America* magazine, Aug 23, 2019).

Characters aren't addressed by name, but by title or formal address – 'Signore', etc. The libertines aren't named (as they are in the Marquis de Sade's text). It's what they embody, socially and politically, that's more important – a Duke, a Banker, a Bishop, and a Judge. (However, some of the victims are named during the round-up, and sometimes the victims speak each other's names).[30]

The male victims include Franco Merli, Claudio Chiccetti, Carlo Porro, Tonino, Sergio Fascetti, Umberto Chessari, Rino and Lamberto Gobbi. The female victims include: Giuliana Melis, Fatimah, Eva, Dorit Henke, Benedetta Gaetini, Renata, Graziella and Antinska Nemour. The collaborators include: Bruno, Ezio, Claudio Troccoli and Fabrizio Menichini. The daughters include: Susanna Radaelli, Tatiana Mogilansky, Liana Acquaviva and Giuliana Orlandi. The storytellers include: Signora Vaccari, Signora Maggi and Signora Castelli. The studs include: Efisio Etzi, Guido Galletti, Rinaldo Missaglia and Giuseppe Patruno.

The libertines are often portrayed as polite (though black-hearted); they sit about drinking coffee and spirits, they discuss their rules, and they comment on how their 120 days of orgies is unfolding. But they also lose it – some of them whip the victims in frenzy, or scream when the rules are broken or when a victim refuses to do something.

THE POLITICS OF *SALO*.

Salò, or The 120 Days of Sodom's set in the short-lived fascist state of Salò (= Italian Social Republic) in Northern Italy (the caption says 1944-45).[31] Pier Paolo Pasolini said it was about fascism and capitalism in the 1930s and 1940s. In *Salò* desire is unbridled, the lust for sex, death and torture is unfettered by social constraints.[32] Nothing impinges from outside on the activities inside the *palazzo*. The aristocrats seem to be free to do whatever they wish (they announce that they are operating without legal restraint).[33]

Salò is a town in Northern Italy on the Riviera Bresciana, and the name of the last republic of Benito Mussolini (following his rescue by the Nazis from the Abruzzi), between 1943 and 1945. Salò is thus employed as a shorthand term for both Italian fascism and German fascism (and European fascism). A journalist, Mussolini (1883-1945)

---

30 As the brief exchange between the libertines and the victims in the round-up shows, some of the aristos have had their eye on particular youths in the region.
31 The sound of planes is mixed behind the action throughout the movie, the cheapest and easiest way of suggesting that the military conflict continues in the outside world.
32 'Pasolini's film is not about sex but the death of sex', noted Naomi Greene, very obviously.
33 The aristocrats are kings who're being waited on and pleasured: they don't lift a finger. Instead, it's their four wives who act as brothel madames and pimps, preparing the victims for the delectation of their masters.

became the leader of the fascist movement in Italy following WWI. King Victor Emmanuel appointed Mussolini Prime Minister; by 1928, Mussolini had aligned Italian politics with fascism, disbanded opposing political parties, and attempted to emulate Germany (Mussolini was in love with the corporate appearance of fascist power at the same time as ruthlessly suppressing any opposition. Mussolini's regime also had an impact on the Italian film business).

It's also the North of Italy as the realm of the father, for Pier Paolo Pasolini personally – Bologna and the North was his father's world – Carlo Alberto Pasolini (he gives one of the characters his father's name; and other names have personal resonances, such as Sergio. There are references to Bologna, Milano, etc).

One of the reasons that Pier Paolo Pasolini said he set the story in WW2 and in Northern Italy was because it was a time and place he knew. It was far enough away from the present to make it convincing, but without it being too fairy tale-ish or allegorical had it been set in the Marquis de Sade's era.

In other words, keeping it real, as they say – for the same reason that other historical movies plump for an earlier era that's not too far from the present day. (Also, thousands of movies go back to the 1920s-1940s, a favourite era for all the obvious reasons. Francis Coppola, Steven Spielberg, George Lucas, Woody Allen, Alan Rudolph and Brian de Palma are some well-known examples among North American directors. Many European *auteurs* also revisit that period).

But the story, Pier Paolo Pasolini also insisted, could be set in any era – humans are cruel, and cruelty has been part of human history since forever. The 1975 film was about oppression, about those who exploit and those who are exploited, and about the disturbing links between oppression and submission. So it could've been set in Ancient Rome or contemporary New York.

'Power is anarchy,[34] says Pier Paolo Pasolini – power would like to abolish history and overcome nature. History and nature can be abolished and overcome through sex,' is how Enzo Siciliano sums up the theme of *Salò* (ES, 387).

For Pasolini, it seems that the theme of domination and submission was uppermost, and more significant than any of the other themes, such as sex, or exploitation, or consumerism, or the decline of modern Italy, or even political fascism. As the maestro explained to Gideon Bachmann:

> The common phenomenon is the instinct of submission, which in man is

---
[34] 'We fascists are the only true anarchists', Blangis boasts.

as strong, undoubtedly, as that of domination. Throughout history there have been stratifications of a social nature based on this dialectic. What we call the class struggle today is only one form of it; it was neither de Sade nor Marx, and certainly not myself, who have invented the tensions between the oppressor and the oppressed; these are as old as agriculture and perhaps as old as hunting. Most likely all our social organization, our pecking order as you might say, is based on it.

As Pasolini noted: 'where de Sade says God, I say Power; he was against the power over man's beliefs, I am against the power over man's body.' This puts *Salò, or The 120 Days of Sodom* into the same critical field as the philosophical debates about the body and slavery that you find in the writing of Michel Foucault[35] or 1970s second wave feminism. In *Salò*, the body is the site of the exploration of the issues of power, domination and submission.

> Louis Valentin: Can love exist without sado-masochistic relations?
> Pier Paolo Pasolini: It is inconceivable. But who started it? Sade or Masoch? It's the old story of the chicken and the egg. The equilibrium of these two forces is the result of human equilibrium. (1970)

When Pier Paolo Pasolini discussed *Salò, or The 120 Days of Sodom*, he talked about power and its abuses, about the impact of political power on the body, about consumerism as the new fascism,[36] and lamented the passing of the old Italy, the old Rome, as it was overwhelmed by postwar affluence, the media, and capitalist consumption.

'In this film', Pasolini noted in "The Lost Pasolini Interview",

> sex is nothing but an allegory of the commodification of bodies at the hands of power. I think that consumerism manipulates and violates bodies as much as Nazism did. My film represents this sinister coincidence between Nazism and consumerism.

And for Pasolini, capitalist consumerism was more insidious than fascism:

> I consider consumerism a worse fascism than the classical one, because clerical-fascism did not transform Italians. It did not get into them. It was totalitarian but not totalizing. (2012)

Director Elio Petri described Italian society as 'the kind of society that absorbs everything and turns it back into consumerism... All is absorbed into consumerism' (D. Georgakas, 56).

---

35 *Salò* is virtually an illustration of Foucault's writings on power and sexuality.
36 For Pasolini, what Adolf Hitler did with bodies in WWII – turn them into things, then destroy them – was what the consumer culture was doing to his beloved Italy.

For Geoffrey Nowell-Smith, Pasolini's films ran out of proposing cinematic and social alternatives to the onslaught of consumerism and capitalism which he reckoned was destroying Italian society:

> The problem was that by the end of his life he had run out of imaginative alternatives to the modernity he increasingly hated. The peasantry, with its closeness to the soil and the seasons and the rituals of death and resurgence, had disappeared as a class throughout the western world. (In N. Power, 2017)

For Lorenzo Chiesa (writing in "Pasolini and the Ugliness of Bodies"), the degradations brought about by capitalist-consumerism affected everyone:

> Pasolini now believes that the hedonistic consumerism and sexual promiscuity imposed by the techno-fascist power of late-capitalism necessarily entails an anthropological genocide which is concomitant with a degeneration of *all* bodies.[37]

As Gary Indiana noted, there have been plenty of movies more explicit, more violent and repulsive than *Salò, or The 120 Days of Sodom* since 1975 (90). True, but few films have been as angry or as extreme ideologically as *Salò, or The 120 Days of Sodom*. There are details and images that might be more explicit in movies after 1975, but no one can deny that when Pier Paolo Pasolini is angry, he is truly scary. (One reason is that *Salò* is rooted in contemporary politics and in recent history; it's fantastical but its horrors cannot be dismissed as fantasy, as so many movies can be).

Ninetto Davoli saw *Salò, or The 120 Days of Sodom* as Pier Paolo Pasolini's reaction to a new era of cynicism, where you couldn't make fairy tales like the 'trilogy of life' movies anymore. *Salò, or The 120 Days of Sodom* for Davoli was consciously angry, intended to show Pasolini's critics what he *really* thought of life in modern Italy. It wasn't a 'negative' rejection of the mediæval trilogy, it was a concerted attempt to do something very different, to move in a very different direction.

Repudiating the 'trilogy of life' movies, Pier Paolo Pasolini veered towards the extreme in the other direction: a movie which would determinedly and ruthlessly avoid/ usurp/ subvert pleasure: *Salò*. A film of death to counter the 'trilogy of life' films, perhaps. A pleasure*less* movie, a movie where desire is negated by excess and torture. A movie in

---

[37] In L. Polezzi, 2007, 107.

which joy would consist in witnessing people utterly without joy.[38] A movie as a jackboot in the face. As Pasolini put aside other movie projects (such as *St Paul*) in order to take up *Salò*, 'his vitality and joy had taken on a deep shadow of mourning', as Enzo Siciliano put it (ES, 366).

In an interview, Rosi Braidotti drew attention to the bogus nature of 'difference', and how it has its roots in fascism:

> I think the notion of "difference" is a concept rooted in European fascism, having been colonized and taken over by hierarchical and exclusionary ways of thinking. Fascism, however, does not come from nothing. In the European history of philosophy, "difference" is central insofar as it has *always* functioned by dualistic oppositions, which create sub-categories of otherness, or "difference-from". Because in this history, "difference" has been predicated on relations of domination and exclusion, to be "different-from" came to mean "less than", to be *worth* less than.[39]

Salò, or The 120 Days of Sodom is also a movie of social rituals, but perverted and deranged: the early rituals, like the joint signing of the document to inaugurate the grand scheme of debauchery, are conducted in a polite, refined manner (the black rulebook is later waved in front of naughty victims who dare to defy the laws the four aristos have composed). But the ceremonies rapidly become truly grotesque once the orgiastic terrors begin. There's a parody of a wedding ceremony, for instance (when Duke Blangis goes nuts and launches himself at the group of naked youths, groping and slathering over them).[40] The guests (the victims) carry white lillies. After their nuptials, Renata and Sergio are ordered to do the deed while the libertines watch, then they're raped. A second wedding feast has shit and more shit and only shit on the menu (yummy!),[41] served by naked maidens on a silver platter, evoking the *Monty Python* sketch about spam, spam, spam (meanwhile, the bride is a boy dressed in white. He looks quite darling).

The social rituals are empty, utterly devoid of their former value or meaning. They are also performed by people who have no relation to them, who are play-acting (it takes Brechtian alienation to an extreme).

The victims are not given much characterization, beyond their

---

38 Gary Indiana notes that none of the libertines appears to enjoy their sex acts, which they do in the Marquis de Sade's text: 'these men exhibit a much more dour and grimly dutiful reaction to their own orgiastic agenda, as if monotonously running through a checklist of obligatory outrages' (53).
39 Quoted in N. Schor, 1994, 45.
40 You can see the actors quaking as Paolo Bonacelli (as Blangis) gets closer and closer to them, as they wait their turn to be groped and slobbered over.
41 The fæces were produced with broken cookies mixed with chocolate, marmalade, olive oil, and condensed milk. *Mmmm!* (If there was merchandizing for *Salò*, like *Star Wars* robots or Reese's Pieces with *E.T.*, edible fæces would be sold).

presence as an actor or an extra (i.e., their naked body). The 1975 movie isn't much interested in who they are or where they came from (tho' when such information can help to titillate the libertines, it is included, such as Renata losing her mom). Another filmmaking team, for example, would've made more of the round-up, and more of the victims.

Take an equivalent Hollywood example. Producers Gerald R. Molen and Branko Lustig, director Steven Spielberg and company, for instance, expanded the liquidation of the ghetto sequence in *Schindler's List* (1993) from the scene in Steve Zaillian's screenplay. The sequence in *Schindler's List* is staggering in its ferocity, its brilliant staging, its masterful editing by Michael Kahn, and its acute, hallucinatory sense of detail. You can see Spielberg and the team thinking in both a broad and a detailed manner, moving from the big view to the close-up view. And you can see the filmmakers improvizing and adding to the scene as they developed new ideas, or hear another testimony from a Holocaust survivor. Zaillian said Spielberg kept coming up with visual ideas.[42]

Salò, or The 120 Days of Sodom is a movie that announces to the audience: *I am going to hit you in the face, then I'm going to do it again, and again, until you are bruised and bleeding. Then I'm going to beat you some more.*[43]

And yet... it's only a movie!

SALO AS 'NAZI CHIC'.

You could say that *Salò, o Le 120 Giornate di Sodoma* is part of a group of movies of the early-to-mid-1970s period which romanticized the National Socialists in Germany, giving them a kind of 'Nazi chic': *Cabaret, The Damned, The Conformist* and *The Night Porter*. Thus was historical fascism reduced to a-historical fashion, the emptying-out of history in postmodern surfaces. (Sidenote: these 'Nazi chic' movies heavily influenced punk rock and post-punk bands, for instance – Joy Division, New Order, Gary Numan, the New Romantics, the 'Blitz' kids and Siouxsie and the Banshees.[44] In punk and New Wave fashions of the late '70s/ early '80s, youths wore swastikas in order to shock, and played around with the imagery of fascism, military clothing and the Third Reich. David Bowie was the most well-known advocate of all things

---

42 *Steven Spielberg Interviews*, University of Mississippi Press, Jackson, 2000, 1982.
43 '*Salò* is not meant to entertain us. Entertainment is a privilege to be enjoyed only by the power mongers in the film', as Renée Brack noted in a 2010 online essay. A recent book on horror cinema (2013) also took this view: *Salò* 'belongs to that select group of works for which issues of entertainment fall into irrelevance, and viewing becomes a question of endurance' (K. Newman, 186).
44 The Bromley Contingent used to adore *Cabaret* (mega-camp Joel Grey and diva Liza Minnelli); they were living the *Goodbye to Berlin* life, according to Berlin, who loved the decadent, Teutonic ambience so much he changed his name to Berlin (J. Savage. *England's Dreaming: Sex Pistols and Punk Rock*, Faber, London, 1991, 184).

Germanic and decadent; Bowie led the Christopher Isherwood/ *Cabaret* lifestyle to the max in Berlin *circa* 1976-77).

Salò, or The 120 Days of Sodom had to be set in the twilight era of Nazism and the war – the audience needed to know that this would soon be over. It would've been 'an intolerable movie' had it been set in the heyday of Nazism, Pasolini said (2012).

SALO, THE HOLOCAUST AND JEAN-LUC GODARD.

It should be noted that *Salò, or The 120 Days of Sodom* isn't *meant* to be a bundle of laughs. Like *The Devils* (1971) or *Schindler's List* (1993), this production seems to be intended as a difficult and uncomfortable film experience.[45] This is, after all, Pier Paolo Pasolini's movie about the Holocaust, about the extremes that humanity will go to in the pursuit of power, pleasure and coercion. *Salò* is unequivocal in its condemnation of the aristocrats and tycoons who stage their 120 days in Sodom and Gomorrah, 20th century-style. But it also, far more problematically, explores the collusion of the victims in this madness (and also the audience's collaboration – this movie doesn't exist without viewers. Everyone's implicated).

Salò, or The 120 Days of Sodom, for all its flaws, does raise fascinating issues about modern history: like, how could a number of Germans exterminate six million people? (Was it 50,000 or maybe 100,000 soldiers and officials running this killing operation? It depends how you look at it: it required hundreds of thousands of collaborators, perhaps millions). *Salò* evokes the everyday mechanics of the Holocaust, how it was actually achieved day-by-day, with its depictions of soldiers with guns herding the eighteen victims, its convoys of trucks and cars. (Documentaries such as *Shoah* (1985) and fiction films such as *Conspiracy* (2001) have explored the mechanics of the Holocaust).[46]

Meanwhile, Jean-Luc Godard has made the Holocaust and World War Two one of his primary topics in his later cinematic and video works. For Godard, the Holocaust *must* be discussed in films, even tho' it's seen as the Ultimate Taboo Subject. The Holocaust and the concentration camps have long absorbed Godard (he relates part of his fascination to his father), cropping up in later works such as *Éloge de L'Amour* (2001) and

---

[45] 'What is depicted in *Salò* is done without alibi, without comfort or saving grace' (Sam Rohdie, 41).
[46] In a 1963 interview, Jean-Luc Godard mused on the possibility of making a documentary about the concentration camps which would focus on the actual organization and means of dispensing with humans on a mass scale. Such a film, which would ask questions like 'how to load ten tons of arms and legs on to a three-ton lorry?' or 'How to burn a hundred women with petrol enough for ten?', would be 'intolerable', Godard admitted, adding: 'the really horrible thing about such scenes would not be their horror but their very ordinary everydayness' (1986, 198).

Histoire(s) du Cinéma, his 1998 history of cinema (in amongst the rush of images in *Histoire(s) du Cinéma,* the footage of the concentration camps overwhelms everything else). The death camps were an event beyond history or above history or rupturing history. An event that couldn't be encompassed. Hence Godard's attacks on those who've tried to depict the Holocaust on film (such as *Schindler's List, Night and Fog* and *Shoah*.[47] No, not even *Shoah* was good enough for Godard).[48]

But the Holocaust should have been filmed, Jean-Luc Godard insisted, and it still must be put on screen. (Godard made similar remarks of the terrorist attacks of 9/11, criticizing French broadcasters for showing the Twin Towers collapsing, but not the people falling to their deaths.)

Cinema should have shown the concentration camps, but no one wanted to see them: this was one of Jean-Luc Godard's recurring issues in his later work. His view was that if the Holocaust had been filmed, and had been *seen*, it might've helped to avert later catastrophes: but 'it started again, so to speak, Vietnam, Algeria – it's not finished – Biafra, Afghanistan, Palestine', Godard remarked in 1995.[49]

ORAL-ANAL/ FREUDIAN-MARXIST.

Salò, or The 120 Days of Sodom is not the easiest film to watch – if you watch it, that is, from the same perspective as other movies. (But there are many ways of consuming movies, and many perspectives). Anyway, taking it straight on, *Salò, o Le 120 Giornate di Sodoma* contains images of brutality, degradation, torture, slavery, rape, murder and a range of sexual 'perversions': flagellation, urination,[50] and coprophilia. There's also sodomy, interracial sex and lesbian sex in there for good measure (as if it's trying to cover all bases). Women are buggered then hung up; captives have their tongues cut off and their eyeballs gouged out; victims are scalped; their skin's burnt with candles; they're covered in filth and left in a tub; they are forced to eat turds; they are sodomized in front of a banquet, and so on.

Among the first acts we witness in *Salò, or The 120 Days of Sodom* centre around homosexuality, under-age sex and the penis – one of the perpetrators is masturbated by a victim, and the storyteller spins a long

---

47 There are hints that Godard would take on the Holocaust in his earlier films – the women who're tattooed with numbers in *Alphaville*, a conversation in *Masculin Féminin*, and the investigator character in *Une Femme Mariée*.
48 Jean-Luc Godard regarded *Shoah* (Claude Lanzmann, 1985) as a failure (even though he later called it 'a very great film'). And *Shoah* is of course one of the very few works about the Holocaust that many critics agree is a worthy attempt at depicting the impossible. But no, not even *Shoah* was good enough for Godard. He attacked Lanzmann in articles, too (such as in 1998). It's as if no film has got the concentration camps right for Godard, not even films such as *Night and Fog* directed by Alain Resnais.
49 In a speech in Frankfurt, when Godard accepted the Theodor Adorno prize (in R. Brody, 564).
50 Hauled into the lavatory, a girl is told to urinate while a perpetrator watches.

yarn of being preyed upon by an old man as a pre-teen (of course, he had a huge ••••). One of the aristos, seemingly already turned on, drags a *ragazzo* impatiently out of the red room, and, when that backfires, he takes a girl.

Salò, or The 120 Days of Sodom is truly an anal film, a film obsessed with the anus, buttocks, sodomy, defecation, fæces, coprophilia, waste matter and urination (the 'civilization du cul', as Jean-Luc Godard put it in *Weekend*, a key filmic forerunner of Pasolini e de Sade). There are so many images of people presenting their asses, people defecating, people eating fæces, sodomy, and lots of talk about *derrières* and *merde*. *Salò* must rank among the most anally-fixated of movies (it shares an anal obsession with other European art films of the era, such as *Last Tango in Paris* (1972),[51] *Blow Out* (1973), *Weekend* (1967), and the cinema of Walerian Borowcyzk).[52]

The 'Circle of Shit' section of *Salò, or The 120 Days of Sodom* is filled with stories of anal and fæcal sexuality: the storyteller (Signora Maggi) talks about a dying man from her youth who wanted to kiss the Almighty Ass for one last time (Maggi bent over and obliged – and shat too for good measure). The story's covered in a single, lengthy handheld shot, as the storyteller dances with the Bishop around the red room (countering the view that Pasolini only filmed in short takes. It's a *very* lengthy shot).

The obsessive anality of *Salò, or The 120 Days of Sodom* ties it in with European intellectual culture which made anal/ excremental discourse prominent: Georges Bataille and *The Story of the Eye*, James Joyce (*Ulysses*), D.H. Lawrence (*Lady Chatterley's Lover* with its talk of burning out the 'deepest, oldest shames' using anal sex), John Cowper Powys (in *A Glastonbury Romance*), Salvador Dali (in his painting *A Young Virgin Sodomized By Her Own Chastity*), Surrealist artist Hans Bellmer (multiple penetrations of orifices in his dolls), Paul Verlaine and Arthur Rimbaud (in their 'Sonnet To the Asshole', for instance), Pauline Réage (*The Story of O*), and most of William Burroughs' fiction (which far-outclasses Pasolini's cinema, including *Salò,* for outrageous homo-eroticism and anal fetishism, and combining sex and death, as well as delivering an apocalyptic scream against many aspects of Western civilization).

Relentlessly polemical, with its Freudian-Marxist-poetic attack on

---

51 Pier Paolo Pasolini had disliked *Last Tango In Paris*: he thought that Bertolucci had sold out to commercialism.
52 Walerian Borowczyk's films have many affinities with those of Pier Paolo Pasolini – Borowczyk attacked 20th century fascism, for instance, in *Immoral Tales*, and bourgeois sensibilities with his controversial *The Beast*.

contemporary, Western capitalist society and morality (an easy target for a veteran iconoclast like Pier Paolo Pasolini), *Salò, or The 120 Days of Sodom* is grim stuff (that is, if you view it solemnly and reverentially). In an interview at the time of *Salò,* Pasolini admitted that he no longer believed in revolution, but acted as if he did.[53]

The style of filmmaking in *Salò, o Le 120 Giornate di Sodoma* is not to everyone's taste, either. The subject matter – a group of degenerate aristocrats abusing attractive youngsters in an Italian *palazzo* – would be 'difficult' enough for many audiences – but the cinematic treatment by Pasolini, Delli Colli, Ferretti, Baragli *et al* – geometrical, painterly *tableaux*, few close-ups, art cinema techniques, sudden eruptions of violence, and no main sympathetic characters to identify with – would likely also put off many viewers. In addition, there's a sly, ambiguous attitude towards the material, a cool, implacable distantiation which further complicates matters. The film refuses to condemn the libertines and their acts, or to offer a firm, moral stance to guide viewers. (*Salò* has 'niche' and 'minority' written all over it, in terms of audiences and markets. *Salò* would never open on 3,500 screens around the world, like a blockbuster movie!).

And yet *Salò, or The 120 Days of Sodom* is also completely silly, and knows it is. It's a black comedy, but with no laughs (and no jokes).[54] It's 'offensive' not in the degradations and excesses that it depicts (and wallows in, to a degree), but in its smug assumption that this is polemical, radical cinema. It's 'offensive' because it's so stupidly reductionist. It's 'offensive' because it assumes a patronizing attitude towards its audience, which starts with the condescending citation of intellectual authors in the credits. (Sam Rohdie suggests viewing *Salò* as burlesque, as a silent movie comedy. Rohdie is one of the few film critics who depart from taking *Salò, or The 120 Days of Sodom* straight).

✻

The first moment of nudity in the 1975 movie is, typically for a Pier Paolo Pasolini movie, not female but male: two youths, Sergio and Franco (one of them is Franco Merli) are ordered to undress in front of the group of visiting aristos, who've come to inspect them, and select their victims. However, female nudity follows soon after (from poor Eva, who's brought in to see the four libertines and stripped by one of the madames).

Franco Merli, by the way, is the object of many of the degradations

---

[53] Even Marxists are consumerists, according to Pasolini: 'all those who consider themselves either Marxists or Communists are consumerists, too' (2012).
[54] 'A comedy masquerading as Theatre of Cruelty' (Gary Indiana, 54).

in *Salò, or The 120 Days of Sodom* – maybe Pasolini and company thought he could handle them, because he had already survived the lengthy, globe-trotting production of *The Arabian Nights* the year before. Thus, Merli is the first of the victims to be undressed; he is the winner of the Best Ass Contest – and has a gun pointed at his head and fired; and he undergoes tortures in the courtyard sequence (having his tongue cut out. Merli is also placed at the front of several other scenes, such as the wedding processions).

The infractions perpetrated by the victims are punished immediately (or noted in the black book). It doesn't matter so much what the misdemeanours are, but that the rules laid down by the libertines have been broken.

The aristos like to stick to their rules (once the rules have been invented, they have to be adhered to), and the rulebook is waved around several times. Regardless of what the rules are, *Salò, or The 120 Days of Sodom* sends up the notion of religiously, stubbornly following them. Occasionally, the perpetrators adjust their rules (such as the collection of excrement).

Let's not forget, though, that in the 'trilogy of life' movies of 1971-1974, a common scenario had sexual play being punished – there were authority figures like knights, kings and priests, and religious institutions such as the Catholic Church. Persecution complexes were everywhere in the 'life' trilogy films, with 'sin' and 'guilt' leading to some excessive punishments. In one scene in *The Canterbury Tales*, participants in homosexual acts were condemned to public execution (in a Cathedral cloisters). So *Salò* sort of continues that social and moral set-up, but exaggerates the stakes, and also links the regime to fascism and World War Two and contemporary Italy.

By the start of the second act of *Salò, or The 120 Days of Sodom* (some 30-35 minutes into the piece), the movie has staged several acts of sexual degradation and exploitation. After this, there is repetition and variation. But the points have already been made. The rest of *Salò* is essentially redundant (indeed, it might be even more powerful if it were cut down 30 minutes: thus, the round-up, the set-up, and the inspection scenes could be curtailed to 7 minutes instead of 20 minutes, leaving time for a single story from Signora Castelli, then a few tortures. That's all it needs. It doesn't need to run to 1h 56m. And if it had been another half-an-hour longer, before the film was trimmed down, it would've been even tougher to sit through).

The scenes of the perpetrators in the ante rooms dressing up or of the storytellers primping themselves before mirrors remind us that this is an act, a performance. (Mirrors are a minor motif in *Salò, or The 120 Days of Sodom* – one of the libertines masturbates before a mirror, for instance – mirror motifs chime with the themes of voyeurism exploited in the final scenes). And notice how the storytellers descend the staircase at the other end of the red room, just like actors walking down to the stage, before they begin their stories, or like Ginger and Fred on a shiny staircase in a 1930s musical movie (they also dance a little, and sing. Folks, we're still waiting for *Salò: The Musical* to open on Broadway!).

In one scene the victims're led into the white room on leashes, barking, like a pack of dogs. Remaining on all-fours, they are fed by the libertines, and treated like animals (begging, barking, eating food off the floor). It's another instance of the in-your-face literalism in *Salò, or The 120 Days of Sodom* (but it's also a brilliant scene).

Late in the piece, the libertines stage a Best Ass Contest (oh so *very* de Sadeian! oh so *very* French! – it's Jean-Luc Godard's 'civilization of the ass'): by flashlight, they inspect the butts of the surviving victims one by one, and the captives crouch in foetal poses on the floor (there is a good deal of discussion about asses and anuses in *Salò, or The 120 Days of Sodom*. The 'lusty fuckers', in true de Sade-style, also ponder on which is the best asshole, male or female).

And what's the Prize for the Best Ass? Instant death, of course! ('Cept this time, it's a tease, and the pistol doesn't fire at the victim.[55] The framing of the scene, featuring poor Franco Merli, seems designed to echo the famous photograph of the execution of Viet Cong prisoner Nguyen Van Lem in the Vietnam War).

✻

In *Salò, or The 120 Days of Sodom,* the film techniques are part of the scheme of representation that the story is an everyday occurrence, a matter-of-fact approach which avoids histrionics, rhetoric, and excessive emotion. So the camera stays back and uses 50mm lenses, with simple mid-shots and long shots, and the staging is again often in a *tableau*-style. The hand-held shots that characterize Pasolini's later style are replaced by the camera on a tripod. It's the normalcy of cruelty, the everydayness of it, the inevitability of it: this is what humans do. They can't help themselves.

Salò, or The 120 Days of Sodom isn't telling us or showing us stuff we don't already know.

We know about World War Two.

---

[55] This was added to de Sade's novel.

We know about the Holocaust.

We know about fascism.

We know that humans are extraordinarily cruel.

Do we need to be told or shown that in a movie? Not really – we don't give a darn.

Salò, or The 120 Days of Sodom comes across as one of those pictures of the era when the filmmakers decided, hell, we are going to go *all out*! In films of this era, you can see Ken Russell doing this with *The Devils*, Jean-Luc Godard with *Weekend*, Sam Peckinpah with *The Wild Bunch* and *Straw Dogs,* Walerian Borowczyk with *The Beast* and *Immoral Tales*, and Bernardo Bertolucci with *Last Tango In Paris*. No holds barred, nothing held back – *no limits*. (It's one of Werner Herzog's mantras: 'I don't believe in limits').

That the horrors in *Salò, or The 120 Days of Sodom* are perpetrated on a group of young Italians is significant: altho' the source may be French (the Marquis de Sade), and the 'official' voice dub may be French (according to Pasolini), and European fascism might be one of the themes, there is no question that *Salò* is set in modern Italy and is about modern Italy and attacking modern Italy. And the victims are modern, Italian kids.[56]

Pier Paolo Pasolini enshrined (nay, idealized) the notion of youth, and the young, vital body: *Salò* is thus a disturbing exploration of the corruption of the young. Nobody can miss the fact that the perpetrators are all middle-aged, and that the victims are all young. Forget fascism or the Nazis, this is also a movie about the eternal issue of youth versus age, the younger generation versus the older generation. It's about the Sins of the Fathers (with the sins this time being highly exaggerated).

The actors playing the victims were born after the war, but the middle-aged actors grew up in the shadow of WWII. Young people in modern Italy were one of Pasolini's preoccupations: he wanted to make them aware of their epoch, of where they stood in history. *Salò* is a message to the youth of modern Italy. Yet, ironically, *Salò* is precisely the sort of niche, arty film that would have a limited audience in 1975, as it would today, and the youth of Italia would not see it. Instead, in 1975, young Italians went to see Hollywood hits such as *One Flew Over the Cuckoo's Nest, The Rocky Horror Picture Show, Shampoo, Dog Day Afternoon* and the behemoth *Jaws,* and all the usual Italian comedies, action-adventures, dramas, *gialli,* costumers, and plenty of thrillers. There

---

[56] Alberto Moravia saw in *Accattone* a link between Pier Paolo Pasolini's 'peasant utopia' (the utopia of the peasants in the past), and his 'homosexual utopia' (in the present day). The peasant world was the youth of the world in the past, Moravia pondered, while the homosexual world is the youth of today.

were many movies to see in Italy in 1975, and *Salò* would be way down the list. Consider the question from a boy to a girl: 'Do you want to see *Salò* tonight, Anna, or *Shampoo*?'.[57]

STAGING, STYLE AND STORYTELLING.

The stories of the Signoras, like madames who preside over a brothel (or like whores who aren't getting paid), are at the narrative centre of *Salò, or The 120 Days of Sodom*; the 1975 picture keeps returning to the scene of Signoras Castelli or Maggi telling stories to the group of aristos and sex slaves who sit around the sides of the enormous 'Hall of Orgies' (which Dante Ferretti and co. have art-directed (and Tonino Delli Colli has lit) in faded reds, the colour of aged, dried blood,[58] of passionless, vampiric sex, of an abattoir). The other main set is a white space, with a marble floor (and a couple of huge, ominous doors at the far end – the Gates of Hell). The rooms're furnished sparsely with large mirrors, Art Deco lamps, and choice examples of age-brown wooden chairs. An enormous staircase and a second stairway also feature, plus several bedrooms and ante-rooms. Paintings by Lyonel Feininger, Oscar Kokoschka and Marcel Duchamp line the walls of the side rooms. The villa[59] might've been confiscated from 'some rich Jew', Pasolini explained – hence the paintings and the *objets d'art* (the villa with its art is a setting boasting wealth, heritage, old money, and high culture).

Altho' *Salò, or The 120 Days of Sodom* is regarded as a political rant in the form of a historical movie, it draws on the cinematic devices of horror cinema and pornographic cinema. These are both cinemas, incidentally, which focus on the human body, and they are both forms which aim for a visceral response from viewers.

The nightmares of the acts portrayed in *Salò, or The 120 Days of Sodom* aren't obscured by shadows or fancy lighting: this is a horror movie that takes place in the light. The stylized lighting by Tonino Delli Colli and the camera team is often bright and all-over, illuminating the whole set. The shadowless, reflected light, from above, reveals the horrors in a clear, matter-of-fact manner. (Other filmmakers might've been tempted to plump for the flickering, shadowy, intricate lighting of Gothic and horror scenarios – which, of course, Italian cinema is famous for). The cinematic approach of *Salò, or The 120 Days of Sodom* results in the 'elimination of feeling, of psychology, of drama, of human interaction, of

---

[57] And if it was still playing in 1976, *Salò* would be over-shadowed by the hits of 1976, such as *Rocky*, *King Kong* and *Logan's Run*.
[58] Recalling the dried blood colours of Mark Rothko's late paintings, including the famous murals of the Tate Gallery and Harvard.
[59] Bachmann saw the design as 'the typically Italian "Imperial" Bauhaus style'.

natural physical functions, and of social values' (G. Bachmann).

Pier Paolo Pasolini said he was 'proceeding more carefully' in filming *Salò, or The 120 Days of Sodom,* taking a more considered approach: 'to make this film with emotion and stylistic flair would make it only banal' (G. Bachmann). As DP Tonino Delli Colli recalled, Pasolini was after a 'crystaline' mood to the film, and originally he wanted to shoot in black-and-white (the producers persuaded him otherwise. Producers, studios, distributors and exhibitors always want colour).

*

Each libertine is surrounded by a small group of armed collaborators and several naked victims sitting/ lying on the floor. Castelli, Maggi and co. (the storytellers) speak of their sexual adventures, of people they've had, of guys who had kids masturbate them, of being groped by old men, of men who loved to eat fæces, of men who worshipped asses, of men who liked women to urinate in their mouths, of men who liked girls to defecate in their mouths then kick them out of a window. *Salò, or The 120 Days of Sodom*'s like a fable or legend, with a storyteller (appropriately, a prostitute) recounting erotic tales (to piano accompaniment, including many classical piano pieces, and some popular tunes. The pianist[60] gamely plinks and plonks throughout the movie, until she can't stand anymore, and throws herself out of a window. Yet the piano player was one of the four older women hired by the libertines at the beginning of the story).

And it's also typical that the star role of the storyteller should be played by Caterina Boratto with studied indifference, not with the gusto and energy you might expect: it's as if Boratto's Castelli knows she's tiptoe-ing on the edge of a volcano: there's an atmosphere of violence just beneath the surface, which might erupt at any moment, but she steels herself to ignore it. (The madame politely listens to the recommendations of the perpetrators, and adjusts her stories accordingly.)

It's also typical of Pier Paolo Pasolini and the team to stage these scenes with an eerie, forced calm: nobody dares to titter, let alone laugh (yet there is plenty of laughter – the jeering laughter of the libertines' lackeys, and occasionally the libertines). No one is allowed to weep. And a girl who can't take it any more and flees is dragged back by a bunch of guys. When the girl Renata who lost her mom can't stop the tears, the Duke finds it especially alluring: she's the one he singles out to eat his filth off the floor.

(Force is always present in *Salò, or The 120 Days of Sodom;* there

---

[60] It's Sonia Saviange who plays the piano in *Salò, or The 120 Days of Sodom.*

are youths with guns always ready to add the element of physical coercion lest any of the captives misbehave. Escapees are machine-gunned down by German soldiers[61] – the scene on the bridge in Marzabott where former political subversive Tonna Ferruca escapes might've come from any World War II action movie – *The Guns of Navarone*, say, or *The Dirty Dozen*. That is, it's a piece of generic, World War II filmmaking, but it does the job of reminding the audience that in war-time everybody is potentially a victim).

Time doesn't pass in *Salò, or The 120 Days of Sodom* – it remains perpetually an overcast day, and, anyway, the exterior world isn't shown much after the arrival at the villa. It could be days, or it could be months (a spell in Hell is eternal, after all). When it's supposed to be night, the scenes're filmed day-for-night (as usual in Pier Paolo Pasolini's cinema), but a day-for-night which doesn't do much to hide that it's day-for-night (again, as usual). Originally, the idea was to take 3 of the 120 days in Sodom from the novel by the Marquis de Sade and film them.

Some scenes in *Salò, or The 120 Days of Sodom* balance the degradations of the victims with scenes of total banality. For example, the artistos are depicted as gentlemanly connoisseurs of outrages, discussing matters over coffee or wine, in a civilized manner, in one of the fancy ante-rooms, as if they're resting after a game of golf (tho' we don't see the victims in similar relaxed moments – they don't have a rec room, only their own dorms). The oddest of the modest scenes featuring the libertines is the one where they are getting dressed for the wedding in women's clothing, carefully primping themselves in front of mirrors.

To get around film censorship, of not showing that dreaded item, the erect p•n•s, *Salò, or The 120 Days of Sodom* invents stand-ins (most usually, as ever in all cinema, guns. Guns for penises... *Yawn*). In one hilarious scene, a clothed, wooden dummy is carried into the red room, so that the girls can be taught how to masturbate men (Giuliana Melis is the victim who's berated for not doing it correctly)[62] If this was *The Rocky Horror Picture Show* or a Walerian Borowczyk romp, it would be an amusing scene. In Pier Paolo Pasolini's hands, it's yet another solemn *tableau* of brutality and coercion, even tho' the company laughs. (Yet the phallus is everywhere in this picture: *Salò* is also about the phallus's relation to aggression, narcissism, and power-gaming. The phallus, that is, as analyzed in second wave feminism and 1970s bio-political analysis).

Unable to depict the p•n•s by film censorship, the solution in *Salò*,

---

61 The round-up occurs in the landscape of the Po Valley.
62 Presumably to get around censorship laws.

or The 120 Days of Sodom is typical of Pasolini's rebellious sensibilities: if he can't show the actual p•n•s, or an erection, he'll ask the special make-up guys at Cinecittà to kit out the actors with prosthetic peckers. And there's a dummy instead of the real thing. And the madames' stories mention genitals often (of course the men's members are large).

※

The colour design of *Salò, or The 120 Days of Sodom* inevitably employs red as its signature hue. Dante Ferretti and the production design team use red throughout the sets.[63] The other two colours are the ones of alchemy, duality and numerous political movements, including fascism and Communism: black and white (there are numerous all-white and all-black costumes, provided by regular Pasolini designer, Danilo Donati). Often the victims're clad in sacrificial white (or they're in white underwear). The libertines're in black suits or dark suits. The collaborators're put in grey, military uniforms (so we have black, grey and white, with grey as a midway point – the collaborators are somewhere between the bosses and the slaves, and they are partly victims, too). No need to add anything about the symbolism of the colours black, white and red in *Salò:* as with everything else in the picture, it is all very obvious and clear.

In this film where the body is foregrounded to such an intense degree (almost overpowering for some viewers),[64] the hair, make-up and costume departments were essential: Danilo Donati was costume designer, Vanni Castellani was wardrobe assistant, and Sartoria Farani designed some costumes; make-up was by Alfredo Tiberi; hair was by Giuseppina Bovino; with wigs and special make-up by Sergio Chiusi and Carboni-Roccohetti).

The Grand Guignol visual effects in *Salò, or The 120 Days of Sodom* are both deliberately cheesy *and* slick, as if sending up the Italian horror genre (Dario Argento, Mario Bava, Lucio Fulci, Umberto Lenzi, Antonio Margheriti *et al*), as well as drawing on it. There's no doubt that *Salò* is part of the cultural shift towards increasingly graphic portrayals of violence, death and gore on screen (from the 1960s onwards), in addition to the more explicit images of sexuality in films of the era. The *gialli* and horror films were a big deal in the Italian film business in the 1970s (i.e., horror/ thriller films were making money). Italian cinema has a tradition of flamboyant, operatic violence and death, as it does in painting, in art,

---

[63] Red also evokes royalty and wealth, and links to Catholic power (such as cardinal's robes), and Ancient Roman architecture (such as Pompeii).
[64] It's the naked human body that's the true star of *Salò*, as Gary Indiana notes (28).

in opera. Look at a famous horror movie made in Italia in the same year as *Salò*, *Deep Red* (Dario Argento, 1975). If you think the punishments in *Salò* are extreme, have a terrified peep through your fingers at the works of Argento, Bava, Lenzi, Fulci and Margheriti![65]

Scalping, eyeball-gouging, stabbing, hanging and all the rest are staples of the Grand Guignol tradition in horror cinema (and they are still staples in the horror genre the world over today). With the participants in *Salò* mostly naked, and in daylight, the practical effects teams and the special make-up artists have to go that much farther to make it all convincing (because there are even fewer places to hide the tricks).

An element of *Salò, or The 120 Days of Sodom* is thus the spectacle of cinema, of cinema as a visual effects medium: the 1975 film foregrounds the fascination that audiences have had with the self-conscious theatricality of the horror genre since the days of the Grand Guignol performances in Paris.

There's no doubt, tho', that the 53 year-old film director was staging the extreme events in *Salò, or The 120 Days of Sodom* with a veteran's eye for Shocks and Startles (this is Pier Paolo Pasolini's horror movie). How, for example, the first victim (Benedetta – Benedetta Gaetani) who tried to flee is revealed behind some doors, which are opened with a stagey flourish; the body is slumped below an altar and a painting of the Virgin Mary. (Benedetta's death is the first one among the victims: dramatically, it's crucial, to show how high the stakes are, and that the perpetrators will be willing to punish the victims with execution).

Disregarding the ideological, political, social, cultural, psychological and philosophical issues evoked in *Salò, o Le 120 Giornate di Sodoma* (which threaten to swamp the movie), one can admire the assurance of the staging, blocking and presentation of the drama.

To encourage actors to perform some of the acts in *Salò, or The 120 Days of Sodom* you'd have to be an accomplished director, or a director who inspires trust, or a director who paid his actors millions.[66] Many of the victims in *Salò* are either young actors or non-professionals. They are required to perform much of the movie naked, and to indulge in some stuff they'd likely never done before in life or on celluloid, and things they'd never do in any other production (!). The requirement for full nudity in many scenes would automatically put off many actors.

The pre-production on a movie like this is essential for the actors – they need to know what they're going to be asked to do, to think about

---

[65] Dario Argento, bless him, has spent years exploring the fiendishly nasty ways in which victims can be dispatched in his movies.

[66] One of the toughest jobs on *Salò, or The 120 Days of Sodom* would be that of the assistant director – Umberto Angelucci. Fiorella Infascelli was second A.D.

it, and to prepare for it. It's not only the nudity (which can be a big challenge for young actors), it's also all of the other acts. Discussing all of that beforehand is very important. *However*, when the actors were *on set*, and actually *doing* those things, it's something else. *Talking about* stripping off is one thing, but really *doing it* in front of thirty actors and forty crew members is something else.

As with the 1970s films of Walerian Borowczyk, I would imagine that many of the actors only appeared in *Salò, or The 120 Days of Sodom* and nothing else (this seems to be the case with many of the performers – *Salò* is their only significant credit). Not that *Salò* put them off acting (tho' it might've!), just that they were not actors in the first place, and did *Salò* for a laugh (!), or because they needed the money (tho' I bet that wasn't great), or they were intrigued by the theme of the movie, or they were keen to work with a cultural legend like Pier Paolo Pasolini (so you could have it printed on a Tee shirt: 'I survived *Salò!*').[67] And *Salò* is very likely one of those movies where some of the actors and the crew wanted to kill the director. (Not really, just kidding!).

Certainly *Salò, or The 120 Days of Sodom* is a tough gig all-round – for the filmmakers, for the actors, for the audience, for everyone involved. It's bleak. It's harsh. It takes no prisoners – it slaughters them.

But Pier Paolo Pasolini is not the only star here – a challenging production such as this requires a dedicated team with veterans in many of the key posts. *Salò, o Le 120 Giornate di Sodoma* was possible partly because of the wonderful group of artistic talents that had been built up around Pasolini over many years, headed up by film producer Alberto Grimaldi. These were the filmmakers who'd survived clambering up Mount Etna in freezing gales, or baking in the heat of the deserts of Africa. (The actors got to do things they'd never done before or since in a Pasolini picture – yes, but so did the crew. Working on a Pasolini movie wasn't like shooting a boring TV commercial for life insurance in Rome).

✦

Salò, or The 120 Days of Sodom seems 'in its vehemence and negativity, its utterly black humour, a repudiation of everything cloying and pretentious in Pasolini's other work', as Gary Indiana put it (11).

Salò, or The 120 Days of Sodom is conceived and delivered as an anti-movie, an anti-drama, an anti-art project. It goes as far as Pier Paolo Pasolini and the production team could go in producing something that

---

67 And of course film crews have had Tee shirts like that produced for movies that proved especially difficult. During *Blade Runner*, for example – the famous Tee shirt wars, when director Ridley Scott had made disparaging remarks in a British interview about U.S. film crews. Scott said that crews in Blighty were polite, and called the director 'guvnor': the Yanks at Warners responded with Tee shirts that read 'yes guvnor my ass'.

went *against everything*. Whatever is enshrined by convention, by tradition, by expectation in cinema and drama, is self-consciously negated. (As Groucho Marx put it, whatever it is, I'm against it).

As Enzo Siciliano noted of *Salò, or The 120 Days of Sodom* and its portrayal of the victims:

> Their passivity as victims is petrifying – since, being victims, they cannot help weaving a poisonously consenting relationship with their executioners. What is frightening is their wavering between consent and refusal. The – highly regulated – anarchy of the situation ensures that in feeling themselves sometimes free, they delude themselves into thinking that they can offer their loving devotion to someone in full freedom. (ES, 388)

MORE PUNISHMENTS.

A change of pace and content follows the 'Circle of Shit' section: now *Salò, or The 120 Days of Sodom* invites us to contemplate a series of sex acts which, in contrast to everything else we've seen thus far, are apparently consensual and maybe even loving (eh? Love? In *Salò*?!). The Bishop is depicted being sodomized by one of the guards; two of the girls're glimpsed in a clinch in bed; and Ezio the Collaborator is shown fooling around with the black maid (a.k.a. the 'slave girl' – Ines Pellegrini).[68]

In the 'trilogy of life' movies, the omniscient narrator might've cut between each of the scenes of lovemaking without a commentary. In *Salò, or The 120 Days of Sodom,* however, the narration is dramatically denser: the Bishop is alerted to some victims breaking the rules (such as no liaisons without the permission of the libertines). Thus, each act leads from one to another, escalating from a photograph found under Graziella's pillow (of a beloved – Claudio Cicchetti), to a lesbian scene (Eva and Antiniska), and finally to an interracial sex scene, with Ezio and the maid. (In common with the 'trilogy of life' films, however, each of these vignettes is of a romantic/ erotic nature, the standard plots of farce).

In another truly preposterous moment in *Salò, or The 120 Days of Sodom* (a movie which seems to have been designed to feature as many middle fingers raised to convention as possible), each of the libertines, armed with pistols, executes the naked Ezio (who defies them with the Communist salute, a classic Pasolinian touch, which takes them aback for a moment), and the maid. (Ezio is given a spectacular, multi-bullet demise – Pasolini does Peckinpah – turning Ezio into a modern St Sebastian, wounded with bullets instead of arrows. But the maid is seen

---

[68] Yes, we have several departures from white, heterosexual sex: homosexual sex, lesbian sex and interracial sex.

off execution-style, mafia-style – with a single bullet to the head, as if she's not worth any more time, effort or ammo).

THE PORNOGRAPHY OF *SALO.*

Salò, or The 120 Days of Sodom's a film of Hell, the Inferno out of Dante Alighieri's *Divine Comedy* (the 1975 film's divided up, narratively, into Dantean 'circles' – (1) 'Anti-Inferno', (2) of manias, (3) of blood, and (4) of shit. Yes, this is a movie with pretentious title cards indicating just where we are among the Circles of Hell). It's a movie of death, sadism and torture taken to new, carnivalesque extremes. A film of the Marquis de Sade by way of Georges Bataille and Jean-Luc Godard. It's a film of distantiation, never getting close to the subject or the actors. Close-ups tend to be avoided, in favour of *tableau* staging, with the camera sometimes thirty or forty feet away from the action, shooting in wide shots (or from high angles). Filming from way back also of course hides the details of bodies which sidesteps film censorship.

There are also, significantly, no central, sympathetic characters to identify with (in fact, the cast aren't 'characters', but functions or tools of the movie). The viewpoint *Salò, or The 120 Days of Sodom* takes up is that of the perpetrators, which further problematizes the film (like other movies about fascism, such as *Schindler's List, The Damned, The Conformist* and *The Night Porter*). But it does also shift the viewpoint to the victims sometimes, as has been pointed out (which further complicates matters for the viewer. *Salò* doesn't 'take sides' in the usual clear-cut manner of most movies depicting military conflict). The ambiguous complicity of the captives adds more ideological and ethical problems (*Salò* isn't just four degenerate aristocrats and their wives perpetrating violent and degrading acts on totally unwilling victims; there is masochism here, too, as in other Pasolini films).

Salò, or The 120 Days of Sodom's a film of people obsessed with sex and death to the exclusion of everything else. They are endlessly fascinated with its rituals, its transgressions and subversions. Sex in all of its multiple possibilities. It's as if Pier Paolo Pasolini and the producers made a list of the acts and ideas that would appear shocking or intolerable to conventional bourgeois views (and what they could get away with showing in the new relaxation of film censorship in the 1970s), so there's lots of sadism (and, even more problematically, lots of masochism), sodomy, homosexuality, coprophilia and torture. Bourgeois rituals, such as marriage, are also mocked and transgressed. In the carnival of rituals in *Salò,* wedding ceremonies are satirically enacted (the bride and groom are made to kiss with shit-smeared mouths). The decadent aristos themselves dress up in women's clothing.

Salò, or The 120 Days of Sodom can be seen as about the pornography of death, rather than being 'pornographic' in itself. There's a lot of sex in the film, but it's not 'pornographic'. *Salò* isn't a 'sexy' film. At all. It's much more about death than sex. Or power. (Ultimately, it has nothing to do with sex whatsoever).

Most of the acts in *Salò, or The 120 Days of Sodom* occur with an audience – someone is looking at someone else for much of the time. And if there's no one around, a mirror will do. Certainly it enhances the suffering of the victims knowing that there are people, including their colleagues, watching all of this. (The libertines have created their own private club of sadomasochism, but the acts always have audiences, they're always partly public).

The 1975 film's also about power, as Pier Paolo Pasolini maintained. Voyeurism is a recurring motif; in many (later) scenes, characters are watching other people have sex or get whipped or tortured. In the final torture scenes in *Salò*, the libertines sit on a throne-like chair (with a wooden eye on its back), looking out of a window with binoculars at the punishments enacted in the courtyard below (the perpetrators take in turns to sit on the perv's pew and observe their buddies in the courtyard hard at work. It's a condensed, film version of Michel Foucault's panopticon). There's a feeling that the movie itself is ambiguously enjoying these scenes, and not wholly condemning them. They're also problematic in implicating the viewer in the aristocrats' voyeurism, which you find in other movies which entangle the viewer in voyeurism – such as *Rear Window*, *Psycho* and *Peeping Tom*. (Meanwhile, the viewing room is another high culture environment, with art clustered around the walls like a museum, which exaggerates the contrast between culture and brutality, masters and slaves).

✼

The courtyard finale in *Salò, or The 120 Days of Sodom* is also preceded by another story. This one is about Tommy the Tortoise; he decides to have a surprise birthday party for his friends Billy the Badger and Rosie the Rabbit. On his happy, smiley way through the sunny, Summery fields to the baker's store, poor Tommy is kidnapped by German soldiers dressed as zombies, blindfolded and sodomized by 160 fairy tale characters. After 1,001 days of unspeakable degradation, Tommy emerges with a grin, shrugs off the experience, declares himself mysteriously purified, and toddles off home for a nice cup of tea.

IN THE COURTYARD.

The lengthy scenes of the tortures in the courtyard[69] (filmed on the backlot at Cinecittà) are among the most disturbing in *Salò, or The 120 Days of Sodom* – if we are still taking all of this straight (yet they also repeat scenes we've already seen, so they are redundant). Naked men hold naked victims face-down while the aristocrats take turns in torturing them: a girl has her head scalped; genitals and faces are burnt with a candle; tongues are cut off;[70] eyes are gouged out; some captives are naked, lying face-down and bound to stakes in the ground while someone sodomizes them; a woman is double-ended then hung from a rope. Some of the guards are the one-time victims, now complicit in the reign of terror.

These graphic scenes are shot with a long lens with a binocular mask attached to it through a window; there's no local sound (of screams or shouted instructions); some of the images are silent (which's creepiest of all); some have jazz music (Ennio Morricone was music adviser) or piano and other music over them; and some have the sound of distant war planes and bombing (this is an inventive (and cheap) way of reminding the audience[71] that this is taking place during WWII – it's 'apocalypse now' everywhere. At times, the sound of bombers is allowed to run underneath scenes for a long time, creating a bizarre, Gothic atmosphere).

Salò, or The 120 Days of Sodom cuts between long lens images through the window, C.U.s of the aristocrats holding the binoculars, and shots taken outside of the tortures.[72] The Duke smiles with devilish delight as the persecutions unfold (and he fondles the guard standing next to him). To heighten the layers of twisted scopophilia, the filmmakers have the Duke turn the binoculars around, so the view out of the window (of the men grappling the woman to the scaffold) is seen in wide angle.

The special make-up team (headed up by Sergio Chiusi, with Carboni-Roccohetti and Alfredo Tiberi), put over-size, plastic penises on the guys, as you do. (But, note, no over-large breast augmentations for the girls). Fake stomachs, fake scalps, fake tongues, fake necks, fake butts, fake nipples and the like were created for the trick shots of afflictions.

The music playing over the images offers the familiar extreme counterpoint to the horrors. Music is the best of humanity, the highest it

---

[69] Prior to the courtyard tortures, the victims, identified by a blue ribbon, have been stripped and told to sit in a bathtub filled with fæces and urine. This is the holding pen before they're taken outside.
[70] This happens to poor Franco Merli, the star of *The Arabian Nights*.
[71] The viewers that have stayed with the film to this point.
[72] The finale of tortures, the culmination of the movie, is also covered in a matter-of-fact style: it's just another day at the office of totalitarianism and insitutionalized cruelty.

can reach, I think, but the horrors enacted outside is humanity at its basest. From bliss to the abyss. During the shooting of the sequence (as the documentary footage reveals), Pasolini encouraged the actors to emote and suffer, only to erase all of those shrieks of agony not only in the dubbing, but out of the film entirely. (One of the perpetrators – the Bishop – shouts hysterically at the victims, and lashes out with a whip. His frenzy is all the more striking because we don't hear a word of it. It's apt that it's the Bishop, a Catholic authority figure, who loses it; the history of Christianity contains many incidents of over-the-top punishments).

The silent scream is one of cinema's most powerful dramatic devices (there are numerous examples). It's especially effective when the rest of the soundtrack dips out unexpectedly. It's an editor's trick – as is the replacement of the local sound with music (editors often cut films to temporary music – no doubt several records or tapes were pulled off the shelves and tried against the images in the cutting rooms in Roma. This part of filmmaking is a 'try it and see' process – you never quite know what's going to work until you actually see it and hear it. And it's striking that sometimes the music you planned to use (or that you thought would work), *doesn't* work; and also that suggestions of music that you reckon would be just silly, *do* work).

And when we cut back to the voyeurs' room in the villa, we see the radio, which reminds us that the music is playing in the room while each of the libertines observes the depredations outside (they remain in a cultured zone to the end – above, apart, aloof).

When one of the guards flips the rado dial to jazz music (provided by Ennio Morricone), it's a clear signal of a switch in generations, from classical music to modern jazz music, emphasizing the generational gap between the arisocrats and the guards (if the film had been set later – in, say, the 1960s – the jazz would be rock 'n' roll).

THE ENDING.

Salò, or The 120 Days of Sodom doesn't end: it stops. That is, it doesn't have an ending. Not a proper, satisfying ending which resolves or addresses (or does *something*) to or in or with the narrative, the plots, the characters, the goals, the motives, the whatevers. It just stops.

Because, after the graphic re-enactments of mediæval tortures,[73] the 1975 movie can't possibly go any further, doesn't want to go any further, and the audience has had enough already. Anyway, what're you going do

---

[73] As if, in the world of torture, you can't come up with anything new.

if you kill all the victims? Go get another six million souls?

So *Salò, or The 120 Days of Sodom* doesn't have an ending, doesn't have any aftermath/ *dénouement* scenes, doesn't show the aristocrats patting themselves on the back for such a Grand 120 Days of Orgiastic Bliss *à la* de Sade (which they would surely do, before climbing into a limo, and driving away in style).

The libertines, bless 'em, get away with it all: there are no scenes of capture, of imprisonment, of punishment for these four freaks, their wives, their daughters, and their militia. No authorities from Italy, Germany, wherever, turn up and castigate the perpetrators. None of the family and friends of the victims gather into a mob and storm the villa. And no Allies enter the frame as 'deus ex machina' figures evoking the liberation of Europe at the end of the Second World War.

Instead, a number of endings to *Salò, or The 120 Days of Sodom* were considered. (1) Ethel Merman bursts into the Hall of Orgies dressed as the Pope and belts out, 'there's no business like show business!' (2) The cast and crew stake out director Pier Paolo Pasolini and producer Alberto Grimaldi in the courtyard and whip them repeatedly. (3) The camera spins round to show the remainder of the audience in the theatre, sprinting for the exits.

Several endings were tried out for *Salò, or The 120 Days of Sodom*, including the cast and the director dancing in the villa which had been hung with red flags (the idea of dancing ends the film, but in a more modest manner); a red flag with the words 'love you' was considered (but rejected for being too hippyish); in another ending, the libertines exit the mansion and considered the morality of their acts.

So *Salò, or The 120 Days of Sodom* closes, bizarrely, with a couple[74] of youths dancing in the voyeurs' viewing room to jazz music on the radio (when one of them switches the station, and the music changes to jazz).[75] Is it a smidgen of 'hope', a glimpse of the possibility that Life Will Continue, after the Apocalypse and Holocaust we've just witnessed? That these kids will leave the villa and go back to their girlfriends? No: because if the libertines have any sense, they will slaughter everyone involved, to make sure none of them squeal.

Is the ending of *Salò, or The 120 Days of Sodom* about 'normalizing' or transcending the degradations of the previous hour and forty-five minutes? So the film shows something modest, non-exploitative, non-violent, to offer a seemingly everyday scene. That kids will still want to

---

[74] One of the boys is Claudio Tròccoli, a kid that Pasolini had met in the village of Chia (Pasolini had bought a tower in Chia where he retreated).
[75] To counter the notion that these boys are not homosexual, but are dancing for the fun of it, one of them asks the other about his girlfriend.

dance and chat about their girlfriends (to them all of this has just been a job, some part-time work which they undertook for a short period,[76] then they'll go back to their lives). Or is it a suggestion not that 'ordinary life' will continue, but that *bourgeois life* will continue? That is, the middle classes will continue to perpetuate their preference for mundane, self-satisfied existence where they can't stop themselves dominating the classes underneath them?

Yet it's also notable that the film ends with a depiction of the youths, not the libertines. That is, the younger generation, not the establishment. (Is the film guiltily handing over the final scene to the idea of youth, to these two youths (loads of people died, but these two survived), after staging numerous scenes where young people're tortured? We know that Pasolini hoped to address the youth of Italia).

THE CRITICAL RECEPTION OF *SALO*.

Salò, or The 120 Days of Sodom certainly does have a compelling power: *Salò* does compel the audience to witness it. Simply in terms of the sensational subject matter (and, of course, the sheer amount of nudity), it's going to guarantee a certain level of attention. In May 2006, *Time Out*'s Film Guide named it the Most Controversial Film of all time.

Salò, or The 120 Days of Sodom is one of those movies that presents a big challenge to a film critic. Because: (1) It can't be dismissed – this is an important work by a major talent. (2) It is a difficult film to describe in words, using the usual apparatus of film criticism. (3) It departs from many of the cinematic norms – in its form, its approach, and its relationship with the audience. (4) It's an art film, it has no stars, and it tackles very heavy material. (5) It instigates a problematic relation between the movie and the viewer. (6) It explores extremes of behaviour.

Inevitably, *Salò, or The 120 Days of Sodom* ran into numerous problems with film censors when it was released (it was withdrawn in Italia 3 weeks after its Dec 23, 1975 release). In some territories (such as Britain, Sri Lanka, Singapore, Vietnam, Malaysia, United Arab Emirates and Oz), it was banned outright (and the subsequent re-submission process of the movie for classification dragged on for decades – who was paying for that?). It wasn't released until 2000 in Albion. As with challenging movies of the era such as *The Devils, Straw Dogs* and *The Beast,* parts of *Salò* were cut out, and several versions have been released over the years. (But that also occurs with 100s of movies, not only the

---

76 It makes a change from a part-time Summer job waiting tables.

'controversial' ones, many of which are completely innocuous).

Even into the 2000s, for instance, *Salò, or The 120 Days of Sodom* was still problematic for the Australian film censors. It was banned in 1976, then passed in 1993, then banned again in 1998. *Salò* was submitted again in 2008, and rejected. It was passed 'R-18' in 2010. Several organizations protested about the film, including the Liberal Party, the Australian Christian Lobby and Family Voice.

In one extraordinary incident, the film canisters of *Salò, or The 120 Days of Sodom* were taken out into the streets of Roma and whipped by Catholic priests and religious zealots in white, pointy hats. No, not really.

Filmmakers such as Rainer Werner Fassbinder, Catherine Breillat and Michael Haneke have cited *Salò, or The 120 Days of Sodom* as one of their favourite films. For Raymond Murray, in *Images In the Dark: An Encyclopedia of Gay and Lesbian Film and Video*, *Salò* is

> an unbelievably bleak and depressing vision of the human condition which shocked audiences with its brutally graphic scenes of sexual degradation and oppressive violence. (108)

For Pasolini expert Sam Rohdie:

> It is Pasolini's most compelling film visually and his least watchable one: the shit his characters eat, the scalping, the tongue-cutting, the castrations, genitals burned, eyes gouged, masturbation, buggery, incest, killings, mouths blooded with razors. (48-49)

Many critics found it difficult to endure: for *TV Guide*, *Salò* was 'nearly unwatchable, extremely disturbing, and often literally nauseous'. Jonathan Rosenbaum called *Salò, or The 120 Days of Sodom* 'very hard to take, but in its own way an essential work'. Geoff Andrew opined: 'it's very hard to sit through and offers no insights whatsoever into power, politics, history or sexuality'. 'The film is essential to have seen but impossible to watch', remarked Richard Brody. For Vincent Canby, *Salò* was theoretically interesting, 'but becomes so repugnant when visualized on the screen that it further dehumanizes the human spirit'. 'What *Salò* frequently looks like is self-revulsion pushed to an insane limit of absurdity, into an absurd kind of self-acceptance', as Gary Indiana put it (20). And Gideon Bachmann remarked, 'every scene attacks, every sensibility is ruthlessly crushed. Every form of sexual, sadistic, and psychopathic depravity is shown, but nothing separates these actions from the every day'.

In the 2013 book *Horror!*, John Coulthart remarked:

> Pasolini's minimal style offers no escape, with spartan sets, *vérité* camera work and an unrelenting march towards inevitable butchery. In the process it steers possibly closer than the director intended to a kind of vicarious pornography that at least ensures that viewers ask themselves why they're watching this parade of atrocities. (K. Newman, 188)

Bruce Kawin and Gerald Mast in *A Short History of the Movies* summarize *Salò, or The 120 Days of Sodom* thus:

> Pasolini fills the screen for two hours with orgies of sexual torture and oppression – buggery, voyeurism, casual murder, pornographic songs and stories (a vital part of the dirty old men's pleasure), mutilation, branding, scalping, the consumption of human feces. (338)

For some (such as David Thomson), *Salò, or The 120 Days of Sodom* is gratuitously violent and indulgent. Gratuitous – meaning, there's *too much*. *Salò* has made its key points by the 30-minute mark. After that, there is *more* – but it's simply *more of the same*. Narrative progression is put aside in favour of variations on tortures, stories, images and music (like ladling more and more filth onto a plate. You get More – but it's More Of The Same Filth[77]). The patterns repeat, again and again, over the 120 days in Sodom and in Salò (it's a time loop of terror, a *Groundhog Day* of nausea). So, one of the libertines rushes into the next room to jerk off... so a girl is ordered to pee while a man watches... so a woman is fed bread (or cake) with nails in it and pierces her mouth...

Once the pattern is established, it revolves, repeatedly, or it looks at itself and repeats, like the big mirrors in the movie. Thus, the central section of *Salò, or The 120 Days of Sodom* could be re-arranged without altering much of anything. The only real narrative development occurs in the first and final acts.

Or does it? Not really: because, actually, the tortures simply carry on, tho', in the final act of *Salò, or The 120 Days of Sodom,* they move outside, and now the victims are being tortured simultaneously. The arrangement of the tortures alters, but not the narrative impact. And the 1975 movie comes to a stop: that is, the producers order the title card 'FINE' to be cut into the print after the scene of the two *ragazzi* dancing.

But the caption 'THE END' is a lie, because the movie *doesn't* end, because torture and coercion and power games *don't* end, because they never have ended, because there have always been bullies and victims, the haves and the have-nots.

---

77 Just as consumerism and capitalism is more and more of the same junk.

Modern fascism, of the European (German and Italian) kind, might be a recent political phenomenon, but fascism is a very ancient political occurrence (and Italy is certainly one of the breeding grounds of the grandest fascisms – the Roman Empire, which was soon followed by the Catholic Church. Italy, you could say, does things Very Big. It makes the two contemporary superpowers, Russia and Amerika, look like puppies).

SALÒ AND THE END OF EVERYTHING.

In this po-faced (poo-faced), Po Valley pantomime, everyone dies. Of course. The victims know that. The perpetrators know that. The accomplices know that. But this is not a prison camp movie, and there are no plans to break out, no concerted efforts to nobble the guards, no digging of tunnels, no attempts at making contact with the outside world, no calling down an air-strike. Sadly, there are no heroes who're going to Save The Day in this 1975 movie, and the entire narrative movement is downward...

...to *d-e-a-t-h*...

So the viewer is *not* rooting for the victims to survive, because, as in a Holocaust movie, the viewer knows all too well (and, bitterly, accepts) that:

1. There Is No Way Out.
2. That Will Be No Redemption.
3. That Nobody Will Be Saved.

Salò, or The 120 Days of Sodom is not a movie where the audience can *pretend* that the victims might be saved. They won't be. *Salò* is not a movie where the audience can look for glimmers of hope. There aren't any. *Salò* is not a movie where the possibility of escape for the victims (or come-uppance for the perpetrators) is entertained. There will be no escape and no come-uppance.

Everyone will die.

Oh sure, everyone will always die, everyone you've ever loved or ever known will die.

Every single one.

But in a movie, a slice of fiction, sometimes you hope that some kinda, sorta redemption or escape or transcendence is at least possible if not feasible.

But in *Salò*: *nothing*. Absolutely damn all.

This pompous, po-faced, poo-filled movie will beat you senseless.

✻

Salò, or The 120 Days of Sodom is a cold, calculating piece of work, self-consciously (even archly) *un*emotional, as if every camera angle and every image were chosen for its lack of emotive power – the opposite of mainstream cinema, of the traditional and modernist cinema of D.W. Griffith or Orson Welles, where everything works hard to enhance the dramatic impact. In the establishing scenes of *Salò*, shots are composed symmetrically, like the architectural, mathematical studies of Piero della Francesca in the Renaissance era (Italy does look lovely, though – the opening shot of *Salò, o Le 120 Giornate di Sodoma* of the lakes and the shore could be used in a tourist guide.[78] Mantua and Verona are famous for their beautiful lakeland scenery, and are well-known vacation spots).

Coldness, iciness, frigidity – these are clichés in art revaluating the fascist eras of the twentieth century.[79] The chilliness means blank expressions in the faces, unemotive acting styles, cool, medium shots and long shots, rectilinear, bland architecture (the courtyards and facades of the buildings which resemble the country estates of land-owners which've seen better days. Again in a Pier Paolo Pasolini movie, the choice of locations is superb, as is the adaptation and art direction of the spaces by production designer Dante Ferretti and company. They have captured a crumbling, decadent feeling of wealth in war-time: paintings line the floor, not the walls, as if just about to be carted away).

Yet *Salò, or The 120 Days of Sodom* is also too much like a lecture for me, too preachy, too obvious: it's Pier Paolo Pasolini admonishing the audience, beating it over the head with the holy spear yanked out of Christ's side. Let's face it, the target – of Western capitalism, of banal but all-pervasive consumerism, of the power relations between the aristocratic class and the peasant/ working class, of fascism in Italy in the 1930s and 1940s, of domination and submission, of power and coercion – it's all too easy or too obvious for a world-weary, veteran film director and poet like Pier Paolo Pasolini. Had *Salò* appeared <u>before</u> *Weekend* or *Persona* or *Battle of Algiers*, we might be celebrating it as a greater work (certainly its influence might've been stronger. Maybe it's a movie that Pasolini should've made five or more years earlier[80]).

And *Salò, or The 120 Days of Sodom* is simply too immature, too adolescent/ high school, too simplistically intellectual in its ideological

---

[78] There are overcast skies and a flat light, evoking North Italy, and not the familiar Italy of Rome and the South.

[79] In *Salò, or The 120 Days of Sodom*'s first act, the descent to the first circle of Hell, all is calm organization as the aristos and their fascist assistants prepare for their vacation orgy. The aristocrats are not sent up, there's a coolness, a politeness, and a feeling of just getting on with a job.

Part of *Salò, or The 120 Days of Sodom* is simply a film about how to organize and stage an orgy (something every 18th century libertine and 20th century *avant garde* intellectual needs to know).

[80] He was certainly getting there with *Theorem* and *Pigsty*, the two forerunners of *Salò*.

analysis – it's like a diatribe from an out-of-work, Left Bank philosopher in Modern Marxism who's still seething because those ignorant dingbats at the Sorbonne cancelled his professorship.[81]

All of the political and ideological points in *Salò, or The 120 Days of Sodom* have been made better (and more economically) in other movies. It is a filmed lecture, a series of animated, photographic slides. You can practically hear Pier Paolo Pasolini's continuous voiceover commenting on the decline and fall of his beloved Italy: if Pasolini had recorded a narration to *Salò,* he wouldn't deliver a voiceover expounding on the action, he would produce one of his lengthy harangues[82] in which he rails against Italy's governments, its authorities (religious as well as secular), the decline of its working class culture, and his nostalgia for and mourning over the peasant way of life he idealized in his youth.

In this view, *Salò, or The 120 Days of Sodom* represents Pier Paolo Pasolini's denunciation of the people and powers he feels were responsible for ruining his beloved Italy and its working class and peasant class with ugly, superficial consumerism (yet, of course, Pasolini can offer nothing in its place, cannot tell us how he would have changed things, and cannot define his utopia.[83] All intellectuals, Marxists, radicals, liberals, philosophers, poets and artists are like this: they can criticize society, deconstruct and lament society and its ills, but haven't got the faintest idea what to replace it with. Pasolini also can't explain away the fact that Italy's working class people *wanted* consumerist culture and Americana).

Pier Paolo Pasolini was the same: he spent an enormous amount of time and effort relating and analyzing the degeneration of modern Italy in fascism, decadence, mis-management, hypocrisy, greed, corruption, capitalist consumerism and all the rest, but could he suggest, in exact, concrete and practical terms, what he would do to fix it? No. Why didn't he spend some of that precious time constructing – in convincing and realistic and achievable terms – just what his utopian Italy would be?

That is, a *far* more compelling movie from Maestro Pasolini would've been a 120-minute statement of exactly what his utopia, his ideal world, would look like, how it would work, and what its societies and politics would be.

Because artists – and philosophers, intellectuals, radicals, rebels and politicians – *can't.*

---

81 When he was caught in the restroom with a student.
82 Which you can hear in other Pasolini works, such as *Love Meetings* or *Appunti per un'Orestiade Africana.*
83 Gary Indiana pointed out that Pasolini's polemics seem to have had more to do with 'proving the virtuousness of the attack', rather than actually trying to change things (18).

MORE ON INTERPRETING *SALO*.

What is *Salò, or The 120 Days of Sodom* about? *Salò* can be unpicked in numerous ways, starting with the simplest: the hunter and the hunted, the exploiters and the exploited, the oppressors and the oppressed, the killers and the killed, the eaters and the eaten. It's about bosses and workers (on multiple levels, including Communist politics), where the bosses are also prostitutes. It's about capitalism as prostitution (a common view in 1960s and 1970s political cinema – Jean-Luc Godard is one of the chief exponents), where we are all slaves, where we all exist in states of coercion, where social hierarchies're strictly enforced, where there's always someone above you (and always someone below you), where you are exploiting someone else – and somebody is exploiting you.

Salò, or The 120 Days of Sodom is a critique of political systems, in particular of Communism, and of the relation of Italian Communism to Italy's political life, and of the relation between Communism and fascism (at both local levels and ideological levels).

All of these ways of looking at *Salò, or The 120 Days of Sodom*, from the political and the social to the philosophical and religious, are built in to the piece, and rendered obvious to all. The best essay you could write on *Salò, or The 120 Days of Sodom* would be to show the movie again. For your M.A. thesis at Princeton University, you simply include a copy of the film (don't forget the legal notice about permissions and copyright, or you might be dragged outside and burnt with candles!).

Yes, *Salò, or The 120 Days of Sodom* is an essay masquerading as a movie, or a movie based on a film script based on a lecture based on an essay based on a series of ideas. A movie of ideas – *Salò, or The 120 Days of Sodom* is so powerful partly because the conception is so strong (in contrast to most movies, and certainly most Hollywood movies of recent times, where a flamboyant, noisy and fussy delivery masks emptiness).

And this is partly why all of the analyses of *Salò, or The 120 Days of Sodom* you've ever read seem completely redundant. Sure, it's interesting (but only mildly) to see what So-and-So thought of *Salò, or The 120 Days of Sodom,* but *Salò* is a movie which contains its own analysis – and *multiple* analyses. So writing 3,000 words, 5,000 words or 10,000 words, whatever, about *Salò* is sort of useless. None of the critical deconstructions of *Salò* you've read tell you anything that can't already be found in the movie itself.

Thus, as with many of the movies directed by Jean-Luc Godard, the best thing is simply to watch the film again.

Critical reviews of *Salò, or The 120 Days of Sodom* tend to say similar things: it's scary, it's confrontational, it's controversial, it's tough to watch, it challenges the film-viewer relationship, it's about power, about fascism, about Communism, about capitalism, about consumerism, about exploitation, blah blah blah.

Every essay or piece on *Salò, or The 120 Days of Sodom* also notes: (1) the death of Pier Paolo Pasolini so close to the film's release in November, 1975; (2) the mystery of the murder, the theft of the film cans, etc; (3) and of course Pasolini's politics, Marxism and homosexuality.

Salò, o Le 120 Giornate di Sodoma is a perfect movie for studying in schools and colleges – because it's one of those films that deconstructs itself, that offers a commentary on itself throughout, and that even includes a reading list in the credits! However, with its outrageous material and controversial status, it likely wouldn't be selected for the classroom! (You can imagine what would happen when little, rosy-cheeked Sally skips home with a *tra-la-la* through the sunny forest carrying the DVD of *Salò* to show her folks what they're studying in school!).

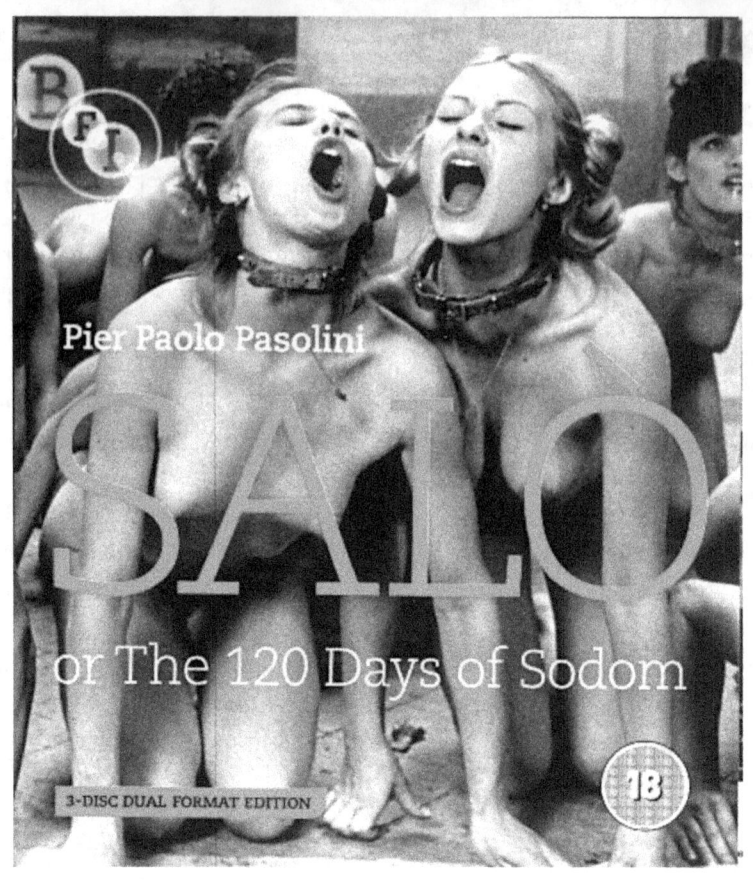

Salò (1975).
This page and over.

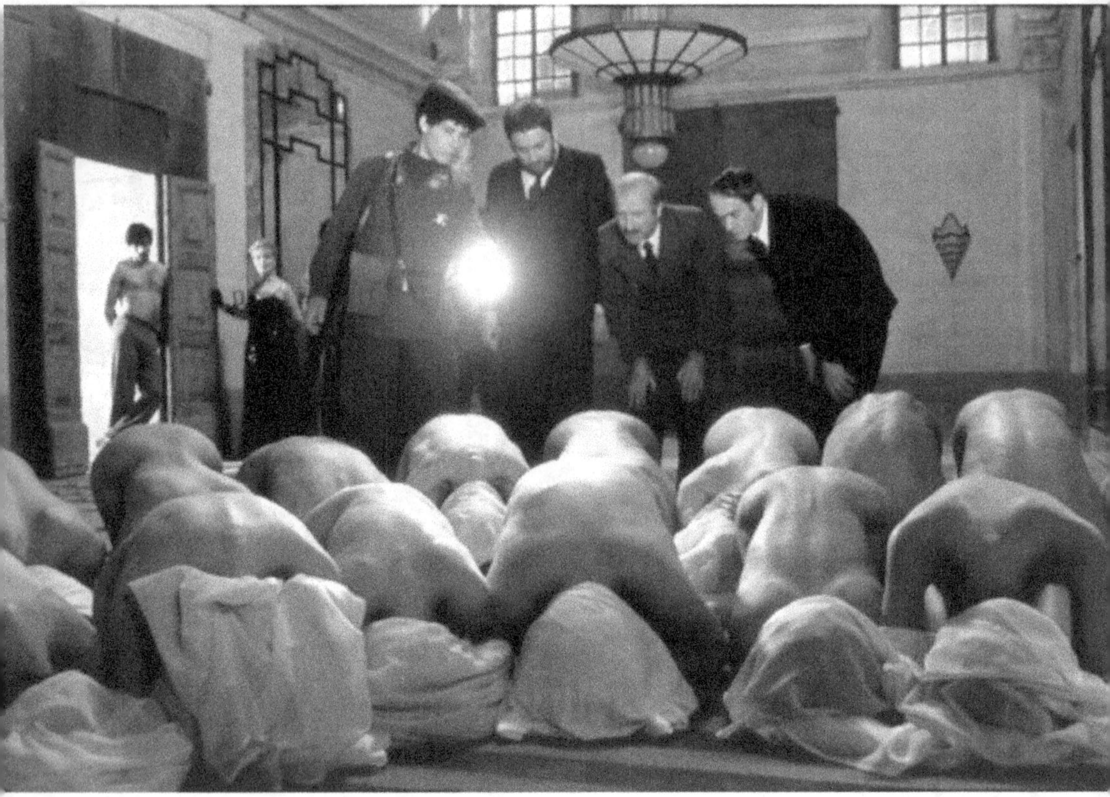

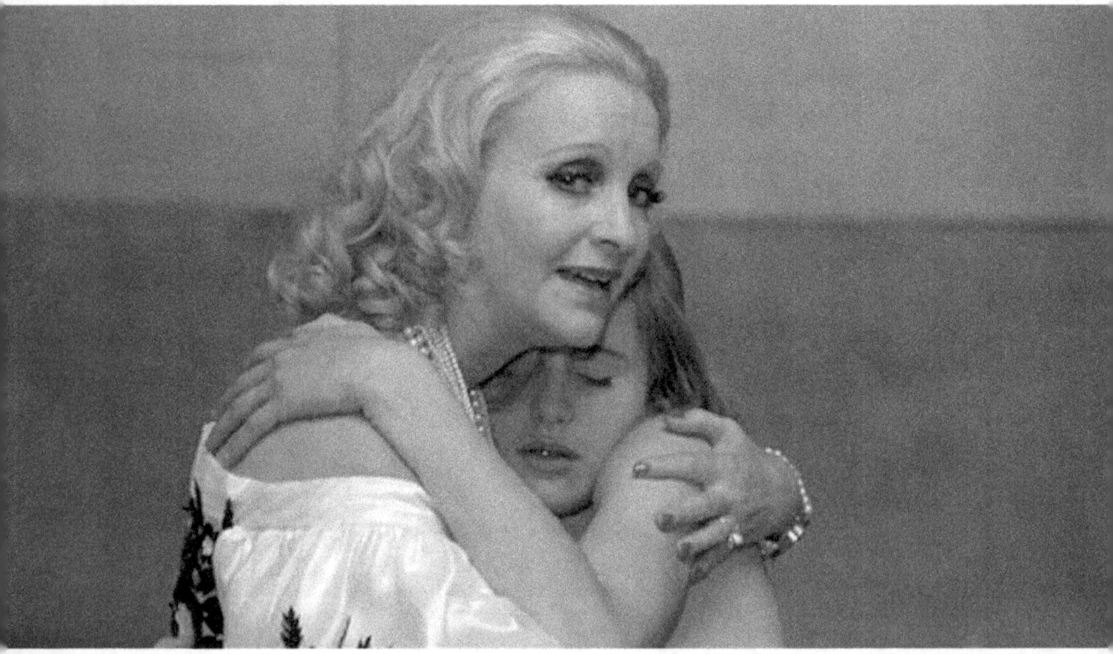

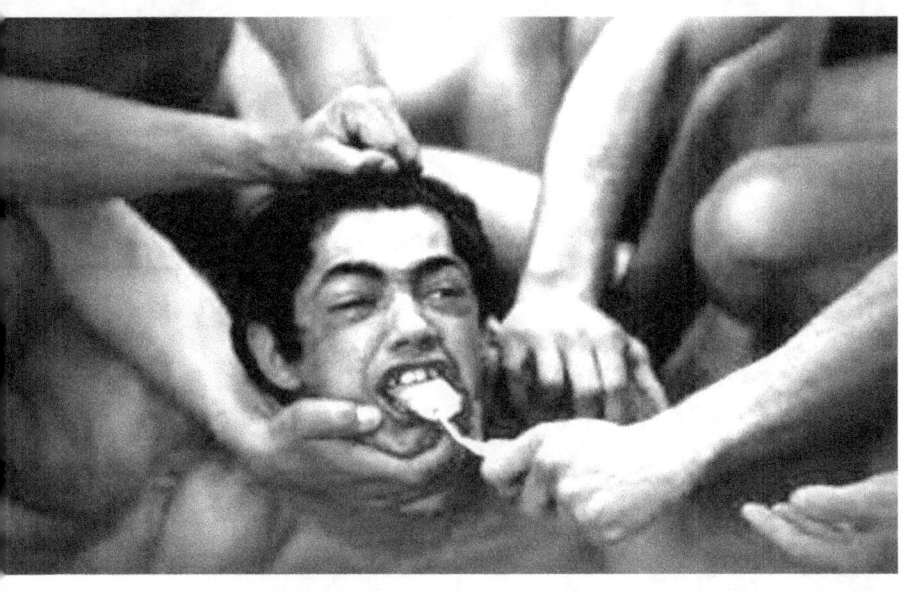

19

OTHER FILMS AND DOCUMENTARIES

I avoid fiction in my films. I do nothing to console, nothing to embellish reality, nothing to sell the goods.

Pier Paolo Pasolini[1]

LA RABBIA

This chapter looks at some of the shorter works and documentaries directed by Pier Paolo Pasolini. *La Rabbia* (*The Anger,* 1963) is a lament, a diatribe, a rant, a political apology focussing on recent historical events such as WWII, the Algerian War, Hungary in 1956, Suez, Cuba, Pope John's reign, Italian prisoners of war, capitalism, Marilyn Monroe's death, and so on. (There's a book of *The Anger*, with Paoslini's poetry and stills from the film).

The Anger comprises newsreel footage (none of it directed by Pier Paolo Pasolini, needless to say) cut together by editor Nino Baragli, with Giorgio Bassani and Renato Guttano reading a voiceover written by Pier Paolo Pasolini. It was made by Opus Films, with Gastone Ferrante producing.[2]

The Anger was made in two parts: the second part, directed by Giovanni Guareschi, became controversial, and the distributor Warners withdrew the movie. According to Pier Paolo Pasolini, producer Gastone

---
[1] P. Pasolini, *The Guardian*, Aug 13, 1973.
[2] Music was by A.F. Lavagnino, A. Sciascia, Simoni, and songs from the Cuban and the Algerian Revolution.

Ferrante wanted a counterpart to Pasolini's leftist view,[3] and commissioned Guareschi to deliver a second film. When Guaresche's section was deemed racist, Warners killed the film. And as Pasolini mused, 'anyway the film was a flop because people weren't interested in such highly political material' (PP, 72). True – and in commercial cinema, at least, they very rarely are. (Enzo Siciliano reckoned that Pasolini was being too naïve in accepting the job, in allowing his name to be wedded to that of Guareschi).

As with other movies culled from existing footage, *The Anger* is very much an editor's movie, and Nino Baragli is the star here, along with the maestro. It was Baragli and his assistants who would've orchestrated the tonnage of celluloid bought from film libraries and TV companies, and also edited the narration into the piece.

Films have been made many times from newsreels and existing footage – some of the famous examples include *F For Fake*, Orson Welles' 1973 masterpiece,[4] and the documentaries of Jean-Luc Godard. Without doubt the most accomplished filmmaker in the world, and in the whole history of cinema, in this field is Godard. What a pity that Pasolini didn't live to see Godard's extraordinary *Histoire(s) du Cinéma*[5] documentary of 1989-1998 (which includes an *hommage* to Pasolini), or his 2001 epic *In Praise of Love*, which both orchestrate a vast army of images from the history of cinema and television.

The Anger was unusual in possessing a voiceover written as poetry: Pier Paolo Pasolini said he had composed poetry specially for the documentary (PP, 70). But it's the imagery that is so powerful in *The Anger*; once you've understood the gist of the poetic narration, you don't really need to listen to it – because the images of humanity in one of its most turbulent centuries are very moving on their own. (Also, you have to admit that the readings by Giorgio Bassani and Renato Guttano are played a little flat).

In fact, *The Anger* isn't as angry as you might expect, or as moving

---

[3] Is it 'Marxist' or 'leftist'? Maybe we've seen quite a few of this sort of documentary or film essay, but the ideology seems more liberal or humanist.
[4] *F For Fake* (1973) was a sleight-of-hand concoction, one of Orson Welles' finest films, with Welles deploying his lightest, deftest touch, as befitting a film about artifice, fakery, lies and putting on a front. It was shot on 16mm and 35mm, written and directed by Welles, produced by Dominique Antoine and Francois Reichenbach, edited by Welles, Marie Sophie-Debus and Dominique Engerer, with music by Michel Legrand.
[5] Jean-Luc Godard produced a survey of cinema in 1989 to 1998, *Histoire(s) du Cinéma*. In *Histoire(s) du Cinéma*, Godard delivered a poetic document of cinema in his highly idiosyncratic style of overlays and endless quotations, a montage style all his own, which combined multiple voices, layers of sounds and music, sound clips from films, and an endless stream of visuals (interspersed with images of Godard at work in his offices, typing or writing or talking). *Histoire(s) du Cinéma* was a super-dense collage of photos, music, sounds and movie clips, taking in prints, paintings (Turner, Moreau, Renoir, Goya, van Gogh, Rembrandt), writers (Rimbaud, Céline, Brecht, Faulkner, Flaubert), newsreel, television, and complex video techniques, such as super-impositions, visual mixes, flash cuts, repeated phrases, and echo and reverb effects on voices and sounds.

as you'd hope. Despite the incredible footage (it's another 'history of the 20th century' survey format), despite a poet of Pier Paolo Pasolini's powers, and despite the inclusion of emotive music (such as the inevitable Samuel Barber *Adagio*), *The Anger* doesn't punch the viewer through the heart and nail them to the wall. It's too smug, too self-righteous, too confident in its right-on left-wing views.

If we don't care, the filmmakers have to *make* us care. If we're not moved by seeing yet another selection of newsreel images of the twentieth-century-as-a-war-torn-era, the filmmakers have to *make* us feel something. If *The Anger* played on Italian TV in 1963, or in a theatre in Rome in 1963, sure, it would've probably been impressive. But not now, not after many other films/ shows/ documentaries have done the rounds.

COMIZI D'AMORE/ LOVE MEETINGS

Love Meetings (*Comizi d'amore*, 1964) is a minor work, of interest only for hardcore Pier Paolo Pasolini fans. Pasolini is the interviewer on the streets of modern-day Italy[6] for this exploration of social and sexual *mœurs* (filmed in Palermo, Calabria, Naples, Po Valley, etc). Nino Baragli was editor, Tonino Delli Colli and Maio Bernardo were DPs, and Vincenzo Cerami was A.D.

Unfortunately, Pier Paolo Pasolini commits one of the cardinal sins of a TV interviewer: he never shuts up. He talks incessantly as he's interviewing people, and his questions are far too long and confusing.[7] You can see the punters being overwhelmed not only by the film crew, but by this forbidding, suave, intense guy with the microphone. Pasolini is a bully, and has to dominate everybody. Nobody can get a word in.

The set-up in *Love Meetings* is crude and manipulative, too. It's a documentary with an agenda, in which the filmmakers have already decided what they want to say, and will shape their interviewees accordingly. Not so much a vox pop documentary as a political diatribe which uses 'real people' to bolster a message.

And later in *Love Meetings,* Pier Paolo Pasolini begins questioning

---

6 *Comizi d'amore* was filmed all over Italy, including the Crotone region (one of the reasons for so much travelling was to seek out locations for *The Gospel According To Matthew*).
7 Instead of questions like: 'tell me about it', or: 'what do you think?', Pasolini asks lengthy, rhetorical questions in which the only answer can be 'yes' or 'no' (students on media courses make the same mistakes).

punters about homosexuals, which he calls 'inverts' or 'abnormal' (in the subtitles). It's a little creepy and sinister, as we know that Pasolini was a homosexual through and through, but his comments during his conversations with interviewees don't acknowledge his own homosexuality at all – and some of the people disclose some violent opinions of gay men, calling homosexuality a 'disease', and hoping that if they had 'abnormal' children they hope they would grow out of it.

One of the curious interviewees in *Love Meetings* is the Italian poet Giuseppe Ungaretti, talking in a mysterious, bewildering fashion about the mysterious, bewildering nature of being human (or, more correctly, of being men). Alberto Moravia, Cesare Musatti, Adele Cambria, Camilla Cederna, Oriana Fallaci and famous football players also appeared.

Love Meetings would be difficult to dub, and subtitles would render it too cold, Pier Paolo Pasolini thought (PP, 65). He was right. The documentary does not translate well – 'you'd lose the accents and the dialects, and the jokes', Pasolini maintained.

But the real problem with *Love Meetings* is that nothing in it is remarkable or even particularly interesting. All of the issues explored have been covered elsewhere far, far better than this. Maybe in 1964, *Love Meetings* might've appeared ground-breaking or amusing, but not now.

LA TERRA VISTA DALLA LUNA/ THE EARTH SEEN FROM THE MOON, FROM *LE STREGHE/ THE WITCHES*

Movie mogul Dino de Laurentiis asked Pier Paolo Pasolini if he'd like to contribute an episode to his anthology[8] picture *Le Streghe* (*The Witches*, 1967).[9] Produced for Dino De Laurentiis Cinematografica and Les Productions Artistes Associés, *The Witches* was released in 1967 (1969 in the U.S.A.). Filmed in Technicolor by DP Giuseppe Rotunno, Pasolini's entry – *The Earth Seen From the Moon* (*La Terra Vista Dalla Luna*) – was edited by Piero Piccioni and Nino Baragli, with costumes by Piero Tosi, sculptures by Pino Zac, music by Ennio Morricone and Piero Piccioni, prod. des. by Mario Garbuglia and Piero Poletto, hair by Maria

---

8 Unfortunately, many of the anthology movies of this period have faded from view, and many aren't easily available. But it's also true that many anthology films contain poor works from great filmmakers (one reason is obvious: they save their best material for their own movies).
9 As Pasolini knew, anthology movies were producer-led projects.

Teresa Corridoni, with Sergio Citti as A.D. (as ever), along with Vincenzo Cerami. *The Earth Seen From the Moon* was filmed in the seaside towns of Fiumicino and Ostia (where the locals have daubed their wooden houses in bright colours).

The other directors involved in *The Witches* were Luchino Visconti, Franco Rossi, Mauro Bolognini and Vittorio De Sica.[10] In the cast of the other stories were Clint Eastwood, Annie Giradot, Alberto Sordi, Massimo Girotti and Helmut Berger; Silvana Mangano appeared in each episode.

Pier Paolo Pasolini's section, *The Earth Seen From the Moon*, was typically eccentric and individual (Pasolini has script and director credit). It was a comedy starring his favourite couple of the moment – Totò and Ninetto Davoli, plus one of Pasolini's cherished actresses, Silvana Mangano (Mangano appears in several of the episodes – the production seems to have been partly designed by producer Dino de Laurentiis as a showcase for his wife). The rest of the cast included Laura Betti, Luigi Leoni and Mario Cipriani.

So, in *The Earth Seen From the Moon,* Totò and Davoli play a father and son (Ciancicato and Basciù Miao) who're searching for a woman to be their new wife and mother (they both sport ridiculous orange hair-pieces/ wigs – Toto with a bald wig with curly side-pieces, and Davoli in an over-size pompadour). The woman in their life has just died – the film opens with the men mourning her loss at her graveside: after weeping hysterically, they immediately begin the quest for her replacement (being able to cook is foremost among their requirements). After several disastrous approaches of suitable women (including a widow in a cemetery and a prostitute), they discover a simple-minded, deaf and dumb young woman, Absurdina Cai, standing in front of a shrine to the Virgin Mary. The moral of this film? Alive or dead – there's no difference. (Or as Lawrence Durrell put it, asleep or awake, what difference?).

The Earth Seen From the Moon, like Pier Paolo Pasolini himself, and like many in the Italian audience, is in love with Totò, and *The Earth Seen From the Moon* is very much Totò's movie. 'Totò is such a human person, he is so credulous, so ordinary, so recognizable and so clownesque', Pasolini enthused (PP, 116). Totò over-acts in his usual manner in *The Earth Seen From the Moon*, but without him the 1967 movie would be less successful (and far less enjoyable). It's silent comedy acting, it's Chaplinesque,[11] it's broad – and the camera can't get

---

10 Few, tho', could recall exactly what those episodes were, despite the calibre of the filmmakers involved.
11 A photograph of Chaplin is duly dug up from the Miaos' home.

enough of it (many of Totò's scenes are filmed frontally, with the clown in medium close-up[12]). Had he lived, no doubt Totò would have been included in the 'trilogy of life' movies, which might've enhanced them significantly.

'I consider it one of the most successful things I have ever made', insisted Pier Paolo Pasolini of *The Earth Seen From the Moon* (PP, 112), tho' many might disagree with him. If you didn't take to *The Hawks and the Sparrows*, you won't take to *The Earth Seen From the Moon* (which is a direct follow-up to *The Hawks and the Sparrows*). Because altho' *The Earth Seen From the Moon* is another of the maestro's attempts at a comedy, it is clumsy and rather irritating. Parts are funny, but this is another example of comedy which hasn't aged well, and hasn't translated well beyond its time and place – Italy in the mid-Sixties. (Once again, comedy finds it tough to cross national borders. Porn, action, horror, thrillers and other genres make it across the barbed wire and checkpoints of national borders, but not comedy).

Again, in *The Earth Seen From the Moon* the Pasolinian method of making comical films comes over awkward at times: for instance, to play scenes in long shot where close-ups would fare better, and, fatally, to allow jokes to run on too long (the shots of the father and son fleeing, for instance, are held and held, as if they're riding guffaws of laughter which won't quit). If the editing is botched in comedy, it wrecks the whole enterprise.

The idea was to improve upon *The Hawks and the Sparrows*, which Pier Paolo Pasolini admitted had been a bit too heavy-handed, and not light and poetic enough (PP, 113). *The Earth Seen From the Moon* would bring back the same team, putting them at the centre of a new story, but jettisoning the ideological tirades (a good move). *The Earth Seen From the Moon* features similar devices to *The Hawks and the Sparrows:* Toto mugging in close-up, Davoli at his goofiest,[13] speeded-up film, the duo running away (used many times), etc.

The Earth Seen From the Moon was to be the first in a series of episodes or fables which together would make up the sequel to *The Hawks and the Sparrows* (PP, 111). But then Totò died, and tho' Pier Paolo Pasolini considered replacing him with Jacques Tati, he cooled about the project. And the problem was, Pasolini acknowledged, that the episode is 'almost incomprehensible' on its own, and needed the other fables to work (PP, 118).

---

12 And yet from time to time the camera stays way back, as if deliberately subverting the usual approach of movie comedy.
13 Davoli performs his customary court jester moves – dancing in front of the newly-weds, playing a harmonica.

While *The Earth Seen From the Moon* isn't as 'poetic' or as mysterious as many of Pier Paolo Pasolini's other movies as director, it does feature the greatest special effect in the history of cinema – the human face. And when that face belongs to Silvana Mangano, even a minor, throwaway piece like *The Earth Seen From the Moon* achieves some magic. When Absurdina stands in the doorway of the Miaos' hovel in a wedding dress (seemingly after death), she is an amazing sight (Totò's reaction, as always, is plenty of eye-rolling and grimacing). Mangano is one of those actors who's made for the camera, for cinema. Quite remarkable. (And in the scene at the Colosseum, Mangano gives Totò some serious competition in comical miming).

The Colosseum episode in *The Earth Seen From the Moon* comes about when Miao senior decides they need a scheme to generate some much-needed Lire (they live in a shabby shack): they persuade Absurdina to pretend to be about to commit suicide by jumping off the Colosseum (they're joined by some friends looking up from the street, who try to start a money collection for the hapless father and son). A pair of tourists (played as grotesque buffoons in drag by Laura Betti and Luigi Leone), toss away a banana skin, and Absurdina tumbles to her doom. This being a comedy, she comes back to life in a send-up of the Resurrection (as all Pasolini characters should). At first the Miaos are terrified, but when they learn that the Absurdina ghost can cook and tup, they go back to being a happy family.

Again the influence of Jean-Luc Godard is apparent in *The Earth Seen From the Moon* – in the humorous names (Miao), the joky, hand-drawn intertitles and the red paint splashed everywhere on the sets (without it being neatly applied and cleaned up, a Godardian speciality). The tombstones at the graveyard include caricature sculptures of the deceased (plus Toto and Davoli). The cartoony approach of *The Earth Seen From the Moon* is very 1960s as well as Godardian – *The Witches* features an animated main titles sequence (a silly, too-long skit).

CHE COSA SONO LE NUVOLE?/ WHAT ARE THE CLOUDS?, FROM *CAPRICCIO ALL'ITALIANA/ CAPRICE ITALIAN STYLE*

Che Cosa Sono le Nuvole? (*What Are the Clouds?*) was an episode in *Capriccio all'Italiana* (*Caprice Italian Style,* 1968). It was produced by Dino de Laurentiis again (for Dino de Laurentiis Cinematografica), Tonino Delli Colli was DP, ed. by Nino Bargali, prod. design by Mario Garbuglia and Jürgen Henze, Sergio Citti (1st A.D.), and Jürgen Henze (cost.). The other directors of *Caprice Italian Style* were: Mario Monicelli, Steno, Mauro Bolognini, Pino Zac and Franco Rossi.

In the cast were Franco Franchi, Totò, Ciccio Ingrassia, Laura Betti, Ninetto Davoli, Adriana Asti, Domenico Modugno, Carlo Pisacane, Francesco Leonetti, Luigi Barbieri, Piero Morgia, Remo Foglino and Mario Cipriani (most of the cast were friends and regulars in the Pasolini Circus).

The gag? A bunch of actors playing puppets put on *Othello* in a small, provincial theatre. And guess who's got the star role as the Moor, in blackface? Nino Davoli! With Totò as the scheming Iago, of course (in green make-up), and the remarkable Laura Betti as Desdemona.

So *What Are the Clouds?* was intended to be an installment in *The Further Adventures of Totò and Davoli* – it was part of a series of skits/ episodes/ fables which would've made up a feature-length movie (another one was filmed for *The Witches*). After Totò died (in 1967), the concept was abandoned.

At the end of *What Are the Clouds?,* which follows the narrative of *Othello* closely, the performance turns into chaos, and the audience invades the stage. Totò and Nino are thrown away as garbage – into the back of a truck, where they're driven to a dump. It's the first time they've been outside, and they marvel at the world, and at the clouds in particular.

What Are the Clouds? is a charming slice of Italian theatrical whimsy, very Felliniesque, with some Jean Cocteau and Charlie Chaplin and Jacques Tati added. We have many Pasolinian regulars appearing in puppet costumes, complete with strings attached (wielded by the puppeteers above the stage, led by Francesco Leonetti).

Thus, part of *What Are the Clouds?* is actually about that perennial of cinema: putting on a show. Wait? Is Pier Paolo Pasolini making a backstage comedy? Sort of – there is a whimsical evocation of theatricality (Pasolini was moving into live theatre at this time). And Totò certainly comes alive even more as a clown when he's got audience.

LA SEQUENZA DEL FIORE DI CAMPO/ THE SEQUENCE OF THE FLOWER FIELD, FROM *AMORE E RABBIA/ LOVE AND ANGER*

La Sequenza del Fiore di Campo (*The Sequence of the Flower Field,* a.k.a. *La sequenza del fiore di carta,* originally titled *Il Fico Innocente*), was Pier Paolo Pasolini's contribution to another omnibus movie, *Amore e Rabbia* (*Love and Anger*, also known as *Vangelo '70,* 1969). The other film directors involved were: Jean-Luc Godard, Bernardo Bertolucci, Carlo Lizzani, Elda Tattoli and Marco Bellocchio. It was produced by Carlo Lizzani. 102 mins.

Written by Pier Paolo Pasolini, from an idea by Puccio Pucci and Piero Badalassi, and aided by the usual Pasolini crew (including Giuseppe Ruzzolini, Nino Baragli, Maurizio Ponai, Franco Brocani, Giovanni Fusco, etc), *The Sequence of the Flower Field* is a twelve minute skit involving Riccetto (Ninetto Davoli) walking and cavorting down Via Nazionale in Roma. As the camera trucks backwards, and Davoli walks towards it, many voices off are heard (including Bernardo Bertolucci, Graziella Chiarcossi, Aldo Puglisi and Pasolini), and a host of tumultuous, politically charged images are superimposed (including American Presidents, the Vietnam War, and of course World War Two).

As Pier Paolo Pasolini explained, the concept for *Vangelo '70/ Amore e Rabbia* was to do something based on the *Gospels* or the parables in the *Bible*. So *The Sequence of the Flower Field* was about the humble, innocent fig tree, and how one cannot waltz thru life without being aware of history and dangerous historical events (PP, 131). One must be aware – and the off-screen voices, including those of God, urge Riccetto to be conscious: 'but like the fig tree he does not understand because he is immature and innocent and so at the end God condemns him and makes him die' (ibid.).

The Sequence of the Flower Field doesn't really work, the elements don't quite gel, and the sight of the irrepressible Ninetto Davoli grinning and monkeying around in amongst the crowds and traffic of downtown

Roma, carrying a giant, red poppy (what happened to the fig tree?), is only vaguely amusing or interesting (this wasn't Pier Paolo Pasolini's concept, however, it was based on an idea by Puccio Pucci and Piero Badalassi).

Show this 12-minute skit to an audience today and assure them that it was directed by one of cinema's great lights, and they will laugh at you. It lectures the audience, and it makes its points in a heavy-handed manner. It's another example of a Pier Paolo Pasolini movie not fulfilling the requirements or the aims of its premise; it is conceptual, needing footnotes or a programme sheet. It doesn't really work as cinema because the filmmakers haven't found a suitably cinematic way of illustrating the ideas.

APPUNTI PER UN FILM SULL'INDIA/ NOTES FOR A FILM IN INDIA

Appunti Per un Film Sull'India (*Notes For a Film In India,* 1969) was another of Pier Paolo Pasolini's filmed preparations for a production (a documentary about a film, he called it, a film about a film). The filmed notes were for a fiction movie focussing on two aspects of India: modern India and historical India, India of the present day and India of prehistory, evoked and explored through the symbolic fable of a Maharaja who dies, giving his body to feed starving tigers (this part of the film would represent ancient India). Following the Maharaja's demise, his family and entourage wander around India, eventually expiring one by one (this would evoke modern-day India).

Gianni Barcelloni produced, Ennio Morricone provided music, Jenner Menghi was editor, the DPs were Roberto Nappa and Federico Zanni, and it was written by Pier Paolo Pasolini and Sergio Citti.

Notes For a Film In India visits several famous spots in India, including the Parliament House in New Delhi, the Ganges River, the palace in Jaipur, and rural spots like Bhavati, etc. As with the *Oresteia* film essay, Pasolini selects people that might represent the Maharaja, his wife and his children; some of the possible settings are contemplated (the Jaipur palace is chosen as the Maharaja's home, for instance).

Notes For a Film In India exhibits all of the elements of the usual

Pasolinian pseudo-documentary: a voiceover from the maestro; snippets from the story of the film that he hopes to make; Pasolini interviewing people on the streets (tho' eliding his presence as usual); dubious ideology and politics; trite sentiments about the 'Third World'; terrible camerawork (this time from Roberto Nappa and Federico Zanni); and a really shoddy technical quality overall.

Pier Paolo Pasolini had visited India in December, 1960, along with Alberto Moravia and Elsa Morante (a book was published about the visit – *The Scent of India*).

Like Pasolini's other documentaries or film essays as notes for potential films, *Notes For a Film In India* is filled with images of people on the streets of India – sometimes gathered around the camera, to be interviewed, and also going about their daily business. As with all of Pasolini's films, it's deemed enough for the camera to linger over faces and bodies. Some guy stares into the camera and Pasolini on the soundtrack explains that he could be the Maharaja in his film. (Maybe – but in Pasolini's fiction films it was always a known actor who played the leading roles).

As with *Love Meetings* and other films (such as the African *Oresteia* documentary) where the director interviews ordinary people on the street, there is something dissatisfying, incomplete and patronizing about the 'interviews'. *Notes For a Film In India* does contain some more conventional interviews, however – with journos from the *Times*, for example, with screenwriters with whom Pasolini might've collaborated to produce his story of the Maharaja, and a representative of the Communist Party in India.

PASOLINI AND THE SHAPE OF THE CITY/ PASOLINI E LA FORMA DELLA CITTÀ

Pasolini and the Shape of the City (*Pasolini e la forma della città* (1974) is a short work (about 17 minutes) directed by Paolo Brunatto, DP: Mario Gianni, editing: Franca di Lorenzo Visco, sound: Tullio Petrioca, with Anna Zanoli credited as creator. Released Feb 7, 1974.

In *Pasolini and the Shape of the City,* Pasolini speaks about his notions of the city (chiefly in Italy, but also in the Middle East).

Visually, *Pasolini and the Shape of the City* comprises images of Pasolini talking (to Ninetto Davoli[14]) while standing beside a film camera (and occasionally peering into it). The film then cuts to what the camera sees – second unit-style images of the Italian towns of Orte and Sabaudia, and towns in the Middle East (there are typical Pasolinian, lengthy pan shots along the horizon). *Pasolini and the Shape of the City* looks like it was filmed in one or two afternoons (some of the images come from Pasolini's travels, including filming the 'trilogy of life' movies).

Pasolini and the Shape of the City is a film-essay in which our man of the moment talks, as only he can. Pretty much throughout the piece, Pasolini is unravelling his thoughts at length about architecture. It's a minor piece, a departure from some of the weightier documentaries in the Pasolini œuvre.

---

[14] Davoli's job is to listen.

20

UNMADE PROJECTS

Who knows what Pier Paolo Pasolini might've directed if he hadn't died in 1975? Certainly the *Socrates,* the *St Paul* and the *Divine Comedy* projects were highly likely. One would imagine that an adaptation of Fyodor Dostoievsky, William Shakespeare, and maybe one of the Romantic authors was very possible, too. Maybe Pasolini would've succumbed to an offer from producers in North America (despite his aversion to 'selling out' and super-capitalism). He might've adapted more of his novels, and also delivered film versions of his plays. (Pasolini might have had a very long career had he not been killed – collaborators such as Alberto Grimaldi and Giuseppe Rotunno both lived until very recently – 2021).

It's not only all of the movies and TV shows and essays and poems that Pier Paolo Pasolini would've produced, had he lived longer, it's also his responses to the contemporary world. Pasolini is one of the most fascinating and insightful commentators among filmmakers, and I would've loved to have heard his reactions to the events of the 1980s, for instance (such as Tiananmen Square, or the fall of the Berlin Wall and the end of the Cold War).

In an interview in Stockholm days before he died, Pasolini asserted that he was going to make two more films then 'dedicate myself completely to literature again' (2012). The two films would likely have been *St Paul* and either *Porno-Teo-Kolossal* or *Socrates.*

In the age of digital filmmaking, where filmmakers can edit their movies on a laptop with software such as Avid or Final Cut Pro (and on set, too, as Tsui Hark has done),[15] Pier Paolo Pasolini might've been able to put together some of his unmade projects, like *St Paul* or *Socrates*. Armed with a video camera and a couple of actors, Pasolini could've filmed rough versions of his unmade scripts. Pasolini was already headed that way with his documentaries and film essays. He could've also edited many different versions of his work, which's easy to do digitally. Some film directors produce many different cuts before they develop the final edit. (However, Pasolini didn't seem much interested in video technology like filmmakers such as Jean-Luc Godard or Tsui Hark, or working in television).

ST PAUL.

Pier Paolo Pasolini had planned to make a film based on a saint, such as St Francis, and a modern-day version of the life of St Paul (to start in Spring, 1969). *St Paul* would be modernized: it would be set in the 1940s to 1970s period. The film would shoot in cities such as Gotham, Paris, Naples, Marseilles, Geneva, Barcelona, Bonn, Vichy, Monaco and of course Roma. (Pasolini might've produced a whole series of films about saints, maybe for television – after St Paul, we might've seen his St Francis, St Augustine and St Sebastian.)

Alberto Moravia said that *St Paul* was lined up as Pasolini's next film project after *Salò*. Pasolini's *San Paolo* would have portrayed the saint as a revolutionary. Pasolini planned to use Paris as Jerusalem, New York as Rome, and Rome as Athens (recalling the 1965 film *Simon of the Desert* (dir. Luis Buñuel), which Pasolini admired, and at one time he was going to produce a companion film to).[16] For Pasolini, New York City had replaced Rome as the seat of power, and Paris would stand in for Jerusalem, as the city of culture. At another time, Pasolini said *St Paul* would be filmed between Roma and Napoli. Biblical events would have contemporary analogies (Pasolini's usual method), so that St Paul standing by at St Stephen's murder would be shot as the Nazi occupation of Paris, with St Paul as a 'reactionary Parisian collaborator who kills a Resistance fighter' (PP, 139). 'But I'm going to be extremely faithful to

---

[15] For example, *Young Detective Dee: Rise of the Sea Dragon* (2013) was filmed with 3-D cameras (5K 3D using RED EPIC cameras (and was converted to 1080p ProRes), and edited with Final Cut Pro X. Tsui Hark was able to edit on set, using Final Cut Pro on a MacBook Pro with Retina display. Cutting the film digitally, the filmmakers were able to send versions of the movie before it was completed to different VFX vendors, the music composer, the sound editor, the marketing team, and the distributors. Tsui commented: 'In addition to consulting with the editor, director assistant, and producer, I sent different versions of the film to many people to get their feedback. Although I know the film I shot very well, the feedback from other people is a good reference for me.'

[16] In *Simon of the Desert*, the narrative shifts from early Christian times (most of the movie involves St Simon Stylites living on top of a column, as saints and martyrs did in the early years of Xianity), to modern-day New York City. The saint winding up in a nightclub, after being assailed by temptations, was a little predictable, but Buñuel pulled it off with his customary grace and wit.

the text of St Paul', continued Pasolini (PP, 140). Instead of miracles, there would be 'some con men pretending to perform miracles, who are then severely punished by St Paul' (PP, 91).

For dialogue, Pasolini would have drawn on the texts in the *Bible* and the *Apocrypha*, as he did with *The Gospel According To Matthew*. But *St Paul* would be more directly politcized: it would have included the civil rights movement in the U.S.A., in the 1960s and Martin Luther King (including his assassination). Figures such as Luke would have appeared.

Like Andrei Tarkovsky's unproduced plans to adapt *The Temptations of St Anthony*, this is one hagiographic film one would love to see.[17] Indeed, one wishes sometimes that Pasolini had left alone one of the 'trilogy of life' movies (the worst one – *The Canterbury Tales*), and forged ahead with his *St Paul* project (or made *St Paul* instead of *Pigsty*).

'I'm now preparing a film on Saint Paul. In the film we bring into question not the validity of the Church but its mere motive of existence', Pier Paolo Pasolini remarked in 1971. Pasolini continued:

> I think that the *Gospel* is one of the many books of religious propaganda that had been written. There will come a time when the *Gospel* will be linguistically incomprehensible to humanity. The *Gospel* is tied to time and its historic place. The Church can only survive if it continues to change and put into continual crisis its own institutionality.

Pier Paolo Pasolini discussed his *St Paul* project again:

> With the simple strength of his religious message, Saint Paul in revolutionary fashion demolished a type of society founded on class violence, imperialism, and above all slavery. And so it is clear that for the Roman aristocracy and the various collaborationist ruling classes, one can substitute by analogy the present bourgois class that has the capital in its hands, while for the humble downtrodden should be substituted, by analogy, the advanced bourgeois element, the works, and the sub-proletarians of today.[18]

The father of Christianity is not Jesus but St Paul. Jesus wrote nothing; St Paul wrote everything, setting down the views of Christianity in that fanatical prose in the *Corinthians* and *Galatians* and *Romans*, which gets so many things wrong about flesh and spirit and marriage. Michael Foucault comments (in *The Use of Pleasure*) on some of the strictures of Christianity:

---

17 It was planned, again, in 1973, and would have been made after the 'trilogy of life' movies. This time, Pier Paolo Pasolini rewrote his *St Paul* script, drawing on the letters of the *Romans*, *Corinthians*, *Philippians* and *Ephesians*. However, the co-operation of the Catholic Church was withheld this time around (possibly because Pasolini had become too controversial a figure by the early 1970s).

18 In Pier Paolo Pasolini, *Saint Paul*, Turin, 1977.

Christianity associated it ['the sexual act'] with evil, sin, the Fall, and death, whereas antiquity invested it with positive symbolic values.[19]

Pasolini condemned St Paul as the instigator of numerous flaws in the Roman Catholic Church and Christianity as it developed out of his writings:

> I violently condemn him as the founder of the Church, with all the negative elements of the Church already present: the sexphobia, the anti-feminism, the organization, the collars, the triumphalism, the moralism. In sum, all the things that have created the evil of the Church are all already in him.

SOCRATES.

Another of Pier Paolo Pasolini's unmade film projects was a life of Socrates, the Ancient Greek philosopher. Pasolini had read Plato's *Dialogues* and had been 'absolutely bowled over by how beautiful they were' (PP, 143).

> I would like my last film to be about Socrates, but let's hope that something will come up between *St Paul* and *Socrates*. To do a film on Socrates I will have to reach a stage where I have completely exhausted all the marginal motives which push me to make movies, and arrive at a totally disinterested cinema, one which is completely pure... I would like to achieve greater purity and greater disinterestedness; I would like a purer relationship with the audience. (PP, 144)

A TV movie (R.A.I.), *Socrates*, was directed by Roberto Rossellini in 1971.

THE SAVAGE FATHER.

An unmade project of the early 1960s would've been about fathers (yet again): *Il Padre selvaggio* (*The Savage Father*, 1963). Because Pier Paolo Pasolini found the *La Ricotta* ordeal too much, too painful, it wasn't made (and Pasolini and producer Alfredo Bini disagreed about the blasphemy case over *La Ricotta*).

The Savage Father would've been another African project, this time focussing on a young, African student called Davidson. It would orchestrate the familiar Pasolinian concerns – of old/ new, primitive/ modern, Africa/ Europe, the Third World/ the Western world, and so on.

GARGANTUA AND PANTAGUEL.

A version of François Rabelais' *Gargantua and Pantaguel* (1532-52)

---

[19] M. Foucault: *The Use of Pleasure*, 14.

was proposed in the early 1970s, with Italian financing from Produzioni Europee Associate, producer Alberto Grimaldi's company; Warners were also interested. According to Ken Russell,[20] who was later offered the project, Pier Paolo Pasolini had pulled out of doing *Gargantua*, 'leaving the producer with a script by Alberto Moravia and no director'.[21]

PORNO-TEO-KOLOSSAL.

Yet another unmade project was written in 1973: *Porno-Teo-Kolossal* was a *Divine Comedy* sort of journey *à la Hawks and Sparrows* which would have featured two travellers (Eduardo De Filippo and Ninetto Davoli) moving thru three zones: Rome (as Sodom), Milan (as Gomorrah) and Paris (Numantia). It would've ended up in India (as Ur). Forget Paris and Milan, tho' – if you want Gomorrah, Las Vegas or New York City in the 1970s would've been much more apposite (or how about Mexico City, or Sao Paolo, or Bangkok, or Calcutta, or Cairo, or Caraccas? – all far wilder than nice, tame Paris and Milan).

It looked as if *Porno-Teo-Kolossal* might've been the next production for Pier Paolo Pasolini following *Salò*: Pasolini had been in discussions with Eduoardo De Filippo and others about it.

THE DIVINE COMEDY.

Had he worked thru further classic texts of the Middle Ages following the 'trilogy of life' movies of 1971/ 72/ 74, *The Divine Comedy* by Italy's national poet would have been a likely adaptation (but please, *not* with Ninetto Davoli as Dante! Or Virgil![22]). Pasolini produced a script version of *The Divine Comedy*. Written between 1962 and 1967, it emerged following the maestro's death as *La Divina Mimesis*.

★

OTHER PROJECTS.

• A film about Charles de Foucauld (1858-1916), a priest who worked in North Africa, was a possibility, tho' Pasolini decided to leave his movies about saints until he'd done his *St Paul*.

• *Bestemmia* was abandoned when Pier Paolo Pasolini opted to do *The Gospel According To Matthew* instead.[23]

---

20 But when Ken Russell saw Pier Paolo Pasolini's version of *The Canterbury Tales*, he was horrified. The director of the excesses of *The Devils*, *The Music Lovers* and *Lisztomania* found *The Canterbury Tales* 'the most disgusting film I've ever since in my *life*!' [ib., 229]).
21 In John Baxter, 1973, 229. If Ken Russell had helmed *Gargantua*, it would have contained plenty of satire on religion and politics (partly taken from Russell's unmade projects *Music, Music, Music* and *The Angels*). The bawdy, phallic elements of *Gargantua and Pantagruel* would have been part of the mix, as well as the construction of the Abbey of Thélème. Locations were scouted in Italy, and Russell got together with designer Derek Jarman to plan the sets and look, but the project didn't go further (*A British Picture*, 102).
22 Maybe one of the damned!
23 Part of *Bettemmia* was published in *Cinema e Film*, 2.

• *Notes For a Poem On the Third World* was planned at the end of the Sixties, but put on hold. It would be a film essay/ documentary made in Africa, the Middle East, India, South America and the ghettoes of N. America.

POSSIBLE PASOLINI PROJECTS.

One can imagine Pier Paolo Pasolini taking up more ancient world tragedies had he lived longer, and also perhaps turning his attention to the plays of William Shakespeare, such as *Macbeth* or *King Lear*. (Pasolini rendering a Jacobean tragedy such as *The Broken Heart*, *'Tis Pity She's a Whore* or *The Changeling* is a very enticing prospect).

It's likely that Pier Paolo Pasolini might've adapted more of his fiction into films (after all, his first production, *Accattone*, had done that). A film essay about his poetry, or a compendium of his poems, perhaps dramatized, might've been considered.

I would love to see Pier Paolo Pasolini taking on a genre picture – science fiction, horror, action-adventure, thriller, etc. Imagine a vampire movie *à la* Pasolini! Or a Western! In the 1980s, Pasolini might've directed Arnold Schwarzenegger in one of the *Conan* movies;. A bizarre notion, perhaps, but they were produced by Dino de Laurentiis; *Red Sonya*, the 1985 follow-up, used Pasolinians such as Danilo Donati and Giuseppe Rotunno. (However, some European art film directors have come a cropper attempting genre pictures – particularly when they try to do them in the North American idiom).

Documentaries – surely Pasolini would've filmed more documentaries, tho' one hopes that R.A.I. TV or some other television company in Italy or France could've handed him a decent budget and crew (because Pasolini's documentaries are really let down by crummy technical work).

One project that cried out to be made by Pier Paolo Pasolini during his lifetime was an autobiographical piece. Pasolini visiting the places where he'd lived and worked, including perhaps film locations (a return to Calabria with the director talking about *The Gospel According To Matthew*, for instance). An exploration of Pasolini's cinema by the film-maker himself... failing that, a very long filmed interview, like the incredible one the British Broadcasting Corporation did with Orson Welles in 1982...

Love Meetings (1964).

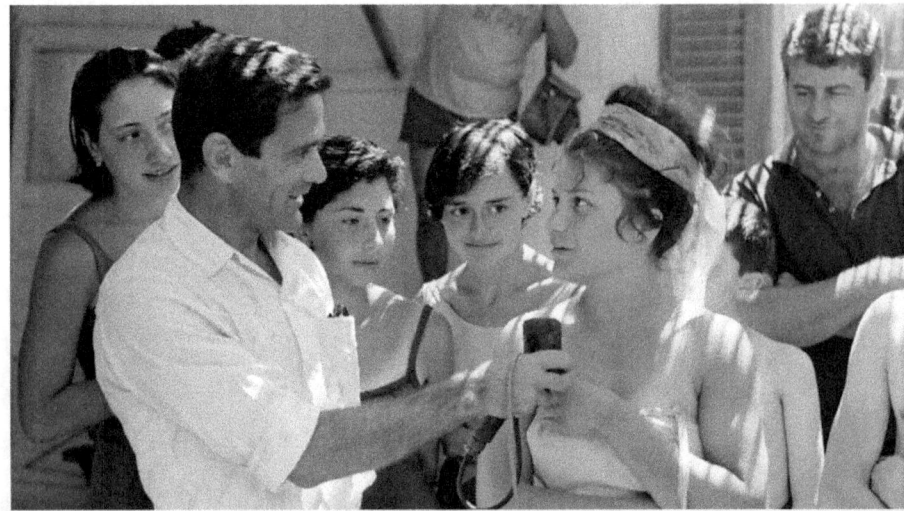

The Witches (1967).

Caprice Italian Style (1968).

Notes For a Film In India (1969).

APPENDICES

QUOTES BY PIER PAOLO PASOLINI

I love life fiercely, desperately. And I believe that this fierceness, this desperation will carry me to the end... Love of life for me has become a more tenacious vice than cocaine. I devour my existence with an insatiable appetite. (1970)

- ...cinema is already a dream

- ...to make films is to be a poet

- One can cheat in everything except style.

- Even a sound image, say thunder booming in a clouded sky, is somehow infinitely more mysterious than even the most poetic description a writer could give of it. A writer has to find oniricity through a highly refined linguistic operation, while the cinema is much nearer to sounds physically, it doesn't need any elaboration. All it needs is to produce a clouded sky with thunder and straight away you are close to the mystery and ambiguity of reality.

- ...a tree photographed is poetic, a human face photographed is poetic because physicity is poetic in itself, because it is an apparition, because it is full of mystery, because it is full of ambiguity, because it is full of polyvalent meaning, because even a tree is a sign of a linguistic system. But who talks through a tree? God, or reality itself. Therefore the tree as a sign puts us in communication with a mysterious speaker.

- When I make a film I'm always in reality, among the trees and among the people; there's no symbolic or conventional filter between me and reality as there's in literature. The cinema is an explosion of my love for reality. I have never conceived of making a film that would be a work of a group, I've always thought of a film as a work of an author, not only the script and the direction but the choices of sets and locations, the characters, even the clothes. I choose everything, not to mention the music. (1971)

-

The cinema is a language which expresses reality with reality. So the question is: what is the difference between the cinema and reality? Practically none.

-

Reality is divine. That is why my films are never naturalistic. The motivation that unites all of my films is to give back to reality its original sacred significance. (1968)

-

I avoid fiction in my films. I do nothing to console, nothing to embellish reality, nothing to sell the goods. (1973)

-

I've never wanted to make a conclusive statement. I've always posed various problems and left them open to consideration. (1971)

NOTES ON RENAISSANCE ARTISTS

MASACCIO.
Pier Paolo Pasolini responded to the flattened perspectives of Early Renaissance art, to the *tableau* approach to grouping figures, and to the separation of foreground and background. Pasolini didn't need to 'quote' particular painters of the Renaissance, or individual paintings, because his visual approach in cinema is already informed by a frontal perspective, which arranges the action (the figures) at right angles to the camera lens.

Each painter in the Renaissance re-shaped space to his/ her own liking. Art historians dutifully record the development of illusionistic space in a progression of artists – from Cimabue and Giotto di Bondone to Masaccio, Domenico Veneziano and Masolino da Panicale, from Fra Filippo Lippi and Fra Angelico through Sandro Botticelli and Filippino Lippi, Giovanni Bellini and Raphael de Sanzio, finding an apotheosis of depth and *sfumato* in Leonardo da Vinci, but deepening in darkness still further with Michelangelo di Caravaggio, and, later, Rembrandt van Rijn.

In the art of Masaccio (1401-28), space begins to open up from the spaceless, golden backgrounds of Byzantine art. The *Crucifixion* from Masaccio's *Pisa Altarpiece* (in Naples) depicts four figures (Jesus and the 'three Marys') against a gold background which suggests, as gold always does in Renaissance painting, power and divinity. With the *Trinity* (in Santa Maria Novella, Florence), Masaccio's space deepens. The evocation of the architecture in Masaccio's *Trinity* is very powerful. He creates a barrel vault between two pilasters, seen from a low viewpoint. The architectonics of the *Trinity* are showy, theatrical, like a stage set. Masaccio monumentalizes his subjects, making God the apex of that strongest of all geometric shapes, the triangle or pyramid.

GIOTTO.

Giotto di Bondone (*c.* 1267-1337) was one of the premier artists in Italy of the 14th century, celebrated by Dante Alighieri, and seen today as one of the key architects of the focus in Early Renaissance art on the human figure. Giotto created works in Naples, Assisi, Padua, Florence and Rome; however, only the famous fresco cycle in Padua (in the Arena Chapel) is recognized as definitely authored by Giotto.

In the art of Giotto, the landscape is still very much a *background*, flattened spatially, so the action in the foreground is not connected with it. Early Renaissance landscape is full of marvellous passages of detail and light, but it is flat and relatively undynamic. In the background of Giotto's *Lamentation*, one of the chief works by Giotto, where the weeping angels swarm like crazed birds in the sky, the landscape is hardly painted in: the suggestions of rocks, a tree, and not much more.

In *The Decameron*, Pasolini cast himself as Giotto (as the artist appeared in the fiction of Giovanni Boccaccio). The Giottoan set-piece in *The Decameron* was a quasi-historical representation of the artist painting a fresco commission in a church (alluding to the Paduan fresco cycle).

PIERO DELL A FRANCESCA.

Piero della Francesca (*c.* 1410/ 20-92) has one of the most special and distinctive forms of space in painting. Piero's sense of space stands out from other painters, as with Paul Cézanne, Rembrandt van Rijn and Mark Rothko. The bright, timeless spaces of Piero are instantly recognizable, and critics sometimes evoke Greek sculpture in connection with Piero's paintings.[1] One might also see in Piero's hermetic, ritualized, timeless paintings the art of Chinese landscape painting, with its evocations of emptiness, which hints at the radical void of Eastern mysticism (in Zen Buddhism and Taoism). Piero's hypnotic art coolly melds science with art, space with spirit, the personal with the cosmic, and history, myth and religion with time.

For Piero della Francesca, geometry, proportion, perspective and mathematics had a magical quality. His art exalts, on one level, a *jouissance* of mathematics and measurement, in which the 'science' of Renaissance perspective is joyously explored. Piero seemed to lean towards the cool, impersonal, impassive scientific inquiry of Aristotlean philosophy, rather than the more sensuous, more obviously mystical aspects of Platonic philosophy: he is regarded by Bernhard Berenson as

---

[1] Like the art of Ancient Greece, Piero della Francesca's paintings rejoice in eternal brilliance, an architectonic precision, and a 'Classical' sense of proportion and harmony. In Piero's epoch, perspective, proportion and geometry attained a fetishistic quality.

'impersonal' (1960, 136). Not a few critics have noted the cool, detached, 'impersonal' approach of Piero's art. R. Vischer calls Piero a 'realist': 'above all he wishes to be a realist, to draw in a realist manner'.[2] A. Stokes regards Piero as the first Cubist, a common view of Piero;[3] while for Kenneth Clark, Piero was a fully 'classic artist'.[4] In his *Tratto della Nabilta della Pittura*, Alberti called Piero 'the greatest geometrician of his age.'[5] F.M. Godfrey was equally breathless, claiming that '[n]ever before has art blended so nobly with a mathematical purity of space-construction'.[6] Other art critics, though, have not been so convinced of Piero's talents. Lawrence Wright pointed out that 'his geometry is by our standards involved and laborious.[7]

MICHELANGELO MERISI DA CARAVAGGIO.

Of the many Renaissance and post-Renaissance painters, including those of the Baroque and Mannerist eras, the art of Michelangelo Merisi da Caravaggio (1573-1610) stands out as having marked affinities with the æsthetics of Pier Paolo Pasolini. Not, in contrast to the Early Renaissance artists, in the sense of space and visuals, but in subject matter, and in a tragic view of life. And Carvaggio's own life: he was a homosexual with a penchant for the rough trade of the streets (which he famously painted); his career was filled with controversy (and occasional violence); he had a troubled relationship with the authorities; he lived much of the time, like Pasolini, in Roma; and he died, like Pasolini, in mysterious circumstances, way before his time. Caravaggio is a Pasolinian personality, ideal for the subject of a biopic (altho' Pasolini much preferred the Early Italian Renaissance artists, like Masaccio and Giotto, to the Mannerists and Baroque artists).[8]

---

2 R. Vischer: *Luca Signorelli and the Italian Renaissance*, 1879.
3 A. Stokes: *The Stones of Rimini*, 1929.
4 Kenneth Clark: *Piero della Francesca*, Phaidon, 1969.
5 Alberti: *Tratto della Nabilta della Pittura*, 1585.
6 F.M. Godfrey: *A Student's Guide to Italian Paintings 1250-1800*, Alec Tiranti 1965, 88.
7 Lawrence Wright: *Perspective in Perspective*, Routledge 1983, 75.
8 The Pasolinian devotee, Derek Jarman, produced a very disappointing biographical movie about Caravaggio in the 1980s.

UNA VITA VIOLENTA AND *LA NOTTE BRAVA*

A VIOLENT LIFE AND *THE BIG NIGHT*

INTRODUCTION.
Before and around the time of the release of *Accattone*, some films were adapted from fiction written by Pier Paolo Pasolini – *La Notte Brava* (1959), *La Commare Secca* (1962) and *Una Vita Violenta* (1962). Producers were starting to take note of Pasolini's fiction (and his work as a screenwriter) – and they recognized that there was an audience among the youth of Italy for these sorts of stories. The films were based on Pasolini's best-known pieces of fiction – *A Violent Life* (1959) and *Ragazzi di Vita* (1955). Both *A Violent Life* and *The Big Night* share some of the same personnel (composer, editor, DP, etc).

The films were marked by young casts, filming on location (in and around Rome), black-and-white photography, jazz scores (both by Piero Piccoli), and a *milieu* of petty crime. These are movies of the 'streets' – young, would-be hustlers and crooks, prostitutes, and drunks. These are movies where a group of young lads and a group of young women hang out together (often at night, often on the margins of the communities); they smoke (*everyone* smokes); they go to bars; they drive around in cars; they get into fights; and they talk (these movies are stuffed with thousands of conversations and arguments). It's a similar social context to Pasolini's first two movies, *Accattone* and *Mamma Roma*.

Censorship is a recurring issue – you can see these films of the late '50s and early '60s pushing against what is acceptable in theatrical movies of the era, particularly in the portrayal of what young people do –

crime, drugs, sex, etc.

The movies are low budget – they have young (i.e., cheap) casts; they are set in the contemporary era (that is, the cheapest to film); they shoot in studio sets, but also make excellent use of existing locations (tho' they struggle to find enough lamps to light them at night – and many scenes are set at night).

And yet, curiously, neither *The Big Night* or *A Violent Life* feel particularly Pasolinian – if we view them in the light of Pier Paolo Pasolini's cinema, that is. As there is nothing quite like Pasolini's cinema, it's difficult to compare regular, mainstream movies to what he did as a film director. Certainly, Pasolini never made a theatrical film as seemingly conventional as either *The Big Night* or *A Violent Life* (some of his documentaries are more conventional, however). Also, even though it's impossible to say for sure, it's likely that if Pasolini had adapted his own novels for the screen, even within a mainstream format, they wouldn't have been like this (definitely no jazz music, for a start!).

THE BIG NIGHT/ LA NOTTE BRAVA

La Notte Brava (Mauro Bolognini, 1959) was based on Pier Paolo Pasolini's 1955 novel *Ragazzi di vita* (it is also known as *The Big Night, Bad Girls Don't Cry* and *On Any Street*). Jacques-Laurent Bost and Pasolini co-wrote the adaptation. It was produced by Antonio Cervi, Antonio Giommarelli and Oreste Jacovini for Ajace Film and Franco-London Film. Carlo Egidi was prod. des., Nino Baragli was ed., cost. by Marcel Escoffier, hair by Adriana Cassini, make-up by Duilio Scarozza, Armando Nannuzzi was DP, score by Piero Piccioni, 1st A.D.: Rinaldo Ricci, sound by Mario Amari and Mario Faraoni. Released: Nov 14, 1959. 95 mins.

In the cast were: Rosanna Schiaffino, Laurent Terzieff, Jean-Claude Brialy, Franco Interlenghi, Tomas Milian, Anna Maria Ferrero, Antonella Lauldi, Mylène Demengeot and Elsa Martinelli.

The cast of *The Big Night* is excellent – note the two young, French turks, Brialy and Terzieff, in the cast (this was an Italian-French co-production). The girls are wonderful together, as are the three lads. For much of *The Big Night*, we are observing these two groups interacting as threesomes, and also hanging out with each other. Forget the background story of selling rifles and petty crime, it's the characterizations and the performances that really pop out of *The Big Night*.

The three actresses – Laudi, Martinelli, Ferrero – are superb as knowing, smart, street-tough hookers, and play beautifully together as an ensemble. The three punks – Brialy, Terzieff, Interlenghi – are convincing as wannabe petty crooks, acting tough but actually possessing little influence in the harsh world of the Roman suburbs (they wouldn't last two minutes in an organized crime outfit).

The emphasis is still on the guys in *The Big Night*, as usual in movies of this period (reflecting the patriarchal bias of society in Italia). However, *The Big Night* generously hands over much screen time to the women, and has them one step ahead of the boys (who cockily reckon they rule the roost).

There are some self-consciously homosocial scenes in *The Big Night*: in one scene, the lads recline languorously in a bourgeois home, listening to records (jazz again),[9] all with their shirts undone and looking like male models (which, as casting directors knew well, was a common look for many young actors in Italia, and the actors are certainly attractive).

A VIOLENT LIFE/ UNA VITA VIOLENTA

Una Vita Violenta (*A Violent Life,* dirs. Paolo Heusch and Brunello Rondi, 1962) was a version of Pier Paolo Pasolini's novel of 1959. It's the same *milieu* as *Accattone*, though it was released after *Accattone*. (*A Violent Life* shares some of the same personnel as Pasolini's cinema, such as Franco Citti, dialogue adviser Sergio Citti, Danilo Donati, costumes, camera operator Giuseppe Ruzzolini, and editor Nino Baragli).

A Violent Life was produced by Moris Ergas for Aera Films and Zebra Film. It was adapted by Ennio De Concini, Franco Brusati, Paolo Heusch, Brunello Rondi and Franco Solinas (five writers, no less! Plus Sergio Citti advising on the dialogue). In the cast were: Franco Citti, Serena Vergano, Alfredo Leggi, Angelo Maria Santiamantini, Benito Poliani, Giorgio Santangelo, Piero Morgia, and Enrico Maria Salerno (the

---

[9] In a Pasolini version, they'd be listening to Bach, and discussing which was the best of the recent recordings of the *St Matthew Passion,* and who was the best conductor of Beethoven – Karajan, Furtwängler or Kleiber.

voice of Jesus in *The Gospel According To Matthew*). Armando Nannuzzi was DP; Nella Nannuzzi edited; Danilo Donati was wardrobe; Luigi Scaccianoce was art dir.; and sound by Fausto Ancillai, Franco Groppioni and Nino Renda. It was filmed in b/w, with a mainly jazz score[10] by Piero Piccioni. Released: Mch 21, 1962. 115 mins.

Like *Accattone*, *A Violent Life* focusses on a youth played by Franco Citti (in *A Violent Life*, however, Citti is playing much younger than his 23 years). Disaffected, rebellious, and drifting towards petty crime, Tommasso is struggling to find his way in the challenging world of postwar Italy.

A Violent Life features numerous Pasolinian scenes and characters, from the Roman shanty town[11] *milieu* to the small-time street criminals. It's all here – the tight-knit group of youths, the *braggadocio*, the prowling about the streets at night in cars in search of fun (or trouble), the fights, and the crammed, working class local scene, a neighbourhood where everybody lives on top of each other.

A Violent Life doesn't shy away from depicting the seedy, cruel sides of life in a poor, Roman neighbourhood – the youths rough up a couple in a car, taking their money, and tormenting the woman, they cruelly taunt a vagabond, they snatch bags, and there are the inevitable street brawls.

And Tommasso, altho' he's the hero/ anti-hero, and suffering a-plenty, is also a boor, raw and crude. He's one of those youths of Existential literature who don't know what they want and don't know how to get it. Nothing in the world seems right for him, and nothing seems to go his way, and he struggles to make things work.

Like many an anti-hero and outsider in Existential, European fiction, Tommasso beats his head against pretty much everything – the State, the society, the Church, the police, even his chums (who might be expected to be on his side). He acts like an oaf with his girlfriend Irene, steals, gets into a fight, goes to jail, has tuberculosis, enters a sanatorium, etc.

A Violent Life is a story of existence in constant decay – Tommasso seems to stumble from one calamity to the next. He's involved in heated brawls on the street, petty crime, weary jealousies, and spends time in prison and in hospital. *A Violent Life* is a kind of 'angry young man' movie, which has numerous links to Neo-realist cinema, and to other films of the period which explored youth culture. The ontological decline continues to the final scene, which is a death scene: the last shot of *A*

---

10 It's not an especially distinctive score, and is marred by too many too-mournful trumpet solos.
11 The film opens with lengthy pan shots around the well-known sights of Roma, moving slowly towards the *borgate*, the side of Rome never shown in the tourist brochures.

Violent Life is of Tommasso expiring.

That the movie accuses sections of Italian society is no surprise – Pier Paolo Pasolini in his writings and movies did that many times. Who's to blame? Or rather, where do you start? No institution, it seems, can really help Tommasso, even tho' he reaches out to the Church and to the State, eventually slipping into the minor criminal underworld. Every social organization seems to abandon him (presumably he left school as soon as he could). Desperation seethes throughout this 1962 film.

What comes across loud and clear in both *Accattone* and *A Violent Life,* beyond the stories and the characters, is the attitude of rebellion, the struggle against disempowerment, the urge towards agency. For these *ragazzi*, prospects seem slim, the older generation (and Italy at large) ignores them, and yet they retain the fierce pride of the downtrodden.

The Big Night (1959),
left and below.
A Violent Life (1962),
bottom.

BERNARDO BERTOLUCCI:

LA COMMARE SECCA

THE GRIM REAPER

The Grim Reaper (*La Commare Secca*, 1962) was produced by Antonio Cervi for Compagnia Cinematografica Cervi/ Cineriz, written by Bernardo Bertolucci and Sergio Citti from a story by Pier Paolo Pasolini, edited by Nino Baragli, photography by Giovanni Narzisi, music by Piero Piccioni, costumes by Adriana Spadaro, and sound by Alessandro Fortini. Released Nov 2, 1962 (Aug 27,1962 in Venice). 88 mins.

The Grim Reaper was produced in the shadow of Pier Paolo Pasolini. It was Bernardo Bertolucci's first film as director (aged 21), but it was very much a work created inside the cinematic world that Pasolini has developed in his first movies, and in the movies based on his stories, *A Violent Life* and *The Big Night*. Many in the production team were from Pasolini's crew (including editor Nino Baragli), and the script was co-written with Sergio Citti, Pasolini's regular collaborator (and lover).

It's no surprise, then, that *The Grim Reaper* was filmed in the Pasolinian mode, with poetic, black-and-white photography (by Giovanni Narzisi), a setting of working class Rome, a story of Roman low life and thieves, and a lyrical soundtrack (by Piero Piccioni, who scored *The Night Night* and *A Violent Life*), which includes plaintive acoustic guitar and whistle (plus some *film noir* jazz, and a selection of Italian pop songs[1]). The influence of Neo-realist cinema is apparent in *The Grim Reaper*, but there's a new poeticizing of the material (reflected in some of the mobile shots).

---

1 Again, it's not the soundtrack that Pasolini would use.

Some of the visuals in *The Grim Reaper* display the elaborate tracking and panning shots which characterized Bernardo Bertolucci's later work. The influence of Orson Welles on the sequence shots, and of Jean-Luc Godard on the long-held close-ups, is obvious. Some of the shots are rather awkward and self-conscious (and even in Bertolucci's mature films, there are many fussy, look-at-me shots).

The Grim Reaper is a companion piece to *Mamma Roma* and *Accattone* (*Mamma Roma* was released in the same year as *The Grim Reaper*) – it's the same world of prostitutes, drifters and thieves, the same colourful characters from Rome's *borgate*, and the same themes of the struggle to survive and taking to crime in order to do so. Thus, many of the locales in *The Grim Reaper* are the same as those in Pasolini's early films. (We spend a *lot* of time in *The Grim Reaper* on the edges of Rome and in the *borgate*, in the grassy, rubble-strewn fields (which have since been built over). In addition, there are scenes alongside the River Tiber, on bridges, and in parks overlooking the city).

✦

The narrative hook of *The Grim Reaper* is a murder mystery – the killing of a prostitute (Wanda Rocci) in Parco Paloino at night where a bunch of characters pass through on the night of the crime. The film follows each character, and includes scenes of them being interviewed by an offscreen cop (sometimes the police interview is heard in voiceover). Robert Kolker in his book on Bertolucci recommends seeing the film twice, to understand how it all fits together (18).

The Grim Reaper isn't interested in the murder as much as the group of characters that are linked to the deed: this is another evocation of the Pasolinian under-class, the small-time crooks and hookers we met in *Accattone* and *Mamma Roma*.

They are people who know how to live but somehow they refuse to follow the usual methods of survival in a modern society. They would rather spend their time pursuing criminal or anti-social possibilities. They are rebels by nature (by birth or by right, you might say), but they lack the *ooomph* to live fully as rebels. They prefer to get what they want by simply taking it (usually in the easiest way).

Masculinity in crisis is another issue found in *The Grim Reaper*, as in some of Pier Paolo Pasolini's films of the period. It's not women and their increasing economic independence and social agency in the early 1960s that exacerbates the uneasy position of men. Rather, it's society itself that some of the young men have difficulty grappling with; social integration is again a sub-issue: this under-class simply refuses to integrate in the usual manner with their community. (However, the playboy figure Bostelli finds his girlfriend Esperia very challenging. She's not going to give up on him until she's squeezed him dry).

Homosexuality is hinted at in some of the vignettes of the people associated with the murder (men lurking in parks at night), though not stated blatantly (this was 1962).

The narrative structure of the vignettes of the characters in *The Grim Reaper* who congregate at Parco Paolino on the night of the murder is bolstered by two narratives frames: one is the series of police interviews with each of the characters; the other is short scenes depicting the murder victim (Wanda Rocci) getting ready for work in her apartment (a rain storm is also included as a poetic refrain – echoes of *Rashomon* or *Francesco*).

✦

First we meet 'il Canticchia' (Francesco Ruiu) and his small-time crooks, who prowl the countryside and caves on the borders of Rome's suburbs, searching for victims to rob. It's typical of Pier Paolo Pasolini (and Bernardo Bertolucci) that their targets are couples making out on the ground (they aim for the purses and radios left nearby). As in Pasolini's early movies, there's a vivid evocation of the desperation and the pathos of stealing at such a petty level.[2] But this is modulated by the rough and tumble camaraderie of the thieves. They may seem to be losers and have almost nothing, and they're scrabbling for existence, but they are also joking with each other. There's a solidarity and loyalty in their low-rent brotherhood.

Canticchia is weak, a loser, a drifter – one of those characters, as with Accattone, who thinks he has nothing but who reckons he deserves everything. Society owes him big, he thinks, tho' for exactly what, he isn't sure (perhaps simply for existing). Canticchia is a king in his mind, but of nowhere, and out of nothing, and nobody else regards him as royalty.

Canticchia is a weasel – when he's caught filching a radio (with echoes of Ettore in *Mamma Roma*), he begs pathetically to the couple to save his hide (rather than be turned over to the police). Once he's out of earshot, he loudly curses the couple in the park who rounded on him.

Another character, Bostelli (Alfredo Leggi), is a small-time (ex) pimp who works with his prostitute girlfriend, Esperia (Gabriella Giorgelli). Bostelli is vain (he has bleach-blond hair and a nice suit), and is an avid

---

[2] There's a lot of effort expended on the thieving, for little return.

consumer (he has a flashy, open-top car[3] complete with a record player so he can have music from 7-inch singles). This section of *The Grim Reaper* (the second part of act one) is filled with characters shouting at each other (Esperia yells at the hookers she's visiting to collect their money, and at her mom and family). So the viewer is sucked into a fifteen minute argument conducted at the hysterical pitch of a street brawl (in the classic, passionate Italian manner, knives are drawn and curses fly as the participants threaten to kill each other. Later, Esperia draws a knife on Bostelli on the street; he flees).

The 1962 movie continues to follow a number of characters for short periods, each of whom is linked to the murder of the prostitute and is interviewed by the police: one is a foolish, simple-minded soldier from Calabria (Constantino Tedoro) who pursues women[4] and loafs around the Colosseum; another is a shifty guy wearing clogs, from Friuli (Natalino – Renato Troiani), who lurks around the park at night; and Pipito and Francolicchio, two young lads who chase girls.

Francolicchio (Alvaro d'Ercole) and Pipito (Romano Labate) are classic, rootless loafers, laid-back, immature, naïve; they hang out, they pursue two girls, and they find they need to come up with 2,000 Lire to buy some food. This leads them to steal a gold cigarette lighter from a guy they meet in the park at night. When they discover that the cops are after them (during a classic, Pasolinian setting – kicking a football around on some waste ground), they flee along the river. Francolicchio tries swimming in the Tiber to escape, and drowns. (One of the ironies of *The Grim Reaper* here is that the police want to bring in the boys to question them about the murder, not for the theft of a cigarette lighter).

The capture of the culprit (clogs-wearing man Natalino) occurs in the Hitchcockian setting of a bar of dancing couples. The witness of the murder of the prostitute wanders amongst the swaying, dancing lovers until he hears the tell-tale clatter of the clogs (a very Hitchcockian device), which identifies the killer.

---

3 The ostentatious car might be another of Pasolini's digs at consumer-capitalism, but he drove one himself.
4 Captured in a striking montage of Teodoro on the streets of Roma following women, all of whom brush him off.

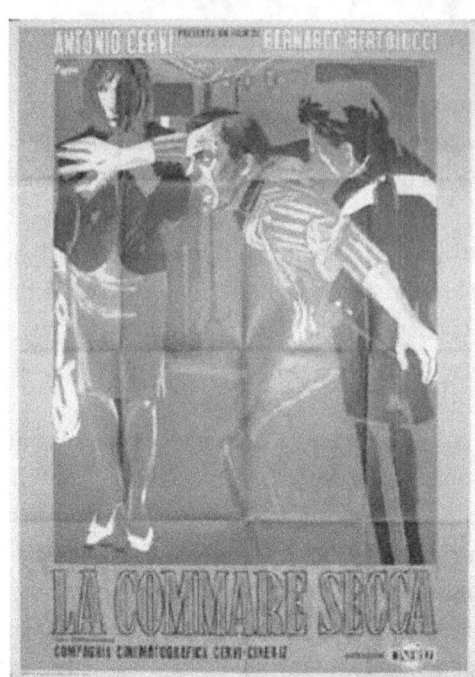

The Grim Reaper (1962).

SERGIO CITTI: TWO FILMS:

OSTIA AND *STORIE SCELLERATE*

OSTIA AND *BAWDY TALES*

OSTIA

Ostia (1970) was produced by Anna Maria Chretien and Alvaro Mancori, written by Sergio Citti and Pier Paolo Pasolini, with music by Francesco De Masi, Mario Mancini was DP, eds.: Nino Baragli and Carlo Reali, prod. des. by Claudio Giambanco, sound by Angelo Spadoni, costumes and set dec. by Mario Ambrosino. The cast included: Laurent Terzieff,[1] Franco Citti, Anita Sanders, Lamberto Maggiorani, Celestino Compagnoni, Nino Davoli, Lily Tirinnanzi, and Settimio Picone. Released Mch 11, 1970. 103 minutes.

    Ostia emerges with numerous links to Pier Paolo Pasolini, including many in the crew and the cast, and themes such as the focus on a group of young men, and the suburban, working class, Italian *milieu*. Sergio Citti, tho', steps out from the shadow that Pasolini casts over *Ostia* as a director: despite its many Pasolinian ingredients, *Ostia* is not a Pasolini film. The opening scenes appear Pasolinian at first – the discovery of a young woman (Monica – Anita Sanders) in the countryside – but soon they become something else. The rhythms and pacing of *Ostia*, for instance, are not Pasolinian, nor is the staging. Much of the movie, too, is filmed in the studio, and focusses on two central characters (it is partly a chamber piece, and a duologue). If Pasolini had taken on *Ostia*, he would've moved his characters out and about much more.

---

1 He was dubbed by Sergio Citti.

Ostia is one of those movies in which nothing seems to happen, in which characters loaf about, and the narrative seems freewheeling. Like: the trio visits the beach... like: Monica goes for a swim... like: the lads make up a story of their childhood which features venal, drunken parents... like: Monica fascinates Rabbino and Bandiera; she's a ray of light or life in their seemingly humdrum lives...

Ostia is not afraid to contemplate some troubling issues, such as attempted rape and incest (centred around the character of Monica). Homosexuality is evoked numerous times in *Ostia*, from the opening scene, where Rabbino and Bandiera wait downstairs, and get drunk, while Fiorino and the other lads are upstairs fooling around with the foundling, to scenes such as some crossdressing (where Monica puts wigs and make-up on the youths).

The influence of Pier Paolo Pasolini is felt in the final reels of *Ostia*, which move into a more mythological, spiritual realm: the lads visit the beach with Monica for a second time, and there's another trip out in a rowing boat. At night, around an open fire, things get ugly when Bandiera discovers Rabbino attempting to make love with Monica, and lays into him (both have fallen for Monica by now). Rabbino retaliates a little too fiercely with a tree branch, and kills Bandiera.

The ending of *Ostia* is a little too contrived and melodramatic, in terms of what happens amongst the characters. More intriguing is the decision to play all of it without dialogue, and accompanied by religious, choral music (the sort of music that Pier Paolo Pasolini puts in many of his films). The music, plus the images of the calm ocean, and Rabbino staring into the void as he takes Bandiera's corpse out in the boat and dumps it over the side, are haunting.

There is also a curiously effective piece of montage (by editors Baragli and Reali) which features visitors to the beach putting up parasols and tables, preparing for a day at the seaside... and Rabbino is sitting next to the cadaver of Bandiera who might be asleep beside him, so no one notices that he's dead.[2]

---

[2] A death at Ostia has sad links to Pasolini's own demise.

BAWDY TALES/ STORIE SCELLERATE

Bawdy Tales (*Storie scellerate*, 1973) is about the closest thing to a Pier Paolo Pasolini movie without being directed by the Master. With Sergio Citti, Pasolini is credited with the story and the script, and the movie was made with many of the same key personnel behind and in front of the camera as Pasolini's movies: Grimaldi (pr.), Ferretti (prod. des.), Donati (cost.), Delli Colli (DP), Baragli (ed.), etc, among the crew, and in the cast: Davoli, Citti, Genovese, Garofolo, etc. Released Oct 12, 1973. 93 mins.

Thus, *Bawdy Tales* is a good example to use as an exploration of just what a director is or does: the conception of *Bawdy Tales,* the way it's filmed, the genre (historical), the technical aspects, the actors and the crew – they're all Pasolinian.

Indeed, Sergio Citti and Pier Paolo Pasolini had worked together so many times, since the mid-1950s, they could've swopped roles (Pasolini working as 1st A.D. for Citti as director, for instance), and directed each other's scripts.

With a script co-written by Pier Paolo Pasolini, *Bawdy Tales* displays all of the familiar Pasolinian touches. One of the most obvious ones is the structure of *Bawdy Tales:* it's based around storytelling, with Ninetto Davoli and Franco Citti as two small-time crooks who tell each other stories (the 'bawdy tales' of the title).[3]

Bawdy Tales has many affinities with the 'trilogy of life' movies, including a similar sort of approach, and some of the same cast (Franco Citti, Ninetto Davoli, Elisabetta Genovese, etc).

Bawdy Tales presents a colourful world of lovers, cuckolded husbands, horny priests and greedy thieves. Indeed, the title may be *Bawdy Tales,*[4] but there is as much here about ruffians and crime. Indeed, the frame story, of Davoli and Citti, has them murdering a guy on their travels (for his loot), and finding themselves caught and imprisoned. Even in jail, they continue to tell tales, and are laughing about their latest yarn on the scaffold, as they're hung.

Bawdy Tales displays the high art aspects of Pier Paolo Pasolini's cinema – the historical settings, the costumes, the Church, the clergy, religion, etc, as well as the crudity, the nudity, the erotica, the groups of virile youths, etc.

Costume designer Danilo Donati makes perhaps his worst selection

---

[3] The thieves meet in a classic, Pasolinian manner – as they hurry away to find somewhere to shit.
[4] The relationships are heterosexual in *Bawdy Tales*, but Citti and Pasolini manage to squeeze in a river full of naked boys bathing (completely gratuitous).

in *Bawdy Tales* when he puts all of the guys in flares. All movies are about and reflect the time of their production, but the early 1970s sees flared pants, big collars, long hair and other aspects of clothing which would look great in a disco in Rome (but haven't aged well).

In the first story of *Bawdy Tales,* we are in Rome *circa* 1800, with a clichéd yarn about cuckolded husbands and their lusty wives. So Caterina di Ronciglione (Nicoletta Machiavelli) has a weak, submissive, older, spoilt husband, Duca di Ronciglione (Silvano Gatti), and fancies something younger and more energetic. While he sleeps, she slips away for nighttime dalliances. In a later sequence, she takes on a whole bunch of *ragazzi* (one of whom is played by Ettore Garofolo, the son in *Mamma Roma*). Fellatio leads to group sex (for an erotic comedy, *Bawdy Tales* is very coy, and cuts away from the deeds).

The alluring Elisabetta Genovese (with her kilowatt smile, seen in *The Arabian Nights* and *The Canterbury Tales*) plays Bertolina, another bored wife in the first story; she has an affair with the local priest, much to her husband Nicolino's (Enzo Petriglia) dismay.

Other stories in *Bawdy Tales* include a thief who frames a priest with the promise of a woman, who then robs him; a long tale (which we return to) of the clergy; another yarn about a betrayed husband, etc.

Bawdy Tales features one of the silliest things that Pier Paolo Pasolini and Sergio Citti cooked up together as scriptwriters: the Chopping Of The Weiner. Yes, the first bawdy tale in *Bawdy Tales* has both wives receiving their punishment. The husband and his pal, armed with knives, burst in upon Bertolina and the priest: Bertolina is stabbed, and dies; then the youths force the priest to cut off his penis. Meanwhile, the furious Duca di Ronciglione commands his wife to undress at home, then drags her down to the basement, hurling her into a room and locking it. And then, before a window overlooking the cell, he slices off his own member in front of his wife, collapsing to the ground in agony.

It's remarkable, perhaps, how unremarkable *Bawdy Tales* is (despite scenes such as weiner removal). The concept and the narrative is wholly clichéd (tho' still sort of new in 1973, in the degree of sexual explicitness). And the story progresses exactly how you'd expect. The comedy, sadly, is rather routine and again suffers from its difficulty in traversing national/ cultural borders.[5]

---

[5] Consider how funny Woody Allen's movies were of this time, which also took on historical genres: *Love and Death* and the first skit in *Everything You Wanted To Know About Sex*. An unfair comparison, of course – because Allen is a comic genius, and the pacing is about 2 million miles-an-hour faster than *Bawdy Tales*.

Ostia (1970).

Bawdy Tales (1973)

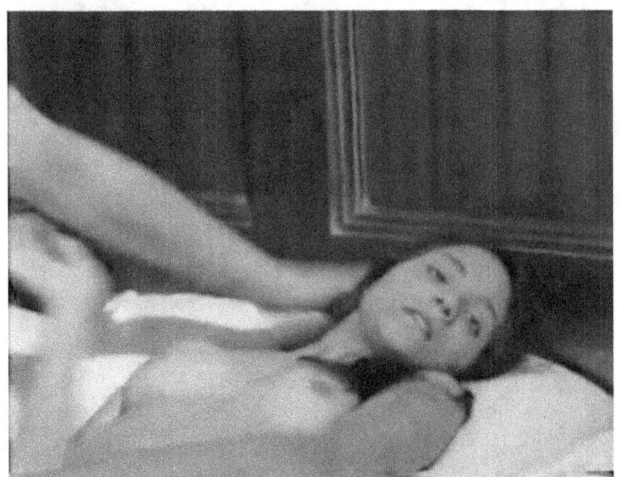

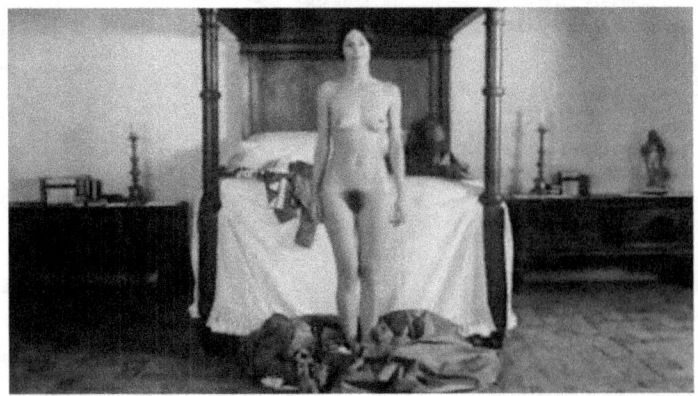

PIER PAOLO PASOLINI

FILMOGRAPHY AND BIBLIOGRAPHY

FEATURE FILMS

Beggar (*Accattone*, 1961)
Mother Rome (*Mamma Roma*, 1962)
Love Meetings (a.k.a. *Lessons In Love*, *Comizi d'Amore*, 1964)
The Gospel According To Matthew (*Il Vangelo Secondo Matteo*, 1964)
The Hawks and the Sparrows (*Uccellacci e Uccellini*, 1966)
Oedipus Rex (*Edipo Re*, 1967)
Theorem (*Teorma*, 1968)
Pigsty (*Porcile*, 1969)
Medea (*Medea*, 1969)
The Decameron (*Il Decamerone*, 1971)
The Canterbury Tales (*I Racconti di Canterbury*, 1972)
The Arabian Nights (*Il Fiore Delle Mille e Una Notte*, 1974)
Salò, or The 120 Days of Sodom (*Salò, o le Centoventi Giornate di Sodoma*, 1975)

SHORT FILMS

The Anger (*La Rabbia*, 1963)
Curd Cheese (*La Ricotta*, episode in *RoGoPaG*, 1963)
The Earth Seen From the Moon (*La Terra Vista Dalla Luna*, episode in *The Witches* = *Le Streghe*, 1967)
What Are the Clouds? (*Che Cosa Sono le Nuvole?*, episode in *Caprice Italian Style* = *Capriccio all'Italiana*, 1968)
The Sequence of the Flower Field (*La Sequenza del Fiore di Carta*, episode in *Love and Anger* = *Vangelo '70/ Amore e Rabbia*, 1969)

DOCUMENTARIES

Location Hunting In Palestine (*Sopralluoghi in Palestina Per Il Vangelo secondo Matteo*, 1965)
Notes For a Film In India (*Appunti Per un Film Sull'India*, 1969)
Notes For a Garbage Novel (*Appunti Per un romanzo dell'immondizia*, 1970)
Notes Towards an African Oresteia (*Appunti Per un'Orestiade Africana*,

1970)
The Walls of Sana'a (*Le Mura di Sana'a*, 1971)
12 December 1972 (*12 Dicembre 1972*, 1972)
Pasolini and the Shape of the City (*Pasolini e la forma della città*, 1975)

SCRIPTS

The River Girl (1954)
Il Prigioniero della montagna (1955)
Manon: Finestra 2 (1956)
Nights of Cabiria (1956)
A Farewell To Arms (1957)
Marisa la Civetta (1957)
Giovani Mariti (1958)
Grigio (1958)
La Notte Brava (1959)
Marte di un Amico (1960)
From a Roman Balcony (1960)
Il Carro armato dell'8 settembre (1960)
I Bell'Antonio (1960)
La Lunga Notte del '43 (1960)
Accattone, F.M., Rome, 1960
La Ragazza In Vetrina (1961)
La Commare Secca (1962)
Mamma Roma, Rizzoli, Milan, 1962
Il Vangelo secondo Matteo, Garzanti, Milan, 1964
Uccellacci e uccellini, Garzanti, Milan, 1966
Oedipus Rex, Garzanti, Milan, 1967/ Lorrimer Publishing, 1984
Requiescant (1967, uncredited)
Il Ragazzo-motore (1967)
Theorem, Garzanti, Milan, 1968
Medea, Garzanti, Milan, 1970
Ostia, Garzanti, Milan, 1970
Storie Scellerate (1973)
Trilogia della vita, Cappelli, Bologna, 1975
San Paolo, Einaudi, Turin, 1977

WORKS AFTER PASOLINI'S DEATH

Laboratorio teatrale di Luca Ronconi (1977)
Mulheres... Mulheres (1981)
Calderon (1981)
Die Leiche murde nie gefunden (1985)
L'Altro enigma (1988)
Who Killed Pasolini? (1995)
Complicity (1995)
Il Pratone del casilino (1996)
Le Bassin de J.W. (1997)
Una Disperata vitalità (1999)
Orgia (2002)
Salò: Yesterday and Today (2002)
Pasolini prossimo nostro (2006)
'Na specie de cadavere lunghissimo (2006)
La Rabbia di Pasolini (2008)
Pilades (2016)

POETRY

Poesie e Casarsa, Libreroa Antiqua Mario Landi, Bologna, 1942
Poesie, Stamperia Primon, 1945
Diarii, 1945
I Pianti, Publicazioni dell-Academiuta, Casarsa, 1946
Dove la mia patria, Publicazioni dell-Academiuta, Casarsa, 1949
Poesia dialettale del Novecento, Guanda, Parma, 1952
Tal cour di un frut, Editizioni Friuli, Tricesimo, 1953/ 1974
Dal Diario, Salvatore Sciascia, Caltanisetta, 1954
Il Canto popolare, La Meridiana, Milan, 1954
La Meglio gioventu, Sansoni, Florence, 1954
Le Ceneri di Gramsci, Garzanti, Milan, 1957
L'Usignolo della Chiesa Cattolica, Loganesi, Milan, 1958/ Turin, 1976
Roma 1950, Milan, 1960
Sonetto primaverile, Milan, 1960
La Religione del mio tempo, Garzanti, Milan, 1961
Poesia in forma di rosa, Garzanti, Milan, 1964
Poesie dimenticate, Società Filologica Friulana, Udine, 1965
Potentissima Signora, Longanesi, Milan, 1965
Poesie, Garzanti, Milan, 1970/ 1999
Transumanar e organizzar, Garzanti, Milan, 1971
Le Poesie, Garzanti, Milan, 1975
La Nuova gioventro, Einaudi, Turin, 1975
Poesie e pagine ritrovate, 1980
Poems, New York, 1982
Sette Poesie e due lettere, 1984
Roman Poems, City Lights, 1986
Poems, 1996
Poems Scelte, 1997
Poesie rifiutate, 2000
La Nuova gioventu, 2002
Tutte le poesie, 2003
Meditazione orale, 2005
Poeta delle ceneri, 2010

FICTION

Ragazzi di Vita, Garzanti, Milan, 1955/ London, 1989
Una Vita Violenta, Garzanti, Milan, 1959
Donne di Roma, Il Saggiatore, Milan, 1960
A Dream of Something, 1962
Roman Nights and Other Stories, 1965
La Divina Mimesis, 1975
Amado mio, Aitti impuri, 1982
Petrolio, 1992/ 2005
Stories From the City of God, 1995
Romanzi e racconti, 1998
Il re dei giapponesi, 2003

Pier Paolo Pasolini in Rome, 1967 (by Franco Vitale).

BIBLIOGRAPHY

PIER PAOLO PASOLINI

Pasolini On Pasolini, ed. Oswald Stack, Thames & Hudson, London, 1969
Entretiens avec Pier Paolo Pasolini, Belfond, Paris, 1970
Interview, *Lui*, no. 1, June, 1970
Empirismo eretico, Garzanti, Milan, 1972
Interview, *The Guardian*, Aug 13, 1973
Con Pier Paolo Pasolini, ed. E. Magrelli, Bulzoni, Rome, 1977
Il dialogo, il potere, la morte: la critica e Pasolini, ed. L. Martellini, Cappelli, Bologna, 1979
"Sopralluoghi o la ricerca dei luoghi perduti" (1973), in M. Mancini & G. Perella, 1982
Lutheran Letters, tr. S. Hood, Carcanet Press, 1987
A Future Life, Rome, 1989
"The Lost Pasolini Interview", C*elluloid Liberation Front*, 2012

OTHERS

G. Aichele. "Translation as De-canonization: Matthew's *Gospel* According to Pasolini", *Cross Currents,* 2002
T. Aitken. "The Greatest Story – Never Told", *The Tablet*, Dec 23, 1995
H. Alpert. *Fellini: A Life*, Paragon House, New York, N.Y., 1988
R. Altman, ed. *Sound Theory, Sound Practice*, Routledge, London, 1992
—. *Film/ Genre*, British Film Institute, London, 1999
D. Andrew. *The Major Film Theories*, Oxford University Press, Oxford, 1976
—. *Concepts In Film Theory*, Oxford University Press, Oxford, 1984
—. ed. *Breathless*, Rutgers University Press, New Brunswick, N.J., 1987
G. Andrew. *The Film Handbook*, Longman, London, 1989
G. Annovi. *Pier Paolo Pasolini,* Columbia University Press, 2017
S. Arecco. *Pier Paolo Pasolini,* Partisan, Rome, 1972
G. Austin. *Contemporary French Cinema,* Manchester University Press, Manchester, 1996
B. Babington. *Biblical Epic and Sacred Narrative In the Hollywood,* Manchester University Press, Manchester, 1993
G. Bachmann. "Pasolini on de Sade", *Film Quarterly*, vol. 29, no. 2, 1975-76
—. "The 220 Days of Sodom", *Film Comment*, vol. 12, no. 2, Mch-Apl, 1976 (and in *Scraps From the Loft*, June 7, 2018)
M. Barker, ed. *The Video Nasties: Freedom and Censorship In the Media*, Pluto Press, London, 1984
—. & J. Petley, eds. *Ill Effects: The Media/ Violence Debate*, Routledge, London, 1997

R. Barthes. *S/Z*, Hill and Wang, New York, N.Y., 1974
—. *The Pleasure of the Text*, Hill and Wang, New York, N.Y., 1975
—. *Image, Music, Text*, tr. S. Heath, Fontana, London, 1984
G. Bataille. *Literature and Evil*, Calder & Boyars, London, 1973
—. *The Story of the Eye,* Penguin, London, 1982
L. Bawden, ed. *The Oxford Companion To Film*, Oxford University Press, Oxford, 1976
J. Baxter. *An Appalling Talent: Ken Russell,* M. Joseph, London, 1973
—. *Fellini*, St Martin's Press, New York, 1993
A. Bazin. *What Is Cinema?*, University of California Press, Berkeley, C.A., 1960, 2 vols
—. "Cinema and Theology", *South Atlantic Quarterly*, 91, 2, 1992
M. Beja. *Film and Literature: An Introduction,* Longman, London, 1979
—. ed. *Perspectives On Orson Welles*, G.K. Hall, Boston, M.A., 1995
D. Bellezza. *Morte di Pasolini*, Milan, 1981
R. Bellour & M. Bandy, eds. *Jean-Luc Godard,* Museum of Modern Art, N.Y., 1992
Maurizio De Benedictis. *Sergio Citti. Lo "straniero" del cinema italiano*, Lithos, 2008
Bernard Berenson: *The Italian Painters of the Renaissance*, Phaidon 1952/ Fontana 1960
A. Bergala & J. Narboni, eds. *Pasolini Cinéaste*, Paris, 1981
R. Bergan & R. Karney. *Bloomsbury Foreign Film Guide*, Bloomsbury, London, 1988
D. Bergman. *Gaiety Transfigured,* Madison, 1991
I. Bergman. *Bergman On Bergman, Interviews with Ingmar Bergman*, eds. S. Björkman *et al,* tr. P. B. Austin, Touchstone, New York, N.Y., 1986
—. *The Magic Lantern: An Autobiography*, London, 1988
—. *Images: My Life In Film,* Faber, London, 1994
A. Bertini. *Teoria e tecnica del film in Pasolini*, Rome, 1979
B. Bertolucci. *Bertolucci By Bertolucci*, with E. Ungari and D. Ranvard, Plexus, London, 1987
P. Biskind. *Easy Riders, Raging Bulls: How the Sex 'n' Drugs 'n' Rock 'n' Roll Generation Saved Hollywood*, Bloomsbury, London, 1998
V. Boarini. *Da Accattone a Salo*, Bologna, 1982
P. Bogdanovitch. *This Is Orson Welles,* Da Capo, New York, 1998
L. Bolton & C.S. Manson, eds. *Italy On Screen: National Identity and Italian Imaginary*, New Studies in European Cinema Series, Peter Lang, 2010
J. Boorman, ed. *Projections 4*, Faber, London, 1995
—. *Projections 4 1/2*, Positif Editions/ Faber, London, 1995
D. Bordwell & K. Thompson. *Film Art: An Introduction,* McGraw-Hill Publishing Company, New York, N.Y., 1979
—. *The Films of Carl-Theodor Dreyer*, University of California, Berkeley, 1981
—. et al. *The Classical Hollywood Cinema: Film Style and Mode of Production To 1960*, Routledge, London, 1985
—. *Narration In the Fiction Film*, Routledge, London, 1988
—. *Ozu and the Poetics of Cinema*, British Film Institute, London, 1988
—. *Making Meaning*, Harvard University Press, Cambridge, M.A., 1989
—. & N. Caroll, eds. *Post-Theory: Reconstructing Film Studies*, University of Wisconsin Press, Madison, W.I., 1996
—. *The Way Hollywood Tells It*, University of California Press, Berkeley, C.A., 2006
—. & K. Thompson. *Film History*, McGraw-Hill, 2010
F. Brady. *Citizen Welles*, Scribner's, New York, 1989
P. Braunberger. *Pierre Braunberger*, Centre National de la Cinématographie,

Paris, 1987
D. Breskin. *Inner Voices: Filmmakers In Conversation*, Da Capo, New York, 1997
R. Bresson, *Notes On the Cinematographer*, Quartet, London, 1986
F. Brevini, ed. *Pasolini*, Mondadori, Milan, 1981
R. Brody. *Everything Is Cinema: The Working Life of Jean-Luc Godard*, Faber, London, 2008
R. Brown, ed. *Focus On Godard*, Prentice-Hall, N.J., 1972
Gian Piero Brunetta. *The History of Italian Cinema*, Princeton University Press, 2009
S. Bukatman. *Terminal Identity: The Virtual Subject In Postmodern Science Fiction*, Duke University Press, Durham, N.C., 1993
P.J. Burgard, ed. *Nietzsche and the Feminine*, University Press of Virginia, Charlottesville, 1994
R. Burgoyne. *Bertolucci's 1900*, Wayne State University Press, Detroit, M.I., 1991
F. Burke and M. Waller, eds. *Federico Fellini: Contemporary Perspectives*, University of Toronto Press, 2002
I. Butler. *Religion In the Cinema*, A.S. Barnes, New York, N.Y., 1969
J. Butler. *Gender Trouble: Feminism and the Subversion of Identity*, Routledge, London, 1990
R. Butter *et al*, eds. *Displacing Homophobia: Gay Male Perspectives In Literature and Culture*, London, 1989
I. Cameron, ed. *The Films of Jean-Luc Godard*, Praeger, N.Y., 1969
A. Carotenuto. *L'Autunno della Conscienza*, Turin, 1985
N. Carroll. *Mystifying Movies: Fads and Fallacies of Contemporary Film Theory*, Columbia University Press, New York, N.Y., 1988
S. Casi. *Desiderio di Pasolini*, La Sonda, Turin, 1990
J. Caughie, ed. *Theories of Authorship: A Reader*, Routledge, London, 1988
—. & A. Kuhn, eds. *The Sexual Subject: A* Screen *Reader In Sexuality*, Routledge, London, 1992
Centro Studi sul Cinema e sulle Communicazioni di Massa. *La Giovani generazioni e il cinema di Pier Paolo Pasolini, La Scene e lo schermo*, Dec, 1989
G. Chester & J. Dickey, eds. *Feminism and Censorship: The Current Debate*, Prism Press, Bridport, Dorset, 1988
M. Ciment. *Projections 9: French Filmmakers On Filmmaking*, Faber, London, 1999
H. Cixous. *The Newly Born Woman*, tr. B. Wing, Minnesota University Press, Minneapolis, 1986
—. *The Hélène Cixous Reader*, ed. Susan Sellers, Blackwell, Oxford, 1994
D.A. Cook. *A History of Narrative Film*, W.W. Norton, New York, N.Y., 1981, 1990, 1996
P. Cook & M. Bernink, eds. *The Cinema Book*, 2nd ed., British Film Institute, London, 1999
T. Corrigan. *A Cinema Without Walls: Movies and Culture After Vietnam*, Rutgers University Press, N.J., 1991
P. Cowie. *The Cinema of Orson Welles*, Da Capo, New York, N.Y., 1973
—. *Ingmar Bergman*, Secker & Warburg, London, 1982
R. Crittenden, ed. *Fine Cuts: The Art of European Film Editing*, C.R.C. Press, 2012
M. Crosland, ed. *The Marquis de Sade Reader*, Peter Owen, 2000
J. Davidson. *The Greeks and Greek Love*, Weidenfeld & Nicholson, London, 2007
G. Day & C. Bloch, eds. *Perspectives On Pornography: Sexuality In Film and Literature*, Macmillan, London, 1988

L. De Giusti. *I Film di Pier Paolo Pasolini*, Gremese, Rome, 1990
T. de Lauretis & S. Heath, eds. *The Cinematic Apparatus*, St Martin's Press, New York, N.Y., 1980
—. *Alice Doesn't: Feminism, Semiotics, Cinema*, Indiana University Press, Bloomington, I.N., 1984
—. *Technologies of Gender*, Macmillan, London, 1987
G. Deleuze & F. Guattari. *Cinema 1: The Movement Image*, Athlone Press, London, 1989
—. *Cinema 2: The Time Image*, Athlone Press, London, 1989
—. *What Is Philosophy?*, Verso, London, 1994
J. Derrida: *Of Grammatology*, Johns Hopkins University Press, Baltimore, M.D., 1976
—. *Spurs: Nietzsche's Styles*, University of Chicago Press, Chicago, I.L., 1979
—. *Writing and Difference*, University of Chicago Press, Chicago, I.L., 1987
—. *Archive Fever*, University of Chicago Press, Chicago, I.L., 1999
G. DeSanti et al. *Perchè Pasolini*, Guaraldi, Florence, 1978
J. Distefano. "Picturing Pasolini", *Art Journal*, 1997
W.W. Dixon. *The Films of Jean-Luc Godard*, State University of New York Press, Albany, N.Y., 1997
J. Dollimore. *Sexual Dissidence*, Oxford, 1991
J. Duflot. *Entretiens avec Pier Paolo Pasolini*, Pierre Belfond, Paris, 1970
R. Durgnat. *Films and Feelings*, Faber, London, 1967
A. Dworkin. *Pornography: Men Possessing Women*, Women's Press, London, 1984
—. *Intercourse*, Arrow, London, 1988
—. *Letters From a War Zone: Writings, 1976-1987*, Secker & Warburg, London, 1988
A. Easthope, ed. *Contemporary Film Theory*, Longman, London, 1993
M. Eliade. *Ordeal by Labyrinth*, University of Chicago Press, Chicago, I.L., 1984
—. *Symbolism, the Sacred and the Arts*, Crossroad, New York, N.Y., 1985
A. Eliot. "*Oedipus Rex* by Pier Paolo Pasolini", *Literature Film Quarterly*, 2004
T. Elsaesser. *European Cinema*, Amsterdam University Press, Amsterdam, 2005
P. Ettedgui. *Production Design & Art Direction*, RotoVision, 1999
Etudes cinématographiques, special Pasolini number, 109-111, 1976
D. Fairservice. *Film Editing*, Manchester University Press, Manchester, 2001
M. Farber. *Negative Space*, Studio Vista, London, 1971
C. Fava & Aldo Vigano. *The Films of Federico Fellini*, Citadel, New York, N.Y., 1990
F. Fellini. *Fellini On Fellini*, Delacorte, New York, N.Y., 1976
—. *Fellini On Fellini*, ed. C. Constantin, Faber, 1995
—. *I'm a Born Liar: A Fellini Lexicon*, ed. D. Pettigrew, Abrams, New York, 2003
A. Ferrero. *Il Cinema di Pier Paolo Pasolini*, Marsilio, Venice, 1977
J. Finler. *The Movie Directors Story*, Octopus Books, London, 1985
—. *The Hollywood Story*, Wallflower Press, London, 2003
John Fletcher & Andrew Benjamin, ed. *Abjection, Melancholia and Love: The Work of Julia Kristeva*, Routledge, London, 1990
K. Forni. "A "cinema of poetry": What Pasolini Did To Chaucer's *Canterbury Tales*", *Literature Film Quarterly*, 2002
G.E. Forshey. *American Religious and Biblical Spectaculars*, Praeger, Westport, C.T., 1992
M. Foucault. *The History of Sexuality*, Penguin, London, 1981
—. *The Use of Pleasure: The History of Sexuality*, vol. 2, Penguin, London,

1987
—. *Politics, Philosophy, Culture: Interviews and Other Writings, 1977-1984*, ed. L.D. Kritzmon, Routledge, New York, N.Y., 1990
J. Franklin. *New German Cinema*, Columbus Books, 1986
K. French, ed. *Screen Violence*, Bloomsbury, London, 1996
P. French et al. *The Films of Jean-Luc Godard,* Blue Star House, 1967
A. Frisch. "Francesco Vezzolini: Pasolini Reloaded", interview, Rutgers University Alexander Library, New Brunswick, N.J.
Diana Fuss. *Essentially Speaking*, Routledge, New York, 1989
—. ed. *Inside/Out: Lesbian Theories, Gay Theories*, Routledge, London, 1991
F. Gado. *The Passion of Ingmar Bergman*, Durham, N.C., 1986
J. Gallagher. *Film Directors On Directing*, Praeger, New York, N.Y., 1989
H. Geduld, ed. *Filmmakers On Filmmaking*, Indiana University Press, Bloomington, I.N., 1967
J. Geiger & R. Rutsky, eds. *Film Analysis*, Norton & Company, New York, N.Y., 2005
J. Gelmis. *The Film Director As Superstar*, Penguin, London, 1974
D. Georgakas & L. Rubenstein, eds. *Art Politics Cinema: The Cineaste Interviews*, Pluto Press, London, 1985
F. Gérard. *Pier Paolo Pasolini*, Seghers, Paris, 1973
—. *Pasolini ou le mythe de la barbarie*, Université de Bruxelles, 1981
J. Gerber. *Anatole Dauman: Pictures of a Producer*, British Film Institute, London, 1992
M. Gervais. *Pier Paolo Pasolini*, Paris, 1973
L. Gianetti: *Godard and Others*, Tantivy, 1975
—. *Understanding Movies*, Prentice-Hall, N.J., 1982
P.C. Gibson & R. Gibson, eds. *Dirty Looks: Women, Pornography, Power*, British Film Institute, London, 1993
Jean-Luc Godard. *Godard On Godard*, ed. A. Bergala, Cahiers du Cinéma, Paris, 1985
—. *Godard On Godard*, eds. J. Narobi & T. Milne, Da Capo, New York, N.Y., 1986
—. *Interviews*, ed. D. Sterritt, University of Mississippi Press, Jackson, 1998
—. *Godard On Godard 2*, ed. A. Bergala, Cahiers du Cinéma, Paris, 1998
—. *Histoire(s) du cinéma*, Gallimard-Gaumont, Paris, 1998
—. "An Audience With Uncle Jean-Luc", *The Guardian*, Feb 11, 2000
J. Gomez. *Ken Russell*, Muller, 1976
R. Gottesman, ed. *Focus On Orson Welles,* Prentice-Hall, Englewood Cliffs, N.J., 1976
P. Grace. *The Religious Film: Christianity and the Hagiopic*, Wiley-Blackwell, Sussex, 2009
D. Graham, ed. *Film and Religion*, St Mungo Press, 1997
B.K. Grant, ed. *Film Genre*, Scarecrow Press, Metuchen, N.J., 1977
—. ed. *Crisis Cinema: The Apocalyptic Idea In Postmodern Narrative Film*, Maisonneuve Press, 1993
—. *Film Genre Reader II*, University of Texas Press, Austin, T.X., 1995
J. Green. *The Encyclopedia of Censorship*, Facts on File, New York, N.Y., 1990
N. Greene. *Pier Paolo Pasolini: Cinema As Heresy*, Princeton University Press, N.J., 1990
Elizabeth Grosz. "Philosophy, Subjectivity and the Body", in C. Pateman, 1986
—. "Desire, the body and recent French feminism", *Intervention*, 21-2, 1988
—. *Sexual Subversions*, Allen & Unwin, London, 1989
—. "The Body of Signification", in J. Fletcher, 1990
—. "Fetishization", in E. Wright, 1992
—. *Volatile Bodies,* Indiana University Press, Bloomington, I.N., 1994

—. *Space, Time and Perversion*, Routledge, London, 1995
B. Groult: "Les portiers de nuit", in *Ainsi soit-elle*, Grasset, Paris, 1975, and in E. Marks, 1981
L. Hanlon. *Fragments: Bresson's Film Style*, Farleigh Dickinson University Press, Rutherford, 1986
S. Harwood. *French National Cinema*, Routledge, London, 1993
P. Hartnoll, ed. *The Oxford Companion To the Theatre,* Oxford University Press, Oxford, 1985
S. Hayward & G. Vincendeau, eds. *French Film*, Routledge, London, 1990
S. Heath. *Questions of Cinema*, Macmillan, London, 1981
—. *Cinema and Language*, University Presses of America, 1983
W. Herzog. *Herzog On Herzog*, ed. P. Cronin, Faber & Faber, London, 2002
G. Hickenlooper. *Reel Conversations: Candid Interviews With Film's Foremost Directors and Critics*, Citadel, New York, N.Y., 1991
C. Higham. *Orson Welles,* St Martin's Press, New York, N.Y., 1985
J. Hill & P.C. Gibson, eds. *The Oxford Guide To Film Studies*, Oxford University Press, Oxford, 1998
J. Hillier, ed. *Cahiers du Cinéma: The 1950s, New-Realism, Hollywood, New Wave*, Harvard University Press, Cambridge, M.A., 1985
—. *The New Hollywood*, Studio Vista, London, 1992
L.C. Hillstrom, ed. *International Dictionary of Films and Filmmakers: Directors*, St James Press, London, 1997
D. Holmes & A. Smith, eds. *100 Years of European Cinema*, Manchester University Press, Manchester, 2000
H. Hughes. *Cinema Italiano*, I.B. Tauris, London, 2011
G. Indiana. *Salò*, British Film Institute, London, 2000
—. "Pasolini, *Mamma Roma,* and *La Ricotta"*, Criterion, 2004
A. Insdorf. *Indelible Shadows: Film and the Holocaust*, Cambridge University Press, Cambridge, 1989
L. Irigaray. *The Irigaray Reader,* ed. M. Whitford, Blackwell, Oxford, 1991
F. Jameson. *Signatures of the Visible*, Routledge, New York, N.Y., 1990
—. *Postmodernism, or the Cultural Logic of Late Capitalism*, Verso, London, 1991
D. Jarman. *Modern Nature*, Century, London, 1991
P. Kael. *Kiss Kiss Bang Bang*, Bantam, New York, N.Y., 1969
—. *Going Steady*, Bantam, New York, 1971
—. *Taking It All In*, Marion Boyars, 1986
—. *State of the Art*, Marion Boyars, London, 1987
—. *Movie Love*, Marion Boyars, London, 1992
A. Kaes. *From Hitler To Heimat: The Return of History As Film*, Harvard University Press, Cambridge, M.A., 1989
E. Ann Kaplan, ed. *Psychoanalysis and Cinema*, Routledge, London, 1990
B.F. Kawin. *Mindscreen: Bergman, Godard and First-Person Film*, Princeton University Press, Princeton, N.J., 1978
—. *How Movies Work*, Macmillan, New York, N.Y., 1987
P. Keough, ed. *Flesh and Blood: The National Society of Film Critics On Sex, Violence, and Censorship*, Mercury House, San Francisco, C.A., 1995
T. Kezich. *Fellini: His Life and Work*, Faber and Faber, New York, N.Y., 2006
G. Kindem. *The International Movie Industry*, Southern Illinois University Press, Carbondale, I.L., 2000
R. Kinnard & T. Davis. *Divine Images: A History of Jesus On the Screen,* Citadel Press, New York, N.Y., 1992
C. Klimke. *Kraft der Vergangenheit: Zu Motiven der Filme von Pier Paolo Pasolini,* Frankfurt, 1988
T. Jefferson Kline. *Bertolucci's Dream Loom: A Psychoanalytic Study of Cinema*, University of Massachusetts Press, Amherst, 1987

P. Kolker. *The Altering Eye: Contemporary International Cinema*, Oxford University Press, New York, N.Y., 1983
—. *Bernardo Bertolucci*, British Film Institute, London, 1985
—. *A Cinema of Loneliness: Penn, Stone, Kubrick, Scorsese, Spielberg, Altman*, Oxford University Press, New York, N.Y., 1988/ 2000
S. Kracauer. *Theory of Film*, Princeton University Press, Princeton, N.J., 1997
L. Kreitzer. *The New Testament In Fiction and Film*, J.S.O.T., 1993
—. *The Old Testament In Fiction and Film*, Sheffield Academic Press, Sheffield, 1994
J. Kristeva. *Powers of Horror: An Essay On Abjection*, tr. L.S. Roudiez, Columbia University Press, New York, 1982
—. *Desire In Language: A Semiotic Approach To Literature and Art*, ed. L.S. Roudiez, tr. Thomas Gora, Alice Jardine & L.S. Roudiez, Blackwell, Oxford, 1982
—. *Revolution In Poetic Language*, tr. Margaret Walker, Columbia University Press, New York, 1984
—. Article in *Art Press*, 4, 1984-85
—. *The Kristeva Reader*, ed. T. Moi, Blackwell, Oxford, 1986
—. *Tales of Love*, tr. L.S. Roudiez, Columbia University Press, New York, N.Y., 1987
—. *Black Sun: Depression and Melancholy*, tr. L.S. Roudiez, Columbia University Press, New York, N.Y., 1989
—. *Strangers To Ourselves*, tr. L.S. Roudiez, Harvester Wheatsheaf, Hemel Hempstead, 1991
A. Kuhn. *Women's Pictures: Feminism and the Cinema*, Routledge & Kegan Paul, London, 1982
A. Kurosawa. *Something Like an Autobiography*, Vintage, New York, N.Y., 1983
J. Lacan. *Écrits: A Selection*, tr. Alan Sheridan, Tavistock, 1977
—. and the École Freudienne. *Feminine Sexuality*, eds. J. Mitchell and J. Rose, Macmillan, London, 1988
R. Lapsley & M. Westlake, eds. *Film Theory: An Introduction*, Manchester University Press, Manchester, 1988
A. Lawton. *The Red Screen: Politics, Society, Art In Soviet Cinema*, Routledge, London, 1992
B. Leaming. *Orson Welles*, Viking, New York, 1985
V. Lebeau. *Psychoanalysis and Cinema*, Wallflower, London, 2001
P. Leprohan. *The Italian Cinema*, tr. R. Greaves & O. Stallybrass, Secker & Warburg, London, 1972
E. Levy. *Cinema of Outsiders: The Rise of American Independent Film*, New York University Press, New York, N.Y., 1999
J. Lewis. *Whom God Wishes To Destroy: Francis Coppola and the New Hollywood*, Duke University Press, Durham, N.C., 1995
—. ed. *New American Cinema*, Duke University Press, Durham, N.C., 1998
—. *Hollywood v. Hard Core: How the Struggle Over Censorship Created the Modern Film Industry*, New York University Press, New York, N.Y., 2000
—. ed. *The End of Cinema As We Know It: American Film In the Nineties*, New York University Press, New York, N.Y., 2002
J. Leyda, ed. *Filmmakers Speak*, Da Capo, New York, 1977/ 84
—. *Kino: A History of the Russian and Soviet Cinema*, 3rd edition, Allen & Unwin, London, 1983
M. Litch. *Philosophy Through Film*, Routledge, London, 2002
P. Livington. *Ingmar Bergman and the Rituals of Art*, Cornell University Press, Ithaca, N.Y., 1982
V. LoBrutto. *Sound-On-Film*, Praeger, New York, N.Y., 1994
—. *Stanley Kubrick*, Faber, London, 1997

Y. Loshitzky. *The Radical Faces of Godard and Bertolucci*, Wayne State University Press, Detroit, M.I., 1995
L. Lourdeaux. *Italian and Irish Filmmakers In America: Ford, Capra, Coppola and Scorsese*, Temple University Press, Philadelphia, P.A., 1990
L. Lucignani & C. Molfese, eds. *Per Conoscere Pasolini*, Bulzoni, Rome, 1978
C. MacCabe. *Godard, Images, Sound, Politics*, Macmillan/ British Film Institute, London, 1980
—. *Godard: A Portrait of the Artist At 70*, Faber, London, 2003
—. *"The Decameron"*, Criterion, 2012
M. Macciocchi, ed. *Pasolini*, Grasset, Paris, 1980
A. Maggi. *The Resurrection of the Body: Pier Paolo Pasolini From St Paul To Sade*, University of Chicago Press, 2009
P. Malone. *Movie Christs and Antichrists*, Crossroad, 1990
R. Maltby. *Harmless Entertainment: Hollywood and the Ideology of Consensus*, Scarecrow Press, Metuchen, N.J., 1983
—. *Hollywood Cinema*, 2nd ed., Blackwell, Oxford, 2003
M. Mancini & G. Perella. *Pier Paolo Pasolini: corpi e luoghi*, Theorema, Bologna, 1982
Mao Tse-tung. *The Little Red Book (Quotations From Chairman Mao Tse-tung)*, Foreign Language Press, Peking, 1967
E. Marks & I. de Courtivron, eds. *New French Feminisms: an anthology*, Harvester Wheatsheaf, Hemel Hempstead, 1981
T. Martin. *Images and the Imageless: A Study In Religious Consciousness and Film*, Bucknell University Press, 1981
G. Mast *et al*, eds. *Film Theory and Criticism: Introductory Readings*, Oxford University Press, New York, N.Y., 1992a
—. & B Kawin, *A Short History of the Movies*, Macmillan, New York, N.Y., 1992b
T.D. Matthews. *Censored*, Chatto & Windus, London, 1994
J.R. May & M. Bird, eds. *Religion In Film*, University of Tennessee Press, Knoxville, 198
—. *Image and Likeness: Religious Vision In American Film Classics*, Paulist, 1992
—. *New Image of Religious Film*, Sheed & Ward, London, 1996
J. Mayne. *The Woman At the Keyhole: Feminism and Women's Cinema*, Indiana University Press, Bloomington, I.N., 1990
M. Medved. *Hollywood vs. America*, HarperCollins, London, 1992
P. Mellencamp & P. Rosen, eds. *Cinema Histories, Cinema Practices*, University Publications of America, Frederick, M.D., 1984
—. *A Fine Romance: Five Ages of Film Feminism*, Temple University Press, Philadelphia, P.A., 1995
M. Miles. *Seeing and Believing: Religion and Values In the Movies*, Beacon, Boston, M.A., 1996
M.C. Miller. ed. *Seeing Through Movies*, Pantheon, New York, N.Y., 1990
Wu Ming. "The Police vs. Pasolini, Pasolini vs the Police", Verso Books, 2016
T. Modleski, ed. *Studies In Entertainment*, Indiana University Press, Bloomington, I.N., 1987
—. *The Women Who Knew Too Much: Hitchcock and Feminist Theory*, Methuen, London, 1988
—. *Feminism Without Women: Culture and Criticism In a 'Postfeminist' Age*, Routledge, London, 1991
T. Moi. *Sexual/ Textual Politics: Feminist Literary Theory*, Methuen, London, 1983
J. Monaco. *The New Wave: Truffaut, Godard, Chabrol, Rohmer, Rivette*, Oxford University Press, New York, N.Y., 1977

I. Moscati. *Pasolini e il teorema del sesso*, Milan, 1995
P. Mosley. *Ingmar Bergman*, Marion Boyars, London, 1981
R. Murphy, ed. *The British Cinema Book*, Palgrave/ Macmillan, London, 2nd edition, 2009
R. Murray. *Images In the Dark: An Encyclopedia of Gay and Lesbian Film and Video*, Titan Books, London, 1998
S. Murri. *Pier Paolo Pasolini*, Rome, 1984
N. Naldini. *Nei camp dei Friuli: La giovanezza di Pasolini*, Pesce d'Oro, Milan, 1984
—. *Pasolini, una vita*, Einaudi, Turin, 1989
J. Naremore. *The Magic World of Orson Welles*, Southern Methodist University Press, Dallas, T.X., 1989
J. Natoli. *Hauntings: Popular Film and American Culture 1990-92*, State University of New York Press, Albany, N.Y., 1994
—. *Speeding To the Millennium: Film and Culture 1993-1995*, State University of New York Press, Albany, N.Y., 1998
—. *Postmodern Journeys: Film and Culture, 1996-1998*, State University of New York Press, Albany, N.Y., 2001
S. Neale. *Cinema and Technology*, Macmillan, London, 1985
—. & B. Neve. *Film and Politics In America*, Routledge, London, 1992
J. Nelmes, ed. *An Introduction To Film Studies*, Routledge, London, 1996
R. Neupert. *The End: Narration and Closure In the Cinema*, Wayne State University Press, Detroit, M.I., 1995
K. Newman & J. Marriott. *Horror! The Definitive Companion To the Most Terrifying Movies Ever Made*, Carlton Books, London, 2013
G. Nowell-Smith. *Visconti*, British Film Institute, London, 1973
—. ed. *The Oxford History of World Cinema*, Oxford University Press, Oxford, 1996
—. & S. Ricci, eds. *Hollywood and Europe*, British Film Institute, London, 1998
—. *Making Waves: New Cinemas of the 1960s*, Bloomsbury, 2013
J. Orr & C. Nicholson, eds. *Cinema and Fiction*, Edinburgh University Press, Edinburgh, 1992
—. *Cinema and Modernity*, Polity Press, Cambridge, 1993
—. *Contemporary Cinema*, Edinburgh University Press, Edinburgh, 1998
C. Ostwalt. "Religion & Popular Movies", *Journal of Religion and Film*, 2, 3, 1998
R. Palmer, ed. *The Cinematic Text*, A.M.S., New York, N.Y., 1989
A. Panicali & S. Sestini, eds. *Pier Paolo Pasolini*, Nuovo Salani, Florence, 1982
E. Passannanti. *Il Corpo & Il Potere*, Joker, 2004
—. *La Ricotta*, Mask Press, 2007
—. *Il Cristo dell'Eresia*, Joker, 2009
—. *La Nudita del Sacro nei Film di Pier Paolo Pasolini*, Brindin Press, 2019
Carole Pateman & Elizabeth Grosz, eds. *Feminist Challenges*, Allen & Unwin, Sydney, 1986
A. Pavelin. *Fifty Religious Films*, A.P. Pavelin, Chiselhurst, Kent, 1990
C. Penley, ed. *Feminism and Film Theory*, Routledge, London, 1988
—. et al, eds. *Close Encounters: Film, Feminism and Science Fiction*, University of Minnesota Press, Minneapolis, 1991
V.F. Perkins. *Film As Film: Understanding and Judging Movies*, Penguin, London, 1972
T. Peterson. *The Paraphrase of an Imaginary Dialogue: The Poetics and Poetry of Pier Paolo Pasolini*, New York, 1994
S. Petraglia. *Pier Paolo Pasolini*, Nuova Italia, Florence, 1974
D. Petrie. *Screening Europe: Image and Identity In Contemporary European*

Cinema, British Film Institute, London, 1992
G. Phelps. *Film Censorship*, Gollancz, London, 1975
K. Phillips. *New German Filmmakers*, Ungar, New York, N.Y., 1984
L. Polezzi & C. Ross, eds. *In Corpore: Bodies In Post-Unification Italy*, Fairleigh Dickinson University Press, 2007
C. Potter. *Image, Sound and Story: The Art of Telling In Film*, Secker & Warburg, London, 1990
N. Power & G. Nowell-Smith. "Subversive Pasolini", 2012-13, ninapower.net, 2017
P. Powrie, ed. *French Cinema In the 1990s*, Oxford University Press, Oxford, 1999
R. Prendergast. *Film Music*, W.W. Norton, New York, N.Y., 1992
S. Prince. *Savage Cinema: Sam Peckinpah and the Rise of Ultraviolent Movies*, University of Texas Press, Austin, T.X., 1998
—. ed. *Screening Violence*, Athlone Press, London, 2000
—. *A New Pot of Gold: Hollywood Under the Electronic Rainbow*, Scribners, New York, N.Y., 2000
S. Projansky. *Watching Rape: Film and Television In Postfeminism Culture*, New York University Press, New York, N.Y., 2001
T. Pugh. "Chaucerian Fabliaux, Cinematic Fabliau: Pier Paolo Pasolini's *I racconti di Canterbury*", *Literature Film Quarterly*, 2004
M. Pye & Lynda Myles. *The Movie Brats: How the Film Generation Took Over Hollywood*, Faber, London, 1979
T. Rayns, ed. *Fassbinder*, British Film Institute, London, 1979
K. Reader. *Robert Bresson*, Manchester University Press, Manchester, 2000
A. Reinhartz. "Jesus in Film: Hollywood Perspectives on the Jewishness of Jesus", *Journal of Religion and Film*, 2, 2, 1998
A. Restivo. *The Cinema of Economic Miracles: Visuality and Modernization In the Italian Art Film*, Duke University Press, 2002
La Revue d'estgétique, special Pasolini number, 3, 1982
J. Rhodes. *Stupendous, Miserable City: Pasolini's Rome*, University of Minnesota Press, 2007
P. Rice & P. Waugh, eds. *Modern Literary Theory: A Reader*, Arnold, London, 1992
J. Richards, ed. *Films and British National Identity*, Manchester University Press, Manchester, 1997
M. Richardson. *Surrealism and Cinema*, Berg, New York, N.Y., 2006
D. Richie. *The Films of Akira Kurosawa*, University of California Press, Berkeley, C.A., 1965
R. Rinaldi. *Pier Paolo Pasolini*, Mursia, Milan, 1982
D. Robinson. *World Cinema*, Methuen, London, 1981
G. Rodgerson & E. Wilson, eds. *Pornography and Censorship*, Lawrence & Wishart, London, 1991
S. Rohdie. *Antonioni*, British Film Institute, London, 1990
—. *The Passion of Pier Paolo Pasolini*, British Film Institute, London, 1995
J. Romney & A. Wootton, eds. *Celluloid Jukebox: Popular Music and the Movies Since the 50s*, British Film Institute, London, 1995
P. Rosen, ed. *Narrative, Apparatus, Ideology: A Film Theory Reader*, Columbia University Press, New York, N.Y., 1986
A. Rosenstone, ed. *Revisioning History: Film and the Construction of a New Past*, Princeton University Press, Princeton, N.J., 1995
R. Roud. *Jean-Luc Godard*, Thames & Hudson, London, 1970
R. Ruiz. *The Poetics of Cinema*, Dis Voir, Paris, 1995
P. Rumble & B. Testa, eds. *Pier Paolo Pasolini*, University of Toronto Press, Toronto, 1994
—. *Allegories of Contamination: Pier Paolo Pasolini's Trilogy of Life*, Uni-

versity of Toronto Press, Toronto, 1996
K. Russell. *A British Picture: An Autobiography*, Heinemann, London, 1989
M. Russell & J. Young. *Film Music,* RotoVision, 2000
V. Russo. *The Celluloid Closet: Homosexuality In the Movies*, Harper & Row, New York, N.Y., 1981
M. de Sade. *The 120 Days of Sodom*, tr. A. Wainhouse & R. Seaver, Arrow, London, 1996
J. Sanford. *The New German Cinema*, Da Capo Press, New York, N.Y., 1982
A. Sarris, ed., *Interviews With Film Directors*, Avon, New York, N.Y., 1969
T. Schatz. *Hollywood Genres,* Random House, New York, N.Y., 1981
—. *Old Hollywood/ New Hollywood*, U.M.I. Research Press, Ann Arbor, M.I., 1983
—. *The Genius of the System: Hollywood Filmmaking In the Studio Era*, Pantheon, New York, N.Y. 1988
Naomi Schor. *Breaking the Chain: Women, Theory and French Realist Fiction*, New York, 1985
—. & Elizabeth Weed, eds. *Differences: More Gender Trouble: Feminism Meets Queer Theory*, 6, 2-3, Indiana University Press, Summer, 1994
P. Schrader. *Transcendental Style In Film: Ozu, Bresson, Dreyer*, Da Capo Press, 1972
M. Schumacher. *Francis Ford Coppola*, Bloomsbury, London, 2000
B. Schwartz. *Pasolini Requiem*, Vintage Books, New York, 1995
P. Schwenger. *Phallic Critiques: Masculinity and 20th Century Literature*, London, 1984
O. Schweitzer. *Pier Paolo Pasolini*, Hamburg, 1986
Bernhart Schwenk & Michael Semff, eds. *Pier Paolo Pasolini and Death*, Ostfildern 2005
M. Scorsese. *Scorsese On Scorsese*, ed. D. Thompson & I. Christie, Faber, London, 1989, 1995
Screen Reader I: Cinema/ Ideology/ Politics, Society for Education in Film & TV, 1977
Screen Reader II: Cinema and Semiotics, British Film Institute, London, 1982
C. Sharrett, ed. *Crisis Cinema*, Maisonneuve Press, Washington, D.C., 1993
D. Shipman. *The Story of Cinema*, Hodder & Stoughton, London, 1984
—. *Caught In the Act: Sex and Eroticism In the Movies*, Hamish Hamilton, London, 1986
T. Shone. *Blockbuster: How the Jaws and Jedi Generation Turned Hollywood Into a Boom-Town*, Scribner, London, 2005
E. Showalter, ed. *The New Feminist Criticism,* Virago, London, 1986
Enzo Siciliano. *Pasolini: A Biography*, tr. John Shepley, Random House, New York, 1982
L. Sider *et al*, eds. *Soundscapes: The School of Sound Lectures 1998-2001*, Wallflower Press, London, 2003
M. Silberman. *German Cinema,* Wayne State University Press, Detroit, M.I., 1995
K. Silverman. *The Subject of Semiotics*, Oxford University Press, New York, N.Y., 1983
—. *The Acoustic Mirror: The Female Voice In Psychoanalysis and Cinema*, Indiana University Press, Bloomington, I.N., 1988
—. *Male Subjectivity At the Margins*, Routledge, London, 1992
—. & H. Farocki. *Speaking About Godard*, New York University Press, New York, N.Y., 1998
P. Adams Sitney, ed. *The Film Culture Reader*, Praeger, New York, N.Y., 1970
—. *Vital Crises In Italian Cinema*, University of Texas Press, Austin, T.X., 1995
S. Snyder. *Pier Paolo Pasolini*, Twayne, 1980

V. Sobchack, ed. *The Persistence of History: Cinema, Television, and the Modern Event*, Routledge, London, 1995
A. Solomon. *20th Century-Fox: A Corporate and Financial History*, Scarecrow Press, Metuchen, N.J., 1988
J. Solomon. *The Ancient World In the Cinema*, London, 1978
—. *The Ancient World In the Cinema*, Yale University Press, New Haven, C.T., 2001
P. Sorlin. *The Film In History: Restaging the Past*, Blackwell, Oxford, 1980
S. Spignesi. *The Woody Allen Companion*, Plexus, London, 1994
George Stambolian & Elaine Marks, eds. *Homosexuality and French Literature: Cultural Contexts/ Critical Texts,* Cornell University Press, Ithaca, 1979
B. Steene. *Ingmar Bergman*, Twayne, Boston, M.A., 1968
—. *Ingmar Bergman: A Guide To References and Resources*, Boston, M.A., 1987
N. Steimatsky. "Pasolini on Terra Sancta: Towards a Theology of Film", *Yale Journal of Criticism*, 11, 1, 1998
L. Stern. *The Scorsese Connection*, British Film Institute, London, 1995
D. Sterritt. *The Films of Jean-Luc Godard*, Cambridge University Press, Cambridge, 1999
P. Steven, ed. *Jump Cut: Hollywood, Politics and Counter Cinema*, Between the Lines, Toronto, 1985
G. Stewart. *Between Film and Screen: Modernism's Photo Synthesis*, University of Chicago Press, Chicago, I.L., 1999
C. Sylvester, ed. *The Penguin Book of Hollywood*, Penguin, London, 1999
Y. Tasker. *Spectacular Bodies: Gender, Genre and the Action Cinema*, Routledge, London, 1993
M. Temple & J. Williams, eds. *The Cinema Alone: Essays On the Work of Jean-Luc Godard, 1985-2000*, Amsterdam University Press, Amsterdam, 2000
—. *et al*, eds. *Godard For Ever*, Black Dog Publishing, London, 2004
S. Teo. *Hong Kong Cinema*, British Film Institute, London, 1997
N. Thomas, ed. *International Dictionary of Films and Filmmakers: Films*, St James Press, London, 1990
K. Thompson. *Breaking the Glass Armor: Neoformalist Film Analysis*, Princeton University Press, Princeton, N.J., 1988
—. & D. Bordwell. *Film History: An Introduction*, McGraw-Hill, New York, N.Y., 1994
—. *Storytelling In the New Hollywood*, Harvard University Press, Cambridge, M.A., 1999
D. Thomson. *A Biographical Dictionary of Film*, Deutsch, London, 1995
C. Tohill & P. Tombs. *Immoral Tales: Sex and Horror Cinema In Europe 1956-1984*, Titan Books, London, 1995
Sergio Toffetti. *La Terra vista dalla luna: il cinema di Sergio Citti*, Lindau, 1993
C. Tonetti. *Luchino Visconti*, Columbus Books, 1985
—. *Bernardo Bertolucci*, Twayne, Boston, M.A., 1994
E. Törnqvist. *Between Stage and Screen: Ingmar Bergman Directs*, Amsterdam University Press, Amsterdam, 1995
J. Trevelyan. *What the Censor Saw*, Michael Joseph, London, 1973
H. Trosman. *Contemporary Psychoanalysis and Masterworks of Art and Film,* New York University Press, New York, N.Y., 2000
F. Truffaut. *The Films In My Life*, tr. L. Mayhew, Penguin, London, 1982
P. Tyler. *Sex Psyche Etcetera In the Film*, Horizon, New York, N.Y., 1969
—. *Screening the Sexes: Homosexuality In the Movies*, Doubleday, New York, N.Y., 1973
M. Valck & M. Hagener, eds. *Cinephilia: Movies, Love and Memory,*

Amsterdam University Press, Amsterdam, 2005
K. Van Gunden. *Fantasy Films*, McFarland, Jefferson, NC 1989
M. Viano. *A Certain Realism: Making Use of Pasolini's Film Theory and Practice*, University of California Press, Berkeley, 1993.
G. Vincendeau, ed. *Encyclopedia of European Cinema*, British Film Institute, London, 1995
—. ed. *Film/ Literature/ Heritage: A Sight & Sound Reader*, British Film Institute, London, 2001
P. Virilio & S. Lotringer. *The Aesthetics of Disappearance*, tr. P. Beitchman, Semiotext(e), New York, N.Y., 1991
—. *The Vision Machine*, tr. J. Rose, Indiana University Press, Bloomington, I.N., 1994
J. Vizzard. *See No Evil: Life Inside a Hollywood Censor*, Simon & Schuster, New York, N.Y., 1970
A. Vogel. *Film As a Subversive Art*, Weidenfeld & Nicolson, London, 1974
A. Walker. *Sex In the Movies*, Penguin, London, 1968
—. *Hollywood, England: The British Film Industry In the Sixties*, Harrap, London, 1986
J. Wasko. *Movies and Money*, Ablex, N.J., 1982
—. *Hollywood In the Information Age*, Polity Press, Cambridge, 1994
P. Webb. *The Erotic Arts*, Secker & Warburg, London, 1975
E. Weiss. & J. Belton, eds. *Film Sound: Theory and Practice*, Columbia University Press, New York, N.Y., 1989
O. Welles. *This Is Orson Welles*, HarperCollins, London, 1992
—. *Orson Welles: Interviews,* ed. M. Estrin, University of Mississippi Press, Jackson, 2002
Helen Wilcox *et al*, eds. *The Body and the Text: Hélène Cixous, Reading and Teaching,* Harvester Wheatsheaf, Hemel Hempstead, Herts., 1990
P. Willemen, ed. *Pier Paolo Pasolini*, British Film Institute, London, 1977
L. Williams, ed. *Viewing Positions: Ways of Seeing Film*, Rutgers University Press, New Brunswick, N.J., 1995
L.R. Williams. *Critical Desire: Psychoanalysis and the Literary Subject*, Arnold, London, 1995
—. *Sex In the Head*, Harvester Wheatsheaf, Hemel Hempstead, 1995
W. Willimon. "Faithful to the Script", *Christian Century,* 2004
S. Willis. *High Contrast: Race and Gender In Contemporary Hollywood Film*, Duke University Press, Durham, N.C., 1997
R. Wilson & W. Dissanayake, eds. *Global/ Local: Cultural Production and the Transnational Imaginary*, Duke University Press, Durham, N.C., 1996
E. Wistrich. *'I Don't Mind the Sex It's the Violence': Film Censorship Explored*, Marion Boyars, London, 1978
M. Wolf. *The Entertainment Economy,* Penguin, London, 1999
P. Wollen: *Signs and Meaning In the Cinema*, Secker & Warburg, London, 1972
B. Wood. *Orson Welles*, Greenwood Press, Westport, C.T., 1990
P. Wood, ed. *Scorsese: A Journey Through the American Psyche*, Plexus, London, 2005
R. Wood. *Ingmar Bergman*, Praeger, New York, N.Y., 1969
—. *Hollywood From Vietnam To Reagan... and Beyond*, Columbia University Press, New York, N.Y., 2003
T. Woods. *Beginning Postmodernism,* Manchester University Press, Manchester, 1999
Elizabeth Wright, ed. *Feminism and Psychoanalysis: A Critical Dictionary*, Blackwell, Oxford, 1992
J. Wyatt. *High Concept: Movies and Marketing In Hollywood*, University of Texas Press, Austin, T.X., 1994

E.C.M. Yau, ed. *At Full Speed: Hong Kong Cinema In a Borderless World*, University of Minnesota Press, Minneapolis, MN, 1998

J. Young, ed. *The Art of Memory: Holocaust Memorials In History*, Prestel, New York, N.Y., 1994

G. Zigaini. *Pasolini e la morte*, Marsilio, Venice, 1987

J. Zipes, ed. *The Oxford Companion To Fairy Tales*, Oxford University Press, 2000

—. *Sticks and Stones: The Troublesome Success of Children's Literature From Slovenly Peter To Harry Potter*, Routledge, London, 2002

—. *The Enchanted Screen: The Unknown History of Fairy-tale Films*, Routledge, New York, N.Y., 2011

—. *The Irresistible Fairy Tale*, Prince University Press, Princeton, N.J., 2012

S. Zizek. *Looking Awry*, Verso, London, 1991

—. *Enjoy Your Symptom: Jacques Lacan In Hollywood and Out*, Routledge, New York, N.Y., 1992

—. ed. *Everything You Always Wanted To Know About Lacan (But Were Too Afraid To Ask Hitchcock)*, Verso, London, 1992

—. *The Metastases of Enjoyment*, Verso, London, 1994

—. *The Indivisible Remainder*, Verso, London, 1996

—. *The Fright of Real Tears: The Uses and Misuses of Lacan In Film Theory*, British Film Institute, London, 1999

Websites for Pasolini-related material include:

pierpaolopasolini.com
pasoliniroma.com
jclarkmedia.com
bernardobertolucci.org

Jeremy Robinson has published poetry, fiction, and studies of J.R.R. Tolkien, Samuel Beckett, Thomas Hardy, André Gide and D.H. Lawrence. Robinson has edited poetry books by Novalis, Ursula Le Guin, Friedrich Hölderlin, Francesco Petrarch, Dante Alighieri, Arseny Tarkovsky, and Rainer Maria Rilke. Books on film and animation include: *The Cinema of Hayao Miyazaki* • *Hayao Miyazaki: Pocket Guide* • *Princess Mononoke: Pocket Movie Guide* • *Spirited Away: Pocket Movie Guide* • *Blade Runner and the Cinema of Philip K. Dick* • *Blade Runner: Pocket Movie Guide* • *The Cinema of Donald Cammell* • *Performance: Donald Cammell: Nic Roeg: Pocket Movie Guide* • *Ken Russell: England's Great Visionary Film Director and Music Lover* • *Tommy: Ken Russell: The Who: Pocket Movie Guide* • *Women In Love: Ken Russell: D.H. Lawrence: Pocket Movie Guide* • *The Devils: Ken Russell: Pocket Movie Guide* • *Walerian Borowczyk: Cinema of Erotic Dreams* • *The Beast: Pocket Movie Guide* • *The Lord of the Rings Movies* • *The Fellowship of the Ring: Pocket Movie Guide* • *The Two Towers: Pocket Movie Guide* • *The Return of the King: Pocket Movie Guide* • *Jean-Luc Godard: The Passion of Cinema* • *The Sacred Cinema of Andrei Tarkovsky* • *Andrei Tarkovsky: Pocket Guide*.

'It's amazing for me to see my work treated with such passion and respect. There is nothing resembling it in the U.S. in relation to my work.'
(Andrea Dworkin)

'This model monograph – it is an exemplary job, and I'm very proud that he has accorded me a couple of mentions… The subject matter of his book is beautifully organised and dead on beam.'
(Lawrence Durrell, on *The Light Eternal: A Study of J.M.W. Turner*)

'Jeremy Robinson's poetry is certainly jammed with ideas, and I find it very interesting for that reason. It's certainly a strong imprint of his personality.'
(Colin Wilson)

'*Sex-Magic-Poetry-Cornwall* is a very rich essay… It is a very good piece… vastly stimulating and insightful.'
(Peter Redgrove)

CRESCENT MOON PUBLISHING

web: www.crmoon.com e-mail: cresmopub@yahoo.co.uk

ARTS, PAINTING, SCULPTURE

The Art of Andy Goldsworthy
Andy Goldsworthy: Touching Nature
Andy Goldsworthy in Close-Up
Andy Goldsworthy: Pocket Guide
Andy Goldsworthy In America
Land Art: A Complete Guide
The Art of Richard Long
Richard Long: Pocket Guide
Land Art In the UK
Land Art in Close-Up
Land Art In the U.S.A.
Land Art: Pocket Guide
Installation Art in Close-Up
Minimal Art and Artists In the 1960s and After
Colourfield Painting
Land Art DVD, TV documentary
Andy Goldsworthy DVD, TV documentary
The Erotic Object: Sexuality in Sculpture From Prehistory to the Present Day
Sex in Art: Pornography and Pleasure in Painting and Sculpture
Postwar Art
Sacred Gardens: The Garden in Myth, Religion and Art
Glorification: Religious Abstraction in Renaissance and 20th Century Art
Early Netherlandish Painting
Leonardo da Vinci
Piero della Francesca
Giovanni Bellini
Fra Angelico: Art and Religion in the Renaissance
Mark Rothko: The Art of Transcendence
Frank Stella: American Abstract Artist
Jasper Johns
Brice Marden
Alison Wilding: The Embrace of Sculpture
Vincent van Gogh: Visionary Landscapes
Eric Gill: Nuptials of God
Constantin Brancusi: Sculpting the Essence of Things
Max Beckmann
Caravaggio
Gustave Moreau
Egon Schiele: Sex and Death In Purple Stockings
Delizioso Fotografico Fervore: Works In Process 1
Sacro Cuore: Works In Process 2
The Light Eternal: J.M.W. Turner
The Madonna Glorified: Karen Arthurs

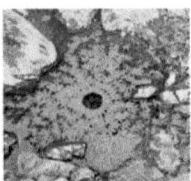

MEDIA, CINEMA, FEMINISM and CULTURAL STUDIES

J.R.R. Tolkien: The Books, The Films, The Whole Cultural Phenomenon
J.R.R. Tolkien: Pocket Guide
The *Lord of the Rings* Movies: Pocket Guide
The Cinema of Hayao Miyazaki
Hayao Miyazaki: *Princess Mononoke*: Pocket Movie Guide
Hayao Miyazaki: *Spirited Away*: Pocket Movie Guide
Tim Burton : Hallowe'en For Hollywood
Ken Russell
Ken Russell: *Tommy*: Pocket Movie Guide
The Ghost Dance: The Origins of Religion
The Peyote Cult
Cixous, Irigaray, Kristeva: The *Jouissance* of French Feminism
Julia Kristeva: Art, Love, Melancholy, Philosophy, Semiotics and Psychoanalysis
Luce Irigaray: Lips, Kissing, and the Politics of Sexual Difference
Hélene Cixous I Love You: The *Jouissance* of Writing
Andrea Dworkin
'Cosmo Woman': The World of Women's Magazines
Women in Pop Music
HomeGround: The Kate Bush Anthology
Discovering the Goddess (Geoffrey Ashe)
The Poetry of Cinema
The Sacred Cinema of Andrei Tarkovsky
Andrei Tarkovsky: Pocket Guide
Andrei Tarkovsky: *Mirror*: Pocket Movie Guide
Andrei Tarkovsky: *The Sacrifice*: Pocket Movie Guide
Walerian Borowczyk: Cinema of Erotic Dreams
Jean-Luc Godard: The Passion of Cinema
Jean-Luc Godard: *Hail Mary*: Pocket Movie Guide
Jean-Luc Godard: *Contempt*: Pocket Movie Guide
Jean-Luc Godard: *Pierrot le Fou*: Pocket Movie Guide
John Hughes and Eighties Cinema
Ferris Bueller's Day Off: Pocket Movie Guide
Jean-Luc Godard: Pocket Guide
The Cinema of Richard Linklater
Liv Tyler: Star In Ascendance
Blade Runner and the Films of Philip K. Dick
Paul Bowles and Bernardo Bertolucci
Media Hell: Radio, TV and the Press
An Open Letter to the BBC
Detonation Britain: Nuclear War in the UK
Feminism and Shakespeare
Wild Zones: Pornography, Art and Feminism
Sex in Art: Pornography and Pleasure in Painting and Sculpture
Sexing Hardy: Thomas Hardy and Feminism

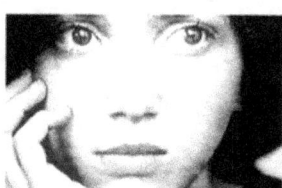

The Light Eternal is a model monograph, an exemplary job. The subject matter of the book is beautifully organised and dead on beam. (Lawrence Durrell)

It is amazing for me to see my work treated with such passion and respect. (Andrea Dworkin)

CRESCENT MOON PUBLISHING
P.O. Box 1312, Maidstone, Kent, ME14 5XU, Great Britain. www.crmoon.com

cresmopub@yahoo.co.uk   www.crescentmoon.org.uk

www.ingramcontent.com/pod-product-compliance
Lightning Source LLC
Chambersburg PA
CBHW060512230426
43665CB00013B/1486